ITALIAN FASCISM'S EMPIRE CINEMA

NEW DIRECTIONS IN NATIONAL CINEMAS
Jacqueline Reich, editor

ITALIAN FASCISM'S EMPIRE CINEMA

RUTH BEN-GHIAT

INDIANA UNIVERSITY PRESS
Bloomington & Indianapolis

This book is a publication of

Indiana University Press
Office of Scholarly Publishing
Herman B Wells Library 350
1320 East 10th Street
Bloomington, Indiana 47405 USA

iupress.indiana.edu

Telephone   800-842-6796
Fax   812-855-7931

© 2015 by Ruth Ben-Ghiat

All rights reserved

No part of this book may be reproduced or utilized in any form or by any means, electronic or mechanical, including photocopying and recording, or by any information storage and retrieval system, without permission in writing from the publisher. The Association of American University Presses' Resolution on Permissions constitutes the only exception to this prohibition.

∞ The paper used in this publication meets the minimum requirements of the American National Standard for Information Sciences—Permanence of Paper for Printed Library Materials, ANSI Z39.48–1992.

Manufactured in the United States of America

Library of Congress Cataloging-in-Publication Data

Ben-Ghiat, Ruth.
   Italian fascism's empire cinema / Ruth Ben-Ghiat.
     pages cm. — (New directions in national cinemas)
   Includes bibliographical references and index.
   ISBN 978-0-253-01559-4 (pbk. : alk. paper) — ISBN 978-0-253-01552-5 (cloth : alk. paper) — ISBN 978-0-253-01566-2 (ebook) 1. Motion pictures—Italy—History—20th century. 2. Imperialism in motion pictures. 3. Colonies in motion pictures. 4. Motion pictures—Political aspects. I. Title.
   PN1993.5.I88B336 2015
   791.430945—dc23
                              2014024935

1 2 3 4 5 20 19 18 17 16 15

For Julia

CONTENTS

Acknowledgments   ix

Introduction   xiii

1. Empire Cinema: Frames and Agendas   1

2. Italian Cinema and the Colonies to 1935   21

3. Mapping Empire Cinema, 1935–1939   43

4. Coming Home to the Colonies   78

5. Imperial Bodies, Part I: Italians and *Askaris*   118

6. Imperial Bodies, Part II: Slaves of Love, Slaves of Labor   167

7. Film Policies and Cultures, 1940–1943   214

8. The End of Empire   243

   Epilogue   296

   Notes   309

   Bibliography   335

   Filmography   369

   Index   375

ACKNOWLEDGMENTS

IT GIVES ME great pleasure to thank the many people who assisted me with this book. I have mentioned those whom I consulted on specific issues in the notes, to make clear their individual contributions. I am grateful to all of you. This study has necessitated the consultation of a variety of film and military archives. I thank Paola Castagna, Emiliano Morreale, and Enrico Daddario of the Cineteca Nazionale di Cinematografia. Silvio Alovisio and Fabio Pezzetti Tonion of the Museo Nazionale del Cinema gave invaluable help at several junctures, and Sergio Grmek Germani and Livio Jacob kindly facilitated my use of the materials of the Cineteca del Friuli's Fondo Genina. I would like to recognize the Istituto Luce's initiative to digitalize its collections and the role of the Archivio Fotografico's Luigi Oggianu in that effort. Decades ago, he pried open a rusted box marked "Africa Orientale Italiana" for me, the images inside relating a history of military and cinematographic collaboration that few had then explored. My study builds on the pioneering work of Mino Argentieri, Jean Gili, and Gian Piero Brunetta in this area. Another exemplary scholar, Adriano Aprà, has been a generous and helpful resource throughout the writing of this book, and I thank him for providing me with materials from his own Archivio Aprà. Raffaele De Berti and Giorgio Bertellini took time to assist me at various stages of this project. Francesco Casetti has been a supportive colleague and friend throughout the years: he will see the influence his lucid and incisive works have had on this study.

At military archives in Rome, I thank Dr. Ester Pennella of the Ufficio Storico della Marina Militare and Colonel Antonio Maria Iannone and Dr. Eleonora Pitaro of the Archivio Storico, Ministero dell'Aeronautica. Angelo Del Boca, Giorgio Rochat, Nicola Labanca, and MacGregor Knox have all patiently answered my questions about military and colonial matters for many years, and this book draws on their pathbreaking scholarship on Fascist imperialism and militarism. The enthusiasm of Geoff Eley meant a lot to me as I took on this obscure topic, and his writings on history and historiography have shaped my thinking. The Collegio Carlo Alberto provided a very hospitable place to write over two summers. I remain grateful for their Italian Studies Fellowship and to Daniela Del Boca for her support and friendship in Torino and New York.

My home base of New York University (NYU) has contributed to this book in many ways. I thank the Humanities Initiative and the dean of humanities for a publication subvention, the Faculty of Arts and Sciences for research funds, and my colleagues in the Departments of Italian Studies and History for encouraging my interdisciplinary explorations. Roberta Garbarini-Philippe and Stefania Pattavina of the former department facilitated my efforts to finish this book while juggling parenting, chairing, and teaching. The work of my graduate students has inspired this study—this book's origins lie partly in seminars I taught on Italian colonialism and on cinema during Fascism. I thank my graduate students for their intelligent engagements with these topics and Alberto Zambenedetti, Franco Baldasso, and Meredith Levin for their research assistance as well. Connor Gaudet of NYU's Digital Studio helped me patiently with the book's many images. I greatly appreciated the enthusiasm and patience of Raina Polivka at Indiana University Press, and I thank her, Jenna Whittaker, Michelle Sybert, and Daniel Pyle for guiding the book through the production process.

My Italian studies writing group read every word of this study, and I so appreciate the camaraderie and invaluable feedback of Ellen Nerenberg, Jacqueline Reich, and Giancarlo Lombardi. So many other colleagues and friends sustained me during the long writing process: I thank particularly Mia Fuller, long an interlocutor on the issues taken up here, and Stephanie Malia Hom: both read the introduction. Lisa Tiersten, Nita Juneja, Mia, Giovanna Calvino, and Diane Coyle offered the gifts of inspiration and the joys of long-lasting friendship over meals and telephone and Skype sessions.

The support of my family in the United States, the United Kingdom, Israel, and France has meant the world to me. I thank especially my father, Raphael Benghiat; my mother, Margaret Spence Robison; my brother, Michael Benghiat; my stepmother, Dušica Savić Benghiat; my sister, Simonida Benghiat; my aunts and uncles, Jack and Brenda Benghiat and Dr. Victor and Viti Benghiat; and my cousin, Shlomit Almog. They showed the kindness of never asking when this book was going to be finished and gave me confidence that I was on the right path. I dedicate this book to my wonderful daughter, Julia.

INTRODUCTION

A soldier gets down from a truck, takes a look around and mutters "Holy crap!" He had imagined a conventional Africa, with tall palm trees, bananas, and dancing women, a mixture of Turkey, India, and Morocco, the dream land of Paramount Pictures' "Oriental" films . . . what he finds instead is a place like home, but even more unwelcoming and indifferent. They had cheated him.

ENNIO FLAIANO's take on the gap between imperial fantasy and reality, written while he was in Ethiopia during the 1935–1936 Italian war on that country, is an apt introduction to a book on Italian Fascism's empire cinema. The allusion to American cinema as the reference for Italian popular imaginings of exoticism sums up the challenges and possibilities Mussolini's dictatorship faced in developing its own imperial film aesthetic. By the mid-1930s, Italy had been in Africa for decades, with the occupation of Ethiopia following those of Eritrea (1890), Somalia (1908), and Libya (1912), as well as the Dodecanese Islands (1912), and each of these colonies had figured in privately funded exploration films or in newsreels and documentaries made by the state-run Istituto Luce. Yet only Libya, Italy's one North African colony, had been the setting for a consistent number of film productions from the onset of Italian control through the slowdown of the Italian industry in the late 1920s. Libya offered a brand of Orientalist scenery made recognizable from Hollywood, French, and other national cinemas, whereas East Africa had no public recall in terms of screen imagery. The perennial imperialist vision of Africa as an "empty space" to be filled in the image of the colonizer's fantasy had particular influence among the Fascist officials and film professionals involved in developing a cinematic profile for the Italian East African Empire so grandly declared in May 1936.¹

In Britain and France as well, film played a key role in engaging national publics with imperial agendas, offering metropolitan spectators experiences of virtual immersion in worlds very different from their own. Even in National Socialist Germany, which had lost its colonies in the 1918 Versailles Treaty, visual culture kept alive the mirage of expansion outside of Europe. Nazi films drew on native traditions (Alpine mysticism) and foreign ones (the American Western) to communicate the thrill of exploration under the safety of hierarchical command.² Fascist empire cinema developed in dialogue with all of these parallel projects, and even during World War II, shared needs to innovate in the realm of film propaganda kept circuits of international influence flowing among Axis and Allied nations. At the same time, Fascism's empire cinema project reflected a collective conviction among officials and film professionals that unfamiliar East Africa could create a market niche for Italy and that North Africa could be depicted with fresh eyes. As one commentator asserted in urging investment in movies about the Italian colonies, such films could speak to the "profound reasons" that people went to see movies in general—"an appetite for the vast world, a desire to expand one's own mental and sentimental horizons"—while showcasing the particularities of Italy's possessions.³

Italian Fascism's Empire Cinema discusses nine features made in this spirit that move among Italy, Africa, and Greece: *Kif Tebbi* (Mario Camerini, 1927); *Il grande appello/The Last Roll Call* (Mario Camerini, 1936); *Lo squadrone bianco/The White Squadron* (Augusto Genina, 1936); *L'Esclave blanc/The White Slave—Jungla nera/Black Jungle* (started by Carl Theodor Dreyer, finished by Jean-Paul Paulin, 1936, and referred to henceforth by its French title); *Sentinelle di bronzo/Dusky Sentinels* (Romolo Marcellini, 1937); *Luciano Serra, pilota* (Goffredo Alessandrini, 1938); *Sotto la Croce del Sud/Under the Southern Cross* (Guido Brignone, 1938); *Bengasi/Benghazi* (Goffredo Alessandrini, 1942); and *Un pilota ritorna/A Pilot Returns* (Roberto Rossellini, 1942). Although some of these works are remembered today because of their stars or their directors, others are virtually unknown. Lino Micciché charged in a groundbreaking 1979 essay that movies made during the Fascist dictatorship (1922–1943) were "the skeleton in the closet" of the Italian film industry. As features supporting Fascist wars and occupations, empire films were at the heart of this uncomfortable film body, and they have remained among the least examined films of this period.[4] *Italian Fascism's Empire Cinema* is the first in-depth study of this group of movies and the fruit of research in film and military archives. Many of the films it discusses are still not available commercially, and some cannot be viewed in their integral and original form even in the archives: *Sentinelle di bronzo,* for example, survives only as an English-dubbed export copy.[5] The holes in linguistic and other knowledge presented by these precarious texts mirror their status as "fragmentary remnants" of national, industrial, and personal histories that were themselves long ignored. Empire and war films gave Rossellini, Mario Soldati, Federico Fellini, Michelangelo Antonioni, Mario Monicelli, and Renato Castellani early experiences in screenwriting, location shooting, and the handling of military technology and extras. Yet all of these histories fell out of memory when empire cinema was placed "in the closet," where it mostly remained for more than a half century after the loss of the Italian colonies during World War II.[6]

Fascist empire cinema may be unfamiliar to some readers as a conceptual category. Italians and those who work on their cinema have preferred to speak of "colonial cinema," leaving "empire cinema" to refer to the British case. I use this term to refer to Italian features and documentaries on imperial themes made between 1936 and 1943. Rarely accorded the status of a film genre, the features I discuss were nevertheless treated as a distinct film corpus by the Fascist-era press. They came out of a distinctive cultural climate, too, one greatly affected by changes in social and international policy that followed upon the Ethiopian invasion. Waging war on a League of Nations member occasioned a global public outcry, Red Cross investigations, and sanctions on Italy; it created image-management problems of a scale the regime had never faced before. This propaganda crisis, as well as the example of Nazi German policies, led to a restructuring and expansion of the Fascist cultural bureaucracy after 1936 to facilitate increased coordination among and controls of print, aural, and visual media. The state's promulgation of racial legislation from 1937 onward also had an impact, affecting features' story lines, reception, and casting. Finally, the Ethiopian War also brought a moment of reckoning in Italy with the political and military utilization of the medium of film. The extensive discussions in the colonial and film press about the relationship of film and war and the different functions of documentary and feature cinema constitute a meta-discourse through which "the cinema was able not only to formulate a certain idea of itself, but also make [that idea] recognizable in the larger public arena," in Francesco Casetti's words.[7]

Highlighting the specificities of this group of films does not mean removing them from ongoing film and colonial histories. I emphasize the relations these sound features and documentaries have with the cinematic traditions of the silent era, which lasted until 1931 in Italy and thus throughout the first decade of Fascist rule. Continuities exist in representations of colonial landscapes and subjects, and the Orientalist plots of the 1920s influenced empire films of the 1930s. Most Italian empire film commissions were given to directors who had begun their careers during the silent era and possessed the experience to handle big budgets and complicated location shoots. Similarly, although the imperial years reveal the weight of Fascist totalitarianism, liberal and Fascist expansionisms shared many tactics and ideologies. From the late nineteenth century through the 1930s, the pursuit of colonies had a huge symbolic as well as geopolitical importance, due to Italy's Roman heritage, its late unification (1870), and its weak power position within Europe.[8] Popular and elite enthusiasm for colonies as stages for the demonstration of Italian modernity to the world began not with Ethiopia but with the historic use of airpower in Italy's 1911–1912 war with Turkey over Libya. Yet Mussolini's obsession with prestige and renewal brought the intertwining of empire with aims of nationalization and modernization to a new level. Most empire films give starring roles to Italian technologies (communication, military, agricultural, and medical devices), and their scenes of mass battle and labor have a political as well as cinematic rationale. They assert the Italians' ability to impose a vision of modernity in sync with Fascist social and military aims, one founded on the regimentation of bodies and the mastery and transformation of terrain.

As the study of empire cinema sheds light on Italian film and imperial histories, it also illuminates histories of Italian mobility. On-screen and in their production practices, these movies engage "the differentiated histories of movement that were central to the imperial process." I set my textual analyses within an account of the intertwined flows of human, material, and filmic resources occasioned by Fascist expansion. My narrative encompasses physical travel—the movements of those who made films about the regime's military occupations—as well as imaginative travel, both the journeys of the protagonists of the films I examine and the journeys of the spectators who watched those films at home and in the colonies. Modernity has been made in these points of crossing and contact, not only those on the ground in the colonies, but those constituted by the meeting of films and their viewers.[9] Fascist visions of empire involved utopian desires to police the former kinds of encounters, minimizing the circulations and cross-cultural fertilizations endemic to war and imperial expansion. The anxieties generated by these tensions between mobilization and mobility found expression through the nomad, a figure that wanders through the films I examine and the Italian and Mediterranean histories they evoke. As a metaphor of mobility, the nomad conjured all that Fascism feared: uncontrolled movement, ephemerality, and the absence of national or territorial loyalties. In empire features, this figure and its values are referenced obliquely but consistently through personages who represent transience and national and biological hybridization. Although they often carry the narrative and the spectacle, they are ultimately removed from the scene, so that the colonies can become ideal "homelands," as described by James Clifford: safe spaces where mobility can be controlled, within and across borders, and where the values of stasis and purity are asserted against the historical forces of movement and contamination.[10]

At the same time, the regime's propaganda machine marketed empire—not least through film—as a project of expansion and inclusiveness for Italians, of participation in "a larger design" that held out the potential for transplantations and resettlements. As I argue, this involved not only the fantasy of an Italian Mediterranean, but something even more grandiose: an imperial-diasporic nation that encompassed Italians in the colonies, the metropole, *and* in Italian communities abroad. Italo Balbo's flights from Italy to South and North America and throughout the Mediterranean in the late 1920s and early 1930s publicized this triangulated national collective. Cinema, along with the airplane and radio, was tasked with sustaining the bonds of patriotism and kinship throughout this *grande Italia*, with Ethiopia soon added to the places where Italians all over the world could "come home" to. The advice columnist in *Cinema Illustrazione* who nonchalantly consoled a lonely reader that "trains, airplanes, and precision rifles have abolished distances" could have added cinema to that list. The mobile medium of cinema allowed Italians to follow Italy's military expansion as it unfolded, but remained there after the guns fell silent to trace the empire's affective dimension, presenting Italian stories that moved from Buenos Aires or Djibouti to Ethiopia. With their themes of travel and their characters who are rarely already in the imperial setting but arrive from somewhere else, Fascist empire films sought out the spectator who had a thirst for mobility, who "did not only want to live stories, emotions, and passions, but also the movements of the world."[11]

Italian Fascism's Empire Cinema also attends to the ways that empire films depended on mobilities behind the camera. Shot partly on location in Ethiopia, Libya, and Somalia in collaboration with the Italian armed forces, with the participation of hundreds (and occasionally thousands) of Italian and colonial soldiers and indigenous extras, empire film productions were marketed as militaristic enterprises. The making of such films became a surrogate form of military service for directors, cast, and crew. As I contend, the production of empire films may be understood within the context of policies of indigenous governance and labor, and film sets in the colonies absorbed the racial and social dynamics of their surrounding societies. Controlled chaos and constant movement marked most colonial film shoots: clans traveled hundreds of miles to reach locations, female prostitutes arrived from the cities to service the troupes/troops, and rain could render carefully chosen locations unusable. These difficult circumstances can be gleaned from press accounts about productions, but at times also infringe on the diegetic world—such as in the unscripted glimpses of uncertainty or sadness in young female extras who were taken from their families to perform in the production. What Laura Mulvey has written for the British case holds for Italian empire cinema as well: "These moments of affect condense time, returning the spectator to their original instant." They call out to the viewer, reminding her of the human costs of the relations of imperial dominance that sustained the making of such movies in Africa.[12]

The directors who made these imperial journeys of the late 1930s had their own histories of movement, including some that Fascist propaganda sought to minimize. With few exceptions, empire filmmakers formed part of the collective migration of Italian film professionals abroad that took place in the late 1920s due to the collapse of the national industry. Circulating among Europe's film capitals, taking work with French, German, and American studios, directors, actors, and technicians gained firsthand exposure to foreign production models and styles in the crucial years of the transition to sound. While all of them eventually returned to Italy, empire films were the work of individuals "who were themselves nomads and vagabonds, who found inspiration above all in the act of *transiting*, in the continual changes of residences and horizons," as Alberto Farassino has written.[13] The relationships forged in these years often outlived political changes, as continuities in Italian-German collaborations from Weimar to Nazi Germany show. Even in years of autarchy, empire films formed part of a web of "international markets, transnational migrations, and image flows." My approach takes account of the mobilities of the film industry—those circulations of bodies, texts, styles, capital, and technologies that took place in and among dictatorships and democracies alike.[14]

The empire films discussed in this book are restless texts stylistically as well. They draw on the American Western, French colonial cinema, international Orientalist and desert warfare films, Nazi German war documentaries, and Allied World War II combat movies. They blend melodrama and realism, theatricality and documentary. This hybridity also marked movies about the French and British empires, and what Charles O'Brien says of French film also resonates for Italian case: "The journeys of the film's narratives often coincide with border crossings at the level of style and mode of address, in which encounters with alterity are signified through transformations of filmic space."[15] I highlight in particular the passages between documentary and fiction within empire films. For reasons of "authenticity" and entertainment, French and British empire features made use of documentary footage of local landscapes, peoples, and customs and used indigenous inhabitants as extras or as actors with speaking parts. Italian empire filmmakers engaged in similar practices, but paid equal attention to Italian military men, featuring real soldiers as actors and extras. Their incorporations of documentary footage and conventions were crucial in these movies' address to the spectator, but also point up the instability of the visual as a category through which the Fascists attempted to mediate Italians' attitudes toward and experience of the colonies. Switching between film forms and quality of stock can be a source of interruption and instability within the text and the confrontation with "the real" an opening to realms of history and emotion of unpredictable effect.

My study contends that by the early 1940s, the close relationship between feature and documentary film had become a hallmark of Italian empire cinema culture: alternating between fiction and nonfiction projects was the norm for most cameramen and some empire film directors. I thus examine empire features within the context of contemporary newsreels and documentaries. As works of collage and compilation, the Istituto Luce's imperial-themed productions form part of an interwar culture of cinematic experimentation (such as Esther Shub's Soviet Russian compilations) and reflection about the role of the archive and the different political possibilities of fiction and nonfiction cinema. Luce created its own vast store of imperial images that were used in photographs, documentaries, and features, but also relied on the still and moving image collection it had acquired from the Colonial Museum of Rome, which dated back to the liberal years and included found footage.[16] By the end of the regime, the intermedial circuits upon which Fascist propaganda depended, and the practices of recycling and sharing footage among different film forms, had created a viewing public and a culture of film criticism habituated to slippages between fiction and nonfiction. Italian neorealism would open a new chapter of these experiments.

Italian Fascism's Empire Cinema also reflects on the relationship of cinema and history during this dramatic time.[17] The Fascists had long claimed that the regime was making history through its bold revolutionary policies, but billed the invasion of Ethiopia as an epoch-making event. Redemption and revenge figured heavily—Ethiopia had defeated Italy at Adwa in 1896—but so did a sense that the country was reshaping its collective destiny: following the Fascist (and Futurist) credo of war as a cleansing and transformative experience, imperial battlefields emerged in state propaganda as laboratories of a new Italy and new Italians. The Fascist official Alessandro Pavolini's account of his air squadron's bombing of Adwa conveys the feeling of a portentous and dense national moment:

> History is a fluid that converges now in one area and now in another according to the times: it fills a vast atmosphere or concentrates on only one point. Right now we feel it focused on what is happening up here among us, in this little aerial cell.... [Galeazzo, Mussolini's son-in-law] Ciano lowers his hand and pushes the little button. We all follow with our eyes the bomb's hit.[18]

Empire film intervenes here, using its audiovisual arsenal to render the transformational energies of mass combat, the epic scale of the imperial endeavor, and the power of the gaze to instantiate the work of destructive creation. The features presented here register the redemptive trajectories of their male protagonists through their story lines and in their treatments of collective destiny and temporality. The sense that the scale of the Ethiopian invasion, and the stories it generated, could not be adequately communicated by traditional means of representation circulated in both the film and the political press. The interest in using film to write these new histories led one critic to call for the creation of "the figure of the cinematographic historiographer" and fostered reflections about the different roles that documentary and feature film could play in this regard, with the documentary considered as "an instrument of propaganda [but] above all an archive for history."[19]

I work from a specific conception of history in my considerations of this theme, privileging movies about the histories then being created by imperial conquest rather than films about remote eras (such as Gallone's *Scipione l'Africano*, 1936). The protagonists of empire films are often in flight from their own pasts; their destinies are fully tied to actuality, to the instantiation of a new era through conquest. Even 1927's *Kif Tebbi*, which takes place during the 1911–1912 Italo-Turkish War over Libya, does not assert itself as a historical film, but uses costumes and settings that reinforce its present-oriented messages about the necessity of fostering Arab collaboration. This focus on the contemporary also motivates the documentary dimension of these films, which incorporate indices of present-day reality to establish their authority as interpreters of current events. Empire films also stage histories that more rarely find documentation. Personal or collective histories, grounded in "embodied knowledge and experiences of the senses," are glossed through resonant material or sound objects, or through iconic images that serve as "condensations, compressed sites of historical 'memory.'" Teshome Gabriel's notion that film, as opposed to historiography, deals with "emotion, loss, the past, relying not so much on full or completed narratives but on collections of fragments," informs this study, as does Robert Rosenstone's contention that film's power as a medium for narrativizing histories lies less in its reconstruction of fact than in its conveyance of "intensity and insight, perception and feeling."[20] As they tell their stories of Italian occupation, empire films also evoke other histories—fraught and forbidden, unrealized or unrepresentable—addressing the spectator through allusions and references flashed on-screen.

Empire cinema's engagement with Fascist violence provides one example. A re-evaluation of Fascism's politics of violence has highlighted the enduring influence of squadrism—the bands of Black Shirts who terrorized Italians from 1919 onward, clearing the way for Mussolini's claim to power—and the crucial role of the Ethiopian War in legitimizing a new wave of squadrist violence.[21] Empire film culture fed this revival of squadrist energies, starting from the number of Fascist officials involved in film policy who had squadrist pasts, who included every minister of popular culture until the fall of the regime; Luigi Freddi, head of the studio complex Cinecittà and the guiding muse of *Il grande appello;* and Francesco Giunta, former undersecretary of state and the producer of *Lo squadrone bianco.* Publicity for empire features channeled the spirit of squadrism, and the Militia (the military organization created in 1923 to house squadrists) was the subject of eighteen documentaries between 1936 and 1942. Empire films traffic in squadrism's symbolic heritage, signaling their participation in the culture of Fascist violence through the display of signs, objects, bodily gestures, and language designed to resonate with spectators in the know: flashes of daggers, flags, trucks laden with soldiers, certain phrases in graffiti or in dialogue.[22] Empire features also register official nervousness about controlling such violence. War scenes sometimes resolve in frames saturated with dust, sand, or smoke, which model a memory politics that left violent acts on the settlements and battlefields of North and East Africa. My readings of these works bring this cloaked violence to light, teasing out what Mulvey calls "imperialism's blind spot"—the residues of a reality "unseen (or overlooked) by its perpetrators," that remained out of vision, like the works themselves, until recent years.[23]

THE PLAN OF THE WORK

Eight chapters and an epilogue compose *Italian Fascism's Empire Cinema*. Chapter 1 lays out the analytical frames and themes of the work, touching on masculinity in empire films, spectatorship, and the positioning of cinema as a technology of imperial conquest. Chapter 2 traces the involvements of Italian cinema with the Italian colonies up to the invasion of Ethiopia, privileging the encounter with Libya in feature cinema through a reading of *Kif Tebbi*. Chapter 3 covers the years 1936–1939 and maps the different film cultures that shaped the making of empire films and their reception in Italy and the colonies. Chapter 4 discusses *Il grande appello* and *Luciano Serra, pilota*, both set in Ethiopia, as empire films that position Italy as a diasporic-imperial nation. I examine the latter film within the Fascist cult of aviation, setting up a discussion that will be continued in Chapter 8.

Chapters 5 and 6 focus on imperial bodies: their depictions in empire films, their utilizations and exploitations behind the camera, their place in Fascist schemes of sensory re-education. Chapter 5 examines empire films about the culture of imperial command and relationships between Italians and *askaris* (*Lo squadrone bianco* and *Sentinelle di bronzo*, set in Libya and Somalia, respectively). Chapter 6 treats two movies set on plantations in Ethiopia and Somalia: *L'Esclave blanc* and *Sotto la Croce del Sud*. These dramas about interracial relationships also engage themes of imperial labor, with the slaveries of love prospected in the films a screen for slaveries of work that will continue long after the forbidden unions are interrupted. Both chapters demonstrate the tensions of empire cinema between the mobilization of the senses and mandates to go beyond the domain of individual desire. This injunction, which surpasses the ethics of patriotism and military duty expressed in contemporary American and European films, lies at the core of Fascist totalitarianism.

Chapters 7 and 8 take place during World War II. The former chapter outlines how Italy's 1940 entry into the conflict affected existing film cultures and policies and addresses the challenges of managing representations of a losing war. I also discuss the "fictionalized documentaries" made by Francesco De Robertis and Rossellini for the Italian Navy Cinema Center in conjunction with the commercial production house Scalera. Chapter 8 examines the features *Un pilota ritorna* and *Bengasi* and argues that the conflict brought the empire cinema formula to an impasse. With empire crumbling, empire film is subsumed into the category of war and propaganda cinema, but Genina's and Rossellini's movies represent a search for new models of political cinema. *Bengasi* takes the empire film into a new kind of narrative—the occupation drama—that Rossellini would make famous after 1945. The epilogue discusses the fate of empire cinema in the aftermath of defeat and the loss of the colonies, from the nostalgic remakes and reissues of the 1950s to their placement "in the closet" of Italian film and imperial history.

NOTE ON TERMS AND LANGUAGE

I have followed current usage of scholars of Africa in my use of Arabic, Amharic, Somali, and Tigrinya terms and place-names, but have retained original place- and other names when quoting from period sources. For a useful lexicon of Italian colonial terms, see Laura Ricci, *La lingua dell'impero*. All translations are my own unless stated otherwise in the notes. Although Fascist-era publications often use the terms "imperial" and "colonial" interchangeably, to recognize the specificity of the years that followed upon the declaration of the Italian East African Empire in 1936, I use the term "colonial" to refer to policies and films made before that date and "imperial" for policies and films made between 1936 and 1943.

ITALIAN FASCISM'S
EMPIRE CINEMA

Empire Cinema
Frames and Agendas

On October 2, 1935, Benito Mussolini stepped out on the balcony of Rome's Piazza Venezia to address the largest rally in the fourteen years of the Fascist regime. Surrounded by microphones and movie cameras, the Italian leader hailed his audience:

> Blackshirts of the Revolution! Men and women of all of Italy! Italians all over the world, beyond the mountains and beyond the seas: listen well! A solemn hour is about to sound in the history of the fatherland. At this moment twenty million men occupy the public squares of all Italy. Never in the history of mankind has there been seen a more gigantic spectacle. Twenty million men: one heart, one will, one decision.

The decision to which Mussolini referred was that of invading Ethiopia, an act that would avenge the Italians' defeat at Adwa by Ethiopian troops almost forty years earlier. The regime had planned the invasion since 1934, and Italian soldiers stood ready at the Ethiopian-Eritrean border even as the Duce told Italians to follow "the wheel of destiny" and avenge their offended honor. The Fascists resembled French and British imperialists in justifying their expansionism with the rhetoric of the civilizing mission, but were perhaps unique in proclaiming the arrogant European, with his history of disregard for Italy, as the enemy along with the African. As Mussolini told his listeners, Ethiopia *and* the Great Powers conspired to "deprive us of a bit of a place in the sun." The League of Nations sanctions scandalously supported "an African country . . . without a shadow of civilization," over "a People of poets, artists, heroes, saints, navigators, and transmigrants (*trasmigratori*) . . . to whom humanity owes some of its greatest achievements." The Italian leader invoked what Avishai Margalit has termed "episodic memory," or the memory of past emotions, such as collective humiliations, as a means of catalyzing Italy: the rationale for aggression rested on the reiteration of a *récit* of national victimization. "*Ora basta!* / We've had enough!" roared Mussolini, declaring war not only against Ethiopia but against an entire international system that placed Italy in a subaltern state.[1]

Although the Duce pledged that the war would not escalate into a European conflict, the Ethiopian invasion set into motion a chain of destructive events that contributed to the outbreak of World War II. It weakened the League's authority, destabilized European diplomatic relations, and flaunted state sovereignty and multiple international protocols, including those relating to chemical weapons. These were used in quantities well beyond military necessity; Italy's massive employment of aviation and gas, along with the industrial scale of the mobilization, made Ethiopia an "experimental field of violence" for the next five years. Six months later, the Italians announced victory in Ethiopia and the establishment of the Italian East African Empire. Entrenched Ethiopian resistance made this "conquest" unstable and incomplete, though, and the new military engagements and occupations (Spain, 1937; Albania, 1939) Italy began as part of the Axis alliance strained its resources to the limit even before the outbreak of World War II.[2] Inside Italy the Ethiopian war was also a watershed event. The country's farther extension into sub-Saharan Africa intensified existing anxieties about the safeguarding of racial purity and the production of Italians who were fit for imperial command. After 1935 the regime's military goals increasingly conditioned every aspect of Fascist policy. The imperial years ultimately ended in a spiral of loss, the fall of the colonies (starting in 1941) followed by Fascist Italy's surrender to the Allies on September 8, 1943.

LOCATING EMPIRE CINEMA

The Mediterranean was the field of action upon which Fascist imperial agendas depended, and it was subject to reinventions and re-imaginings that are visible in the realm of empire film. Control of the Mediterranean, Mia Fuller observes, held the key to achieving Italian autonomy from Europe and to reversing a history of marginalization within the continent by making Italy the vital hinge between Europe and Africa. This notion of Italian influence extending through and beyond the Mediterranean connected to the revival of Rome as a model of imperial power. Rome and the ideology of *romanità* served the Fascists as a "utopia of the past" that supposedly differentiated Italy's imperial vision from that of contemporary powers while providing a historical justification for Fascist expansion.[3] This Fascist construction of the Mediterranean as *mare nostrum*, a space "saturated with a timeless Roman and Italian essence," required its elision as a site of "cultural crossovers, contaminations, creolizations, and uneven historical memories." In Fascist propaganda, this meant splitting off of the "Roman" Mediterranean from the "Oriental" Levant. In the case of the Dodecanese Islands, this translated into an intention to "reclaim" Rhodes and other territories from Turkish influences, the Turk standing in for a history of Oriental backwardness and lassitude. Yet this "other" Mediterranean surfaces in Fascism's empire cinema, which is haunted by the basin as a "fluid and unstable archive" of the kinds of wanderings and intercultural fusions the Fascists so feared.[4]

Empire films bear the marks of such tensions, despite the heavy political demands upon them relative to the rest of Fascist-era cinematic production.[5] Designed to placate the international community by highlighting the humanitarian aspects of Italy's colonization, empire films also asserted Italian military strength. They aspired to compete with Hollywood and other foreign productions for the attentions of audiences abroad as part of a strategy of achieving influence through "two peaceful but very potent arms: culture and commerce." By demonstrating the benevolence and the authority of Italian rule, they aimed to convince inhabitants of occupied territories to collaborate with the regime. And they were to mobilize Italians at home and in Italian communities abroad for combat and settlement in the colonies, creating a constituency for empire and expanding the scope of Italians' national allegiances and imaginaries. This was no small matter, considering that in the early 1930s, after ten years of Fascism and forty years of Italian colonialism, fewer than forty-five thousand Italians had settled in the colonies, out of a population of forty million. Although the occupation of Ethiopia and a mass transfer of twenty thousand Italians to Libya in the late 1930s increased these numbers to more than three hundred thousand by the end of the decade, the vast majority of Italians never set foot in Africa. *L'Oltremare* remained just that, a realm "beyond," even for those who considered the Mediterranean "our sea." This situation, along with the restrictions on movement and the relative provincialism of Italian culture, clarifies the regime's particular investment in film as a window on the colonies and creator of imperial consciousness.[6]

The multiple propagandistic agendas and markets of empire films, their politically sensitive nature, and the substantial capital investment they necessitated meant that most of them took shape at the very vertices of the regime. The Duce's son Vittorio Mussolini, the director of *Cinema* and a pilot who served in Ethiopia and Greece, played a central role in empire cinema culture. His name appears as producer, screenwriter, supervisor, and investor, and he also acted behind the scenes as an influential liaison with censors and other officials. And empire features benefited lavishly from the new financial incentives and assistance the regime offered filmmakers after 1935: *Il grande appello, Lo squadrone bianco, Bengasi, Un pilota ritorna,* and *Luciano Serra, pilota,* all received production advances. Empire productions also could count on state-orchestrated publicity campaigns, including visits by journalists to sets that were celebrated as sites for the reinforcement of martial and authoritarian values. Finally, empire films lay at the heart of the regime's agenda of building a distinctively Italian cinema that would woo Italian and foreign spectators, strengthening national identity at home and exporting national culture and Fascist values abroad.

Market conditions, as well as political fervor, lay behind this financial and symbolic investment. By 1936 cinema accounted for 79 percent of all national spending on spectacle (including music, drama, sport events, exhibitions, and fairs), and this increased to 91 percent by 1941. But American movies accounted for most of that cinematic consumption. In 1927 nearly 80 percent of the films Italians saw came from American studios, and even in 1938, in the full flower of the racial and autarchic campaigns, Hollywood films accounted for 73.6 percent of Italian box-office receipts.[7] Empire films figured heavily in the strategies devised by Fascist officials to remedy this situation. As films of conquest set in exotic locales, they would have the appeal of popular American genres (adventure and war films, Westerns, melodramas) and the allure of Orientalist films. Yet they would tell uniquely Italian stories, publicizing a colonial experience that was little known abroad. They would also draw on the genres that had made Italian production internationally famous since the silent era, such as large-scale costume pictures, while satisfying the regime's desire for features that directly engaged with Fascist imperial campaigns and ideology.[8]

The corpus of empire films reflects this diversified mandate, highlighting the clash between the regime's nationalizing ambitions for film and the cosmopolitan nature of the interwar film industry. Their settings and actors may be "national-imperial," but these movies display influences of and affinities with foreign film traditions. Such cosmopolitanism marked empire films everywhere, and Italian thinking and practice were shaped through an ongoing critique of British, French, and American nonfiction and feature films. Although the regime held up the banner of cinematic autarchy, in practice it continued to tacitly encourage assimilations of foreign styles in the interest of creating compelling spectacles that would please Italian, international, and colonial audiences. The fact that *Lo squadrone bianco* was based on the French novel *L'Escadron blanc* by Joseph Peyré did not prevent it from winning the Mussolini Cup at the 1936 Venice Biennale for "best Italian film."

EMPIRE FILMS AS TECHNOLOGIES OF IMPERIAL CONQUEST

Most Italian empire films are war films: they stage dramas of conquest and occupation and, during World War II, dramas of defeat as well. Battle scenes, sometimes of mammoth scale, figure in all but one of the films discussed in this book, and real military men, rather than actors, make up the rank-and-file combatants seen on-screen. These men utilize weapons and matériel on loan from the armed forces, which also supplied consultants to verify the accuracy and feasibility of the directors' envisioned military maneuvers. Empire films provide a means of investigating the relationship of war and cinema during the later years of the Italian dictatorship. Both feature and documentary films on imperial themes diffused a new mode of seeing, born during World War I, that united the gaze with the potential to inflict violence and positioned the camera operator alongside the bomber and machine gunner as a force for the creation of history. Aerial warfare had great importance in this regard. The prominence given to aviation within many empire films mirrors its importance within Fascist culture as a realm where older fantasies of movement and conquest came together with the new cultures of violence made possible by changes in military technologies. Pavolini was one among many who exalted the creative destruction made possible by the airplane and long-range combat, with the military commander's "clear eye, its precision multiplied by binoculars and calculations" replacing the view of the poet or painter. Empire features and documentaries showcase these strategies of visual domination, celebrating them as the first stage of the conquest and transformation (*bonifica*) of indigenous peoples and their terrains.[9]

The production process of empire films in the colonies also reinforced cinema's function as a technology of conquest and governance. Shooting on location in the colonies, in close collaboration with the Italian military, offered occasions for film professionals to vaunt their own martial experiences and virile qualities. For directors and their assistants, who often were in charge of hundreds or thousands of Italian and *askari* soldiers and indigenous extras, it provided a chance to have their own experiences of colonial command. Alessandrini, who utilized twelve thousand Eritreans for battle scenes in his 1939 film *Abuna Messias*, recalled in the 1970s that the scale of these productions, and the risks involved, often made the production of the film more compelling than the film itself. Comparing his directorial actions to those of a military authority, he mused that it was often "hard to remember that you are there to tell a story." At times, as in the case of Marcellini and other Luce documentarians, filmmaking coincided with and formed a component of their military service in Africa. Michael Geyer's description of the militarized European societies of the interwar period as ones in which "war ascribed status to individuals and lent meaning to the 'work' of those who participated in it" fits the culture and character of the world of Italian empire cinema, with its blurred lines between military and cultural practice.[10]

Filmmaking in Libya, Somalia, and Ethiopia also relied on and formed part of larger systems of military governance and colonial labor, with

FIGURE 1.1.

The camera as weapon, I, Ethiopia, 1936. Used by permission of Luce Cinecittà, Archivio Foto Cinematografico

indigenous participation in films subject to the same practices of surveillance and exploitation that marked Fascism's African occupations in general. *Askari* soldiers were in fact the largest source of film extras and were preferred by directors for the linguistic and obedience training they had received from their military experiences. A chain of service obligations links indigenous participation in real battles, cinematic re-creations, and appearances in parades and colonial exhibitions in the metropole and colonies. On-screen, indigenous characters with speaking parts not only act as "ethnic specimens," broadcasting their colony's human resources and visual attractions, but also advertise Fascism's abilities to domesticate and orchestrate its native populations. Hassan Mohamed, the Somali lead of *Sentinelle di bronzo,* whose character alternates military service with duties at a colonial exposition in Italy, received prominent billing in the credits and in publicity materials, as did Berclè Zaitù Taclè, the female lead in *Abuna Messias*. The making of empire films proved difficult and divisive for many tribespeople, though. Transporting entire clans long distances from home disrupted local economies, and large productions sometimes "inundated and occupied an entire indigenous village," in the words of the director of production Franco Cappelletti. Italians' insensitivity to local rivalries often exacerbated bad feelings, especially when warring groups were asked to act as allies, although it was also dangerous to assign warring peoples to act as enemies: Alessandrini had to issue the Galla and Amhara wooden weapons during the making of *Abuna Messias* after a series of real-life woundings.[11]

Empire film sets were thus shaped not only by Italian production cultures but also by imperial social and economic relations in all their complexity. Sites of exploitation, intimidation, and resistance, these shoots also became spaces of informal socializing, where blacks and whites forged working and other relationships. In their situations of racial imbalance, too (hundreds or sometimes thousands of indigenous men directed by a few whites), they register the colonies' everyday realities. This extends to the question of interracial sex and socializing in the face of the 1937 racial laws. The hyper-masculine production culture of empire films encouraged amorous encounters between black women and white men, even on the sets of movies whose plots warned against such entanglements. Far from forbidding such encounters, colonial officials acted as procurers: the governor of Asmara sent prostitutes for the crew of *Sentinelle di bronzo*, and the governor of Somalia rounded up local beauties for nude screen tests in front of *L'Esclave blanc*'s makers. The journalist Ettore Mattia, who was present on the set of *Abuna Messias*, which utilized thousands of indigenous men and women, later remembered this production fondly as offering men a respite from racial laws that criminalized their relationships with native women. Fuller's comment that "Italians displayed a partial indifference to difference" certainly holds true for the culture of empire filmmaking.[12]

Careful readings of accounts of empire film productions can uncover clues to how Italian attitudes and behaviors may have been received by African actors and extras. The diplomatic phrase "much patience was required," often used by observers, suggests resistances to filming beyond African superstitions or fears of technology. Delayed production schedules or mistreatment provoked threats by some African actors and extras to abandon the set, while others refused to act if they discovered they had been tricked into performing under false pretenses. In such cases scenes had to be re-shot with replacements. On the set of *L'Esclave blanc,* indigenous actors had to be paid extra to interpret the part of the enemy, since they did not want to be portrayed as losing to the Italians, and their recalcitrance to re-enacting their defeat persisted during filming. African translators and guides played intermediary roles here, conveying actors' objections as well as suggestions about correct ways to portray their rituals and dress. Although Italian film professionals sometimes presented the camera to native actors as an extension of Mussolini's gaze, on many sets the Duce might not have liked what he would have seen, whatever the ideological message of the finished film.[13]

MOBILITY AND GENDER IN EMPIRE FILMS

The movements tracked throughout this book encompass various categories of crossings and travel (emigration, colonization, military service, tourism, wartime dislocation), as well as virtual voyages made by the film viewer. Fascist empire films channeled those histories of movement, inviting the spectator to enter into what Jean Duvignand calls a "'vehicular universe" that privileges "the journey, displacement, translation." Mussolini gave political form to such dreams of mobility, from his original roving squads, to his integration of the Futurists' exaltation of speed into Fascist ideology, to his investment in the air, rail, and road networks in Italy and the colonies.[14] Empire films contributed to this glamorization of mobility, and it is telling that the Scalera production house got its capital from the giant commissions for imperial roads awarded to its founders. In practice, mobility had many constraints: the imperial years saw an expansion of state attempts to control the movements of the population in and around metropolitan and colonial cities (and regulate interracial contacts in the latter), and widespread poverty among Italians meant that labor and military service represented the first opportunity many had to gain firsthand experience of foreign territories, languages, and customs. Walter Benjamin's wry observation that "never has freedom of movement stood in greater disproportion to the abundance of means of travel" fits most Italians under Mussolini. Commercial films of the 1930s register this situation, with an errant protagonist experiencing the frisson of new places, only to ultimately renounce all fantasies of geographic and other mobility. The year 1938's *Partire/Departure* (Amleto Palermi) is symptomatic: it begins with an unemployed Neapolitan gazing wistfully at departing ocean liners and ends with him settled happily in the Italian countryside.[15]

These histories of movement and desire create narrative and spectacular tension in empire films, shaping their plotlines, moods, and characterizations. Mediterranean crossings figure in every film I examine, and they initiate travelers into unstable realms of cultural translation and personal transformation. In fact, the personages of these films about transit, conquest, and settlement never really settle. Drama comes from their confrontations with their new surroundings—both people and landscapes are protagonists here—and in their struggles for self-mastery. Duty, whether familial or political, wars with the pull of adventure and the various libidinal temptations that could lead to the Mediterranean swamp of decadence and colonial dissolution. In staging these conflicts, empire films are revealing of the "driving symbols, desires, and tropes" that undergirded the Italian imperial project. What Charles Burdett has written of travel writing to the colonies and elsewhere of the Fascist period—"it is precisely in the presentation of the travelling subject that one finds the most concentrated engagement with the prevailing belief systems of the period"—is equally valid for films structured around voyages of flight across the Mediterranean.[16]

The traveling subject privileged in this book is male, since military men are the protagonists of almost all of the films I examine. Both on- and off-screen, that male subject bore the burden of Fascism's ideological tensions: he had to be daring and aggressive yet ready to submit to his superior and unafraid of personal sacrifice. Mussolini was the model here. He was celebrated as a virile hero, but also as a frugal person who worked hard, ate little, and drank less. The regime called both dimensions of Fascist manhood into play in its imperial politics. As Giulietta Stefani and Alessandro Bellassai have argued, the colonies served the cause of national renewal by acting ideally as sites of "therapy for masculinity." The frontier nature of colonial life would allow men to reclaim a physicality and camaraderie imperiled by contemporary urban existence. Proximity to temptation, female and other, was part of this physicality and colonial service's appeal. In empire films, the primacy of the homosocial is asserted by plotlines that ultimately remove the Italian woman from colonial space and dramatize the intensity of male engagements. Hierarchies of dominance take shape through visual exchanges, occupation and movements through space, aural cues, and bodily appearances that resonate with extra-cinematic Fascist male iconographies.[17]

Screen masculinity provides a useful lens to approach the meeting of foreign and national cinematic traditions in empire films and the tensions between the agendas of political and commercial filmmaking. Hollywood remained the template for male stars, and Italian actors had to compete with its leads for audience loyalty; Amedeo Nazzari was presented to Italian audiences as the Italian Errol Flynn. Still, Italian stars were constrained by official ambivalence about that aspect of the Hollywood model, and all male stars existed in a subordinate relation to Mussolini, the supreme divo of the Fascist era. The Duce attended to his own fan base by sending out signed "postcards," including a summer image of him in his bathing suit looking through a movie camera, which appeared in the August 1935 issue of *Lo Schermo*. In practice, stars were necessary for commercial reasons, and they also figured in the regime's pedagogical ambitions to use movies to model the behaviors and language of male command. Empire films had an important role in this regard, and they launched the careers of major leads such as Nazzari and Fosco Giachetti.[18]

The uniformed male body stood at the center of the particular cult of masculine appearance fostered by empire cinema. Maurizia Boscaglia has argued that the interwar period saw the consolidation of a new kind of male corporeality in Europe—powerful and "either uniformed or unclothed"—which accompanied and encouraged the flow of new circuits of consumer desire. This development had special impact during the later dictatorship, where ubiquitous civil and military uniforms symbolized a larger militarization of society. On-screen, the uniform fashioned the rituals of militarized masculinity, disseminating the fetishized male body of Fascist iconographies. The uniformed body had a pedagogical and spectacular value in its address to the viewer (who, if male, was likely often uniformed himself) and its place as a bridge between the filmic and material worlds. Drawing on positivist and racial thinking, the Fascists drew connections between appearance and behavior, and the outfitting of Italians in a burgeoning array of civilian and military uniforms took part in a larger agenda of totalitarian transformation that began with the body. Uniforms would not only "recall the wearer to a proper comportment," but would act, in Pinkus's words, as a kind of "armor," a symbol of "self-restraint against desire itself, against the libido, whether this is understood as a force coming from without or from within the body."[19] The uniform also helped men assert a command profile on the ground. Fascist authorities' private worries that Italian civilians' filthy attire "presented quite an un-imperial spectacle" translated into exhortations in colonial manuals that Italian men "take care of your clothing; err on the side of vanity.... If you have to receive dirty or rag-clad natives, dress elegantly, as though you were going to receive a beautiful woman." The uniform minimized such problems, and its standardization of body surface also aided the abstraction of the individual into the category of "governing authority," reinforcing political and racial boundaries. Hildi Henrickson's contention that colonial encounters constitute "a particular kind of semiotic event in which a visual language of bodily forms is especially critical" is affirmed by the prominence of the gleaming white uniform within the frame of empire films.[20]

Empire films also base their spectacle and emotional appeal on displays of male abjection, be it the shame of paternal failure, female domination, or the humiliation of the emigrant's life. Such treatments of threatened masculinity make for compelling spectacle, and they are designed to call forth in the viewer the kinds of emotions Mussolini exploited so ably in his construction of a cult of Italian victimhood. In this diegetic world the Italian colonies are sites of recovery and redemption: not merely settings, but active catalysts of these "dramas of conversion," as Marcia Landy terms them. Transformations register at the bodily level, through an evolution of voice, carriage, gesture, and a mastery of space that also reveal cinema's imbrications with Fascist spectacle. The male bodies inhabiting these films are "social bodies," as theorized by Pierre Bourdieu, in which learned bodily postures, expressions, and emotions reflect and reproduce social hierarchies and relations. Often, the journey from abjection to transcendence is accomplished through "the elimination of the road that leads to personal freedom and pleasure." Sometimes this elimination is absolute, in that the narrative ends with the struggling protagonist's martyrdom. Not all men could be regenerated: older male protagonists, too tainted by their experiences of abjection during the liberal era, find salvation only through sacrificial death on the battlefield, their soldier sons the ones to embody the Fascist "new man."[21]

Other times the arrival point is the sublime realm of homosociality, and then the resolution is often more ambiguous, connecting to other, homoerotic, histories and journeys that were part of the colonial experience and imaginary but could not be openly expressed. In several films examined here, those intense interactions include manifestations of male-male desire. In discussing such moments in Italian literature set during this period, Derek Duncan asks, "To what extent did the nature of Fascism compromise the homosocial contract or construct on which it was based by spilling over into the excluded realm of the homosexual?"[22] Empire films offer openings onto this other realm, under the guise of male camaraderie, in the show of bodies at battle, or in the nostalgic performances that have long been a staple of emigrant and military life. To get at these diverse journeys, I attend throughout the book to the importance of the performative dimension of masculinity: the gestures, forms of speech, and visual exchanges between men and women and men and men that enact the norms of manliness prized by the regime. The men of these films bear traces of the "amorous or hostile struggle[s]" experienced during their travels, but their ultimate journeys and battles are interior in nature as they seek to purify the body, rendering it serviceable for Fascist goals. In these films the frontier is thus not only a space "composed of interactions and interviews," as Michel de Certeau describes it, but also a space of interdictions.[23]

Such journeys across the Mediterranean had very different outcomes for men and women, both on- and off-screen. In terms of their European populations, the Italian colonies were predominantly male spaces, especially outside major cities such as Addis Ababa, Asmara, and Tripoli. The regime tried to remedy this situation, which ran counter to its settler-colony ambitions, by importing white females to work as nurses or secretaries, instituting "pre-colonial camps" for young women, and advertising Italian Africa to women as a place that "can satisfy every kind of taste, fulfill all desires, yield to the needs of all temperaments." Yet white women remained scarce, and films set in Africa register this situation, since Italian women are often present only remotely—as the mothers who must have produced the men on-screen, as the authors of letters delivered to the battlefield.[24] Indigenous women, instead, abound in empire films as pseudo-ethnographic subjects, landscape elements, and, in features, as objects of desire. Arab and sub-Saharan African women received very different treatment at the level of representation, with the Orientalist veils of the former (over)determining their depiction as sensual, silent, and statuesque, while the partial nudity of the latter licensed fantasies of unbridled sex available for the asking. The colonial labor system allowed such fantasies to materialize off-screen through a parallel indigenous sex-worker universe in North and East Africa that included city brothels, traveling units, and, before 1937, a certain degree of tolerance for longer-term involvements and cohabitations. Even after the criminalization of interracial sexual unions, the paucity of white women in the Italian colonies meant that most sexually active Italian men had intercourse with indigenous women.[25]

Fascist empire films resemble their continental counterparts in staging white male desire for exotic women, but stand out for their mandates that white men must overcome their susceptibility to women of *any* race to continue in colonial service. A number of these movies had been conceived with very little space for women characters, and the presence of strong female leads in them speaks to the triumph of production and profit imperatives. Female glamour is given a negative association, though, with Cristiana of *Lo squadrone bianco* and Mailù of *Sotto la Croce del Sud* standing for boudoir and ballroom and Levantine excess and artifice, respectively. The rigor of the colonial male world ultimately leaves no room for either: the white uniform vanquishes the white telephone in both its metropolitan and its colonial articulations. With the white female protagonist of *L'Esclave blanc* an exception, women of all races have exited that world by the end of the narrative. But along the way, for viewers, there is the charge of the interaction. Spectacles of bad behavior and beauty competed with these films' political messages and behavioral injunctions. Robin Pickering-Iazzi and Giuliana Bruno have emphasized the special appeal of movies about journeys and expansive landscapes for female spectators, who are invited to enter into states of *transito*, defined by Bruno as "circulation that includes passages, traversals, transitions, transitory states, spatial erotics, (e)motion."[26]

Desert spaces form the backdrop of these journeys of expansion and exclusion. For both men and women, deserts are unstable places, and journeys of domination can quickly degenerate into experiences of spatial dislocation. European colonial discourses often romanticized the nomad and mythologized deserts as anachronistic spaces where the rhythms and customs of an earlier, simpler, era lived on. The North African desert had particular popularity in the interwar years as "the great decompression chamber of Western civilization" for both sexes, and the nomads who inhabited it were a source of fascination. Desert spaces had been a particular escape for wealthy European women, since they allowed for a sartorial and sexual freedom (dressing and acting like a European or Arab man, dressing like an Arab woman) unknown at home. The spectacular appeal of such costuming was not lost on film producers, who cast such Hollywood stars as Marlene Dietrich in Orientalist movies such as *Morocco* and *The Garden of Allah*. The racial and masculinist concerns that inform Fascism's imperial culture skew its screen productions with respect to these Euro-American productions. Dietrich's serenades to an interracial nightclub crowd in a man's top hat and tuxedo in the former film would be unthinkable in Fascist empire movies, as would the story line of *Princesse Tam-Tam* (Edmond Gréville, 1935), in which a white French writer brings his Tunisian paramour (Josephine Baker) back to Paris. Certainly, these movies usually right the gender and racial wrongs they create: Dietrich ends up trailing through the desert in the company of goats, behind her Legionnaire lover, while Baker is dispatched back to Africa when her lover returns to his white French wife.[27] Female nomadism is how Fascist empire films express anxieties about female mobility. Two female leads are nomads who have been forcibly separated from their clans (*Kif Tebbi* and *Sentinelle di bronzo*), while others have a rootless heritage and temperament (*Sotto la Croce del Sud* and *Giarabub*), or embark on tourist vagabondages across the Mediterranean (*Lo squadrone bianco*). Above all, these movies resolve differently. Female leads are either literally driven out of colonial spaces or restored to the authority of their families when Italian victory is ensured. And homosocial bonds are proposed less as a temporary substitute for female affection, as in many French and British films, than as a different path, a sign that Fascism's re-education of the body and senses has been successful in teaching men to go "beyond women" altogether. It is this dimension that sets Fascist empire films apart from their foreign counterparts, as well as the identification of nomadism as a political as well as moral and gender threat.

EMPIRE FILMS AS EXPERIENCES OF VISION AND AUDITION

As the Fascists recognized, the cinema is itself possessed of nomadic qualities, from the transnational circulations of texts, people, and capital that lie behind its productions to the movements of desire it stages on-screen and enables in the body of the spectator. Empire films reveal the contradictions of a Fascist filmic project that offered spectators the virtual enjoyment of "travelling, crossing borders and countries, and the encounter with diversity," but also taught that the body must be overcome as "the material site of desires, the senses, happiness." This anaesthetic agenda made for a deep uneasiness about the embodied viewer, a subject who has come in for renewed critical attention in light of recent appraisals of "the basic tactility and viscerality of cinematic experience." My book follows this critical move in treating the spectator as an active agent in the making of filmic meaning through embodied experience and knowledge as well as through extra-filmic cultural references.[28]

The realm of sound plays a central role in my examination of empire cinema's diversified address to the spectator and its operation as Fascist propaganda. Film sound can stabilize the viewer, anchoring him or her within the field of constantly changing images. As employed in empire fiction and nonfiction movies, it conveys Fascist intentions to "restructure sense perception, contain spontaneity, and recast cultural difference as incompatible alterity." At the same time, it guides viewers' affect and attention, often speaking for the on-screen protagonists, as in the many empire features with a melodramatic component. Sound travels across narrational boundaries between the spectator and the character, asking us to hear but also, at times, to "identify with someone who will hear for us." As such, it is integral to cinema's interpellative dimension. Yet the aural realm offers many hints to the insecurities of Fascist rule. Mirjan Schaub's observation that "whereas the eye searches and plunders, the ear listens in on what is plundering us. The ear is the organ of fear," is particularly appropriate to the use of sound in the operation of imperial film propaganda.[29]

The voice plays a particular role in this solicitation of the spectator, not least for its quality of displaying "what is inaccessible to the image, what exceeds the visible," in Mary Ann Doane's words. Pitch and timbre communicate the inner life of a character and evoke corporeal responses in the viewer. The prominence of commanders in empire films gives them a special role in disseminating models of male vocality. Mussolini's distinctive style of speaking offered an obvious template. Officers frequently echo the Duce's rhetorical style, while radio scenes reproduce the everyday experience of hearing disembodied authoritarian speech, with its harsh and telegraphic delivery. The study of empire cinema suggests how the "space of the encounter between a language and a voice" became a political space during the dictatorship. That space was a highly unstable one. In both feature and documentary empire films, the presence of untranslated dialogue, and of exotic or unsettling vocalizations by unseen indigenous subjects, glossed that blend of alienation and attraction that lay at the core of Fascist imperial ideology, but also produced a high degree of unintelligibility for audiences with respect to French or British empire films. This was, in part, a calculated strategy by a regime that limited Italian-language instruction (and did little to facilitate Italians' knowledge of the native languages of their colonies), especially in sub-Saharan Africa, where assimilationism was feared as harmful to prestige. Both documentary and feature films support Giorgio Bertellini's assertion that sound and speech, no less than visuals, reveal the Italians' "remarkable uneasiness about confronting the African antagonist, the colonized Other, and an inner conflict centered on dilemmas of self-representation."[30]

For its abilities to touch the emotions of spectators through sound and image, and for its potential as a carrier of political messages under the guise of entertainment, cinema stood at the heart of the regime's attempts to utilize high and mass culture to transform Italian behaviors and values. Empire films did not act alone here, but as part of a larger colonial culture, and they also reinforced the modes of spectatorship encouraged by Fascist political spectacle. Colonial-themed fiction provided an important touchpoint, providing images and idioms: three of the movies I examine, *Kif Tebbi, Lo squadrone bianco,* and *Sentinelle di bronzo,* had their origins in novels or stories.[31] Fascist officials and cineastes singled out the potential of moving images to convey colonial experiences, though, due to their illusions of proximity and reality and their capacity for sensory stimulation. One month after the declaration of empire, an editorial in *Lo Schermo* argued that "the screen, more than the press, is the best means of acquainting Italians with the aspects of this new war, which will take on an epic character for the immensity and configuration of Ethiopian territory." Three years later, in the wake of a half-dozen empire films filmed in Somalia, Libya, and Ethiopia, *Cinema* sustained this view: "The screen can expose to the eyes life in those faraway lands as it unfolds freely and integrally with a concreteness that is unattainable by the writer or the ethnographic collector."[32] Still, empire cinema did its work in partnership with imperial literature and ethnography and had meaning during the dictatorship as an ensemble of texts, sights, and sounds that related to extra-cinematic domains.

I build here on Casetti's notion of the film text as "a medium for the exhibition and exchange of proposals" that often come from other realms of knowledge and experience. Studies on National Socialist and Italian Fascist cinema have pointed up the porous boundaries between film fiction and the material world and the movements of images among different media and different forms of spectacle. Such studies acknowledge the importance of textual contradictions and ambivalences, as does this book, but they also emphasize the interaction of cinematic and extra-cinematic elements as they affect film's power as a "centripetal force" for the mobilization of affect. My film readings emphasize the imbrications of figural strategies, modes of address, iconographies, and sound with nonfiction cinema and with the broader ideologies and configurations of power that structured Fascist society. Such an approach can be of particular value in studying the cinema of a regime that Emilio Gentile has described as an "experiment in political domination" characterized by ambitions of interconnectedness between the public and private spheres and among the state agencies charged with mass persuasion.[33]

At the center of this network of discourses stands Mussolini, as father figure, director of spectacle, and "superdivo protagonist of audiovisual communication." The image of the Duce—his stage name—structures the public representation of all other men in Fascist Italy, from his fellow officials to male stars, male figures in advertisements, and the "ordinary Italians" who appear in both fiction and nonfiction cinema. Mussolini channeled the silent film strongman Maciste (Bartolomeo Pagano) in his bodily stances, gestures, and physical showmanship for the camera, but language and vocality played a key role in his reach to his public, whether "live" at a mass rally or as heard on radio and film. While repeated audition of his voice was key to the hold and legitimation of his authority, the Duce also protected his uniqueness, limiting other officials' direct speech to the cameras on official occasions. Like Maciste, they were mute, spoken for by the homogenized and mechanical tones of the announcers, as if to intimate that they, too, were replaceable.[34] Mussolini's writing style, and his famous pithy turns of phrase—fruit of his journalistic experience and talents—also found mass reproduction. His mottos and sayings circulated throughout Italy and the colonies via graffiti on buildings as well as the many products of the mediatic, cultural, and educational apparatus. Mussolinian language and style also had indirect expression through its influence on the slogans and graphics of advertising, including film posters and other publicity.[35]

This 1936 photograph of Via Montenapoleone in Milan offers a glimpse of how Fascist tropes and iconographies migrated throughout the public sphere, how Mussolini's image was consumed in an intermedial context, and how the Fascists wove their messages about imperial conquest as the redress of national injury into the fabric of everyday life. Reading the image from left to right, we see the outsize *M* of the Motta advertisement, which honored the Duce; a cannon-like stick of butter blasting out of a *panettone*, labeled "Victory"; a poster for the film *Non ti scordar di me/ Forget Me Not* (Zoltan Korda, 1935), starring the Italian tenor Beniamino Gigli; and, above Gigli, a Mussolini who also urges Italians not to forget, or, rather, to continue to remember the infernal date of November 18,

FIGURE 1.2.

Imperial propaganda, Via Montenapoleone, Milan, 1936. Used by permission of Gruppo Lactalis, for Archivio Storico Galbani

1935, when the League of Nations levied sanctions against Italy. This juxtaposition of media stars encapsulates the cultural climate within which empire films developed, the cosmopolitan world of the tuxedo-clad Gigli co-existing with the truculent world of Fascist spectacle. The next chapter leads up to this dense moment, tracing the involvements of the Italian film world with Italian colonial enterprises from early cinema to 1935.

2

Italian Cinema and the Colonies to 1935

This chapter offers an overview of the imbrications and encounters of Italian cinema with the colonies up to 1935. I focus on the 1920s, a decade that has been slow to receive attention in accounts of both Italian colonial and filmic enterprises. During those years, the Fascists developed the ideologies and strategies of conquest that would serve them in Ethiopia and during World War II, quelling active rebellion in Somalia and carrying out a ruthless repression of resistance in the Libyan regions of Tripolitania and Cyrenaica. In the realm of cinema, the 1920s is normally considered a period of crisis and retrenchment, due to the collapse of production and distribution structures. Tenacious research has revealed a variegated filmic landscape, though, one characterized by a good number of colonial and exotic-themed productions.[1] I bring these imperial and filmic histories together in my reading of Camerini's 1927 work *Kif Tebbi*, which is located within the Orientalist genre that flourished internationally in the decade after World War I. My discussion of this Italian narrative of masculine redemption emphasizes the ways it sets the tone for empire films, but also highlights Orientalist elements that found less favor in the militaristic climate of later Fascism. This chapter also explores the notion of cinema as an "eye of the war" as it emerged during the Italo-Turkish War and World War I. Empire film culture of the late 1930s builds on the militarization of the cinematic apparatus and celebrates the new images made possible by advances in military and optical technologies during these years.[2]

CINEMA, WAR, AND EMPIRE: ITALIAN BEGINNINGS

The history of cinema is bound up with the history of imperial expansion and with the history of the technologies of movement that made that expansion possible. Cinema pioneers Georges Meliès's and Louis Lumière's early works include not only the well-known footage of trains arriving in Lyon and Joinville, but also shorts on slave-trading, harem dances, and Ashanti women and children who had been brought via boat and train to France for the 1897 Lyons Exhibition. Early cinema's fascination with rail travel and with the journey as an optical experience for the passenger-spectator was soon harnessed to the cause of colonial exploration and the camera's discovery of indigenous bodies to be studied in situ.[3] In the African interior, where the train rarely traveled, the camera was a primary emblem of a mobile modernity. Although the Italian case is less known, Luca Comerio, Giovanni Vitrotti, and Roberto Omegna were as active as Hans Schomburgk and other Europeans in enshrining cinema's place in the culture of empire as an instrument of documentation and political propaganda. Exploration and ethnographic films, often sponsored by Italian geographical societies, experimented with the panoramic shot and the long shot to highlight the "emptiness" of targeted landscapes, even as they documented close encounters with the inhabitants of those landscapes. This "reciprocal legitimation of the cinematic and ethnographic gaze" laid the foundations for interwar European colonial cinemas' engagements with the bodies and cultures of colonial subjects by affirming the modernity of the film apparatus, establishing the authority of the cameraman, and justifying his "ocular aggression" as necessary to the work of the civilizing mission.[4]

Comerio's extensive oeuvre is key to understanding the range of the Italian cinema's engagement with imperialism. He documented Italy's pioneering aerial bombing missions and other military operations of the 1911–1912 Italo-Turkish War, most famously in *La battaglia delle due palme/The Battle of Two Palms*, but also celebrated the parallel conquests of Italian radio technology (*L'inaugurazione della stazione radiotelegrafica di Tripoli/The Inauguration of the Radio-Telegraphy Station in Tripoli*) and the work of Italian colonial troops (*La vita degli ascari eritrei/The Life of the Eritrean Ascari*—all films from 1912). Soon after, he returned to Africa to film an expedition led by Baron Raimondo Franchetti. For decades to come, Comerio would be a protagonist of war and colonial cinema. His 1929 documentary *Dal Polo all'Equatore/From the Pole to the Equator*, composed of footage that spans a period from the early 1900s to the late 1920s, anticipates many of the themes that run through Italian empire cinema: the camera as weapon of war, the ability of modern technologies to tame and vanquish nature, performance as a lens on the essence of the "primitive," and the privileged position of the cinematic apparatus and its operator in registering all of this. There is also the positing of a chain of prosthetic sight—the camera aimed repeatedly at the targeter, with the lens pointed at the back of his head—that implicates the camera in what is being filmed. As Casetti has observed, this dynamic, in which "the observer partakes in the destiny of the observed," was integral to the emergent modern(ist) condition. It would also find articulation in totalitarian schemes of political visualization then in development.[5]

The Italian war against the Ottomans for Libya is often overshadowed due to its proximity to World War I, but it constituted a landmark event for Italy. It was unified Italy's first national war, its first foray into colonial conquest after the Adwa debacle, and its first chance to use such conquest as a stage for the demonstration of Italian modernity to the world, which was achieved through the first use of airplanes in battle for reconnaissance and for day and night bombings. At stake here was not merely the acquisition of a "fourth shore" for Italy across the Mediterranean, as Gabriele D'Annunzio (another early aviator) termed it, but the overcoming of a legacy of feelings of inferiority and backwardness with respect to the more powerful nations of Europe.[6] This preoccupation with modernity and prestige meant that Italian colonialists demonstrated little of the "melancholy discourse of nostalgia" for the disappearing exotic Other that Ali Behdad has found in the French case. Any "belatedness" that haunted Italians was largely about their late start at colonization with respect to other Europeans. The investment in technologies of movement and communication that marked Italian expansion from the liberal through the Fascist period, and the primacy given to aerial warfare and, later, to gas bombing, proclaimed to the world that Italy could overcome the shame of Adwa and prevail as a modern imperial power. Although Italy's large Socialist Party decried the Libyan occupation, Nationalist intellectuals from

D'Annunzio to the Futurists to Giovanni Pascoli lauded it in precisely these terms. Italy, "the great proletarian nation," was nonetheless "the first to beat her wings and rain death upon her enemy's camps," exalted Pascoli in 1911, referring to its bombings of Libya from the air.[7]

The Italo-Turkish War also launched the engagement of commercial cinema with Italian imperialism. At the close of the war, sensing an expanded market for features and documentaries on colonial and exotic themes, Comerio opened a branch of his production company in Tripoli. He was not alone. The Italian occupation of Libya produced more than a dozen fiction films, many of which were exported. Directors ranging from Elvira Notari (*Guerra italo-turca tra "scugnizzi" napoletani/The Italian-Turkish War among the Neapolitan "Street Urchins,"* 1912) to Gennaro Righelli (*L'eroica fanciulla di Derna/The Heroine from Derna*, 1912) celebrated the war in their own fashion; even the popular comic figure Kri Kri was conscripted (*Kri kri reduce d'Africa/Kri kri Veteran of Africa*, Giuseppe Gambardella, 1914). Some of these films presented the war as a racial encounter (*Negri comici/Comic Negroes*, 1912, or *Bianco contro negro/White against Black,* Ubaldo Maria Del Colle, 1913), while others catered to European male fantasies of the Arab female (*Bidoni e l'araba/Bidoni and the Negress*, 1914). Black and Arab characters become foils for an Italianness still in the making and deeply divided on regional lines. Such early feature films deserve further study as part of a tradition of racialized representations within the Italian cinema that carry on to and beyond the Fascist era.[8]

The start of World War I provided a new arena for military practices and strategies of violence utilized in the colonies and brought out cinema's potential as an arm of war. Newsreels and documentary films intended for mass distribution contributed much to the "mobilization of the imagination" that Jay Winter sees as one of the features of total war. They also affirmed a new mode of seeing, one characterized, in Paul Virilio's words, by "the fusion and confusion of eye and camera lens [and] the passage from vision to visualization." World War I's erosion of distinctions between home front and combat zone, and its "mobilization of all the country's resources, human and material, for the practice of violence," departed from existing concepts of how to wage war. It legitimized different ideas about war's function within society, encouraging utopian schemes of using war as a force for the remaking of race and nation. Between the 1909 Futurist exaltation of war as the "only hygiene of the world," and fascist mobilizations of entire societies for war understood as a form of social therapy, lay a conflict that inflicted years of "shock and dislocation" on a mass scale, on and off the battlefield.[9]

Innovations in military technologies also played a large role in the diffusion of new modes of perception that affected conceptions of temporality, space, and the individual within them. Although "the contact battle of physical encounter" continued, the long-range weapons deployed in land, air, and sea battle zones increasingly removed the enemy from direct sight. Aerial warfare, which brought the biggest changes in this regard, continued its prominence within Italian military strategy; by 1916 the Italian High Command's photography and cinematography unit had hundreds of operatives, Comerio among them. Aerial photography and film produced landscapes devoid of traditional points of orientation, within which "the human figure... is no longer the measure of things," as well as a different concept of the camera's relation to the reality represented. Bernd Hüppauf argues that during and after the conflict, "war was no longer the mere object of the lens; it reconstituted the very position of the camera and the photographic process within reality." In this lay its importance as a military arm *and* as a bearer of the consciousness, and conscience, of modernity.[10]

The formal integration of the cinematic apparatus into the armed forces occasioned new reflections and regulations regarding the representation of war for cameramen who remained on terra firma as well. The visual mastery of the aerial bomber was denied to those on the ground: the mobility of the camera and of its operator was limited, and grand battle scenes such as those staged in the fictional cinema were rarely possible to film. Such restrictions and the absolute novelty of the scale and nature of this first total war did spawn new cinematographic techniques and technologies. The handheld camera, the telephoto lens, and the development of more efficient viewfinders all came out of a war that offered "a great moment of experimentation in terms of the possibilities of the gaze." This collective experience of audiovision was as formative of modern taste as speeding trains and bustling cities, and films about the war diffused a modern temporality associated with "assault, acceleration, and speed."[11]

The "imperial eye" of the colonies found a deadly assist in the new military technologies that came out of World War I and the collapse between the functions of the eye and the weapon that they engendered.

Unsurprisingly, the Futurists were among the first to complain that the commercial cinema had yet to exploit the new aesthetic visions offered by the conquest of time and space. The 1916 manifesto *Futurist Cinematography* charged that the cinema, despite being a new art, had inherited all of the "literary garbage" of the novel and the theater. The future lay in films about "travel, hunting, and wars" that would give full expression to the thrill of modern mobility. Italy's film industry then ranked among the most important in the world in terms of quality and quantity: its historical colossals (Giovanni Pastrone's famous 1914 *Cabiria* chief among them) and melodramas had robust national audiences and global market placement, as did its flourishing regionalist genres. But the inflation and political unrest that followed World War I left the state and the private sector with little ability to engage in capitalization, and the first attempt to bring production, exhibition, and distribution under one aegis (the Unione Cinematografica Italiana [Italian Cinematographic Union], founded in 1919) failed in 1922.[12] Paolo Cerchi Usai has argued for a less pessimistic view of the 1920s. More than 1,300 films appeared between 1920 and 1931, with production especially robust in the first half of the decade. "Strongman" movies were popular: Camerini and Brignone directed Maciste films in the 1920s.[13] In 1927 Turin entrepreneur Stefano Pittaluga revived the silent-era powerhouse Cines, and a protectionist law that year required foreign films to be dubbed into Italian and theaters to reserve one-tenth of their programming for Italian productions. Yet the industry remained undercapitalized and without adequate exhibition and distribution networks. Even Pittaluga could not forego income from importing American sound films into Italy. So the downward spiral continued, and the 500 feature films Italy produced in 1909 fell to 144 in 1922 and 20 by 1929. Italians went to the cinema in ever-growing numbers—50 percent of leisure activity revenue went for films in 1927—but they consumed mostly foreign films, the majority of which hailed from Hollywood.[14]

Nonfiction film presented a much better situation, in part because Mussolini saw its potential for mass propaganda. Trained as a print journalist, Mussolini held entertainment films in disregard early on, classifying them with "wine, women, and chicken" as opiates the Left promised to the working class. Ignoring pleas for state subvention of the feature film industry, he invested almost exclusively in nonfiction cinema, founding the Istituto Luce (1924) and ensuring distribution for its newsreels by making their projection obligatory in commercial theaters (1927). Before radio's mass diffusion in the mid-1930s, Luce films were the main way the regime reached an adult population with still-significant rates of Italian-language illiteracy (20 percent in 1930). Luce newsreels and documentaries, such as 1926's *Dux*, were also essential in these years in establishing the Duce as Italy's preeminent male media presence, one sometimes compared to Valentino in the American press. Fascist officials also channeled resources into educational cinema, so much so that Italy was held up as a model at a 1927 international conference in Bâle on the subject and then became the host country of the new League of Nations–sponsored International Institute of Educational Cinema (IICE). Although King Victor Emanuel II funded it, Mussolini insisted that its headquarters be located in Villa Torlonia, his private residence, allowing his screening room to be outfitted with state-of-the-art equipment from Zeiss and General Electric.[15]

Although Italian nonfiction film has been less studied with respect to commercial production, it had a central role in the operation of Fascist propaganda and ideology. The practice of recycling footage among nonfiction films (and between these and feature films) and the wide array of venues that showed newsreels and documentaries (exhibitions, mobile screenings, commercial theaters, schools, parishes, mass organizations, as well as consulates and Case d'Italia abroad) meant that audiences viewed its content multiple times. Especially in the first decade of the regime, when few empire feature films were made, documentaries had particular importance in staking Fascist imperialist claims and enabling fantasies of mobility and adventure in the colonies; they presented the viewer "with a world different from his own, at a time when few people travelled." Such films also familiarized Italians with foreign-held lands (or untamed regions within Italian possessions) that *were targeted to become* part of the Fascist empire. They functioned as a type of reconnaissance film, a preamble to martial action. This is one meaning of the little Italian flag seen in *Aethiopia* (1924), which chronicled Guelfo Civinini's expedition to Ethiopia's Lake Tana ten years before the Ethiopian invasion. The 1929 expedition film *La spedizione Franchetti nella Dancalia etiopica* / *The Franchetti Expedition to Ethiopian Dancalia* also falls into this category. The choice to show *Aethiopia* at a 1925 high-profile gala for five thousand that inaugurated the Istituto Luce is telling of the prominent role the regime intended to give to colonial-themed cinema.[16]

KIF TEBBI, THE CONQUEST OF LIBYA, AND THE ASSAULT ON THE NOMADIC

Just a few years after its inception, the Istituto Luce had secured its role as the "filmic arm" of Italian colonial expansion. A group of Libya-set documentaries issued in the late 1920s, such as *Il nostro esercito coloniale/ Our Colonial Army* (1928) and *Il gruppo meharista al commando del Duca d'Aosta/The Meharist Group at the Command of the Duke of Aosta* (1928), offers a case in point. Emphasizing Libyan collaboration with Italians and offering spectacles of orderly command and desert beauty, they masked the realities of a brutal military repression of rebellious tribes in the country's interior. Although Libya held the most promise among Italian colonies as a touristic and resettlement destination, fierce local opposition had prevented the Italians from expanding beyond the coastal region. The advent of Fascism opened a path for the ruthless suppression without fear of public outcry. The brutal tactics of General Rodolfo Graziani resulted in the control of northern Tripolitania and the Saharan hinterland by 1925, but resistance in Cyrenaica persisted, thanks to the skill of the nomadic and semi-nomadic Bedouin fighters whom the Sanussi employed as their ground troops. In 1927 Mussolini had thus approved the biggest Italian military operation since the Italo-Turkish War—including more than ten thousand Italian, Eritrean, and Libyan soldiers; dozens of aerial fighters and bombers; and poison gas—and the new wave of Luce productions appeared in tandem with this onslaught.[17]

These weapons of industrial warfare proved ill matched to the stealth guerrilla tactics of the Bedouin, but the regime's solution—deporting more than one hundred thousand nomads and their allies to concentration camps deep in the desert—had its origins in ideology as well as military strategy. Graziani wished to strike at the nomad for symbolic and practical reasons: "[The nomad is] anarchic, a lover of the most absolute liberty and independence ... who uses his mobility and ease of displacement to roam immense desert territories.... [N]omadism must be considered an imminent danger, one that must be rigorously and definitively stopped and controlled."[18] The existence of colonial concentration camps, like the deportation of dissidents, dated back to the liberal period and marked other European powers' repressive strategies. But the Fascists' camps stood out for their magnitude—more than twenty-five thousand tents that housed a half-million animals and men, women, and children who were let out only to perform forced labor—as did the 185-mile barbed-wire fence that sealed off Cyrenaica from Egypt. The indigenous workers who completed the fence in four months were "trained for maximum output," as the Fascists boasted. This public pride in mass repression is also notable. Far from hiding the human tragedies they were creating deep in the desert, the regime advertised them in publications and newsreels as proof of its organization and modernity. Alessandro Lessona, undersecretary for the colonies, brought Italian and international journalists to what a 1931 Luce film termed an "encampment of nomadic tribes." The restless camera flits from extreme long shots to capture the endless rows of shabby tents to medium shots of crowds of the camp's inhabitants, but there is no mistaking the feeling of chaos and misery.[19] The camps and fence also inspired 125 pages in the glossy work *La nuova Italia d'oltremare/ The New Italy Overseas*, which justifies them as "a warning to all those who were directly or indirectly involved in keeping the rebellion alive that *this time* we intended to see this through to the end and that nothing would stop us from achieving our aim." As usual, the French and British, Italy's rivals in the region, were among the audiences for this totalitarian statement, along with Italians and Libyans. The last endured the losses. In 1931 the regime hung the resistance leader 'Umar al-Mukhtar in front of twenty thousand of his supporters, marking Cyrenaica's "pacification." Most surviving notables took the path of exile, their cultures marked for generations by "the dispersal of tribes and the provoked disintegration of collective memories."[20]

Italian empire films set in Libya mask these messy realities, trafficking in the romantic appeal of the nomad at the level of their aesthetics even as their plots settle restless Arab and Italian characters. The Orientalist trend of filmmaking that flourished internationally in the decade following World War I privileged Saharan settings and themes of mobility, and my analysis of *Kif Tebbi* within this framework explores for the Italian case "the ways Orientalist texts relate to their historical moment and/or generic formulas." Influenced by the Rodolfo Valentino vehicle *The Sheik* (George Melford, 1921) and the colonial colossal *L'Atlantide* (Jacques Feyder, 1921), Orientalist films of the silent era generally follow the male protagonists who stand for the superiority of Western civilization as they save the female lead from the lascivious or brutal Arab or African. The male hero may be a European (*Maciste contro lo sciecco/Maciste against the Sheik*, Camerini, 1926; *La sperduta di Allah/Allah's Lost Soul*, Enrico Guazzoni, 1929; *L'Esclave blanche/The White Slave*, Augusto Genina, 1927), a Europeanized native (*Kif Tebbi*), or a native who turns out to be European (*The Sheik*). In their mise-en-scène and costume design, these movies draw on an older history of Orientalist representation as enshrined in paintings, photographs, and literature.[21] Yet their dramatic tension as films also develops as they map out racial and civilizational hierarchies through encounters among woman, native man, and European man.

Considering the Camerini films *Maciste contro lo sceicco* and *Kif Tebbi* in relation to *The Sheik* can isolate how Italian features stood out from international formulas in their portrayals of masculinity and mobility. Valentino was a racially and sexually ambiguous figure in the context of silent American cinema: he may have rescued aristocratic white women, but he was himself an erotic object, and his Oriental pictures brought forth his feminization and otherness. In *The Sheik*, Valentino plays Ahmed, a Sahara desert chieftain who saves the intrepid British explorer Lady Diana, who has been kidnapped by a rival sheik. Ahmed is both titillated and irritated by Lady Diana's independence, and he soon makes Lady Diana into "a helpless captive in the desert wastes," forcing her to dress *à l'arabe*. Valentino looks at his prisoner with gleaming, lascivious eyes, but the arrival of a French friend, Raoul, calls him to his conscience. He cannot act "like a savage"—like the other sheik, who has no such scruples—because, as we find out at the close of the film, he is actually European, even sharing an English genetic patrimony with Lady Diana through his father. We have here a double set of triangulations: between good and bad Arab over the woman, and among the three men, who represent stable and unstable models of civilized Western masculinity (Raoul and Ahmed-Valentino) and Arab barbarity. Raoul is an unassuming male physical presence, the better to offset the robed splendor and dramatics of the figure of Valentino; both men claim the desert and wanderings through it as a male space and a male prerogative.[22]

The Italian iterations of this genre inherited the dilemma of dealing with the overwhelming screen presence of Valentino. Released in Italy in 1924 as *Lo sceicco*, *The Sheik* was the film most responsible for Valentino's popularity there. One solution was the path of imitation, incarnated by Marcello Spada's star turn in *Kif Tebbi*; the other was rejection, as embodied by Pagano in the tellingly titled *Maciste against the Sheik*. The latter film, shot partly on location in Tripoli, reprises the narrative of a young aristocratic woman (played by Cecyl Tryan) at the mercy of an evil sheik. Maciste is a sailor who saves her honor, but it is his partner, a young aristocrat disguised as a fellow sailor, who has physical contact with the noblewoman during and after the rescue. Pagano is an imposing strongman, but one devoid of any lustful tendencies. He is, rather, a tender giant, ministering to the ill captain on board; a good uncle, puffing contentedly on his pipe whenever the young couple shows tenderness toward each other; and the populist everyman. Clad in a sailor's undershirt for much of the film, the former dockworker's raw but benign masculinity stands out amid the theatrical costumes and settings. As an icon of national manhood, Maciste is indeed against the sheik: not only the one in his film, who represents Oriental barbarism, but also the one played by Valentino, whose ambiguous sexuality and open appetites rendered him unfit to embody Fascist masculinity. Pagano had no such problem: he served as a model for Mussolini's own stylings of Italian masculinity. The physical resemblances (strong jaw, intense eyes, imposing torso, balding heads), the populist ethos combined with imperious and imperialist gestures, and the displays of strength and athleticism all made their way from Maciste's commercial films to Duce-centric documentaries. But Pagano's star waned as the cult of the Duce consolidated: the Maciste series ended its run in 1926, a victim of the difficulties of the Italian industry, its star already forced to work periodically in Berlin.[23] That same year, Valentino suddenly died. While 20th Century Fox launched a massive search in Italy for his replacement, newcomer Spada was shooting *Kif Tebbi,* resurrecting Valentino's persona of the culturally conflicted Arab.

Kif Tebbi foregrounds the struggle between personal desire and collective duty and the temptations of the nomadic that will mark empire films made a decade later. While its acting styles, plot, and shot sequences testify to the transnational nature of the Orientalist genre, it marks a transition to a new filmic era in Italy marked by the quest to convey a national colonial imaginary and sensibility: it was one of the first features to enjoy a subsidy from the Fascist regime. Shot mostly on location in Tripoli, and adapted by Camerini from Luciano Zùccoli's 1923 novel of the same name, it putatively takes place (like the novel) during the 1911–1912 Italo-Turkish War but also pays homage to Graziani's assault on Tripolitania in the early 1920s. Zùccoli traveled with Graziani's troops while researching the book, and its title, which translates to "as you wish," conveys a fantasy of colonial obedience achieved through repression.[24] On the eve of a massive escalation of this repression, Camerini's film reminds audiences of the value of Italy's original civilizing crusade. Through the shifting cinematic subtext and intertext of Spada's character, it also advocates for a militarized masculinity. As the notable Ismail decides to do his military duty, casting his lot with the Italians, his masculine bearing becomes less that of Rodolfo than that of Benito, his Oriental softness exchanged for a harder manhood appropriate for war.

At the start of the film, Ismail is a man caught between two cultures. The son of a Tripolitanian notable, he has just returned from a transformative trip to Europe. Wearing an Italian suit and smoking a cigarette, he paces restlessly, at peace only in front of the altar to his continental journey he has created inside his father's compound. The camera lingers on the portrait of a European woman, the bottle of French cologne, the photograph of the Eiffel Tower, and the gramophone, all of which relate a series of losses: of an amorous attachment, of the sights and sounds of European culture, and of Ismail's identification with his own culture. We see the impossible backwardness of his surroundings through the servant who gapes at the gramophone and the tribal elders who shake their heads at the warships depicted in Ismail's Italian magazine. Ismail's "recollection objects" reference not just nostalgia for Europe, but an experience of modernity that all Libyans can share by accepting the guide of the Italian

FIGURE 2.1.

Ismail as moody cosmopolitan, *Kif Tebbi*. Author's collection

colonizer.[25] The disjunctions of time and space that come with cultural dislocation are evoked when Ismail flees from his oppressive home, riding his horse to a nearby desert dune. As he sits lost in thought, embellished by his ornamental cape, a close-up channels the ghost of Valentino.

Yet we quickly drift away from the sheik into Ismail's own affective world in which the desert is a prison rather than an exotic escape. Dull light and foreshortened perspective depict a barren landscape of empty dunes, countering the conventional Saharan dramatics achieved in Euro-American films through extreme long shots and chiaroscuro effects. This image is then overlaid with an undulating sea—the gateway to Ismail's memories of his Italian sojourn. A montage of documentary footage of busy construction sites, bridges, speeding trains, and the blur of wheels in movement transforms the sands into a mirage of mobile modernity. This sequence reflects not only the sensibility of Camerini, who was fascinated by modern transportation, but also that of the documentarian Corrado

D'Errico, who served as assistant director. A caravan of camels marching by rudely interrupts Ismail's reverie. The innovative tracking shot of the camels' hooves in the sand garnered Camerini praise for its evocation of the rhythms of the desert, but its function is to convey the dislocation between Ismail's inner world and his immediate surroundings.[26] The young Tripolitanian is a figure lost in translation, afflicted by a malady that only collaboration with the Italians will cure.

In reality, three models of culture interplay here—Italian, Libyan, and Turkish—all of which are presented through the lens of masculine values and behavior. European modernity offers the supreme standard of civilization, and as in *The Sheik* it is associated with male self-control and the overcoming of Oriental lasciviousness. "When an Arab sees a woman he wants, he takes her," declaims Valentino, as Ahmed, in *The Sheik*. Spada's characterization of the Arab in *Kif Tebbi* rebukes this. His restrained gaze and body language, like his noble actions, offer an enlightened model of Arab manhood, to be contrasted both with the less civilized Rassim (a rival tribal leader closed to all Italian influences and the film's hirsute "bad Arab") and with the barbarous Turks.[27] The Turks maraud and plunder, carriers of a brand of Islam that brings out the worst Arab tendencies. In the movie's key ethnographic scene, the Ottoman declaration of a holy war against the Italian infidel brings forth "strange processions of fanatics" among Marabouts. Men shot at close range dance and chant ecstatically; others gyrate suggestively, with eyes rolled back and ritual objects hanging from their mouths; still others engage in self-mutilating rituals (such as gouging the eye with a huge knife). Such scenes were not uncommon in the colonial cinema of other countries—Julien Duvivier's 1931 *Cinq Gentlemen Maudits/Moon over Morocco* offers another example—and minus the eye-gouging, they also mark Luce films of the era set in Libya, such as *Festa religiosa araba in Tripolitania/Arab Religious Festival in Tripolitania* and *I Berberi e gli italiani/The Berbers and the Italians*. In *Kif Tebbi* the tribal display symbolizes the destructive underbelly of Islam, reminding viewers of the barbaric energies that can erupt at any moment without Italy's firm and enlightened rule.[28]

Competition for the female nomad Mné brings out the confrontation between styles of manhood and civilization most clearly. Stalked by Rassim, Mné initially hides from Ismail, but she soon warms up to him.

The film does not neglect the play of gazes and allure of the veiled woman that form part of the appeal of this genre, but the tone is playful rather than erotic. At their first meeting, Ismail gazes at her uncovered sandaled foot, but when she tracks his gaze and hastily withdraws her foot under her tunic, they both laugh heartily. Camerini also defuses things by mocking the Orientalist trope of forbidden looking: when Rassim, who is plotting to kidnap Mné, is hanging about her tent, hoping for a glimpse of her, Mné whets his appetite by rustling the tent's opening, only to present him with a braying baby goat instead. While Rassim represents traditional "uncivilized" Arabic mores with respect to women, it is the Turk who poses the greatest threat. After seizing Mné's caravan, a Turkish soldier spies the young woman and from his perch on his horse leers at her, leaving no doubt as to her fate if he takes her. His face, shot in close-up, evokes criminality and otherness (hooked nose, frizzy hair, beady eyes, lascivious expression) in its Levantine and later Semitic iterations. As a soldier, he is also a negative model of armed manhood—the Italian southern bandit-rapist, with attendant mustachioed and swarthy physicality—that had no place in Fascist Italy. Fascist censorship forbade the full expression of this criminality, by cutting out the scenes of the Turkish sacking of Gasr Garabuli, but the suggestion remains. The Turk, in this film, is more than the enemy in the struggle for Libya: he is a symbol of all that Italy must disavow and disallow in its refashioning of Italy and the Mediterranean.[29]

As against Rassim and the Turk, Ismail plays the role of Mné's savior, modeling a disciplined manhood. Ismail's particular mix of paternalism and passion, and the emphasis placed on the mutual nature of the bond between Mné and Ismail in *Kif Tebbi,* has its origins in the need to discourage sexual and other plunder among the next wave of Italian occupiers, as well as in the conventions of screen romance. When the couple hug and kiss, Spada's gaze and gestures evoke Valentino, but the intertitles let viewers know that this is a romantic partnership. "You belong to me and I belong to you" (*Io ti appartengo e tu mi appartieni*), Mné murmurs to him as they embrace. The film deviates from Orientalist fantasies of female slavery, and it also leaves out the novel's many episodes of male physical violence against women, including a scene in which Ismail whips Mné. But Zùccoli's Mné is no wallflower, either: she beats a servant and slaps and threatens to strangle her blind sister, Gamra. Although Ismail kills two men in the course of *Kif Tebbi*—Rassim, during a duel over Mné, and a Turkish officer—it is ritualized violence, done in the name of female and Italian honor.[30]

This face-off between Occidental and Oriental models of masculinity has a political dimension. Much of this movie's dramatic tension comes from Ismail's transformation from a romantic estranged from his surroundings to a tribal leader who mobilizes his men for battle. When he is acclaimed as the new *capo* by Rassim's *mehalla*, he says gravely, "I am proud to take command of you. We will leave as soon as possible!" Shot first in profile and then from a three-quarter angle, he is imperious in his ornamental cape. The visual and verbal referents for his persona are no longer Valentino, but Mussolini, who had visited Tripolitania the year before. Initially, Ismail goes off to fight for the Turkish cause, but his philo-Italian sentiments soon earn him a death sentence. He escapes from prison by the end of the film, just in time to see the Italians triumph and know he will be able to reconcile his two worlds, serving his people and his colonial masters as an enlightened leader and warrior. From his initial existential dilemma, born of rootlessness—"no longer Arab, but unable to be European," the novel glossed it—Ismail becomes the perfect colonial intermediary.[31] Nor will he have the distractions of romance: with Mné returned to her family, his only object of desire will be his Italian commanders, a plot resolution that will be respected in future empire and military films. Mné, too, has learned a lesson: wandering through the desert is a male privilege. Ismail saved her from harm, but he also put an end to her nomadic existence, confining her indoors in the manner of the women of settled Muslim populations. When her mother arrives to take her back to her *cabila*, her response—"*Kif tebbi* (As you wish)"—brings an order to the film's gender politics that matches its political and cultural messages: now Tripolitania will be able to pursue its Roman heritage without nomadic or Levantine threat. It should not surprise that a partly sonorized re-edition of the film was released in 1932, the year the regime declared Libya officially "pacified."

The experience of virtual travel offered by Orientalist films depended, in part, on their success in soliciting the senses, whether through the lush luxury of their costumes and interiors or their desert landscapes. Italian reviewers saw Camerini's extensive location shooting and his choice of a

FIGURE 2.2.

Ismail as Roman leader, *Kif Tebbi*. Author's collection

"fresh and natural" female protagonist as renewing this filmic formula, freeing it from the "preciousness and literary atmosphere" that afflicted many movies of this type. *Kif Tebbi* stood out for its exploitation of the cinema's specific abilities to evoke proximity. In the words of one critic,

> *Kiff tebby* is so dramatically and scenically effective that while it lasts it makes us completely forget our Western life. *Kiff tebby* really brings us to the desert, making us feel its infinite poetry. We hear the wail of Arab songs brought by the Eastern wind, we follow the regular paces of the camel, and we seem to truly feel the sweet relief of the shade when we enter the oasis after a long walk on the burning sand.

Nor were the film's political message and timing lost on reviewers, who professed feelings of patriotism and pride for the original 1912 victory and its universal message: "Only the tricolor flag can bring a breath of civilization (*civiltà*) among such barbarous people." *Kif Tebbi* also served Fascism well abroad, receiving good reviews from the American press, including the *New York Times* (which were proudly excerpted by Italians). Appearing at one of the lowest moments in post–World War I production, *Kif Tebbi* appeared as a ray of hope for the Italian industry, as well as a model for future imperial-themed works.³²

FILM NOMADS: ITALIANS ABROAD IN THE CRISIS YEARS

The release of *Kif Tebbi*'s anti-nomadic message coincided with the start of itinerant existences by those behind the camera, Camerini included, who could no longer make a living in Italy. Many film professionals circulated among the production capitals of Europe for at least five years, with most absent until the early 1930s, when increased government support for features and the opening of the Cines studio created more work at home. Elite directors who had busy careers abroad, such as Camerini's older cousin Genina, could afford to wait for the right opportunity, and high-profile empire films, with their big budgets and guaranteed publicity, occasioned some of the last repatriations in the mid-1930s. For the rank-and-file directors, actors, and technicians who had been the backbone of Italy's prolific silent film industry, the late twenties meant the start of peregrinations among Paris, Berlin, Budapest, London, and Vienna, earning a living through co-productions, Italian versions of other European films, and master classes. Only a handful went to the United States: the director Alessandrini spent a year in Hollywood, and the actor Antonio Centa, a protagonist of *Lo squadrone bianco* and *Sotto la Croce del Sud*, worked from 1931 to 1933 for Paramount, after spending years as a builder and artisan.³³

Most Italians passed through the international film centers that specialized in multiple editions of films in various languages (Foreign Language Versions, or FLVs). Joinville, the Paramount studio complex outside of Paris, produced more than three hundred FLVs in its four short years of operation (1930–1933). Camerini arrived there in 1930, after years in Italy during which he alternated filmmaking with adapting and translating French and German films for Italian screens. There he joined European and American colleagues who often communicated in the local French-English patois known as "le Paramount." The Joinville practice of setting up a scene and then shooting it around the clock, in anywhere from three to fourteen languages, gave film professionals a firsthand view of how the same script was adapted to a variety of national traditions and acting styles. Joinville and other foreign studio complexes involved Italians in practices and process of cultural translation, offering daily lessons in how texts could travel (or not) across frontiers and political contexts.[34]

Such sojourns abroad also exposed Italians to technological innovations connected to the advent of sound film. The spread of dubbing throughout Europe in these years spelled the demise of FLVs, but brought new professional opportunities for Italians working outside of Italy. In Hollywood Alessandrini supervised the dubbing of Metro-Goldwyn-Mayer (MGM) films into Italian; many took similar jobs within Europe. Since not all of the many foreign films that entered Italy could be dubbed, at first Italian censors merely suppressed the dialogue (intertitles allowed spectators to follow the narrative), leaving sound and music intact. A series of measures created the beginnings of a dubbing industry in Italy, fostering more repatriations: as of 1931, all foreign films entering Italy were required to have dubbed dialogue, and a 1933 law imposed tariffs on films dubbed outside of Italy.[35] While dubbing remained a controversial practice among Italian film professionals, it fostered a keen sense of differences in national tastes and mentalities among Italian film professionals. From styles of humor to the question of regional and class accents and the lexical and tonal qualities attributed to "good" and "evil" characters, dubbing necessitated thinking through two cultures, in order to discern what could and could not be "of both." The collective migrations of the 1920s and early 1930s also left stylistic legacies. Joinville and other smaller production centers were not just film factories that produced FLVs of variable quality, but bold attempts to forge "a synthetic transnational diegesis" built on exchanges and fusions of American and European cinematic traditions. This "international style," with its emphasis on "flights, journeys, encounters abroad," influenced Joinville veterans Genina and Camerini as well as Marcel L'Herbier and Paul Fejos. Italians, as well as Russians and Germans, formed part of the world of film migrants, displaced by economic or political circumstances.[36]

By the early 1930s, the continued absence of national talent, coupled with the domination of American movies in Italy, led the regime to assist and protect the feature film industry. The decrees on dubbing made sure that Italians increasingly heard only Italian at the movies, whatever the national origin of the films they watched, but a 1931 law mandated that one-tenth of films in Italy screened had to be Italian and set the parameters for what constituted a "national" film production. Source stories had to be of Italian origin or adapted by Italians, a majority of film professionals involved in the production must be Italian, and the film had to be shot on Italian soil. Such "national" films would also now be rewarded for their profitability, with government subsidies forthcoming for those garnering the highest box-office receipts. A law of October 1933 rewarded quality as well as profitability, subsidizing Italian movies that "show particular artistic dignity and technical expertise" and upping the minimum quota of Italian films screened to one-quarter of total feature film projections.[37]

Such national films also had to be competitive on the international market, and thus in step with the most popular international styles and genres. The Fascist official Giuseppe Bottai reminded Italian filmmakers that their movies had symbolic and economic importance as an "act of resistance" against the hegemony of foreign entertainment films, but had to win over a "public [that] wants to be amused." The regime thus listened to requests from critics and others to "remain in contact with the best of world production and possibly learn something from it," instituting a variety of venues where Italian cineastes who were not working abroad could see uncensored and undubbed foreign films (film schools; the Biennale, which added a film competition in 1932; cine-clubs; and the cinema sections of the Gioventù Universitaria Fascista [GUF, Young University Fascist] organization). In truth, though, both elites and the general public of spectators could not help but gain an international cinematic education: in 1932 only 26 of the 225 films shown commercially in Italy were Italian, most of the others being products of the strong American (139), French (16), and German (47) industries. Even the content of the Luce newsreel programs shown with feature films was only half Italian: the rest originated from foreign news services.[38] This exposure to foreign fiction and nonfiction also framed discussions about the aesthetics, scale, and type of production and target audiences for empire cinema.

The early thirties also marked a shift in Fascist attitudes regarding the organization of culture under the dictatorship that had important consequences for the cinema industry. The example of the German National Socialists counted here—the Reich Film Chamber had been set up soon after Hitler took power in 1933, and Joseph Goebbels extolled the merits of state intervention on a visit to Italy that year—but so did Fascists' admiration for the American studio system. Luigi Freddi, a former Fascist Party propaganda chief, had spent two months in Hollywood in 1932 and worried that Fascism's relatively laissez-faire approach would result in a national industry that "imitated—badly—what others have already done well." His 1934 reports to Mussolini, which asked for a centralized office that would promote "an original, Italian 'type' of cinematography" and regulate film planning, patronage, and censorship, resulted in the Direzione Generale di Cinematografia (General Directorate for Cinematography, 1934). Headed by Freddi, and tellingly placed within the Fascists' new Sottosegretariato di Stato per la Stampa e la Propaganda (State Undersecretariat for Press and Propaganda), it facilitated state intervention in the entire arc of the moviemaking process, from the treatment phase through postproduction through the orchestration of films' reception.[39]

Over the course of 1935, as preparations for the invasion of Ethiopia took shape, the regime extended its control over the film industry. Film censorship was further politicized, with "lay" members of the state censorship commission (such as professors and a mother) now replaced by representatives from the GUF and the State Undersecretariat of Press and Propaganda. While the Istituto Luce member also lost his spot, Luce gained something more valuable: the right to invest in the commercial film industry, an arrangement made operative later that year with the foundation, with mostly Luce capital, of the Ente Nazionale Industrie Cinematografiche (ENIC, National Agency for Cinematographic Industries). Charged with regulating the acquisition, sale, production, and distribution of films and headed by Luce president Giacomo Paulucci di Calboli, ENIC would distribute a quarter of all Italian films by the end of the regime and control more than one hundred movie theaters throughout Italy and the Axis bloc. The state also formalized its financial assistance to filmmakers in 1935, through advances (up to one-third of the estimated costs) and loans (a credit bureau at the Banco Nazionale del Lavoro gave up to 60 percent of expected expenses), with box-office receipts taken into account only as of 1941.[40]

The impending war influenced Fascism's film culture in myriad ways. A lavish commemoration in March 1935 of the fortieth anniversary of the invention of cinema putatively celebrated France's pioneering role in the medium. Lumière himself was present; his first shorts were shown in French, as was Julien Duvivier's *Poil de carotte/The Red Head* (1932), and Sorbonne students sat with Italian GUF representatives at the gala screening for three thousand at Rome's Supercinema. Of course, the event also intended to remind the French, and the international press, of the Italian contribution to the development of cinema. The program also included two compilation films, including one by D'Errico, that asserted *Cabiria*'s influence on *Intolerance* (D. W. Griffith, 1916) and the Italian origins of lighting and montage techniques. Behind this show of Franco-Italian friendship lay imperialist intentions: just two months earlier, Mussolini had signed an accord with French foreign minister Pierre Laval that gave him tacit approval to invade Ethiopia. Many of the men in the audience, captured on film for a Luce newsreel in their Fascist Party uniforms and tuxedos, would be serving in Ethiopia by the end of the year.[41]

3

Mapping Empire Cinema, 1935–1939

"Roads and bridges, hospitals and pharmacies, electricity and cinema: all at once Fascism has given the subjugated populations all the bounties and conquests of progress and civilization," exalted the young militant Giuseppe Lombrassa, writing from the newly conquered town of Adwa. Marveling at the presence of the "white screen and luminous camera in the Adwa piazza" as "the good subjugated Tigryna" watched their first Luce newsreel, he praised the "representational and persuasive powers of the cinema . . . where the word is not enough, the cinema moves in to hit the target." Lombrassa's comments sum up several of the major themes of this chapter: how films were envisioned as "machines of war" and aids to governance, how cinema's particular expressive language could be exploited in imperial propaganda, and cinema's importance in raising the profile of Italian modernity at home, abroad, and in the colonies. An air of optimism pervaded the industry in the wake of the Ethiopian invasion. The Axis alliance increased commercial and production opportunities, and most expatriate film professionals had returned home. Even if the retrospective claim of the screenwriter and director Mario Soldati that "after the [Ethiopian] victory, almost everyone became a Fascist" may be exaggerated, Fascism's empire inspired amateurs and film professionals. Scripts and story ideas for films on military and colonial themes "flooded in and are still flooding in now, from every part of Italy and even from abroad," wrote Freddi in June 1936.[1] This chapter maps the sites within Fascist film culture that shaped empire cinema, influencing its aesthetics, production practices, marketing, and reception. I examine the spaces of opportunity and control created by the increasing militarization of Italian society, the need for more image management and coordination, and a changing international situation. Nonfiction film took on new prominence as an interpreter of a new imperial history in the making, and I examine the closer relationship between documentary and feature film in these years.

The spectator of empire film is present throughout this chapter, sometimes as a phantom figure influencing Fascist film discourse and policy, sometimes as an explicit reference. The declaration of empire not only brought forth debates over the social function of film, but also inaugurated a lively debate about the formation of a national-imperial audience that influenced how empire-themed films were conceived and received. I pay particular attention to the role of film sound in soliciting spectatorial interpretation and affect. The body-voice connection of cinematic characters is central to sound's anchoring function for the viewer, but voices also "inhabit an intersubjective acoustic space" that make the listening *context* equally important to the process of making meaning from films.[2] That context grew more problematic when officials and critics contemplated how to best reach the heterogeneous audiences of the colonies, composed of individuals of very different linguistic abilities and cultural understandings than viewers in the metropole. The Italians did not subtitle the films they showed in the colonies, and the uncomprehending native spectator raised the specter of larger misunderstandings, mockeries, and refusals of Fascist rule.

FILM POLICIES AND CULTURES, 1935–1939

The invasion of Ethiopia began a new era of cultural policy making that placed new political demands and constraints on the Italian film industry, as well as creating new funding and artistic possibilities. In 1937 the Istituto Luce, together with the General Directorate for Cinema, came under the control of a new Ministry of Popular Culture (MCP), headed by Dino Alfieri, a former journalist and squadrist and an admirer of Goebbels.[3] The MCP intervened in every stage of the filmmaking process. It vetted ideas; offered financial advances; applied preventive censorship that included checking the political, national, and racial credentials of cast and crew; and recommended attention to (or neglect of) films in ways that heavily influenced publicity during production and reception upon release. Such state intervention combined with a commercial mandate meant to challenge the hegemony of American films at home and abroad. Freddi, who had remained in charge of the General Directorate of Cinema, discouraged openly propagandistic films as well as openly avant-garde or "high art" ones. His openness to Italian adaptations of the American studio model also reflected his desire to steer Italian film culture away from the path of modernist experimentalism to a consistent qualitative and quantitative norm. Freddi's strategy is often judged a success: 43 Italian films were made in 1936, 77 in 1939, and 106 in 1942, making the Italian industry one of the most productive in Europe during World War II. In the meantime, Alfieri concentrated on the expansion of state control over distribution and exhibition. His granting of a monopoly to ENIC for the distribution of foreign films in Italy after 1938 prompted the major Hollywood studios to withdraw from the Italian market in protest, but ENIC had other sources of income: the entity controlled ninety-seven Italian cinema venues by 1941.[4]

The 1937 creation of the Cinecittà studio complex, which was designed in part by a Hollywood-trained Italian engineer, with early input from the American trade consul John McBride, was the most visible sign of the regime's bid to compete with Hollywood for domestic and European markets. Fully half of the films made in Italy between 1937 and 1943 were shot there, and Cinecittà became a major crossroads of the international film trade. By 1939 more than one-fifth of Italian productions were the work of foreign directors or part of FLV packages. The eventual integration of the Istituto Luce and Cinecittà into one architecturally modernist cinematic zone on Via Tuscolana recognized the Fascists' view of the symbiotic relationship between nonfiction and feature cinema. The stage set for Cinecittà's inauguration, which featured the slogan "The cinema is the strongest weapon," reiterated the expectation that commercial cinema would contribute, in its own fashion, to the regime's social and other agendas, while the giant mockup of the Duce looking through a movie camera warned that the institution of cinema would itself be a subject of scrutiny. Fascist spies had free rein in Cinecittà, with Soldati, Alessandrini, Genina, actress Doris Duranti, and Freddi himself among the legions of film professionals denounced for anti-Fascism, corruption, or personal "irregularities" ranging from homosexuality to extramarital affairs.[5]

The shifts in international alliances that resulted from the Ethiopian invasion had significant repercussions for European film politics. Although Italian consumers preferred Hollywood and, increasingly, French films, Mussolini's alliance with Hitler led by the end of the decade to an Axis film bloc (Germany, Spain, and later Japan and Axis satellites) and a counter-"cinematographic Axis" composed of "Paris-London-Hollywood." The German film industry was an obligatory reference point in the late 1930s and early 1940s, and Berlin's studios were as busy as those of Rome with multiple versions and co-productions. Itala Film had a Berlin branch to facilitate these, as did the German production house Tobis in Rome.[6] With the exception of Rossellini, whose filmmaking experiences abroad were limited to Ethiopia, all of the Italian directors discussed in this book worked in either Germany or Spain during this period. Such collaborations often continued contacts Italians made when they worked abroad in the 1920s, before Hitler came to power.[7] The history of the International Film Chamber (IFC) highlights how Axis film projects influenced Italian policies, and in particular the development of the Biennale Film Festival. Founded by Goebbels in 1935, the IFC had two main goals: to counter the supremacy of American cinema on the continent by promoting intra-continental co-productions and distributions of European films and to ensure Germany's leadership of this process. It was finalized at the 1935 Venice Biennale, and the histories of the IFC and the Biennale closely converged for the remainder of the 1930s. Although the first IFC president, Franz Scheuemann, was also the head of the Nazi domestic Film Chamber, initially the IFC did further the cause of filmic internationalism. France took over the presidency in 1937, and the Biennale's juries, which had been entirely Italian, now included members from France and Sweden as well as Germany. By 1938, though, this had begun to unravel. The signing of the Italian-German Cultural Accord that year made clearer the outlines of an alternative project of continental domination, and the awarding of the top Biennale prize *ex-aequo* to *Luciano Serra, pilota* and Leni Riefenstahl's *Olympia* that year prompted the French to withdraw formally from the Biennale and found their own "democratic" film festival at Cannes.[8]

This institutional breach did not prevent Italian and French film cultures from having many points of contact and cross-pollinations. Coproductions, double versions, movies made in Italy by French directors, and French outposts of the Italian production houses Lux and Scalera built on relationships forged in France during the period of emigration. French features arguably had more influence within Italian film culture. The desert aesthetics of French colonial films provided a model for Fascist empire cinema, and the poetic realist works of directors such as Carné and Renoir had a particular impact on younger Italians such as Luchino Visconti, Alberto Lattuada, and the critics of the review *Cinema*. Yet Argentieri's characterization of the French-Italian rapport as one of "affection and diffidence" rings true. Admiration for French filmmakers' poetic sensibilities and bravura mingled with mistrust of their freer morals and cosmopolitan attitudes. This divided attitude may be seen in Italian reviews of the major French films of the period, such as *Le jour se lève/ Daybreak* (Carné, 1939), seen as "excellent as film" but spiritually "sick and morbid."[9]

Hollywood served as the foil for all these European cinemas, although the lack of firsthand experience there among Italian film professionals made America a very different case. Without the familiarity built up through proximity and years of collaborations, Hollywood remained a screen myth, a place consumed only through the virtual travel afforded by the culture of images. Of the directors treated in this book, only Alessandrini spent any time there. Still, Hollywood was the dominant film culture of Fascist Italy for its enviable market shares and influence on popular culture. In 1937, 190 American films screened in Italy, as opposed to only 31 Italian ones, and took in 73.5 percent of box-office receipts of all films screened the following year. America also had the most films at the Venice Biennale between 1936 and 1938, with France, Italy, and Germany alternating for second place. American cinema set a standard for the Italian film industry in terms of technical prowess, the definition of genres, and the intertwining of star and consumer culture.[10] Whether this standard was appropriate for Italy was open to debate. Although Vittorio Mussolini saw American films as a means of "emancipating" Italian movies from a lingering theatrical inheritance, others, such as Luigi Chiarini, viewed the mission of the national film industry as that of "detoxifying the public from the subtle poisons of films made in the USA." Insufficient Italian production and the lure of profit led pragmatism to triumph over ideology, though. For most of the dictatorship, Italian public and private authorities facilitated Hollywood's inroads into Italy, to the benefit of America's "market empire."[11]

The regime's decision to take a more proactive approach to the creation of a national cinema tested the "limited partnership" between Italy and America. Mussolini knew that his decision to grant ENIC control of American film distribution would anger the major studios, and a desire to legislate national taste as well as increased profits lay behind this measure. In this sense Hollywood's boycott was indeed "a critical moment," as Vittorio Mussolini called it in *Cinema*, not just for the Italian-American relationship, but for the regime's promotion of a certain model of popular culture. In early 1939 director Francesco De Robertis reported an "atmosphere of uncertainty and perplexity among Italian producers after the latest unexpected measures," and even the philo-American Mussolini did not hide his trepidation about the effects of Hollywood's absence from Italian screens, but rather applauded the "totalitarian" measure against "the Communist-Jewish central that is Hollywood." As it turned out, the exit of the American majors, coupled with the financial incentives for the Italian industry provided for by the companion Alfieri law of 1938, helped to redress a longstanding imbalance. From 1938 to 1939, audience share for Italian films jumped from 13.7 percent to 35.1 percent of box-office receipts, and Italian spectators could choose from 50 Italian films as opposed to 60 American ones. American films did not completely disappear from the market, since minor Hollywood companies struck deals with the Italians to distribute their films, and Hollywood remained the matrix of spectators' fantasies about glamour and modernity. Hollywood's predominance in Italy should not obscure the fact that films from many other countries also circulated, with the range of national cinemas *expanding* in the years of autarchy. Even in 1942, fully half of what Italian spectators saw was foreign in origin. Film's authority in the interwar period lay in its ability to provide a script for reading the modern experience, and its interpretative gaze was also inherently a disciplinary one. In the case of Italy, that guided perspective on modernity was more often than not a foreign perspective, even at the height of Fascism's imperial-autarchic phase.[12] In this sense, too, going to the cinema was often a virtual voyage into a negotiation of that modernity, with the body as meeting point and filter for the foreign and national sounds, gestures, and visions that emanated from the screen.

FILM SOUND: VOICES OF THE IMPERIAL NATION

Although the aural dimension of Fascist film has received relatively little attention, it too figured in projects of collective (re)education. As Michel Chion argues, the "audiovisual contract" of cinema assigns sound the role of binding the flow of images, bridging narrative gaps, and establishing atmosphere. Producing aural signposts to guide the viewer's interpretation of individual characters, settings, and events, sound traces an emotional map for the spectator, even as it elicits an embodied response that has its own autonomy. Film music acquired a greater prominence in the filmmaking process after 1936, with Freddi recruiting well-known composers to write for the screen. Antonio Veretti, Genina's composer of choice on *Lo squadrone bianco* and *Bengasi*, praised the magical results of true collaboration even as he flagged the many challenges. Composers often had to do multiple rewrites of their scores, with very little notice, and the expedient of using documentary clips of ethnographic musical performance was sometimes a function of the difficulties of recording directly on location. Empire films were particularly complex audio creations, and sound helped to set the tone for Fascism's particular imperial culture and style of governance. Musicologists or folklorists who came to the colonies for military or civilian service, such as Gavino Gabriel, became important translators of indigenous music into the world of documentary and fiction film and helped to shape radio programs of indigenous music that were heard throughout the empire.[13]

The voice also came in for new scrutiny in these years by a regime that sought to maximize cinema's interpellative potential. Debates about the use of the voice on-screen reveal the importance of the aural realm in managing affect and attention, as does the employment of vocality in general. For the power of the voice is not confined to language: ululations and chanting, for example, which figure in documentary films and in features such as *Luciano Serra, pilota* and *Lo squadrone bianco,* simultaneously estrange and fascinate, perhaps unsettling the spectator more than the sight of indigenous costume that had been present on national screens since the days of silent film. In 1937 critic Ettore Allodoli noted that sound films spoke to the basic human desires to "say, speak, yell, scream, laugh and cry ... and the overwhelming need to hear."[14] Emotional and sensory liberation was hardly what the regime wished to encourage through the cinema, though. Rather, sound in empire films is meant to facilitate a re-education of the senses that aimed to produce imperial subjects who would further Fascism's social and political goals.

Sound also came in for attention for its potential to provide linguistic education. But what kind of Italian should be diffused on-screen? For critic Paolo Milano, a more modern tongue: noting American English's informality was crucial to the popularity of Hollywood films, Milano argued that "the creation of an everyday Italian language" should be a priority among the industry. Others disagreed, contending that sound cinema had already been complicit in spreading "the worst neologisms and North American idiocies." Behind some of these objections lay the campaign for linguistic purism then shaping up in Italy. Spearheaded by the Royal Italian Academy, it aimed to remove all foreign terms from Italian. Other manifestations of "linguistic autarchy," such as the banning of the supposedly foreign-derived Lei form of address, reflected the desire to militarize Italians and inculcate in them a culture of imperial command. And even Allodoli, who shared Milano's preference for a new Italian marked by "simplicity and freshness," lobbied for the institution of a *revisore,* a kind of linguistic censor, who would be acknowledged in the credits for his protection of the integrity of the Italian language on-screen. Many foreign words and phrases remained, though, due to their ideological and commercial utility. In comedies and romantic dramas about contemporary life, foreign words such as "cocktail" and "tennis" appealed to the spectator as the sonoral equivalents of the white telephone and the evening gown, cueing a glamorous modernity known only on-screen. And as in *Il grande appello* and *Bengasi,* foreign speech often counted in the characterization of negative figures, facilitating audience estrangement. Anti-dialect policies also found uneven application, since dialects could be useful in showing the national scope of populist enterprises (as in the Risorgimento-themed *1860* or in *Il grande appello*). By the late 1930s, though, with knowledge of standard Italian increasing, heavy accents and recognizable single words usually stood in for dialect speech as a means of conveying regional affiliation.[15]

The desire to create an imperial-autarchic culture and consciousness also informed policies and debates about dubbing in these years. The dubbing of foreign (and after 1941 Italian) voices offered a measure of political control over a mass cultural product with huge influence over a rising generation of Italians. Dubbing a film is always an act of mediation as well as of translation, but here the interventions were often of an ideological nature. Censors suppressed or altered objectionable dialogue and changed proper names and geographical settings. Film titles were loosely translated when necessary, starting with the first film ever dubbed inside Italy, *A nous la liberté* (René Clair, 1931), which became the more cautious *A me la libertà*. Under pseudonymic cover, screenwriter Giacomo Debenedetti lamented the difficulties of working with a government that sometimes halted a wrapped film for yet another round of sonoral modifications. The dialogist of a dubbed film, he wrote, must be attentive from the start to "involuntary 'double meanings'... or foreign proper names whose sound resembles other words which could cause hilarity at the most political moment of the film." Even as dubbing made the foreign more familiar, by providing an acoustic filter that was "consonant with the culture and experience of the spectator," it opened the way for interventions meant to silence the politically unacceptable.[16] The opportunities for linguistic and vocal standardization through dubbing were not lost on officials and ideologues, who saw in the disciplining of the vocal sphere a complement to their aims of reshaping bodily and emotional regimes to suit the demands of war. The Italian heard in dubbed features of the late 1930s increasingly resembled the language of Luce nonfiction in its anonymity and lack of accent or local color. In Fabio Rossi's words, dubbed language tended toward "a strong normative identity ... and an evident stylistic neutrality." Despite this, purists derided dubbed language, especially in American movies, as a degradation of Italian through its retention of American terms and its creation of senseless neologisms. But Gilberto

Altichieri pointed out the disconcerting effects for spectators when purist inclinations won out over realism, as when Italians heard street urchins fighting in proper, even aulic, Italian.[17]

Altichieri had put his finger on another problem: dubbing severed the body-voice connection that is central to sound's stabilizing effects for the spectator. What Roland Barthes called "the grain of the voice," meaning the voice's capacity to evoke emotions and the senses, is tied to its quality of embodiment, to the sight of "the materiality of the body speaking its mother tongue." Thus did another commentator complain of the disjuncture between the audition of an Italian voice and the vision of a "face and person that could only belong on Broadway, or on the Siberian steppes," and of characters condemned to speak "with a voice that is not even theirs, and which does not correspond, as it naturally and truly should, to the person who speaks, who was born and will die with his own voice."[18] Yet by the end of the 1930s, audiences no longer expected to hear the star's real voice. Only the elite got to see films in their original languages, at film schools and festivals or special screenings. Everyone else related to their favorite foreign stars through the mediation of a national voice, and since the most in-demand dubbers often represented several major stars at once (Tina Lattanzi was the voice of Greta Garbo, Marlene Dietrich, and Rita Hayworth, Emilio Cigoli that of Gary Cooper and Cary Grant), that voice became a very familiar one. As Rossi notes, the mass public, with its uncertain reading skills, not only welcomed the absence of subtitles, but grew used to "the correspondence between a certain vocal timbre and a certain physiognomy or character." In fact, Italians were disoriented when American films first appeared undubbed, with Italian subtitles, just after World War II, and then were upset if new voices replaced the old ones when dubbing returned. Dubbing shaped the national ear, habituating Italians to differences in timbre, accent, and tonality that were associated with particular traits of morality or sexuality. The vocal and aural registers that were developed though dubbing for foreign screen characters served as the foils for their Italian equivalents: a Fascist commander in Ethiopia or Libya had to sound, as well as look and act, quite different from the voice of the enemy. Vocality, as well as visuality, establishes masculine dominance and hierarchy, and there is an aural dimension to the ensemble of actions and interactions that represent gender identities.

Whether dubbed or not, the voice exceeds signification, and the voice also has a greater weight than other sounds in the film frame, such as music and noise. As Chion writes, "The presence of a human voice structures the sonic space that contains it."[19]

No one intuited this more than Mussolini, who was perhaps the only male star in Italy who was never dubbed. The Duce was a skilled orator, using concise and memorable phrases, binary and ternary sentence structure, varied rhythms, and liberal use of pauses to solicit affect and applause. His rhetorically powerful speeches provided many "slogans" that circulated throughout the public sphere, and his pacing and pitch fostered imitators among radio, newsreel, and sports announcers. His voice was central to his personal appeal and to his strategies of mobilizing his listeners at the emotional level as well. Mussolini's vocal performances aimed less to impart information than to "to convince [his listener] to act, to persuade or dissuade him, to curb, incite, and rouse him," argues Augusto Simonini, who gives the example of the Duce's October 2, 1935, speech. Delivered at dusk, at the end of a daylong rally, it lasted just thirteen and a half minutes, with silences occupying nearly half of that. The vast majority of those gathered in Piazza Venezia only *heard* him, through loudspeakers, and this visual absence (which is respected in the Luce newsreel of the event) reflected his acousmatic presence in Italian life. Although his image saturated Italy, the Duce was just as often experienced "live" as a voice without a body, not least through the radio, delivering sound that had the properties of "ubiquity, panopticism, omniscience, and omnipotence."[20] His vocal signature haunts empire cinema, and the pitch, phrasing, and diction of its male protagonists are calibrated to evoke or contrast with Mussolini's inescapable aural presence.

Empire films also offered a linguistic profile of the ideal indigenous subject, one that rested on the use of a pidgin Italian that was heavy on infinitives ("tu sparare"). Although purists lambasted this practice as giving rise to "a barbaric and ridiculous caricature of the limpid and clear Italian elocution," pidgin Italian persisted because it so effectively conveyed the supposed inferiority of the indigenous. In this, too, empire cinema related to Fascist policy: although the French and the British had long diffused knowledge of their languages as an instrument of colonial governance, from the inception of colonial rule in the liberal period, the Italians held an ambivalent attitude toward the education, linguistic and other, of their colonial subjects. By the late 1930s, racism had further reduced Italian instruction for sub-Saharan Africans, although Dodecanese Greeks, Italy's "white" colonial subjects, received education in Italian throughout the Fascist period. Libyan Arabs fell in between, due to attendance of Italian schools and Fascist colonial youth units such as the Gioventù Araba del Littorio. Overall, though, the ubiquity and persistent use of pidgin Italian in the densest spaces of interaction—commerce, labor, and the army—testify to how prestige mattered more than intelligibility to the Italian dictatorship. Language in empire films reinforces these priorities: the Italian actor (Cesare Polacco) who played a Libyan soldier-aide in *Lo squadrone bianco* was forced to learn pidgin Italian for his role. Such staged juxtapositions of the standard Italian of the occupier and the crude linguistic approximations of the Arab or African are acts of "linguistic arrogance," to use Emily Apter's phase. They obscure the often poor and dialect-ridden Italian of the colonizer along with the linguistic prowess of the colonized.[21]

For their hybrid linguistic nature and variable quality and type of sound, empire films stand out for their disruptions of the classical operation of sound and image and of the body-voice connection. The prominence of extra-linguistic sounds, vocalisms (such as ululations), and large amounts of untranslated foreign speech made for a greater measure of unintelligibility than in other types of commercial cinema. The frisson of exotica provided by such speech and vocalisms was surely part of empire films' sensory fascination and one basis of their ethnographic authenticity. Empire film scores usually placed their Orientalist motifs within a comfortingly familiar romantic frame, though, so it was through untranslated dialogue, live performance, and "elements [that] escape a strictly verbal codification" that these movies rendered the colonial experience at the sonoral level. Exigencies of both documentation and spectacle probably lay behind Alessandrini's decision in *Abuna Messias* to alert viewers in the credits that "the dialogue of the indigenous has been translated only when deemed indispensable to the clarity of the narrative." Unintelligibility in empire films also cued audience sympathies, marking intended zones of emotional estrangement with respect to Italian-speaking characters of all races whose motives and body language could be contextualized through language. As Thierry Millet reminds us, the sphere of sound involves not only acoustic phenomena, but also "the listening subject and that which he accepts or refuses to integrate, name, or comprehend."[22] I now turn to that listening subject, and to the culture of Italian spectatorship, to examine empire films' intended publics and contexts of consumption.

SPECTATORS IN AND OF THE COLONIES

By the time of the Ethiopian invasion, watching movies, whether in parish halls, plein air screenings, or commercial cinemas, was by far the most popular leisure-time activity in Italy. Economics explained part of this appeal. With the exception of first-run theaters in big cities, films cost less than many other mass entertainments, and well into the 1930s a cinema ticket often included *varietà* (a category that encompassed dance troupes, magicians, singers, comics, and so on), offering up to five hours of diversion. Cinemas were also spaces of socializing and socialization as well as spaces of fantasy. Some newer urban cinemas marketed themselves as modernist palaces where spectators could experience for themselves the kinds of luxurious settings they saw on-screen.[23] Movies' ever-increasing popularity brought them in for scrutiny by Catholic and Fascist authorities. The church did its part to curb the influence of films—its Centro Cattolico Cinematografico (Catholic Center for Cinematography), founded in 1934, had a rating system that told families which films to avoid—and in 1936 Pope Pius XI issued the encyclical *Vigilanti cura* to warn of cinema's dangers to the emotions and the mind. The encyclical sparked debates in cinema journals on the morality of films and filmgoing. Psychologist and film scholar Father Agostino Gemelli warned that movies destabilized the spectator by activating "dreams, unsatisfied hopes, and unrealized desires," gradually "remov[ing] the spectator from his own world until, at a certain point, his forgets himself and no longer has control of his own life."[24] These concerns about film's corrupting influences magnified when Italian critics and authorities considered the colonial subject as film spectator. Vittorio Mussolini signaled the importance of the theme by featuring an article by Maurizio Rava (former governor of Somalia and vice governor of Tripolitania) in the inaugural issue of

Cinema. Rava extolled cinema's potential as a "potent arm of peaceful persuasion" among African spectators, but warned that it could easily become "a boomerang that returns against the one who launches it." Such trepidation also reflected film's enormous popularity in the colonies. As in the metropole, movies trumped all other forms of popular entertainment, with venues ranging from outdoor screenings to commercial theaters to schools, missionary institutes, and *Case del fascio*. In Libya, at theaters such as the Miramare in Tripoli, films shared space not only with *varietà* but with belly dancers and Arabic musicians from throughout the region. The Miramare, the biggest theater in Italian Africa before 1936 with eighteen hundred seats, expanded further in 1938 to meet the demand.[25]

Film programming and spectatorship in East Africa show the effects of Fascist ideologies of racial segregation and the practical considerations that made such separatism difficult to sustain. The absence of a tourist industry and other entertainment options, the presence of a large population of Italian soldiers, and the relative ease with which one could operate a movie theater due to lax regulation all contributed to cinema's outstanding popularity. In 1939 Italian East Africa had forty public cinemas, with a total of thirty thousand seats; just one year later, that number had risen to fifty-five cinemas and sixty thousand places. Mogadishu's Benadir cinema (fifteen hundred seats) and Addis Ababa's Supercinema Teatro Italia (twelve hundred) were quickly dwarfed by Asmara's Impero and Augustus, which had twenty-eight hundred and two thousand places, respectively. In all, Asmara had eleven commercial cinemas, with a total of six thousand seats.[26] Only one of those was restricted to black Africans, since most Eritreans could not afford regular cinema attendance; even the owner of a cinema in the busy Teclè Haimanot indigenous quarter of Addis Ababa complained about low profits in asking Luce to send him documentaries and newsreels for free. Urban cinemas such as the Cinque Maggio in Addis Ababa resorted to mixed screenings, restricting black Africans to the last rows and disinfecting the theater after such performances. Others had separate screenings for Italians and black Africans (black African notables could often attend Italian screenings, although they had to sit in designated areas). Assab's Imperial Cinema, which opened in the wake of segregationist legislation, had twin indigenous and "national" theaters connected by a corridor of shops that included cloth-

FIGURE 3.1.

Supercinema Teatro Italia, Addis Ababa. Used by permission of Luce Cinecittà, Archivio Foto Cinematografico

ing stores, a perfumery, hairdressers, and a veranda bar. The inevitable interracial contact before and after the movie in the complex's common spaces highlighted the difficulties of making the practice of cinema-going reinforce Fascist dictates to "maintain the exclusion of the indigenous element from locales frequented by whites." A new round of racial laws in 1940 prompted some owners to end mixed screenings: the Benadir, in Somalia, exiled black Africans to a new dedicated theater in the indigenous zone, and an article in *Cinema* on audiences at Addis Ababa's Cinque Maggio no longer made mention of an indigenous public.[27]

Like their French and British counterparts, the Italians made use of traveling cinemas in the colonies. Operating in Libya as of 1929 and East Africa after 1936, these free screenings sponsored by Luce and the Opera Nazionale Dopolavoro (National Leisure Organization) (the latter's vans had roamed Italy since 1927) had the most success in reaching African audiences. They showed films in rural villages, remote military outposts, and small towns without cinemas, delivering up to seventy-five programs a month. As in the cities, these outdoor projections brought together Italians and Africans. Especially in rural settings, the physical and technological aspects of the experience of cinema spectatorship were seen as crucial to the work of "trampling" and disarming the credulous black spectator. Luce circulated both still and moving images of its screenings, such as these shown from the Ethiopian countryside in 1937. The spectacle began not with the film screening but with the assemblage of the projection equipment, and Luce's own films headed up the program.[28]

Despite this outlay of resources, several factors hindered the regime's attempts to use film as a weapon of propaganda in the colonies. The lack of adequate venues for sound film viewing and spotty film distribution channels meant that demand often exceeded supply, and the relatively low output of the Italian film industry until World War II translated into more time given to American and other foreign films than in French and British territories. In the last three months of 1938, filmgoers in Asmara saw sixty-eight American, eleven Italian, eight French, and six German films, whereas Roman spectators saw twenty-eight American, thirteen Italian, two French, and two German films. As in British India, American Westerns were very popular with both Italian and black African viewers, and having Gary Cooper, Clark Gable, Bette Davis, or Myrna Loy as stars of movies of any genre ensured a big crowd, although Nazzari kept pace, as did Vittorio De Sica. The Cinque Maggio did a brisk business due to the preeminence of American movies among its programming, but the critic Mattia took pains to point out that its proprietor, Giovanni Licati, had only a tenuous connection to Italy, having lived his entire life in the colonies. In general, enthusiasm for the rapid expansion of the cinema industry in Africa outweighed concerns that most of what Italians saw

FIGURES 3.2 AND 3.3.

Mobile film screening, Ethiopia, 1937. Used by permission of Luce Cinecittà, Archivio Foto Cinematografico

there was not Italian, although critic Enrico Fiume reminded his peers that film would ideally "remind [nationals in the colonies] of the face of their mother country," perhaps with the example of Licati in mind.[29]

The impact of such cosmopolitan programming on indigenous audiences proved even more worrying to officials and critics. The common European perception of the black African's inability to distinguish illusion from reality informed recommendations by Vittorio Mussolini, Rava, and others to avoid showing "bad whites," "loose women," and gangsters, although organized violence, in the form of war, met with approval, since "war is always understood, even when it is of a type unknown to the indigenous, since all African peoples have war in their blood." Others aired fears about the power of images to foster imitation, as when an Italian colonel based in Adrigat complained to the army command in 1938 that Eritrean *askaris* and civilians had reacted to scenes in the Risorgimento film *1860* of Italians being taken prisoner by foreign troops. The anxieties that permeate these articles hint at the insecure base of Italian colonial power in Ethiopia, especially in the countryside, where rebellion still raged.[30] Italians who observed black African spectators directly also worried that cultural differences were complicating the reception of feature films, obstructing or even subverting their intended meanings. Italian conceptions of the dramatic and the comedic had little validity in Africa, they reported: films that featured heroic deaths and love scenes met with open derision, and, most disturbingly, the audience often rooted for the "wrong" protagonists. Most felt that sentimental comedies and melodramas should be avoided in favor of Westerns, combat and adventure films, and documentaries. Rava took a long view in counseling extreme selectiveness. He saw the Italian colonization of Ethiopia as an opportunity to "educate the eyes and the spirit" of an entire population that had never before lived under European rule. "In Abyssinia the indigenous must be slowly habituated to understand or, more precisely, to 'see' the screen." Such education of the eye was especially important when Italian films were involved, for reasons of indoctrination and colonial prestige. Mattia warned that the entertainment provided by Italian films was often at the Italians' expense, with colonial dramas often bringing the most laughter and criticism, especially those like *Sentinelle di bronzo*, which featured black African actors in prominent roles.[31]

To be sure, some of these audience "misreadings" stemmed from linguistic limitations that were partly of the Italians' own making. Dubbing meant that Italians did not subtitle their movies, and they rarely provided simultaneous oral translations for a population that had been systematically excluded from the level of Italian instruction necessary to understand a film. Nothing came of proposals to make features in local tongues especially for indigenous audiences, nor of a 1938 agreement between the Ministry of Italian Africa and Luce to produce documentaries in Arabic and in East African languages. Cultural differences, and lack of familiarity with the cinematic medium, redoubled the effects of this linguistic impasse. An old colonial hand noted in *Cinema* that in Somalia and Eritrea, where the local populations had had more exposure to the Italian language and to cinema, public comments attended more to the story line, while in newly colonized Ethiopia, audiences had a more vivid emotional and physical reaction. Another commentator admired the "authenticity" of such responses, noting that Africans "give free expression to those 'base' sentiments of human nature that we repress," but the spectacle of uncontrolled outbursts by groups of mostly male black African spectators made most Italians uncomfortable.[32] Some Italians saw audience laughter as a rebuke to Italian dignity, and through their vocal responses to film projections black African spectators became the authors of a sort of parallel soundtrack, with Italians in the audience experiencing the film through the filter of such mockery. It is telling that one Italian critic writes of attending mixed-race screenings in which Ethiopian notables stifled their laughter with their hands or their robes: such gestures only highlight the subversive significance of laughing at rather than with the colonizer. It was this possible destabilizing of authority, as well as the staging of negative models of Italianness and whiteness, that made the Fascists so nervous about showing their subjects feature films. In his monthly column on empire film, Fiume repeatedly aired such worries, citing the "political errors" the British made in India by thoughtless or inappropriate programming that placed the indigenous "on guard against anything made in the West." Fiume warned his peers that Indians had changed from a "dumbfounded and silent [audience]" to a viewing public "ready to rise up against anything that can offend its country and religion," a message echoed by an anonymous writer: "The cinema is a very powerful weapon whose utility is equaled only by the damage it can do if it is employed inappropriately or in bad faith." Such trepidations led many to support the documentary as the safest kind of film to show indigenous audiences. As Vittorio Mussolini contended, the documentary offered a reality to be taken at face value, without complicated narratives and characterizations to distract and mislead. The "power and greatness of Italy" could come through intelligibly and directly, facilitating submission to Fascist rule.[33]

NONFICTION FILM AND EMPIRE FILM

Steven Ricci has argued that three interactive bodies of film proved most influential in shaping the "particular historical matrix" of Italian spectators during the Fascist era: Italian features, American features, and state-produced nonfiction. Empire feature films took shape amid discussions about the respective roles that fiction and nonfiction should play in developing a new national-imperial imaginary. The allocation of resources for big-budget empire films after 1935 had a parallel in state investments in nonfiction film: the two developed in tandem and in dialogue with each other. Thirty documentaries were made on the Ethiopian war alone, twenty of which were shot on location, as was the special series *Cronache dell'impero/Chronicles of Empire,* all of which supplemented regular newsreel production.[34] Some directors of empire films, such as Genina and Gallone, had made military documentaries during World War I, and many of the younger generation, such as Marcellini and D'Errico, moved back and forth between empire features and documentaries, as did camera operators such as Craveri. The loose relationship between feature and documentary filmmaking on imperial and military themes, and the need to produce more effective propaganda, facilitated this dialogue among film forms. But this same body of work conveys anxieties about the incomplete and tenuous state of Italian rule in East Africa. Cameos of angry notables and uncomfortable female subjects channel a climate of non- or reluctant cooperation, opening doors to "psychological and somatic forms of intersubjectivity between viewer and social actor" that ran counter to Fascism's imperial governance.[35]

The closer relationship of Italy's military and propaganda apparatuses that followed upon the Ethiopian invasion encouraged the sharing of film footage among newsreels, documentaries, and feature films. As Virilio has noted, such practices dated back to World War I, which produced a vast image bank of military footage that was "recyclable within the film industry itself." Luce seemed to benefit more from such practices than the military did: in 1934 the head of the Press Office of the Royal Navy had complained that the Istituto Luce often bypassed him in releasing images of naval maneuvers to the press.[36] The security and propaganda needs related to the Ethiopian war mandated better cooperation, and Luce's new East Africa Unit (Luce AOI) was created in August 1935 in conjunction with the armed forces. By July 1936 the eighty cameramen working for Luce included men who were doing their military service as embedded operators in the Italian Army, Air Force, Militia, and Navy, further blurring the lines between images captured for combat training versus propaganda. Yet Major Guido Bagnoni complained in *Cinema* in August 1936 that Luce material was too heavily edited to be of use for military pedagogy and asked that the army's new cinematheque appoint more men with film training. In effect, Luce's closer ties with the armed forces gave the regime greater access to military images, and tensions from the military side over this situation persisted until the fall of the regime.[37]

The greater intertwining of civilian and military filmmaking reflected one of the key themes of Fascist film culture in the imperial years: the militarization of the cinematic apparatus. Nonfiction cinema should not only document the war, but help to wage it, going beyond the external perspective of traditional combat journalism ("eye on the war") to become "the eye *of* the war" (*l'occhio della guerra*), in Bagnoni's phrase. Such discussions carried forth World War I–era ruminations on the modes of seeing inaugurated by industrial warfare. The regime censored any reflections on the human toll of such warfare, privileging celebrations of the dazzling modernity and military potential of the mechanically assisted gaze. Commentators praised the interoperability of cameras and machine guns on aerial bombers, and inventions such as the *cinemamitragliatrice*, or "cinema-machine gun," which shot images at the same pace as bullets. Documentaries such as *Sulle orme dei nostri pionieri/On the Tracks of Our*

FIGURE 3.4.

The camera as weapon, II, Ethiopia, 1936. Author's collection

Pioneers (Luciano De Feo, 1936) and *Il cammino degli eroi* liken the camera to a weapon, its open lens assimilated to the lethal blackness of cannon and gun barrels. Fascist empire cinema elevated the camera to the status of another "prosthetic instrument that extends ideology and visions of history into the depth of the human body, leaving the dead and the depicted in its wake."[38]

Off-screen as well, Luce AOI became a symbol of Fascism's abilities to place technologies of mobility and vision in the service of its imperial goals. Alfieri had given Luce AOI the mandate to "offer the public an immediate visual chronicle of the marvelous deeds of our soldiers and workers in East Africa," and critics and functionaries publicly praised the unit's ability to send images to Italy as early as three hours after the conclusion of a battle. The emphasis on the speed with which events could be transformed into spectacle and the ability of audiences to follow the making of histories as they occurred created a space for cinema as the superior witness of war and the privileged medium of mass communication. The shortened time frame between the event and its consumption by viewers became a further guarantee of the veracity of newsreels and documentaries such as *Da Adua ad Axum: Le tappe dell'avanzata italiana in A.O./From Adwa to Axum: The Stages of Italian Advance in East Africa* (1936), which was advertised in *La Provincia di Bolzano* and the *Rivista del cinematografo* as the fruit of the mobile laboratories and other elements of Luce's AOI's modern infrastructure. "This is why cinematographic actualities such as those we can see tonight can be projected in Italian theatres so soon after the events they show have taken place," enthused the former paper. This celerity in image production and distribution, and its claim to represent modern temporalities and actions both in front of and behind the camera, were as important to Luce's authority as a purveyor of documentary reality as the actual content of its films, which were often dated in their visual and aural rhetoric.[39]

The weaponization of the cinematic apparatus and the climate of permanent mobilization also brought new visibility and relevance to the figure of the cameraman. After 1935 Luce operators such as Craveri became minor stars in their own right, garnering and granting interviews in the film press. As described by Luce's D'Errico, Luce cameramen were "eager and devoted servants, conscious of their high mission, silent, tenacious, sensitive, ready to face discomfort and sacrifice as much as their companions in uniform"—in other words, paragons of Fascist militarized manhood. The slippage between the roles and qualities of the wartime cameraman and the soldier dominates Craveri's 1936 autobiographical article, "An Operator among Wars and Revolutions," which relates his experiences in the early 1920s as part of an anti-resistance military unit in Tripolitania, his work on Hollywood and Italian Orientalist features set in Libya, and the armed clashes with bandits that marked his filming of Baron Franchetti's 1928 Ethiopian expedition.[40] These celebrations of male heroism behind the camera, and the added value given to the figure of the camera operator within empire film culture, compensate for Luce's mandate that its productions bear an anonymous and collective "eye." As David MacDougall reminds us, the body behind the camera also forms part of a film's repertory of corporeal images, but Luce's industrial aesthetic asked that body to disappear, subordinating its voice to that of the war machine. Luce newsreels replaced the sensibility of the lone documentarian and his or her rendering of raw experience with that of the editor whose skill lay in distilling that experience into a highly mediated "reality at second hand." The minimizing of individual subjectivity in favor of the anonymous voice of collective history and the reliance on the archive recall 1920s Soviet experimental compilations that formed part of a turn away from the avant-garde. As we will see, D'Errico's own artistic trajectory conformed to this path, and he, like many of his peers, prized his parallel feature film career as a space for that individual artistic expression largely banished from "Luce style."[41]

Adding to the cameraman's challenges was the fact that much of the combat in Ethiopia could not be represented on-screen. Although almost one million men were mobilized by early 1936, the main facilitator of the regime's rapid advances in Ethiopia—the massive use of chemical weapons—could not be depicted, and visually compelling aerial warfare also carried many restrictions. Moreover, Ethiopia's mountainous terrain favored guerrilla warfare, which was famously difficult to film, rather than the mass battles that made for good cinema. A *Cinema* editorial charged that instead of conveying the epic nature of the Italian enterprise, Luce newsreels focused on "the minute chronicle of secondary events." The Ethiopian war's limitations as a cinematographic event did not escape Luce officials, who faced heavy demand for war images. When MCP head Alfieri complained to Paulucci di Calboli that much of Luce combat footage lacked the large-scale battles necessary for spectacular effect, the Luce president replied: "I have the impression that our colonial war . . . rather than presenting mass conflicts, is basically an endless series of isolated actions . . . and even if we film as many of these as possible, which would be a great service to historical documentation, we would not succeed in giving the public a more dramatic representation."[42]

All of these constraints translate into newsreels that emphasize moments of collective mobilization and indigenous submission rather than actual warfare. The binding figure is the demonstration of collective assent through forward physical movement that gains aural reinforcement by martial music and high-pitched arrangements for strings that provide tension and suggest beehive-like activity in the service of the regime. The often frenetic pace of the images, the filling of space with massed bodies, and a camera eye that takes up the point of view of the anonymous viewer of Fascist events communicate the logic and mobility of total war—movement between and in the metropole and colonies. The rigorous attention to the collective also reflects the idea of empire building as an agent of Italian nationalization, with mobilization for the war presented as the instantiation of a national destiny. Within each imperial newsreel, as within the corpus of Luce texts, "the split between the continuist, accumulative temporality of the pedagogical and the repetitious, recursive strategy of the performative" maps the production of a nation reborn under Mussolini's lead. The telegraphic tones of the narrator, who is usually the only voice (other than the Duce) heard in Fascist newsreels, provide the former dimension, while the mute choreographed bodies enact the latter: together, they offer a visual record "of the history that is being written every day" on the battlefields and work sites of the empire.[43]

The newsreel's limitations led the documentary to emerge as a testing ground for new models of propaganda and the assertion of a greater degree of artistic individuality. As screenwriter and critic Jacopo Comin observed, the documentary also offered the filmmaker space to insert "a strictly subjective dimension, an interpretative and therefore artistic vision of reality. The choice of a point of view takes on the value of a creative act." This perception, along with the documentary's much lower costs with respect to feature film, accounted for the great interest among younger Italians in this form of cinema. Young men and women took advantage of the 16mm film production units that the regime provided in increasing numbers to GUF centers, and in 1938 the government authorized a rival agency, Incom (Industria Corti Metraggi), which encouraged innovation and greater authorial recognition within the documentary form. Fascist officials had been encouraged by the public interest shown during the Ethiopian war, when documentaries on imperial themes were sometimes advertised more prominently than commercial films and rivaled them in popularity. As critic and screenwriter Corrado Pavolini had remarked in 1937, "The predilections of film audiences were reversed: the four hundred meters on the African war were the big draw, and the spectacular film was the 'side attraction,' as the saying goes. And the theatres were packed as never before." The use of modernist aesthetics in the fonts and graphics of titles, charts, and maps added to the sense of dynamism. By 1939 one critic termed the documentary a "lifesaver" for the Italian film industry due to the formal and authorial innovations it encouraged.[44]

The eight films from 1937 that make up the *Cronache dell'Impero* series come out of this experimental climate. Falling in between the newsreel and the documentary in length and style, they combine the conventions of the tourist film (showing labor on coffee plantations, market scenes, local landmarks, and daily rituals) with the maps and didactic narratives of standard Luce documentaries. The aural signatures of these movies tag propagandistic priorities that were arguably shared by other imperial powers: the display of technological superiority, the legitimation of the colonizer's authority (the narrator and the martial music), and the evocation of the alterity of the indigenous (exotic local music and untranslated speech and vocalisms).[45] Two things in this body of work speak to the particularities of Italian imperial culture. First, the prominence of aerial settings and aesthetics, from the starring sonoral role given to airplane motor noise in many films to the sheer amount of time we spend in the air, with the pilot and his cockpit sometimes meriting a closer look than any colonial subject. This preference for the aerial point of view also suggests a fundamental insecurity of rule in Ethiopia, as does the avoidance of direct or frontal engagement with indigenous civilians. We are never already on the ground in these films, but mere visitors who, along with the narrator, fly in and presumably out, even in long-held Eritrea (as in *Eritrea-Asmara*). The instability that marked Italian reality in Ethiopia also comes through in film sound: in *Governo dell'Amhara—Gondar*, the aerial drone and driving symphonic music of Italian imperial command give way to ambient noise made up of barely intelligible indigenous male shouting, which is further disorienting for being out of sync with the images of market life and Muslim men praying. It is the sound of tumult, of the uncontrolled native male crowd, and while it is swiftly undone by martial music that synchronizes the steps of obedient marching *ascari*, it remains as a kind of sonoral specter of what lies outside of vision, below the reach of the aerial imperial eye. Praised for their "optimum cinematographic effect," the dense and quick *Cronache dell'Impero* still had the stain of the newsreel for *Bianco e nero*'s critic: "The true and proper documentary of this immense, very interesting, and very important material has still to be made," he felt.[46]

The hopes placed in the documentary also rested on its abilities to solicit emotions and desires as it fulfilled its didactic duties. "The documentary image functions in relation to both knowledge and desire, evidence and lure," writes Michael Renov, with the real a source of spectacle as well as information. Imperial documentaries engaged this double address through their recalls to adventure or melodramatic feature film narratives. One observer noted approvingly that the Italian Army's documentaries on mass mobilization often resembled feature films, while another boasted that many Italian documentaries were produced "like true and proper spectacular films," from the script through shooting to sound editing. Giorgio Ferroni's Spanish Civil War documentary *España, una, grande, libre!/Spain, United, Great, Free!* (1939) integrates a fictional film into its narrative.[47] A case in point is *Sulle orme dei nostri pionieri*, which combines lively pacing and innovative visuals, including animated charts, with a heavy-handed rhetoric and pedagogy designed to rouse nationalist sentiments and resentments. The film justifies the Ethiopian occupation as a continuation of Italian explorations of Africa from ancient Rome onward, but also as an armed response meant to correct Italy's subjection to "the rapacious demands of rich peoples." Although De Feo directed the League of Nations–sponsored International Institute of Educational Cinema, the Great Powers are as much the enemy as the Ethiopians in this film that celebrates cinema as a mobile technology. Moving images, juxtaposed with an antique-looking letter, suddenly bring a map of Africa to life, alluding to Fascism's visual and political reach across the Mediterranean and its ability to be a portal of the new. Statistics and maps about Italian emigration trace a history of national abjection that, like the old letter, can now be archived, with the new history of Fascism's imperial conquests to be written by moving images. The film's staging of Italian victimhood certainly struck a chord with critic Mario Milani, who acknowledged the formal "novelty" of De Feo's work before turning his review into a diatribe on the coalition of plutocratic powers that sought to block Italy from having "the place it deserves in the world."[48]

Luce's positioning of its films as interpreters of Italy's imperial epic did not preclude the press from highlighting their micro-historical relevance. The Fascist press exploited the potential local and personal resonances of imperial documentaries' spectacle of the real, which often included quick cameos of actual workers and military men. *La Provincia di Bolzano* advertised the release of *Da Adua ad Axum* as "an event of particular interest for our city, since the Gavinana Division, which was responsible for the taking of Adwa, includes soldiers from our province." Special screenings

FIGURE 3.5.

An Ethiopian tribal leader, 1936. *Da Adua ad Axum*. Author's collection

were arranged for schoolchildren, with the expectation that they might recognize a brother or father at war, and such assists to audience identification likely encouraged what Sobchack calls the "dynamic and labile" nature of spectatorship. Yet only military officials and Galeazzo Ciano merit a frontal pan: the rank and file are subsumed into a fast flow of images. A tribal leader on horseback receives the most sustained attention. Although he is presented as among those who ask for protection from the Italians, his gaze, aimed directly at the camera, speaks on its own, offering spectators a "flash of wordless intuition of reality," at odds with the martial music and narration.[49]

The imperial documentary's "spectacle of actuality" also encompassed the pleasures of seeing the world laid out by others, who, like Luce and Incom narrators, "know for me." This passive spectatorial disposition was much encouraged by Fascist nonfiction, which aimed less to convince the viewer about the truth-value of the film than to present that truth as inevitable, part of a historical process that was impossible to stop. These documentaries communicate the convergence between the desires of the Italian people and the Duce for empire through figural strategies, dynamic editing and narrative construction, driving martial music, and the rapid-fire delivery and staccato cadence of the off-screen commentators. As D'Errico summarized the traits of "Luce style," "in front of the facts all discussion is useless, and the screen brings the facts to the most incredulous eyes, impartial, suggestive, 'photographic.' ... [I]t is with the documentary that film takes on its true historical function." In the imperial documentary, Fascists' anxieties about their place in the world and the belatedness of their empire translate into configurations of past and present history as pre- and over-determined. In this way, they participate in a broader Fascist culture that sought to "substitute scrutiny of its policies with an aesthetically mediated belief in their inevitability."[50]

D'Errico's hourlong Luce documentary on the Ethiopian War, *Il cammino degli eroi* (1936), narrates this history in the making as an encounter with modernity, celebrating the war's industrial scale and the mobilities that made it possible. Made for international distribution, with graphics and French and German intertitles dividing the film into chapters, this compilation film is an experiment in propaganda. D'Errico had come from the ranks of an Italian cinematic and theatrical avant-garde fully in step with contemporary European developments. In 1929, after assisting on *Kif Tebbi*, D'Errico scripted Camerini's feature *Rotaie/Rails* and made his first documentary, *Stramilano/Supermilan,* a meditation on performance and glamour that would not have been out of place in Weimar Berlin. The city film aesthetic also marks his 1933 *Ritmi di stazione/Rhythms of the Station,* an ode to the flows of people and machines occasioned by train travel. The Italian station referred to in the title is embedded within international networks of transit and communication, but D'Errico reminds viewers that in Italy mobility also serves the specific ends of Fascism, by featuring a large "W il Duce" sign on a train being used to take children to a sea resort. His focus on movement continues in his first feature film, *La freccia d'oro/The Golden Arrow* (1935, co-directed with Piero Ballerini), which is set inside a high-speed luxury train. The all-Italian cast of this jewel heist drama did not stop the critic of the populist *Popolo d'Italia* from complaining about its deracinated plot and style: "Who knows what country this luxury train is passing through. Perhaps, in the author's mind, the same big world as Baum's Grand Hotel." The reference to Vicki Baum's 1930 novel, on which the famous Greta Garbo film vehicle was based (*Grand

Hotel, Edmund Goulding, 1932), took issue with a cosmopolitanism that would also mark many empire films.[51]

In *Il cammino degli eroi,* mobility enables political socialization, not individual liberation. Although it draws on the Weimar machine aesthetic and Russian constructivism, it repudiates modernist contingency and fragmentation in favor of a Fascist aesthetic of hierarchy and overdetermination. It also furthers narratives of Fascist innocence, presenting the Ethiopian War as a defensive response to "bloody aggression" by "savage hordes." This need to disavow Fascist violence, and the restrictions on combat coverage, meant that only two of the twelve chapters focus on the armed conflict between Italian and Ethiopian troops. This film about total war differentiates little between those making and those bearing arms, with endless footage of smoothly running machines and regimented bodies proof of the "great organizational capabilities of our people," as Paulucci di Calboli described the project. The mass embarkments for Africa appear as an act of blind faith, an appointment with national destiny, as well as a humanitarian intervention. In Ethiopia the frenetic movement continues, with roads built and bridges erected, but against a landscape that recalls the Western. In one of several chapters devoted to aviation, a pilot flies low over an expanse of brush-dotted plains, with drumbeats in the musical accompaniment conjuring Indians and caravans of tanks standing in for covered wagons.[52]

D'Errico follows his two aviation segments with one devoted to the work of Luce AOI and its cameramen-soldiers. We witness the setting up of the giant camera-as-weapon (footage shared with *Sulle orme dei nostri pionieri*) and the camera as part of a totalitarian circuit of surveillance that ends, of course, with Mussolini, who stars in an open-air screening prepared by a Luce mobile projection unit for an Ethiopian audience (the same projection referenced in figures 3.2 and 3.3). The internal film, which shows the Duce parading on horseback in Rome, cheered on by huge crowds, guides a relay of gazes between spectators in the colonies and those in the metropole. The audience in the cinema watches the Ethiopian audience sitting in the dirt, which watches the Italian audience on the Roman streets watching the Duce—who looks back at everyone. Throughout the Luce segment D'Errico engages with Soviet compilation practices, and with Dziga Vertov's experiments with "baring the device," and it is not surprising that a 1939 article cited *Il cammino degli eroi* (along with *Sulle orme dei nostri pionieri*) as a pioneering attempt to use cinema to write history, with the Luce archives as a primary source. D'Errico's highlighting of the cameraman's work draws attention to the way the raw material of that archive is captured. For him, the documentary's authority lies not only in the image, but in its assertion of what is anterior to that image: the binding and controlling powers of the gaze.[53]

The field of empire features hosted its own experimentations, in this case with the use of nonfiction clips and documentarist aesthetics. Two areas of criticism and practice informed discussions about this issue. First, the realist aesthetics that appealed to some Italian film professionals in the early 1930s as a possible foundation for a new national cinema. Filmmakers such as Giovacchino Forzano (*Camicia nera/Black Shirt*, 1932), Raffaele Matarazzo (*Treno popolare/Popular Train*, 1933), and Camerini (*Gli uomini, che mascalzoni!/What Scoundrels Men Are!*, 1932, and *T'amerò sempre/I Will Love You Always*, 1933) integrated documentarist conventions (filming on location, utilizing nonfiction clips and non-professional actors) as a means of grounding their fictional narratives in history, rendering Italy's particular articulation of modernity, and forging a model of cinema that would differ from both European art cinema and Hollywood. This tendency found increasing official support in the imperial years for films made in both metropole and colonies. Ciano championed the cinematic exploitation of the Italian landscape in a 1936 speech to Parliament, and *Lo Schermo* announced the formation of a state-financed production company, Etrusca Films, that would specialize in films shot on location. A hybrid feature-documentary aesthetic offered a path forward for the Italian cinema, but it presented considerable challenges. "How to blend the strictly 'documentary' and narrative parts? How to obtain a stylistic unity?" director C. L. Bragaglia asked in 1937. This question would be up for debate after each appearance of an empire film.[54]

The use of realist conventions in contemporary foreign films on imperial or exotic themes, whether British empire and desert films, French colonial movies, or Hollywood features, also provided a frame of reference for empire cinema. Hollywood productions served as negative models for Fiume, who often lambasted American movies for their falsity. "Two palm trees, a little sand, a lot of whiskey and a few nude women: this is the mannered Africa created by American rhetoric." Fiume had plenty of company in this opinion: the film professionals who contributed to a *Bianco e nero* review of the American blockbuster *The Lives of a Bengal Lancer* (Henry Hathaway, 1935) all agreed that the film was effective entertainment but lacking in authenticity. "Everything is typically Made in U.S.A. [sic] so that the spectator will at the most feel like he is inside the British Indian pavilion (Military Section) of the Los Angeles Exposition," complained set designer V. N. N. But Hathaway was accused of "an unjustified use of the documentary... Everyone knows that in an entirely 'constructed' film, an arbitrary use of [the documentary], purely for setting [*ambientazione*], always creates a visual, rhythmic, and photographic dissonance," charged Jacopo Comin.[55] British and French imperial features also fused documentary and fictional conventions, but political concerns and Fascist resentments of perceived British imperiousness often colored the Italian reception of British empire movies. And Fascist repudiations of Gallic decadence led them to disavow French colonial films' large aesthetic influence. Yet formal and stylistic commonalities can be found among French, British, and Italian empire films, starting with the ways that documentary realism is also a source of instabilities and interruptions within the film text. Charles O'Brien has argued that in using such referential material, especially of an ethnographic nature, French colonial films evoke aural and other phenomena that "exceed the representational capacities of the official culture." The use of nonfiction footage and indigenous actors in Fascist empire films suggests that the same can be said in the Italian case.[56]

The history of such formal experiments within the silent and sound Italian cinema on colonial themes includes features such as *Alima* (Gino Cerruti, 1921) and *Fiamme abissine* (Gino Cerruti, 1922), both filmed in Eritrea with all-indigenous casts, and *Siliva Zulu* (Attilio Gatti, 1927), shot in British Zululand. Fruit of a collaboration between Gatti, Vitrotti (cameraman), and anthropologist Lidio Cipriani (technical consultant and screenwriter), *Siliva Zulu* has been labeled "an African (melo)drama," and its tribal love-story plot owes something to Orientalist cinema. But the narrative breaks down often in the service of the film's real aim: the demonstration of customs and rituals by its all-Zulu cast. The ambiguous formal and stylistic profile of Gatti's film is captured in its publicity tag: "*Siliva Zulu*. A novel of life as it is lived in Zululand."[57] Italian empire features of the late 1930s build on these domestic and foreign traditions in their aesthetic experimentations. In their awkward passages from documentary to fiction, from location to studio shooting, and from professional to non-professional actors, as well as in the critical conversations they generated, they form part of a collective search to find a new formula for topical filmmaking that would earn Italy a niche on the international market. These political and commercial expectations also brought them in for heavy attention, with every missed opportunity severely judged. Until the end of the regime, Fiume groused in his column about the history of failed "hybrid fusions" in which feature filmmakers "realizing the profit possibilities ... inserted a weak adventure or sentimental narrative into a documentary frame."[58] The promulgation of the racial laws added another level of scrutiny, with anxieties about political stability and white male hegemony in the colonies factoring into critical discussions. Shooting on location and including indigenous actors and documentary footage mattered little if the film was discernibly false to colonial audiences or harmful to Italian prestige. Both *Sotto la Croce del Sud* and *L'Esclave blanc* would be lambasted for their depictions of the loss of white male dignity, despite their ample use of realist conventions.

The use of ethnographic material in Fascist empire features reflects tensions between distance and desire within imperial ideologies and practices, as well as the complicated provenance of the sources themselves. As in *Siliva Zulu* and French and British empire films, alterity is performed through ethnographic scenes that can seem to have little diegetic justification. Yet such scenes were essential to and expected of empire films, and not only for concerns of authenticity. The staging of the primitive through song, dance, and ritual confirmed, for Western audiences, the primacy of instinct and the body in the colonized culture, justifying a civilizing process to which the camera contributed through its own disciplinary gaze. Whether re-created by the filmmaker or inserted from documentary footage, ethnographic scenes in empire films depended for their evidentiary value on their recalls to an intertextual chain of colonial images that encompassed still images, advertising, and the live displays of colonial exhibitions.[59] Photography may be singled out for its importance in this chain of image circulation, with the Istituto Luce a main conduit. Its still images were often extracted from the same film negatives that produced newsreels and documentaries, with 350,000 colonial images produced in the nine months of the Ethiopian War alone, taken from the negatives from 80,000 meters of film. As Michael Zyrd has written, the reuse of certain images contributes to their iconicity. Italians vaccinating babies, tribal rituals, bare-breasted African women: these images stand in for a colonial politics of prestige and exploitation, with their historical and metonymic powers enabled by their repetition through various media. The use of ethnographic documentary clips and re-creations in feature films was rhetorically efficient: even as it operated as spectacle, it also referenced hierarchies of colonial power and knowledge beyond the film frame.[60]

The military sphere constituted the other main entrance point of realist elements in empire features. As war films that reach their dénouement in battle scenes, imperial movies made ample use of military resources, from indigenous and Italian soldiers who served as actors and extras to military footage and military consultants who vetted plot points and combat scenes for authenticity. Battle scenes also allowed for the display of Italian technology on a grand scale: aerial footage took center stage here, reflecting Italy's primacy in that area, but the operation of communications technology is also much in evidence. Telegraphs and radios in feature films also remind the viewer that the chain of colonial authority always leads back to the patria, with the radio serving as an aural equivalent of the movie camera in its interpellative role. Whether of anonymous soldiers on foot or in tanks, planes flying in formation, or disembodied fingers and voices conveying information, nonfictional inserts add energy and historical grounding to the fictional film, soliciting that "sensory excitement" so central to the experience of modernity. As Virilio argues, a cinematographic consequence of World War I had been the "accidental invasion of the picture show" by military documentary images. By the late 1930s, though, this was no accidental invasion, but a common practice of Italian filmmakers, one that would carry on after World War II.[61]

With respect to nonfiction clips of military operations, the vision of real soldiers performing actions they engaged in off-screen had a different valence, one that permits us to probe how empire films worked within the larger frames of imperial culture and Fascist spectacle. Although the majority of real soldiers played anonymous extras, filmmakers showcased those with voices and visages that suited their ideological intentions, whether those involved the demonstration of regional diversity or the chiseled beauty of the new Fascist man. Real soldiers could be scripted to serve as models of a militarized masculinity that echoed beyond the film frame. This performative dimension extended to the screen presence of real *askaris,* who not only added to the film's exoticism but allowed for the re-creation of situations of colonial submission and the reinforcement of masculine and racial hierarchies. The presence of real soldiers, whether in documentary clips or re-created battles, also sustains the rhetoric of victimhood that ran through Italian imperial ideology, by enabling violence to be partitioned off from the actions of the fictional protagonists. Whereas Ismail is shown committing acts of violence in 1927's *Kif Tebbi,* by 1936 showing direct aggression by an Italian protagonist was less acceptable. With the title character of *Luciano Serra, pilota* an exception, close-up killing is often assigned in empire films to anonymous male soldiers—troops on foot, bomber pilots in the air—leaving the actors in speaking roles, with whom the audience has presumably forged a bond, unblemished. Even the pilot Rossati in *Un pilota ritorna,* who drops bombs from the air, becomes a hunted man on the ground in the second half of the film. Thus do empire films further a "historiography of excuse" that simultaneously glorifies and externalizes violence.[62] But the spectacle of the real in empire cinema also gestures toward other histories that could not easily be narrated: histories of desire that accompany imperial conquest and histories of oppression and compromise on set and behind the camera.

Coming Home to the Colonies

A specter haunted Italian nation building and the imperial histories entwined with it: the emigrant, emblem of a poor country's inability to provide for its citizens. Other European powers, too, had unprecedented levels of mobility in the late nineteenth and early twentieth centuries due to migrations and colonial expansions, but the Italian state saw mass defections on an unparalleled scale. Thirteen million Italians left between 1880 and 1915, with two to four hundred thousand more emigrating every year until the end of the 1920s, a global dispersion that has led scholars such as Donna Gabaccia to label Italy a "diasporic nation." The immensity of this loss shaped Italian imperial ideologies, from their emphasis on the colonies as sites of demographic development to their inclusion of Italian communities abroad along with Italy's actual territorial possessions in visions of Italy's global reach. Although a number of emigrants returned to Italy during the dictatorship, the existence of this "nation outside the Nation," as one Fascist official called it in 1935, allowed the regime to reinvent the Italian nation as a potentially transnational entity, with communities of "Italians abroad" held together by affective ties and modern communications technologies. Thus did Mussolini appeal to "Italians all over the world" in his October 2, 1935, speech as "transmigrants"—a term that captures the sense of living among and between more than one country. The Ethiopian War consolidated this imaginary, with East and North Africa posited as homelands outside Italy that offered an alternative to emigration, and empire as a solution to a vexed history of flight from the patria.¹

This chapter explores how films about emigrants and their returns "home" articulate the emotional and political geographies proper to Fascism's empire. *Il grande appello* and *Luciano Serra, pilota* present the Italian colonies as redemptive spaces for their male protagonists, whose lives abroad (French colonial Djibouti and Brazil, respectively) were marked by loneliness and humiliation. Both films contrast these itinerant men with their militarized sons, commenting on the passage from a generation of migrant laborers to a generation who went only where the Fascist state sent them and from an impulsive individualism to a mind-set devoid of personal desire. The body registers this transition within Italian masculinity. The physically imposing fathers (Camillo Pilotto and Amedeo Nazzari) fill the screen and carry the story: they are the poles around which these films rotate as spectacle. But they must give way, through death, to the era of the uniform and uniformed body, one unscarred by the trials of emigration and suitable for Fascist mass warfare and collective life.

There are cracks in this cinematic armor, though, through which other states and realities can seep. *Il grande appello* and *Luciano Serra, pilota* showcase the liminal mentalities and situations that characterized colonial life but were in theory discouraged by the Fascist regime. From the blurred boundaries between the homosocial and the homoerotic to the sexual and other allures of the cosmopolitan spaces that lay outside the Italian national-imperial realm and to the colonies as sites for practices of violence associated with squadrism, these movies tap into the underside of the colonial fervor that swept Italy in the wake of the Ethiopian invasion. Both films also emphasize the tears to the family fabric that come with emigration, but ignore the separations imposed by military service, presenting the colonies instead as sites where fathers and sons can reunite. Italian women are pointedly excluded from these male havens, as are, eventually, the tainted fathers, who die on the battlefield. This time the paternal absence will be permanent, and these films send an ambiguous message about the worth and place of this generation of absent fathers within the totalitarian state, offering Mussolini and the military as a different kind of father and family.

In examining how these films give voice and body to those experiences of loss that were among the legacies of mass emigration, I draw on Laura Marks's study of how film can express "the disjunctures of space and time" that characterize the experience of emigration or diaspora. In *Il grande appello* and *Luciano Serra, pilota*, objects such as straw-covered Chianti bottles, accordions, and heritage foods solicit the spectator, serving as emblems of the national, appealing to his or her "nonvisual knowledge, embodied knowledge, and experiences of the senses." The display of technology also figures in here: shots of radio towers transmitting signals, telegraphs in operation, and planes swiftly crossing territory not only advertise Fascism's modernity and map the country's transformation "from an Italian to a global force," but also reduce the effects of physical distance and facilitate communication. Sound also bridged Italian eras and places in these movies, with Italian traditional songs, airplane motor noise, Fascist anthems, and nightclub music circulating among the metropole, Italian communities abroad, and colonial homelands. Following Iain Chambers's observation that "the history of place is itself an archive of sound," I explore how in empire films place is rendered not only through landscape but also through aural means.[2] Finally, I explore how tensions between an ethos of (re)settlement and one of movement played out behind the camera, as empire filmmakers adjusted to circumstances in Fascist Italy and the different kinds of circulations (the colonies, the Axis bloc) encouraged by the establishment of empire. *Il grande appello* and *Luciano Serra, pilota* may assert the Italian colonies as resting places for Italians, but they also reflect the cosmopolitan backgrounds of their directors. Much of their narrative force and drama comes from the consequences of uprootings and transits, from the "elsewhere" that plagues their protagonists, and from their presentations of states of mobility that Fascist imperial spectacle sought to exploit and to control.

IL GRANDE APPELLO

Mussolini's global imperial project aimed to exploit the "de-centered, lateral connections" proper to the Italian diaspora, and invitations to fight for the patria in Ethiopia were directed to Buenos Aires as well as to Bologna.³ Other lateral influences proved more troubling for the Fascists, such as those coming from French colonial culture. France's hold in North Africa not only complicated Italy's domination of the Mediterranean, but also testified to Italy's failure to retain its citizens. Until the early 1930s, more Italian emigrants settled in French colonies than in Italian ones, and throughout the 1930s many of the eighty thousand Italians still leaving Italy every year continued to relocate to French territories. The French colonial holding of Djibouti, where half of *Il grande appello* is set, was a particular sore point for Italians: it was Ethiopia's unofficial port city and had a direct rail connection to Addis Ababa—one built by the French back in the 1880s, when Italian colonial expansion was just beginning.⁴ Within Italian imperial culture, France was usually cited as a negative model of governance due to the French emphasis on assimilationism, and *Il grande appello*, which is set in Djibouti and in Ethiopia, participates in an intermedial presentation of French colonial space as threatening racial, gender, and national hierarchies. The film articulates this logic of differentiation through sound, models of masculinity, and forms of spectacle. *Il grande appello* appeals to the senses to call forth an expanded notion of Italianness in the spectator, soliciting desires that motivated men to come to the colonies but worked against Fascist mandates for sexual and racial order.

Il grande appello's intertwined stories of masculine and national redemption center on the transformation of a dissolute expatriate, Giovanni (Camillo Pilotto), into a devoted father and martyr for the national cause. The pull of paternal feeling sets in motion Giovanni's rediscovery of his Italianness in the colonies, and the film places intimate ties in relation with sentiments of national belonging in positing a transnational and trans-colonial emotional geography. While Giovanni is depicted as completely deracinated, when he hears from an Italian naval officer that his son's mother has died, he journeys to Ethiopia to find Enrico (Roberto Villa) and bring him back to Djibouti to take over the family business— the "Hotel Orient" in Djibouti, which has become a haven for anti-Fascists and exiled Ethiopians since the start of the Italian occupation. Enrico, an army communications specialist, never really accepts him, but the older workers and soldiers see him as a *paisan*, and in Ethiopia he exchanges French champagne for Chianti and sings long-forgotten Italian songs.

Shaken by Enrico's wounding in an ambush by the Ethiopians, Giovanni repents and during a battle between Italians and Ethiopians he blows up a smuggled shipment of arms meant for the Ethiopians, fatally injuring himself. While Giovanni has come "home" from the alien atmosphere of French colonialism, there is no on-screen reconciliation of father and son, and his death signals the passage of a generation of defectors out of the scene of national history.

As we saw in chapter 2, the exigencies of reconciling propaganda and entertainment became more important than ever in the wake of the Italian occupation of Ethiopia. Camerini's experience filming in the colonies for *Kif Tebbi* and his past box-office successes probably counted in Freddi's choice to give him the big-budget commission. The idea for the film had been Freddi's own, and the treatment prepared by Soldati and Piero Solari was shown to Mussolini before receiving the green light. The first feature film shot in Italian Ethiopia, *Il grande appello* had lavish funding from the Ministry of Press and Propaganda and the Ministries of Colonies, Aeronautics, and War; almost one-third its expenses were advanced by the state. Soldati sits uneasily in this official milieu. Because of his contacts with Italian anti-Fascist exiles abroad, he was under close surveillance during the film's production. Fascist spies read his mail and followed him around Italy and France, and the police repeatedly questioned him. Yet Soldati's 1935 book *America, primo amore/America, First Love*, about his attempt to resettle in America in 1929–1931, inspired the film's anti-emigration politics. The pressures that weighed on Soldati in this period may account for his framing of his book as a cautionary tale. In a preface that was removed from most postwar editions, he characterizes his flight from the nation as a "youthful error." "During my American stay I believed it was possible to evade: to change one's country, one's religion, one's memories and one's conscience," he wrote, announcing his intention to stay in Italy forever, "ringing the bells, singing in churches and taverns, burying the dead." Soldati's denunciation of his own emigration acts as a paratext of *Il grande appello*, since it influenced Soldati's and Freddi's public statements about the film during and after its production. Summarizing the story in *Lo Schermo* in June 1936, Freddi attributed Giovanni's flight to "youthful instincts of evasion." In Djibouti, Giovanni had been seduced by an "individualist utopia," losing "all sense of country and family" and becoming an "adventurer without patria." Soldati then echoed Freddi on the occasion of the film's release, characterizing Giovanni as "corrupted by the individualist mentality of an adventurer without country or family," who is changed by his contact with "the pure, strong, and heroic environment of our workers and troops in East Africa." Both men located the drama of the film in its contrasts between two worlds and two generations, between Italy's past and its future in the making.[5]

Into this ideological mix comes Camerini, who uses humor and a light touch to draw audiences into this drama of injured masculine and national pride. At the start of the film, two navy officers arrive in Djibouti to inform Giovanni about the death of Enrico's mother. They evoke Laurel and Hardy in their physical contrast, and the short one, who carries a copy of Marinetti's tract *Come si seducono le donne e si tradiscono gli uomini/ How to Seduce Women and Betray Men* (1916), embodies the comic figure of the *inetto*, or inept male. At the outdoor bar of the Hotel Orient, the short officer approaches a pair of Ethiopian women. He is in his undershirt, having soiled his uniform, and the women, who are dressed in European clothing, laugh at him in a language he does not understand and demand that he buy them champagne. Their unintelligible speech may be meant to estrange Italian audiences, but the scene holds potential for extra-linguistic understandings, including on a gender basis (Italian female spectators relating to the African women), that work against colonial ideologies of differentiation.[6] Things grow serious when the tall officer discovers a cache of arms meant for the Ethiopian enemy, and a bar brawl ensues between the Italians and Giovanni and his Spanish arms smuggler associates that recalls the fight among Foreign Legionnaires in Julien Duvivier's 1935 *La Bandera/Escape from Yesterday*. Hustled away by black colonial policemen, the tall Italian officer consoles his companion that more beautiful women await in their next port. Using a visual language taken from French cinema, *Il grande appello* reminds Italians that military service brings possibilities of interracial liaisons in exotic places, even as it depicts French Djibouti as a nefarious "world turned upside down" (blacks arresting whites, black women laughing at Italian officers, interracial couples).

As its name indicates, the Hotel Orient is the colonial version of the Grand Hotel's mélange. It is one of many such cosmopolitan and modern spaces in Camerini's oeuvre and Giovanni one of a series of interrelated protagonists who drift through them. "Dissatisfied and nomadic, Camerini's characters reappear from one setting and film to another," writes Guido Fink, and often those characters communicate the director's ambivalence about modernity's effects on traditional social relations and values. *Il grande appello*'s stark characterizations do not figure in Camerini's earlier metropolitan movies, though, and its provisional title, *Rinnegato* (meaning one who denounces or disowns, in this case his nationality), references the heavier political climate that followed the Ethiopian invasion. What does continue is Camerini's mobile aesthetics and use of advertisements, emblems, and objects with extra-cinematic recall, all of which embed the film's fictional narrative in actuality. "The cinema is a visual thing, and the most useful examples are graphic in nature. In this field a few signs almost always say more than many words," wrote Camerini during the film's production. While he referred to the storyboards that he published in *Cinema*, the director's use of signs, both semiotic and literal, is important to the rhythm and energy of his style and to the outlining of the two polarized worlds that he presents to the spectator.[7]

The first is that of the Hotel Orient, which we encounter when Giovanni tours the premises speaking English, German, Spanish, French, and Amharic. He greets Red Cross nurses, African notables, and others who transit through as refugees, exiles, merchants, and travelers. It is a fitting "home" for Giovanni, whose wanderings as an itinerant laborer through New York, Australia, Brazil, and Shanghai before settling in Djibouti have left him seemingly without any fixed identity. He no longer sees himself as an Italian—he refers to Italians as "voi altri" when speaking to the naval officer—but neither does he retain the regional or local affiliation that sustained so many Italian emigrants who identified, say, with Brooklyn and their native *paese*. Giovanni is not only the diasporic Italian who was forced into a degrading emigration by an incompetent state, but the quintessential nomadic subject of modern cosmopolitanism. Fittingly, Giovanni's Hotel Orient is less a resting place than a space in the sense intended by de Certeau—a dynamic place of passage formed by "intersections of mobile elements." A cacophony of visual and verbal messages stuns the senses. Plays of light and shadow from blinds and fluttering fans formed part of the colonial aesthetic of classical narrative cinema, from *Morocco* (Josef Sternberg, 1930) to *La Bandera* and *Casablanca* (Michael Curtiz, 1942). Here they take part in a larger (over)loading of the film frame, sometimes through depth of field, other times through a plethora of signs and objects, so that the eye cannot rest on any one thing or person without obstruction. Ads for Vichy water, Schweppes beverages, and Texaco motor oil fill the walls, with Italian products notably absent. They frame the characters, adding to their distraction, and distract the audience from them as well. The aesthetic of excess extends to the treatment of the body and the emotions, and verbal and physical arguments abound among the Hotel Orient's inhabitants. From the Spanish smugglers (who include Giovanni's companion Deborah and Deborah's lover Salvador) to Giovanni, who is fulsome in body and temper, the protagonists are always uncomfortable and irascible, always about to explode: Fascist uprightness and self-mastery have no place here.[8]

The use of sound in *Il grande appello* reinforces the sense of incipient anarchy. The Hotel Orient is a Tower of Babel. The languages its residents speak often have nothing to do with their countries of origin, and almost everyone is multi-lingual, often switching tongues in mid-sentence. Although we are in French territory, Spanish and Amharic are heard as often as French. The soundtrack in the Djibouti scenes is similarly complex, with music coming from a mix of diegetic and non-diegetic sources, accompanied by indigenous background noise. The Hotel Orient enacts linguistically diffused anxieties about modernity's dilution of national sentiment and Mussolini's dire prophecy that without Fascism, white European civilization would arrive at "a senseless disorder." With its "singular linguistic fabric," marked by a flow of incomprehensible sounds, *Il grande appello* gestures toward an aural realism even as it develops a kind of sound film spectacle that "relativiz[ed] speech" by inscribing it in "a visual, rhythmic, gestural and sensory totality."[9] But Freddi had a precise political aim in permitting so much foreign language to be heard in Djibouti: to unsettle and distance the viewer, preparing him or her for a linguistic "homecoming" in the film's Ethiopian scenes.

FIGURE 4.1.

The Hotel Orient, *Il grande appello*. Author's collection

Sound also provides occasions for the insertion of authoritarian discourse and vocal style into the film. Radio does the work here, since *Il grande appello* lacks an officer protagonist. It calls to Italians in Italian and foreign colonies and reaches enemy ears, facilitating the "oceanic spread of the national breath" throughout the national-imperial body and its expatriate extensions. In this and other empire films, engagements with Fascism's aural community, either as listener or as operator, become patriotic and political moments. Here the radio sparks an altercation between Fascists and anti-Fascists that is also a fight over political and linguistic authority. A Fascist journalist sitting in the bar (played by the real Fascist journalist Ercole Patti, whose experiences in Djibouti were one source of the story) turns up the radio's volume when the Fascist news bulletin comes on, drowning out all other sound. As the metallic voice narrates Italian successes, the journalist glares at the exiled Ethiopian notables who have just read aloud their own bulletin, in French, detailing heavy

FIGURE 4.2.

Giovanni, the volatile expatriate, *Il grande appello*. Author's collection

Italian losses. The Ethiopians protest angrily in Amharic, prompting him to exclaim, "I don't understand a word!" as he pushes them away. The radio silences all other speech, performing a "ballistic speech act" in keeping with a language politics that privileged one-way communication, even at the cost of efficient governance.[10]

Sound acts as a bridge between the cinematic and the extra-cinematic in other ways as well. After the bar brawl prompted by the Italian officers' discovery of the smuggled arms, Salvador puts on an upbeat record, which turns out to be "Giovinezza," or, rather, a cover done with a notable Latin inflection. "Te gustera mucho," Salvador tells Giovanni, as elegant multi-racial couples dance, unaware that it is a Fascist anthem. But Giovanni recognizes it immediately and responds by smashing the record, prompting a jump cut to Luce documentary footage of masses of Italian soldiers flowing onto ships headed for Ethiopia and to the martial sounds of "Giovinezza" done right. This scene also borrows from *La Bandera*. In that film, Jean Gabin's character, Pierre, who has joined the Spanish Foreign Legion after murdering a man in Paris, is tormented by the French music a fellow French Legionnaire (who knows Pierre's secret) insists on playing on the bar gramophone to remind him of his past. There the musical provocation is a private one, whereas in *Il grande appello* it is collective in nature, a desecration of a Fascist icon. The cut to the documentary insert silences this strange world in which "Giovinezza" is danced as a tango, carrying the spectator into Italian territory and the "normality" of Luce footage that by then had been seen and heard by Italian spectators countless times. The awkward and abrupt transition from the fictional setting to the documentary calls attention to the film's own artifice, though. The "redoing" of the diegetic "Giovinezza" as an auratic external voice, together with the evident shifts in image quality, cues a passage from the subjective voice of the director to the objective voice of the regime.[11]

The theme of contrast between the falseness of French-controlled Djibouti and the authenticity of Italian Ethiopia continues during the film's second half, which, as the film's credits state proudly, "was entirely made in Italian Africa." Expansive landscapes replace the crowded and claustrophobic interiors of the Hotel Orient, and Italian masculinity, stifled and disrespected in Djibouti, has free reign: no European women are ever seen, and African women are glimpsed only at a distance. The film's own production culture had set the virile tone: *Il grande appello* marked the first collaboration in Ethiopia between the military and film establishments. The young Renato Castellani, stationed in Ethiopia for his military service, had little problem "transferring" his duties so he could join the production. The filmmakers also emphasized the masculine character of their decision to film in the colonies. Soldati boasted that besides Pilotto, the film was shot "entirely without actors, that is with real workers and soldiers found on location" an enterprise "that would have made anyone's pulse race." The "maximum respect toward reality" that dictated casting, scenography, and sound in this half of the film may be read as an attempt to create a sober and "tough" model of film spectacle that reflected the realities of life in the empire.[12]

The scenes of the Italian encampment in Ethiopia hold great interest in this regard. The open spaces first disorient Giovanni, who is habituated to cluttered and chaotic interiors. And they are meant to startle the viewer as well. *Il grande appello*'s natural setting is not that of Sahara dunes, which were well known from French and Italian movies set in North Africa, but an untested Ethiopian landscape, seen by then in innumerable quick takes during Luce films but never in the slower pans and paces of features. Orientalist codes give way here to those of the Western and that genre's stagings of masculine conquest and renewal ground the film's solicitations of the spectator. Giant cacti dot the rocky clearing that is home to the encampment, with arid mountains in the distance. In this spartan space the soldiers and workers have re-created the basics of modern Italian life. Hand-lettered signs *"gran bar," "spaccio/*canteen" rebuke the glossy confusion of the products featured in the Hotel Orient. Meals are taken outdoors, cooked over an open fire, consolidating the frontier mood and appeal. As in the Western, the mountains and expansive landscape give a sense of stillness and solidity, in contrast with the fluttering nerves and fans of the Hotel Orient. The use of such conventions encouraged spectators to read Ethiopia as a new frontier, casting Italian workers and soldiers in the roles of pioneers of a new imperial history.[13]

The sense of the encampment as a male vanguard community frames Giovanni's first encounter with his son in the radio shack. Enrico's commanding officer has clearly become a father figure, and he stays with him during the reunion, allowing the workers to watch from outside. This denial of privacy is maintained throughout the Ethiopian scenes: the men are always seen together as they drink, comfort one another, and labor the harsh land. Giovanni stands apart here, especially with regard to Enrico, the new man of Fascism, who shares neither Giovanni's commanding personality nor his father's prepossessing physique or knowledge of the world. Enrico's horizons and affective connections are limited to his radio, his comrades, and his (now dead) mother in Italy. Soldati described Enrico rather ambivalently as "completely closed in and ardent for his nationalistic ideals," yet he is brave, saving his comrades during battle while telegraphing while wounded, whereas his cosmopolitan father cowers at the sound of a gunshot.[14] The campfire celebration the commander puts on to celebrate the father-son reunion brings us back to the film's interpellative function, to its "great call" to Italians abroad to return to national territory. As darkness falls, and the accordion, the Chianti bottle, and *minestrone al pesto* appear, Giovanni is brought back to the Italy of his youth. Such objects stand for an iconic (and internationally recognizable) Italianness, but they are also anachronisms that channel Italy the way Italian emigrants may have remembered it. Sound collaborates in this bridging of time and space. The middle-aged workers sing traditional songs, and one gives a solo performance of the Ligurian popular song "Cinque Minuti O Di Piacer/Oh, Five Minutes of Pleasure." Gesturing awkwardly, his bare arms thin but muscular, he invites the listeners to "leave your mother and come with me.... [I]f you want to make love with me, come at four, at five, at three."[15] As in the Western, the natural setting and campfire performance convey nostalgia for woman and family while affirming the pleasures of a temporary "home on the range." No less than the material objects in the scene, the song transports Giovanni to a young manhood spent in Italy, and perhaps to his seduction of Enrico's mother.

The setting and style of this performance also allude to other possible pleasures. The singing cowboy of the classic Western was often a well-known actor (such as Gene Autry), and his campfire performances were normally directed to an off-screen audience as well as on-screen companions. In *Il grande appello,* though, a anonymous worker is filmed mostly with his back to the screen audience, with occasional shots from a three-quarter angle or side angle: this serenade is meant for the special homosocial community of the encampment. As opposed to the emphatic heterosexuality of the Djibouti sequences, this male desire is open-ended. In keeping with Fascist male and combat ideologies, this scene plays on the ambiguous situations created by the circumstances of collective labor and combat. Alluding to furtive couplings (five minutes of pleasure) as well as traditional romantic longing, the performed song accesses a history of male interactions that had little record within written histories. As it channels nostalgia for home, *Il grande appello* also evokes the unrepresentable, inviting spectators to journey to their own spaces of desire and memory.[16]

Sound and speech are also integral to the film's logic of contrasts between the moral and aesthetic environments of French Djibouti and Italian Ethiopia. A minimalist communication style among uniformed men at the encampment replaces the chaotic aural climate of the Hotel Orient. Enrico speaks little, and his words carefully echo Fascist propaganda, even in the emotional scene when his father discloses his paternal wish

FIGURE 4.3.

Fascism's new man, *Il grande appello*. Author's collection

FIGURE 4.4.

The male enclave, *Il grande appello*. Author's collection

that Enrico leave Ethiopia and take over management of his hotel. "We are off track," Enrico responds. "I have made a commitment here, and I did it at a moment when the Patria..." It is only when Giovanni interrupts him, saying in a mix of French and Italian "Oh, the Patria... La patria c'est moi! Moi et toi..." and tells him his hotel is smuggling arms to the Ethiopians that Enrico loses his composure. For the duration of the film, Enrico refuses to speak to his father, even after he is wounded, and there is no father-son reconciliation within the space of the film. Giovanni is punished not only for his linguistic internationalism but for his linguistic excesses—too many words, and the wrong ones—whereas Enrico has learned how to be silent and cut off the enemy.

One thing carries over from the Djibouti scenes: the staging of the Italians' linguistic imperialism. As Giovanni arrives in the encampment, he hears "I don't understand!" spoken, this time by Italian soldiers who are being asked by Ethiopians to have their children seen by the doctor. Giovanni immediately intervenes as a translator, but his knowledge of Amharic is unwelcome. In all colonial contexts, translation politics reflect the need to conserve asymmetrical power relations, but the Italian Fascists were particularly assiduous in restricting the possibilities on both sides for genuine communication.[17] In this way, too, Enrico is a Fascist emblem. Unlike the older workers, who speak with heavy regional accents, his Italian is standardized, like the parlance of the radiotelegraph he operates. In the autarchic world of Italian Ethiopia, ignorance of other languages is a virtue: it filters out competing loyalties and tendencies to humanize the enemy. The exception is the tongue of technology, which is presented in empire films as the only language besides Italian that Mussolini's subjects need to speak. As a radio operator, Enrico is the new elite. He saves the unit by wiring for reinforcements and then is saved when a field doctor operates on him via radioed instructions from a specialized Italian surgeon in Asmara. Radio brings things in—soldiers, the latest science, and the Duce's voice—and links Italians to the patria wherever they are in the world.

Il grande appello does make use of various dialects and regional accents to tag the national scope of the imperial enterprise. Although the display of dialect was frowned upon in films, regional speech functioned here as an aural equivalent of the Chianti bottle, a sign of home to the emigrant and the metropolitan Italian alike. This kind of code-switching—between dialect and Italian—was acceptable to the Fascists, unlike the multinational Babel of the Hotel Orient. It is no accident that language is Giovanni's portal into Italianness: soon after he enters into Italian territory, he is given a ride by two soldiers with heavy Brescian accents, who pepper their speech with dialect terms and songs. These performances featured in pre-release publicity as an example of Camerini's skill in getting the most out of non-actors by tapping into their "popular and regional souls. Songs, phrases, jokes in their native dialects were enough to achieve the poetic atmosphere necessary for filming," Soldati attested; the Brescians were "continuing to live, during the filming, as they would in their normal lives." Sound acts as a bridge to the extra-cinematic, personalizing the mass endeavor of colonial conquest and grounding the film's fictional plot in real-life stories. What Koepnick calls "linguistic sampling," referring to the use of dialect in excess of plot requirements, was an integral part of the film's appeal to the viewer as spectacle and current history.[18]

This authenticity did not extend to the representation of Africans in the film. While *Il grande appello* is unusual for the range of depictions of the enemy (soldiers and officers, the population living around the encampment, the exiles of all social ranks in Djibouti), the "Ethiopians" in the film were almost all Eritreans, recruited in Asmara, since Italian rule was too tenuous and contested in Ethiopia to permit reliable extras to be found. Camerini does not play up the primitivity of the indigenous, as he had in *Kif Tebbi*, but emphasizes the Ethiopians' modernity. They are either Europeanized exiles who drink whiskey at the Hotel Orient bar or well-armed, almost equal military opponents; there are many close-ups of soldiers aiming powerful rifles at their Italian targets. The shot sequences and scale of the action in these scenes channel the Western, but a long mourning scene that places the action within the frame of Fascist history. Such scenes often figured in Foreign Legion and desert films—*La Bandera*'s is a close referent—but the inclusion of a roll call, where the Italians stand at attention, answering "Present" for their dead comrades, connects to a world of Fascist ritual and martyrology well known to any Italian spectator of the time. The aurally and visually effective and affecting scene provides yet another interpellative moment, bridging, at least in its intention, the emotional and physical distance between a desolate area in Africa and the viewing and bodily space of the spectator in New York or Milan.[19]

Such intimacy is lost in *Il grande appello*'s final scenes, which rely on long shots and panoramic camera work to render industrial-scale combat, complete with tanks, airplanes, and hordes of Italian and East African extras. Camerini had Ministry of War backing and the funds to shoot the climactic battle from scratch rather than rely on Luce documentary footage, but featuring real soldiers had propagandistic advantages. These anonymous men, whose collaboration was advertised in publicity and the credits, modeled a militarized masculinity that echoed beyond the film frame. Perfect physical specimens, they have the burden of mass killing and aggressive onslaught through technology, leaving the ragtag middle-aged fictional characters in the safer roles of beleaguered individuals who act only in self-defense. As the first film shot in Ethiopia, *Il grande appello* helped to establish this formula: its workers take up arms only when ambushed by the Ethiopians, and Enrico and his commander are both shot, begging the question of the Italian occupation that provoked African firepower in the first place. This partitioning off of violence from the protagonists of the fictional story externalizes Fascist violence from the "recognizable" national body, preserving narratives of Italian innocence.

Unlike other empire films, *Il grande appello*'s libidinal draw does not depend on a handsome male star, a tormented love story, or the exploitation of colonial exotica in the conventional sense. Rather, its spectacle lies in the exercising of its visual, aural, generational, and political tensions, in the oscillations from the "artificial" to the "authentic." As we have seen, the movie also makes recourse to the realms of memory and the senses in soliciting Italians to come home to the colonies, holding out the prospect of ambiguous forms of male camaraderie. This variegated address to the spectator perhaps contributed to its box-office success and to the cautionary rating (excluded for children) it got from the Catholic Church. Some critics were favorable. *Cinema* admired its use of contrast: *Il grande appello* combined the demonstrative merits of the documentary aesthetic—"a full adherence to the whole reality of things"—with the dramatic force of a fictional narrative. At a time when the empire film was seen as a testing ground for the reconciliation of propaganda and entertainment, this reviewer concluded that the movie showed that "it is possible to make political art." Others showed more skepticism, finding the film "disconnected (*slegato*)," and wondering why the Djibouti bar scenes, which were of such high political relevance, featured foreign languages "incomprehensible to the masses." Journalist Telesio Interlandi took the harshest attitude, asserting that Camerini's film served anti-Fascist politics by showcasing a character (Giovanni) with an "absolutely deplorable and dated mentality," whose negative opinion of Italy "put the entire Patria on trial." Disputing the conversion narrative that underlay the movie, Interlandi asked, "Is it possible that in Italy, in Fascist Italy, you can only be a patriot if you have first been a smuggler and an assassin?"[20] Freddi had been worried about the character of Giovanni from the start, and he had given the film scrupulous attention, showing it to high Fascist officials, the king, employees from the Ministry of Colonies, the movie studio, and Ethiopian War veterans. Interlandi's diatribe thus struck a sensitive nerve. Fascist ideologies of victimhood and regeneration required the staging of such male conversions, though, and similar plotlines marked virtually all empire films until World War II.[21]

In the postwar period, both Soldati and Camerini expressed remorse at having made *Il grande appello*. Soldati traveled to Addis Ababa to "confess" his "guilt" to Haile Selassie as part of an Italian TV program he made in 1974, while Camerini singled out the Interlandi episode, partly in order to frame the film as politically daring: "I remember the film as being rather fair until the breaking of the 'Giovinezza' record. What interests me, in terms of my personal defense, is the article by Interlandi in *Tevere*, the most Fascist paper. I was happy that he attacked me. Interlandi was very intelligent, he had understood everything."[22] The space between Camerini's first two sentences holds the attention here, as he jumps from his claim that the film is not pro-Fascist *until that point* to the implicit acknowledgment that it would be interpreted as such. By eliding mention of his use of the Luce footage that enters the film at that moment, Camerini begs the question of what it meant to incorporate an official point of view within his movie. At issue is also the larger question of the pressures the regime placed on the film industry in those years: the "great call" of the film's title was also a request that film professionals put aside their own physical and creative peregrinations and travel, like Enrico, only within a Fascist-approved political geography. This dimension was naturally left out of Freddi's own postwar recollections, as was the ultimate goal of these Italian homecomings, as stated by him in 1936: "to return a sense of ITALY even to its most long-lost and dispersed sons: and obtain from them, if necessary, the sacrifice of their lives."[23] Behind Mussolini's call to "Italians beyond the mountains and the sea" lay a totalitarian state's need to execute its imperial conquests, with bodies that came from Rio and Little Italy as well as Rimini.

LUCIANO SERRA, PILOTA

Made two years after *Il grande appello*, *Luciano Serra, pilota* represents the peak of the Fascist investment in empire movies as experiments in the blending of entertainment and propaganda. The story of an Italian pilot who spends fifteen years in South America before coming "home" to Ethiopia to fight with the Fascist Militia, its aviation theme helped to make it one of the biggest box-office successes of the regime. Aerial acrobatics, bombing scenes, and transatlantic flights provide compelling visuals and advertise Italy's advanced technology in this sector. Yet the airplane has other meanings in this emigration movie: it brings people together, bridging the gaps that afflict divided families. Nazzari, as Luciano Serra, is not only the virile pilot, but the vulnerable Italian abroad, a father separated from his wife and son. The film appeals to the spectator by foregrounding an emotional geography that parallels the physical map of Italian peregrinations. Indeed, *Luciano Serra, pilota* starts out as a family (melo)drama. In 1921, unable to provide for his family, Luciano accepts a job in commercial aviation in South America, but jumps at the chance to return home with his pride restored, ten years later, at the helm of a spectacular transatlantic flight from Rio to Rome. When the internationally advertised project is jettisoned, just when Luciano's son Aldo (again played by Roberto Villa) sends notice that he too wants to be a pilot, Luciano attempts the flight on his own, only to crash into the sea.[24]

The plunge to his presumed death marks a series of transitions in the film. As in *Il grande appello*, a narrative ellipsis brings us from foreign to (colonial) national territory, from studio-shot interiors to mostly outdoor spaces, and from a life of individualism to one given meaning by a military collective, in this case the 221st Legion of the Militia, which Luciano joins under an assumed name. "The war saved many. And it saved me too," Luciano tells the military chaplain. Ethiopia is also the scene of father-son reunion, and it is in saving Aldo on the battlefield that Luciano is fatally injured; his old friend Colonel Morelli (Mario Ferrari) will father Aldo in the future. Two of the film's trajectories are completed here: the end of the emigrant's physical alienation from his family, rendered by the greediness of the dying Luciano's touch for his son, and his moral rehabilitation. But other histories of violence and belonging, connected to Fascist aviation and the Fascist Militia, haunt *Luciano Serra, pilota* and are signaled in the text and the paratextual apparatus. Both figure in the regime's strategies of reclaiming Italian emigrants from the Americas, and both had the Fascist official Italo Balbo as promoter and protagonist. As we will see, Luciano's history is entwined with that of Balbo as star aviator—and star squadrist.

Luciano Serra, pilota dramatizes emigration to South America, where millions of Italians had settled by 1926, the year Foreign Minister Dino Grandi decreed that the term "emigrants" be replaced by "Italians abroad." Brazil, where the fictional Luciano settled, had smaller Italian communities than Argentina, in large part due to a 1902 ban on subsidized emigration that followed persistent reports of mistreatment. All over the Americas, prejudice and continued poverty coexisted with the comforts of large numbers of compatriots. The Fascist regime made political capital from this unfortunate situation, encouraging movies such as Brignone's *Passaporto Rosso/Red Passport* (1935), which depicted Italians in Argentina as victims of labor exploitation and generalized corruption. The *fasci all'estero*, or Fascist groups abroad, provided solidarity and political organization for emigrants, and during the Ethiopian war they recruited Italians to fight in Africa in a special *fasci all'estero* legion organized by the Fascist Militia. With many middle-aged men as members, the value of this emigrants' legion was less military than symbolic. Bringing together men from every continent on the basis of their Italian origins, the legion stood for an identity "bound by distance" that could be mobilized in times of national urgency.[25]

This legion, which gave the fictional expatriate Luciano Serra a "home" in Ethiopia, had been the subject of a 1936 documentary, *Legionari del secondo parallelo—Diario di un milite*, by the empire filmmaker and Militia member Marcellini.²⁶ Loosely following an emigrant's journey from Buenos Aires to fight with the 221st legion in East Africa, it provides a frame for *Luciano Serra, pilota* and highlights the different ways documentary and feature cinema engaged with this subject. Fifteen years younger than Camerini, Marcellini never lived abroad, and his career developed entirely within the regime's film and military structures. He advertised his documentary as chronicling the emigrant-soldiers' "acclimation and training for war," boasting that it developed "on the ground," out of discussions with his fellow Legionnaires in their tents. Marcellini's status as a paragon of the militarized film professional comes through in this account of the film's production by journalist Sisto Favre: "Shooting [the film] went on among the whine of friendly and enemy machine guns, sometimes caught between two lines of fire, one had to suffer thirst and hunger, bivouac, and pass hours and days drenched by torrential rains, braving the same toil, discomfort and danger as the humble and heroic Legionaires."²⁷ These tough conditions meant that much of the footage deteriorated due to the heat, so the movie made liberal use of Luce inserts, as well as of material re-shot by Marcellini. *Legionari del secondo parallelo* was a compilation film in fact, if not in intention, and "Luce style" prevailed over auteurist tendencies. Cold-toned omniscient narration and hammering martial music drive the action forward, with the subjects speaking only through on-screen writing, whether the diary entries referred to in the film's title or messages Marcellini finds on lorries, on docks, and even on safari helmets: "*Donne e motori/Gioia e dolori. New York—USA*," one man has inscribed on his.²⁸ The diary entries speak of hardships ("Sand, wind, and heat"), track temporal and spatial passages, and serve as historical grounding ("Graziani wants to speak to us"). Close-ups of the author's hand writing his entries suggest a space for the personal within the industrial scale of warfare, yet the putative Militiaman protagonist merits only fleeting medium shots. Marcellini keeps the emphasis on the collective nature of the Ethiopian War and the aggregate value of the men "who came [to Africa] from all over the world" to recover their Italianness—or perhaps just to find the next lucrative opportunity. "Afgoye: this seems like a garden, not a battlefield. I will return here with Marietta. *This* is America!" reads one diary entry.

Movement is the true subject of this film and the source of its action: most of the film documents the struggle to move through the land. As in

Il grande appello, Ethiopia is an empty space to be conquered, a frontier forged by pioneers. At times the Western inflects Marcellini's imperialist vision—there are campfires and majestic landscapes—but Fascist war and masculinist ideologies prevail. Currents of raw virile energy run through the film, massing in groups of bare-chested males, and Graziani speaks to the legion, via the narrator, praising it for redeeming "the humble and neglected Italy of the emigrants." As these men strike the enemy, they also kill their own histories as defectors from the patria, and recurring images of hands raised in Fascist salutes make clear that this is a journey of political re-socialization. We also see Ethiopians supposedly submitting to Italian authority, although most of the notables who are filmed as they attend Italian lessons refuse to look at either the teacher or at the camera. The shift to high politics at the close of the film—ceremonies involving uniformed officials, none of them returned emigrants—leaves all of those humble histories on the battlefield, largely unexplored, awaiting their dramatization in feature films such as *Luciano Serra, pilota*.

Alessandrini characterized *Luciano Serra, pilota* before its release as a film "of much pathos," and the aim of soliciting spectatorial empathy for and identification with the male protagonist influenced its portrayal of the Italian emigration experience. Unable to make enough offering tourist flights over Lake Maggiore to maintain his family, Luciano loses his wife and son (who go to live with her father) and then his home as well, opening the door to his emigration. We are, crucially, in the last year of the liberal era, and the film sets up the coming of Fascism as a solution to this waste of masculine energies. Luciano is no deterritorialized nomad, like Giovanni in *Il grande appello*, but a reluctant exile, and his departure from Italy begins a chapter where both father and son think and feel transnationally, as did so many Italians. The son remains fiercely loyal to his father, and Luciano dreams of being able to return home to him. The intimate ties that bind them over fifteen years of apartnesss are crucial to the film's narration of the human drama of Italian emigration and to its address to the Italian spectator's own history of family separations.[29]

Supervised by Vittorio Mussolini, whose father, the Duce, suggested the film's title, *Luciano Serra, pilota* was an official creation. In some ways its protagonist embodies a Fascist fantasy of the Italian emigrant experience. Although Luciano's job in commercial aviation turns out to be degrading—he flies a circus lion from continent to continent—he works hard at it. And although Grandi and other officials worried that Italian emigrants might undergo "a violent and total assimilation into other civilizations and races," Luciano remains seemingly unaffected by his surroundings. Despite ten years in Rio, he seems to have learned no Portuguese, his only friend there is an Italian mechanic, and he never shares screen space with a Brazilian woman. Linguistically and sexually, Luciano is Fascism's autarchic "armored body." Italy is his reference point throughout his diasporic existence of "living here and remembering/desiring another place." This same object of desire—Italia—appears at his most desperate hour, in the form of a neon hotel sign outside his window, galvanizing him to steal the plane and return to his country.[30]

Luciano has a dark side, however, which is signaled in this key scene by his framing in chiaroscuro, with the flashing sign and rotating fan blades lending his figure an air of drama and mystery. In gangster and Foreign Legion films, such plays of light often cue characters operating in a zone of marginality, and in fact Luciano is about to embark on an illegal enterprise. The narrative has set up this moment, though, calling attention from the start to Luciano's impulsivity and attraction to risk. After his family leaves him in the film's early scenes, Luciano puts on his tuxedo and goes to the Grand Hotel in Stresa, where he meets an American aviation tycoon and charms the American's platinum-blonde wife, earning the job offer that leads to his departure, rather than work as *un impiegato,* or functionary, in his father-in-law's firm. "Mine is an escape," he tells Morelli. In Rio his job in commercial aviation does not satisfy his urges for freedom and action, leading him to accept the daring transatlantic flight. A montage of newspaper titles and shots of telegraph and telephone operators and radio towers buzzing about his fate communicates his new status as a media subject. Back in Italy, Aldo reads about his father and asks Morelli to be admitted to Fascism's Aeronautics Academy, As Morelli, Ferrari anchors the movie for spectators, his rectitude a foil for Luciano's unpredictability, and in his past military roles (*1860, Villafranca, Cavalleria, Ettore Fieramosca*) delivered authoritarian messages with a clipped delivery and harsh tone. Here he gives audiences a dose of propaganda about Fascism's success in turning aviation into an arm of the state. When Aldo's grandfather questions Aldo's decision to be a pilot, Morelli assumes the favored arms-akimbo stance as he tells the older man that today's flyers "are more careful than your accountants.... Today we are no longer the pilot. Today we are the Air Force. Today it's not enough to be courageous to be part of our family, you need the clearest and highest sense of discipline." The contrast with Luciano—who has always lacked such discipline—is evident, and Morelli's speech carries an implicit critique of Luciano's individualism, which would prevent him for joining the air force "family" even if he were present.

The critique of spectacle purveyed in this spectacular and star-driven film reflects its supervisor Vittorio Mussolini's ambivalent attitudes toward Hollywood. The film took shape at the peak of the younger Mussolini's infatuation with American cinema, which he advocated as a model that would "emancipate" Italian cinema from its silent film and stage inheritances. In 1937, as *Luciano Serra, pilota* started production, he traveled to Los Angeles to form a production company with Hal Roach. Three Luce newsreels document his journey, including one in which he speaks some English during a visit to the set of Roach's "Our Gang."[31] Alessandrini's experience in Hollywood at the start of the decade no doubt contributed to his gaining the commission, as did his work with Nazzari in *Cavalleria* (1935).

Made as a response to "overseas colossals," *Luciano Serra, pilota* contains many signs of Hollywood influence: the use of lighting and mise-en-scène to set mood and character, ways of filming action and battle scenes and landscape, and the purveyance of a certain model of modernity and consumer culture. *Lo Schermo* had advocated in 1936 that empire films feature "the immensity and configuration of Ethiopian territory," and Alessandrini and his collaborators make use of a Western-derived repertoire of framing and composition to that end.[32] As in Camerini's and Marcellini's movies, we have Ethiopia as a new frontier and the empire film as a space to experiment with that tension between the known and the new that is fundamental to the operation of genre cinema.

Yet it is equally significant that the most "American" moments of the film—which are staged in ways that appeal to the Italian spectator's expectations of how Hollywood films should look—correspond to situations of moral liminality. In fact, like scores of Fascist ideologues and intellectuals, Vittorio Mussolini admired American films and rejected American social and political values in equal measure. The scenes at the

Stresa Grand Hotel provide one such moment. Its Hollywood-inspired elegant dancing couples, platinum-haired women, white columns, and ballroom floor led Antonioni to mistake Stresa for Hollywood in his review of the film; he stated erroneously that Luciano first went to North America before landing in South America. At the same time, this Grand Hotel could be located anywhere; indeed, its indeterminacy is key to its extra- and inter-textual recall. And it is precisely in this non-place that Luciano's distancing from his own place begins.[33] An interracial boxing match that Luciano attends in Rio offers another example: it channels the 1935 fight in New York between the Italian Primo Carnera and the African American Joe Louis. Brazil was also a multi-racial society, and Carnera had toured South America victoriously in 1934, but he had been defeated in New York by Louis, whereas here the black man wins only because the sports promoter has paid the white man to lose. The film thus offers viewers the visual pleasure of the boxing match without the displeasure of the racial insult—we are in 1938, when race laws were in force in Italy and the colonies. The Rio scenes are central to *Luciano Serra, pilota* as a model of marketable entertainment that also reinforced the regime's ideology.

Nazzari's presence within *Luciano Serra, pilota* may be understood within this framework. His star power within Italy approximated that of a Hollywood male lead, and his performance as Luciano guaranteed the film's box-office success while satisfying nationalist and political demands. Fascist officials and critics held divided opinions about stardom as a whole, and Mussolini's status as uncontested divo of Italy made the issue of male stardom particularly delicate. The greater export and ideological demands placed on the Italian film industry in the imperial years made male stars indispensable, though, and the imperial years saw a heightened interest in actors that also reflected the greater emphasis on the male body as a vessel of Italianness and militarized masculinity. *Bianco e nero*'s 220-page special issue on the subject was merely one of several discussions going on while *Luciano Serra, pilota* was in production. De Feo argued that actors must reflect "our character" and not be "bad copies" of American stars. "In terms of makeup, photography, and costume, we must have in mind the characteristics of our people and only our people." Whether those paragons of national identity should be allowed to be stars remained up for debate, but all agreed on the importance of finding actors who would connect with the spectator to the point where he "no longer has his own point of view, but sees with the eyes of the character," as one commentator wrote.[34]

Nazzari's importance lay exactly here, in his ability to connect with male and female spectators through an emotional expressiveness that was balanced by his virile physicality. Known as "the Italian Errol Flynn" for his physical resemblance to the Australian American actor, his star persona was partly marketed and received as a translation of American film culture. Yet he was also considered a very Italian figure. Tall, broad-shouldered, and elegant in both a tuxedo and a military uniform, Nazzari was the arguably the most successful product of a Fascist-era film culture that, as Marcia Landy writes, "had an eye on Hollywood as well as on Fascist gendered iconography." Nazzari possessed the "physique, imperious diction, militaresque bearing, [and] cult of the positive hero" necessary to carry films of combat and conquest, and he starred in three of the eight features discussed in this book. He played a key role in disseminating the commanding body but also in staging the disappearance of that body. Both *Cavalleria* and *Luciano Serra, pilota* resolve in a "sacrifice and transcendence of the body for the nation through technology" that reinforced Fascism's "abstract moral imperatives of heroism, patriotism, and family honor."[35]

Nazzari was no Futurist hero, though. His popularity with audiences stemmed from his qualities of humanity. He often played struggling, abject characters and cried on-screen. This expressiveness, as well as his confident masculinity, led the critic Puck (Gianni Puccini) to praise Nazzari as a "strong and Italian man," a corrective to "our anemic roster of faces and figures." But Nazzari's impact, for Puccini, also lay in his familiarity: his was a face "that we know [and] which represents a prototype which is extraordinarily close to us ... an everyday face." The regime's populism, its desire to differentiate Fascist films from Hollywood ones, and impulses toward a greater realism in Italian film all led to a critical preference for male and female stars "with an ordinary face, not exceptional or unrepeatable," and Nazzari seemed to fit the bill in this regard as well. In any event, within Fascist culture the privilege of being exceptional and unique in physiognomy and history was reserved for one man only: Mussolini. Giuseppe Gubitosi has argued that Nazzari's star persona had

FIGURE 4.5.

Luciano at the Grand Hotel, *Luciano Serra, pilota*. Author's collection

a complementary relationship to that of the Duce, with the actor representing a more humane Mussolini. On-screen, Nazzari was akin to the Italian leader in being the authoritarian father, "protective, understanding and yet firm and severe," while also being—quite unlike Mussolini—a devoted and loyal spouse.[36] Nazzari's dialogue in *Luciano Serra, pilota* emphasizes this approachability. His deep, warm voice fills the screen; he uses colloquialisms; and his sentences are brief and tend toward simple tenses. In all this Luciano contrasts markedly with Morelli, who moves stiffly in his uniform and speaks in Fascist sound bites.

Vittorio Mussolini had characterized *Luciano Serra, pilota* before its release as "a film of youth," and at an early point there were plans to center the film on Aldo becoming a pilot, with Nazzari, the absent emigrant father, appearing only in a photograph.[37] Box-office considerations counseled against such a move, since Nazzari drew in that younger generation of Italians, men and boys who were Fascism's target audience for military recruitment as well as a main source of film revenues. Like *Il grande appello, Luciano Serra, pilota* is a film about generational change, with errant fathers making way for disciplined sons. Unlike Giovanni, though, Luciano is a man of action who knows the language of technology. In 1935's *Cavalleria*, Nazzari played a young cavalry officer who transitions to aviation; as the middle-aged Luciano, he struggles against a new era in which movement—of aviators and emigrants—is highly regulated. Nazzari's star turn as an aviator also had a political rationale. It connected the movie to a culture and industry of aviation that were a source of national pride and aesthetic innovation. *Luciano Serra, pilota* stands as an example of the partnership that peaked in the imperial years between cinema and the cult of Fascist aviation, a partnership motivated by the demands of military conquest as well as those of spectacle.

Fascist propaganda of the late 1930s and early 1940s celebrated the airplane as a showcase of Italian ingenuity and power, a means of winning wars quickly, and a means of publicizing an imperial-diasporic nation that extended beyond Italian territorial possessions. *Luciano Serra, pilota* showcases and references all of these dimensions of Italian aviation. As we saw in chapter 2, the Italians had pioneered reconnaissance and bombing day and night flights during the Italo-Turkish War, and strategic bombing continued to have priority in Italian military strategy during World War I, under the influence of General Giulio Douhet, who contributed to the design of the Caproni precision bomber. Balbo championed Douhet's ideas as undersecretary (1926–1929) and then minister of aeronautics (1929–1933), ensuring that bombing technology played a key role in Fascist colonial conquest. Libya alone endured more than six thousand missions during the years 1922–1931. Balbo also invested massively in aviation infrastructure, clearing the way for the creation of the commercial airline Ala Littoria, which after 1936 had a dedicated "Empire" route that flew to Djibouti, Cairo, and Khartoum as well as the Italian colonies. Ala Littoria became the centerpiece of a civil aviation that by 1939 ranked third worldwide for range of destinations and for volume of goods and people transported, with twenty-eight international and twenty-four domestic airports in the metropole and colonies. Twenty-five foreign air forces trained pilots in Italy, thirty-nine nations imported Italian aeronautics products (including the lightweight Avia movie camera), and the Italians held 110 world records for distance, altitude, speed, load, acrobatics, and more.[38]

A pilot himself, Balbo had put Italian aviation on the global map with collective flights that traced a map of Italian influence in the western and eastern Mediterranean (1928 and 1929) and the Americas. His "mass cruises" to Brazil (1930) and the United States (1933), which involved dozens of planes and hundreds of people, advertised Italians' cutting-edge aviation technology, with Italian and Italian American products featured prominently in publicity materials. The imperial dimensions of Balbo's flights come through in Craveri's documentary of the Italy–Brazil trip (*Lo stormo atlantico/The Atlantic Flock*, 1931), which blends aerial cinematography with exploration-film footage from refueling stops in French and Portuguese colonies.[39] The destinations in the Americas (Rio, Chicago, and New York) all boasted large Italian communities, and Balbo's flights there charted bonds of intimacy and nostalgia that bound a dispersed Italian population. One year later, the Fascist government celebrated aviation's role in forging this sense of belonging with a 1934 stamp, printed for use in Cyrenaica, which celebrated the advent of long-haul postal flights between Italy and South America. The triangulation of Libya-Italy-Argentina asserted an Italian imaginary founded on kinship and patriotic sentiment rather than sovereignty. Balbo's pilot persona was crucial to his role in creating such an imaginary for public consumption, along with his commitment to strategic bombing: he embodied every aspect of the culture of Fascist aviation. It was in part Balbo's doing if in the 1930s "the great pilots were loved and admired like the *divi* of the cinema." The filmic character Luciano takes much from Balbo's bravado, even though he is largely a negative shadow of the Fascist official, and probably only Nazzari, with his strong physical presence, could approximate the larger than life Fascist official, who took on an imperial role as governor of Libya after 1936.[40]

From Comerio onward, the cinema had been present to record the successes of Italian aviation, and the mobility of the cinematic apparatus also lent itself to aesthetic experimentations in capturing the experience of flight. The rapid montage, sudden high and low views, exploding graphics, and the prominence of noise in Craveri's Balbo documentaries would all feature in imperial fiction and nonfiction. In the late 1930s, an intertextual chain of images that sought to represent flight's compressions of time and space, the pilot's unique view on the world, and the marvelous strangeness of landscapes seen from the air linked documentary and fiction cinema, photography, and Futurist *aeropitture*.[41] The Fascist investment in bomber technologies created many opportunities for image capture, and the sinuous lines and chromatic effects of reconnaissance and bombing photos—the one shown in Figure 4.6, taken in Somalia by Masoero for the *Disperata* bomber squad, was published in Pavolini's 1937 war chronicle—find an echo in empire movies with aviation themes. Underlying this work of representing flight was a belief in the creative and military synergies of the movie camera and the airplane: as "mythopoetic machines of modernity," both were crucial to the Fascist epic of imperial expansion. The copious attention given in the press to the military and aviation experience of empire cameramen and directors has its origins here, in the value placed by a militarized culture on the collapse of sighting and shooting functions and on cinema's integration into the Fascist arsenal.[42]

Luciano Serra, pilota comes out of this alliance and intertwining among aviation, film, and imperial interests. The movie's financial backers included the National Association of Industrial Motors and Aircraft, and it advertises the producers of some of the aviation technology it displays on-screen. The film's *équipe* included aerial photographer and cinematographer Filippo Masoero, who co-authored its original treatment with Alessandrini while serving as the head of the air force's cinema unit in Africa. Masoero's special status as a paragon of the Fascist cameraman–military operative comes through in Pavolini's Ethiopian War chronicle, *Disperata*: "[Masoero] accompanied us frequently [and] documented almost all of our bombings, giving precious material to the command. That day . . . a bullet grazed his temple, wounding him, but he continued on in his duty to film, just as the others filled their duties to pilot or to shoot."[43] Craveri, by then one of Luce AOI's top operators, also figured in the crew. He had recently completed work on the feature *L'Esclave blanc* (discussed in chapter 6) and on Marcellini's Spanish Civil War aviation documentary, *Los novios de la muerte/The Grooms of Death*. Although Ubaldo Arata substituted for him during the actual production, Craveri's presence, along with that of Masoero, gave the production's aerial profile credibility, not only with critics but with spectators who could assimilate

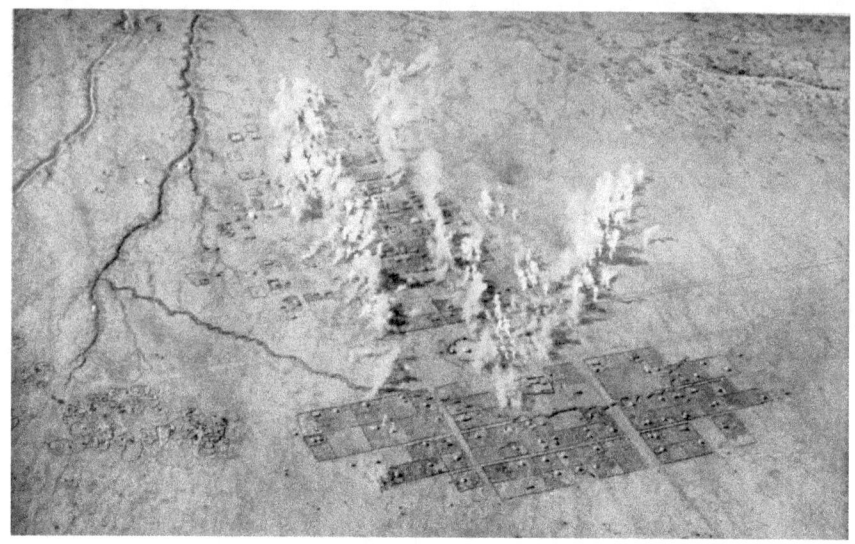

FIGURE 4.6.

The *Disperata* squad bombs Gorrahai, Somalia, 1935–36. In Alessandro Pavolini, *Disperata* (Florence, Vallecchi, 1937), 176–177

the images to those they were familiar with from Luce AOI films. Craveri's extensive location and background footage for *Luciano Serra, pilota* was in fact slotted to become a freestanding documentary, made by Rossellini, before the latter became busy co-writing (with Alessandrini) the script.[44]

Vittorio Mussolini, himself a pilot and the movie's supervisor, had brought this all-star imperial filmmaking team together. Mussolini Jr.'s own ideas about war's cinematic potential were shaped by his bombing runs as well as his consumption of Hollywood cinema. Both influences are evident in his 1937 war journal *Voli sulle Ambe/Flights over the Mountains*, which extols aerial bombings' aesthetic "effects," along with Ethiopia's aesthetic failings as a field of combat. The Ethiopian War lacked "huge explosions like those in American films," he complained, and the absence of any Ethiopian aviation excluded the craft-to-craft battles that were the stuff of many aviation films. The younger Mussolini thus defended the risky practice of strafing as an antidote to the antiseptic combat that came with industrial warfare's increasing abstraction of the enemy. "We too have the right to see the faces of our enemies."[45] Fiction film compensated for such privations: his *Luciano Serra, pilota* featured spectacular strafing and acrobatics *and* on-the-ground physical encounters. It may seem surprising that Vittorio Mussolini chose Alessandrini for this important commission. The director had no prior colonial film experience, and moreover he was the consummate cosmopolitan, studying at Cambridge as well as in Italy before starting his film career in Rome and Paris. His first movies were either remakes of or heavily influenced by Weimar German cinema (*La segretaria privata/The Private Secretary*, 1931, based on a Wilhelm Thiele movie, and *Seconda B*, 1934, which drew on Leontine Sagan's 1931 *Mädchen in Uniform/Girls in Uniform*). Yet he also had firsthand experience with the Hollywood studio system and a talent for approximating Hollywood spectacle, and he even had African origins, having been born and partly raised in Egypt. Although comedies would continue to be part of his repertoire, from 1935 on Alessandrini mostly made films on military and missionary themes.

Alessandrini proved well suited to empire film culture. His vaunted return to his natal continent, coupled with his personal "fame as an adventurer," set the tone for the production process as itself a martial endeavor. The director's declarations during *Luciano Serra, pilota*'s production emphasized the physical and logistical challenges and the heroic scale of the enterprise. In *Cinema* he boasted of the ninety-three hundred miles he, Craveri, and producer Franco Riganti flew in "magnificent Ala Littoria aircraft" and Capronis to shoot documentary footage and scout locations, enduring 120-degree temperatures and sudden floods. Throughout, they were accompanied by the air force officer who served as aviation liaison and guarantor of the fidelity of the movie's military maneuvers. "[In combat], as is known, columns of soldiers advance with a network of scouts at their side and the vigilant eye of aviation above them," Alessandrini wrote, giving his trip the feel of a military reconnaissance mission. Alessandrini's fame came from his mastery of mise-en-scène and studio-shot cinema, but here he echoed Camerini in associating his use of location shooting with a commitment to masculine authenticity. *Luciano Serra, pilota* would be distinguished from older colonial films in which "Africa is present only through banana leaves and where the things done and said could be out of one of those novels read by schoolgirls who are sick with Oriental romanticism because they saw Ramon Novarro dressed as a sheik."[46] Novarro, like Spada, was among the inheritors of Valentino's exotic persona, and Alessandrini's distancing of his picture from the films these men made claimed Africa for a new kind of spectator: less young women than the young men targeted as the next generation of Fascist flyers and fighters.

Other members of the production echoed this paramilitary and masculine tone, presenting the making of *Luciano Serra, pilota* as an opportunity to live (and sometimes re-live) their own war stories and flight experiences. Riganti, as producer, compared his experience in managing this "difficult undertaking" to fighting a battle, with 25,000 machine guns employed, 550 bombs exploded, and 40,000 rifle shots fired, as well as a near-fatal plane crash he was involved in during some of the 640 hours of flying time that accrued during filming. Arata called it "the kind of job that makes the veins pulse," while Ferrari reminded readers that his role as a pilot and air force commander drew on the real combat he had experienced as an aviator in World War I. "But this was only a film ... what a shame," he lamented. Even the young and shy Roberto Villa confessed that he had gotten the flying bug while on set—"I jumped onto the fuselage"—inspired by Riganti, Alessandrini, and the other amateur aviators in the troupe. Only Nazzari, who did not join the troupe in Africa, distanced himself from the chorus of masculine celebration, praising instead the "real pilots" and "real inexhaustible legionaries who did the long African marches."[47]

Nazzari's mention of the Italian military men who played themselves in *Luciano Serra, pilota* reminds us how empire film productions reinforced colonial labor policies and racial ideologies. Italian soldiers were paid for their time, in that acting counted as part of their military service, but such was always not the case with the indigenous, especially if they were not already in the colonial military. These extras often traveled long distances from their homes, neglecting family, tribal, and labor obligations. For Italians, productions that involved thousands of Africans offered the thrill of imperial command, with the submission of the indigenous to the will of the director and the camera standing in for obedience to Fascist political authority. Press coverage of the making of *Luciano Serra, pilota* highlighted Italian power to orchestrate the indigenous and control their bodies. *Cinema* made Alessandrini's rough handling of a young Galla woman the visual centerpiece of an article, and Alessandrini himself highlighted how the same army major (De Sarno) who had convinced

Galla tribesmen to fight alongside the Italians during the Ethiopian War now helped him to choose four thousand of these "magnificent warriors, who are celebrated throughout the Empire for their courage and valor" and "get them used to the camera." These men, and the Eritreans, acted alongside one thousand "Abyssinians from irregular bands," cavalry squads from Godo Fella, and one thousand Italians borrowed from the army. That these collaborations came with many difficulties is alluded to in Alessandrini's remark that he preferred to work with more "adaptable" Eritrean *ascari*. "They already were in the habit of obeying and when they heard commands they accepted them almost with pleasure." One wonders what success De Sarno had on his next mission, which started when the shoot concluded: transitioning the Galla into the next phase of colonial labor, "transforming men who only know how to plunder into a peaceful mass of farmers."[48]

As in the extra-filmic domain, the Italians depended on colonial interpreters to act as intermediaries who kept things calm as they transmitted commands from the authorities. De Sarno worked closely with an Ethiopian translator named Osman in dealing with the Galla. Alessandrini, who knew Arabic, spoke directly to Muslim Eritreans but in keeping with Italian colonial practice used only what he termed "senseless Italian" (*italiano balordo*) with the *askari* and had to hire the Eritrean Zainù Soliman to make his commands intelligible. The director kept to pidgin Italian when he thanked his translator publicly in the review *Film*: "Zainù how is you, I well, thank you to say hello to everyone, tell your ascari they do 'theatre' very good" (Zainù comi stai, io bene, prego te salutare tutti tuoi ascari dire loro avere atto "teattru" molto buono). Zainù, he added for Italian readers, had been invaluable on set for his ability to "yell like a lion," conveying commands, instructions, and imprecations in "all the dialects of the Empire." The tensions, resistances, and everyday violences that marked this complex production can also be gleaned by *Cinema Illustrazione*'s attempt at humor in presenting an African extra ordered to play a victim: "And here, finally, is a . . . cadaver. Authentic, of course. This is a war film and as such it's necessary once in a while to cover the ground with numerous victims."[49]

That Italian aggression is the subject of the closing pages of my analysis, which looks at *Luciano Serra, pilota*'s battle scenes and the film's relations with histories and memories of violence that go beyond the film frame and beyond the colony. The war scenes are among the film's most effective in terms of their dramatic force. Here Luciano's rescue of his wounded son Aldo is paralleled by another plotline: the need to save Italian civilians who are stranded in a train. This plot twist recalls the iconic 1924 John Ford film *The Iron Horse,* but the shots of Ethiopian soldiers descending upon the train, intercut with panicked faces of Italian men, women, and children, conjure Fascist propaganda's denunciations of Ethiopians' rapes, decapitations, and castrations of their enemies. Sound also established Ethiopian barbarism, through the ritual chanting that accompanies a scene of sabotage to Italian railway tracks. The train scenes also justify a shift to large-scale battle and the showcasing of Italian aerial bombing and other technology. Although well armed with machine guns and knives, and far outnumbering the Italian forces, the Ethiopians cannot match the airplanes that save the day, just in time, the equivalent of the cavalry in the Western. The bombings create huge smoke effects much like those described admiringly by Vittorio Mussolini in his pilot chronicles, and the sequence resolves in a skillful montage of scattering Ethiopians, dust, and smoke, until our vision is obscured completely, opening a transition that is also an ellipsis, as it places us back in Italy, with Aldo and Morelli, at a ceremony honoring Luciano after his death. Here Luciano's history undergoes a cleansing: he is praised as a veteran of World War I, a civilian pilot, and a Legionnaire in Ethiopia, but his long years outside the nation are elided. The regimented scene hews to a Luce model of political spectacle as it asserts the right of the state to rewrite the past, replacing stories of flight from Italy for economic reasons with narratives of homecoming that answered the needs of the Fascist war machine.

The end of the battle sequence acts as a smoke screen in other ways as well. As we have seen, *Luciano Serra, pilota* enters into the history of Italian aviation, referencing (and reversing) Balbo's Italy–Brazil journey. Luciano, however, acts as Balbo's doppelgänger, less in terms of direct physical resemblance than in his doing wrong what Balbo did right: whereas Balbo's flight came with the benediction of the state, and involved a disciplined collective, Luciano's flight was the fruit of misguided individualism. "I'm leaving anyway," he says when told that taking the plane to Italy was illegal and carried a high risk of death en route. Even in Ethiopia, Luciano is unable to fully toe the line of collective discipline: there, as in Rio, he shadows not only Balbo the media star and aviator but Balbo the former squadrist. The Militia, which had become famous for its marauding activities in Ethiopia, provided the perfect home for someone of Luciano's hot-tempered character. Stefani's observation that Militia service in Africa "provided an organized context within which [men] could experiment with camaraderie and collective violence" found euphemistic expression in journalist Favre's comment that "one has a clear sense of the squadrist origins of the large Black Shirt army." This spirit of masculine freedom and transgression, which is also present in Marcellini's *Legionari del secondo parallelo,* pervaded the culture of imperial conquest at the highest levels. Ciano and Pavolini's bomb squad, Disperata, took its name and emblems from the Florentine band of squadrists formed in 1919. Balbo was among the founder of the Militia, and his fame also remained tied to his squadrist identity. A 1936 Luce newsreel of a parade held in his honor as governor of Libya singled out a Militia dagger held proudly, asserting the continuity of squadrist identity from early Fascism to the imperial years.[50]

In its characterizations, iconography, and publicity, *Luciano Serra, pilota* channels this squadrist spirit. Nazzari's Luciano goes from one liminal situation to another, driven by a "force of will, rough energy, and severe frankness," and confesses to the chaplain that he is one of many Legionaries to have signed up with a false name and identity. Luciano's remark associates the Fascist Militia for audiences with the French and Spanish Foreign Legions, which were depicted in films such as *La Bandera* as places "to erase the blackboard and start over again." In Marcellini's documentary the 221st Legion "repatriates" and nationalizes emigrants, but in Alessandrini's feature it also allows Italians to shed their pasts, with no questions asked.[51] His individualistic nature asserts itself when he abandons his unit in the heat of battle to reach the wounded Aldo. A white-robed Ethiopian soldier garners close-up treatment as he struggles with his gun and then unsheathes a long knife. Although hand-to-hand combat and intense physical violence were largely banned from Fascist screens, we see him and Luciano writhe together on the ground, locked in mortal combat, before Luciano takes out his own knife and stabs him to death. The standard-issue Militia dagger (*pugnale di marcia*) is another kind of memory object, less comforting than the Chianti bottle but equally part of Italian history: its force, like other such objects, lies in

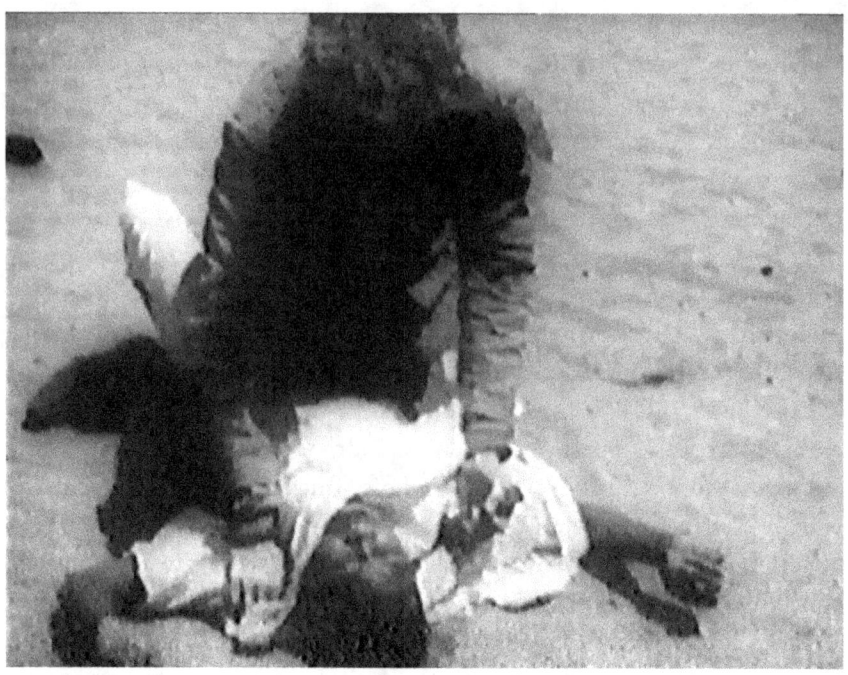

FIGURE 4.7.

The Militia dagger in action, *Luciano Serra, pilota.* Author's collection

"the unresolved traumas embedded in them [and] the history of material interactions that they encode."[52] As it conjures a past of squadrist violence, the knife prepares Luciano's own fadeout from Fascist history, as glossed by the smoke-obscured screen. He too has been fatally wounded, and in any case this new Italy has no place for him, as it has no place for Giovanni in *Il grande appello*. But here it is not only his tainted past as a neglectful father and emigrant at issue, but his rogue mentality. His death is that of the rogue who acts outside the group, of the Militiaman whose violence is needed but not officially sanctioned, and of all Italians who were flight risks, in every sense of the term.

The double path walked by the film with respect to this vexed history of Fascist violence registered in the film's critical reception and publicity. Unlike Giovanni in *Il grande appello,* Luciano's trajectory from emigrant to soldier seemed a plausible representative of "Italians' most recent history," although Nazzari's great popularity and virility undoubtedly helped in this regard. The extensive location shooting and use of real Italian and

FIGURE 4.8.

Fadeout in *Luciano Serra, pilota*. Author's collection

African soldiers also aided *Luciano Serra, pilota*'s claims to historical authenticity. Critics felt that it offered "a truer reality" than had been seen before, due to Nazzari's performance and the film's "genuine and direct" way of narrating its story. De Feo focused on Alessandrini's layered presentation of that history and his use of ellipses to speak about charged national moments, noting that the movie concealed as much as it revealed about the history it presented. "The discourse is often indirect," with the history "subtly veiled behind the case of the protagonist." This "modesty" meant "the zone of history's allusive second level is fused and assimilated."[53] In that zone lay the violence that could not be represented but had to be evoked to reach the film's target audiences, tell the story of this Militia legion, and sell Ethiopia as a home for all Italians, no matter what they had done in the past.

The film's marketing displayed greater transparency, sometimes playing up the squadrist ethos behind the film. One poster advertised *Luciano Serra, pilota* as "the film of Italian daring" (*Il film dell'ardimento italiano*) referring to the *arditi* shock troops who were a nucleus of squadrism, and Alessandrini played up his film's "daring and heroic atmosphere" (*atmosfera ardita e eroica*). This double frame is implicit in Antonioni's description of *Luciano Serra, pilota* as "a work that sums up the ideals and passions, the torment and the spirit of this Fascist era, of this Italian era."[54] And it was precisely in the slippage between Italian and Fascist history, picked up by Antonioni, that the film spoke to spectators, exalting and disavowing violence and asserting the regime's right to determine individual mobilization and mobility. Even fathers can be expendable, *Luciano Serra, pilota* warns, if they are not in tune with the regime's collective institutions and goals. Fascist military encampments were the new hearth, and the colonies the new home, for their sons' generation. Through the death of its emigrant and errant pilot protagonist, *Luciano Serra, pilota*, like *Il grande appello*, stages the diasporic Italian nation *and* its fantasy demise. Luciano did live on in the paratextual realm, reuniting with his son in a *cineromanzo* (serialized comic-book) version of the story. And Nazzari's rise to most popular male actor in Italy after this film (according to a poll of the public done by *Cinema*) may be seen as another kind of afterlife, since his later military roles existed in relation to his iconic star turn here. But, as befits a doppelgänger, Luciano's first "death" in flight presaged Balbo's own: the Fascist official perished during a 1941 air mission Claudio Segrè has characterized as "reckless, despotic, impulsive."[55]

Gabriel has compared the experience of seeing films that deal with memory and migration to "an excavation ... of one's culture, of one's cultural memory." Both *Luciano Serra, pilota* and *Il grande appello* engage the spectator's senses, not only in terms of the colonial fantasies they directly or obliquely evoke (the cosmopolitanism of colonial life, the ambiguous joys of male camaraderie, the thrill of flight, or the ecstasy of killing) but in their dramatization of the disjunctures of space and time and the pull of intimate ties "elsewhere" that marks the life of the emigrant. Autarchic agendas drive both of these films, with the colonies presented as sites of purification from foreign as well as female influence. Roberto Villa's Enrico and Aldo share the limited horizons, submissiveness, and faith in the language of technology proper to the new generation. These characters are neither distracted from duty nor distracting to the spectator, and their absent libidinal impulses are reflected in the bland way in which they are filmed. It is their fallible migrant fathers who carry the films, their volubility an integral part of the spectacle, their histories of movement an integral part of many spectators' lives. In the face of Fascist desires for emigrants to "come home to the colonies," both films remind us of how "transnational movements of bodies, objects, and images transform concepts and experiences of home and belonging," making the tension between "elsewhere" and "here" a permanent state. They place Italian Ethiopia within a broader network of sites of Italian belonging that the Fascists would never conquer, whether in South America or the French colonies.[56]

The airplane, which in *Luciano Serra, pilota* flies to both Rio and Addis Ababa, highlights these tensions of empire and the contradictions of Fascist attitudes toward mobility. Although relatively few Italians flew in these years, the airplane had a special meaning in the interwar period due to the prestige of Italian aviation and the large percentage of Italian nationals who lived overseas. Like the movie camera and the radio, the airplane collapsed distances, facilitating affective connections as well as the diffusion of ideologies. Alessandrini again made it a protagonist in his 1939 feature *Il ponte di vetro/Bridge of Glass*. In it an Ala Littoria commercial plane is forced to land in a deserted area en route to Tunisia, placing a surgeon's wife in a compromising situation with the handsome pilot. Although conjugal affairs are righted in the end, the movie highlights how travel to the colonies opens up realms of possibility and desire that are both liberating and destabilizing. The empire films of the next two chapters develop these themes further, exploring Italian settlers' and officers' discoveries of the intimacies and attractions of colonial life. Male sexual desire for the indigenous woman or man features here, but so does the assertion of a higher form of male fellowship based on a Fascistic submission to authority. As we will see in the next chapters, the camera enables its ethnographic eye, probing the indigenous body for purposes of spectacle, only to settle on its real fetish object: the Italian man as master of colonial space and agent of Fascist imperial conquests made possible by the sublimation of desire into hard labor and the joys of military command.

Imperial Bodies, Part I
Italians and *Askaris*

The narratives of empire film, like empire itself, revolved around the management of imperial bodies. Both colonizers and colonized had value as a productive force (infrastructure, agriculture, conquest). They reinforce, and sometimes transgress, social and racial hierarchies and are marked by the displacements and journeys occasioned by Italian wars and occupations and by the encounters, for all races, with alterity. The films of chapter 5 and 6 stage the relations of intimacy, estrangement, and exploitation that marked these encounters. The titles of chapter 5's two films, *Lo squadrone bianco* and *Sentinelle di bronzo*, limn their putative homages to Libyan *meharisti* and Somali *dubat*. These narratives of military advance are twinned with dramas of sentimental attachment that complicate masculine comradeship among both Italian and indigenous men. Chapter 6's movies, *L'Esclave blanc* and *Sotto la Croce del Sud*, focus on attractions between white men and black and "Levantine" women on plantation settings in Somalia and Ethiopia. In most of these films, flows of white desire for women interfere with military duty and governance of the indigenous. In all of them, the nomad and the nomadic feature as the Italian empire's internal enemy, whether in the form of indigenous tribes, wayward female temperaments, or the *mal d'Africa* that afflicts their male protagonists.

A series of contradictions revolve around the imperial body, influencing the ways it is filmed, its place within a larger network of images and ideologies, and its relationship to the bodies behind the camera and in the movie theater. The films examined here proclaim Italian dominance and superiority with respect to the occupied populations, but reveal the degree of Italian dependence on those populations for conquest, governance, labor, and sexual satisfaction. On the ground, the small size of the settler population made colonial intermediaries such as foremen, interpreters, and *askari* leaders indispensable, but contributed to a sense of insecurity that registers in feature and nonfiction film. Language is a measure of this. Lacking much knowledge of local tongues, Italians relied on these intermediaries to convey their commands, whether on agricultural fields, battlefields, or film sets. The indigenous man performing the act of translation, set apart from the rest of the native labor force, was a common sight in Fascist propaganda, but the scant knowledge of indigenous languages among Italians meant that the content of the translation very often remained a mystery. A 1930 article had acknowledged this problem, calling the interpreter an "unreliable and sometimes dangerous intermediary... who constitutes a grave *unknown* (*incognita*) as far as the honesty and impartiality of the very delicate work that he is given."[1] This incognito persists in empire features, with their untranslated speech by interpreters and others, whereas Luce nonfiction replaces native speech with the narrator's gloss on the action, leaving the colonized to speak through their bodies.

The mix of alienation and attraction that came with the audition of untranslated speech marks the more general use of ethnographic elements in empire feature films. The demands of "authenticity" and spectacle led to the use of documentary conventions to showcase exotic peoples and landscapes. Such practices were not unique to Italy, and Fascism's empire cinema entered into a filmic field already crowded with American and British desert films, French colonial films, and a new generation of Orientalist sound films emanating from Hollywood. Fascist officials such as Freddi were well aware of this other dimension of Italian belatedness. The emigration films discussed in chapter 4 constitute one approach to the particularity of the Italian experience; enabling the ethnographic eye was another. Officials and cineastes engaged in public discussions about how to visually exploit the specificities of Fascism's territories, highlighting their "little known lands, unusual and diverse races [and] undiscovered customs" for Italian and international spectators.[2]

Fascist empire films shot in North and East Africa present divergent profiles in this regard. As part of North Africa, Libya was assimilated to other Sahara desert landscapes and Maghrebian settings that had featured in international features since the silent period. The Italo-Turkish War had given rise to silent features shot partly on location, and even a specialized production company, Libya Films, which made *La figlia del deserto/The Daughter of the Desert* (A. Di Natale, 1923), photographed by Craveri but released only in Tripoli and Bengasi. More successful features included Camerini's *Maciste contro lo sceicco* and *Kif Tebbi* and Guazzoni's *La Sperduta di Allah/Allah's Lost Soul* and *Myriam*, both from 1929. By that year, a critic for the review *Kines* complained about "the usual tedious commonplaces proper to films with an Arab-Muslim setting ... a setting already very exploited in every way ... (the desert, the camels, the caravans, all things which, oh God! we have seen an infinity of times on screen)."[3] Such concerns about originality and international market share may account for the surprisingly small number of Italian sound films set in Libya. In the imperial years, Libya was an arguably safer place to film than Ethiopia, and Balbo, as governor of Libya, promoted tourism. Yet *Lo squadrone bianco* was the first such feature in seven years to be shot in Libya, and six more years would pass before 1942's *Bengasi* and *Giarabub*.

Fascist racial mandates might have contributed to this situation, by censoring the kinds of exotic indigenous performances, such as belly dancing, Italian audiences were accustomed to seeing in Hollywood and French films set in North Africa. Such spectacles existed in Libyan clubs that attracted European tourists and local elites with performers from across the Maghreb. But the moral and pedagogical pressures placed on empire films prohibited the showcasing of "degenerate" venues that hosted such performances—harems, nightclubs, and brothels—despite their popularity. The bare breasts and lascivious dancing by white women that marked the club scene of Blasetti's 1935 naval drama *Aldebaran* had no place on Italian screens by 1937, when Fascist officials called for a ban on "the folklore of nudes, full moons, long caravans and ardent sunsets, of mad love with the faithful and humble indigenous woman," all of which perpetuated "a mentality that is absolutely not Fascist." Genina, the director of two of the four Libyan sound films released during the dictatorship, avoided all of these elements, putting his own authorial stamp on the Saharan tradition and using sound and characterization to assert the Italianness of his North African production.⁴

East Africa, in contrast, offered the visual and aural novelties of sub-Saharan black populations and a niche for Italian empire films in the international marketplace. Mirroring its role in imperial politics as the major source of *askaris*, Eritrea served mostly as a staging ground for film crews and a source of reliable extras: no feature films were set there during the imperial years. Ethiopia posed problems of political instability for filmmakers, but its importance as the heart of Italy's empire and the need to attract volunteers and settlers mandated that its attractions be showcased. As in *Il grande appello* and *Luciano Serra, pilota*, filmmakers highlighted the country's majestic landscapes in ways that recalled the Western, playing into Ethiopia's frontier appeal, but they also exploited the exotica of tribal rituals, bodies moving in unfamiliar ways, and textures of flora, all integrated with varying degrees of diegetic relevance. Coptic Christian rituals, which offered a blend of the familiar and the strange, figured in all features set in Ethiopia and in many Luce newsreels on Ethiopia as well. Somalia, the setting of *Sentinelle di bronzo* and chapter 6's *L'Esclave blanc*, seemed to hold special promise as a cinematic commodity. Although it had been an Italian colony since 1908, Somalia had never been featured in a silent or sound fictional production and had a fainter presence in Luce nonfiction with respect to the other African colonies. Men such as Quadrone (screenwriter and guiding spirit of *L'Esclave blanc*) and Marcellini saw rich commercial and aesthetic opportunities in this situation. Quadrone asserted that Somalia offered "a sincere and straightforward Africa, very different and no less moving than the one the Americans generally construct in Hollywood," while Marcellini focused on physiognomy, culture, and casting: "These [Somali] blacks are infinitely more noble and civil than the Negroes and Negroids of Harlem.... [W]e have a new, exclusive, and unconventional black product to launch on the market."⁵

Fascism's racial mandates and preoccupations affected these commercial preoccupations. Racisms of various sorts informed the colonial films of all countries: even in French films made during the Popular Front, interracial unions are rarely unproblematic. And Italian films incorporated older and broader Euro-American visual and literary traditions of depicting alterity, whether of an Orientalist or sub-Saharan African articulation. Still, these movies came out of a dictatorship and were made in the first flush of a new level of racial anxieties caused by the mass influx of white Italians into black Africa. Starting in 1937, legislation directed first at the colonies and then at Italian Jews in both colonies and the metropole attempted to regulate interracial contact and preserve white Christian hegemony and Italians' putative racial purity. These imperatives produced new attention and significance to the corporeal realm, on- and off-screen: as body surface, with appearance treated as an index of moral character and, for some, biology; as the locus of the senses; and as an entity establishing hierarchies of power through interactions with other bodies in space. As one commentator argued in the wake of the racial legislation, an African setting was no longer sufficient: a true "colonial cinema" must dramatize "the domination of one people over another and therefore the real comparison [raffronto vivo] of two diverse races."[6]

The double edge of the ethnographic in empire films has its origin here, in the need to simultaneously show engagement and mastery, collaboration and repudiation, attraction and discrimination. The ethnographic register can abstract the bodies of the colonized, as was often the case in Luce nonfiction, but the camera's abilities to collapse distances enabled moments of voyeurism and proximity that had a spectacular and sensual value. What an air force specialist in aerial photography exalted as the camera's capacities to "suck out the secrets of the earth as the bee does with the essence of a flower" became, on the ground, part of a larger Fascist imperial project devoted to "the domination of space, to the appropriation of bodies that move through space, to the recuperation of the 'hidden' private lives borne by those bodies."[7] The ways bodies are filmed in these movies facilitate these violations, bringing the audience closer to the colonial subject in ways that may have encouraged fantasies of possession as well as estrangement.

As an example, empire films make spectacle not just of military and ethnographic costume but also of the absence of costume—exposed skin—and their viewers saw more skin than in other kinds of movies made in Fascist Italy. Pinkus has commented on the emphasis placed on epidermal smoothness within the cult of the black female within advertising and the Fascist press. In the sub-Saharan African movies examined here and in chapter 6, skin is not only a marker of racial difference and an aesthetic element, but a bridge between the body on-screen and that of the spectator. *Sentinelle di bronzo*, *L'Esclave blanc*, and *Sotto la Croce del Sud* all feature male and female nudity and Italians and Africans with wet gleaming skin. Somalia had a special place here, as its inhabitants had always been regarded in the Italian colonial press as having a particular beauty, with their faces and bodies freer of the supposed physiognomic deformations and corporeal odors that characterized other sub-Saharan peoples. "Our Somalis are in fact black by pure chance," Quadrone maintained. "Their very regular profiles betray their very pure Semitic origins, and if they had white skin, they would not seem dissimilar to the *selezionati* and elegant Europeans." Yet their non-white skin was at the core of their aesthetic fascination for Westerners, particularly if they were female. Somali women placed at the top of this aesthetic pantheon, due to their "tiny steep breasts," "perfectly hollowed" backs, and, above all, their "silky skin, [which is] not only on their legs, but on their entire body, like a sweater."[8]

The reference to black skin as costuming is not incidental, given the presence of racial masquerade within Fascist empire films, which usually took the form of casting white Italian actresses to play indigenous objects of desire. Such practices figured heavily in British and Hollywood films on imperial and exotic themes as well: it was seen as more economical to darken the faces of white actors than to import indigenous peoples or train them to act. Racial masquerades in empire films allowed fantasies of interracial intimacies to be staged without infringing on official interdictions, and indeed the Fascist press highlighted the practice. The July 1936 issue of *Cinema*, which appeared in the first flush of empire, featured a white man spray-painting a white woman black. The man's lab coat placed "science" behind the idea that the colonizer could whiten or blacken at will and that skin color indexed degrees of cleanliness and civilization. At the same time, the illusion of proximity created by the focus on exposed skin worked against Fascist mandates for Italians to channel libidinal desires into combat or work, given that in empire films both agriculture and battle bring races together and occasion bodily display. The movies here and in the following chapter address the tensions that arise on sites of battle and settlement, where whites and non-whites worked together, modeling "allowable forms of intimacy," within imperial society.[9]

As in *Il grande appello* and *Luciano Serra, pilota,* the movies examined here and in chapter 6 stage conflicts within their male leads between individual fulfillment and collective duty. For Giovanni and Luciano, the frontier appeal of the colonies is tied to the possibility of forms of adventurism (war profiteering and the practice of violence). *Il grande appello* also alludes to the pleasures of male comradeship in the desert, a theme also explored in *Lo squadrone bianco.* Here, though, the focus is on younger Italians' struggles to master their emotional and bodily passions as part of growing into a position of command. *Sentinelle di bronzo*'s indigenous lead, the *askari* official Elmi, is spared such inner turmoil, having already assumed his place within a male chain of colonial labor, with his commander the object of his admiration. Probing the indigenous psyche in ways that admitted of *Kif Tebbi*–like ambivalence had no place on-screen by 1937, and indeed Elmi dies in battle—confirming the expendable nature of his racial cohort—whereas the white Italian leads of *Lo squadrone bianco, L'Esclave blanc,* and *Sotto la Croce del Sud,* once liberated from temptation, assume their duties as the newest members of the imperial elite. Their political socializations and character transformations register at the level of the senses: the men in these movies look and are looked at, act and are acted upon, hear and are heard—and, equally important for Fascist purposes, learn when not to look, not to act, and not to speak.

The importance of bodily control to the militarized masculinities of empire films comes through in the acting style of Giachetti, the top-billed male lead in this chapter's movies and, along with Nazzari, one of the most popular male stars of the imperial years. Although directors exploited Giachetti's sex appeal by showing him in his undershirt, like Gary Cooper's officer character in *Lives of a Bengal Lancer,* his screen persona revolved around a highly stylized use of the body that leaned less on Hollywood and more on the Duce and the stage (or the balcony) for its inspirations. Giachetti's officer characters modeled the martialized Italian body, and the actor was often photographed in a hard light that brought out the sculpted quality of his features. His "stoic, reserved, and restrained masculinity," conveyed through a sharp voice and controlled bodily gestures, rebuked the "Oriental softness" of Valentino and an earlier era of colonial film. Seemingly uninterested in women, and devoted only to duty and other male commanders, this "autarchic divo" served empire film culture as an emblem of a stern Italian manhood with Roman roots and pretensions.[10]

Giachetti's assertive virility contrasts with the hesitant and sensitive presence of Antonio Centa, the co-star of *Lo squadrone bianco* and *Sotto la Croce del Sud*. Seven years Giachetti's junior, Centa had been discovered by a Paramount producer while working as an artisan in America, but was not an obvious leading man for Fascist Italy. He had a nervous and scattered manner, moved awkwardly in his slender frame, and his nasal and high-pitched voice communicated tension rather than sexual magnetism or authority. He never obtained Giachetti's aggressive domination of the frame, even in his roles as an official, but his "ordinariness," and struggles with women and his own impulsiveness made him approachable and believable to his own generation. He also had squadrist credentials, having participated in the March on Rome, as *Lo Schermo* took pains to note in placing Centa's eight years away as an emigrant in the best possible light. "In 1935, tired and full of nostalgia, he returned to the Patria, intent on helping his salesman father," the review volunteered.[11]

The male leads in empire films must also gird themselves against female temptation. The features examined here and in the following chapter have strong white or indigenous women characters that exert power over the protagonists, distracting them from their military and other duties before they are removed from the narrative. Significantly, most of these women have nomadic roots or tendencies. In *Lo squadrone bianco*, Cristiana's nomadism is first that of the spirit—she is always "elsewhere," desiring the man she is not with at present—and then takes material form as she embarks on an extended tourist journey across the Mediterranean. Dahabò of *Sentinelle di bronzo* belongs to a nomadic tribe, in the tradition of Mné from *Kif Tebbi*, while *Sotto la Croce del Sud*'s Mailù has no clear origins and lets her soul "to go where it will." Doris Duranti, who played both Dahabò and Mailù, made her career from playing such willful nomads. Her dramatic features lent themselves well to exoticization, and she appeared in a large number of films on imperial themes (bit parts in *Aldebaran* and *Lo squadrone bianco* and leading roles in *Sentinelle di bronzo*, *Sotto la Croce del Sud*, *Giarabub*, and 1940's *Il Cavaliere di Kruja*, set in Albania and directed

FIGURE 5.1.

Giachetti as imperial commander, *Lo squadrone bianco*. Author's collection

FIGURE 5.2.

Centa as imperial commander in training, *Lo squadrone bianco*. Author's collection

by Carlo Campogalliani). "The Empire came to me, in a way, and in my own fashion I conquered it," she recalled in her memoirs. The half-Jewish Duranti's air of difference accounted for her appeal, but also brought her an uneasy place within Fascist-era film culture. Although she had status as the lover of the Fascist official Alessandro Pavolini, she ran counter to autarchic demands for fresh-faced and easily legible leading ladies. A *Cinema* poll of 1941 found that Duranti was less popular with spectators than the blonde ingenue Alida Valli, even with soldiers stationed in Africa, who, according to journalist Mattia, preferred stars who reminded them of their girlfriends back home. Duranti's significance within Fascist film culture lay elsewhere: both erotic and remote, her characters expressed the dynamics within imperial ideology between attraction and estrangement, desire and its denial. Within the male-oriented universe of empire films, the women played by Duranti and other white and black actresses are bodies that matter: it is their materializations of femininity, more than the fatigue of battle and agricultural toil, that bring out weakness and crises in men.[12] The abjection of the emigrant male staged in the films of chapter 4 gives way in the films of chapters 5 and 6 to the torment of male desire for an unobtainable, mobile, or forbidden woman—until that woman is expelled from the colonial scene, allowing that desire to be redirected to further the causes of imperial conquest and labor.

Both *Lo squadrone bianco* and *Sentinelle di bronzo* approach imperial negotiations of intimacy and distance through a focus on the relations among Italian officials and *askaris*. Indigenous soldiers had given an essential assist to the Italian Army since the early days of colonialism, and as in other colonial contexts it was a relationship of dependence and exploitation. Whether in East Africa or Libya, the Italians relied on *askaris* for their knowledge of local terrain and languages and for their fighting styles built on "mobility and individual action" rather than the industrial warfare the Fascists initially favored. One hundred thousand colonial soldiers from Libya, Somalia, and Eritrea fought in the Ethiopian War, with two hundred thousand mobilized by World War II. While the Fascist government made a show of awarding prizes to the most valorous, in general *askaris* were treated as an expendable element of colonial labor and remained an "unknown and unintelligible mass" even to Italian soldiers. That labor was not confined to the battlefield, but included taking part in colonial exhibitions and marching in parades in the metropolis, traveling with officers as their personal valets, and appearing in features and documentaries filmed in the colonies and being available for documentaries.[13]

Whether it was the Somali *dubat* in his distinctive white turban, the white-wrapped Libyan *mehariste*, or the Eritrean foot soldier, the *askaro* by the late 1930s was an iconic image that sent a reassuring message about Italian control and prestige. Their display on the streets of Italy, on work and battle sites, and in the mass media stood in for a larger imperialist politics that asserted the right to regiment, resettle, and exhibit the body. In Luce newsreels, long-shot coverage of military exercises can rapidly shift into close-up ethnographic inquiry: the camera very slowly pans up and down the bodies of *dubat* standing at attention, displaying their slim muscular physiques, while a Galla warrior gets the same probing treatment, until he unsheathes his knife, prompting a quick cutaway. Fascist racism dictated a different treatment for the Libyan Arab than the sub-Saharan African, with the former thought to be more civilized than the latter. Less subject to animalization and commodifications that conflated them with colonial products (coffee, bananas, cacao), North African soldiers also had a greater aesthetic value: they were Italy's entrée into an Orientalist marketplace dominated by images of French *meharistes*. They did not always cooperate in their utilization by the Fascist media, however. In a 1936 newsreel devoted to the Libyan oasis of Ghadames, which was being marketed as a tourist destination, *meharisti* are tagged along with other indigenous men and women "who accept to pose for the camera, although with some reluctance."[14]

Colonial soldiers were often infantilized. Stefani has found that "a strong pietist and paternalistic" attitude dominated their portrayals by Italians, along with an appreciation of their courage, physical elegance, and fidelity. Such paternalism acted as a palliative for insecurities about the degree of colonial control on the ground, lending the Italian commanding officer the aura of a father figure. The feminization and sexualization that marked representations of indigenous soldiers of the British empire had little place in Fascist propaganda. Colonial soldiers were, however, subject to the same processes of abstraction and disembodiment that marked Fascist-era mediatic treatments of Italian soldiers and workers. The latter's "featureless faces," hidden by their helmets, found an equivalent in the quickly panned cinematic "lineups" of *askaris*, in the barely sketched faces and bodies in print media, and in the silhouettes that obliterated the body's materiality altogether. The productivist imperatives of the Fascist colonial labor system, together with the dictatorship's homogenizing imperatives, conspired to reduce both colonizers and the colonized to "multiple semi-mechanical serial productions," devoid of any individuality.[15]

These massed groupings of soldiers and *askaris* served as the foil for the singular authority and visual splendor of the imperial officer. Although the maintenance of colonial hierarchies required the cultivation of distance, officers lived in relations of intimacy with *askaris,* who attended them in their private quarters, bringing them coffee in bed in the mornings, and served them as aides, guides, and translators in the field. The hybrid form of the officer's Sahara uniform—Western dress and decoration with North African sandals and white scarf—was not only a typical military appropriation of the colony in the interest of practicality, but a gesture to the shadings of culture and feeling between the Italians and the *askaris* they depended on. Military life not only bred patronizing attitudes but also created situations where the lines between homosocial and homoerotic feeling blurred, as officers' memoirs and diaries testify. The films in this chapter play on this panoply of affect, with the show and sheen of bodies in battle and the intensity of feeling among military men threatening to break through the armor of the uniform. That uniform has itself a role of protagonist in empire films, its sharp contours guiding the body through its military rituals, encouraging the "repetition of stylized movements in performance" that enacted masculinities of command for both Italian and colonial officials.[16] The uniformed man also reminds us that body surface was the main interface for practices of colonial domination that reached far beyond relations of officers and *askaris:* especially in the Italian context, which was so fraught by situations of linguistic blockage, it spoke more clearly than language ever could.

LO SQUADRONE BIANCO: FASCIST COLONIAL STYLE AND BODILY RE-EDUCATION

Lo squadrone bianco brings us to the heart of several tensions that marked Fascism's empire in its political and filmic manifestations: between the needs of the marketplace and those of ideology, between mobility and settlement, and between the national and the transnational. Farassino has called the film "an example of cosmo-colonialism... more European than Italian," and it may be located within an international matrix of Orientalist visual culture, Foreign Legion movies, Anglo-American desert warfare films, Fascist imperial iconography, and French colonial cinema. As with *Luciano Serra, pilota,* empire films posit the Militia as the Fascist equivalent of the Foreign Legion. They retain the notion of that military service as a space of male reinvention while eliding the visits to brothels and mercenary spirit that marked Legionnaire culture and the pessimism about the utility of war seen in many French films on the subject. *Lo squadrone bianco* has a particularly close relation to Foreign Legion films and French colonial culture, and not only by virtue of its Sahara setting: it was adapted from the Foreign Legion novel *L'Escadron blanc* by Joseph Peyré, who also contributed to the script. As such, it provides an opportunity to investigate the processes of cultural translation and censorship that intervened to give a "national" inflection to works that took shape within a broad intertextual web. In *Lo squadrone bianco,* the action moves from Algeria to Libya, and the vicissitudes of the Italian officers in command of the *meharisti* stand in for the Foreign Legion's "cocktail of adventure, conquest, internationalism, romanticism, rebellion, interior laceration [and] desire for annulment."[17] As in the novel, and as in influential desert films such as *The Lost Patrol* (John Ford, 1934), the near invisibility of the enemy rebels keeps the focus on male interactions among officers, between officers and indigenous troops, and on the physical and mental challenges presented by extended time in the desert, especially for the inexperienced junior officer who is the film's co-protagonist. Yet that younger male expires midway through the French novel, foreclosing possibilities of male redemption and generational turnover that are integral to the Italian film. As we will see, the play of absences and presences between novel and film is revealing of Fascist ideological and market agendas as well as of the broader international trends that informed plot points, aesthetics, and audience expectations.

Genina's own professional peregrinations make him a good subject for an investigation of such shadings of the national and international. Although most directors of empire films had worked in France during the crisis years, Genina had been there the longest and had enjoyed the most success, above all with his 1930 Louise Brooks vehicle *Prix de beauté/Miss Europa*, which was produced by Georg Wilhem Pabst and written by Pabst and Clair. This work features the rapid montage and nervous cinematography inherited from the avant-garde and its city films and uses original framings of crowds and close-ups together with unsettling noise and sound to create situations of psychological unease.[18] Its tragic ending—the newly anointed beauty queen, Brooks, is killed by a boyfriend jealous of her autonomy—also testifies to an interest in modernity's impact on gender identities and relations between the sexes that will shape *Lo squadrone bianco* as well. The closest antecedent to Genina's 1936 film, however, is his lost 1927 French-German co-production *L'Esclave blanche/Die Weisse Sklavin/The White Slave,* which won Genina praise for his "poetic" treatment of the Sahara. The "white slave" in question is a British woman who relocates to North Africa with her Muslim sheik husband, only to find he has a harem, another wife, and expectations that she will live a cloistered life. Her flight from the desert back to Europe, after having tried to free the sequestered first wife, ends with the death of the sheik and her finding love with a French doctor. The narrative arc of racial and cultural transgression and its correction conforms to Orientalist conventions, as does the mix of metropolitan and desert costume scenes. Stylistically as well as in terms of its cast, it was "an international film down to its bones," and although Genina was also active in these years in reviving the Italian film industry (with his younger cousin Camerini and others, he founded the ADIA consortium that produced *Kif Tebbi*), his base in the late 1920s and early 1930s remained the French capital. It is no surprise that the empire film made by this "very Parisian Italian" was based on a French novel. Genina was a marquee name who also answered the film industry's desire to exploit the talents of Italians who have "travelled, read, seen, in a word who have a thorough knowledge of how one lives in the different environments of different countries" to make movies that would be popular abroad.[19]

Lo squadrone bianco's establishing scenes let us know that this cosmopolitan world of constant mobility will also be put to critique. Music and camerawork convey a sense of recklessness and danger as a young Mario Ludovici (Centa) speeds down a highway in the middle of the night, desperate to see his lover, Cristiana (Fulvia Lanzi), who has failed to show up for their rendezvous. Cross-cutting reveals that Cristiana is out dancing with another man, and subsequent scenes at her home identify her with a Hollywood-inflected Italian glamour and artifice, complete with glossy modern furniture, expensive jewelry and gowns, and even a white telephone, which she uses to hang up on him when he calls demanding to see her. When she finally lets him in he attempts to strangle her until her maid intervenes. "I'm crazy, crazy about you... I feel capable of anything and everything... I am afraid of myself."[20] The site of male abjection is not the emigrant's foreign land, as for the older stars of chapter 4, but Mario's own metropolis: military service in Africa offers a seemingly easy escape.

This preamble to the colonial setting marks the first significant difference with Peyré's novel. There, we start and end in the Sahara, in the thick of the action, with the commander Marcay indignant at having to take on the young Kermeur, who is "an officer of dance halls and carousels," with no desert or military experience.[21] Kermeur is a neutral character, without Mario's past of romantic humiliation, and the desert crisis that leads to his death is born of illness and a sense of existential isolation unconnected to any female figure. In the novel, women are virtually absent: Marcay has a "little indigenous spouse," but neither she nor the female villagers who live near the fort have much diegetic relevance. Peyré's narrative is a story of male interactions: among Legionnaires, with their *meharistes,* and with the memory of a fallen commander who will hold importance for Genina's film as well. Cristiana and her very watchable metropolitan settings are thus products of the transition from novel to film, from a Francophone reading public to an international market of cinema spectators. Cristiana also has a moral function within the movie as providing the source of the male dis-ease that the colonies will cure, and she is eventually exiled as the movie charts Mario's path of freedom from sexual dependence and libidinal desire. The film's staging of the longing both characters experience at different moments as a result of their Italy-Africa separation is an important part of its affective reach to the spectator and provides some of its most poetic as well as commercially viable moments. Finally, Peyré's book does not share the movie's strong pedagogical slant. The Algerian Sahara tests male character, but is not a site of male regeneration, nor of the creation of new elites, since it is the junior officer who dies there

FIGURE 5.3.

Cristiana, *Lo squadrone bianco*. Author's collection

without having learned much of anything. And while the film respects the novel's depiction of desert warfare against the rebels as ongoing, it does away entirely with the air of pessimism about the human costs of war that marks *L'Escadron blanc*'s ending. As in other Fascist films, war has a value beyond territorial acquisition: combat makes men better, and the desert brings forth male loyalty to each other and to the greater cause of empire.

As we have seen, the Fascists intended through the cinema to diffuse the elements of an Italian colonial style, meaning not only outward appearance and dress but also modes of interaction and comportments suited to imperial command. *Lo squadrone bianco* is the empire film most preoccupied with such issues, and it makes explicit the connections among exterior style, strength of character, and effective governance of Italian and indigenous soldiers. The film presents viewers with various exemplars of Italian colonial masculinity, who, as in the novel, live together in a fort at the edge of the desert. There is the retired Captain Donati, with a Balbo goatee, who is a father figure to everyone; there is the Lieutenant Fabrizi, unhappy to be in Libya, who treats his servants badly and shirks his military duties; there is Mario, who arrives without the proper Sahara uniform and immediately puts out Cristiana's photograph, prompting his Libyan aide, El Fennek, to observe, "Our life is in desert. In desert man forget everything"; and there is Captain Santelia (Giachetti), splendid in his desert whites, with his erect carriage, decisive tone, mastery of desert warfare, and knowledge of Arabic, all of which bring him the respect and admiration of the "white squadron."

The preoccupation with authority and prestige comes through clearly in Santelia's review of his *meharisti*. The interaction is highly stylized, from the lines of soldiers at attention to the immaculate white garb of all parties and the language used to address them. The cadence and pitch of Santelia's speech closely resemble Mussolini's, down to the enunciation of key words such as "heroes" and "combat," as does the body language, including the jutting jaw. Speech, here, is an aural equivalent of the uniform. The swiftly moving traveling shot makes a 360-degree tour, often shooting the commander from below to emphasize his authority, but also probing everyone, including Santelia, from every angle, calling attention to the camera's ability to survey and the performative nature of the gathering. A second troop review soon after underscores Santelia's domination. As he passes by his men, they straighten up as though poked from behind, their bodies resembling marionettes suddenly rearranged by their master. Earlier he had told Mario that "here the cut of your clothing has no importance. Here it is the suggestion and example of the *capo* that counts." Yet outward appearance is fundamental to Fascist colonial governance as advanced in this movie, body surface being the interface with the colonized and the outward sign of strength of character.[22] The sandals and sharp baton that form part of Santelia's Sahara uniform, which receive close-up attention, signify the imperial dance of appropriation and alienation, the colonizer's simultaneous move toward and exploitation of the indigenous, and the threat of violence in case of insubordination.

As in the novel, the virile commander's vulnerability saves him from caricature. He suffers from the recent desert death of his own comrade and commander, Bettini (a Corsican of Italian origin in the book), whose photograph he displays prominently on his desk. The silent partner in the relationship of Santelia and Mario, Bettini is to the former what Cristiana is to the latter: an absence that sends the spirit elsewhere. In *L'Escadron blanc*, too, Marcay cannot easily speak about Bettini—"there was a silence around the memory of the dead leader," Peyré notes—but the married Frenchman does not carry his feelings for Bettini into this new partnership.[23] Santelia, on the other hand, lives in an all-male world, with no outlet for his sentiments beyond the photo he looks at so frequently. The removal of the commander's indigenous wife in the translation from novel to movie tinges Santelia's intense interactions with Mario with ambiguity. Santelia's irritation with Mario is limited not to the latter's lovesickness, juvenile nature, and lack of preparation, but also to Mario's persistent refusal to accept anything from him, be it food, drink, advice, or company. "In sum you really don't want anything from me!" he explodes during a night they spend in the desert, having earlier told Mario off for his distraction: "Your past does not belong to me, but your present does. I have a right to it. And I demand to own all of it, understand? All of it!"

These words assert the claim of a totalitarian state on the mind and the body that goes beyond the normal military chain of command, but they also reference an affective hold, one that references the kind of full immersion male experience Santelia apparently enjoyed with Bettini. As in *Il grande appello,* the younger generation does not seem to seek out that kind of male liberation: Mario tells his *capo* that he does want one thing from him: his respect and, even as he sits at his feet, accepting his subordinate position, moves further away. Earlier, Donati has told him that he and Santelia "speak different languages. You don't understand one another." Given the diversified audience the film wished to reach, which included military men and former squadrists, that language, like Santelia's physicality with Mario, lends itself to multiple interpretations. In *Lo squadrone bianco,* the dead Bettini, and his relationship with Santelia, haunts the film, filling the screen with his non-presence, just as memories of Cristiana haunt Mario before his blackout. Genina's film about public history in the making also evokes what remains off the public record: private longing and recollection. It is, in spirit, a "ruin," in Gabriel's sense: as "mobile, shifting, [and] nomadic" as the desert sands where Santelia, killed in battle, will join his mate Bettini.[24]

Although Santelia's death will complete Mario's evolution from abject male to self-sufficient commander, the younger male's struggle to free himself from Cristiana's hold on him propels the plot forward for much of the movie, cross-cut with Cristiana's distress over losing Mario to Africa. His transformative crisis comes deep in the desert, during a risky anti-bandit mission that leaves the squadron short on water and increasingly disoriented. As in the novel, the young officer is unfamiliar with the desert, and he soon falls ill with fever, but hides his state to prove his worth to his superior. In the book, though, Kermeur's hallucinations are indicative of the worsened state that leads to death, while Mario's are part of a process of regression and rebirth. His crisis manifests as a crisis of the senses: he collapses the next day during a sandstorm, going blind before he loses consciousness and is rescued by Santelia. The swirling sands that fill the frame signal Mario's plunge into oblivion, but also the Sahara's cleansing potential. The theme of desert crisis as a test of manhood, and Africa as a place to "start over," marks empire and Foreign Legion films in their British, French, and Hollywood iterations. *Lo squadrone bianco* conforms to this narrative model, but here the symbolic burial triggers a reconstruction of character that alienates those parts of Mario's self that are not in keeping with Fascist ideology. Rather than facilitating the forgetting of an unpleasant episode of one's past, as in these foreign works, it enables a flight to nothingness that kills off impulse and libido, emotion and memory, leaving the body surface as shell. When the tormented Cristiana finds him at the fort, he tells her that "Mario no longer exists, I left him down there, under the sand . . ." The new Mario is an uncharismatic copy of Santelia, with none of his vibrant virility. Mario has learned the gestures of authority, as his tentative arms-akimbo stance testifies, but his command style will be colorless, though, like that of the young officers played by Villa in *Il grande appello* and *Luciano Serra, pilota*. Significantly, the main lesson he learns from his aide, El Fennek, is to close his mouth. The injunction is to avoid taking in sand, but it references a lesson about what Cecilia Boggi calls "Fascist Italy's colonial dream of incorporation": that cultural influence was to flow in one direction only, with the rhetorical model less a dialogue than an oration and silences used to affirm one's power, as in Mussolini's October 1935 speech.[25]

Lo squadrone bianco's sonic dimension plays an important role in this bodily and sensory re-education and in the mapping of colonial hierarchies based on racial and cultural difference. With a filmography dating from 1912, Genina belonged to a generation challenged by the coming of sound, but he quickly learned to use noise and music to innovative effect. The plays between sound and silence in *Lo squadrone bianco*, which reinforce Genina's visual poetics of absence and presence, develop out of this long-standing interest in creating acoustic environments and "unified

FIGURE 5.4.

Fadeout in *Lo squadrone bianco*. Author's collection

sound fields" in which music, voice, noise, and silence all play a part.²⁶ Antonio Veretti's score ranges from melodramatic to elegiac to triumphal in tone, mirroring Mario's journey from inner turbulence to a man who grows into his capacity to command. Genina commented that in *Lo squadrone bianco*, music often takes the place of "verbal clarification," and director and composer collaborated closely. Rather than presenting Veretti with a finished film, Genina periodically sent footage to Rome, and Veretti traveled to Libya to have "direct contact" with the desert and its musical cultures. Empathetic music defines the scenes of the squad's movements through the desert, where tempo matched to the camels' plodding and the use of a low *ostinato* add to the feeling of time suspended. Music has a binding function with respect to the images and with respect to the spectator's immersion in the audiovisual spectacle, living up to Veretti's ambition that the two should achieve "a magic equilibrium."²⁷

Music also aids in the differentiation between metropolitan and colonial models of spectacle. In the Italian-based scenes, diegetic instrumental music acts as an auditory signature of Cristiana's character, with on-screen performances of band and symphonic music. Silence and Arabic instrumental and vocal music set the tone in the Libyan scenes, but even diegetically relevant music is acousmatic in nature. Its source is never shown, even when it is commented upon, as when Donati and Fabrizi are playing cards and Arabic music being played outside pours in loudly through the open windows, leading the latter to declare that he finds it intensely irritating. Here the dialogue explicitly refers to the music, which continues in response to what has remained unsaid: Fabrizi's anxiety at being surrounded by an alien culture and his wish—common to the colonizer— that the colonized would just disappear. You may not be able to see us, but we are here around you, says the music, speaking for the local Libyan population. Similar unseen sounds sweep in when Mario arrives at the fort and opens the window of his room, which looks onto the vast desert. Although Mario is alone and does not comment on the music, its prominent entrance into the scene inserts the spectator into a key moment of Mario's transition to Africa, with sound acting as a bridge between the hearing body on-screen and the hearing body of the viewer. The strategy of having Italians in Libya "hear for us" throughout the film also solicits our identification with their feelings and their corporeal experiences of attraction and alienation. Even as it adds to the exotic appeal of the Italian colony, it reminds Italians on- and off-screen that distance is essential to maintaining boundaries between the thinly staffed Italian fort and an surrounding indigenous culture they were continuously absorbing, by aural and other means.[28]

Noise and vocality also convey the uneasiness of precarious political situations, such as that created by two Italian officials leading dozens of trained Libyan soldiers on a hunt for their rebel compatriots deep in the Sahara, far from the reinforcements and trappings of Italian authority. In the desert, while the familiar Western symphonics of the score hold things together for the viewer, other kinds of sounds convey the unsettling and uncontrollable aspects of colonial and desert life: brayings of camels, winds so strong they disorient vision and render speech impossible, and native chanting, begun as an accompaniment to the labor of setting up camp but continuing off-screen as a strong, breathy vocalizing that mimics the rhythms and sounds of copulation. Such amorphous, "untraceable" sound figures in *Luciano Serra, pilota*, and also in some Luce documentaries, and here too it is less a question of sound substituting for speech than sound referencing what cannot be said: the horror and fascination of primitivity and the libidinal urge, and the undoing of everything in the event of racial insurrection. The power of the unintelligible in empire cinema, and the voice's ability to exceed signification, is again manifest. Even and especially when untethered to an individuated body, the voice elicits "corporeal reactions of desire and fear, pleasure and disgust, fascination and shame" that also marked colonial interactions on the ground.[29]

The dance of domination and dependence between Italians and the indigenous comes through most clearly in the regulation of *askari* speech. Here a military culture of linguistic discipline—speak only when ordered to—meets Genina's minimalism to produce a near muteness on the part of the troops that ultimately aids in their reduction to a "visual accompaniment," as Bertellini terms it. It also sidesteps the issue of dependence on translators, although this figure has an important role during Santelia's Duce-like stiff address to the *meharisti* in which he characterizes Bettini's "heroic death" as a "fulgid example and a noble incitement." The Libyan official's relay of this invitation to die for the occupier into Arabic is an integral part of the ceremony. Such officials were sometimes resented by ordinary Italian soldiers, one of whom remembered that the job of translator conferred an intimacy with the commander "and a power which even we did not have."[30] The staging of translations also showed off bilingual abilities among Libyans that few Italians possessed, countering warnings by the Fascist minister of education that "obvious considerations of prestige require us to avoid making the indigenous equal in mastery to us." Scenes of translation in this and other empire films maintain the fiction that the colonized could speak only pidgin Italian. The translator silently listens to the official's proper Italian and then speaks only in his native tongue to his peers. So invested were the Fascists in this linguistic "strategy of containment," to use Apter's phase, that Cesare Polacco, the Italian actor who played Mario's aide, El Fennek, with darkened skin, had to learn pidgin Italian for his part.[31]

The place of silence in *Lo squadrone bianco* stands out within this sound profile. Genina had flagged his film's unusual linguistic economy in an interview given during filming, asserting that "the dialogue will be reduced to a minimum. . . . [T]he director should use lines as one uses words in a telegram sent to America: knowing that every word costs 100 lire." Such linguistic efficiency came with its base text: Peyré's novel is parsimonious with dialogue, portraying the ability to be silent as a sign of male strength and part of Legionnaire culture. Italian military culture commanded silence as well, for disciplinary and commemorative purposes, and Fascism's particular re-education of the body advanced its own control over the right to speak. Not surprisingly, the Roman salute made obligatory by the 1938 "reform of customs" was a silent gesture, meant to replace a verbal salutation. Mario's evolution from Cristiana's love slave to commander of men and of himself can be charted by his linguistic evolution from nervous barking and volubility to an individual who learns the power of silence and non-verbal communication as part of the art of governance.[32] Silence also has aesthetic value within the movie's poetics of presence and absence. Genina had long been interested in the place of silence within sound film, and the Sahara setting offered a chance to experiment. As Béla Balázs observed, silence is both a spatial experience and an "acoustic effect," and the active silence of the desert gives it the status of sonic landscape rather than setting. In the desert scenes, which as Bertellini has observed have the feel of a religious procession, with "Santelia" at its head, there is a near absence of dialogue, and the minimalist score produces a hypnotic and elegiac atmosphere. The frequent use of silence creates a sense of stillness and builds on the trope within international colonial visual culture of the Sahara as a dreamscape outside of Western space and time.[33]

Finally, silence functions as the sonic equivalent of Genina's narrative use of ellipsis. As used in the sequences of the desert campaign, it elides the messiness and suffering of war, present in the book through the screams of an insubordinate *mehariste* who is left to die in the desert. *Lo squadrone bianco*'s battle scenes allow the entrance of the sounds of military technology, with machine-gun fire echoing among the dunes. Yet speech is stilled in much of the scenes of the march through the desert, leaving only sound and the score to underscore empathetically the bravery and endurance of the *askaris* who search for an unseen and unheard enemy. The close-ups of the indigenous soldiers humanize them, showing the toll of their service in the Sahara etched on their faces, but their muteness also allows them, at other points, to be aestheticized as silhouettes against the sky. While Genina includes no documentary footage in his film, he makes use of a visual language about the Sahara common in both Luce and international nonfiction that privileges the flattened corporeal presences achieved by long-shot cinematography. At the same time, as Germani and Martinelli have written, Genina's style expressed his own "need to subtract, to search for a vanishing point," which in *Lo squadrone bianco* collaborates with Fascist ideologies of male conversion and a spiritualism of both Catholic and Fascist inflection to take us into the realm of a silence that is increasingly disembodied, the equivalent of the "gaze without a subject" that closes the film.[34]

Yet Genina, who had directed more than seventy films by 1936, does not let the body go easily. On the contrary, he repeatedly calls attention to the emotional and corporeal dimensions and effects of spectatorship. One such moment is his isolation of the "irritating" Arabic music the officers hear, which places the focus on point of audition, bridging the spectator and the on-screen character through the act of hearing. Cristiana's attendance at an alfresco performance in the Basilica of Maxentius is another. Her longing for Mario carries her inward, away from her lover who sits beside her, setting her apart from the sea of faces paying rapt attention. The focus on point of audition, here, merely throws into relief the rival "soundtrack" coming from within and the ways that spectatorship is also a private and voluble situation, sometimes occasioning journeys to intimate spaces unrelated to the performance at hand. The musical choice, the "Largo" from the "Winter" concerto of Vivaldi's *Four Seasons,* is telling: it gives voice to the search for a home for the soul, something that Cristiana, despite her luxurious lifestyle, decidedly lacks. The concert, in fact, sets her on an emotional voyage that leads to physical peregrinations around the Mediterranean that will likely continue after her ejection from Mario's desert domain. Such attention to the ways sound travels between screen and spectator also forms part of Genina's traveling aesthetics.[35]

This meta-reflection extends to the visual sphere. Here there is a more openly pedagogical dimension, with the emphasis on watching and being watched in line with the regime's emphasis on Fascist colonial style as an outward sign of internal discipline. When a jealous Mario charges toward Cristiana early in the movie, gripping her neck, the camera cuts to a view from outside of the room, allowing spectators to watch the action through a transparent windowed partition of modernist stamp upon which Afri-

FIGURE 5.5.

One of the "White Squadron," *Lo squadrone bianco*.
Author's collection

FIGURE 5.6.

Genina's Saharan imagery, *Lo squadrone bianco*.
Author's collection

can statues are displayed. We watch the statues watch, openmouthed, as Cristiana screams, the primal sound expressive of "the unthinkable inside the thought, of the indeterminate inside the spoken, of unrepresentability inside representation," in Chion's words. The African objects' presence undoubtedly references the eruption of the primitive within Mario, as Boggi contends, but their placement also emphasizes their status as silent witnesses who anticipate the rows of *askaris* Mario will encounter in Africa. Indeed, as Santelia reminds Mario in admonishing him to act like a *capo*, the *meharisti* are, together with Italian soldiers, the audience for officials' performances of masculinity and imperial domination. The eyes of the indigenous on Italian behavior are also alluded to in the circular traveling shot of the first troop review, and in the scenes of the indigenous women and children who turn out to watch the squadron depart for the desert. The unknowable thoughts of the veiled women, like those of the marching soldiers and the unintelligible Arabic vocals and speech in the film, are reminders of the tenuous nature of the colonial collaborations this and other films in this chapter celebrate.[36]

Publicity for *Lo squadrone bianco* focused mainly on a different kind of collaboration, though: the return to the national fold of the most successful of Italy's filmic expatriates. Unlike the other directors of empire movies examined in this book, Genina did not alternate foreign projects with Italian-based ones: he had not made a movie in Italy for almost ten years. Moreover, it was public knowledge in film circles that Genina had offered the project to French backers and then to Alexander Korda's London Film, which had just produced the empire film *Sanders of the River*, before accepting to make it in Italy. It does not surprise that an Italian reviewer termed *Lo squadrone bianco* "an important film which is, shall we say, not exactly tied to our traditions" and Genina someone who "occupies a special position ... not classifiable by the same standards [as other Italian directors]."[37] This cosmopolitan background, and the exogenous nature of the base story, made the role of the regime's propaganda machine and the involvement of officials more crucial than in most empire films. Political guarantors did not lack: Balbo lent his camel troops and military advisers, and Francesco Giunta, the film's director of production, had been an undersecretary of state and even more famous as a squadrist leader in Trieste. Giunta's paramilitary past figured positively in the press from the start of *Lo squadrone bianco*'s production. A spread in *Lo Schermo* the next month, entitled "Squadron on the March," explicitly channeled squadrism in likening the shoot to a military occupation, even including a map of the troupe's/troops' movements. "There is an air of war and a smell of gunpowder at 'Rome Film' these days," gushed journalist Giv., recording Giunta's frenetic requisitioning of rifles, tents, and camels and the prominent place of books by Graziani in his office. This "rough, tough, linear" movie would be a testament to the values of "mindful discipline and meditated courage," distancing it from the "desperate" tone of *La Bandera* and *The Lost Patrol*. *Lo squadrone bianco*'s ending might disappoint those hoping for a romantic love story in the desert, he concluded, but it "will not surprise old squadrists and will please young Fascists."[38] The Libyan "white squadron" and its Italian leaders stand in for the Italian "black squadron," and the suspect French Legionnaires of the novel are substituted by a military force organic to Fascist history.

Other interventions in the Fascist colonial and film press toed this same line during production. *Lo Schermo* asserted that a special military official "competent in colonial matters" would join the troupe to guarantee its "military exactness," and a "Libyan Italian" named Sanino Nahum, possessed of "a perfect knowledge of the Arabic dialects," would act as translator. The Italian Libyan newspaper *L'Avvenire di Tripoli* called attention to the "tent city" set up in the fort of Sinauen for the troupe, which included one hundred camel troop extras relocated for the filming, and to the "perfect organization" that allowed Genina to send rushes to Italy by auto and then airplane. And a lavishly illustrated article in the popular magazine *Cinema Illustrazione*, written after filming in Libya had been completed, let its readers know that hundreds of people had endured "discomfort, sacrifices, labors, and disillusionments" while shooting in Africa. Genina, doing his part, told a journalist during filming that *Lo squadrone bianco* would be "an Italian colonial film: a heroic and virile film with a light love story on the side." National-international and political-market tensions are negotiated in these various declarations, which frame the film as a man's picture and begrudge the female presence, even though Cristiana's transformation into a tourist tied in well with the regime's current marketing of Libya as a vacation destination. Luce's newsreel on *Lo squadrone bianco*'s production tried to cover all bases, displaying the "tent city" as a marvel of efficiency but also a place of intercultural encounters with "authentic *meharisti*" and exotic animals.[39]

These tensions persisted after the release of the film, which won the "best Italian film" cup when it premiered at the Venice Biennale. Sandro De Feo, the critic of the populist *Il Messaggero,* praised it as "a completely Italian film" in story and style. Like other commentators, he lauded a linguistic and narrative strategy that had allowed the director to avoid both the picturesque (when portraying Arabs) and the rhetorical (when portraying Italians). Even uniforms did not have a merely decorative value in this film, De Feo noted approvingly, but signified inner qualities proper to each character. The director "has managed to do something with nothing," added *Cinema,* specifying "'nothing' does not mean emptiness, but masculine renunciation of specious effects, colorful digressions, and gossipy suggestions." This "moral and narrative austerity" with all of its masculinist connotations, along with its squadrist framing, was Genina's point of entry into Fascist culture and into the developing lineage of empire films. A "prologue" of intertitles strengthened the film's political credentials with its dedication to the duke of Aosta's troops "who brought Libya back to Rome," a reading that Genina encouraged by declaring that his film honored "all the force and power of the Italians who fight in the name of *civiltà* in the African colonies." For Filippo Sacchi of the *Corriere della sera,* that fighting was almost beside the point: Genina had made "a strong, vital, masculine, and very personal film" that did not depend on the scenes of desert combat for its efficacy. Yet such combat formed part of the formula of empire cinema. A 1937 letter from a French friend alludes to the director's private unhappiness at the triumph of the homosocial war story over the kind of romantic tale that had figured so heavily in his European work and evidently in the original treatment or script as well. "As we already know, the love story with this woman who vaguely evokes Greta Garbo has been forcibly sacrificed.... But the whole desert part is a masterpiece of filming," Maurice De Kobra consoled him. As it was, other Italian reviewers found Cristiana's presence corrupting and intrusive: "She has nothing in common with Italian women," Ferruccio Bonfiglio complained, and she lent an unwelcome "melodramatic and sentimental" tone to the movie. Genina's past tendencies to "fall into the courtesies of a delicate sentimentalism" had to be expurgated for him to become the poet of Fascism's imperial enterprise. For the director, as well as for his character Mario, the Sahara was to act as a "redemptive force."[40]

French reviewers treated Genina as one of their own. Playing the movie's military and desert dimensions up or down according to their political leanings, French critics lauded his skill in translating Peyré's novel in ways that accentuated the possibilities of the cinematic medium. Genina had dared, "at the risk of monotony," to render the majestic slowness and silence that make up "the rugged poetry of the desert." The real protagonist, for some, was this "sumptuous desert, with its violent light," not the soldiers with their ideals of "military virility." For Peyré, though, the movie's values of "individual and collective discipline, obliteration of oneself, friendship and duty" were universal ones, as he emphasized in print and in a prologue to the French edition. At least one of his compatriots agreed with him. Comparing it to *The Lost Patrol*, Maurice Bardèche asserted that *Lo squadrone bianco* bore neither a specific political nor a geographical mark of origin: it could have been made anywhere.[41] In fact, the film did well in the capitals of both democracies (London, Paris) and dictatorships (Berlin). The exception was Italy, where ticket sales did not match critical enthusiasm. Given the official investment in the film, and its awarding of the top prize at the Venice Biennale, few Italian-based critics wanted to draw attention to its tepid reception among Italian audiences. But the Italian exile G. B. Angioletti had no such qualms: writing from Paris, he complained that Italians' lack of a colonial culture and puerile attachment to romantic comedy made them unable to appreciate the movie's austere poetics and its linguistic and bodily minimalism. And indeed, the colonial style advanced by *Lo squadrone bianco* was one that displayed the body only to renounce it, with the play of estrangement and attraction resolved through death—of Bettini, of Santelia, of El Fennek, and, symbolically, of Mario, too. By the end of the film, Mario has freed himself from his enslavement to the senses, but his banishment of Cristiana is also a banishment of all carnality in the name of a faith that marries Catholic and Fascist mysticism. Differently than in French and British desert films, the Sahara becomes a sacralized space, its mirages and endless silent horizons an entrée into a transcendental realm not only beyond women, but beyond the body as well.[42]

THE BREACHED BODIES OF *SENTINELLE DI BRONZO*

With *Sentinelle di bronzo*, we move from the "white squadron" to the "bronze sentinels," from the blindingly clear spaces of the Sahara to the lush vegetation and flowing waters of Somalia's Shebelle River, and from a master stylist to a young documentarian-journalist shooting his first fiction film. *Legionari del secondo parallelo*, which was discussed in chapter 4, was symptomatic of Marcellini's nonfiction work, which focused on the imperial campaigns of the Italian Air Force and the Militia. Marcellini had also served as an assistant director to Gallone on *Scipione l'Africano*, though, and his alternations between documentary and feature moviemaking hold interest in light of his attempts to blend the conventions of the two film forms to create an original national screen aesthetic. *Sentinelle di bronzo*'s experimental qualities lay in its use of documentary techniques (it was shot entirely on location, with mostly indigenous actors) within an "industrial production," he contended. In Marcellini's view, studio re-creations of Africa were false and financially impractical, given the limited resources of the Italian industry, nor was "the usual formula of adventure films like *Eskimo* or *Trader Horn*" (location shooting mixed with studio shooting and stock footage) suitable to truly render the feel and look of the Italian colonies. Doing away with the studio as much as possible, Marcellini aimed to suffuse the entire movie with a documentary spirit, offering "a new and very modern orientation for certain types of productions... and bring fresh air, not only to the Italian cinema."[43]

Marcellini's reference to W. S. Van Dyke's 1931 and 1933 films was not incidental. The Italian public's seemingly insatiable appetite for American films loomed large in the minds of all Italian film professionals, particularly those who wished to inaugurate a new cinematic current. We can recall that in 1937, the year *Sentinelle di bronzo* was released, Hollywood films took in more than 65 percent of box-office receipts in Italy. The public writings of Marcellini and others involved in Italian empire film culture reflected a real resolve to do something different, for ideological and aesthetic reasons as well as market share. As Chiarini wrote that same year, the Italian imperial film could not just be driven by "commercial preoccupations," like its American counterparts, offering merely "an hour of diversion." It had to have a moral value, reflecting "the principles of duty, heroic adventure and the spirit of camaraderie." Marcellini, an ardent Fascist, shared this view, arguing that empire films represented opportunities to "bring the Italian cinema industry in line with the new imperial project" *and* to "approach this project from a truly political spirit and perspective." Casting figured heavily in this alternative film model. Rather than utilizing professionals such as "Lotus" (Lotus Long, the half-Hawaiian, half-Japanese actress) and "Mala" (Ray Mala, the half-Inuit star of *Eskimo*) who are "true and proper film actors, with Hollywood contracts, cars, and mentalities," who played a variety of ethnicities, Marcellini featured anonymous indigenous men and women proper to the territories depicted on-screen. Duranti's presence as a lead, alongside the Somali Hassan Mohamed, was a concession to commercial concerns—and pressures by the film's producer Eugenio Fontana, then Duranti's lover.[44] Marcellini's training meant that nonfiction provided the starting point, and *Sentinelle di bronzo* builds on a tradition of Italian docufictions such as Gatti's *Siliva Zulu*. Terzano, the cinematographer, had experience with empire documentaries (*Dall'Italia all'Equatore/From Italy to the Equator*, 1923, which he also directed) and features (*Aldebaran, Il grande appello*, and *Lo squadrone bianco*).

Marcellini's will to originality, and his use of a documentary style to maximize Somalia's visual and aural novelty for viewers, make the Western and Orientalist influences in *Sentinelle di bronzo* notable. His film builds on Orientalism's themes of intertribal conflict, female kidnappings, and displays of exotic customs and costumes. It also shows a heavy debt to the Western, from the frontier spirit of the encampment to the staging of battle scenes and to the portrayal of landscape. Both are enmeshed in a Fascist war story that progresses, in typical fashion, from a narrative driven by characterization and ethnographic display to industrial battle sequences populated by anonymous soldiers who have little or no relation to the film's named personages. The prominence of the body in landscape and bodily surface within the frame provides continuity here: gleaming black skin, wet from the river, gives way to gleaming white skin, wet from the sweat of battle. The body also stands at the center of the movie's rhetorical and historical figurations, for *Sentinelle di bronzo* is a story about the threat and substance of violations. National, familial, and individual bodies are breached and cut, as is, eventually, the membrane of cinematic illusion. Although Marcellini later rued the title of his work as something imposed by the producer, "which had little to do with anything," skin, as boundary and contact zone of the body, has everything to do with this empire film.[45]

The movie's original title, *Marrabò*, which translates from Somali as "I don't want to," was undoubtedly deemed unsuitable for a work meant to celebrate the fidelity and valor of the *dubat*. Yet the imperative of refusal has both a political and a dramatic rationale in the film, which dramatizes a December 1934 clash between Ethiopians and Italians at Wal Wal that was used by the Fascists as an excuse for the invasion of that country. Located in the Ogaden border region that was then part of Ethiopia, Wal Wal, with its hundreds of wells, had long been coveted by the Italians, who sent *dubat* there to guard it as early as 1930, posing as the protectors of the Ogaden Somali nomads who depended on its water. *Marrabò* thus referred to the Somali nomads' unwillingness to submit to Ethiopian rule. This macro-history is the setting for a story of familial conflict featuring the beautiful nomad Dahabò, who is kidnapped from her *cabila* by the brutish Ibrahim (Abdul Omar), brother of the *askari* official Elmi (Hassan Mohamed). As in *Kif Tebbi*, which vilified the Arab Rassim as well as the Turks, there is an internal as well as external threat, and it is Dahabò who speaks the word *Marrabò* in objecting to her seizure by Ibrahim. Elmi plays the hero in this tribal drama, and Dahabò favors him for his gentleness. Notice of an impending Ethiopian attack sends Elmi on a mission to the Ogaden borderlands to convince his father, head of their nomadic tribe, to collaborate, but his influential brother remains pro-Ethiopian until Elmi dies in battle, whereupon he offers his *cabila*'s services to the Italian outpost's commander, Captain Negri (Giachetti), and releases Dahabò. Tank and aerial reinforcements secure this Italian victory, but only the occupation of Ethiopia and a continual supply of indigenous troops, nomads among them, will stabilize the situation.

Robert Hess argues that Somalia's main imperial value for the Fascists lay in its shared border with Ethiopia. Somalia had no Roman heritage or direct Mediterranean connection, and only 10 percent of its land was suitable for settled agriculture. In both the liberal and the Fascist periods, undercapitalization and a low rate of Italian migration reflected a lack of official direction about its function within the pantheon of Italian colonies. Like Libya, Somalia had been conquered in phases. Direct rule of the entire country occurred only after the Fascist takeover, with the acquisition of the Jubbaland region in 1926 and a military onslaught that quelled the most militant resisters by the end of the decade. And as in the case of Libya, securing Italian rule entailed confrontation with tribal and clan structures: the state exploited intertribal factionalism, gave some autonomy in religious and tribal justice matters, and solicited paid collaboration through military service. Yet the outcome differed, in part because Somalia was targeted neither for Libya's mass tourism and population transfer nor for the benefits and burdens of imperial citizenship. If Libya was the "fourth shore," Somalia was "the Cinderella of the Italian colonies," beautiful and full of potential but largely neglected.[46]

The regime's contrasting treatments of nomadic peoples in Libya and Somalia leave traces in the two films, which engage differently with this sensitive political theme. The absence of any direct reference to nomads in Genina's film registers their physical removal to concentration camps in the desert, but nomads are also the unseen adversary of the Saharan interior. In Somalia most nomadic tribes, including those of the upper Shebelle River area depicted in the film, had been disarmed in the mid-1920s, but the regime's attempts in the 1930s to settle them by imposing boundaries for the movement and grazing rights had little effect. In fact, the continued mobility of nomads ended up serving the regime's purposes, since protecting roaming border tribes from attacks from Ethiopians provided one excuse for the expansion of Italian power in the region. Nomads remained a source of nervousness, though, which *Sentinelle di bronzo* exploits with its re-creation of the precarious situation before the Ethiopian invasion and its setting in the border region Ogaden, which is billed as a "no-man's-land" in the credits. Ibrahim and Elmi come from this labile space, and they represent the different trajectories of Somali nomads: finding a physical "home" in the Italian Army and an affective dwelling in one's ties to one's superior (Elmi), siding with the Ethiopians (Ibrahim, early on), or placing your tribe at the Italians' disposal (Ibrahim, later).

Italian-proficient *askaris* and other colonial intermediaries had greater prominence and responsibility than in Libya because of their relative scarcity. Somalia had the smallest budget for instruction of all the Italian colonies. Until the 1930s, the Italian government had left education (limited to primary school) entirely in the hands of religious institutions, and even in 1938, with many missionaries replaced with state-appointed teachers, only 896 African students attended ten government schools in the country. Thus, relatively few Somalis learned Italian outside of military service, and far fewer Somalis served as *askaris* with respect to Eritreans. The absence of a Somali written language further complicated communication. Somalia, "the furthest away of all of our overseas colonies," as a Luce documentary termed it, also remained perhaps the least understood.[47] *Sentinelle di bronzo* registers this situation in various ways. Elmi's Italian is far better than that of El Fennek in *Lo squadrone bianco,* and Giachetti's officer character, who could speak some Arabic directly to his soldiers in Genina's film, relies heavily on Elmi for communication. The scenes of troop review make clear Elmi's abilities as Negri's aide, translator, and the fort's ranking *askari*. His ideological value, as expressed in his repetition of Negri's orders, is as "the shadow able to imitate (imperfectly) the actions of the colonist." His translations are not neutral communications, but interpellations of other Somalis by an already socialized colonial subject. As in *Lo squadrone bianco,* Negri is virtually alone as he commands an outpost in an area known for enemy activity; long shots show a fort in the midst of an immense desert plain. Strutting about in his officer's whites, barking orders in a brusque tone, Giachetti performs the gestures and speech of imperial masculinity more forcefully than in *Lo squadrone bianco*.[48] We learn nothing about his history or his inner life: he lives in the present moment. His armature protects a threatened masculine body—his own, and that of the Italian nation, vulnerable to breaches of its territory by Ethiopian marauders.

Such power relations and Italian insecurities shape the paternalistic model of colonial relations that guides Elmi and Negri's interactions. While El Fennek was something of a desert sage, his face lined with years of experience, Elmi seems little more than a boy, despite his years of faithful service to his commander. His youthful appearance and childlike manner are key to his suitability as an indigenous male lead, as they desexualize him and forestall any masculine competition with Giachetti's robust character. Marcellini asserts a proprietary relationship between commanders and their faithful *askaris:* Elmi served with Negri in Libya and then in Italy, at a Colonial Exposition, before coming to Somalia. The reference to the exhibition places the *askaro* within a broader chain of colonial labor that demanded the black body for both battle and display and gives the audience a context for his third kind of colonial service: working in empire films.[49] Paternalism also governs the relationship of a second man-boy pair meant to provide the film's comic relief. The gruff and bumbling Sargent Amato (Giovanni Grasso), who is a kind of Fascist Oliver Hardy, spars constantly with the fort's mascot, calling the Sabu-like figure *faccetta nera* (little black face) and *mezza cartuccia* (good for nothing). The relationship between Negri and Elmi is clearly the didactic template, however, and they are set apart from the ranks of indigenous and Italian soldiers by their costume and comportment. Although some publicity for the film portrays Elmi as similar to other *dubat*—as an extension of the Somali landscape, with the shadow of tree branches on his face—his uniformed body marks him off from the mass of half-naked Somalis who are scrutinized by the camera in *Sentinelle di bronzo* and Luce nonfiction alike.[50]

Elmi's journey home to his tribe, to the borderlands between Ethiopia and Somalia, brings the viewer into the world of the indigenous. Marcellini's documentary predilections dominate in this part of the film, where an all-native cast (with the exception of Duranti, who plays Dahabò with darkened skin) inspires a looser narrative that allows for the display of Somali customs and social practices. Africa is a paradise of the senses, with lush foliage, tea rituals, vocalizations, and gleaming skin, but also a barbarous place of intra-African bodily violations that justify Italian intervention as humanitarian rescue. The absence of Italians in these scenes of violence makes the black African the persecutor of his own kind, resolving the colonial dilemma of how to carry out repression while preserving the fiction of benevolence. Tribal justice showcases this contrast between savagery and enlightenment. Early in the movie, Negri acts as a kind of sheriff, adjudicating local grievances; his hands twitch on his sharp baton, but his rulings involve no corporeal punishment. In Ogaden, instead, the body is repeatedly mutilated, first by the Ethiopians, who cut off the ear and then the penis of a traitor—the latter alluded to by shots of the bare torso on the ground, the raised knife, and screaming—and then by Elmi's own tribesmen, who flog a thief. The latter is organized violence,

FIGURE 5.7.

Elmi as colonial intermediary, *Sentinelle di bronzo.* Author's collection

as it takes place at a tribal gathering presided over by Elmi's father, Islam (Mohamed Agi Ali). Italian policy allowed for the exercise of Muslim and Somali customary law through Indigenous Tribunals, but Marcellini displays the whip's branding of the skin as an index of primitivity. The body is "a critical site for maintaining alterity and enacting governance," and this one reaches out to the Italian and indigenous spectator through an afflicted corporeality that is also a warning. Significantly, the scene closes with Elmi relaying Negri's request for the tribe's collaboration with the Italians against the impeding Ethiopian assault.[51]

The regulation of speech is a prominent theme throughout the film. It formed part of Fascism's re-educative projects for Italians and the indigenous, but religious and tribal institutions also legislated the right to speak. In empire films set in Libya and Somalia, the veils of Muslim women speak to the silence tacitly imposed on them in the public domain by local gender politics and Western expectations. They vocalize, in the form of

FIGURE 5.8.

The breached body in *Sentinelle di bronzo*. Author's collection

ululations, but they have little dialogue; their un-individuated voices form part of Somalia's sonic landscape. Not so Dahabò, who is introduced as Ibrahim shoves her off his horse and presents her as his war booty. Throwing off her veil, she establishes her independent nature with her first words to the tribal leader: "Islam, since when do warriors kidnap women? Your son has stolen me away from my *cabila* and from my father. Is Dahabò a slave?" Ibrahim responds in a mocking manner—"Woman, I could make you my slave. Instead I will make you my wife." Dahabò replies, "Never," and although Islam dismisses her outburst, saying, "Women's words are like footprints of the shepherd, swept away by the wind," he gives her into the protective care of the women of the clan.[52] Dahabò cannot be confined, though: again infringing the rule against women speaking in public, she appears at the tribal meeting and warns the nomads of Amhara cruelty against her own *cabila*, urging them to flee to the desert.

Dahabò's testimony also affirms the instabilities created by the sound experiments of empire films. *Sentintelle di bronzo* presents a hybrid sound profile, mixing direct sound and speech with studio sound and dubbed voices and featuring a variety of Somali dialects and accents. Dahabò, like Ibrahim and Islam, speaks only in Somali throughout the film, with subtitles relaying the meaning of her words. Although Duranti is dubbed by a Somali actress, hers is an embodied and intelligible voice, which facilitates audience identification, as does her sympathetic role in the film. It is also the vessel of alterity. The guttural and unfamiliar sounds (for viewers in Italy) that emanate from Dahabò's mouth have an emotional charge that complements her visual exoticism, yet go beyond the screen image. As Kaja Silverman observes, the voice is situated in the interstices between the biological body and the social body, and in this sense, too, the character Dahabò is unplaced: removed from her clan, she becomes a woman with masculine pretensions to speech. Her voice is that of the nomad who refuses domination and settlement, both in its symbolic form of language regulation and as forced marriage.[53]

It is fitting that Duranti's body, as viewed on-screen, is also the result of a transfer: from white to black and into the skin of the other. Skin, no less than voice, exceeds signification, and such masquerades could disrupt as well as reinforce racial hierarchies. Duranti's performance upholds racial propriety—audiences desire someone known to be a white woman—while allowing for transgressions in gender roles. Dahabò's defiance and strength, and her verbal directness, are tolerated precisely because she is an artificial creation. Costumes that grow more exotic over the course of the film evince this theatricality, and Marcellini's realism gives way here to the imperatives of stardom and spectacle. Although his scenario posited Dahabò as a minor character, just another "reason for disagreement" between Elmi and Ibrahim, Duranti ends up often dominating the picture, as was probably the hope and intention of Fontana. Blackened skin in empire films makes the white performer into a kind of intermediary, invested with the job of translating one race to another. Duranti recalled that she relied on her double, actress Alima Christina, to teach her "how a girl of color moves, squats, looks, and sits" and to wash off her blackness every night, "restoring my white appearance . . . and returning me to my race."[54]

Other instabilities and infractions to the operation of fictional narrative mark the sequences of *Sentinelle di bronzo* devoted to ethnographic display. The courtship of Elmi and Dahabò justifies some of these scenes,

FIGURES 5.9 AND 5.10.

Ibrahim and Dahabò: Orientalism in *Sentinelle di bronzo*.
Both author's collection

which take place on the banks of the Shebelle River, often billed as Italy's Nile. Dahabò is a queenly figure, with her female guardians ladies in waiting, and Elmi her elegant suitor who is an intermediary between native culture and modernity: he teaches the women to smoke and explains the telephone. Yet his demeanor is that of a brother rather than that of the romantic lead, which is also why he is allowed into the women's private space. Throughout their scenes together, Duranti dwarfs him, and she claims in her memoirs that she had to teach Mohamed how to kiss.[55] Native proverbs, a lot of untranslated dialogue, and the evocation of the sounds, smells, and tastes of tribal life offer an ethnographic panorama completed by the sight of a trio of fully naked women entering the river, laughing and splashing one another. Sunlight illuminates their wet skin, with gleaming buttocks prominently displayed as the women playfully wrestle. The lighthearted score infantilizes these three African graces, as does the cut to children nearby. Dahabò and her companions join the group, but Duranti preserves her bodily mystery. Such an exuberant display of Muslim female skin, which is nowhere found in Libya-set movies, sustains the mythology of sub-Saharan African female sexual availability and the white fascination with black body surface. These frames conjoin the legacies of the Hottentot Venus with the cult of the silky Somali, soliciting what Marks terms a "haptic visuality"—a sense of touching through the eyes—perhaps calling up "tactile memories" for male spectators who had spent time in Africa. Although they do not advance the war story or the love story, they affirm the gender-bifurcated scheme of Fascist colonial labor: the *askaro,* "who loves to fight more than American blacks love to sing," and the "smiling Negress," as Pinkus has termed her, who beckons with none of the complications Italian women posed back home.[56]

The tribal dance scene that flows from the river sequence has greater diegetic justification (it celebrates Elmi's homecoming), but it, too, enacts a fantasy of "direct, unmediated visual access to the native body." The mating ritual, which features lines of men and women facing one another and moving in what many Western viewers would consider a suggestive manner, is a staple of empire films for its efficient means of portraying the strange and primitive nature of African sexuality. And something is indeed off: the men do their job competently, but the probing close-ups show that the youngest girls kept their gazes averted, their discomfort also suggested in the way one of them breaks character and looks at the camera. Such reactions run through the photographic record of Italian colonialism, countering its eroticization of the female black body, and moments of fear and anger punctuate the stream of Luce representations of the indigenous as well. The timorous glance that travels out to the viewer in Marcellini's feature jars the happy fictional occasion and the very fabric of cinematic illusion. These "fragmentary moments of visible reality," as Sigfried Kracauer identified such instances generally, function in the colonial context to remind us of the mortification that could accompany filmic and other colonial collaborations. As MacDougall writes, flashes of raw emotion, which are not uncommon in documentary reenactments, can lead the spectator to relate to "objects and gestures, attitudes and social behaviors, [in ways that] that often elude the intention of the director." The moment is certainly made more poignant by the anempathetic march-style music that accompanies the scene.[57]

Like other empire films, the production of *Sentinelle di bronzo* relied on and furthered a system of colonial labor that occasioned abuses and intimacies, displacements and dependencies, and ambivalence—that defining colonial condition—seemed to govern the attitudes of both filmmakers and indigenous actors. Duranti recalls how casting calls for extras, done through village chiefs, brought out "tall and dignified men, wrapped in their white robes, silent, who remained motionless for hours.... [I]t was not clear if they were looking for work or just keeping an eye on us." Later, when the interpreter explained the filming process, some listened with "a severe and closed expression that was like a reprimand." Marcellini's accounts of filming, published in the Fascist press, take a quite different tone. True to the Luce ethos, he emphasizes the intimidating effects of the technical apparatus of moviemaking on Africans and interprets their participation as a form of subjugation, with the camera eye standing in for that of Mussolini. When the "big cars" carrying the moviemaker and his troupe roared into their villages, even the "pure and noble" Majeerteen people fled into their huts:

> The movie camera, surrounded by Black Shirts, was not very reassuring, it seemed like a weapon. No one was in sight. The head of the tribe, an elderly man with a white beard, plucked up his courage and came forward.... [Marcellini asks] "You know Mussolini?" Yes, he knew him

FIGURE 5.11.

Young girl performing, *Sentinelle di bronzo*. Author's collection

well: he be great Leader, everyone here his people, and we his soldiers. "Merere people be good, and Mussolini want to know. This be his faraway eye" and I pointed to the lens of the LUCE apparatus. This was all true, and he was immediately convinced. He called all his people, and they let themselves be filmed, and even rounded up their animals.[58]

Other collaborations seem to have been more complicated. The initial credits of *Sentinelle di bronzo* boast that "the actual Aberghidir, Abhal [Abgal], Avadiè, Macannè *cabilas* and the Dagabur detachment appear." Although the Aberghidir clan had recently lent tribesmen for the filming of *L'Esclave blanc*, those with speaking roles apparently had to undergo a "quite delicate and sensitive moral and psychological preparation." Some clans had traveled long distances, leaving their lands and animals untended, and one group of hundreds of tribesmen, after riding 125 miles, turned around to leave again after finding a rival clan there: only sacks of sugar and flour added to their normal pay convinced them to stay. Filming during the rainy season also meant that many fell ill from standing for hours in the water. Duranti remembers "the terrible rain and discomfort" and that Giachetti, who had his own car and driver, refused to sleep in a tent. The governor of Asmara sent Italian-speaking African prostitutes to the set to cheer up the Italian men, but this did nothing for Duranti's mood, and Marcellini admitted that conditions were "pitiful" for all involved. Resistance to collaboration also took the form of withholding the performance of the distinctive rituals necessary to the director. The women who allowed Marcellini to film them naked in the river refused for a long time to let their voices and ululations be recorded. Whatever their motivation, their actions imposed limits on the utilization of the body for colonialist aims, interrupting the translation of local knowledge necessary to the film's ethnographic dimension. As it was, most of the Ethiopians depicted were Eritreans, due to ongoing political volatility, and Marcellini noted obliquely that the degree of collaboration given to him by Somali peoples was not possible with the Amhara, who "would not have the same spiritual reactions even though as individuals they could reach the highest levels of cinematographic performance." The split between the good Somalis and the bad Ethiopians in the film also gestures toward this political reality.[59]

Marcellini had more control with his film's stylistic development. Orientalist elements are tamed by a documentarian's sensibility. The almost total absence of interior space in the movie and the lack of a strong romantic male lead do away with some of the preconditions for Orientalist decadence, leaving the exotic Dahabò, kidnapped by an evil Muslim, to draw in viewers attentive to such themes. Interior space in Italian empire films is also the scene of white male abjection, with sweeping African landscapes acting as recovery zones, but *Sentinelle di bronzo* departs from this model. White men do not interact much with black women, and the only male conversion involves Ibrahim's decision to collaborate. Exterior landscape holds sway here as a place of male defense, through the encircled Italian fort; a place of male conquest, through the many scenes of Italians and *askaris* charging through terrain; and a space, in de Certeau's sense, that is traversed by many but owned by none.

Marcellini relies heavily on the Western to depict this play of spaces and places, whether in his treatment of bodies and animals moving across

FIGURE 5.12.

Somalia as Western landscape, *Sentinelle di bronzo*. Author's collection

landscape or in his narration of battle scenes. The director had publicly dismissed the genre as "exhausted" and related to a type of standard production "that cannot interest us," but it is central to the operation of an imperial ideology that depended on the mix of the familiar and the unknown. The flight of the nomads into the desert, on Dahabò's warning, offers the visual elements of the Western, from the big sky to the difficult crossing of the river and to the herded animals, but the cattle are mostly camels, the pioneers Somali clanspeople, and the riders flashing by under the clouds white-turbaned *dubat*. The 1930s English-language dubbers of the extant version of *Sentinelle di bronzo* can be forgiven for turning the movie into an aural Western, with Giachetti as sheriff and words like "varmint" and "shoot-out" peppering the dialogue.[60]

The river crossing takes us back into "Italian" territory, where the Western feel continues as a showdown shapes up between the Ethiopians and the Italian forces. As in other empire films, the former are well armed, with a lot of machine guns, cars, and modern uniforms, and they ambush the nomads, killing Islam, before Negri and his *dubat* arrive. Rather than the slow, hypnotic trekking of the "white squadron" of Libya, indebted to a Saharan mystique, there is the frontal charge of the "white turbans," framed in the tradition of the Western and of British desert films. Back at the fort, the *dubat* fight bravely, Elmi among them, but they are outnumbered, and it takes the arrival of Italian tanks and airplanes to eventually vanquish the enemy. Whereas the beleaguered males of Genina's film (and many Foreign Legion and desert films) rarely see their enemy, the visibility of the evil Ethiopian offsets both the goodness of the *dubat* and the dangers posed by nomads such as Ibrahim, who could wander in either direction. Ibrahim comes over to the Italian side, galvanized by the killing of his father, but his conversion is sealed only when he sees the power of Fascist military force and military kinship—Elmi waits to die until Negri arrives. Elmi's death scene symbolically reconciles the disparate social actors in this colonial drama: the *askaro,* the male and female nomad, and the anchoring force of Italian authority, represented by the doctor and portraits of Badoglio and Mussolini.

The presence of the handsome Italian doctor at Elmi's deathbed flags the transition to the movie's final part, which is dominated by the display of Fascist technology in action. The flowing river, with its bathing beauties, gives way to an aesthetics of hardness and the thrill of targeting the enemy. What does continue is the display of gleaming skin, this time that of the white men who are paragons of the militarized masculinity desired by the regime. A sequence involving a trapped encircled tank—a staple of the war film—articulates the importance of the body in *Sentinelle di bronzo* as erotic spectacle as well as instrument of colonial conquest. Marcellini cuts between long shots of *dubat* advances and the drama unfolding inside the tank, where the shirtless, sweaty men endure enemy fire. The sight of the commander holding his men's faces, pouring the last water into their mouths, offers one of the more homoerotic moments in Fascist-era cinema and, at the very least, a testament to the male camaraderie promised to those who volunteered for Africa. Enclosed in their metal container—the only fully interior space shown in the film—their muscular bodies are never trespassed by others. As in other empire films, airplanes enter at the right moment, forcing an Ethiopian retreat, and

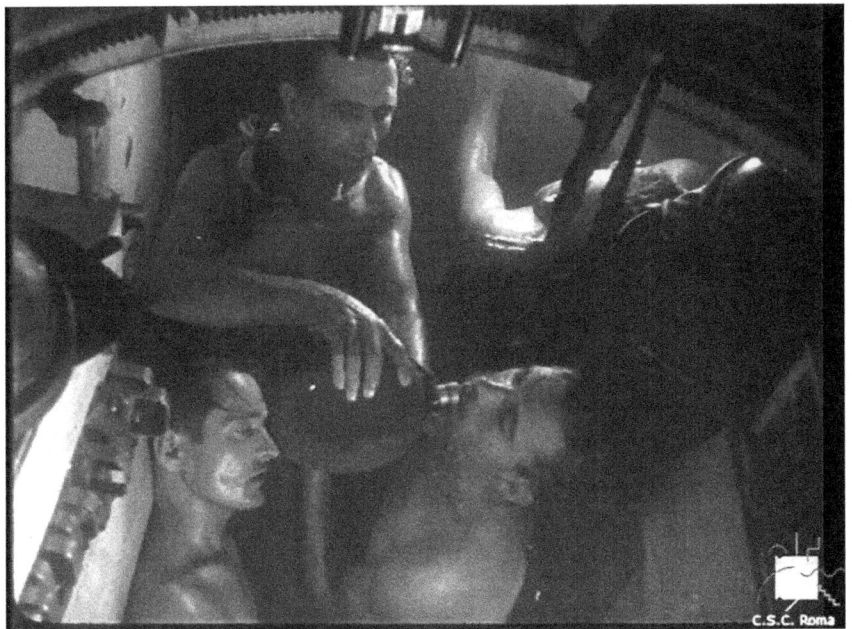

FIGURE 5.13.

The male enclave in *Sentinelle di bronzo*. Author's collection

ululations cheer on the *dubat*, with Negri at their head, as they ride back to the fort.

As perhaps befits a film that marries a tribal drama to a war film, *Sentinelle di bronzo* has two endings. In the on-screen resolution, we return to our starting point of the fort and its two officials. As Amato recuperates from his battle wounds, Negri salutes him against the backdrop of a small Fascist flag that shows a skull and crossbones, Fascism's symbol in its squadrist days, next to an image of Mussolini in his battle helmet. This conjoining of images of early and current Fascism posits Africa as a place where the energies and violence of squadrism may find expression. When Amato worries aloud about the ongoing Ethiopian threat to Italian security, the camera closes in on Negri as he reassures his comrade that another incursion will not be tolerated. "Now we begin. Right here," he says firmly as his face expands to fill the screen. The shot channels Mussolini, but goes beyond Marcellini's fetish of male authority. The face without a body represents an obliteration of the senses in the name of blind and dumb devotion: the tunneling of vision from the expansive Somali landscape of the film's start to the face of Fascism affirms Gilles Deleuze's insight that the face is not just an image but a product of a machine of "faciality" that stratifies power relations and secures majoritarian interests.[61] The "year zero" posited by Negri's whiteout of context alludes to the birth of empire to come, to the foundation of a new political and territorial body whose boundaries will be secure.

The film's other ending connects to its moments of rupture and openness and its treatment of the nomads who occupy the interstices of the Italian-*askaro* tale. "Nomadism is not about fluidity *without* borders, but the precise awareness of the non-fixity *of* borders," writes Rosy Braidotti, and it was this nomadic consciousness that had to be defeated for the "no-man's-land" of Ogaden to become the "one-man's-land" of Mussolini, and Ethiopia and Somalia Italian homelands. Dahabò has the most open-ended trajectory in this regard: given Elmi's rifle by Ibrahim as a sign of respect, she disappears from the film. Presumably, she will return to her father's tribe, but perhaps she will just wander, armed, throughout the desert. In the world of Fascist empire films, it does not matter: it is enough that she is off-screen, allowing the diegetic world to recover its integral maleness before the film concludes. The male nomad has no such luxury: closure is achieved by Elmi's death and his clan's submission to the Italian military. For Mohamed, the actor who played Elmi, Marcellini's film brought another kind of endpoint. As part of emphasizing his departure from the American studio model, the director proudly noted that "the indigenous actors of *Sentinelle,* after taking part in the film, did not have illusions [of stardom], but ... returned naturally to their normal occupations, in *cabile,* in the bush, or in bands of *dubat*. ... [C]inematography brought no agitation or discontent." Such was not the fate of Mohamed, who during the filming coughed up blood and was diagnosed with late-stage typhus. "We were barely able to finish the film," Duranti recalled, "and he died in hospital at Asmara," this time unattended by Giachetti, one supposes.[62]

The challenges of filming in the Somali bush, with a cast composed almost completely of indigenous actors, did not escape Italian critics, who expressed admiration for Marcellini's tenacity. The director was a gen-

FIGURE 5.14.

The face of Fascist aggression, *Sentinelle di bronzo*. Author's collection

eration younger than Genina, Camerini, and Alessandrini, and his youth skewed the commentary toward appreciations of his film's newness and vivacity. While *Sentinelle di bronzo* was felt to share the same weak story problems of other empire films, it had the merit of "spiritual freshness, immediateness of sensation, impetus, ardor and abandon." The prominence and spontaneity of native actors, Marcellini's own knowledge of Africa as a soldier, and Terzano's use of filters to achieve "a sense of the burned, the ardent and the violent" all contributed to a sense of "*sprezzatura*, courage, sincerity [and] love of seeing clearly." The *Corriere della sera* commented on "the freshness of vision and action that penetrates everything, the landscapes that expand around the figures, as the skies do around the landscapes," qualities that *Bianco e nero* identified with the film's "faint smell" of the Western, but the reference was less to high Hollywood productions than to "the early American 'cowboy' films: in which the most realistic document of lived life had fantastic and almost mythic tones."[63] *Sentinelle di bronzo* also gave new impetus to discussions over how empire films might reconcile documentary and fictional conventions. Ferruccio Bonfiglio termed it an "experiment of undisputed audacity" in this regard, but literary critic Giacomo Debenedetti found it unsurprising that the documentarian Marcellini would reduce the fictional narrative to little more than "journalistic reportage." For Debenedetti, its value lay in its expressiveness as "reflexive testimony, interpretation, 'state of mind.' ... [I]t is rather a lived film: what distinguishes it from the documentary is precisely the difference between things seen and things lived." Fiume, the foe of studio re-creation in empire films, praised Marcellini for shooting entirely on location, but another critic warned that documentation was not sufficient to solicit the emotional involvement of the spectator: "Undoubtedly people like to see unfamiliar lands, unusual and diverse races, unknown customs. ... Rendering this environment with the greatest scruples of truth, exactness and information: this is a necessary preoccupation. But let's not forget that the colonial film must be first of all a film and not a documentary: this is the point."[64]

The anonymous critic of *Bianco e nero*, who saw beyond the debate over the film's realism, produced perhaps the most perceptive intervention. Like Debenedetti, he felt that Marcellini's film was not really a fictional documentary, despite a "realistic surface that is determined by a truly documentary background. We are in a quite different field ... in a form of mythicization of the real. ... The episode becomes legend, [and] the legend becomes epic: and for this reason is highly and poetically human." Cinema, here, is less an agent of documentation than of figuration, and indeed Marcellini's movie plays into Fascism as "oneiric expression" as well as "political project."[65] The justification of violence forms part of this mystification and mythologization, with Negri's disembodied face at the end proclaiming the beginning of a new era of invulnerability, achieved through the defeat of the Ethiopians. In a different way from Genina, Marcellini, too, goes beyond the body; instead of Mario's singular redemption, we have here the nation as a whole saved from threat. Chapter 6's films problematize this invincibility, staging Africa as a place of sensual temptation, with the body not always able to obey the dictates of white male command.

6

Imperial Bodies, Part II
Slaves of Love, Slaves of Labor

Chapter 6 moves from films of military conquest to films of colonization and from bodies bound by martial duty to corporeal encounters occasioned by everyday life on Italian agricultural settlements. Both *L'Esclave blanc* and *Sotto la Croce del Sud* make spectacle of the dangerous passions sparked in white Italian men by the proximity to non-white women in Somalia and Ethiopia, respectively. Strong father figures in both films anchor the masculine trials and travails of the young male protagonists, which, in *Sotto la Croce del Sud*, shade into melodrama. Yet the real internal work on these plantation-style settings goes beyond resistance to sexual temptation: at stake here is the integrity of "a series of behaviors, practices, and attitudes" designed to reinforce the superiority of white and Italian Fascist civilization. Distance, bolstered by the cultivation of a "colonial disgust" that reacts to the indigenous as dirty and primitive, grounds this imperial culture, yet proves difficult to enforce. The labor needs of colonial capitalism, the interracial intimacies of colonial domestic life, and the inherent cosmopolitanism and mobility of imperial formations all conspire to foster a "carnal knowledge" born of close observation and, often, physical contact, whether of the whip or the fingers.[1]

Filmed partly on location in Somalia and Ethiopia, the movies examined here build on the image of Africa as sensory paradise. Brignone had a long history of engagement with cinematic theatricality, and both he and Paulin play with conflations of African landscapes and bodies, calling attention to the politics and erotics of the gaze. True to the empire film lineage, these works assert a historical specificity through realism, as manifested in the prominence of indigenous actors, untranslated language, and exterior scenes. Yet drama prevails over the documentary in these moral parables of the damages wrought by miscegenation to white *and* indigenous cultures and to the stability of the imperial order. In many empire films, *Lo squadrone bianco* among them, the African sojourn brought "the experience of new emotions and seductions and perhaps the discovery of oneself." In these movies, however, the new emotions and seductions lead to a loss of (white) self. In Paulin's film, Georges becomes not merely the "white slave" of the title, but a *décivilisé*, cohabitating with the Somali beauty Faye in the bush, while Paolo in *Sotto la Croce del Sud* becomes obsessed with the exotic Mailù. Both men are temporarily lost for the labors of Italian colonization, until other whites intervene to reclaim them. Such transgressions lay at the core of a colonial nostalgia, often known as *mal d'Africa*, which was active long before the loss of the colonies.

The "colonial situation" also occasioned other kinds of encounters that inflamed the senses. Chapters 4 and 5 raised the issue of the intense male relationships that accompanied military service in Africa, but cohabitations on plantation settings also permitted non-heterosexual intimacies of varying duration and degrees of consensuality. I am thinking here of the white master of the house and his *diavoletto*, or boy, and of the white foreman and the black worker, the latter kind of encounter barely traceable even in private notations but glossed, through the gaze, in *Sotto la Croce del Sud*. But it was the white man/non-white woman model of embodied encounters that colonized the national imagination, starting with its enshrinement in "Faccetta nera." That song remained an emblem of the Ethiopian war's conquest fantasies, with its fantasy of an Italian "slavery of love" that would replace Ethiopia's system of indentured service. The reference to labor as well as sexual bondage is telling. The Fascist claim to have abolished slavery in East Africa, announced at the start of the Ethiopian War, hid a history of measures by Ethiopian emperors through Haile Selassie to phase out this ancient institution. In Somalia, where slaves constituted one-third of Mogadishu's population in the early 1900s (even nomadic tribes owned them), the liberal government had already banned slaving and had negotiated the freedom of thousands of slaves between 1900 and 1914. The persistence of slavery allowed the regime to advance abolitionism as a moral justification for invading Ethiopia, even though propaganda and labor needs rather than any humanitarian values lay behind this stance. Freed slaves served as a main source of the forced labor pool the Fascists used on agricultural settlements and elsewhere in Somalia. Addressed to a "slave among slaves," "Faccetta nera" channels this history of bodily suffering and everyday humiliations.[2]

My analyses of *L'Esclave blanc* and *Sotto la Croce del Sud* set their stories of forbidden passion into this broader framework, arguing that behind these slaveries of love lie slaveries of labor, both black and white, which are rarely remembered or recorded. The *mal d'Africa* of the chapter's title— *mal* translating as "pain" or "misfortune"—is not just Italian nostalgia for Africa's various sensual offerings, but also experiences of bodily and psychological injury. The empire films discussed in this chapter enable both of these dimensions, delivering fantasies of the regimented laboring body along with those of sexual possession. At the same time, they are "contradictory texts," both stylistically and in terms of their allusions to the limitations of Italian domination. The whip and the burning hut encode histories of Italian and African violence, referencing the insecurity of Italian rule, Italian dependence on Africans for sex and labor, and the incompleteness of the project of "feeling and becoming colonial" on both sides.[3] The next section provides some context for these cinematic renderings and compressions of current events, surveying the unstable situations created by the work of colonization. The Fascist empire mobilized both Africans and Italians on a new scale, creating the conditions for interracial intimacies and exploitations in the cities and on remote construction sites and plantations.

IMPERIAL MOBILITIES AND THE DEFENSE OF RACIAL PRESTIGE

In *Mudundu*, the 1935 mix of fantasy and reportage that served as the base text for *L'Esclave blanc*, Ernesto Quadrone recounts how his film troupe, going inland on a lorry from Mogadishu, got stuck in the mud for six days and nights along with "three indigenous, an Abyssinian woman, a *'sciarmuta'* [prostitute] of Mogadishu, a little nun, and four whites." Such "frightening promiscuity," as Quadrone termed it, formed part of everyday life in the colonies: Italian civilians who traveled throughout the empire had unpredictable experiences, involving journeys of fortune, unforeseen bedfellows, or no beds at all. Many polyglot "Hotel Orients" of the type denigrated in *Il grande appello* flourished in the Italian Empire. The cast and crew of *Sotto la Croce del Sud*, in Addis Ababa on their way to the countryside, stayed at the Pensione Mimosa, which Duranti remembered as "something between a local tavern and a bordello." Duranti arrived in Addis Ababa via the British-controlled Port Said, but many Italians who came to Africa passed through Eritrea's Massawa, a "cosmopolitan Red Sea hub." The confusions of race, nation, class, and *métier* that marked everyday life in the colonies—the white Italian nun sleeping near the black Somali prostitute—posed a dilemma for a regime that sought to control all kinds of interracial mixings and circulations.[4]

Gian Luca Podestà has termed the Italian Empire an "experimental laboratory" for the realization of economic and social policies that reflected the ambitions of a totalitarian state. Ethiopia, the only East African country occupied during Fascism, became a test case for a model of governance based on practices of segregation, rather than the mix of associationism and assimilationism that had characterized Italian policies elsewhere on the continent and in the Dodecanese. After 1936, urban planning in Addis Ababa, Gondar, and other Ethiopian cities aimed to keep races apart in daily life to avoid "familiarities between blacks and whites, from which followed intimacies and fusions that certainly could not confer prestige on the white man." The differentiated seating for "nationals" and the indigenous in cinemas, discussed in chapter 3, constituted one component of a wider politics of separation that included dedicated bus lines, housing and market areas in imperial cities, and agricultural settlements envisioned as enclaves of white Italianness.[5]

The Fascist legislation of 1937–1940 that sought to defend "racial prestige" responded to two specificities of Italian imperial rule. First was the sudden creation of large white populations in East Africa. One million Italian men were mobilized during the nine-month war on Ethiopia. Addis Ababa absorbed the most, but Asmara's Italian population mushroomed from five to sixty thousand between 1936 and 1938. As Barrera notes, in the absence of preparation for colonial life, legislation stepped in with its own norms and guidelines to "protect" Italians by urging them to privilege ideology over profit or desire and maintain the physical and mental distance necessary for effective rule.[6] The humble origins of much of the Italian population—the second distinguishing factor—made that distance hard to attain. The "empire of labor" was supposed to resolve Italy's land and employment problems, luring poor peasants from the Veneto or Sicily and Italian emigrants from apartments in Brooklyn with the promise of landownership. But many Italians worked as road builders, since at first many Ethiopians preferred military service to such demeaning and difficult activities: foreign observers labeled these Italians as "white slaves" for the chain gang–style organization of this labor and their dire appearance, the result of infrequent pay, twelve-hour days, inedible rations, and precarious housing in tents or shacks.[7] Others plied the trades they knew from home. In Asmara more than 50 percent of Italians worked as laborers, craftsmen, and tradesmen alongside and sometimes for Africans, exchanging money and goods and sometimes sharing food. The most indigent lived in *tukuls* alongside natives: economist Giacomo Guiglia wrote of the "heartbreak to his white dignity" suffered in seeing Italians selling trinkets from their "poor and dirty" huts. A 1938 decree that banned Italian workers from performing the same jobs as natives and mandated separate lodging and meals implied a high degree of interracial mingling. Le Houérou's study of men who immersed themselves in indigenous society shows that the trigger of their *insabbiamento* was not the romantic pursuit of a black female but pauperization. The emphasis on bodily appearance and self-control in colonial propaganda—from empire films to colonial manuals—derived from a real worry about colonial authority.[8]

Finally, the racial laws also addressed the higher degree of contact due to African mobilities occasioned by the Ethiopian invasion. Rural Eritreans, Ethiopians, and Somalis flooded the cities, looking for work as servants, *askaris,* day laborers, or prostitutes. The nervousness caused by these displacements comes through in Lessona's August 1936 request that Fascist officials pay special attention to "the question of 'nomadism' and 'sciarmuttism,' [which is] to be confronted with extreme rigor."[9] This linkage of prostitution with nomadism, which informs *Sotto la Croce del Sud* and other empire films, sees miscegenation as a catalyst of rootlessness as well as racial pollution. Here, too, the Italian case is distinguished by the immediate and concentrated shift in official attitudes toward mixed-race relationships that were both common and long-standing in colonial life, numbering more than ten thousand in Eritrea alone in 1935. From the liberal era onward, to discourage displacement and prostitution, the Italian government had encouraged freed female slaves to remain in domestic servitude, where they received room and board but no pay. These arrangements were the source of some of the unions that had produced a de facto *métis* class of children in Eritrea and Somalia, who had been allowed, through a 1933 law, to obtain Italian nationality.[10]

The huge influx of Italian white men that came with the Italo-Ethiopian war promised to create many more such relationships. The regime imported white prostitutes for city brothels and mobile sex units, tried to regulate black prostitution, instituted a sex police (*la squadra del madamismo*), and tried to get more single Italian white women to settle in the colonies, training more than one hundred thousand for colonial life through colonial preparation courses and allowing women's magazines to advertise the professional opportunities possible in fields such as nursing and education as well as "the splendors of the unknown" colonial existence could provide. Yet white women remained scarce in the Italian colonies—only ten thousand Italian women resided in all of Italian East Africa in 1939, and five thousand of those lived in Addis Ababa—and the same climate of sexual conquest that produced "Faccetta nera" encouraged real-life "slaveries of love": Indro Montanelli, in Ethiopia as a soldier, boasted of buying (and later selling) a twelve-year-old girl to be his concubine. Fascists remained in a permanent situation of white dependency on the indigenous for sex as well as for labor, and the criminalization of unions as a means of forcing changes in Italian and African behaviors was neither realistic nor effective.[11]

These situations carry over to the rural settlements that are the settings for *L'Esclave blanc* and *Sotto la Croce del Sud*. East Africans' preference for military service over the remote locations and difficult work of agriculture and mining made labor shortages the norm. In Ethiopia the continued resistance to Italian occupation translated into work refusals, even with the promise of high wages. Italian-owned platinum mines such as that depicted in *Sotto la Croce del Sud* produced only half of what they had before the Italian invasion. In Somalia a 1929 law requiring workers to commit to shifts of two to three weeks and live on concession premises with their families had only partially solved the problem and had also fostered prolonged and troubling proximities between the relatively small groups of Italians and the large indigenous labor force.[12] After 1936 the Fascists chose another route: forced labor. *L'Esclave blanc* is set in the fertile Jubba River area of southern Somalia, precisely where ex-slaves were relocated to Italian plantations to continue their bondages under another name. Military barracks and frequent whippings characterized this *kolonya* system, as locals called, it, which subjected newly liberated slaves to a new form of bondage, creating a world of "impoverished and malnourished villagers living on the edge of starvation alongside large state-supported Italian plantations." The contradiction between such practices and Fascism's celebration of its humanity in abolishing slavery led Fascist supporters to dig deep into their rhetorical arsenal. One justified forced labor as "a thrust to backward peoples to overcome their millennial torpor," but warned that the interracial cohabitations it required partly mitigated its "moral force."[13] This history of labor and sexual bondages leaves its traces in *L'Esclave blanc* and *Sotto la Croce del Sud*. "Faccetta nera" may be considered an intertext of these films, not only for its celebration of the black woman but also for its threat of violence against her by Black Shirts who promise to "vindicate the heroes who fell liberating you." In both movies, the removal of the distracting non-white female lead allows for the restoration of Italian prestige and the domination and exploitation of all of the regime's subjects—black and white.

WHITE SLAVE TO WHITE MASTER: *L'ESCLAVE BLANC*

The syndrome of "black fascination" lay behind the making of *L'Esclave blanc*, as its creator, Quadrone, freely confessed at the outset of his *Mudundu*, which combines an account of the film's production with a fictional story of an Italian's *décivilisation*. "The black continent agitated my soul with all its potent force of attraction," luring him to Somalia as a journalist, after his last adventure, flying to the Americas with Balbo, had left him at loose ends. *Mudundu*'s story within a story on this topic was the basis for a screenplay, *L'Homme ensablé,* which Quadrone co-wrote with the Danish director Dreyer, who left the production during its location shoot due to creative differences and malaria. Both titles disappeared when Jean-Paul Paulin stepped in to finish the film as an Italian-French co-production, made in two versions, with different lead actresses. My discussion of *L'Esclave blanc* reconstructs the film's paratextual history from Quadrone's *Mudundu* to Dreyer and Quadrone's *L'Homme ensablé* and onward, attending throughout to what is lost and what is gained in this chain of literary and image transfers.[14] Quadrone's tale of an Italian lawyer who ends up happily living in the Somali bush becomes, on-screen, a story of a young white Italian who starts down this path of white slavery to an African woman, only to be saved by a white woman who helps him realize his racial and colonial destiny. The tangled backstory of *L'Esclave blanc* offers a reflection on how Italian empire films figure into a broader European colonial culture. By 1937, when the film appeared in Italy, *L'Esclave blanc* had become a taboo title, and not just for its Orientalist associations: it conjured not only a newly criminalized miscegenation but Fascism's exploitative labor practices. It was far better to direct viewers' attention to the black collective, as the Italian title, *Jungla nera,* did, leaving white agency out of play.

Although Quadrone was not a film professional, he provides the sole element of continuity in this project, as author of the original story and scenario and as director of production for both Dreyer and Paulin. He also shared the desire of Marcellini and others to develop an original Italian model of empire film, one built on location shooting rather than Hollywood-style studio re-creations, and *Mudundu* asserts his ambition to make "a small film [that lies] between the document and the novel." In this, he partly succeeded: for most critics, the documentary aspects of the film proved the most compelling. Like *Sentinelle di bronzo,* which it predated and probably influenced, *L'Esclave blanc* was shot entirely in Somalia, with indigenous actors in major roles, and Craveri, as cinematographer, experimented with natural light in exterior scenes. The finished film by Paulin is highly theatrical, though: Paulin's sensibility here, on partial suggestion of Dreyer's script, is not a realist one.[15]

"The Story of Gall, White Man," which was the loose basis for Dreyer and Quadrone's screenplay, took shape from Quadrone's desire to narrate "a real history, a human documentation: the life and adventures of a *uomo insabbiato*/man 'gone native'" and from his quest to understand why some men "let themselves be taken little by little by the fascination of Africa" to the point of losing their racial and personal identity. Quadrone took issue with texts such as the novel *La Maitresse noire/The Black Mistress* (Louis-Charles Royer, 1928) that depicted men who had liaisons with indigenous women as drunkards and petty criminals. For him, *insabbiamento* was something larger: a "pathological and physiological phenomenon" that led to a giving up on the white male civilizational drive. Civilization is a thin veneer for Quadrone and whiteness relative and situational: both can be lost, if both the body and the soul are not adequately defended.[16] One of the first settlers of Italian Somalia, the fictional Gall had sworn to return to Italy only after having won his "colonial battle," but a string of bad luck, including the death of all of his livestock from tsetse flies, plunges him into indigence—in every sense of the word. But his relationships ended badly: the first reversed his initial revulsion to black skin, but caused the shaming of his Somali companion, while his next lover was murdered by her tribespeople. The theme of the deleterious social and moral consequences of mixed-race unions for both parties will be preserved in the film, as will the idea of *insabbiamento* as a gradual process. *Mal d'Africa,* Quadrone writes, is a slow contagion. "Gall 'buries' himself sweetly, he indigenizes himself (*si indigenisce*), becoming 'black' with a pleasure that amazes him," this inner transformation matched by an epidermal darkening caused by his work with coal. But the story's ending—Gall's final mixed-race union produces many children and a happy conjugal life—could not translate to the screen, especially when Quadrone reveals that Gall is based on a real man he met in Somalia, who overcame his early tragedies to buy a house in Brava and parent eight biracial children with a third partner. As a text appearing during Fascist rule, "The Story of Gall" was as subversive both for its reveal of economic realities as for its florid treatment of the delights of black women. Quadrone's declarations in *Mudundu* that the movie in production would publicize "the Fascist government's efforts and accomplishments in the colonies" rang a bit hollow.[17]

The postwar story of the film's production from this starting point is largely one of denial of influence, with Paulin seeking to avoid the taint of Fascist propaganda and Quadrone hardly mentioning Paulin's contribution. Denis Scoupe's work with the Dreyer archive gives Dreyer most of the credit for the screenplay written with Quadrone, but minimizes the carryover of this text to the finished film. In fact, the passage from Quadrone's writings to Dreyer and Quadrone's script, and onto the film as finished by Paulin, sheds light on commonalities of European imperial ideology that rested on the assumption of the superiority of white civilization, although Dreyer's contributions to this co-production tested the limits of what could be said about both French and Italian colonial regimes.[18]

The film's cosmopolitan production culture made its Fascist lineage easier to ignore. While *L'Esclave blanc* was shot in Somalia in 1936, its genesis dated from before the Ethiopian War and official desires to invest heavily in films about the colonies. After failing to find any Italian financing beyond a sponsorship by *La Stampa,* Quadrone sent a scenario to the French producer Jacques Grinieff, who had worked with Dreyer on *The Passion of Jeanne d'Arc* (1927) and knew Dreyer was looking for opportunities after a series of box-office failures, including the horror film *Vampyr* (1932). Quadrone recalls Dreyer as professional but remote and indifferent to the hospitality Fascist officials showed him in Somalia. "He did not even appreciate the picturesque salute given us by hundreds and hundreds of indigenous people who were arranged along the roads by concessionaries who wished in this way to celebrate our arrival," Quadrone complained decades later.[19]

The script Dreyer worked on with Quadrone added a political gloss that would prove to be too anti-colonial for either French or Fascist screens. In this version, a colonial pioneer and Resident and his second in command, Florio, clash over the treatment of the plantation's labor force. The starving workers, who are identified as Banta people—the group of ex-slaves commonly used for forced labor in Somalia—protest their treatment, but the Resident, described as "tough and a slave of rules," refuses to give them any extra food. Florio responds, "Poor hungry people should be pitied, whether black or white," and later asserts that whites should leave the blacks to their own country. Ordered to leave the plantation when the

Resident discovers his love affair with his daughter, Florio stops at the hut of the Somali beauty Faye and her companion Nur to sleep and asks Faye to go off with him to build a new life. After Faye has a shaman prepare a potion to erase memories of the past, Florio adopts indigenous garb and manners. "It is as if something has broken with me, like a barrier between me and others," he tells his white lover when she tries to convince him to return. As in Quadrone's story, the Somali transgressor is punished with death by her tribe, but here the white man, too, is targeted. The Resident and his daughter rescue Florio just before his killing, during a ritual knife dance, but a political rationale lies behind the Resident's forgiveness: the need for all available white bodies. Dreyer and Quadrone's script adds a parallel story line tailored to Italian Fascist specificities: an external threat from "Abyssinian rebels" who cross the Somali border and attack the plantation workers' village when Florio was away. In a scene labeled "three years later," the young couple tour the land, with Florio presumably ready to assume control of the plantation when her father can no longer rule.

Although much remains of Dreyer's work in Paulin's movie in terms of plot, set design, and frame composition, what is altered permits the fault lines of Fascist ideology to emerge. The anti-colonial outburst of Florio (now Georges) disappears, along with all references to the workers' hunger and mistreatment. In their place come elements consonant with Italian empire cinema: the primacy of technology, a montage of documentary footage of plantation work performed by anonymous and abstract figures, and a rehabilitated young male ready to assume his place in the colonial hierarchy. We are in the period anterior to the racial laws, and the unclothed black female body stars along with the unclothed white male body. Yet the movie's assertion of a politics of separatism, its worries about continuity of governance and control of territory, and its displacement of Italian colonial violence onto other Africans resonate with Italian empire cinema. Like *Sotto la Croce del Sud*, *L'Esclave blanc* draws its dramatic tension from its demarcation of boundaries that are subsequently transgressed. The movie's pedagogical thrust comes through its characterizations, which explore a range of attitudes toward colonial dependency and distance. While the unfolding interracial romance of Georges and Faye provides much of the spectacle, the movie also addresses spectators at the level of epistemology. What should they know about Italian Somalia in order to uphold the colonial order? What can or should not be known to protect their whiteness? The film approaches these questions through its splits between the registers of realism and theatricality and through the use of sound to heavily mediate viewers' engagements with screen events. By repeatedly thwarting or containing the direct experience of Africa it purports to offer the viewer, the film attempts to manage colonial anxieties regarding experiences of proximity.

The opening frames foreground *L'Esclave blanc*'s dual nature. As with *Sentinelle di bronzo*, we are near the border with Ethiopia in 1934, before the stabilization of Italian authority in the region. Titles tell us the film was shot "entirely in Italian Somalia," and the camera shows lush foliage and the flowing Jubba River until a close-up of Georges and Simone (Georges Rigaud and Jeannette Ferney) blots out this historical specificity, as do the titles:

> In this country, where time does not matter, life is simple and rough, passions violent and tenacious. White men engage in a ceaseless struggle against the climate, fever, and isolation (...)[20]

We are in the realm of colonial romance, but, as the ellipsis suggests, not only of the white romance so aggressively asserted, but of other possible passions. The ellipsis also lets viewers know that what they will see is not the whole story. In calling our attention to that which is absent, it reflects the place of interracial sex within the Fascist colonies: officially banned and un-narratable, but there for those who know where to look.

As we have seen, the strong father figure and his relationship with a younger leader in training feature centrally in most Italian empire films, reflecting Fascist ambitions to refashion national manhood. Here this figure takes the form of the Resident and plantation owner (Egisto Oliveri) who, as in the script, is feared by his workers and intolerant of crossings of the color line. The successful owner of a banana and cotton plantation on the banks of the Jubba, the Resident embodies the colonist who lives in defensive mode. He leaves his land only when fortified by his auto and other technology and his omnipresent whip. Although suffering from malaria, the Resident stays tough and virile throughout the film; he is the anchoring senior male required by Italian empire features. In this he contrasts with Georges, a young man of imposing physical vitality whom

FIGURE 6.1.

Georges and Simone, *L'Esclave blanc*. Author's collection

we meet as he attends an indigenous festival. From the start, Georges angers the Resident by ignoring the imperial attitudes that come with the role of the colonizer. Shaking hands with the tribal leader, Nur, and his veiled companion, Faye, his skin is less a barrier than a porous membrane, receptive to the touch and regard of others.

In this Georges also differs from the Resident's daughter Simone, who journeys to Somalia from Italy to see her father after ten years' absence. She is the vehicle for the film's touristic moments, but she has no desire to understand her new surroundings. Her frame of reference and sight lines remain thoroughly European. Upon arriving at the plantation, she avoids any notice of the native workers laboring before her eyes, and she laughs throughout a scene that evokes a slave market when Georges takes her to the plantation's village to find her a chambermaid. Able to shoot and drive, she is the perfect colonial woman, but her real value lies in her capacity to see selectively and block out realities she does not want to know. Her priority, beyond her father's well-being, remains the preservation of colonial order. Ferney's bright acting style and smart city clothing accentuate this willed lack of assimilation: her affect seems more suited for a Paris-based sentimental comedy. Fiume may have had in mind her performance when he complained about Italian empire films in which "a white actor moves like a tourist, with female attire that is too stylized or even 'too obviously colonial,'" thus undermining the movie's claims to authenticity.[21]

In fact, Simone's artificiality in the Somali context serves several purposes in the film. She retains Western notions of rationalism that Georges loses over the course of the film, unflappably assisting in emergencies, but she is also the referent for the film's high theatricality. Her flat screen persona is key in a film whose depth and texture come less from the realm of the emotional (as in Brignone's melodrama) or the ethnographic (as in *Sentinelle di bronzo*) than the scenographic. Simone's presence in an exterior scene often preludes the entrance of the picturesque, a comforting frame for viewers and for Simone herself, who takes refuge there to avoid an authentic apprehension of what is going on around her. Among modes of colonial representation, Jessica Dubow observes, the picturesque enacts "a notion of present sight as 'seeing through' . . . a view of nature recognized in a background stock of perceptual knowledge." A scene in which Georges takes Simone to see a flower-covered pond on her father's property illustrates this well. As Georges goes off to gather some flowers, drumbeats are heard in the distance, startling her. Georges reassures her it is just a bush wedding, but she drowns out the tribal music by singing a French song. Framed by the flora, trilling like a bird, Simone is in Somalia but also far from it, in a European romance story already well known. Caught up in her soulful song, she somehow manages not to see that Georges is completely naked in the pond but for a strategically placed bouquet. That spectacle is reserved for the eyes of Faye, who spies on him, jealous of his affection for Simone, before a leopard attacks her. The scene ends with a Hollywood screen kiss between Georges and a girlishly frightened Simone, but Georges has revealed his inner primitive, and "Africa" lies in prey.[22]

The prominence of the picturesque in this film bears the mark of Paulin's aesthetic, much more than Dreyer's. Paulin came to the cinema after working in the furniture department of the Bon Marché department store, and his early movies do resemble set pieces at times, as do *L'Esclave blanc*'s plantation interiors. The treatments of landscape in *L'Esclave blanc*, instead, bear the mark of his formation among the many impressionist painters his sculptor father, Paul, frequented, but Paulin also seeks to reassure viewers by preserving the ocular distance of the colonizer, whether by placing his European subjects in moving vehicles or by buffering them with foliage, creating spaces of Western refuge and intimacy.[23] The African bush offers no real privacy, though: someone is always watching, be it Faye or Nur, whose intrigues lend the movie its Orientalist tinge, or the Resident, who spies on Georges and Simone at night and then banishes Georges from the plantation to break up their relationship. On and off the plantation, huts and houses are porous, letting in the sights and sounds of outside and letting audiences know that their own actions in the colonies will not go unnoticed.

As in the example of Simone's spontaneous singing, film sound, and music in particular, plays a key role in the articulation of the film's theatricality, directing and containing the experience of alterity. The film score, which utilizes mostly Western instruments and tonalities, supports the picturesque visual mode by setting moods that range from the pastoral to the frolicking. The attempt to make Somalia "legible" for Western viewers produces scenes of high artificiality, as when Georges, now a *décivilisé*, leads a leopard hunt. Quadrone brought in Boni (Aweer) hunters and their dogs from Afmadow to play themselves in the film, but the documentary feel disappears when a soundtrack of horn blasts and barking hounds adds the aurals of an English fox hunt. The use of Western amplified sound as a means of drawing European spectators into the tensions between the familiar and the exotic that mark colonial ideologies also figures heavily in the night dance scene that seals Georges's devolutionary destiny. Cast out from the plantation, Georges seeks advice from an Italian who has detached himself from white society, who takes him to the plantation's village so he can find a native woman. As the *insabbiato* inspects women—we have, again, the echo of the slave market, and one woman protests loudly at being handled—off-screen drumbeats distract the men, leading them into a hidden clearing and into a reality normally out of (white) sight and knowledge. Fully dressed young women dance as a man with a stick lightly whips their buttocks, as a group of indigenous musicians,

FIGURE 6.2.

Music in *L'Esclave blanc:* Harlem/Paris in Somalia. Author's collection

Nur among them, plays along. Close shots linger on the bare-chested men, making them part of the spectacle, but a brass-heavy big band soon incorporates their drums into its own score, shifting the aural gravity offscreen, to the dance clubs of Harlem and Paris and their African American musicians.

The entrance of this Western music marks a shift into a mode of looking that has little to do with the picturesque. We are in a danger zone, and the fantasy of close contact is rendered by a haptic visuality: a man's hand around the waist of a woman in a white dress whose buttocks gyrate wildly; a bare breast, seen in close up from the side, as it would be from the point of view of another dancer; and a long hold on the bare neck and upper back of a man whose tribal jewelry evokes a slave collar, setting the tone for Georges's loss of agency, as Faye leads him out of sight. Music acts as ringmaster of this cinematographic evocation of sensory overload, where the film most closely realizes Quadrone's account of the onset of

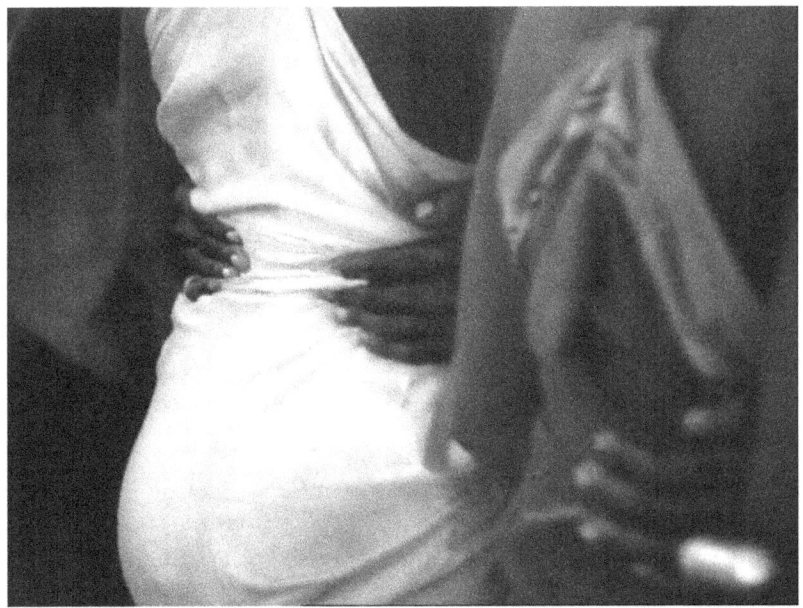

FIGURE 6.3.

Dance in *L'Esclave blanc:* Fantasies of proximity. Author's collection

mal d'Africa: "One starts to fall prisoner to the African soil for the colors. Then you yield to the odors . . . and the soft passionate sheen of black skin" until, one day, Africa "will envelop you, with the captivating and irresistible slowness of an embrace." As it happens, that embrace is kept off-screen. Throughout the film, although Georges and Faye embrace and are seen naked together, they sleep on separate mats in their hut, and a boy (Dig Doro) who followed them from Faye's village is usually with them. Any physical crossing of the color line is referred to the spectator's imagination, left in the realm of things that are present but cannot be narrated. As in the script, Faye has a shaman "prepare the forgetting potion for my white friend," making him the victim of an "African illness." As they enter deeper into the forest, Georges loses whatever imperial eye he once had, appearing as a sleepwalker. The mental cleansing is also the work of the forest itself, which in European fantasy and Quadrone's *Mudundu* is a primeval place, outside of time, a "shadow of civilization," as were its black inhabitants. The frenzied big band gives way to slow funereal music that alludes to the death of Western time and place, as Georges becomes a slave, less of the gentle Faye than of Africa's soul.[24]

The scenes of Georges as an *insabbiato* highlight the importance of outward behaviors and attitudes in communicating authority and protecting prestige—and in the performance of racial identity. Eating with his hands, wearing only a tribal cloth, spearing a leopard, Georges has forgotten not only Simone but also how to be white. A scene in which Faye and Georges laugh and dress together in the morning offers viewers not only ample vision of their skin, but the knowledge that Georges has become the happy primitive, like Gall in Quadrone's *Mudundu*. When Simone arrives and asks what is keeping him in this life, he responds, "Everything," gesturing to what most Western spectators would consider nothing—the simple hut in the forest. Rousseau is the French director's reference here, not only the philosopher Jean-Jacques's praise of the state of nature, but the painter Henri, whose naive style in paintings such as *The Dreamer* (1910) is evoked in a scene in which Georges washes Faye. Her supple figure, as silhouetted against the shining river and framed by foliage, makes for an image that is less sensual than painterly, despite the sight of her wet skin. We are back in the realm of cinema as window, a mode of seeing that underscores distance and power of observation rather than proximity.[25]

We are not the only ones observing Faye and Georges. Nur shoots an arrow to end their idyll, prompting Faye to utter her first words in French, "J'ai peur" (I am afraid). Up to now, Georges and Faye have communicated through eye contact, gesture, and the bilingual Dig Doro. Unlike Simone, Faye is permeable: as her outburst in French indicates, she has absorbed what is around her. She is as much a destabilizing force in her culture as Georges is in his, and she is killed by her tribe for abandoning Nur, and Georges is tied to a tree as the men begin the ritual knife dance that preludes his killing. Quadrone brought the Aberghidir clan of warriors from far away to guarantee the ritual's authenticity, but its oneiric feel and staging recall Dreyer's horror aesthetic in *Vampyr*, while close-ups of the bound Florio channel Orientalist fantasies in gender reverse. Music speaks during this silent scene, with high-pitched *ostinatos*, low rhythmical chords mimicking drumbeats, and strange whimpering sounds expressing white horror at the unleashing of the murderous urges

FIGURE 6.4.

Georges as *décivilisé*, *L'Esclave blanc*. Author's collection

FIGURE 6.5.

The return to nature, *L'Esclave blanc*. Author's collection

that lie beneath the surface of colonial collaboration. Low shots make the men and their double-edged knives look even bigger as they lurch toward the bound Georges, taunting and occasionally cutting him, with intermittent reverse shots putting the spectator in Georges's position. His skin grows sweaty and feverish until he faints, not before one man sucks the blood from a large cut on his arm. This is the underside of the forest and its inhabitants and the outcome of Georges and Faye's unthinking passion. Interracial relationships are destructive for both the "white slave" and the "black jungle," this film contends.

The shift in the film to violence is matched by developments on the plantation, which in the meantime has been attacked by "nomads" who sack and burn the workers' village. Although these particular fires destroy Italian property, the burning native hut was a positive symbol in Fascist imperial propaganda, part of the "purifying reclamations" the regime undertook in East Africa. In *Mudundu* Quadrone praises the "burning to the ground" of Mogadishu's diseased *meschinopoli* (wretched-opolis) and its inhabitants' relocation to "concentration camps" outside the walls of the city. As so often in Italian empire films, it is the history behind the screen image that begs its own narration, with the "nomad" antagonist a projection of Fascism's hidden histories of violence, forced displacements, and hybridity.[26] The film's ending traffics in this history of coerced mobilities and labor exploitations. The Resident and his men rescue Georges, and his memory of his white self returns when Simone revives him, allowing for their reconciliation. This plot resolution respects the script's finale, which marks off *L'Esclave blanc* from other Italian empire films, which cast off all women, white or black, for a life of colonial duty. Mario's collapse in *Lo squadrone bianco* annihilated his past as a desiring subject tout court, whereas Georges's blackout merely erased his tendencies to "blackness," keeping his emotional core and colonial knowledge intact. The Resident's change of heart about Georges holds a message for future Italian colonizers: every white man counts in the black jungle, as long as he is infused with the ideology of white superiority.

But while Dreyer's ending placed Florio and Bianca on a peaceful stroll through nature, Paulin's concluding montage sequence offers a Fascist-inflected romantic fantasy. Anempathetic pastoral melodies accompany fast-paced documentary footage of rows of workers digging trenches, car-

FIGURE 6.6.

Fadeout in *L'Esclave blanc*. Author's collection

rying crops, and driving machinery. Clock wipes brush aside the workers to make room for more. Such Fascist representations of black *and* white laborers as "a chain of copies... a series of automata forming a harmonious pattern" had an intermedial resonance from advertising to Luce films about Somali plantation labor. This figuration of history as a continual racial cleansing comments on the aggression engendered by the Italian dependency on blacks for labor, just as the death of Faye allows Georges to overcome his reliance on black women for sex and companionship. That dehumanizing blacks is necessary for secure colonial governance is made clear from the superimposition of the smiling faces of Georges and Simone, future colonial rulers, on the anonymous laboring black bodies. Superimpositions can call out fantastic or dreamlike states, as André Bazin observed, and so does *L'Esclave blanc* warn viewers that white prestige and happiness rely on them not looking too closely into black reality, beyond its potential as a labor pool. The cinema can act as their screen, telling them everything they need to know about Africa. The last theatrically lit and posed frames of their faces banish the workers altogether, bringing us back into the fictional realm, which was perhaps Paulin's way of having the final word.[27]

The production of *L'Esclave blanc* participated fully in the practices of debasement referenced by the film's documentary segments. Quadrone was fascinated by slavery—in *Mudundu* he comments on the "black worms" (ex-slaves) who "prefer to crawl secretly at the feet of their former owners who accept them and feed them." Not only did Quadrone set the film in the precise area where plantations made use of forced labor by ex-slaves, but he used these same ex-slaves as the film's extras. He also dates the Resident's arrival in Somalia to 1924, associating him for Italian audiences with a group of Fascist militants who arrived that year and became notorious for their extreme violence toward the indigenous. Dreyer's script and storyboards referenced that reality, but its only echoes in the finished movie are the sticklike bodies who labor in the final documentary segment, only to be periodically "wiped out." *L'Esclave blanc*'s production bolstered Fascist colonial labor and social policies in other ways as well. Quadrone went to great lengths to observe canons of documentary authenticity, traveling widely to convince clans known for certain rituals or practices to appear as themselves in the film. Although he emphasizes that all actors were paid, his account in *Mudundu* accents the coercive nature of the recruiting process. As he boasts, using a term (*prelevare*) often associated with police actions: "I went to round up the Bardera singers from their religious 'university,' forcing them to take a 'walk' that totaled eight hundred kilometers there and back, in order to feature them in only one frame of the film." As would be the case with *Sentinelle di bronzo*, other participations proved more difficult. Some clans, like the Majerteen, who were used in dance scenes, "were more difficult to capture than panthers." Even ex-*askaris* had to be paid more to act the part of nomad warriors turned back by the Italians, and their recalcitrance to portraying the defeated persisted during filming.[28]

The most delicate negotiations in a largely Muslim country involved female participation. One whole chapter of *Mudundu*, entitled "Twelve women on the terrace," is devoted to the difficulties Dreyer, Quadrone, and Craveri had in finding the right female lead. Governor Rava did his

FIGURE 6.7.

Plantation labor in *L'Esclave blanc*. Author's collection

part, hosting the filmmakers in his palazzo and arranging for "all the beauties of the capital" to be brought for nude inspections and screen tests filmed by Craveri. Among these was Alima Christina, who would serve as Duranti's tutor and understudy in *Sentinelle di bronzo*. Former slaves from the Shebelle River clans had their bodies ruined early by work, but had the merit of being "as docile and obtuse as sheep," dropping their robes on command: "You could slaughter them on the spot and they would pose no resistance," marveled Quadrone, anticipating the silent screen bodies effaced by the wipe at the close of his movie. In the countryside, the filmmakers attended indigenous dances to scout for women, only to meet with hostility from clan chiefs, shamans, and older women, "who put up a soundless and invisible war and gave us 'bad press.' . . . [A] web of diffidence was drawn around us." It was not surprising that a certain Ascia, whose photograph is included in *Mudundu*, was hastily removed from the screen tests by her mother, but the filmmakers were upset when a fellow white, a Swedish missionary, refused to give over his fourteen-year-old servant.[29] As for Fai, the young woman chosen to play Faye, Quadrone had met her on an earlier trip to Somalia and had promised to make her "a diva of the cinema," taking her "out of the forest and lying her, flattened and magnificent, on the screen." His evident infatuation may have been why Dreyer imposed a veto on any contact between her and members of the crew, including Quadrone. The troupe's "bad press" attests to the climate of film sets in the colonies. The making of *L'Esclave blanc*, like the film itself, registers the intertwinings of imperial sexual, film, and labor politics and the complicated relationships produced by white dependency on blacks in all of these spheres.[30]

As for the film's reception back in Italy, even the most charitable critics, who were always eager to add another title to the growing empire film tradition, judged *L'Esclave blanc* (seen in the Italian version) a disappointment. Ferruccio Bonfiglio remarked darkly in articles written just after its release that some Italian films, which had been shot entirely on location, "could have been produced more economically and much better in the studio," with his praise for *Sentinelle di bronzo* making clear he was not referring to Marcellini's movie. Roberto Savarese refused to consider it a real colonial film, which for him was "a propaganda film, made for the masses, able to awaken the imperial and colonial conscience of Italians." The film relied instead on "more or less provocative bronzed nudes, with various 'touches' of sensuality and morbosity and lots of journalistic-style folklore," to reach the spectator. It was best thought of as a "tropical document," an opinion shared by other critics, one of whom focused on the more politically acceptable moments depicting "the harvest of bananas, the labor in the concessions, the leopard hunt," leaving out the interracial romance entirely.[31]

This had also been the tactic of the filmmakers in their application to the Ministry of Popular Culture for censorship approval. The summary that passed in July 1937 excised that romantic relationship completely. Here, the white male protagonist is thwarted by his employer in his intention to marry the daughter, but leaves the plantation to make his own fortune with his employer's blessing. The Faye he meets at a dance in the jungle is a slave of the "evil Negro" Nur and follows him only to get away from Nur's tyranny, "offering him her help as a guide to find appropriate lands to create his own concession." We return, here, to the "Faccetta nera" fantasy of the Italian who liberates Africans from bondage, but here both the "slavery of love" that follows for the woman in the song and the white slavery of the bewitched man are excised in favor of a platonic colonial collaboration. This censored summary may have worked with the censors and set the tone for most critics to ignore the interracial romance, but not for Filippo Sacchi, who questioned the moral value of a white protagonist who "does not seem able to distinguish between race and race" and takes a black woman as a consolation prize. Like the other critics, Sacchi recommended the film be seen as "exclusively a document of Italian Somalia," which at least allowed one to praise its "scrupulous preoccupation with respecting geographic and ethnographic truth."[32]

The lack of cohesion and consistency in the style and story undoubtedly reflected the fragmented production process and the differences of sensibility among Quadrone, Dreyer, and Paulin, but a common European colonial *habitus* does emerge. The story of Georges's devolution, across Italian, Danish, and French interventions, ends up as a story of the affirmation of whiteness through encounters with blacks whose differences are not just skin deep but civilizational. The protagonists of French colonial films may forget their pasts in the desert, but they rarely forget their race. Paulin's theatrical mise-en-scènes betray his discomfort with the drama he inherited and perhaps with the documentary spirit that had become part of the formula of Italian empire movies. The only co-production among Italian empire movies, and the one with the fewest official connections, *L'Esclave blanc* also departs from that formula in significant ways. The union of the romantic couple at the end of the story has no equivalent in other Italian films, where the woman is always removed. Paulin's film also lacks the ambiguous shadings of masculine interactions. Although the movie features more male nudity than any other movie of its type, the sight of Georges's muscular body is reserved for scenes with women. There are no emotionally hot moments among men, no meaningful silences and gazes (as in *Lo squadrone bianco*, *Il grande appello*, and *Sotto la Croce del Sud*), and no stagings of a charged male corporeality (as in *Sentinelle di bronzo*), differences that return to Duncan's point about the unstable relations within Fascist representation and practice between the homosocial and the homoerotic.[33]

The film's ending traces a model of white-black proximity that speaks to Fascism's specific separationist priorities: the white slave has become the white master, armed with a whip, overseeing hordes of workers with whom he has no personal relationship. It is significant that Georges never utters a word of Somali during his time in the forest, although he masters many indigenous practical skills. This rejection of linguistic assimilationism distinguished Italian from French colonial policy. Even the most notorious French *décivilisé* of the era, the Timbuktu missionary Auguste Dupuis-Yakouba, was admired for his rare linguistic skills, which he continued to place at the service of French authorities after he left the church to live in indigenous society.[34] Insecure domination and Fascist racism made the Italians' priorities in East Africa revolve around segregation, not communication, giving rise to fantasies of wordless obedience by workers like the one that ends this film.

SOTTO LA CROCE DEL SUD: CHARTING THE RACIAL BOUNDARIES OF THE "EMPIRE OF LABOR"

In a March 1938 article in *Cinema*, Fascist film functionary Jacopo Comin announced his intention to broaden the subject matter of Italian empire cinema: "Until now, there have been colonial films such as *Il grande appello, Squadrone bianco,* and *Sentinelle di bronzo* whose predominant themes have been the war. I would like to make the film of the postwar. The Italian people mobilized because they needed land and work: it is logical that, having conquered the colony, they begin the war of work, itself full of hostile elements they must battle against." The "colonial adventure film" Comin envisioned, *Sotto la Croce del Sud,* would draw its drama from strong men "taking possession of the land" and making it fertile for the "new families" they were creating in Italian Ethiopia. This was "adventure in the elevated sense of the word," Comin cautioned, with romance and spectacle subordinated to a moral end. The popular review *Cinema Illustrazione* saw things differently. Its articles on the production centered on a large photograph of a reclining Duranti, who was advertised not only as the female lead but the pole star "around [which] three men move": Marco, a pioneer in Ethiopia; Simone, "a Levantine adventurer"; and the young Paolo, "trying his hand, after the war, at the adventure of colonization." In the space between the two interpretations of "adventure" given by Comin and by the fan magazine lie the contradictions that marked not only *Sotto la Croce del Sud,* but the entire project of Italian empire cinema. Here, ideals of political moviemaking meet up with the demands of the market, in ways that, in part, we have seen before. As in *Lo squadrone bianco* and *Sentinelle di bronzo,* the female lead grew larger and more glamorous than the script's intentions, magnifying her unsettling effects on men and dwarfing the role of the Italian colonial wives, who would be relegated on-screen, as they already were in *Cinema Illustrazione,* to "a background part."[35]

Yet Duranti's character changed in ways that *Cinema Illustrazione* did not anticipate. "Finally we can savor [Duranti] without black face paint or dyes. This time she must play a white woman, a beautiful woman," the magazine exalted, only to find her on-screen as a "Levantine." By then, Brignone had taken over the film's direction, and Comin's desire to continue along the path of realist experimentation would be folded into a melodramatic frame that distinguishes this movie from others in the tradition. It is a frame well suited for the articulation of those "hostile elements" that threaten the colonizers, which, as we will see, are here not so much the Africans as "an Esperanto humanity," who, by 1938, had become Fascism's latest nomadic internal enemy. Duranti's progression from the Somali Dahabò to the Levantine Mailù registers the broadening preoccupations of Fascist racial policy. Italians' new official designation as "Aryan Mediterraneans" made the non-Aryan Mediterranean the focus of anxieties about mobility, loyalty, and cultural alterity. The conveniently broad category of the "Levantine" included not only the Jew, but peoples of the eastern basin, including the Turk, who had surfaced in *Kif Tebbi* as the true enemy. The entry point for these racial preoccupations is probably less Brignone than Comin, who remained on as lead screenwriter throughout the project. An early Fascist, film censor, and member of the Direzione Generale di Cinematografia, Comin did not follow the production to Ethiopia in the spring of 1938 due to a new assignment, one in tune with such political sensibilities: coordinating Luce's coverage for Adolf Hitler's May 1938 visit to Italy. As we will see, the colonists in *Sotto la Croce del Sud* aim not only to exploit the plantation's human and natural resources—black workers, coffee beans, the fertile land—but also to purify it of all that is artificial and foreign. The collaboration of blacks and whites in this task sets the film apart from its predecessors, foreshadowing a different kind of racial persecution that continued on after Fascism's empire was lost.[36]

In its positioning of the colonies as Italian homelands, *Sotto la Croce del Sud* does connect with *Il grande appello* and *Luciano Serra, pilota,* continuing the narratives of those films from the phase of conquest into that of colonization. In Comin's script, the workers were emigrants coming "from all the meridians, from Brazil to Australia . . . who everywhere strengthen your pride in being Italian." Brignone's 1935 *Passaporto rosso* treated Italian emigration to Argentina. Pilotto, who played Giovanni in Camerini's film, had been the original choice for the role of Marco, before the similarly large and gruff Giovanni Grasso, late of *Sentinelle di bronzo,* took it on.[37] The finished film does away with such origin stories, limiting the diversity of provenance among Italian workers to the regional level, thus placing the burden of foreign experience and affiliation on Simone and Mailù. The world of unreliable wanderers is no longer safely "outside," in Djibouti, but rather installed in the heart of the Italian collective. The only relevant fact of these workers' past is their participation in the Ethiopian War, which is Marco's criterion for granting them an interest in the plantation. All are "ex-combatants," ready to alternate the spade and the rifle, in keeping with the blurred civilian-military divide in Italian East Africa.

Sotto la Croce del Sud also breaks with the male-only Italian presence in Ethiopia that marked *Il grande appello* and *Luciano Serra, pilota.* A 1936 editorial in *Lo Schermo* had asked for features that would "create familiarity among Italians and Ethiopians so that he who departs does not do so as a solitary emigrant but brings his wife and children with him. This will avoid the plague of 'madames' and mixed-race children and all contacts with the indigenous population that could result in a lessening of our prestige."[38] The film's inclusion of wives responded to the mandates of demographic colonization, constituting one of the "elements of propaganda" Comin flagged for future viewers. Brignone finds drama in a different direction, though, in the difficult work of managing desire in the majority who came alone to Africa. Mailù presents a challenge in this regard, when she is discovered living illegally on the plantation with her shifty partner, Simone: the men neglect their work to stare at her or engage in idle fantasies. Chief among these is the engineer Paolo (Antonio Centa), whose evident infatuation gives Simone the idea to order Mailù to encourage Paolo's interest so they may remain on the plantation, allowing him to continue stealing platinum from its mines. The unlikely plot point of Marco agreeing to host the squatters makes the plantation into a microcosm of Italian Africa, as it was in *L'Esclave blanc,* with labor and living situations requiring constant interracial interactions. It also sets the stage for forbidden passion to develop. Mailù, who identifies herself to Paolo as being of a different race, stands in for all non-white women, although she is, crucially, not a sub-Saharan black, or even a half-black, as critics who have labeled her a *métis* make her out to be.[39]

Although sexual desire for the exotic woman (and man, in one case) lies at the heart of the film's spectacle, its threat is the distraction it poses from the film's true obsession: labor. "Bisogna lavorare" (We need to work) is the film's mantra, expressed countless times when frustrated libidinal urges create friction or distraction among the men. The "war of work" necessitates discipline, and the film follows other empire movies in engineering the removal of the offending female influence. Like Cristiana in *Lo squadrone bianco,* Mailù is literally driven away at its end. By then Simone has perished in quicksand, freeing the black laborers he exploited to be utilized by the Italians. "Paolo, let's go and work," the film's unsurprising last bit of dialogue, registers the accent on labor as the next phase of the Fascist imperial epic. Yet histories of slavery and subjugation, told through the figures of Simone and Mailù, encroach on this "master" narrative, leaving it on shaky ground.

Sotto la Croce del Sud narrates these intertwining stories through a combination of realism and melodrama, a coupling not uncommon in international imperial productions. As John Parris Springer writes, melodrama's effectiveness is maximized by "a recognizable world with tangible threats and dangers," such as those unstable colonial environments easily provide. The British "imperial romances" studied by Jaikumar blend documentary conventions with stark morality plays and suffering male protagonists to situate anxieties about disorder and dissolution in a precise historical reality. The colony substitutes for the home—the traditional setting for the form's female protagonists.[40] Melodrama had a robust history in Italy from the silent period forward, but Fascist critics and officials routinely denounced the presence of melodrama in foreign films set in Africa, objecting to the lovesick white men and larger female presence, whether black or white, that fueled "turbid passions." But Brignone was undaunted. The director of some forty movies from 1915 onward, he had a reputation as a versatile director of genre cinema and had made at least four melodramas during the sound period.[41]

The credit sequence at the start of *Sotto la Croce del Sud* cues the viewer that this empire film will differ from those that preceded it. A pan of the landscape quickly shifts to a stormy sky, chiaroscuro effects, and ominous music by the young composer Renzo Rossellini, all of which signal a choppy emotional climate that realism will be unable to fully narrate. As in most melodramas, music plays a critical role in articulating feelings, pointing up the limitations of verbal language, and often speaking for the character. Mailù's theme, the romantic song "Under the Southern Cross," played on her gramophone, is the first diegetic sound we hear. Its slow-tempo sadness and lament of a "nostalgia deep as the sea" sign her emotional world. Mailù listens as if in a daze, gazing at times out the window up at the stars. Her glamorous costuming and her habits (drinking, smoking) associate her with Cristiana and other metropolitan female antagonists of Fascist-era films, but her exoticism places her beyond the nation, in a cosmopolitan nowhere also evoked by her boudoir's eclectic décor. As it was for the nomadic Ismail of *Kif Tebbi*, who was "no longer Arab but not European," the gramophone is an emotionally charged object that has accompanied her on her peregrinations. Ismail, however, found a "home" as an intermediary within the Italian colonial order, whereas Mailù, as a woman who also comes from outside the empire, has no such option. Her refuge is the song, its "bath of affect" speaking to and for her.[42] A shouted order by Simone, who is weighing platinum in the next room, to turn off her music interrupts her reverie, bringing us into the reality of her oppressed existence: we are in melodrama's unhappy domesticity.

The character of Simone has occupied the few scholars who have written about *Sotto la Croce del Sud* mainly in function of his liminal racial status. Identifying himself on-screen as Simone Aeropoulus and as a

FIGURES 6.8 AND 6.9.

Mailù and Simone, Levantine intruders in Ethiopia, *Sotto la Croce del Sud*.
Both author's collection

Levantine, he is nonetheless referred to by Italians during the film as a "bastard" and "*meticcio.*" Although his classification as an outsider is central to the film's tracing of racial boundaries, his character has multiple functions within the film's libidinal and labor economies. Enrico Glori, the Neapolitan character actor who portrayed Simone, was another product of the Italian filmic emigrations: he had lived in France since 1930 and would have been known to Italian viewers largely as a villain of French cinema, having made more than a dozen films with directors such as Pierre Chenal, Jacques Feyder, Marcel Carné, and Abel Gance. He returned to Italy only in 1937 to make the Italian-French coproduction *Il fu Mattia Pascal* with Chenal and remained in a burst of professional activity that placed him in eight other Italian movies in 1938 alone. Brignone exploits Glori's reputation for playing negative and violent characters by casting him as a crook who swindles whites, exploits and whips blacks, and manipulates and intimidates those around him, including Mailù. This long performance history outside of Italy facilitated the apprehension of his character as not only untrustworthy but tinged with the foreign, certainly as opposed to his screen adversary, Marco, played by an actor (Grasso) who came from Sicilian regional theater and had played only Italian populist roles such as the blustering sergeant of *Sentinelle di bronzo*.

Brignone follows classic cinema's conventions for signaling shady characters from our first encounter with Simone in the credits. Simone is mostly shown in interior settings, enhanced by high-contrast illumination that shadows him and his omnipresent cigarette. He stands for the colonial version of the metropolitan criminal: his white fedora is tattered and made of straw, he carries an African whip as well as a knife and a gun, and he wears a trench coat and drives a big black car in his getaway scene through the African bush. Astute and ruthless, with a history of flight after deals gone bad, Simone represents the underbelly of the Italian colonies, which, like all colonies, attracted criminals and speculators who took advantage of both blacks and whites. But Simone is also, according to the script, specifically a "Levantine adventurer," and as such his character lends itself to various readings, especially in its 1938 context. While *Sotto la Croce del Sud* was starting production, openly anti-Semitic sentiments appeared in the film press to prepare Italians for a new set of racial laws that now included Jews within the non-white category. Writing in *Bianco e nero,* Giulio Cogni called on filmmakers to help Italians understand their "Nordic-Mediterranean" roots by training them to "understand the bodies and faces of men to uncover the truth." Brignone's treatment of Simone plays into this climate. Connected to screen stereotypes of criminality, Simone's dark hair, eyes, and skin are also readable as the face of a racial outsider, in keeping with our knowledge that he has a Greek name but is also of another affiliation, quite possibly the Jewish one. Although close-ups of Mailù also follow the dictates of female stardom, the vagueness of her ethnic affiliation ("Levantine") warrants scrutiny by the audience. Simone and Mailù embody those "rootless and cosmopolitan beings" who had always irked Fascists but now could be presented in a different frame.[43]

The murky and theatrical atmosphere of these scenes shifts abruptly to its opposite: clear light, broad views, and Italian workers' arrival at the plantation. As in *L'Esclave blanc,* the scene of Italian arrival is used to set the plot in a precise historical context, and the stream of information given by each of the men about their war service contrasts with the elliptical communications of Simone and Mailù. Throughout the film, realism allies with rhetorical efficiency and honest labor, and the productive temporality of Fascist expansion, while melodrama is the realm of secrecy, parasitical relations, and, in the case of Mailù, the suspended time of melancholy and fantasy. Neither Simone nor Mailù have such moments of self-disclosure: our knowledge of Mailù's history comes through suggestion and allusion and that of Simone through the statements of the Africans who denounce him to Marco. What is made clear is the past of mutual exploitation that ties them—"You serve me, as I served you before"—Simone tells Mailù, holding over her the threat of telling the Italians that "you are not my wife, and where you come from." The film's two formal registers thus correspond to two moral and linguistic regimes, one of legitimacy and truth, the other of illegality and deception.

Sotto la Croce del Sud differs from other East Africa–set empire films in placing the Ethiopian workers in the first camp within this Manichaean scheme. The plantation laborers' improbable loyalty to Marco is based on their hatred of Simone, who treated them with brutality and trafficked in slaves as well as platinum. "Simone very bad man. He whip all blacks," the caretaker Yusuf tells Marco. Italian benevolence brings out the end of bondage: Marco proclaims to the entire indigenous village, "There will be no more slavery. Work will be fairly compensated." This ostentatious repudiation of forced labor in Ethiopia registered a fragile grip on power and local hostilities that translated into refusals even of waged work. As Shelleen Greene has observed, the putative renunciation of rule by violence places the accent on language as a means of governance, and Marco, who speaks no Amharic, prefaces his abolitionist announcement with an aside to an Ethiopian intermediary to "translate what I say." The verbal tagging of the moment of translation affirms Marco's position as resident *capo*, making him equivalent to the uniformed officers who give orders through translators in *Lo squadrone bianco* and *Sentinelle di bronzo*. Ethiopians with speaking parts all communicate in pidgin Italian, affirming their subordinate status, but *Sotto la Croce del Sud* contains less untranslated indigenous speech than other empire films, opacity being the monopoly of the third party—the Levantine—who has come into the equation.[44]

As in *L'Esclave blanc,* montage sequences of documentary footage trace out the tensions of this approach to labor governance. Frantically paced shots of blacks chopping down trees transition to superimpositions that mingle the trees with the endlessly renewing motions of workers, implying that these may themselves be chopped down if necessary. At first the Italian workers stand apart, supervising, but they too end up in the mix, so that black and white labor and the land become one hive of activity. As Bazin observed, superimpositions can efface perspective, which is why, as in Paulin's picture, scale is used to establish hierarchy. Instead of the ghostly faces of Simone and Georges, though, we have the apparition of Marco, who rises above all as the symbol of authoritarian order. The leveling of races in the name of a common work ethic and destiny has sense within the film's triangulated logic, but channels the specter of "white slaves" toiling next to blacks in Ethiopia. Whether on racial or aesthetic grounds, it greatly irritated the critic of *Bianco e nero,* who denounced it as "one of the worst superimposition montages the cinema has ever produced."[45]

Even as the black workers are emancipated by the Italians, Paolo falls into a slavery of his own. Centa once again plays a junior colonialist who is tested by Africa before realizing his leadership potential. As an engineer, he represents modernity and control of technology, but he is also the most sensitive of the group, responsive to Africa's visual and aural attractions. As in *Il grande appello,* the men drink Chianti and sing about their women at home to mark their arrival, but here there is competition from Mailù's own theme song, which lures Paolo to her veranda. In melodramatic fashion, Mailù communicates more through "scenic effects" than "semantic units," and she answers Paolo's questions about her background vaguely and minimally. Her face is a mask, her body hidden and immobile under layers of clothing. Such costuming, as out of place in the African bush as Simone's trench coat, distinguishes her both from the Italian wives, with their simple peasant clothing, and the African girls with their bare skin. Her enigmatic beauty has an effect on Paolo. When Marco offers to host a celebration of their arrival, Paolo says, "Tonight we're going to have an orgy!" to which the men reply, improbably, "Boys, tonight we drink!"[46]

Elsewhere, *Sotto la Croce del Sud* is blunt about the problem of desire of white men alone in the colonies, with sex talk posited as compensation for action. Georges in *L'Esclave blanc* went off with a black woman but did not talk about it, whereas the workers speak openly about Mailù as a fantastic creature they can never have. "She has a marvelous mouth. And what eyes, boys ... You'd like it, wouldn't you, old man?" they taunt each other in their barracks. Marco, the sage father figure, attempts to assuage their frustrations by allowing drinking sessions. In the Ethiopian-based *Il grande appello* and *Legionari del secondo parallelo,* the sharing of wine is presented as a means of forging homosocial bonds and taming homesickness, a little bit of Italy in Africa. Although the straw-covered Chianti bottle does function, as in *Il grande appello,* as part of an autarchic economy of "Italian" objects (versus the whiskey favored by Simone and Mailù), wine drinking, here, figures as a futile attempt to calm their senses and is often followed by scenes of another compensatory activity: physical labor. More often, though, fantasy overcomes everything, and the mere passing by of Mailù stops the labor of colonization in its tracks, prompting sighs and gazes probed in close-up.

The passions of Paolo and Mailù take shape against this charged background. The Ethiopian landscape, with its lush flora, speaks for the flowing desire between the two, as does their matching white clothing. His enchantment with her is palpable:

Paolo: I have the impression that you have a poetic soul.

Mailù: I don't know, maybe I have a vagabond soul. I close my eyes and let my soul go where it will.

Paolo: That could be dangerous.

Mailù: Yes, it can happen that the soul is attracted by some unknown force, and then it's like looking into an abyss. But I recognize it immediately when it happens and command my soul to change course.

Robin Pickering-Iazzi has argued that Brignone's use of "panoramic space and movement" engaged with contemporary appeals to Italian women to experience the expansive life of the colonies, as do the characters of Cristiana in *Lo squadrone bianco* and Simone in *L'Esclave blanc*. Mailù's wandering also places her in this category, but she differs in mentality from these purposeful metropolitan women. "I lose myself willingly in dreams. It is my race," she told Paolo earlier, explaining her immersion in worlds "elsewhere," and other indices of a nomadic sensibility. She is also saddled with her unspeakable and inescapable past and origins: biology is destiny for this non-Aryan character. Mailù's state of captivity is underscored by the restrictions of her costuming: a heavy robes, tight bun, and tweezed eyebrows. Her prison house is "a history that can never be completely expressed," one narratable only by melodrama, with its privileging of the extra-linguistic.[47]

As we have seen, empire films posited the colonies as places of potential sensory overload, with the blackouts experienced by their male subjects an integral part of their conversions. Indigenous dance scenes, as observed by white men on-screen, can precipitate that sensory flooding, leading to a temporary loss of their agency. Such re-created ethnographic scenes are also rhetorically efficient: as they entertain, they proclaim the cinema's abilities to domesticate and probe Africans. The ritual rain-dance sequence in *Sotto la Croce del Sud* contains all of these elements. It continues the story of Ethiopians' acquiescence to Italian benevolence, since it is prompted by Marco's announcement that all labor will henceforth be paid. Performed by "the most beautiful virgins" of the plantation's village, it renders sub-Saharan black culture as titillating but strange. But the camera does not keep its distance for long. Over the course of the ritual,

FIGURE 6.10.

Ethiopia as sensory paradise, *Sotto la Croce del Sud*. Author's collection

it moves from the position of observer to that of participant, emphasizing its presence. An abrupt cut to hands drumming and the sound of chanting sets the scene, as very young bare-chested girls and men face each other in parallel lines. The focus is on the faces and breasts of the girls, and one of them breaks rank to look around, including at the camera, before she is singled out for a rather sad cameo. The men dance toward the women, moving in ways that simulate copulation, bobbing up and down and brushing their lips over the women's noses. The camera returns to the girl as it moves into extreme close-up, so we are just inches from her and her partner, who looks at her while she keeps her gaze down. Holding here, with all else removed from the frame, Brignone leaves Marcellini's ethnographic eye far behind and also goes beyond Paulin in offering spectators the fantasy that they are witnessing—or engaging in—a "private" erotic act with a very young African woman. The big-band accompaniment of *L'Esclave blanc* kept the viewer to more familiar aural territory, but here

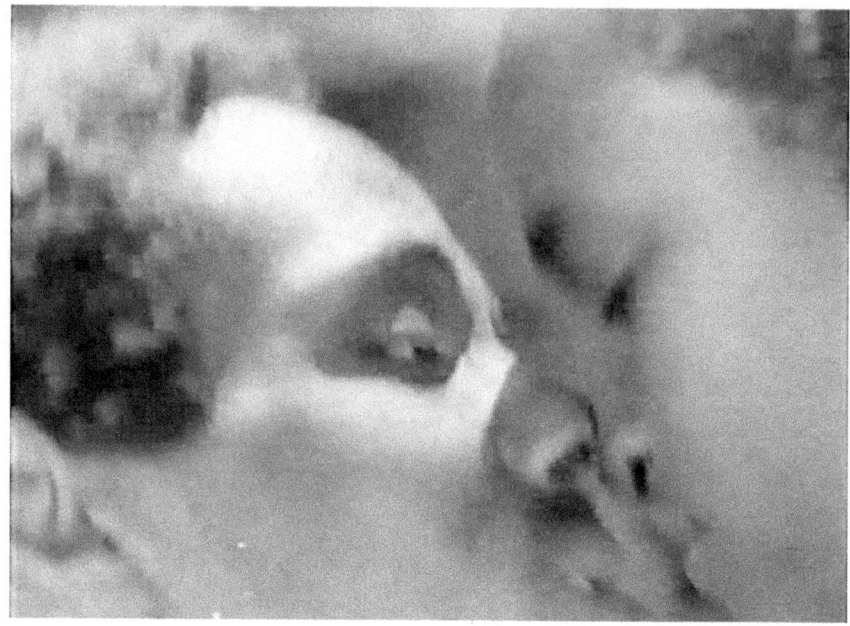

FIGURE 6.11.

Dance in *Sotto la Croce del Sud:* Fantasies of proximity. Author's collection

the strange tonalities of the single chanting voice, accompanied by drums, heighten the sense of alterity and intimacy. Chanting, writes Balázs, is "an aural close up," and the ear is drawn to the grain of the voice, which mimics the frenzied rubbing in evoking the frisson of Africa, the absence of a point of audition referencing a world of free-floating desire.[48]

Three groups watch this spectacle. Reverse shots interspersed throughout the ritual show the reactions of the married men who mostly ignore it as they drink wine and eat pasta with their wives, the single men who drink wine and comment directly on the action, and Paolo and Mailù, who watch separately. "What does all this nose-rubbing mean?" asks one worker, before the conversation shifts to Mailù's own exoticism. "A pretty wife, a house in the sun, beautiful children, this is what allows one to work," says another, whose sentiments will be repeated later with an old Italian folk phase that took on new meaning in a climate of racism and autarchy: *moglie e buoi di paesi tuoi* (take wives and cows from your own villages). *Paese* translates as both "country" and "village," and the Levantine Mailù can belong to neither. This does not bother Paolo, who is by now in a state of arousal, as is Mailù, who reclines on her veranda, breathing heavily, and soon they are kissing passionately. Looking, the film reminds us, is an embodied act, and life in Africa requires strong defenses against the allures of the senses. With the kiss, realism recedes in favor of melodrama. Simone has a jealous fit and threatens to expose Mailù, a conversation overheard by Paolo, who renounces his tainted lover. Marco decides to banish both Levantines after Simone is caught giving alcohol to the workers, but the lovesick men are upset when they hear of Mailù's departure. One worker even asks to hear her theme song, demonstrating his aural colonization: Mailù's world has drifted into his own.

The threat of breached boundaries also finds expression in a scene of a different kind of longing. The chanting of the rain ritual returns as Ethiopians clad in loincloths pound coffee beans, supervised by an Italian. The off-screen sound lends a hypnotic feel to the rhythmic pounding of the beans with a long wooden pole. A close-up isolates one of the Ethiopian men, lingering on his face in three-quarter profile, sun illuminating his hair and skin and the glint of his earring. The man keeps his eyes on his work as a triad of shots links the movements up and down into the hole created by the stick, his face in extreme close-up, and then the desirous gaze of the Italian foreman, who averts his eyes with some effort. The tactile quality of these shots limns the desire for contact. This empire film mobilizes the senses to "express the inexpressible": male desire for another man.[49]

Until now, this particular Italian has had a low profile in the film. Neither married nor besotted with Mailù, he speaks little, other than to inform us at the film's outset of his martial credentials. The colored scarf he wears throughout the entire movie is his only outward mark of difference. Brignone's inclusion of this stolen moment of pleasure is consistent with a form of narration that privileges what cannot be communicated through language and calls on the spectator to put together the fragments that are offered. In this respect the movie differs from *L'Esclave blanc*, which told its story of interracial passion through the voice and eye of epistemology, framing and ordering knowledge of Africa for the viewer. The

FIGURES 6.12, 6.13, 6.14.

Male desire in *Sotto la Croce del Sud*. Author's collection

melodramatic *Sotto la Croce del Sud* operates like Mailù's nomadic soul, soliciting the viewer to go where he or she will, before Brignone imposes boundaries through a plot resolution that protects the Italian collective.

The showdown between good and evil that marks melodramatic narratives operates at the film's end to emphasize the unity of the Italians and Ethiopians against the Levantine outsiders. Simone sets fire to the supply warehouse, stabs Marco when he is discovered stealing money, and flees into the bush. The night fire scene, its drama heightened by Renzo Rossellini's swirling minor-key melodies, was among the few scenes that Fascist critics liked for its display of Italian male heroism. The African workers are absent from this sequence—perhaps fire was too hot a topic, given the uses the Fascists usually made of it—but soon serve the Italians by chasing Simone, with spears raised, until he falls into quicksand. Yusuf watches as he flails about and finally vanishes into the mud, an *insabbiato* of a different sort. Mailù also vanishes, saying, "These are good people who must work. My presence here is a like a poison." The fire has also purified the plantation from Levantine contagion, leaving blacks and whites to labor in peace together. As Yusuf shuts the gates of the property behind the car that takes Mailù away, Paolo grows in stature, now filmed from below in the tradition of imperial commanders. The return to a cloudless sky, as Marco suggests they get back to work, completes the autarchic fantasy of *Sotto la Croce del Sud*. Mailù's departure is also the expulsion of melodrama, understood as "the transfer onto the body of film of the tensions (*turgori*) and excesses that emanate from the body of history." These are not only the exploitations of the black body for labor, and the humiliations of the working-class white, but the effacement of the violence that accompanied the occupation of Ethiopia—and the onset of Jewish persecution at home. The figure of Mailù, woman and Levantine, bears the burdens of the consequences of Fascist crossings of the Mediterranean into Africa: forced displacements, slaveries, interrupted love stories, interracial mixings, cultural hybridizations. Her *mal d'Africa* is the unspoken dimension of Italian imperialism, all that had to be excluded from its representation and memory.[50]

Premiering at the 1938 Venice Biennale along with *Luciano Serra, pilota*, *Sotto la Croce del Sud* met with almost universal hostility that is revealing of the political as well as cinematographic climate. The most charitable or diplomatic critics, cognizant of Comin's role in the project, underscored the "distance" between the "healthy Fascist ethic" of the original story and the finished film, especially with regard to Duranti's character, which had gone from a "slave (*succube*)" of modest appearance in the script to a costumed "'Oriental,'" representative of "a vampirism out of place and time." It was Mailù's fault that the Italian colonists "cut a terrible figure," coming across as "ridiculous" wine guzzlers who ogled the actress and "the robust breasts of the black girls." Brignone had brought in Comin's wife, Marisa Romano, billed as "the first female screenwriter in Italy," to bring "a female perspective" to the story, but the (male) critical reaction to a film that granted a non-white woman such power within the narrative made *Sotto la Croce del Sud* a low point in the history of women within empire films. In the wake of these critiques, the regime forced Brignone to make cuts before it was approved for theatrical release, and one can imagine that Duranti's role was further minimized. The director later protested these "misunderstandings" of his film, which had left him "bitter and disillusioned." He had wished to give a realistic picture of the temptations Italian men would face when they came to the colonies, as a means of admonition: "In Africa one must always remember that one is white, and even more, Italian and Fascist," he stated, perhaps trying to set his political credentials right.[51]

Among the most telling reactions to the film in this regard was that of Càllari, who asserted in 1940 that *Sotto la Croce del Sud*'s deficiencies as a narrative about the Italians' "colonizing spirit" lay in its overemphasis on "adventure, love, passion, and the very delicate racial problem." Given the easy collaboration between blacks and whites in the film, including in the task of removing the Levantines from the plantation, it is possible to wonder which racial problem Càllari refers to here. By then anti-Semitism had joined other themes as a "normal" element of Fascist propaganda, and racial legislation had ejected Italian Jews from public schools, confiscated their assets, and forbidden their unions with "Aryan" Italians. But no Italian film had appeared that expressed openly anti-Jewish sentiments; the *Jud Süss* (Veit Harlan, 1940) of Nazi Germany had no Italian equivalent. Whether this was due to export considerations or other factors is hard to say. But it is telling that other critics avoided parsing the "Levantine" issue, and the reviewer of *Bianco e nero,* in calling Mailù an "'Oriental,'" used internal quotes to indicate the open and variable significance of the term.[52]

What *is* clear is that Brignone's movie touched a sensitive chord about Italians' weak will as well as the realities of life in the colonies. Critics worried about Italians seeing foreign films such as *S.O.S. Sahara* (Jacques de Baroncelli, 1938) and *La Bandera* that presented the colonies as gathering places for "a mob of adventurers, of escapees from the prisons of the Patria, of disreputable women in an environment where crime and vice are the order of the day." Simone and Mailù implied that such people existed also in the Italian territories, an idea that Fascist propaganda could not allow. Ironically, the movie's troupe seems to have been exposed to exactly such an environment, lodging in Addis Ababa at the Pensione Mimosa, run by a German as "a kind of *zona franca* where one met white Russians, Chinese smugglers, German spies, Italian countesses in search of adventure, international scoundrels, and deserters from every flag," according to Duranti. The plantation used for filming was little better: according to Duranti, its owner was a Belgian drunkard who was raising a biracial child, the kind of outcome of extended colonial residence *Sotto la Croce del Sud* hints at by showing the availability of wine drinking and interracial sex.[53]

Coming on the heels of *L'Esclave blanc*, *Sotto la Croce del Sud* prompted calls in the film and colonial press to avoid the depiction of "adventures, amorous passions, the picturesque, the exotic," all of which contributed to "useless fantasizing by the fatigued minds of our workers." Luigi Balestrazzi reminded his peers of cinema's social function within imperial propaganda, warning that "we will do the biggest damage to ourselves if, while we are engaged in the battle for the defense of the race, we act in another realm against our fundamental principles." The appearance of *Equatore/Equator* (Gino Valori, 1939) did nothing to quell such worries. Produced by Giunta (of *Lo squadrone bianco* fame), with a young Mario Monicelli as assistant director, the movie drew early praise for the decision to circumvent "the technical superiority of the American studios" by filming "almost everything on location." Yet upon release it was criticized as harmful to Italian prestige and received a one-star rating, for films judged "a mistake," from *Cinema*. Although it supposedly took place in the corrupt British colony of Kenya, it was filmed partly in Ethiopia, and its plot points of adultery, black insurrection, febrile white men assisted by black nurses, and intra-white fraud and intrigue struck too close to home. In this climate, is not surprising that Blasetti failed to get funding for a film project about "five defeated and deluded men" living in a state of "abjection and rot, which is realistically described," even if the director's intent was to make "a very Fascist movie" that focused on the process of their redemption.[54]

By the end of the decade, debates over the Italian empire film had not placated. The issue of how to integrate "*il romanzesco*"—a term that refers to fictional narrations, but also to a spirit of romantic adventure—with the need for authenticity *and* the ever more stringent demands of propaganda continued to preoccupy critics and film professionals. Some felt the empire film's failing lay in Italians' "lack of a concept of colonial cinematography," while others pointed out that the best colonial films were made by a people with no African colonies at all: the Americans of Hollywood. And American Westerns were a model, even for directors who positioned themselves in opposition to the Hollywood studio system. Yet Italian empire films had their differences: the investment in location shoots as starting points of the production, rather than as a supplement to studio-shot scenes; the integration of documentary conventions ranging from nonfiction footage to the extensive use of Italian and African non-professionals; and the inclusion of film in Fascism's arsenal of imperial conquest and governance, which determined the militarization of its production culture. All of this became part of the formula of Fascist empire films, and the critic Fiume's vigilance about authenticity reflected his desire to protect an emerging brand as well as Italians' investment in the imperial enterprise. Until the very end of the regime, he was empire films' toughest critic, denouncing "African" films made in Turin, excessive or awkward use of documentary footage, and "African" foliage "that could easily belong to any number of Roman villas." Without a credible African "atmosphere and ambience," not only would the workings of cinematic illusion be compromised, Fiume feared, but "the public will no longer *believe* in that Africa or that colony that the cinema wanted to represent."[55]

The issue of reception returns us to the way "extra-textual and cultural knowledge" figures into the ways the spectator "takes up the image," in Sobchack's words. Imperial visual culture brought the realms of fiction and nonfiction together, recycling images and framings of the colonies across film forms and onto advertising and photography. Highlighted through empire movie's publicity, authorial declarations, and reviews, this mingling of the two film forms came to define empire films for spectators and critics by the end of the 1930s. Although films come to the viewer already indexed as fiction or nonfiction, as Noël Carroll argues, Fascist empire film culture played on the tension between the two, so that critics could recommend to audiences that they view a fiction film through the lens of documentary, as happened in the case of *L'Esclave blanc,* or documentaries through the lens of features, as would be the case of the films by De Robertis and Rossellini examined in the next chapter.[56]

It is telling in this regard that the tentative genealogies of the Italian empire film a few critics traced at the end of the decade included both fiction and nonfiction. Balestrazzi dated the tradition from Comerio's Libyan documentaries during the Italo-Turkish War, finding nothing after that worthy of note until the Orientalist works of the late 1920s. His comments testify to the hardening attitudes toward racial mixing: he lambasted Guazzoni's *La sperduta di Allah*, which included a union between a British woman and an Arab sheik, while finding *Kif Tebbi* marred by "an absolute incomprehension of indigenous psychology," perhaps due to the space it gave to Ismail's dilemmas of loyalty and identity. Balestrazzi applauded the development of a Fascist film bureaucracy that had allowed the empire film to come into its own, but warned obliquely of the need for strong stories to combat the threat of the rhetorical that surrounded all propaganda movies. Càllari, too, found the origins of empire film in early war and exploration documentaries. Although he praised Camerini for shooting *Kif Tebbi*'s exteriors in Africa, that work did not constitute an Italian colonial film "understood as an exaltation of our race," and neither did *Il grande appello*, with its focus on the Hotel Orient's "clientele of ill repute." Like Balestrazzi, Càllari took the Ethiopian War to be a turning point in the depiction of the Italian colonies. Despite a discouraging tally of five good films (*Kif Tebbi, Lo squadrone bianco, Sentinelle di bronzo, Abuna Messias*, and *Luciano Serra, pilota*) versus four bad ones (*Sotto la Croce del Sud, Uragano ai tropici, Equatore*, and *Il grande appello*) Càllari reasoned, "Today we are only at the start, we have only recently created a colonial environment." Empire remained "a grand horizon toward which the Italian cinema must look even more than it does now." To this end, he asked Italian directors the following questions: "Have you ever been in Africa? Do you believe in the cinematographic appeal of the African continent? Have you ever thought about making a colonial film? How would you make it?"[57]

Although the poll offered directors an opportunity to publicly affirm their investment in Fascism's empire, officials were probably not pleased with the results. The topics that interested the majority had a high potential for veering in the wrong direction. D'Errico reminded everyone of the eighteen documentaries he had made in Africa for Luce, but his idea to set a film in Libya because "the landscape speaks for itself, with a language that needs no commentary," recalled Genina's *Lo squadrone bianco*. Alessandrini expressed pride in his *Luciano Serra, pilota*, terming it "my best work," but reflected obliquely, "My excessive love for Africa has sometimes brought me more bad than good." As for Camerini and Palermi, the former wanted to interweave stories about two families, one white and one black, while the latter wished to dramatize the situation of "Abyssinians who find themselves faced with the *fait accompli* of our almost fulminating Ethiopian conquest." Neither was likely to find much official encouragement. Oreste Biancoli cautioned that in filming his story about a family of colonizers, "I would not want limitations [posed] on the encounters between white and colored men. I would resolve the racial problem with the instinctive repulsion the races have for one another, and let my characters act exactly as they really do in those regions"—not a reassuring prospect. Brignone used his response to complain about *Sotto la Croce del Sud*'s reception. He admitted that "the fascination of Africa really exists, and it is a sweet pain (*un dolce male*) that enters in your blood and you can no longer free yourself from it," but said he would accept a future colonial project only "with the understanding that they would leave me to act without limitations."[58]

The "they" Brignone refers to is, of course, the dictatorship's film bureaucracy, whose interventions would become only greater after Italy entered World War II, a month after this article appeared. The empire born from the Ethiopian War, still in a phase of creation, now had to be defended. It is not surprising that Càllari closes his article with the passage from Pavolini's *Disperata* that honors Masoero, the cameraman–military operative who continues to film as the bullets fly. The special relationship of cinema and aviation Masoero had helped to shape now began another, more complex, phase, which is examined in the book's final chapters. The features by Rossellini and Genina examined in chapter 8 retain the obsession with the display of technology and the ideals of militarized masculinity, but there is less time for journeys of redemption. The drama of these films comes less from within than from without, from everything falling apart around their protagonists. Whether set in Greece or in Libya, they bear the weight of Fascist imperial propaganda and policies as they struggle not with the management of individual desire but with the shame and disaster of collective defeat.

Film Policies and Cultures, 1940–1943

On June 10, 1940, Mussolini once again stepped onto his balcony in Piazza Venezia. Ending Italy's nine months of "non-belligerence," he declared the country's entry into World War II alongside "its great ally Germany." His speech, which he delivered in the arms-akimbo stance beloved by Fascist authorities, covered familiar themes in justifying intervention: Italy defending its existence against "the reactionary and plutocratic democracies of the West"; Italy suffocated in its own sea, the Mediterranean; war as defensive yet inevitable. Yet this is not the same Mussolini as in October 1935. A Luce documentary captures a Duce who barely moves as he speaks, his hands seemingly glued to his thick belt. Whereas he was barely seen in the October 1935 newsreel announcing the Ethiopian invasion, now his solid and massive presence anchors the screen as it flits around Italy, sequencing each time the name of the city, the sleek white Marelli loudspeakers blaring his voice, and the packed piazzas. And Luce operators keep more distance from the crowd: there are no close-ups and slow pans here, just distant sober and uncertain faces that belie the cheering soundtrack. The contrast between Luce's mobility and Mussolini's statuesque presence highlights the importance nonfiction cinema had come to have in creating a sense of Fascist omnipotence, especially within a state that revolved around one person who could only be in one place at a time.[1]

The role feature films could play in shaping affects and allegiances would also be clarified in the dense and dramatic years that followed. By the time of Mussolini's speech, Italy had already occupied Albania and would soon invade Greece, Yugoslavia, and France, even as East Africa (1941) and then Libya (1942–1943) fell into British hands. Two years into the war, with Italian East Africa defeated, New Order Europe became the focus of Fascist planning and the Balkans the last outpost of the imperial project. "The cinema depends closely on war, and its future is often tied to war. Markets respond to the progress of [military] operations, occupations, and alliances," observed one critic in 1942.[2] This was above all true for empire films, which take those operations and occupations as their subjects: Albania and Greece, as well as the Russian front, now replaced Ethiopia and Somalia as settings. This chapter examines the challenges that marked this final round of the Italian cinema's involvement with the Fascist war machine, preparing the ground for the discussions of the features *Bengasi* and *Un pilota ritorna* in chapter 8. Tensions between the Fascists and their Nazi allies, the void left in the Italian features market by the exit of American movies, and the need to produce films that would engage audiences in Tripoli, Athens, Split, and Trieste all determined the parameters of film policies in these fraught years.

This chapter also examines how the propagandistic needs of World War II led to an intensification of the ties between feature and documentary film, and the fate of the category of empire cinema when empire was fast disappearing. The military component almost all empire films shared made it easy to subsume them under the rubric of *cinema di guerra* (war cinema). The blend of "the pure documentary of battles" with "the histories and dramas of the characters that take part in them" that marks military features draws on empire cinema traditions, as do the mix of real soldiers and divas, use of Luce footage, and investment in an "approach to a documentarist style" as Italy's signature within the international features market.[3] But the war necessitated the abandonment of one of empire film's main features: shooting on location. *Il cavaliere di Kruja/The Cavalier of Kruja,* which was filmed in Albania and starred Doris Duranti, was one of the last such movies to be filmed on site. Although the martially minded Alessandrini insisted on risky reconnaissance shots in Libya for *Giarabub,* the actual production, like that of *Bengasi,* took place mostly in the studio, with set designers relying heavily on Luce documentaries and photographs for accuracy. And *Un pilota ritorna,* set in Greece, was filmed near Viterbo. "The retreat of Italian war cinemas into the studios is the best mirror of how the conflict went. Cinecittà ... became the 'Giarabub' of cinema, a fortress in which to close oneself up and defend oneself," Farassino observes. The vicissitudes of the war also changed the face of empire cinema's labor pool—*askaris* no longer being available—although not its need for masses of extras: five thousand Italian soldiers were "stationed" at Cinecittà while they participated in *Bengasi,* and American and Greek prisoners of war worked on *Harlem Knockout* (Gallone, 1943) and *Un pilota ritorna.*[4]

Italy's participation in World War II is often reduced to a catalog of military failures, but this does not render the mix of hope and ambivalence that many Italians, including high officials, felt toward the war effort, nor the devastating and lasting effects of the Balkan occupations. Mussolini entered the conflict against the advice of his military and economic advisers: five years of mobilizations (including participation in the Spanish Civil War) had nearly bankrupted Italy, the colonies continued to drain state finances, and the armed forces were not equipped to wage industrial warfare on multiple fronts. And not a few in the political hierarchy viewed Hitler from the start as a deeply unreliable ally. Already in 1941, Ciano noted in his diary that even Italy, "the lady of the Mediterranean," would end up at best a junior partner, if not an eventual province, of the Third Reich. But the Duce had delayed Italy's entry until he was sure France would fall to the Germans (which it did a week later), which allowed the Fascists to advertise the conflict as a short and easy war—and also ask the Nazis for long-desired or formerly Italian French territories (Savoy, Tunisia, Nice, Djibouti, Corsica). Such potential gains off the French enthused many Italians, as did the master plan for the future empire: control of the Mediterranean bolstered by the Adriatic and the Red Seas, the Red Sea secured through acquisition of the British-held Suez Canal and Egypt, and Italy at the center of a new geopolitical configuration, "Eurafrica." World War II would complete the trajectory of national redemption begun in 1922 and advanced with the occupation of Ethiopia: no longer spectators of histories "that took place without their participation and against their will and rights," Italians were "protagonists" who would "decisively and definitively transform Europe and the world."[5]

In other ways, too, Fascists saw continuities of this war with Italy's previous imperial mobilizations. Battle with the Allies extended the regime's campaign to redeem humanity from slavery, whether as practiced in East Africa or "the gilded but none the less barbarous and bloody [slavery] of the City and Wall-Street." Drawing directly on their imperial experience, the Fascists would introduce "a new concept of war: that of a war-colonization" that would made conquest merely the prelude to the work of economic exploitation. This modern war would rely on proven practices of violence. For Ferdinando Loffredo, squadrism remained the model: "The rush of the trucks, amidst the drone of land and aerial motors, the crackling of machine-guns, and the din of artillery... takes the concept of the punitive expedition to the level of the supreme clash between peoples. It is the tradition of squadrism, powered by the latest means of struggle... and bolstered by a will to imperial greatness."[6] More broadly, as Davide Rodogno and Mark Mazower have observed, Fascism's colonial experiences in North and East Africa provided a template for the military tactics and politics of violence of the Balkan occupations. As they had in Libya, the Fascists removed entire populations of Greeks, Slovenians, Croats, and Serbs to concentration camps and bombed and set fire to whole villages, as they had in Ethiopia. Militia and army forces roamed the Greek and Yugoslav countryside looking for partisans, taking on the role of the nomad, as described by Duvignand: "pass through, burn, and continue on your route." Back in Italy, the war had unleashed mass movements of a new scale and urgency, with Italians now the targets of the strategic bombing so celebrated by the Fascists. The Allied bombings of urban centers in the North that began soon after Mussolini's speech escalated over the next years, forcing huge numbers of Italians to evacuate to the countryside and almost daily visits to shelters for those who remained. Duranti recalls how the constant onslaught gave Italians "a knowledge of war that we never imagined we would possess," one that greeted sunny days (perfect for bombing) with trepidation and looked forward to cloudy, rainy skies for the relative peace they offered. The displacements of the home front undid Fascism's twenty-year attempt to control mobility. In 1933 art critic Ugo Ojetti had praised the Fascist government for removing the unaesthetic sight of "swarms of starving people in movement from one city to another." Now the hungry and dispossessed appeared everywhere in the metropole. Calvino recalls his encounter as a young Avanguardist with the first evacuees at a relief center: "Their shabby appearance, as though hospital bound, made me as anxious as if I were arriving at the front line."[7] As the war progressed, these refugees included waves of Italian settlers who were repatriated by the British as each African colony was lost. As we will see in chapter 8, both *Bengasi* and *Un pilota ritorna* register these grim realities, with their refugee and prisoner-of-war protagonists who are bombed and mutilated, the ravaged landscapes of Libya and Greece also standing in for the destruction ongoing in Italy.

THE "CINEMATOGRAPHIC AXIS," 1940–1943

Italy's German ally figures in both features examined in the next chapter and in ways that evoke the range of sentiment Italians held toward the Axis alliance. Cultural and military accords between the two dictatorships from 1936 onward supported myriad joint initiatives and exchanges. Expanding to include each new satellite of the Axis bloc during World War II, they traced a map of a new European Order to be realized in the cultural realm as well. Italians who embraced the Axis saw it as a chance to defeat ideologies of "cultural internationalism" that had long menaced Italy. Pavolini, soon to be minister of popular culture, reassured his compatriots that Axis culture would be different, its goal being not to erase national differences, but to allow each power to contribute its own strengths to the New Order.[8] Cinema became a primary site of the collaborations and tensions that marked the Axis alliance. Co-productions between Germany and Italy flourished—at least 15 between 1941 and 1943, including the much-maligned *Giungla/Jungle* (Nunzio Malasomma, 1942), which had a bi-national cast. Axis initiatives to mount a continental filmic front to challenge Hollywood's hegemony built on earlier attempts to create a "Film Europe" and met with support from many Italians, given the dire situation: in 1940 Germany and Italy together had produced 172 features as opposed to Hollywood's 479. Axis collaborations would produce that "European cinematographic consciousness" necessary to mount a successful defense "against the invasion of American cinema." The markets for Axis films encompassed Eastern and Western Europe, the Mediterranean basin, and Argentina. The addition of that Italian stronghold in South America shows how this new vision of the empire incorporated older Fascist schemes of influence based on kinship as well as territorial conquest.[9]

The wartime history of the International Film Chamber offers a case in point. That project of Axis domination and response to competition by American films resumed its activities in 1941 after a hiatus due to the outbreak of war. The power politics of the new situation, and the Biennale's subordination to its political orientation, comes through clearly in its new name, as of 1942: the Italian-German Cinema Exhibition. Although the IFC leadership assured the Axis occupied and satellite countries that the chamber intended to help their film industries increase their own markets, the pillaging and dismantling of Polish and other industries by the Germans did not inspire much trust. This filmic imperialism translated rather starkly into Biennale jury decisions: after 1936 military and empire films took home the "best Italian film" awards every year but one, and from 1938 onward German films won "best foreign film" every year. By 1942 Antonio Pietrangeli worried aloud that the loss of American films, coupled with the fact that "only certain energies are presented at the Venice proving ground," could isolate Italy.[10]

The IFC's president, Giuseppe Volpi di Misurata, spearheaded Fascist Italy's own aggressive pursuit of film and economic interests in areas of direct rule (Dalmatia, Greece, Croatia) and in satellites such as Hungary and Romania. The head of Confindustria, former governor of Tripolitania, and major investor in the Balkans since the early 1900s, Volpi di Misurata envisioned Italy's film exports as a means of consolidating Italian influence. To the consternation of Goebbels, the Fascists pursued this brand of expansionism vigorously and made inroads into Eastern European markets that had generated little revenue for the Germans. In Bulgaria and Hungary, Italian military movies often garnered more attention and profits than German ones. In Romania, the Italians bought interests in studios and established joint-venture production companies. Italian imports rose sharply (90 Italian films came into Romania in 1942 as opposed to 30 the year before), and export sales increased threefold between 1940 and 1943. Many of these co-productions were made at Cinecittà, more than ever a major crossroads of the international film trade. In 1939 Antonioni had noted with pride the number of foreigners working in Italy's film studios, and although Italy's entry into the war deprived the country of certain presences—Jean Renoir, there to film *Tosca*, had to leave in haste in June 1940—Axis-bloc productions filled in the gap. Goebbels's irritation at this situation surfaces periodically in his diaries. "The Italians are creating every sort of difficulty for us. They want a piece of the pie at all costs and on this subject there is no reasoning with them," he complained in June 1941.[11]

A flourishing Italian industry made such successful competition possible. Production increased from 83 films in 1940 to 119 in 1942, fueled by steady state investment (loans and advances for productions and reward for good box-office performance) and profits made by Italian films in countries such as Bulgaria, Romania, and Hungary. Distribution societies appeared in each Axis satellite, with ENIC furnishing all films. Italians also made inroads into markets never accessed before, such as France, where Italians became the major shareholders in French production houses and studios, even before the Fascists expanded their empire to cover seven *départments*. France also gives an example of how territorial occupation as part of the Axis allowed the Italians to expand, through force, what had been started in the late 1930s: the attempt to balance an international flow of films and profits that had been decidedly negative for Italy. In 1939 only 2 Italian films had been distributed in France versus 42 French films in Italy. By 1942 the relationship had been almost equalized, with 18 Italian films in France and 20 French films in Italy. Nonfiction's increased international reach mirrored this trend. By 1941 the 9 foreign editions of Luce's *cinegiornale*, which were translated into the relevant local languages (Spain, Portugal, Slovenia, Croatia, Swiss, Bulgaria, Romania, Albania, Greece) represented one-quarter of total copies released.[12]

The market for films also increased inside Italy. Theaters increased from 4,822 in 1940 to 5,236 in 1942, and cinema took in 75 percent of all entertainment revenues in 1942, despite frequent blackouts and bans on outdoor showings in bomb-threatened cities. Soldiers received free tickets to special soldier-only screenings of war and empire films, and actors, film journals, and production houses donated blocs of seats to show their support for the war effort. For audiences outside the cities, the government planned to add 200 mobile cinemas to its fleet managed by the Opera Nazionale Dopolavoro and Luce, although wartime shortages of tires and gas and hazardous conditions often limited their use, both in Italy and in the occupied territories. The regime made less progress with national audiences' appetites for foreign films. Market tastes and insufficient national production meant that Italian films made up only half of what spectators saw that year.[13] Despite the American majors' boycott of the Italian market as of 1939, Italians (including Italian soldiers stationed abroad) continued to see old American films and those from minor production houses until the United States entered the war at the end of 1941. *Lo Schermo* claimed that the exclusion of new Hollywood films had changed Italian audiences, who "no longer boo [our films], as they used to do, but crowd the theatres and often applaud our own stars which have become as popular as their defunct brothers and sisters from overseas." In fact, Hollywood remained the matrix of spectators' fantasies about stars, film glamour, and screen modernity, and the absence of American movies figures in Italian popular memory as one of the many deprivations of the World War II period.[14]

A variety of national cinemas filled this programming gap. French films gained in popularity: in 1940 they took in almost as much revenue as Hollywood ones. Many Fascist critics condemned poetic realist movies as defeatist and pessimistic, but these proved influential among younger Italians for their mix of realism and tragedy. The twenty-five-year-old Alberto Lattuada lauded the bleakness of films by Carné and others as reflecting the current continental mood "of being cursed and condemned to pain." Renoir's *La grand illusion* may have been denounced for its attitude toward war, but was studied for its contributions to the military genre, with special screenings held at the Biennale and Milan Triennale.[15] Nazi war documentaries were popular, and German feature films also performed decently with Italian audiences, helped by massive publicity campaigns and their frequent Biennale awards. The German-speaking Bolzano area provided a natural market. The anti-British colonial drama *Ohm Krüger* (Hans Steinhoff, 1941) enjoyed a gala opening in a theater decked out with Fascist and National Socialist flags, while the anti-Semitic *Jud Süss* did well enough for *La Provincia di Bolzano* to urge spectators to attend afternoon performances "to avoid excessive crowding in the evening."

Both films also sold well in Florence. The former film stayed in theaters for 83 days, well above the average 74.9 for Italian films, and the latter for 70 days, as opposed to 48 and 73 days for *Un pilota ritorna* and *Bengasi*, respectively. As in all mobilized countries, the cinema—of whichever nation—provided consolation, entertainment, and respite from the grim realities of war. This last function of film perhaps lay behind the mediocre showing of many Fascist military and empire features, especially as the war situation worsened for Italians. Rossellini's final Fascist war movie, *L'uomo della croce/The Man with the Cross*, set on the disastrous Russian front and released two months before Mussolini's ouster, stayed in Florence theaters only 22 days.[16]

Whether Italians watched Emil Jannings, Viviane Romance, or Doris Duranti, the voices they heard were not the stars' own. As we saw in chapter 3, the regime's decision to dub all foreign movies stemmed from nationalist and xenophobic preoccupations (a desire to spread knowledge of Italian and minimize the audition of foreign speech) as well as pressures to create work for the Italian film industry. The spread of post-synchronized sound in Italy in the early 1940s led many Italian stars to now be dubbed as well, leading to another round of debates on the subject. Antonioni lambasted dubbing in *Cinema* as a "mere acoustic surrogate" that favored technical prowess over the voice as an expression of the soul. When proponents of dubbing protested, the review polled film professionals and ordinary spectators on the pros and cons of the practice. This "inquiry on dubbing" found the latter group (which included lawyers, artisans, civil servants, housewives, shop owners, and students) more favorably disposed, although even those who were for continued dubbing asked for a greater variety of voices, so that a particular star would have his or her distinctive vocal profile. Those against dubbing suggested subtitles or a summary at the start of the film as substitutes, but by 1941 the Italian Academy's campaign for linguistic autarchy was in full swing. More filtering of the foreign at home, not less, was the order of the day.[17] Anglophone soldier characters, whose dialogue was often untranslated, constitute an exception and a new addition to the soundscape of empire cinema. Whether English or Australian, their exaggerated accents emphasize their foreignness, and their Italian speech, while usually grammatically correct, is rendered almost as caricature, to better offset the familiarity of the "true" Italian voice. Such portraits would disappear with the fall of Fascism, when the German soldiers emerged as Italians' persecutors and American liberators the main voices of Anglophone speech.

THE SPACE OF NONFICTION

The outbreak of World War II and the period of "non-belligerence" threw empire features into a holding pattern. Already, the appearance of films such as *Sotto la Croce del Sud* had brought some desire for reassessment of this kind of cinema, which threatened to go in directions the regime did not welcome. The stance of neutrality amid rapidly changing military and sovereign situations in Europe also dictated a moment of caution and reflection among Italian production houses, leading Fiume to complain that no empire feature had been released in 1940.[18] Nonfiction film filled this void. The regime expanded the structures established during the Ethiopian invasion, based also on its study of the efficacy of Nazi German practices in this sector. The Istituto Luce remained the main protagonist in this sector and kept its monopoly on newsreels, but Incom, the Ministry of War, the Ministry of Popular Culture, and the Cinema Centers of the Armed Forces were also authorized to make documentaries. Luce's new headquarters in Rome, which began operations in 1940, had state-of-the-art production and editing facilities, but Luce never had the resources of the Nazis, who sent hundreds of camera operators into battle—sixty was Luce's high number, in 1942—and it stayed a civilian organization (unlike the Nazi film propaganda corps). Seventeen units dispersed among the army, navy, air force, and the governorate of Libya, along with that of Luce Africa Orientale, composed Luce's troops/troupes, who worked alongside and sometimes equally for the Armed Forces Cinema Centers and occasionally on commercial releases. Luce's *équipe* included Craveri and many other veterans of empire cinema: an article in *Cinema* emphasized that its war units include "the same operators who have already given us effective and lively documentations of our wars in Africa and Spain and of the occupation of Albania." As an air force official, Craveri also worked for that military arm's Photocinematographic Center, along with Marcellini (now an air force captain) and Vittorio Mussolini.[19]

This commingling of personnel reflect not only an initial shortage of qualified operators, but a conscious decision to further centralize propaganda operations, ending the relations of competition that had marked the Ethiopian War years. Henceforth, footage from all theaters of war arrived in Rome, to be edited into coherent films by Luce operatives working alongside military advisers and censors. This immense image bank of film negatives provided for military training films, newsreels, documentaries, and still photographs, increasing practices of sharing and recycling and the regime's control over these intermedial exchanges. Cinema Centers of the Armed Forces did have the autonomy to make their own films. The army's made training movies and documentaries (Lattuada got his start here), while the air force's had come to prominence during the Ethiopian War, when it was headed by the aerial photographer Masoero, and participated in the making of *Il grande appello; Lo squadrone bianco; Luciano Serra, pilota;* and *Un pilota ritorna*. The prestige of Italian aviation, its central role in warfare, and the popularity of aviation footage with spectators led to an expansion of that center's resources, with movie cameras now installed directly on airplanes. The navy's cinema center had the biggest influence on the film world, though, thanks to the commercially released films by its head, Captain Francesco De Robertis, who gave Rossellini his start in feature-length cinema and whose own full-length "novelized documentaries" will be discussed below.[20]

The Luce newsreel, that bedrock of film propaganda, underwent a modernization of form and content. The government had not forgotten the numerous complaints of the late 1930s about audience saturation with Luce's repetitive films, and even as Italian newsreels circulated more within Axis and neutral Europe, they decreased in frequency within Italy. UFA, Luce's German equivalent, gained more screen time, accounting for almost one-third of all foreign newsreel footage. Under D'Errico's guide, Luce updated its emblem, replacing the imperial eagle with a more playful Roman wolf with her cubs, and reorganizing the newsreel's structure in ways that borrowed from the newspaper. For Lando Ferretti of *Lo Schermo*, these reforms would appeal to "millions of men who are no longer content with reading a newspaper or listening to the radio ... but want to see in action the glorious and humble heroes of the multitudinous daily events." The celerity of production vaunted since the Ethiopian War further improved, due a more centralized editing process and the faster speeds of airplanes that "float almost on invisible wires, transporting reels of film from one continent to another." Only the movie camera had the agility and speed to capture "the lightning war" and deliver it to spectators, Càllari contended: "There is no conceiving of modern war without the cinema, especially a war of velocity like the one we are fighting now, which adopts the tactic of the *Blitzkrieg*, which makes facts old by the time they are recounted [and] can only be followed and recorded with the radio and the camera lens."[21]

The conditions of World War II did consolidate the militarization of the cameraman, and camera operators were lauded as "combatants among combatants who ... put aside one weapon (because the movie camera is a weapon) to take up another." This was not mere rhetoric: as the war effort worsened, and battlegrounds became more hazardous, many cameramen lost their lives or received medals for bravery. As one nonfiction filmmaker complained, these same conditions made the cameraman into a mere operative, charged only with getting as much footage as possible and staying alive. Luce editor Fernando Cerchio thus defended the creative contributions of cameramen, who were not just technicians, but "thinking and functioning mind[s]" who made expressive and individual choices in deciding how to film prescribed events. Editors had a different kind of agency, which was expressed in the structure they gave the newsreel as well as in their "very innocent small tricks," such as changing the location of footage—making a cannon that fired in France seem to fire in England or passing off a clip of military maneuvers in Italy as real battle operations. "What matters is what I say ... with that apocryphal, reconstructed clip," he asserted. The Luce newsreel undoubtedly "spoke to the crowd," but its heavy propagandistic burdens, compressed format, and the range of events it covered—scenes of Italian and German battlegrounds combined with home-front activities and gala film premieres—constrained its ability to make sustained connections with spectators. At any rate, Luce had a captive audience: newsreels had long been an obligatory part of feature film programming, In November 1941 war documentaries were added to this mandatory mix, in keeping with the regime's added investment in a film form that offered different propagandistic possibilities.[22]

The heightened interest in the documentary during World War II spanned national boundaries. In America, Britain, and continental Europe, the lessons of the best politically engaged filmmaking—whether John Grierson's "creative elaboration of actuality" or Communist and fascist compilation films—inspired a new round of experimentations, including by filmmakers who came out of the crucible of interwar modernism. Alberto Cavalcanti, author of the avant-garde-influenced city film *Rien que les heures/Nothing but Time* (1926), worked for the British Ministry of Information's Film Division during World War II. The Ministry's Crown Film Unit made feature-length "narrative-documentaries," which integrated studio shooting and other elements of commercial cinema, not unlike those made in Italy. In Germany, Walter Ruttmann's modernist to military film trajectory resembled that of D'Errico: he made *Berlin: Die Sinfonie der Grosstadt/Berlin: The Symphony of a Great City* (1927) and shorts for the Nazi Bureau of Labor before turning to war documentaries. Nazi war documentaries were often newsreel compilations, which, as Hilmar Hoffman has argued, show the influence of Russian montage theories. Highly regarded films such as *Feuertaufe/Baptism of Fire* (Hans Bertram, 1940) and *Sieg im Westen/Victory in the West* (Svend Noldan, 1941) were studied closely not only by Italians, but also by the British and the Americans. By 1942 a chain of mutual stylistic influences and citations linked the nonfiction military films of allies and enemies.[23]

The war occupied about one-quarter of Italian documentary production. Even more than Nazi films, Fascist war documentaries—most of them compilations—posed the problem of engaging a public already saturated with Luce footage. "The director of the documentary must interest and win over his public, by making what has already been seen, at least three times, appear to be brand new," one commentator asserted. The need to transform that raw footage, shot by multiple cameramen, gave rise to reflections about the editor's role in producing Fascist war propaganda, especially since battle scenes sometimes had to be re-created behind front lines. Cerchio, who had by then passed from editing newsreels to making and editing Luce documentaries, put the accent on creating a "narrative and spectacular" flow that would allow the spectator to "not only perceive but examine" the image, which was less possible with the rapid-fire shots of Luce newsreels. Feature films could also provide models in their uses of sound to bring out audience emotion, as opposed to the aural assaults of Luce's "total and continual rather careless mixage of sounds, music, and speech," but Cerchio also cited the German war documentary's inclusion of choral music.[24]

The reference to German war documentaries was not incidental. Such films enthused and haunted Italians for their dynamism: they captured events from many camera angles yet placed "every element into a whole of a great dramatic action." But the Nazis' military film operations had the same advantages as their military, with respect to the Fascists: more men, better technology, and greater mobility. Writing from Berlin soon after the fall of France, after seeing a program of war documentaries at the Gloria-Palast Theatre, Giuseppe Isani admired how their effects went well beyond those of informative propaganda. In following the progress of the German armed forces, audiences could "relive their own dreams and escapes and enter into the events presented." His fellow spectators had been moved, in the emotional and physical senses: watching those documentaries "was like accompanying the troops, via an unreal means of transportation that takes us by land, sea and air.... [T]his is the greatest merit of these filmed war chronicles: their progression, their unfolding, their *racconto,* we would be tempted to say." When the lights went back on, Isani perceived the difficulty some had to tear their eyes from the screen, with the transition from virtual voyage to immediate reality "almost like a return from a long and very dear journey that continues on in our desires and minds."[25]

This ideal immersive state had long been an aim of Italian empire features shot on location, but "Luce style" and Luce's resources worked against it in the realm of nonfiction. As Pavolini himself would admit in a special issue of *Film* published in 1942 for an Italian-German readership, Fascism's war had been "less spectacular" and too often offered spectators only a limited viewpoint, especially with regard to naval battles. He tipped his hat to "our German friends and allies, masters in this area," but mentioned Italy's own skill in the realm of war features, referencing *Luciano Serra, pilota* (which had done well in Germany) as a model for forthcoming pictures such as *Un pilota ritorna*. Not everyone was as diplomatic as Minister Pavolini. In an article not translated into German from that same issue, De Franciscis objected that the different nature of Fascism and Nazism made comparisons of their documentaries invalid. Italians' greater humanity and spirituality led them to be more objective about war's hardships and more focused on the Italian soldier, as opposed to Germans' focus on "giant collective moments in which man has importance only as a unit of the bureaucratic machine." A year earlier, Luce's director Giuseppe Croce had made the same observation on cinematographic grounds, pointing out that "Italian war documentaries must be judged according to the characteristics of 'our war.' . . . Mass movements, large employment of armored and air power, the very proportions of overwhelming victories like that over France, are just not part of the reality of our war, and thus not translatable into images."[26]

Two documentaries from 1940 suggest how imperial nonfiction negotiated these constraints as it experimented with this film form. *Il primo colpo all'impero britannico. La conquista della Somalia Britannica/The First Blow at the British Empire: The Conquest of British Somalia* (1940) relates the acquisition of a territory heavy with symbolic weight. Since the early 1920s, Mussolini had railed against the Great Powers; now, Fascist forces had defeated the haughtiest member of that club, annexing its lands to their own Italian East African Empire. The narration is accordingly heavy-handed, but the cinematography, by Renato Sinistri, is lively, and includes animated graphics. Sinistri, one of Luce AOI's original cameraman, also worked occasionally on features and had assisted Craveri on *Luciano Serra, pilota*'s aerial shots. In *Il primo colpo all'impero britannico*, images of preparation for and waging of ground and air warfare alternate with long-range shots that evoke Orientalist views of the desert landscape. Pace is everything in this twenty-five-minute film: the spectator has time to scrutinize what is presented on the screen, whether an officer looking at his bandaged foot, a soldier showing the bullet holes in his ambulance, or a bomb being loaded onto an airplane. The human scale is further evidenced by the numerous acknowledgments of the presence of the camera: by *askaris* who file by on their way to battle, by soldiers traveling on dusty roads, by a wounded soldier whose gaze makes contact with the man behind the camera as well as with the spectator. Although the documentary features compelling aerial footage, it also projects its own path to the narration of military victory, making up for the lack of large-scale majestic onrushes of troops and the storming of famous foreign capitals.[27]

Il primo colpo all'impero britannico's musical score also shows relations with fiction film. Luce's trademark hammering music gives way to lyrical, exoticizing, and lighthearted symphonic melodies that structure the movie, cueing suspense for the fate of Italians in the final battle and indifference to the fate of the enemy, as when tunes that evoke a day outing in the country accompany British prisoners of war to a concentration camp. The musical and cinematographic sophistication shown in *La conquista della Somalia Britannica* garnered it praise above and beyond its story of victory. Mino Doletti noted its "impeccable filming and editing," while *Film* placed it in the tradition of the best fictional empire films. "[Sinistri] sends us the reels of film that are impressed with real history, with the new history of our conquest; and, while waiting to see them projected, we like to think that this whole war in Africa is a continuation of the epic of *Luciano Serra*."[28]

La battaglia dello Jonio/The Battle of Jonio, which was made by Luce in conjunction with the Navy Cinema Center and supervised by D'Errico, constitutes an Italian response to the German model. It covered a historic event: the first clash between the Italian and British navies near Taranto (also known as the Battle of Punta Stilo) and was to be a showcase of Luce's modernization. The government assigned an unusually large number of camera operators to the film; hired Guido Notari, Luce's most famous voice, as the narrator; and gave cameramen more autonomy of movement to secure the best vantage points. But bomber planes dominate the beginning of the movie, giving us by then familiar shots of targeting technology, with battleships emerging as the cameras' focus only a quarter way through and the battle itself much later than that. As becomes clear, the film has a difficult task: manufacturing dramatic tension from a showdown with an invisible enemy. Security concerns required a distance between the fleets that prohibited any "direct image" of the British; maps with moving graphics, and the narrator, could provide only "an approximate idea" of the enemy formations. As one of the cameramen admitted when interviewed by *Film*, the British were just "a tiny point, a puff on the horizon. It was impossible to film them." This film about a naval battle becomes a meditation on modern warfare's abstraction and remove: although the Italians' ships receive abundant coverage, binoculars search the empty horizon for enemy ones. The British position is known only from aerial reconnaissance and communicated wirelessly, through radio towers, without any materiality. Even in the heat of battle, billowing smoke in the foreground (the result of a British hit of an Italian warship) and wisps of smoke in the background (Italians' own hits) stand in for war's violence. "More than war documentaries, Italy seems to specialize in documentaries about and around the war," writes Marco Bertozzi in reference to this and other films.[29]

Sound works overtime to compensate for these visual deprivations. Along with Notari's abundant off-camera narration and droning airplane noise, a driving martial score alternates with playful or melodramatic orchestrations to add variety and drama. Music mourns the twenty-one Italian dead who are never mentioned by the narrator, and as the ships return to port a male chorus sings softly and the narrator speaks the prayers of the sailors, officers, and cameramen aboard ("Lord, bless our faraway homes... Bless we who keep an armed watch..."). The chorus that continues as the images cease contrasts sharply with the hammering music at the start of the film, the openly religious character of the sequence marking Italian Fascist difference with respect to the Nazis' use of such vocalisms. As in *Luciano Serra, pilota* and *Lo squadrone bianco*, the repeated images of smoke clouds not only screen war's violence, but also gesture toward a kind of existence "beyond the body" that will reappear in many war features released in 1943, during the final disastrous year of Fascist battle. Press coverage of *La battaglia dello Jonio* reflected its status as a kind of test case for the new Fascist war documentary. As with empire features, the martial nature of those behind the camera became part of the film's overall value within Fascist film culture. Here, though, the battles were real, and six of the *équipe* received military honors for continuing to film under attack. *Film* helped along public interest with an article in which each of the cameramen spoke about their role and its dangers, recalling the publicity efforts expended for *Luciano Serra, pilota*. This did not prevent Càllari from critiquing the film's limited battle coverage. Still, the footage shot for the film had an abundant afterlife, not least in Rossellini's commercially released naval docufiction *La nave bianca* (1941).[30]

I turn now to that film, and to De Robertis's 1940 *Uomini sul fondo*. These commercially released *documentari romanzati* (novelized documentaries), which were a joint production of the Navy Cinema Center and Scalera, mark a bold push forward in the meeting of imperial and war fiction and nonfiction, and they occasioned another round of the debates about the melding of feature film and documentary aesthetics that had accompanied empire cinema since its inception. Now a shrinking empire threw that category of film into jeopardy, and *Lo Schermo*'s call for a "war cinema ... that unites documentary footage with a story that can be filmed in the studio," made in the aftermath of the loss of Italian East Africa, uses new terminology to extend an ongoing critical conversation and tradition of filmmaking practice.[31] The newness of De Robertis's and Rossellini's films lay rather in their documentary and military origins—they approached the coupling of feature and nonfiction from the other side—and De Robertis had been nervous about finding a backer "willing to take on the burden of making a non-normal film." Scalera proved to be a willing partner and could afford to take chances: formed in 1938, with capital from imperial sources—the Scalera brothers' construction companies built airports and the famous highways between Asmara and Massawa and Tripoli and Benghazi—Scalera became one of the most prolific production houses during the war. Its releases for 1940, the year *Uomini sul fondo* appeared, include genre cinema by Brignone, Alessandrini, and D'Errico, as well as Renoir's *Tosca*. Scalera would also produce *La nave bianca*, but that film had the added promotion and scrutiny by the regime's new Committee for War and Political Cinema, which began in 1941 to exert more control over features. Rossellini's film counted in the committee's packet of planned "films of spectacle or of documentary-spectacle," and the casual mention of this category of hybrid works shows how far this strain of cinema had come since 1936.[32] The stakes were even higher now, though: putting a positive spin on often-devastating circumstances. Instead of the forward march of conquest in Africa, these films are about holding ground and containing loss. It is not surprising that *Uomini sul fondo* and *La nave bianca* take place almost entirely inside safe "national" spaces: a submarine and a hospital ship.

The inward-facing story of *Uomini sul fondo,* which recounts the drama of sailors whose damaged submarine has sunk to the seafloor, is deceptively simple. Made with a cast of full-time naval operatives, it promised in its opening titles to "make known the great renunciations, mute heroisms, and silent joys" of the military life. And linguistic and gestural minimalism does dominate the movie. While De Robertis uses sound effectively to communicate the texture of life on a submarine, he does away with the verbosity of most empire films, as well as with the kinds of charged gazes and actions that, as in *Lo squadrone bianco* and *Sentinelle di bronzo*, filled in their occasional silences. Such turbulent air is absent from the metallic closed world of the submarine, which models masculine subjects not in struggle with themselves, but men who simply desire to do their job in the best way possible, even in situations of grave emergency. This linguistic profile corresponds to an emphasis on collective rather than individual psychology. Although the commander receives the most screen time, neither he nor his men are developed as characters beyond the minimum necessary for audience identification. Even when the submarine is sinking, alarmed gazes and accelerated movements are the only human registers of the disaster, leaving music and editing to convey any distress felt by these men. When they do speak, their voices are low and calm, and the news of their possible rescue merely elicits a laconic "Finally." But technology talks often, or rather informs, in the tradition of empire films. When the submarine's drama is broadcast to the public, a mother serving dinner freezes, her hand stopping in mid-air; a family turns wordlessly in unison toward their radio. Technology bonds Italians of all classes to the human drama: even the rich follow the radio's updates throughout the night. The aural sphere becomes the main means of conveying the comforts and commands of authority, including an unseen priest, who, when all seems lost, recites in voice-over the same prayer heard in *La battaglia dello Jonio*. By World War II, the acousmatic is Fascism's preferred sound type: it is everywhere and nowhere, like Fascist power and Mussolini himself. From the bottom of the sea, respecting chains of command in tenuous or no contact with any authority, De Robertis's real naval operatives demonstrate they have internalized its messages.

A similar restraint in the film's mise-en-scène offers a point of contrast with empire features. The small and dark spaces of the film made for lighting contrasts that owe something to the silent cinema, where the movie's artistic director, Giorgio Bianchi, had gotten his start. But documentary style reigns through a liberal use of horizontal and other pan shots that frame individuals within their social context—the submarine and its technology. The extreme heat of their watery prison means that sweat and naked torsos feature throughout the movie. Yet the taut and muscled bodies are, filmed as "unremarkable," part of quotidian submarine life, than eroticized. The exception is the body of a sailor marked out from the film's inception as fragile: he has a crippled hand and, as De Robertis shows us in an unusual sustained close-up, a scarred torso. Although this sailor announces that he "does not believe in women," his passage is not to men but to martyrdom. His fiancée is shown as already in mourning, clinging to the locked gates of the port. *Uomini sul fondo* excludes women from the male enclave of the sunken submarine, but neither pathologizes them (as in *Sotto la Croce del Sud*) nor views them as traitorous (*Il grande appello, Lo squadrone bianco, L'Esclave blanc*): they are civilians who wait, with children and the elderly, for news of the submerged vessel. This shift has its origins in World War II's practical and patriotic needs and will mark the features examined in chapter 8. Needed for myriad types of work, as well as for consolation and sustenance, female characters could no longer be driven away or otherwise dispatched off-screen, as they are in many films shot and set in the colonies. They may be on the margins of the action, but they are part of the national community.

Uomini sul fondo also parted ways with past imperial documentaries, since its careful advance production process—treatments, script, and storyboards, which I discovered in the Italian Navy archives—had more in common with that of feature films. Although De Robertis sought to film "the most normal and common story possible . . . devoid of all rhetoric," his movie meant to exemplify his belief that "a film about the Navy must be *a film about atmosphere*."[33] In these ambitions De Robertis was in step with trends in international war documentaries. That same year, Britain's Crown Film Unit made a similar film, *Men of the Lightship* (David MacDonald). Produced by Cavalcanti, it uses a real lightship crew as actors and narrates the story of a lightship sunk to the bottom of the sea after an attack by the German Luftwaffe. In this film, though, there is no happy ending: the crew escapes, but all of them drown when their lifeboat turns over, and unlike in *Uomini sul fondo* a voice-off narrator introduces the characters, fills in the story, and serves as the father figure and anchor for

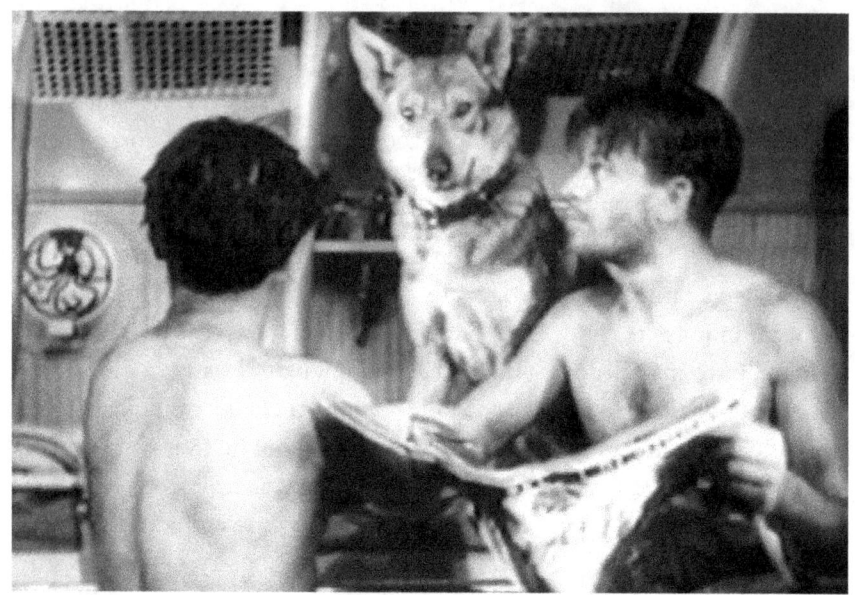

FIGURE 7.1.

The male enclave in *Uomini sul fondo*. Author's collection

the audience throughout the tragedy. There is also an off-screen chorus, similar to that in German documentaries and in *La battaglia dello Jonio*, that begins and ends the movie. *Uomini sul fondo* is more technocratic and admits of no such blandishments: military hierarchy and self-control regulate the action. De Robertis's emphasis on equanimity and composure, and the break with empire features' stories of male abjection, pleased Italian critics who had denigrated movies in which men in service to the state were distracted by their passions. Ugo Casiraghi also admired the movie's restrained sound profile, so different from Luce's films that "bombard the spectator with parades, battles, and aggressions that end up invading the microphone and thus the soundtrack (and our very delicate ears) with shots, screams, and lamentations." Others praised the filmmaker for working "the thorny terrain of propaganda" to produce "a classic" that reflected "an Italian heart, an Italian eye, an Italian of our times."[34]

De Robertis can also claim partial paternity of Rossellini's *La nave bianca*, since both films came out of his 1939 treatments.[35] Political considerations long distanced Rossellini from this movie, but it is best seen as a joint work that issued from a highly collaborative environment (the Navy Cinema Center). Rossellini's work as assistant director and co-screenwriter on 1938's *Luciano Serra, pilota* had introduced him to the craft and culture of empire films: he directed battle scenes in Ethiopia, logged hundreds of flight hours, and consolidated his friendship with Vittorio Mussolini, who henceforth served as his informal patron. After the success of *Luciano Serra, pilota,* producer Riganti employed him as a screenwriter, even as he began to experiment with nature documentaries. He had a contract with Scalera Films to make ten shorts when he was tapped to make *La nave bianca* under De Robertis's supervision.[36] Unlike *Uomini sul fondo, La nave bianca* was made after Italy's entry into the war. It was shot on location at Jonio, on a warship and a hospital ship, but the command bridge was reconstructed inside Scalera's studios. Security and budget concerns mandated the recourse to Luce clips and the documentary *La battaglia dello Jonio* for some of the battle footage that features heavily in this film. The filmmakers exploit the convenient anonymity of such footage in the initial titles, which boast that "the battle scenes were actually filmed (*riprese dal vero*) during combat at Punta Stilo and Capo Teulada": what mattered was not who shot the footage, and for what purpose, but that it was "real." The cinematography and plot points of this self-described *racconto navale* are mostly guided by similar imperatives of documentary display—of naval and medical technology; of the professionalism of the real military men, doctors, and nurses who feature in this film; and of "the simple humanity of those sentiments that constitute the ideological world of each of them," as the first titles announce. The actual white ship materializes only forty-five minutes into the film, after the viewer is familiar with the duties and personalities of the sailors (who are individualized, to a greater degree than in *Uomini sul fondo,* through body type and regional accent), with the competence of the handsome officers, and with Fascist mottos—"Men and machines work together as one"—that will guide them when the ship is attacked.

Rossellini follows the empire cinema formula in privileging the sight and sound of the operation of combat weapons, but the direct hit the ship has taken also adds something new: the direct vision of the physical toll of war. The sanitized woundings of the protagonists of *Il grande appello, Sentinelle di bronzo,* and *Luciano Serra, pilota* give way to burned skin and open wounds, which are mirrored in the battleship's own damage. Sound contains these visual disturbances. No verbal outcries of pain accompany the men's injuries: Renzo Rossellini's music speaks for them, through repeating four-note string motifs, in a minor key and accentuated by drums on the first count, that develop those of *Sotto la Croce del Sud* and rehearse the score of *Roma città aperta*. The muting of the voices of victims and the insistence on the collective frame keep melodrama at bay; the focus remains the shows of camaraderie and the operation of sophisticated emergency protocols that range from rescue actions to surgeries performed under enemy fire. Sound also tracks the habituation of the sailors to an ethos of duty and sacrifice over the course of the film. The sailors have abundant dialogue early on, to establish their characters and the jocular atmosphere on board. But when battle begins authorities speak for and to them, as do the Fascist slogans placed strategically throughout the ship. As Enrique Seknadje-Ashkenazi argues, such graffiti act as prompts for the performance of actions on-screen; they are interpellative rather than decorative in nature.[37] But the body also speaks, and Rossellini communicates its vulnerability, in anticipation of *Un pilota ritorna*, not least in a scene where a helpless bandaged soldier is led by a nurse to see the doctor and immobilized by both of them as his eye is probed in ways that recall the surrealist film *Un chien andalou/An Andalusian Dog* (Luis Bunuel, 1929).

Rossellini and De Robertis also give viewers one of the most open homages to Axis collaboration of any Fascist empire or military film. A long scene has patients and staff gathering on the hospital ship's deck for some air. Germans materialize in uniform, some with bandages but many without, and everyone sings a German song, accompanied by Italian and German patient-musicians. This scene has no diegetic value—in the sense that none of the leading characters feature in it, nor in the scene of a collective Fascist salute that immediately follows it. One could attribute an allegorical value to an early shot in the deck scene that shows a dog and cat warring for food out of one bowl—most likely a Rossellini touch—and observe that not everyone participates in the salute. But those scenes are there, despite postwar critics' best attempts to avoid commenting on them, and they assert the coordination of the regime's filmic and political projects beyond the world of Luce. Indeed, the last glimpse we have

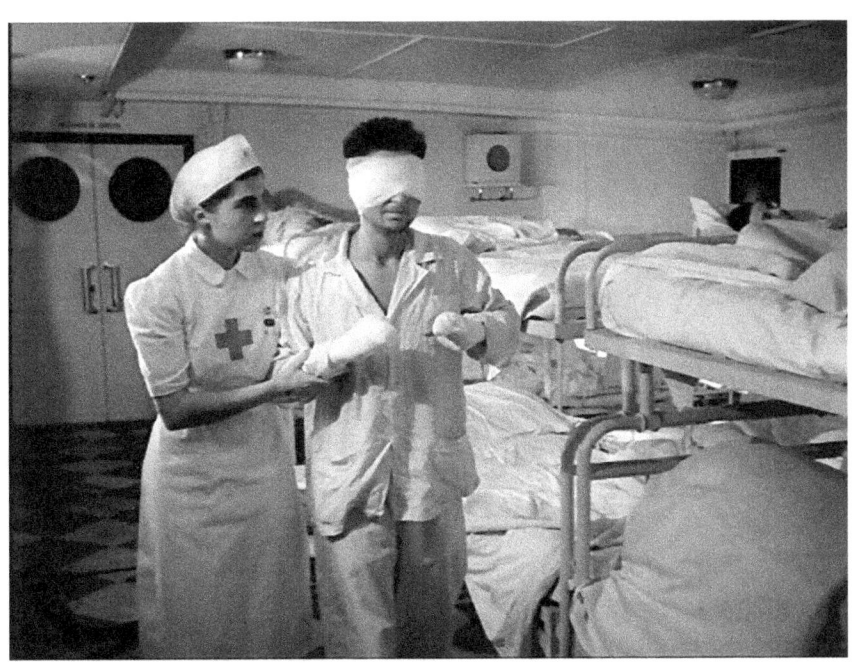

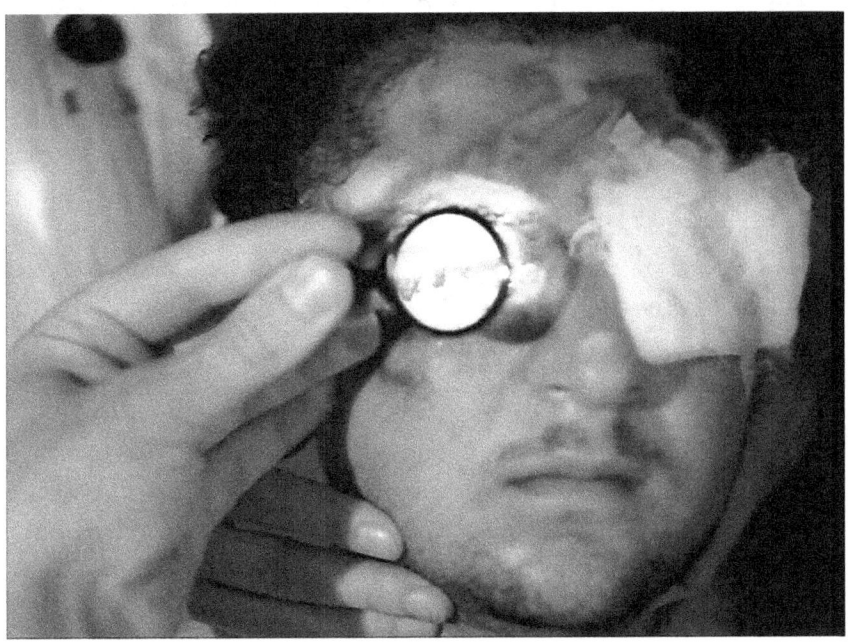

FIGURES 7.2 AND 7.3.

The breached body in *La nave bianca*. Author's collection

of the sailors limns their transformation from a rowdy diversified group, filmed dynamically, into a lineup of mutely saluting wounded, able to be captured by the horizontal pan favored by Fascist *and* Nazi spectacle.

Standing a bit apart from this group are the pair who star in *La nave bianca*'s subplot about a sailor who has an attachment to his *madrina di guerra*, or pen pal, who works as a volunteer Red Cross nurse. De Robertis regretted the inclusion of this relationship, writing in a 1943 issue of *Cinema* that it contaminated his "simple story of a wounded man," taking away "the ethical and stylistic purity that was severely respected in *Uomini sul fondo*." Yet his 1939 treatment had made space for "emotional conflicts" and "so-called theatrical elements ... to satisfy the public's curiosity and passion," and Scalera produced it on that basis. De Robertis did win out on one point, vetoing an on-screen marriage in favor of a plot solution that respects empire films' assertions of duty above desire. Except here the woman has the agency: she recognizes Augusto as her amorous correspondent, but disguises her feelings and identity out of a refusal to favor him over other patients in her care. As their last frame together suggests, their love story sublimates into a relationship of mother (or *madrina*) and child. Although Elena's self-sacrifice is undoubtedly typical of the ideology of "pure-mystical-repressive fascism," in Maria-Antonietta Macciocchi's words, *La nave bianca*'s gender politics differ from those of earlier films we have examined: the woman continues her work, while the man ends up an invalid.[38]

De Robertis's refusal of the romantic happy ending holds interest for its clarification of the fault lines of this new brand of "fictionalized documentaries" with respect to empire films. For De Robertis, these danger zones involved the presence of female characters, but also a world of affects and emotions expressed through a freedom of the body and language that were anathema to his stark and moralistic military mindset. Although apportioning credit for the film is difficult, De Robertis' storyboards and the precedent of his *Uomini sul fondo* allow his influence and sensibility to be individuated in *La nave bianca*. The spareness of dialogue, the attention to detail and to quotidian actions, the clipped montage that emphasizes the navy's efficiency, the displays of masculine self-control in times of emergency, and the interactions of men and machines in the service of the war show his hand. Yet *La nave bianca* is also recognizable as Rossellini's work. An attention to formal composition, which is present from the first Eisenstein-influenced frames of a warship's guns pointing at the viewer; a more expansive mise-en-scène in the film's second half, which works with the slower pace of the scenes featuring Alfredo and Elena; the use of music to signal changes of tempo and mood; and cinematography (long takes, high-angle shots) that takes an interest in the big picture of this total war.[39]

Rossellini's imprint also manifests in the space given to the iconography and doctrine of Christian humanism. Elena is a carrier of rectitude and charity as well as a romantic interest. The movie's last frames reinforce her symbolic status: as the camera holds on the red cross on Elena's uniform, voiding the screen of all reference to surrounding reality, only to superimpose a dedication to "the stoic sufferings and unchanging faith of the wounded of all the armed forces. To the silent abnegation of those who attenuate their sufferings and nourish their faith." The centering of the phrase "silent abnegation" emphasizes Elena's own choice to stay quiet for the putative good of the patria. It also underscores the consolatory ideology that pervades *La nave bianca,* which was made during a war that had already produced a devastating number of Italian casualties and the temporary loss of half of the Italian battleship fleet before Rossellini even finished his picture.[40] One theme cuts across the contributions of both men: the presentation of Italy as an aggrieved rather than aggressive party. As in *La battaglia dello Jonio,* unseen enemies attack Italian vessels, including those supposedly protected by the Red Cross. During the course of World War II, uneasiness about Italy's weak military position added Italy's own German ally to the list of forces that could threaten Italians' autonomy. While this 1941 film paints a cheery picture of Axis relations, the mood will grow darker in *Un pilota ritorna,* when German Stuka bombers threaten the film's Italian protagonist. It is telling that the last image of De Robertis's film is the slogan MARE NOSTRO, while the final image of Rossellini's is that of the cross. In between, the East African empire had been lost.

As one of the first works promoted by the Committee for War and Political Cinema, *La nave bianca* received special attention upon its release. It had two premieres: one for civil and military officials, including two thousand naval officers, and a more traditional opening at the Biennale, where it won the Fascist Party Cup. Critics praised its homage to "military

FIGURE 7.4.

Axis harmonies in *La nave bianca*. Author's collection

duty," but were especially struck by its stylistic innovations. Massimo Alberini, who frequently wrote about nonfiction film, noted Rossellini's break with the Luce model in which "the fast rhythm of the editing and music overwhelm the documentary and its didactic functions." He liked the absence of rhetoric in the portrayal of a battle "in which nothing exceptional happens," yet everything about life on board a ship is understood. He wondered how to label the film, though: is this a documentary, he asked his peers, or something more? Others concurred that *La nave bianca* could not be evaluated according to conventional categories, as it "made use of elements that are entirely new for its genre" and termed it, along with *Uomini sul fondo,* as something in between, a "fictionalized documentary." These films offered an expanded storytelling space within the documentary frame and also showed a new usage of documentary images, which, as Guido Aristarco observed, were "not a mere background, but a fundamental and active factor in the narration."[41]

Empire films had also elicited such praise and quizzical reactions, and some critics placed *Uomini sul fondo* and *La nave bianca* in the tradition of *Lo squadrone bianco* and *Luciano Serra, pilota*.[42] But these movies also looked different. For one thing, they seemed more cohesive. The all-Italian, mostly anonymous casts removed the juxtapositions of Italian stars, with

FIGURES 7.5 AND 7.6.

The consolations of faith, *La nave bianca*. Both author's collection

their large screen presence, with indigenous actors and extras, as well as the language barrier that rendered empire films partially opaque to the vast majority of Italians. *La nave bianca* and *Uomini sul fondo* continued these films' formal experimentations and use of real military operatives, but took away the famous stars *and* the foreign settings, showcasing everyday Italians in or close to metropolitan territories. As Adriano Aprà observes, they also countered the Hollywood model of spectacle in terms of editing and casting that was visible in films such as *Luciano Serra, pilota*. In this they responded perfectly to their times: to the regime's need to broadcast the patriotic exigencies of wartime, to popular desires to see their own military men at the center of the action (as opposed to *askaris*), and to critics' requests for "a true and proper cinematographic story (*racconto cinematografico*)" whose dramatic tension came "not from outside" (as in the exoticism of foreign peoples and landscapes) but from the vicissitudes of everyday Italian life during wartime. And those critics, like the officials who approved their reviews for publication, now had a different eye, one informed by the development of documentary culture and by years of seeing non-professionals, including military men, on the screen. Reviewing the Italian offerings of the 1941 Biennale, Enrico Fulchignani found deep commonalities between the best war documentaries and films like *Uomini sul fondo* and *La nave bianca:* both express "the same spiritual need" to find "in a rigorous cinematic language the right path forward for 'our' cinema, for 'our' art." Chapter 8 turns to the other element in this equation, examining some of the last empire features produced during the regime.[43]

8

The End of Empire

From 1936 to 1941, the Fascist government's investment in commercial empire films had been largely on an ad hoc basis. While some features had official or semi-official origins (*Il grande appello; Luciano Serra, pilota; Sotto la Croce del Sud*), others had come to Italy as a last resort or depended on foreign financing (*L'Esclave blanc, Lo squadrone bianco*). The propagandistic exigencies of World War II made this situation unacceptable. In the spring of 1941, even as Emperor Haile Selassie returned triumphantly to Addis Ababa, the Ministry of Popular Culture formed the Committee for War and Political Cinema to exert greater control over features. Films on imperial themes now came under this aegis. The committee took over preventive censorship duties, examining all war-themed treatments (twenty-two of seventy were approved) and drafted a multi-year production plan for movies that would celebrate specific units of the armed forces on the war's major battlefronts. Films for children and historical films "with reference to actuality" figured in the mix, such as "a great historical anti-Jewish film" that would presumably compete with *Jud Süss*. That film was never made, probably for reasons of the export market, but Pavolini reminded the industry that Italian cinema was "a cinema at war, in war, that is, with the Jews of Hollywood, with the filmic slavery that comes from having foreign lifestyles impoverish our land through the screen."[1]

With more stringent controls came new patronage opportunities for commercial film directors. Pavolini boasted that twenty-five new directors were scheduled to debut in features then in planning or production. Such new energies and youthful points of view were needed to tackle the difficulties of making features that would encourage young men to fight even as losses mounted. An article by Fascist journalist Asvero Gravelli about the making of the Libyan-set war film he co-scripted, *Giarabub* (Alessandrini, 1942), gives an idea of the creative costs of committee jobs and how the regime intended to use films to manage public knowledge of a dire situation, in this case the desperate stand of Italian troops against the Allies in the oasis town of Jarabub. Military advisers monitored its authenticity as a combat film, but propaganda points determined its plot, above all the mandate to showcase "the masterful performance of the Royal Italian Army" during a state of siege. The mandate to portray the fort's commanding officer (played by the sturdy and jovial Carlo Ninchi) as "an active, strong-willed, reflective and calm" *capo* rather than as "a yelling and hysterical individual" translated into a strategy of linguistic minimalism, with "every word weighed and relevant to [a] situation" that Gravelli summed up starkly: "We are reduced to the bone" (*siamo all'osso*). Perhaps Ninchi overcompensated: one critic found him fatherly but "grey and indeterminate" as a protagonist.[2]

This is one endpoint of the militarized screen masculinity discussed throughout this book. As we have seen, empire films were structured around stories of male abjection and redemption that moved them beyond the desiring body. The plots of World War II films largely subtracted such conversion story lines. The dramatic tasks of leading men revolved around holding their ground, in fending off the threats that came from a war going badly. Although the display of military and communications technology continued, the body that controlled such technologies was increasingly vulnerable, its own movements severely constricted. By 1942, when the committee films *Bengasi* and *Un pilota ritorna* were made, the breached boundaries dramatized in *Sentinelle di bronzo* had become a reality. In the final years of the regime, the Italian leading man staged a different story, that of the violation and dismembering of Fascist Italy and its empire, as rendered by imprisonments and mutilations of white as well as black bodies.

Against this backdrop, female protagonists acquire a new mobility and agency. Doris Duranti, banished from the plantation in *Sotto la Croce del*

Sud, reappears as a nomadic figure in *Giarabub,* her story line placing her among the many Italian residents of Ethiopia who fled to Libya after the fall of Italian East Africa. Stranded in the death trap of the Jarabub fort, she transforms herself from a prostitute with a fake foreign name (Dolores) into a nurse who cares for the many and growing wounded. While *Cinema*'s critic complained about the clichéd nature of this transformation, another reviewer defended her presence. "Whoever knows colonial warfare knows the importance of a woman's smile amidst the desert dunes, which is sometimes greater than that of bread and water." The aggressive homosociality of empire films did not disappear during World War II. The original story of *Un pilota ritorna* had no female characters, and *Giarabub*'s second female protagonist, also a prostitute, was eliminated at the last minute. Yet women characters could not easily be excluded from representations of a total war that breached boundaries between military and civilian, public and private—and women spectators were the fastest-growing part of cinema audiences. Both *Bengasi* and *Un pilota ritorna* showcase female bravery and, like contemporary German films, make space for "war women" who shared the hardships of male characters.[3] But women also have the burden of manifesting the psychological crises of the mutilated men who populate the empire film in its wartime iteration. By 1942 their role is less that of generating life for the future than preserving life in the present national emergency.

UN PILOTA RITORNA: THE END OF THE IMPERIAL EYE

From the early 1930s onward, the emblem of Fascist manhood had been the aviator, reflecting the importance of flight for the regime as a vehicle of international prestige and as a means of charting the imperial-diasporic nation. Italian military pilot Giorgio Cannonieri had evoked both in 1937, writing that "aviation is the eye, the arm, the immediate means through which empires are conquered and held [and] the tie that binds those close by with those far away," but the aerial photograph he placed on the cover of his Ethiopian memoir emphasized its bellicose uses.[4] By the early 1940s improved imaging technologies had given such photographs a larger military role, even as their anaesthetic quality continued to account for part of their aesthetic appeal: abstracting inhabited territory, eclipsing individuals, they allowed for the myth of an imperial expansion over empty land that incurred no real victims, "allowing a perceptual distance between beholders and the scene of ruination." Italian Air Force photographs from 1941 that record the aftereffects of bombings in Albania, Greece, and Yugoslavia maintain that perceptual distance by depicting depopulated spaces, with the occasional donkey the only sign of life. One year later, the air force established a dedicated unit (the Autonomous Aerophotographic Section) to interpret images for the purposes of reconnaissance and assessment of strategy and bombing efficacy. All combatant powers had such units, but this one felt the effects of a losing war. Of the twenty-seven flights the unit sent to North Africa between March and May 1942, only seventeen were able to take any photos due to constant attacks by enemy aircraft. *Cinema* gave the unit a two-page spread, though, celebrating its efficiency in terms usually reserved for Luce operations: "When the aircraft lands, all the material filmed during the flight is already ready for editing." Mesmerizing aerial images of targeted and actual imperial possessions circulated publicly throughout the war, not least through Luce documentaries such as *Ali fasciste: Attività della nostra aviazione nel Mediterraneo orientale/Fascist Wings: Our Aviation's Activity in the Eastern Mediterranean* (1940), which closely anticipates the shot sequences and framings of *Un pilota ritorna*'s aerial scenes.[5]

Un pilota ritorna appeared at the peak of the Fascist cinema industry's second "aeronautical moment," with makers of empire films prominent in this new wave of movies. The success of *Luciano Serra, pilota* and Luce aviation documentaries had led to initiatives such as 1939's *La Conquista dell'aria*, the Italian version of the docufiction *The Conquest of the Air* (Alexander Korda, 1936), which reenacted the history of attempts at flight from Icarus onward. Marcellini, fresh from his aviation documentary *Los Novios de la Muerte*, directed the movie, writing the script along with Comin (*Sotto la Croce del Sud*) and Freddi (*Il grande appello*); Craveri and composer Veretti (*Lo squadrone bianco*) also participated. Aerial themes engaged established feature directors (Alessandrini and Camerini) as well as newcomers from the sphere of documentary (Giorgio Ferroni, Gianni Franciolini); Comerio's early aviation films were restored by young documentarian Domenico Paolella; Mondadori issued *Mussolini aviatore/Mussolini Aviator*, a collection of the Duce's air-themed speeches; and the naval stalwart De Robertis even sketched a project for an aviation film. The Committee for War and Political Cinema planned three films on flight (*Un pilota ritorna, Piloti,* and *Sentinelle azzurre/Blue Sentinels*), and although only the first was made, the title of the last signals the effects of the loss of Africa on empire film culture. With no more *sentinelle di bronzo* to command on the ground in Somalia, and imperial landscapes costly to re-create in Italy, attention shifted to Italian aviators—the vanguard of Italian imperialism—and to the spectacle provided by aerial battlegrounds, which looked the same wherever they were filmed.[6]

As had been the case with African-set empire film at its peak, Italian critics culled Italian cinema to trace genealogies of aviation movies. *Luciano Serra, pilota* was a focal point for R. G., who credited the surge of interest to the "dramatic actuality of the air war," but the paucity of Italian features meant that the author cited many Luce films and foreign productions ranging from German war documentaries to features by King Vidor and Howard Hawks. This critic saw aviation films as an international genre, starting with civil aviation documentaries that showed resemblances "in their open propaganda, their techniques, their sequences and their editing," regardless of their country of origin. As for features, although American films were no longer shown in Italy, he mentioned the "competition" from Hollywood films such as Michael Curtiz's *Dive Bomber* and Mitchell Leisen's *I Wanted Wings*, both from 1941.[7]

It is telling that inset into this article, as a kind of centerpiece, we find an homage to Rossellini written after seeing an early edit of *Un pilota ritorna.* Here and elsewhere, *Cinema* made it clear that this film would be Fascist Italy's major entry, after *Luciano Serra, pilota,* into this crowded international market and that both films stemmed from "the same necessity... to entrust to the screen the glorification of Italian aviation." This "correlation" extended to a replication, in part, of the *équipe* of the earlier film: Vittorio Mussolini reprised his role as supervisor and muse (the script took off from his story based on his bomb squad service, this time in Greece) with Franco Riganti and Luigi Giacosi again in managerial roles. But now Rossellini was director, charged with representing a war that, unlike Ethiopia, could not be won by dropping tons of chemical weapons on a population without its own aviation. And *Un pilota ritorna*'s creative group now included men of a younger generation (screenwriters included Antonioni and Massimo Mida), who wished for another model of spectacle, one that would narrate landscape not only through the magic of cinema—long takes, high shots, aerial views—but through the perceiving and feeling subject. A two-page spread on the movie asserted that this aviation picture would be guided by an ethos of realism rather than "the rhetoric and falsity" of similar American movies. "What we want to say is that *Un pilota ritorna* is a film of youth.... [I]ts principal merit is its truth: the truth of things that really happened, reality of places and actions. It was really shot in the skies of war, with real actions and pilots, and real soldiers as extras, as well as real English and Greek prisoners, and the flight scenes were shot by Roberto Rossellini himself, with his valorous helpers, at 4000 meters' height." This declaration places Rossellini's film in the tradition of empire cinema, which proclaimed its "truthful settings and action" as a way forward for Italian film on the international market, took the performances of its makers during production as a form of military service, and advertised its use of imperial subjects—now Italy's prisoners of war—in films as evidence of their domination.[8] Now those real settings were much harder to come by. Although the air-base scenes were filmed in situ, Viterbo had to stand in for the Greek countryside, and the air battles were all fought in the metropole. But, as we will see, this loose truth aids in the articulation of another order of reality, one arguably just as important to Rossellini: the emotional and human truths that emerge in situations of war. Italy is not only Greece: Greece is also an Italy marked by bombings, the wanderings of refugees, and wrenching separations.

Like many of the Fascist empire films that preceded it, *Un pilota ritorna* is structured around a series of journeys, these occasioned by the Italian campaign to conquer Greece in 1940–1941. We meet the film's protagonist, an air force pilot (Rossati), as he arrives by car at his new post, and follow him on his first bombing missions, until British airmen shoot down his plane and he becomes a prisoner of war in Greece. There, he falls in love with Anna (Michaela Belmonte), an Italian doctor's daughter, who assists Italian civilian refugees. But Rossati is at the mercy of his British and Greek captors, who shuttle him, along with other soldiers and civilians, through a series of shelters and concentration camps. The real masters of his movements, though, are the bombers of various nations who appear everywhere the ragtag group stops for rest. Bombs determine mobility in this narrative, their arrival repeatedly signaling the need to move to safer ground. The chaos of a night bombing attack allows Rossati to escape and steal the British warplane that carries him back to his Italian base, but his love story has no happy ending: he and Anna have been separated by the same vagaries of war that brought them together.

The journeys narrated in *Un pilota ritorna* were not unique to Italians. Allied airmen had similar on-screen fates. The conceit of the stolen enemy aircraft appears in the Errol Flynn vehicle *Desperate Journey* (Raoul Walsh, 1942), and the vicissitudes of the flyer stuck behind enemy lines occupy *One of Our Aircraft Is Missing* (Michael Powell, 1942). A chain of shared images, plot points, sounds, and the mixing of actors and real military men binds Allied and Fascist productions, with their bomber jackets, blondes, officer's clubs with jazz music, canteen jocularity, cockpits buzzing with engine noise, and interrogations by threatening enemy officers. We can recall the linkages of African-set empire films with the Western, British desert films, and French Legion pictures. World War II combat and occupation films likewise show the traces of a Euro-American cosmopolitanism born in the days of transition to sound, its common ground the fruit of the influence of American cinema throughout Europe, the European roots of Hollywood directors such as Michael Curtiz, and the European and American experiences of Italians such as Alessandrini and Genina. Rossellini had a different trajectory. A generation younger, he never worked abroad, and Fascism's documentary and empire film cultures provided his apprenticeships. This lack of firsthand exposure to foreign studio models left him perhaps freer to develop his own distinctive style of narrating war within a common store of characterizations and images.[9]

Within this international framework, *Un pilota ritorna* tells several Italian stories. One is about Fascism's Greek occupation. The Italians had controlled the Dodecanese Islands since 1912, but mainland Greece had remained an elusive prize throughout the Fascist period. Mussolini's 1940 invasion had intended to broadcast Italy's autonomy within the Axis, but the power of Greek resistance led to Fascist retreats. Italy ended up dividing the country with the Germans who intervened to secure victory, and both powers subjected Greek soldiers and civilians to concentration camps, burned villages, and everyday humiliations. *Un pilota ritorna*'s original story alluded to the lack of food in Greece (Italian policies had caused a famine) and joked about the fraternizations of Italian men and Greek women, but had no female character. The finished film subtracts Rossati's hunger (he is seen eating several times in Greece) and adds a love interest, but makes her Italian, so that she may fulfill her patriotic function.[10]

The other Italian story told by this film, that of a journey back to the senses by a young man educated for war, turns the empire cinema formula on its head. The conversion narrative of those features presupposed a state of male abjection made manifest, among other ways, by wayward movements of desire and the physical body. Rossellini's hegemonic male needed no such reclamation. Perfectly bland and *bello* at the start of the film— "Dear Mamma, I am here. I am all tanned from the sun. We lead a very peaceful life," he writes to his mother before his first bombing mission— his journey to Greece is rather an undoing of a Fascist perfection based on years of learning what not to see, hear, and say. Anna is the catalyst for this evolution, since it is through Anna that Rossati is drawn into experiences of war, suffering, and love that go beyond what he knew before. Critics sometimes compare Anna to Elena, the nurse of *La nave bianca,* and both do spend their screen time helping the sick and the wounded. But Elena hides a truth from her sailor (that she is his epistolary love), and her carnality behind her white uniform, while the eighteen-year-old Anna is as open as the bodies she attends. "War is a condition of non-translatability or translation failure at its most violent peak," writes Apter. The bilingual Anna never translates for Rossati, but her actions suggest ways of relating to others that overcome those failures and clash with the Manichaean universe and cult of invincibility that supported the Fascist war machine.[11]

Rossellini narrates these two intertwining stories by shifting between two notions of temporality and history. One is the time of imperial conquest, measured out by instrument panels, countdowns, and time logs. It is tracked on-screen through whizzing tanks, planes cutting through the sky, newspaper and radio propaganda, and driving musical motifs. This accelerated time mimics "Luce style," with its figures of convergence and inevitability. The other is an undirected time, tied to realms of nostalgia and memory—as in Rossati's scenes with Anna—but also to war's downtime, as in a scene in which aviators ride bikes in circles on the tarmac between bombing missions. The former temporality adheres to histories of forward movement, tracked by empire films; the latter limns a history that was not being written, or at least not by the victors. As one would expect from a film of the Committee for War and Political Cinema, the temporality and history of conquest belong to Rossati and his Italian comrades. Early in the film, Rossellini's documentary temperament translates into an attention to the quotidian, with a focus on the privileges of the officer's life. Rossati's first words are commands; valets unpack his bags; food, drink, and pretty women abound; and the modernist architecture of the air base, like the neat formations of fighter planes, is far from the messiness of war. During bombing missions, the film manifests the time of war not only through the expected means of "action" footage (dynamic cross-cuttings among the plane's exterior, its instrumentation, the pilots, and the landscape they target), but also through references to that peculiar slowing down of time experienced by aviators. A slow traveling shot of the cabin, repeated cuts to a clock whose hands show the passing of the minutes, and the buildup to the dropping of the bombs bring to mind Pavolini's sense of an appointment with destiny as his Disperata squadron targeted Adwa in 1935.

As with many nonfiction and feature works of empire cinema, *Un pilota ritorna* links the ability to make history to the possession of advanced technology and the visual vantage point. The scenes in the bomber plane emphasize the optical moment, whether it is Rossati learning to "read" the aerial landscape, watching for enemy craft, or Rossellini placing the spectator in that chain of gazes familiar from D'Errico's *Cammino degli eroi* and many other Luce documentaries. The eyes are the first link in a chain of violence that is here dematerialized, disembodied, its effects mere smoky scars on a distant landscape. The absence of non-mechanical sound and minimal dialogue also keep the focus on the faculty of sight. Rossellini hews to an aural as well as a visual realism here, but the missing human voice also signals a set of priorities. These barely individuated men have importance in function of their ability to fly and bomb, and the "white noise" of the airplane is a familiar aural presence. The pairing of this war footage with a dramatic story also adheres to the tradition of empire films, most notably *Luciano Serra, pilota,* another film featuring a plane stolen by an aviator anxious to return to Italy. Rossellini apprenticed as a feature

FIGURES 8.1 AND 8.2.

The time of conquest: Targeting Greece in *Un pilota ritorna*.
Both author's collection

filmmaker on that movie, which became one of the most profitable films of the later Fascist period, spawning several Axis versions by the time *Un pilota ritorna* went into production. A montage of documentary footage of tanks and troops moving across terrain, newspaper headlines, and the wing of a plane emblazoned with *fasci* locates this footage in a precise historical reality, channeling *Luciano Serra, pilota* and other empire films.

Yet Rossellini's unconventional mode of storytelling, with its choppy and awkward transitions, moments of disconnect between sound and image, and camera work that calls attention to the cinematographic apparatus, works against the illusionistic qualities that were the aim of classical cinema. A director like Marcellini, who also came from the realm of the documentary, may not have identified with the goal of seamlessness, and this book has argued that empire cinema provided a space to test out aesthetics that were in opposition to the Hollywood model. Yet even Fiume, who acted as a watchdog for the authenticity of empire films, argued that effective propaganda needed a smooth and continuous spectatorship experience: "that 'atmosphere' in which the public feels transported without discerning an effort or clear confines between reality and the scenic fiction." Rossellini's difference emerges here: his testing of the formula happens rather at the level of craft. *Un pilota ritorna* comes out of Italian discussions about editing, the relations of documentary and feature film, and dubbing, with at least one participant in those discussions—Antonioni—involved in this production. As Aprà notes, Rossellini's is an "elliptical and laconic film, with abrupt changes in rhythm and rich with disjunctures and rejoinings" that challenge and sometimes disorient the viewer.[12] But what is the aim of this atypical narration and of its jarring disturbances of the work that sound and image do together? One answer lies in *Un pilota ritorna*'s preoccupation with ontology. *L'Esclave blanc* and *Sotto la Croce del Sud* traced the boundaries of what it was safe to know about the Other and asserted what could not be known due to racial differences. Rossellini, too, asks what we can know, but his Other is other Italians; his interest is less ethnographic than existential. Above all, he asks *how* we can know others, calling our attention in myriad ways to a sensory and emotional intelligence.

It is in this reach to the spectator as a sensate rather than sensual being that Rossellini breaks most clearly with empire cinema. There are no objects of desire in the diegesis, other than Italy. Rossati's love for Anna has nothing carnal about it; there are no dangerous passions, no bodies filmed in an erotic or homoerotic light. The senses are re-awakened rather than ignited and then denied. In part, this stems from circumstances: like *Bengasi*, *Un pilota ritorna* depicts a state of emergency in which energies are mobilized for survival, not seduction. But Rossati's trajectory also reflects Rossellini's ambivalent attitude toward Fascism's war culture, one that was shared by others of his generation. On the ground in Greece, without the armored shell of his plane, Rossati begins to learn another way of seeing and hearing. And Rossellini experiments with another kind of spectatorial address, one that uses audiovision not to cultivate the classical cinema ideal of an "untroublesome viewing subject" who remains largely unaware of "the technological nature of film discourse," but to call attention to the man behind the camera and to the power of the gaze, from the perspective of the targeted as well as the targeter. It is this double-sided reflection that distinguishes *Un pilota ritorna* from empire film culture and gives it the status of a transition film.[13]

These meditations on audiovision within the movie begin almost at the film's inception, well before Rossati take his first journey. During his very first words with the officer who greets him at the air base, a truck drives by, drowning out their voices, which then overlap as each tries to continue the conversation. This exchange may mirror quotidian linguistic occurrences, but it startles in its roughness, as does a scene soon after that leaves the spectator in the dark, disoriented, until it is revealed that the flashes of light are made by the pulling back of curtains in the foyer of a theater. The scene of the officers' relaxation with the dancers provides an example of how this flagging of what we choose to see and hear can sometimes tread a fine line between undercutting and underscoring the work of Fascist propaganda. A woman picks up a newspaper, telling the pilots, "There's an article in the paper that talks about you." As soon as she begins to read, taking on the voice of the regime at its most rhetorical, the camera leaves her, starting an almost 360-degree pan that reveals the reactions of her listeners (flirtation, boredom, impatience), its abrupt movements also making its own presence known. Point of audition sound—a sudden increase in the volume of the diegetic popular music—also flags the listen-

FIGURE 8.3.

Listening in Italy, *Un pilota ritorna*. Author's collection

ers' distraction from the voice. Against this background, the woman reads, or tries to:

> Woman: You who are the winged heroes who plough the sky, bringing victory and glory through your hearts and your planes, offering without limits, beyond all human possibilities. You, cavaliers of . . .
>
> Officer 1, interrupting: I'm not even a cavalier.
>
> Woman, continuing: . . . modern times, who offer all of yourselves, your houses, your spouses, and your destinies. Because the future has finally . . .
>
> Officer 2, interrupting: Don't bore us with this stuff.

The camera never returns to the speaker, who is left in the everywhere-and-nowhere realm of the acousmatic with respect to the concreteness of her listeners. In one way, this scene furthers the ethos of Fascist militarized masculinity as also purveyed in De Robertis's and Rossellini's previous films: these officers are interested not in talk, but in doing their job. Yet Rossellini stages a disconnection here between ideology and its reception, between public and institutional narrative and private experience that will return again in the film.[14]

The entrance of ominous music as the second bombing mission begins signals the end of this world of masculine command and privilege. That excursion ends with the death of an Italian pilot, and the next—which is one of the most skillfully shot aviation battle scenes in Fascist cinema—concludes with Rossati parachuting out of his ravaged plane into the Greek countryside. We do not actually see his passage from one temporality to another; an ellipsis takes care of that. Rossati is suddenly surrounded by a swirl of Greeks and untranslated Greek language and quickly taken to a British military outpost. The British officers treat him decently: they are by-the-book warriors who are there to do their job, which is to "make a desert in front of the enemy." As he will in *Paisà*, Rossellini humanizes the enemy. "So you were there as well," Rossati says to a British officer while they drink whiskey and share war stories. "Of course, we were there too. It was a hard fight, very tough combat. It was our last action before we came to this awful place," the officer replies in a mix of Italian and English. After an unsuccessful escape attempt he is transferred to a decrepit country property guarded by Greeks. There he meets Anna and is exposed to the consequences of war "on the ground." As he mixes with bedraggled Italian civilians and wounded soldiers, he begins to take the full measure of the spectacle of human suffering and resilience around him. The dramatic music that accompanies the second pan of the film, this one a full 360 degrees, limns this emotional deepening.

Enrique Seknadje-Askenazi sees in this moment the birth of Rossati's capacities to be a witness, but recognizes his ambiguous position: "He is a spectator of the drama of war [and] spectator in that drama." Certainly, Rossellini highlights Rossati's growing sensitivity to the emotional and physical pain of others, as when a frame transition superimposes Rossati's pensive downturned face and the ear of an ailing soldier over a young Italian boy running to his mother: they know that the boy is about to find out that his father has died. As Rick Altman contends, the marking of an internal auditor on-screen is an effective way of "luring the spectator into the diegesis," since "we are asked not to hear, but to identify with someone who can hear for us." *Un pilota ritorna* fulfills its propagandistic burden, soliciting viewers' emotions about the plight of Italians who are in Greece but could be anywhere (the property strongly resembles a *casa colonica*). The film's Italian spectators can feel for Rossati, who takes in the suffering

FIGURE 8.4.

Listening in Greece, *Un pilota ritorna*. Author's collection

not of the (Greek) other, but of other Italians: his care—and theirs—is also a patriotic act.[15]

The scene in which Rossati assists Anna and her father in amputating his comrade's leg takes his participant-observer role to a new level. Music designed to play to the emotions grows more somber over this ten-minute scene, most of which builds tension around the horrific act that is to come: a man whose leg must be cut off while he is awake, cushioned only by a bit of painkiller and cognac. The camera draws back as the moment nears, setting up a tableau that places a Greek guard in the foreground. We experience the moment of the cut not only through the patient's virile grunt but also through the guard's reaction: he cringes and covers his eyes. This scene drew complaints from De Santis that it slowed down the main narrative, but it is one of the most fundamental of the film in terms of its engagement with the spectator. It carries forth a larger history of the spectacle of the body's violation by technologies that include the cinematic apparatus, a history Walter Benjamin drew on in comparing the filmmaker to a surgeon while discussing cinema's "shock effects." It also initiates a reflection about the ethical dimension of the acts of watching and producing images that will be developed in future Rossellini films (most famously *Roma*

FIGURE 8.5.

The breached body in *Un pilota ritorna*. Author's collection

città aperta, in which the viewer watches a priest watching an Italian Resistance operative being tortured by the Germans).[16]

The spectacle of bodily intervention staged here works to the advantage of the Italians. Although they are the occupiers, it is the Greek who hears the effects of the mortification of Italian flesh, and his empathetic reaction validates Italian victimhood. But the guard's placement in the scene also draws audiences into the spectacle of a suffering humanity that is presumably beyond boundaries of ally and enemy. Rossellini's film also opens here to a humanitarianism that pits the state, any state, against its servants, exposing the gap between "institutional histories of the body as a productive, politically worthy laboring instrument, and histories of subjectivity that examine the ways in which the human body is understood as a locus of pain, suffering, and injury."[17] We have seen lacerated suffering bodies before in this book: in *Sentinelle di bronzo*'s whipped and castrated men, in Georges's knife wounds, and in the embedding of the squadrist dagger in flesh in *Luciano Serra, pilota*. Those were indigenous bodies, though—or bodies that had crossed the color line—as were the bodies shown in the montage sequences of *L'Esclave blanc* and *Sotto la Croce del Sud*, which modeled slave labor to be used up by the regime and wiped out/off-screen. Italians bear the burden of both kinds of histories in Rossellini's film—they are the only injured people seen in the film—but the director also comments, through those Italians, on the war's brutalizations of soldiers and civilians of any nation.

While Rossati remains intact and in his bomber jacket throughout most of the film, he, too, becomes more exposed and vulnerable. During the next leg of his journey, Italian soldiers and civilians, led by Greek soldiers, form one ragtag crowd that streams through the wrecked Greek countryside, with Rossati carrying his amputee comrade on his back. Longview and panoramic shots emphasize the material and human toll of war: decimated villages and smoking ruins replace the abstract geometries of Greece as seen from aerial viewfinders. Rossati bears the burdens of the war directly, often carrying his amputee comrade on his back. Rossellini places these Italian peregrinations within a larger international flow of wartime mobilities. Everyone is on the move in this film, regardless of nationality, yet we see no Greek civilians. The men, women, and children who trudge through the Greek countryside are marked as Italian nationals by their unaccented, fluent speech (the Greek prisoners of war who played the Greek military roles speak Greek or heavily accented Italian or English in this picture) and by Fascist newspaper headlines that protest the British taking of Italian "civilian hostages" in Greece. Yet Rossellini often shoots these nationals at a distance, which universalizes their plight as people lost in a destroyed landscape. The parents worried about their sick son become any displaced family, the tattered domestic belongings in the wagons become any refugee's, and Anna is the Samaritan who goes where he or she is needed, the woman who puts aside her needs for the good of the wartime collective. This setting, and proximity to Anna, bring out Rossati's humanity. As he listens to an old pocket watch, he tells her, "My father used to let me listen to its tick-tock, holding it to my ear," and enters into the space of intimate memory and into a different temporality than the countdown to violence tracked by the clock in his plane. Anna's connection to that alternate and private realm is sealed toward the end of the film, when she tells Rossati, "I will wait for you forever."

FIGURES 8.6 AND 8.7.

Other temporalities: Ruin and memory in *Un pilota ritorna*.
Both author's collection

Yet another bombing attack interrupts this reverie, and Rossati warns of its German origin, yelling, "Stukas, Stukas!" as British, Greeks, and Italians all endure a harrowing and lengthy strafing. The film's original story also featured a Stuka bombing, and instructions to stage its deadly effects on the landscape—"Nature itself seemed shocked amidst so much destruction"—but also includes a friendly encounter with German troops that begins with a Heil Hitler and Viva Mussolini and ends with a shared cognac. In the movie the Germans do not share in the hardships of war; they only seminate death, and the bomber is the only time Germans are seen or mentioned. The universalizing tendencies of Rossellini's representations complicate the apportioning of victory and victimhood along national lines, though. The close-up we see of the British bomber who downed Rossati's plane has nothing "British" about him. His body surface shows just the bare necessities of the bomber's craft. The German bomber inside the attacking Stuka is a different kind of abstraction: we never see him, but only take up his target position. These two shots, though distant in the film, combine to stand for all bombers, who operate in a Greece-Italy that is also the Everyman's land of war.[18]

Rossati's desire to return to Italy guides the last segment of the film, in which he escapes from his final confinement space and flies home in the stolen plane. This stop at Pargas concentration camp also occasions one last sound-image scramble. Rossati sees comrades from his downed plane, but as he tries to reach them they are all caught in a swirling, pushing crowd that fills the frame. Voices and visions of the protagonists of this scene fade in and out, but the dubbed voices also separate from their speakers, as though the dubbers had grown careless here. It is probable that Rossellini wished to simulate in spectators the experience of being part of that chaotic action, but the effect is to reveal, rather than conceal, the apparatus at work. Chion has written of dubbing as a kind of doubling: "Sound loiters around the image like the voice around the body.... [D]ubbing produces a palimpsest beneath which there runs a ghost-text." And Rossati's dialogue here does contain a haunting ellipsis, "It's been eleven days since ... so many things have happened," elides not only his capture but his immersion in another world. Soon after, amid shrieking sirens, he asks Anna to flee with him to Italy, but both must do their duty—she to her father and his patients, he to his country. Rossati arrives at his

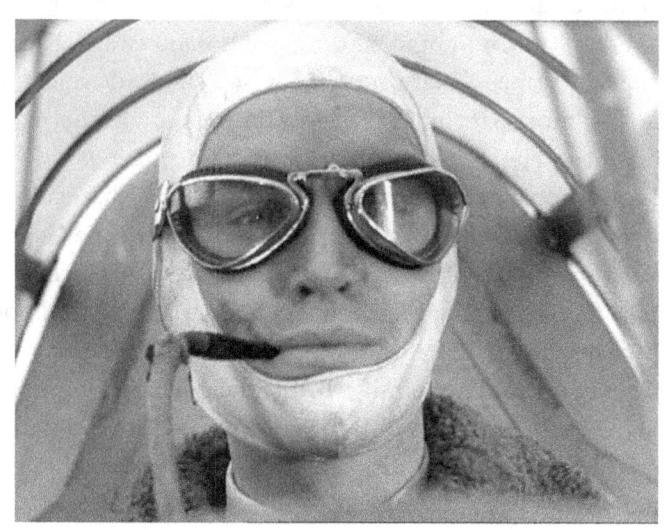

FIGURES 8.8 AND 8.9.

Unmarked enemy, uncertain victor, *Un pilota ritorna*. Both author's collection

home base safely, but wears an ambiguous expression in the movie's final frame. Is he torn by his love for Anna, exhausted by his flight, or haunted by what he has experienced on the receiving end of the war machine? It is left to the spectator to make that interpretive leap, but under his uniform Rossati has changed: part of him is "elsewhere," despite his reunion with the patria.[19]

In the tradition of empire films, the regime's publicity machine framed the production of *Un pilota ritorna* as a martial endeavor. Screenwriter Rosario Leone painted Rossellini as an imperial warrior who had already logged "two hundred flight hours in the skies of Africa, Italy, and the Mediterranean." On this shoot, Rossellini "always shared with the pilots assigned to the film those flight risks that no one would ever think belonged to the profession of film director." Since those scenes took place in the skies above Viterbo, the risks came from the making of the film, not from battle; three soldiers lost their lives transporting explosives to be used in the production. Publicly, though, the film press tried to capture some of the excitement that inhered in past productions shot in Africa, speaking of sleepy Viterbo's exposure to "the enormous motors of our airplanes that glorified the pages of heroism written by Italian pilots during the recent combat." And as with other films associated with the Committee for War and Political Cinema, its launch was a highly orchestrated event, featuring many high political and military dignitaries and free screenings for air force personnel and soldiers. It did fairly well at major first-run theaters, remaining two weeks at the Supercinema in Rome, but was among the least successful committee films among Florentine audiences, staying only forty-eight days in theaters there, as opposed to an average of sixty-three days for its other films released in 1942.[20]

Most critics did not comment on the narrative and technical unconventionalities of *Un pilota ritorna*. Instead, they lauded what was by then familiar from empire films: the use of non-professional actors, the understated affect of the officers, and the anti-rhetorical qualities, as well as what was new: the humanity of his portrayal of war.[21] Two reviews stand out for their contrasting views of Rossellini's distinctive mode of filmmaking. Càllari's represents a reaction from within the culture of empire cinema. He praises Rossellini's abilities to make the war "relived, rather than seen" for spectators and his renunciation of "any and all rhetorical concessions."

By the spring of 1942, Italian East Africa no longer existed and parts of Libya had fallen into Allied hands several times. Càllari's review focuses on the director's style more than on its subject. With Greece represented by Viterbo, the crafting of "pure and essential cinema" is what counts, not ethnographic authenticity:

> Rossellini is a synthetic director.... [D]ialogue, action, and camera movement seem to have an intrinsic rather than functional value for him.... [H]e goes right to the point, he does not fall in love with the frame, forgetting about the film.... [H]e keeps to the essential triad of camera, actor, and script ... and is able to illuminate and focalize (not through the camera lens, but through the mental and emotional world of the spectator) a character who tells a story [through] the expression of his face [or] with just one word.

Càllari looks beyond empire films, to the future of Italian filmmaking—De Sica is among the other "new forces in our cinema" he discusses—ending with an exhortation to Rossellini to pursue his particular path: "Attention to your next film: no commercial concessions, please!" [22] That next film, *L'uomo della croce,* stepped back from these audiovisual experimentations, but its religious themes and melodramatic touches would carry over in Rossellini's work from imperial to anti-Fascist culture, as would his brother Renzo's music: the dramatic motifs sketched in *Sotto la Croce del Sud* took further shape in *La nave bianca, Un pilota ritorna,* and *L'uomo della croce,* developing fully in *Roma città aperta.*

Un pilota ritorna provoked a more critical reaction from De Santis, who was a generation younger than Càllari and an opponent of Fascism's imperialist ventures. De Santis formed part of a group of intellectuals who looked to realism as a way forth for the Italian cinema. Rather than the documentary aesthetic rooted in Fascist reality that inspired empire and war cinema, the realism of De Santis and his peers was anchored in the "poetry of man" and took Giovanni Verga's literary *verismo* as one model of "a revolutionary art inspired by a humanity that suffers and hopes." The titles of the articles by De Santis, Pietrangeli, and literary critic Mario Alicata in *Cinema* ("The Language of Relationships," "For an Italian Landscape," "Truth and Poetry: Verga and Italian Cinema") lay out a program for an Italian cinematic aesthetic based not on technology's hard gazes, remote aerial landscapes, choreographed bodies, and conquest narratives but on a compassionate and human-centered view that privileged small stories and quotidian actions. This cinematic and political sensibility guided De Santis's reaction to *Un pilota ritorna*, which suffered from a lack of "human penetration," as manifested in its superficially drawn characters. Rossellini might have followed Renoir's inspiration in *La grande illusion*, another prisoner-of-war feature, or continued with nonfiction, since at least Luce documentaries, "in bringing us clips of real war, raise the 'documented' reality to the level of epic expression by virtue of a perfect balance, certainly spontaneous, between subject and object, form and content." Instead, Rossellini had made a fiction film weighed down by a "documentarism [that] does not manage, if not in rare frames, to become transfigured into essential poetry."²³

De Santis did not like or understand Rossellini's technical experimentations. The list of the latter's "defects, limitations, and errors" in this film included technically deficient sound, digressive sequences, the recourse to spectacular "effects" to manipulate the public, and conflicting representations of temporality. Above all, De Santis had a different conception of the political function of cinema, which in his mind involved the creation of "a general conscience, without restrictions, so that every man would feel indissolubly linked to others in a relation of rights and duties with others ... reawakening hope and knowledge in troubled souls." The severity of De Santis's comments about Rossellini suggests a sense of anguish at a missed opportunity by someone who could be a kindred spirit. Rossati's awakening in *Un pilota ritorna* is undercut at the end: he returns home to his air base, and he will certainly bomb again. De Santis's reference to the film's subject matter as "that particular splitting open of history/ *squarcio di storia*" expresses his distaste at the imperialist violence that it glorifies. All these feelings lay behind De Santis's public exhortation to Rossellini to reflect on the path he was taking by making films for the Committee for War and Political Cinema: "Each one of us will feel the precise duty to contribute everyday one small stone toward the construction of that future for which we should all feel responsible promoters; he will be conscious of this before he becomes involve in a tumultuous struggle that risks dragging his soul to a place devoid of any clear direction. The laws that lump humanity together, giving the intellectual the same functions as the soldier, are difficult to understand, if not beyond scrutiny altogether." Here De Santis also takes on the militarization of the filmmaker that characterized empire cinema culture since the Ethiopian invasion. As we have seen throughout this book, Vittorio Mussolini served as éminence grise of that culture, and De Santis pointedly directs his review-manifesto not only to Rossellini, but to all "the authors of *Un pilota ritorna*" who, as everyone reading *Cinema* knew, also included the Duce's son.[24]

We have arrived at a quite different moment from the optimistic days of the Ethiopian invasion. By 1942 Italy's weak military position was all too evident. Instead of *mare nostrum,* the Mediterranean had become "a sea of fear," and the staged bombings Italians fled in Greece-Viterbo alternated with real bombings that afflicted all of Italy. We may return here to Gabriel's contention that films may constitute an alternate historiography, one that narrates through fragments and the evocation of feelings and fears. *Un pilota ritorna* is a film of fragments, and in the space between these fragments looms the specter of loss: this pilot returned, but many others did not. Rossellini's film, and De Santis's critique of it, testifies to a new climate that developed in 1942, a year in which mounting civilian and military deaths, on top of the loss of East Africa, called into question the dictatorship's imperial causes.[25] *Bengasi,* the last film I examine, also grapples with the crumbling of empire and the end of the cult of the invincible male body. Although Genina's movie disappeared quickly from Italian screens due to Italy's defeat in North Africa, in it empire cinema transitions into the occupation drama. It would fall to Rossellini to take its lessons, and those of his own Fascist war trilogy, and make *Roma città aperta* at the close of the war.

BENGASI OPEN CITY: MOBILITY AND THE UNDOING OF EMPIRE CINEMA

Bengasi offers a study in paradoxes. It represents the apotheosis of imperial filmmaking as a heroic male endeavor, yet it is a film about the crisis of Italian male agency. Conceived as a dramatic feature about actuality, done in a documentary style, it became an entirely studio-shot movie, when "Benghazi" had to be re-created on empty land near Cinecittà due to the loss of the city to the Allies while it was in production. It celebrated the heroic resistance of Italians during the British occupation of the city between February and April 1941, but Benghazi was definitively lost soon after it appeared. And although in terms of state investment this Scalera production marked the peak of the Fascist-era studio system, *Bengasi* departed from the conventions of that system and from imperial stories that rotate around the vicissitudes of one of two hegemonic males. Nazzari and Giachetti have major roles, but the female leads receive equal billing and visual treatment in the film's publicity and equal weight in the film's four storylines. These involve Enrico and Clara (Giachetti and Maria De Tasnady), a married couple who lose their child in a bombing; Filippo and Giuliana (Nazzari and Vivi Gioi), an Italian intelligence operative and a professional woman stranded in Benghazi who start a relationship; a prostitute, Fanny, who hides the Italian soldier Antonio (Laura Redy and Felice Gentile); and a peasant mother and Giovanni, her blind soldier son (Amelia Rossi and Carlo Tamberlani). This narrative structure means that Nazzari and Giachetti do not dominate the screen, but are simply part of a fresco of life during a total war that places civilians and military, women and men, together on the same plane of patriotic service and suffering. This departure from the empire cinema formula answered desires for portrayals of "life as lived by civilian populations in one of the most terrible conflicts in recorded History," but Genina took a gamble in making an imperial film without an anchoring officer. *Bengasi* includes Italian authority figures, including the Podestà of Benghazi, but they do not wear military uniforms for most of the film. Although military films were made until the fall of the regime, this work marks the end of the costumed male body of Fascist empire cinema and, with it, the certainty of imperial rule as celebrated from Genina's own *Lo squadrone bianco* onward through choreographed bodies, male-only spaces, and chains of command. As it celebrates Italian resilience and courage during the British occupation, it also communicates the chaos and dejection that came with military defeat and the loss of imperial control through images of ragged crowds, crammed into shelters and apartments; men and women in flight from bombs and the British; families separated; and an indigenous population left on its own between Italians and British who come and go.[26]

Genina was perhaps the best suited among Italian directors of empire films to take on this difficult project—making a film about military victory in a context of military defeat. The director's filmic curriculum was much longer and broader than the Fascist cinema industry, which made him the object of admiration and resentment. *Lo squadrone bianco* had done much better abroad than in Italy, and the French origins and tone of that film left critics wondering, years later, if Genina were not just "a happy seeker of picturesque motifs like the white *meharists* of Africa." After the critical and box-office success of his Spanish Civil War film *L'assedio dell'Alcazar/The Siege of Alcazar* (1940), his career had been the subject of several assessments that grappled with his long expatriate period and the mark of foreign tendencies within his cinematic aesthetic. Puck concluded that Genina was in a different class than other Italian directors, but others persisted. "Who is this new Genina [who] runs like Caesar from continent to continent, wherever the horn of war sounds?" asked Eugenio Giovannetti in November 1941, as *Bengasi* was in production.[27]

L'assedio dell'Alcazar had made Genina an Axis star, and the regime was ready to invest in him and in another Libya-based project. Libya had been strangely absent from Italian screens since *Lo squadrone bianco*. Balbo's buildup of the tourist infrastructure, and the successful transfer of tens of thousands of Italian colonists there in 1938–1939, should have made Libya attractive as a location. East Africa rather than North Africa was the regime's filmic priority, though, and even as Libya was incorporated into Italy in 1939, a commentator complained that "for the Italian cinema Libya does not exist, which is very sad to acknowledge for those of us who live and work on the Fourth Shore." Attention shifted to Libya when it became Fascist Italy's only remaining holding in Africa, but by then military circumstances made filming on location there risky. Genina had enough political capital and box-office clout for Scalera and the government to agree to see the project through, at whatever cost, but other productions set in Libya did not see the light. Gino Talamo, director of the ill-received 1939 empire film *Uragano ai tropici/Hurricane in the Tropics*, took his troupe to Libya late in 1942 to make *I cavalieri del deserto/The Cavaliers of the Desert*. Axis forces had re-conquered the country in January, but a month into filming the Allies triumphed again, and the production had to flee back to Italy. The project, which adapted an Emilio Salgari novel, involved empire film veterans such as Vittorio Mussolini (co-screenwriter), Renzo Rossellini (music), and Angelo Jannarelli (photographer and supervisor of the documentary *La battaglia dello Jonio*) as well as a new entrant, Federico

Fellini, who wrote the treatment and the script together with Mussolini Jr. Years later, Fellini recalled the dangerous passage through "that piece of *mare nostrum* which was no longer really ours" as a dramatic introduction into the realities of film production and Italy's military situation. Talamo never finished the production, which in any case showcased a land soon to be lost for good.[28]

Genina faced a different order of difficulty in shooting *Bengasi*. As he had for *L'assedio dell'Alcazar*, which was shot partly on location in Spain, he and his team did extensive background research. They interviewed hundreds of former Benghazi residents to "awaken in them memories of every particular, even those of apparently little importance," and read informers' reports and correspondence to gain an idea of the psychological and political atmosphere during the months of British occupation. This preparation came in handy when Benghazi fell to the Allies, ending plans for location shooting and necessitating the re-creation of the city on land near Cinecittà. Genina dispatched four photographers to Benghazi, who spent four months documenting every detail, down to the pattern of the tile on the floor of the municipality, where some key scenes take place. Luce still and moving images from Benghazi also took on new importance. Many reviews, as well as the film's press book, testify to its status as one of the largest and most costly Italian productions since *Cabiria*: tens of thousands of workers used sixty miles' worth of wood to build the sets through which passed fifty tanks, one hundred trucks, and twelve airplanes. The production defined 160 distinct roles for actors and utilized fifty thousand extras and five thousand Italian military men. In the tradition of empire films, there were colonial and military consultants, among which we find Masoero, the former head of the Air Force Cinema Unit who had worked on *Luciano Serra, pilota*.[29]

That the economically strapped dictatorship went ahead with a gargantuan production that took human and other resources away from the war is a measure of how important the cinema had become for the Fascists. Within the Axis bloc they had proved their worth as avenues of international influence and prestige. At home, and for Italian troops abroad, they stepped in to manage a national drama of wartime devastation. By 1942 the on-screen spectacle of bomb-ravaged Benghazi, with its soup kitchens and shelters, was also the off-screen spectacle of metropolitan

Italy: the film has a double address to and for the national spectator. At the same time, it tells stories of life in an imperial "open city" that could not be told in an Italian setting, at least not until after July 1943. *Bengasi* offers the vision of Fascist officials displaced from power, suspected spies beaten up by the populace, and prostitutes acting as patriots. In staging the loss and recapture of the last piece of Italian Africa, this film addresses transitions of identity and sentiment at the national, familial, and personal level.

Empire filmmakers had always asserted the authenticity and historical relevance of their works in positioning them as the chroniclers of Fascist imperial expansion. Here, too, we find the accent on documentation and the enormous efforts made to ensure accuracy. But *Bengasi* aims to connect with the spectator through emotional as well as ambiental realism. The setting of each of the four stories of interpersonal drama and intrigue in a broad collective framework and the prominence of women characters in the movie both work toward this emotional connection, as does the Manichaean division between good Italians and reprehensible British and Australians. Such stark divisions bespeak the presence of melodrama, as does the use of high-contrast lighting and music to express psychological states and the creation of situations of pathos, in which spectators have privileged knowledge of characters' desolations and share in their apprehension (in both senses of the word). Composer Renzo Rossellini lauded Veretti's use of music to delineate character and to voice "passions which are lived entirely internally." Francesco Pasinetti highlighted *Bengasi*'s attempts to "pull at the sentimental cords of the spectator, bringing to experience anxiety, surprise, deep feeling, and enthusiasm" and saw the film as the *summa* of Genina's intimist *and* propagandist persuasions. The efforts taken by the filmmakers to achieve an accurate rendering of the reality of Benghazi under British occupation are thus legible in function of the prominence of melodrama in the film: spectators' belief in the indexical quality of what they are seeing heightens the impact of what is not shown but referenced through gesture, music, vocality, and mise-en-scène. The melding of personal and public dramas is also made possible by the war's destruction of the private sphere. Conflict-ridden encounters take place not only in family dwellings, as in traditional melodrama, but in bomb shelters, stairwells, and gardens. And those story lines are themselves interwoven, since those dwellings are now shared, with intimate and domestic dramas open to the eyes and advice of others. This is why many critics saw the film's true protagonist as "the crowd," its many visages melding into "a single face lined with tears," its many trials stemming from a single fact: Italians' victimization by foreign invaders.[30]

Yet *Bengasi* differs from previous empire films that sought to mobilize Italians. The Italians retake the city, anchoring Fascist imperial macro-history, but the four micro-histories are mostly left *in sospeso*, their protagonists nowhere to be seen in the film's final triumphant sequences, which feature thousands of anonymous civilian extras that flood the streets, carrying Italian and Nazi flags. The unresolved fate of these leads haunts this celebratory ending, but continues a theme of present absences that runs throughout the film and is manifested in the missing limbs and senses of mutilated male characters and in the loss of place and historical purpose of an entire population. The rigorously collective finale also reaffirms the movie's emphasis throughout on the universal sentiments and situations contained in the historical particular. Many of the male characters of the four story lines connect to a history of imperial figures that are traceable in previous empire films and their intertexts (military commanders, owners of agricultural concessions), while female characters reference archetypes of womanhood (mother, wife, prostitute). New characters also emerge in this film of 1942 that depart from empire cinema but connect to broader wartime cinematic trends inside and outside of Italy: the child, seen as a victim of family strife and war; the single professional woman, seen in a positive light; and the ambiguous male operative, outfitted in civilian clothing. My analysis departs from the film's gender characterizations and poses broader questions of how *Bengasi* engages with the visual and aural practices that characterized many past empire films and how it registers the crisis of Fascist imperial history and cinema's place as that history's privileged interpreter.

Let us begin with the figure of the peasant mother: celebrated by the regime for her fecundity, essential for the success of Fascism's "demographic colonization," and excluded from previous empire films. This unnamed woman of limited horizons has traveled from her farm to Benghazi to look for her soldier son and stands for generations of tenacious women who migrated to the colonies, raising children now called to military duty.

She finds her son, only to discover he is now blind, and then returns with him to their farm to find it ruined by the Allies and her husband dead. Genina tells this colonial and family tragedy through realism tinged with melodrama and by moments of visual apprehension that, as elsewhere in the film, mark a turning point in the story line. This one comes when the mother spots her son by chance in a hospital garden. Genina tracks the instance of recognition and the rush to reunion, but foregoes close-ups for frames that keep the open-air setting and Giovanni's wounded comrades in the picture, as befits the depiction of the war as a collective drama.

The realist feel continues on their journey back to the farm, with the focus initially the natural setting, until sound steps up to express war's horrors. We cut to the patriarch Piero assailed by rowdy Australian soldiers who destroy the property, shooting his pets and sacking his house in search of liquor and valuables. The strapping men speak indistinctly among themselves, laughing at Piero's remonstrations in an Italian they do not understand. Their cruel laughter constitutes a sound act that parallels their physical acts of deturpation, and the soundscape of mockery it creates echoes throughout this sequence. They shoot him dead when he resists with a spade after they begin to wreck his plants, saying, in true peasant fashion, "No. Not the earth." When the mother and son arrive, the spectator is privy to this awful story and to the burden the mother assumes when she chooses not to say anything to her son. But as Giovanni settles into his home garden, blissfully embracing a tree, she races through the devastated property, calling frantically for her husband. Soon she is off-screen, but her echoing voice, less a feminine scream than a powerful yell, continues, as does the spectacularly anempathetic pastoral score. The pathos lies here, in those horrors the spectator already knows about and the horrors yet to come: finding the body, shattering Giovanni's illusions, going on with no husband and an impaired son. The story line ends here, but there is nothing silent about this vocalization, which reverberates beyond the episode and beyond the frame, expressing the ruination of decades of peasant toil and imperial aspiration and the desperation of all mothers. Sound makes vain the titles' promise to show the viewer how women "bear the most profound sacrifices of the war with the most silent faith."[31]

A different play of sound and image informs the story line devoted to Fanny, a prostitute who hides the wounded soldier Antonio in her lodg-

FIGURES 8.10, 8.11, 8.12.

A mother's love, the enemy's mockery, *Bengasi*. All author's collection

ings at great personal risk. *Bengasi* gives to Fanny, and not to an Italian man, the conversion narrative that informed past empire films. Over the course of the movie she sheds her makeup and her French-tinged name and gains the hope of a legitimate life. But Fanny becomes every Italian woman in wartime, standing in line for soup. Antonio shares war stories with her, but tells her, "You are a woman and you cannot understand certain things." *Bengasi* assigns women and men firm places in the community of suffering created by the war, but also suggests that the present need for female nurturing should overrule moral judgment. Women must bear the consequences of male silences, though, expressing through their voices and bodies what Fascist wartime masculinity does not allow to be made manifest. As men lose their limbs and their senses, women become the repositories of their phantom sights and feelings. Thus do the mother's vocalizations express what Giovanni cannot see and refuses to acknowledge; and thus does Fanny somatize a war trauma that is not only her own but that unexpressed by Antonio.

Australian brutality against men is once again the trigger for a female crisis. During a surprise search of Fanny's house, Antonio hides in a closet covered only by a thin curtain, and Fanny sits in a chair, pretending to be ill. A carousing Australian soldier, drink in hand, shoots into the curtain, and although Antonio emerges unharmed after the intruders depart, Fanny is petrified with fear; Genina holds on her terrorized figure. The film's reviewers focused on the bravery and goodness of "una povera Fanny qualunque" (a poor anyone-Fanny), but the aftereffects of her patriotic performance are equally important. Overcome by nerves, she cries and laughs hysterically. Antonio lays her on the bed to calm her, lending an intimacy to the intense scene that, in other circumstances, might resolve in a kiss. Here, though, faith steps in, and we witness a conversion in some respects similar to that undergone by Mario in *Lo squadrone bianco*. In that film, a blackout in the desert led to the casting off of desire for Cristiana and the embrace of a life beyond the carnal realm. Here the protagonist renounces a life guided by desire and avidity, rediscovering a lost innocence. Whispering "God has helped us," Fanny tells him that her real name is Maria. The subsequent cut to the bomb shelter, where women chant "Ave Maria," underscores the religiosity of the national crusade to resist the foreign invader and the hope any woman can have to transcend her past and gain forgiveness through patriotic action. This wartime Madonna will give up her nomadic ways and return to her childhood home, in Italy, to wait for Antonio. This plot resolution puts female wartime heroism in its place, revealing anxieties about the new mobilities engendered by the conflict.[32]

Anxieties about the management of femininity that surround many melodramatic narratives come to the fore in a story line about the troubled marriage of Clara and Enrico, the latter a harsh military officer who cares only about their young son. "If it weren't for the boy I would have left long ago for my mother's in Hungary," she retorts to a local doctor who blames her for not leaving Benghazi earlier, as Enrico had ordered her to. Unlike Mailù, whose heavy robes in *Sotto la Croce del Sud* mimed her sense of constriction but offered a visual display, Clara's simple black garments efface the body, allowing her hands, her eyes, and high-contrast lighting to communicate her inner tensions and sorrow, especially when her child, Sandro, is killed after she accedes to Enrico's second attempt to get her to flee the city. Fearful of Enrico's moods, Clara cannot bring herself to tell him about the death, even when she visits him in the hospital. Veretti's score signals her distress as she rushes to find him. Pizzicatos combined with a tremolo that increases in intensity communicate the unbearable tension, with a sudden full stop when Clara and Enrico finally lock eyes. When she realizes that his arm has been amputated, she throws herself upon him, crying, and the spectator knows that her tears are not only for his fate, but for the shared loss her husband does not yet know about. When Clara returns home the doctor and other men tell her she failed in her "duty" to tell her husband, but Clara knows that Enrico will blame her for the death—as happens when he comes home, unannounced, and finds the empty crib. Unlike the mother and Fanny, she stays silent not just to protect a wounded soldier, but also to protect herself—and therein lies her transgression.

Enrico represents Genina's last iteration of the Fascist imperial officer, and his character offers a means of exploring the endpoints of Fascist militarized masculinity. Giachetti loses his uniform very early in the movie, adopting tattered civilian clothing after he becomes an underground operative. For the rest of the film, as he hides out in an abandoned building, his pristine armored self—familiar to spectators through his previous

FIGURES 8.13 AND 8.14.

War's toll on Fanny and Clara, *Bengasi*. Author's collection

empire films—remains present only in photographs that Clara keeps in their apartment. In *Lo squadrone bianco,* the picture of the officer Bettini that Giachetti, as Santelia, kept on his desk glossed that film's preoccupation with private longing and memory. In *Bengasi* the photograph of Enrico as he was signs a collective nostalgia in the making for a lost time of imperial confidence and control. Genina, long a chronicler of changes in gender roles, gestures with this film toward a different model of masculinity, one fitting a war of civil resistance fought in an urban context, where the boundaries between civilian and military participants are difficult to decipher. *Un pilota ritorna*'s male protagonist mixed with civilians, but remained in his bomber jacket throughout the movie. Genina's occupation drama takes things further, making of Enrico, and of Nazzari's Filippo, the harbingers of an armed masculinity disconnected from the Fascist uniform, if not yet from the Fascist credo.

This different masculinity, along with the conditions of total war, is accompanied by a shift in attitudes that mirrors the shedding of military dress. Enrico's combat vicissitudes cut back and forth with those of his marriage and his coming to grips with the death of his child. His reconciliation with his wife remains off-screen, but at the end of the film he admits to the doctor that his intransigent attitude toward Clara in commanding her to leave Benghazi makes him "the true guilty party" in Sandro's death. Genina also uses the child to comment on the effects of an education to Fascist imperial masculinity. Sandro plays with outsize toys of tanks and cannons, with his uniformed father watching in the photograph, and when Enrico returns Sandro tells him that their African maid is mean to him. He asks Enrico to "call the Carabinieri and have her arrested" and proceeds to sing "Vieni con me, bella bimba bruna" (Come with me, beautiful brown girl), the opening lyrics of a popular song. At five years old, Sandro has learned the Italian man's way of interacting with the colonial female population: seduction and repression. His death is the interruption of a Fascist colonial masculinity celebrated in past empire films. Genina had long explored the male potential for brutality—*Lo squadrone bianco*'s Mario took himself away to the desert after he tried to strangle Cristiana—but by the time of *Bengasi,* there was no escape from oneself or from the female universe. The shedding of the uniform, although dictated by necessity, becomes a first step in rehumanizing the

FIGURES 8.15 AND 8.16.

Enrico: Imperial officer to underground operative, *Bengasi*.
Both author's collection

Fascist man. Even at the end of the film, when the British begin to retreat and it is safe to take out arms again, most men stay in their civilian attire.

Nazzari's Filippo, who appears in uniform only in a photograph, is in theory the clearest sign of such transitions in the practice of Fascist manhood. Yet his double-agent character lives under the sign of ambivalence. Probably only Italy's most popular male actor could have played such a character, since the affective bond he enjoyed with audiences could not be easily breached. Nazzari had often played men who suffer, as in *Luciano Serra, pilota,* but not in *Bengasi:* never in crisis, nor in tatters, Nazzari is at the heart of the civilian resistance, but also somehow above the fray. The male attire he favors—a fedora and a trench coat or leather jacket—had been used in past empire films to mark negative characters (such as Simone in *Sotto la Croce del Sud*), and he is accused of spying and beaten up by the populace for his public fraternization with the British. Yet throughout the film he is lighted in a way to emphasize his *solare* and trustworthy qualities—whereas his accuser in the bomb shelter, although speaking "for the people," looks sinister in his black shirt. Filippo also stands apart as an agent of modernity with respect to the other Italians: he arrives in the ancient war-torn city of Benghazi as an engineer (his cover) and speaks perfect English, which allows him to pose as a collaborator and translator for the occupiers. Yet he is also the perfect gentleman and *cavaliere*—a role he had played at the outset of his career—showing an old-fashioned courtesy, paternalism, and nobility of spirit. As Gubitosi notes, Nazzari's persona rested on "a concentration of the positive qualities that were thought to be typical of the Italian man." He, and not the Podestà, charts a path for the future of Italian national history.[33]

As we have seen throughout this book, Fascism's empire had acted, in theory, as a container for a masculinity rendered anxious at home by female emancipation. Empire films such as *Il grande appello, Sentinelle di bronzo, Lo squadrone bianco,* and *Luciano Serra, pilota* offered comforting scenes of a male camaraderie unbothered by Italian female presence and, as in *Sentinelle di bronzo, Sotto la Croce del Sud,* and *L'Esclave blanc,* the fantasy of non-white female companionship and sexuality. In *Bengasi,* though, the empire is in shambles and its male bodies in crisis, rendering gender roles "in flux and unpredictable." Filippo's relationship with Giuliana showcases this anxiety. A chemist by training, Giuliana fled her job in Asmara after the fall of East Africa and lands in Benghazi by chance after her plane is attacked. Clad in smart, professional clothing throughout the film, Giuliana represents a female mobility enabled by empire. Giuliana differs from Fanny or Mailù, who depend on men to support themselves, and from the rich and idle Cristiana, who comes to Libya as a colonial tourist. Simone of *L'Esclave blanc* was a capable colonial administrator, but remains throughout the film under the protection of her authoritarian father. Genina's predilection for sympathetic portraits of the modern woman, expressed in early films such as *Maschiaccio/The Boyish Girl,* (1917) and *L'Ultimo Lord/The Last Lord* (1926, which features a woman dressed as a man), had been discouraged by Fascism's misogynistic atmosphere, and the character of Giuliana has no precedent in empire films. The image of her flagging down Filippo's car, running through the desert with suitcase in hand, beckons to a modernized femininity to be developed in postwar cinema.[34] When Filippo brings her a cigarette case ("[Smoking] is a vice I picked up in the colonies," she has told him), telling her

> Filippo: My duty is to take care of you,
>
> Giuliana: I think I'm capable of taking care of myself...
>
> Filippo: So you really don't trust me at all?... We are men, are we not?

The Giuliana-Filippo story line also gives a new political edge to Genina's poetics of silence and his treatment of language as a mode of symbolic domination. Giuliana sees Filippo accused of spying, offering another moment of witnessing, this one rendered in melodramatic close-up, which occasions a turning point in the narrative. Filippo has witnessed her dismay, and his need to set things right with her leads him to go to her apartment, resulting in his arrest. As will be the case with occupation films made after the fall of Fascism, the silences imposed by political action take their toll on personal relationships. Filippo is not at liberty to tell Giuliana what she needs to hear—that he is not really a spy for the British—and trust, along with empathy, must fill in for verbal communication. Through the character of Filippo, *Bengasi* also comments on the relationship between the command of language and the command of people and on the politically ambiguous role of the translator. In Genina's *Lo squadrone bianco* and other empire films, indigenous soldiers and civilians performed

FIGURES 8.17 AND 8.18.

Giuliana and Filippo, *Bengasi*. Author's collection

the task automatically, their political fidelity seemingly never in doubt. In *Bengasi,* though, the indigenous population is out of the equation, and the Italians play the role of the occupied people. Long stretches of English dialogue mark a scene in which Filippo dines with British officers, with Italian audiences left out of the joke (but admiring, perhaps, of Nazzari's linguistic abilities, since it is his voice we hear), bolstering the sense of the arrogance of Italy's colonial occupiers. When Filippo says, in English, "You're beginning to speak Italian very well," the lead officer demonstrates his prowess using mundane objects on the table—"fruit," "spoon," "glass"—finishing with a loaded statement in Italian: "I have to learn Italian to give . . . to give orders to the Italians." "What did he say?" asks another British officer in English. "He wants to give orders to the Italians," a third responds.[35]

Genina's ambivalent realism is fully enabled here. The director takes great care to achieve an accurate sound and vocal profile, reproducing the mispronunciations and halting pace typical of new English speakers of Italian. Yet he also calls attention to the unfaithfulness of language, to what lies behind and around verbal communications, as he flags as hypocritical the British officer's linguistic efforts. He also critically reflects on Fascist linguistic policies that, for reasons of prestige, discouraged language apprehension beyond that necessary to give and take orders—giving the figure of the translator an arguably greater role than in the British and French empires. It is telling that the scene's diegetic purpose is to illustrate the popular Italian maxim "Traduttore-traditore" (A translator is always a traitor), since Filippo is observed during this meal by Italians who are disgusted at his apparent collaborationism. And the British eventually realize that Filippo may speak their language perfectly, but he is not their friend. In the face of language's unreliability, Genina asserts the ethical value of silence, as in the scene of Filippo's interrogation by the British after his arrest. Although he is shown photographic evidence of his military affiliation, he refuses to give up his true identity, even when he hears he will be handed over to the War Tribunal. "I remained silent when Italians spit in my face. And you think I am going to speak now?" Filippo's status as a patriot and gentleman is sealed through this act of linguistic resistance: his last words are "I have done my duty. You are free to do yours."

Bengasi restores to view an individual agency and sovereignty eroded by the dictatorship, linking it to the right to determine when to remain silent. Women have a new prominence, and burden, in this regard, whether it is Clara's decision not to tell Enrico about their son, the mother not telling her blind son the property has been ransacked, or Fanny refusing to tell the British about the soldier she is hiding. The erosion of masculine authority can be tracked in the many instances where the fate of men depends on the actions of women and where Giovanni and other men are left in the dark. Men have lost the imperial eye and ear crucial to the issuance of imperial speech, and it is telling that communication issues plague Italian military radio operators throughout the film, Enrico among them. Filippo again constitutes an exception. As befits an intelligence operative, he is in command of the chain of communication, and his uncertain destiny at the end of the film allows him, the only man to keep his body and attire intact, to remain the agent of an Italian history in transition.

The importance of this open ending to *Bengasi*'s commentary on Italian imperial history can be further clarified by the other dramatis personae who, along with the leads, make up the diegetic space of the film: the indigenous crowd, the Italian crowd, and the Italian leader, in the person of the Podestà. In a departure from previous empire films, Libyans are mere *comparse,* or appearances, who watch silently as trucks carry the Italians and British in and out of their city. The attentive treatment given to the *meharistes* in Genina's desert film has given way to a wary distance.[36] This lessening of cinematic interest is in keeping with *Bengasi*'s transition from empire to occupation film. It is Italians, not Libyans, who hold Genina's camera. A final scene in the bomb shelter signals the shift. The worn faces of nationals now receive the same dignified treatment as *Lo squadrone bianco*'s colonial troops; instead of colonial troops lost in the desert, the subjects are the *popolo* made rootless from bombs and defeat. As in *Un pilota ritorna,* the shelter is also a refuge for Italianness in a hostile environment. As such it encompasses the institutions of Italian daily life: the church, through a scene of elderly women chanting "Ave Maria," lined up as though facing an altar; the family, through tableaux of mothers with their babies; and the piazza, through scenes of debate about Italy's future under British occupation. All of this brings to mind Blasetti's Risorgimento film *1860,* as does the moment of British retreat, when men unearth their weapons hidden in the shelter in an atmosphere of collective purpose and energy. For most of the film, though, the dramatically lit shelter is a space of a people who have become victims, their horizons of imperial possibility reduced to confinement in interior spaces.

The suit-clad Podestà is putatively a benevolent father figure to this wrecked populace, but Genina's portrait of him raises questions about the status of Fascist authority. Introduced on the occasion of his removal, he is never seen without an entourage, and he is defined through acts of translation that comment on his lack of agency: unlike Filippo, he does not know English and must have others speak for him. But in the first balcony scene of the film, when the actual transfer of power is being conducted, the Podestà refuses to read the translation of the general's statement of Italian capitulation that the British have prepared for him:

Officer: You will read this afterward (handing him a sheet)

Podestà: I refuse to read this.

Officer: As you wish, we have interpreters.

Podestà: Make them read it then.

When the Podestà abruptly leaves the balcony, the voice of the British translator follows him, its heavily accented Italian a further mockery. In his memoir–travel narrative *A Cure for Serpents,* Alberto Denti di Pirjano, who was governor of Tripoli when that city fell to the British, recounts that the body often spoke involuntarily on such occasions. During that power-transfer ceremony the Podestà's nervous tics were out of control, and "he kept one eye closed, as though taking aim. Fortunately I was not able to see what kind of show I was putting on." In *Bengasi,* the Podestà is one of many men who are not able to see, or do not want to see, what is happening around them: only Filippo remains clear-eyed and clearheaded.[37]

The juxtaposition of Filippo and the Podestà as models of Italian manhood reaches its peak in the concluding scenes of the film. Tensely awaiting the rumored arrival of Italian troops, the crowd in the shelter is rocked by blasts: the British have mined Benghazi as a parting gift. Huge explosions destroy the sets that Italian audiences knew took so much time and money to build: buildings crumble to pieces, and smoke fills the screen. Genina winks at film tradition here—most notably the imperial debris created in Griffith's *Intolerance*—and this is also the last of those foggy ellipses that in empire films model a politics of oblivion. Here it screens out the end-of-empire (melo)drama that has occupied the film in favor of a form and content taken from Fascist spectacle. The eight leads are notably absent among the Italians who stumble into the streets to celebrate the end of British occupation, but other presences make themselves known: Nazi flags, which join with Italian flags as an impromptu parade heads to the Municipality, with the open trucks of squadrist lore whizzing by. Soon the Podestà appears with other authorities, all wearing black shirts underneath their uniforms. This highly ritualized balcony scene openly channels the Luce aesthetic, a task helped by the employment of Luce narrator Guido Notari in the role of Podestà. Notari reproduces Mussolini's body language, leaning on the balcony toward his audience, and the exact pace and pitch of the Duce's delivery.

We may ask why the Duce figure has been rendered in such a literal manner. Together with the signifiers of a Nazism nowhere else represented in the film, the balcony scene gives the ending the feel of an add-on done out of political exigency. It is worth noting that by 1942 Fascist mass spectacle mostly existed on the screen: relentless bombings made outdoor gatherings risky, and the Duce himself had been uncommonly silent, giving only six public speeches during the period between Christmas 1940 and mid-May 1941. The government's inability to deal with the consequences of the war Mussolini had insisted on entering eroded the trust many Italians had placed in the Duce. His stylized "doubling" in *Bengasi* by the voice of Luce newsreels, on a false balcony of a reconstructed city, is a nod to the self-referentiality of Fascist propaganda and an acknowledgment of the inaccessibility of the real-life imperial vistas that had inspired empire films since the 1920s. *Bengasi* knows Fascism's enemies and feeds off the same anti-British wellspring as contemporary Luce newsreels, but anticipates a coming void of positive models of authority. As in *Un pilota ritorna,* the real local power politics are un-representable—here, the Germans as the true agents of the retaking of Benghazi. Whereas Rossellini opts for abstraction (the faceless German bomber), Genina adopts an emphatic theatricality. In leaving Filippo and the other protagonists of his decentered narrative outside of this solution, he flags *Bengasi*'s ambivalent relationship to the tradition of Fascist empire cinema.

FIGURES 8.19 AND 8.20.

Fadeout and Fascist Spectacle in *Bengasi*. Both author's collection

Bengasi marks a transition from empire films in other ways as well. Genina proposes a trove of visual images—hideouts, rooftop escapes, well-dressed ambivalent characters—found elsewhere in international wartime cinema but normally associated with Italian films that appeared after the fall of the dictatorship. Many scenes in *Bengasi* give the feel that something new is happening on-screen with respect to empire cinema and other Fascist-era commercial productions—as do the Greek scenes of *Un pilota ritorna* (and De Sica's 1942 *I bambini ci guardano/The Children Are Watching Us* and Visconti's 1943 *Ossessione*). This sense of freshness that critics often attribute to the presence of a new realism lies more specifically in a new relation of realism and melodrama. In *Bengasi* this melodrama is measured and contained through setting and cinematography, but used expressively to communicate the interpersonal and existential horrors of war and the challenges of popular resistance to foreign occupation. Thus, we have Giachetti and Nazzari, the two paragons of Fascist empire cinema, one in rags and the other in a trench coat and fedora, hiding in a bombed-out building and then escaping across city rooftops; the stairwell of the city apartment building as a place of danger and intimate encounter; the rhetoric of civilian resistance to the foreign invader—and the emphasis on the gendered boundaries of that resistance; the British occupiers who see Italian territory through the lens of the picturesque; the emotional toll of the destruction of private and domestic space; the otherwise faultless resistance operative whose passion for a woman causes his arrest; and the interrogations of patriots by enemy invaders who keep a map of the city behind their desk.

Like the abandonment of a unified narrative centered on a uniformed male protagonist, the above images and figures signal the start of a transition in the language of Italian cinema facilitated by the war's debilitations of Fascist authority and revivals of individual agency and perception. Mobility, as a sign of this agency, also gains a different kind of prominence: with the exception of Fanny and Antonio, all the leads are seen in moving vehicles, fleeing or returning to their homes, transiting in Benghazi for work or necessity, leaving as prisoners of war or escaping captivity. Most of these vehicles are open-air, and landscape as seen from them takes on a new value with respect to many earlier empire films. *Bengasi* features no touristic or Western vistas and no aerial hieroglyphs. The surrounding desert, glimpsed from the speeding trucks, seems empty but is far from neutral. It has become a terrain of destruction and of fear—ruled by British bombs, Australian soldiers, and the Libyan nomads who are never shown but now came back to reclaim their lands from Italian settlers. It is telling that Marcellini's Libyan documentary from this period (1941's *Piloti e fanti nel deserto sirtico/Pilots and Infantrymen in the Sirte Desert*) presented what Fiume called "an apocalyptic landscape" in which Italian soldiers "seem paralyzed and absorbed by the sea of sand." In *Bengasi*, too, the desert has become a place of no exit: instead of the mystical infinite horizon of *Lo squadrone bianco*, we have the desert as Italian tomb.[38]

In the meantime, though, the regime's massive investment in *Bengasi* translated into equally massive publicity, with dozens of premieres in Italy and throughout the Axis bloc and coverage in every major and small Italian publication. *Bengasi* won honors at the 1942 Biennale: Mussolini Cup for Best Italian film and Volpi Cup for Best Actor to Giachetti, whose role as a father, husband, mutilated officer, and resistance operative covered all the bases of Italian screen masculinity in its World War II iteration. Some critics saw Genina's film as continuing the achievements of *Lo squadrone bianco; Luciano Serra, pilota;* and the films of Rossellini and De Robertis, all of which proved Italians' skill in a difficult genre that "blends history and chronicle, politics and documentary, fantasy and reality." Fiume applauded its fidelity to actual events and its ties to empire cinema, but saw it as a product of a war that had spared no one "privations and suffering," creating protagonists who are "surprised and trampled by wartime events." Benghazi was the real protagonist of *Bengasi*, and the signs of the war were everywhere visible, "like immense wounds open on its body of Gebel white stone." Others praised the leads but labeled *Bengasi* as a "choral" film, seeing "the crowd" or "universal humanity" as this film's real star. "The passion of Bengasi becomes our passion," one concluded.[39]

Genina's film also produced a new round of reflections on the relationship between cinema and history that had engaged commenters on the imperial documentary a few years earlier. The young Giorgio Almirante felt that *Bengasi* should be a model for feature film's role in producing "histories written by the cinema," while *Film*'s critic contended that only a director with roots in the silent era would have had the courage to "take on, in the middle of a war, a film about that war, when things are still redhot and men still pained by facts that are still alive in everyone's memory." For others, that closeness to the present and those documentary pretensions were also weaknesses; their criticisms echo those made of Rossellini's film. "Vice" observed that Genina's wish to deliver "the chronicle of the nude facts of war and the human condition of war (one can think of certain crude and terrible cinematographic reportages) ... which has not yet become history" had made casualties of his characters, who lacked depth, and his sets, which had no warmth and vitality. Another cautioned that *Bengasi*'s battle scenes risked boring a public "exposed every day to war documentaries." By late 1942, the surfeit of Luce productions and two years of war had quelled appetites for those combat re-creations and Luce inserts that were the staple of the empire films of the late 1930s.[40] Another contingent of critics found fault with *Bengasi* as a commercial drama. Some could not adjust to the absence of a central male protagonist and labeled Genina's film as "fragmented" and "episodic," while others showed uncertainty about the stark divisions between Italians and the British: "All of us are good, and all the others bad," wrote Vice skeptically. Writer Guido Piovene accused Genina of depicting "an overly fertile world of mothers and fathers of children who die, of Ave Marias, of tearful peasant mothers ... and of prostitutes who dream of the church of their childhood." Yet such polarities are crucial to the address of melodrama, and the critic of the popular weekly *Illustrazione italiana* found them perfectly appropriate: "[*Bengasi* is] an excellent film of polemic and propaganda ... that contains all those elements necessary to elicit in the public pity and disgust, love and hatred." Pietrangeli felt that the presence of "celebration, gratuitous exaltation, formalistic conviction ... and insipid rhetoric" harmed the film's efficacy as propaganda.[41]

In the end, it was Vice who delivered the most devastating opinion, observing that *Bengasi* stood out for its emphasis on "quantity"—of people, resources, and scale of action. "Genina is not a poet, but rather a narrator of collective atmospheres.... [H]e's not an artist, but an artisan," with "a full consciousness of his material and himself." The anonymous critic was on to something, for quantity stood out in the film's publicity materials, starting from a full-page advertisement in *Bengasi*'s press book, entitled "Technical Data," that listed exactly how many thousands of pieces of wood, nails, extras, and everything else had been employed in the production. This was not just boasting, but went to the heart of *Bengasi*'s standing as an empire film released in the twilight of empire. Genina's film expresses the psychological disposition of *horror vacui*—a fear of the void that is often compensated for by the filling up of space. The lists of the sheer quantity of people and objects involved in the making of *Bengasi* stand in sharp contrast to the loss of everything. Presented as a Fascist imperial colossal, *Bengasi* is a monument to a ruin, not only of empire but also of a certain model of cinema that is blown up at the end, its artificiality made evident in the scenes of its destruction. "Bengasi, pearl of our Mediterranean," is already lost, its uniformed men relegated to photographs in Genina's film.[42]

Critical doubts did not keep audiences away from this cinematic extravaganza. *Bengasi* trailed only the Russian-themed blockbuster *Noi vivi/ We the Living—Addio Kira* (Alessandrini, 1942) among films made under the auspices of the Committee for War and Political Cinema. In Florence it remained in theaters for seventy-three days, which was about average for melodramas, comedies, and other popular genre films. Producer Franco Bassoli ecstatically telegraphed Genina in October 1942: "98 cinemas principal Italian cities started Bengasi today with delirious success. Box-office receipts beyond estimate representing an absolute first of all time." Similar reports of success followed the many premieres throughout the Axis bloc, with Maria de Tasnady's starring role making the Budapest opening particularly lively. Genina attended that gala event, as did Italian, German, Japanese, and other Axis diplomats. Hitler's Reich represented a notable exception to these Fascist festivities: angered at the exclusion of Nazi troops from the story of the city's recapture, Goebbels banned *Bengasi* from German screens.[43]

Bengasi also had a print afterlife, in the form of a companion text by Genina's research assistant, Alberto Bargelesi. Part reportage, part novel, *Bengasi. La città murata*, features photographs of the real Benghazi taken during pre-production. Like the *cineromanzo* version of *Luciano Serra, pilota*, Bargelesi's book extended the film's popular reach. Published by the Institute for Book Propaganda, many of its 364 pages are devoted to diatribes against Italy's enemies. As in the film, the Australians are depicted over and over again as drunken and thieving barbarians and the British officers as full of "selfrighteousness [sic] and arrogant and violent with foreigners." Although Bargelesi references "indigenous thugs," Arabs are mostly collaborative in this story: the Levantines are the real source of trouble in Benghazi. The Greeks spy on the Italians and provide the British with photographs of suspected underground members; and the Jews are greedy opportunists, part of a larger "Judaic-Masonic rabble of the decrepit plutocratic democracies" that conspires against Fascism, in Libya as in the metropole. Here Roman Catholicism brings Italians together against these enemies. The blind soldier character—who has no mother—has a religious awakening, and the book ends not with a triumphant parade of civilians but with a mass celebrated in Benghazi's Cathedral. As the war went from bad to worse, the consolations of faith featured more heavily on-screen as well, as in the 1943 movies *I trecento della Settima/The Three Hundred of the Seventh* (Mario Baffico), *Quelli della montagna/Men of the Mountain* (Aldo Vergano), and Rossellini's *L'uomo della Croce*. But the Ministry of Popular Culture rejected as "inopportune for the current moment" a proposal that year for a theater adaptation of *Bengasi* that featured a miracle: the blind soldier Giovanni regaining the faculty of sight when the Italians re-conquered the city.[44]

In the meantime, it is the *Bengasi* press book, and not the film or its print companion, that renders the situation in what remained of Italian Africa most clearly: it features an impressionistic painting of a crowd of Italian men, women, and children, running away from a smoldering city. Most of the people wear expressions ranging from the terrified to the grimacing, as though they are being pursued by a phantom. Some of the subjects are smiling, as though they are running toward someone; several men in uniforms have their arms raised, as though in a Fascist salute. Perhaps these Italians were greeting the British forces, as did the real-life soldiers and civilians who posed for British military cameramen after the fall of Tobruk, during the Allies' Operation Compass that would soon also take Benghazi. Perhaps the soldiers among them made it all the way to Tripoli, like the ones Mario Tobino encountered as they fled Cyrenaica, enacting "a triumphal march in reverse." Some of them could have returned to Italy on the same white Italian Red Cross ships that Rossellini had immortalized, which the regime had already employed to rescue Italians from East Africa. In any event, the image proved prescient, since

FIGURE 8.21.

Illustration from *Bengasi* press book. Used by permission of the Cineteca del Friuli, Fondo Genina

the film's commercial release came shortly before the city fell definitely to the British, creating thousands of refugees. The reviewer who characterized *Bengasi*'s true subject as being *la fuga* (escape or flight) was right on target.[45]

Bengasi and *Un pilota ritorna* prospect the end of empire and, with it, the end of those films that promoted imperial conquest and the institution of cinema as its privileged interpreter. To the notion of war as generative of Italy's future, these movies posit war as the undoing of everything. To a present rendered eventful and meaningful through permanent mobilization, they oppose a time of waiting under siege and panicked flight. Rossellini represents both temporalities, both shapes of history, while Genina's charge is to convey the drama of a victimized people, but also to separate that popular history in the making from official representations. The year 1942 closes the parabola started with the Ethiopian invasion in cinematic terms as well: it is another moment when "cinema developed a

FIGURE 8.22.

Italian captives, *The Fall of Tobruk* (1941). Used by permission of the Imperial War Museum Film and Video Archive

direct or indirect commentary on itself," this time to signal the exhaustion of one model of cinema and the birth of others. The attention both directors pay to the function and relation of sound and image and the emphasis on the unreliable nature of language, and on the act of seeing and its consequences, communicate the possibility of a different kind of cinema—and a different kind of spectator. Both Rossellini and Genina set up situations in which the viewer is drawn into the acts of witnessing and caring that happen on screen, rather than positing the spectator as a passive recipient of Fascist spectacle or an accomplice in the objectification of the indigenous. This was not yet a political break—both directors were solidly in the Fascist studio system—but a restlessness, or uneasiness, with reigning formulas and sensibilities.[46]

In any case, with most of Italian Africa gone, empire cinema had little reason for being. Fiume continued to write his column on colonial cinema until the very end of the regime, but almost all of the elements upon which that cinema depended were now out of reach. Dark-skinned people were more difficult to come by—not every black prisoner of war wanted to act in a Fascist film—and often not of the ethnicity needed for the film's setting. Nor was the expedient of stocking crowd scenes with masses of blackened white extras and placing a few authentic blacks in front an ideal solution. And with African jungles and deserts off-limits, Fiume could only exhort peers to make their re-creations filmed in Frascati (or Cinecittà) as authentic as possible. Where to set those films also proved to be a problem for the industry, and by summer 1943, in what proved to be the last issue of *Africa italiana*, this exigent critic had relaxed his standards to include a film about the South Seas (*Inferno giallo/Yellow Inferno*, Géza von Radvanyi, 1942) in his column, perhaps because it starred Giachetti. Like a number of Italians, Fiume remained confident that Italy would return to Africa, and he reminded his readers that national audiences now included many thousands of Italians with firsthand colonial experience. "Every reconstruction carries with it a great responsibility, and we will have to assess our current practices to make sure our future colonial cinema does not repeat the same errors."[47]

In June 1943, with the Italian war effort in shambles, journalist Sisto Favre, who had cheered the development of empire cinema since the Ethiopian invasion, fell back on the core of Fascism as a motivation for future works. "The war film, whether as direct documentary or documented dramatic feature, must teach and instill hatred," a sentiment that the "noble and generous" Italian people did not adequately possess. Lattuada disagreed. In 1941, as he began his own military service, he had published a book of photographs with a preface that denounced the effects of years of Fascist education to violence:

> The absence of love brought many tragedies that might have been averted. Instead of the golden rain of love, a black cloak of indifference fell upon the people. And thus people have lost *the eyes of love* and can no longer see clearly; they stagger in the obscurity of death. Here are the origins of the disintegration of all values and the destruction and sterilization of conscience: it is a long chain that is anchored at the devil's feet.[48]

Lattuada's eyes of love translated into images of men, women, and children living in poverty in his native Milan, washing their ragged garments and selling humble objects. And this, too, was an outcome of Fascist empire cinema, and one that would have important cinematic consequences at the close of the war: the turn away from the exotic and the futuristic and the desire to look anew at one's own surroundings and engage with the struggles and poetry of daily life.

For men older than Lattuada, the Ethiopian invasion had represented the start of a decade spent in uniform, fighting in North and East Africa, in Spain, and on the multiple Fascist fronts during World War II. By 1945, 4.5 million of them had served in the Italian armed forces or the Militia or had fought for the Resistance or the Republic of Salò (1943–1945). Some 300,000 of these combatants had lost their lives on the battlefield, and another 1.2 million had been sent to concentration camps as prisoners of war around the world. The homecomings of these captives, which often concluded long after Italy was liberated from Fascism in the spring of 1945, were among the last links of an extraordinary chain of mobility set off by Italy's imperial engagements. Few Italians, including non-combatant men, women, and children, escaped some form of dislocation or separation from home. The naïf curiosity of the teenaged Calvino at the arrival of the first Italian refugees to his native La Spezia in 1940 had transmuted, by 1945, into weary habituation to journeys of fortune and encounters with men and women from every part of Italy and the world. Bombed-out families searching for shelter, Fascists in flight, anti-Fascists and Italian Jews returning from the Lagers, settlers returning from the colonies: the movements of all these people were a visible legacy of the defeat of Fascism and its imperial ambitions. During and immediately after the war, Italians did return to being the "navigators and transmigrants" evoked by the Duce. Yet the landscapes they traversed were ones of ruin and loss, worlds away from the sense of plenitude and expectation captured by Luce's cameras during the Duce's speech of October 1935.[49]

Epilogue

By 1947 "Aethiopia: Notes for a Little Song," the jocular annotations Flaiano had penned during the Ethiopian war, had become a novel whose title (*Tempo di uccidere/A Time to Kill*) expressed the problems of memory Fascism's empire now presented. Its protagonist, an Italian officer in service in East Africa, is haunted by a crime he committed. Having accidentally wounded an African woman he had sex with, he kills her rather than get her medical assistance, so as to avoid discovery of his transgression of the racial laws. Although his crime is never discovered, he is unable to escape from his thoughts and becomes obsessed with the traces of his guilt that he finds everywhere: a cut on his hand that will not heal (a sign of the leprosy he thinks he has contracted from her), a letter addressed to him that appears in the desert. His guilt plagues him even after he leaves Africa; his "time of killing" remains alive inside of him.[1] Flaiano won Italy's first Premio Strega for this work, but it remained an anomaly in its direct engagement with Italian crimes in the former colonies. Shame over Italy's defeat and the desire to avoid an accounting with its violence made Fascist imperialism an uncomfortable subject. In the late 1940s, the Mediterranean was a sea of regrets for Italians, but also a barrier against colonial phantoms—albeit an unreliable one. In the tellingly titled *Vivere in pace/To Live in Peace* (Luigi Zampa, 1947), which relives World War II from the point of view of an Italian village, one such phantom disturbs the peace of an old peasant. When a black American soldier enters his home, he screams, "An *askaro!*" clearly frightened at this apparition that evokes his time in Africa.

This wish to bury memories of Africa coexisted with longings to return there—which films of the immediate postwar period could and did not address. Some of the more than four hundred thousand Italians who "repatriated" had never set foot in Italy before, and they were at times regarded with suspicion in a democratizing Italy. These ex-settlers took hope from the intense lobbying by Italian politicians of every political party (except the communists, but including the anti-Fascists Benedetto Croce and Carlo Sforza) with the Allies for Italy to keep its colonies acquired during the liberal period. At stake here was the enduring dream of Mediterranean influence, as well as "the legitimate *amor proprio* of a great people," in Sforza's words. The 1947 Paris Peace Treaty dashed these hopes. It finalized Italy's loss of its North and East Africa territories and gave the Dodecanese Islands back to Greece and the Istrian and Dalmatian territory to Yugoslavia, leaving Italy with only the promise of an eventual trusteeship of Somalia (1950–1960). The Paris Peace Treaty left Italians *a terra* in another sense as well: its Article 64 established a limit of 350 national aircraft, devastating a sector that had enjoyed a favorable balance of trade and international acclaim for a half century. The release of an aviation-themed occupation drama with a nostalgic title (*Ultimo amore/The Last Love*, Luigi Chiarini, 1947) only underscored the loss of this emblem of Italian prestige.[2]

The hardships of the immediate postwar period and the perception of the loss of the colonies as an offense to Italian national pride did not encourage a reckoning with Fascist abuses and criminality. Goals of national unity led Italian Communist Party chief Palmiro Togliatti, as minister of justice, to amnesty Fascist criminals in 1946. The Allies fully supported this measure. Their worries about social unrest had earlier favored a minimalist approach to sanctions for Fascist violence—wherever it had been committed—and no action was taken on the charges the Ethiopian, French, Greek, and Yugoslav governments filed with the United Nations War Crimes Commission against Italians for atrocities committed during Fascist occupations. The Italians lost their colonies, but they also avoided official censure for what they did there. As in Flaiano's

Tempo di uccidere, their imperial crimes remained unresolved as well as unsolved.[3]

A decade earlier, Pavolini had warned his compatriots of the untamable relationship between Italian memory and Africa. Writing on the eve of his return to Italy, his Ethiopian war military service at an end, he asked,

> What is this *mal d'Africa:* a spiritual amoeba that will make us suffer for many years in the future, making certain things indispensible? And what if for us those things are *ambe* [Ethiopia's distinctive mountains] and date palms, instead of certain cigars and old dressing gowns? Or is it rather a change Africa makes within us, in the first months after we leave it? A gravitation toward horizons, toward deserts? It is through introducing Africa into memory that you feel how enormous it is: it does not fit neatly, but presses on you, and overflows.

The parameters of this messy overflow have been paradoxically well defined from the fall of empire onward. Memories of African women fit neatly: the nostalgia for *faccette nere* is a core component of colonial memory. As Ruth Iyob and Sandra Ponzanesi have shown, the images of black women that circulated so frequently throughout Fascist visual culture had their own afterlife.[4] But memories of the persecution of those women, and of African men, had no place in republican Italy. Thus could Montanelli boast publicly of buying an East African girl to keep as his mistress, but deny that the Italian armed forces used gas as a weapon in the colonies. As this book has argued, behind the idea of slaves of love so central to *mal d'Africa* stand slaves of labor, black and white, whose bodily mortifications have been largely erased from the historical record but which surface in empire films. Those films also laid down other vectors of colonial memory that were respected in the post-Fascist period, from the screens of fog and sand that protected amorous and violent relations among men on the plantation and the battlefield to the presentation of Italians as benevolent colonial masters. Exploring these configurations of memory through the lens of cinema confirms the value of Derek Duncan and Jacqui Andall's call to investigate not only colonial amnesias but "the ways in which Italy held on to memories of colonial rule and ambition."[5]

And what of the Fascist film industry that had funded and promoted empire cinema? In some ways, its fate paralleled that of other state sectors in which the transition from dictatorship to democracy saw continuities of institutions and personnel. The major actors and brands of that industry (Luce, Incom, the CSC, the Biennale, ENIC) continued their activities after the fall of Fascism—some after a transition phase or under new management—as did larger studios such as Scalera. The ubiquity of Luce, the entity most identified with imperial and Fascist propaganda, ironically guaranteed it safe passage to a new political reality. The urgency of mass re-education after decades of dictatorship and a civil war, along with the lack of funds, did not allow for the creation of a new propaganda structure: "The State already has its own institution, that of the Istituto Luce," Prime Minister Ferruccio Parri reasoned in June 1945. One month later, the first *Notiziario Luce Nuova/New Luce News Digest* appeared, with politicians now in civilian clothing and commentators adopting a warmer tone—even Guido Notari, who continued to narrate Luce and Incom productions. One critic still spied "the shadow of the old Luce," though, and the montage of peasants and workers that preceded the first edition would not have been out of place during the Fascist regime.[6] Nor would have been a 1946 Luce newsreel about Italian colonization in Libya, in which Libyans industriously work the land, with a few machines and a lot of oxen; an Italian foreman appears for one second only. As in the films about imperial labor discussed in chapter 6, the workers are pushed onward by editing that includes superimpositions and by strident music that mimics the footsteps of laboring men and animals. The film even invokes the double enemy ingrained in Fascist discourse, denigrating the British and the indigenous. Yet something has changed: Luce presents the footage as an unusual archival find, as something that emanates from a remote past. A narrator with a pointedly youthful and cordial voice tells viewers: "The cinematographic document we present to you today is among the oldest and rarest (*fra i più antichi e rari*), because it relates with mute but irresistible eloquence the tough early days of Italian colonization in Libya. And how Italians educated the nomadic and lazy Arab (*l'arabo nomade e fanullone*) in the school and civilization of labor. We dedicate this document to all those who presume to be masters of colonization despite having degraded and destroyed entire civilizations with alcohol and the rifle." This assertion of Italy's long presence in Libya certainly reflects the campaign then going on to retain control of the colony. But it also positions Libya, seen through the veil of this shaky mute footage, as a memory object. And indeed it continues Fascist empire cinema's own memory politics, by which corruption and violence are displaced onto others or left behind in the colonies, remaining on the margins of representation, much like the Italian overseer who flashes on- and off-screen.[7]

The features realm illustrates best the difficulties of the Italian film industry after the ravages of the war and fall of its main patron—the Fascist regime. Production in 1945 returned to pre-1936 levels (twenty-five films); many small production companies appeared and quickly failed, and the lack of capital, studios, and equipment forced Italians to look elsewhere for funding (such as American investors and the Vatican). This had also been the case before 1936—Quadraro had resorted to foreign funding to make *L'Esclave blanc*—but the range and amount of Fascist assistance (advance loans, subsidies based on box-office performance, preferential publicity, and so forth) and Axis benefits (co-productions) Italians had enjoyed for seven years after that could not be duplicated.[8] Cinecittà's conversion into a refugee camp by the Allies in 1944 speaks most eloquently to the ways the war and the fall of Fascism affected the world of Italian cinema. Instead of stars like Duranti and Nazzari, Cinecittà's sets and spaces now hosted Italians repatriated from the colonies and Dalmatia, as well as Displaced Persons under United Nations Relief and Rehabilitation Administration (UNRRA) authority. Disease, violence, and malnutrition marked the Italian and UNRRA camps, where thousands lived on the soundstages in tiny cubicles made of cardboard and wood—and materials from the sets of past Cinecittà productions. Although the film press mobilized for "the children of Cinecittà," as it had for imperial causes a decade earlier, Steimatsky relates that the Italian film world mostly disengaged with this instance of humiliation. It was, in fact, a double blow: an Allied takeover of what had been the symbol of Italians' success in reviving their movie industry and an occupation of the key site of Fascism's cinema of empire by survivors of the collapse of that empire. "Today the reality that the dignitaries of yesterday's cinema did their utmost to exclude erupts violently in the old stately center," the magazine *Film d'oggi* wrote ruefully. Genina's blowing up of the colossal sets of the fake imperial city he had constructed in Cinecittà for *Bengasi* had foreshadowed that reality. In this universe of ironies it should not surprise that Luce used the Cinecittà refugee camp as a setting for a feature it co-produced with UNRRA to demonstrate its alignment with new international realities (*Umanità/Humanity*, Jack Salvatori, 1946).[9]

We may ask how the creators of empire cinema navigated this ruinous territory as they made their own transitions to a postwar world. Empire film's location as the heart of the "skeleton in the closet" that was Fascist cinema dates from this period, when directors of big-budget films on imperial themes were singled out by the Allied Commission for the Purge of Directors, Assistant Directors, and Screenwriters set up after Rome's liberation in June 1944. The choice of Gallone, Genina, and Alessandrini for a six-month ban on filmmaking may seem puzzling. Gallone had made just one such film (*Scipione l'africano*) out of more than thirty Fascist-era releases, whereas purge commission member Camerini had made two (*Kif Tebbi* and *Il grande appello*). Gallone had made no films for the Committee for War and Political Cinema, whereas Rossellini, who was not targeted by the commission, had made three, more than any other director.[10] But the empire films of Gallone, Genina, and Alessandrini most openly modeled Fascist political spectacle, from their stagings of the leader-crowd relationship to the uniformed bodies and Fascist vocal signatures of their male commanders. In 1941 Alessandrini had publicly regretted a former "inebriation" that had led him, in filming *Abuna Messias*, to "act more like a general than a director": that movie, like Genina's *Bengasi*, included a balcony harangue from an authority figure. The themes of mobility set out in this book may suggest a secondary reason. These directors were the most prominent Italian filmmakers to leave Italy during the crisis of the mid- and late 1920s and the ones who had enjoyed the most successful careers abroad. Gallone and Genina had been gone for almost a decade, and Alessandrini had spent several years in Hollywood, the only Italian director of his generation to do so. As we have seen, the cosmopolitan backgrounds and predilections of these men engendered suspicion as well as admiration, even as they produced empire films that sold well abroad. All three of those purged had a history of having one foot outside of Italy—something that could not be said about Rossellini, Marcellini, or De Robertis.[11]

Brunetta comments that the relatively light punishment meant that Gallone, Genina, and Alessandrini returned to work without having to provide "any gesture of condemnation concerning the past," and it is true that this reflects a lack of desire to raise the stakes in a climate of collective complicity.[12] There were other ways to speak to one's peers, though—and to the Allies. As during the Fascist period, filmmaking had a performative dimension, and the choices directors made in terms of film projects and locations broadcast political loyalties, connecting them to certain networks and subcultures that could cushion the passage to a new identity. Religious subjects appealed to several empire film directors: as gestures of penitence, for the consolations of faith amid so much disaster, and perhaps for the availability of Vatican funding. Marcellini could point to a proven record here. In 1942, while he made his Luce Libyan films, he also shot a documentary on Pius XII (*Pastor Angelicus*, 1942), for which the Vatican granted him six months of access to the pope. Marcellini lay low during the years of foreign occupation, but emerged in 1945 to make a documentary about the Vatican's anti-war efforts and assistance to refugees. In *Guerra alla guerra/War on War* (1946), the director repudiates the imperialist credos that had informed his entire oeuvre during Fascism, labeling war as an offense to Christ's teachings.[13]

Genina also sought the solace of religion, but his project for a film about Saint Francis drew a negative reaction from some of his peers. An anonymous critic blasted Genina's temerity in portraying a saint identified with pacificism: "The honest workers of the cinema know that today it is finally possible to clean our environment of all the dregs that fascism had thrown in it, of all the accomplices of Mussolini, Hitler and Franco.... [T]hey will therefore not work with this gentleman. If he wants to lay siege to Assisi, he should look for mercenaries." Genina made no films between 1942 and 1949, when he chronicled the short life of the canonized girl saint Maria Goretti in *Il cielo sulla palude/Heaven over the Marshes*. Rossellini would be the one to depict Saint Francis, in *San Francesco, giullare di Dio/ The Flowers of Saint Francis* (1950). Alessandrini also had trouble bringing new projects to completion, and he seemed to struggle to find his place in the new filmic climate of postwar Italy. Most of his immediate postwar releases featured nomadic protagonists who are in flight or cannot settle anywhere, such as *Chi l'ha visto?/Who Has Seen Him?* (released in 1945, but shot at Cinecittà in 1943, with Fellini among its screenwriters), about a vagabond actor, and the 1948 drama *L'Ebreo errante/The Wandering Jew*, which adapts Eugène Sue's novel to a World War II setting. The latter tells the story of a married but restless French Jew (Vittorio Gassman) who is deported to a Nazi camp but escapes with his lover, only to voluntarily return to face his death to save the lives of five hundred other Jews. Guido Fink finds that Alessandrini's boldness in being the first feature filmmaker to portray the camps is offset by the undercurrent of traditional anti-Judaism that structures the plot. Through the improbable fate of a Jew who agrees to return to a death camp, Fink contends, the film raises the prospect of Jewish guilt, positing the Holocaust as a means of "settling accounts" for the Jews' deicide.[14]

Other directors made features that articulated anxieties about the new kinds of mobilities and encounters brought by the war, building on concerns about the integrity of the Italian national community that informed their earlier works. Brignone made two films that echo *Sotto la Croce del Sud*'s concern with social policing. The melodrama *Lacrime di sangue/ Tears of Blood* (1944, with Craveri as photographer) dramatizes the plight of a woman cast out from society, this time not because of her race but because she is an unmarried mother of a child resulting from rape. And in *Canto ma sottovoce/I Am Singing Softly* (1946), about a wealthy family who flees Rome to escape the Germans, a father does not allow his son to wed an unmarried mother. In 1945 Camerini and Rossellini both released anti-Nazi occupation dramas set in Rome, the former's unjustly unknown (*Due lettere anomine/Two Anonymous Letters*), the latter's justly famous (*Roma città aperta*). *Due lettere anomine* examines the breakdown of trust among Italians due to collaborationism, informing, and female infidelity. Issues of language and signification, always dear to Camerini, manifest here in instances of crossed and threatened communication (a printing shop is a center of the Resistance), and there is a nod to *Bengasi* in the attention to translation as a political act. Both Camerini's and Rossellini's movies divest language, gesture, bodies, and objects of the meanings they had taken on during Fascism. The emergence of the witness—presaged in *Un pilota ritorna* and *Bengasi*—figures in here as a means of modeling the reawakening of civic and humanitarian sentiments. The "desensitized, uniformed, and uniform" subjects of Fascist empire cinema give way in the movies of these years to emotionally and physically ragged Italians who are learning the values of *pietà* and *tenerezza* (tenderness).[15]

Among empire and war film directors, De Robertis faced perhaps the trickiest situation: his genre was the military film, and he had also supported the Republic of Salò. As this choice placed him outside of the jurisdiction of the Allied purge committee, he faced no sanctions; he continued to make naval pictures, albeit with titles that alluded to a lost glory (*Fantasmi del mare/Phantoms of the Sea*, 1948; *Marinai senza stelle/Sailors without Stars*, 1949). It is De Robertis's non-naval picture *Il mulatto/The Mulatto* (1950) that merits attention here as an example of how the war's foreign occupations created a new arena for the expression of older racial anxieties. Made under the auspices of the International Union of Catholics, *Il mulatto* treats "one of the most delicate HUMAN PROBLEMS [sic] created by the war," that of the children born from unions between white Italian women and black American soldiers. This fictional case ascribes the union to force and does away with the mother, in empire film fashion (she dies in childbirth after having been raped by a black G.I.), leaving her husband, Matteo, to discover the truth about a son he has longed to see during five years in prison. The film purports to narrate a conversion narrative suitable for republican Italy: Matteo's internal journey from "physical repulsion" to wanting to care for Angelo. The body of the film belies this humanitarian journey "from hate to pity to love." The supposedly kindly character Gennaro, whose mantra is "we are all equal," repeatedly tries to wash off Angelo's blackness "so the whiteness of the mother can emerge," and Matteo's future is foiled by Angelo's presence. A walking reminder of Matteo's cuckolding, the child occasions continued humiliations—Matteo is forced to perform the popular song about such biracial unions, "Tammurriata nera"—and his new love Caterina declares Angelo to be "an outsider (*estraneo*) . . . one of a different race. The child divides us and will always divide us."[16]

Salvation arrives in the form of the black G.I.'s brother, who comes to Italy to check on Angelo's well-being (the soldier himself having died in battle). Angelo is mesmerized by a performance the African American visitor gives and clings to the stranger with skin like his own. The two leave for America together, but by then the film's segregationist message has found graphic expression in a scene where Gennaro carefully separates white bread crumbs from fragments of black crust. "Each one to his own" (*Ognuno per il fatto suo*) is his, and De Robertis's dictum. *Il mulatto*'s plot resolution reproduces imperial racial legislation, labeling mixed-race children "outsiders" even if they are half Italian. It is fitting that this film was produced by Scalera, the production house financed in the past by imperial labor, and also that the American brother is played by a Libyan, Muhammed Hussein, who speaks pidgin Italian in the film. The insertion of this imperial language into the mouth of a black American character furthers the film's racist message—all dark-skinned people have the same linguistic (in)capacities—and also functions as an aural trigger of nostalgia for a lost dominion. Two years after making *Fantasmi del mare*, De Robertis conjures and then exiles an imperial phantom, on the grounds of that same "colonial disgust" that suffuses the narratives of many empire films. *Il mulatto* is symptomatic of the state of imperial sentiment in the late 1940s and early 1950s, when the Paris Peace Treaty's purely legal solution—subtracted land—caused a volatile cultural, social, and psychological situation to remained unresolved.

This sense of an Italian imperial history that had been suspended or interrupted, rather than concluded, also manifests in this period through the appearance of other kinds of imperial ghosts: re-editions of the empire films discussed in this book. Alessandrini's *Abuna Messias* was re-released in 1947, after two years of lobbying by its producers to the Allied Psychological War Board and the Italian undersecretary of state; Brignone's *Sotto la Croce del Sud* (1950) Alessandrini's *Giarabub* (1952), and Genina's *Bengasi* (1955, released as *Bengasi anno '41/Benghazi Year '41*) followed. These films usually do not appear in their directors' filmographies, since they are often the work of production houses and can involve significant alterations to the original. They cut and change footage and dialogue to suit political circumstances, sometimes shooting some new footage with new or original actors. Daniela Baratieri has studied the case of 1955's *Bengasi anno '41*, which brings the relationships and themes of the original film into the present. Giuliana, Fanny-Maria, and Antonio reappear (played by the same actors, now fourteen years older), the latter now married to each other, as was the promise of the 1942 film, the former still mourning the loss of Filippo, despite the presence of Charles, her British companion. The symbols of Fascism are gone, but Giuliana, the narrator, seems frozen in the past, refusing to marry Charles because he was "on the other side." Still, Benghazi, and *Bengasi*, is a mobile *lieu de mémoire*: new sequences are set in the El Alamein cemetery, which had become the principal point of Italian sacrificial memory in North Africa by the 1950s. We do see Filippo's grave—the reason for Giuliana's pilgrimage—but

Charles shows Giuliana the graves of Allied soldiers also buried there, inviting her to leave behind her grief and animosity. There is no mention of the contributions of colonial soldiers, though, and *Bengasi anno '41* also elides the female mobility and independence that marked the original film. Fanny-Maria, now a mother, has buried her former libertinism, and her prostitute character story line is excised completely from another post-1945 version of the original *Bengasi*, released in this period. As for Giuliana, the Benghazi she mourns is a ruin—as Genina had left it in his 1942 film—and *Bengasi anno '41*, with its original footage from that film, has the value of an artifact: it forms part of what Stoler terms "the political life of imperial debris." At the same time, the dual temporalities of this film at the narrative and material level gloss the feeling of a lack of resolution, testifying to "the uneven pace with which people can extricate themselves from the imperial order of things."[17]

And what of the imperial debris left by Fascist empire film culture in the former colonies? Many movie theaters erected by the Fascists remained in place, put to new uses or retained as venues during the British Military Administration and after. In Somalia the Cinema Italia, built in 1936 and reserved for Italian elites, became the Cinema Hamar in 1956; like the Cinema Benadir and Cinema Eel Gaab, which had been created for indigenous-only audiences, they were in use during the Italian trusteeship and hosted the productions of the fledging Somali industry after independence. In Asmara, where the Italian architectural and cultural heritage was best preserved, the Cinema dell'Impero continued to show movies, as does the restored Cinema Roma today. Other traces of empire cinema are found beyond the built environment, in the stories passed down orally in families of those who worked as interpreters or guides of film crews. These stories form part of an archive of sound, or "acoustic debris" of empire, to use Nancy Rose Hunt's term—that also encompasses the songs and sayings ("Faccetta nera" being both) by which Italians filtered their interactions with the indigenous; words from Somali, Amharic, Arabic, and other languages that entered into standard Italian (and vice versa) and that colonial lingua franca, pidgin Italian.[18]

As material objects, empire films emanated from fraught and difficult environments. Heat, humidity, and the journeys of fortune that accompanied location shoots often ruined film stock, necessitating re-shoots or the expedient of documentary inserts. What Càllari said of Luce war films—that they were the fruit of "a work of stitching together"—characterized imperial features as well. Conceived in offices and salons in Italian cities, often at the suggestion of men at the highest levels of the Fascist bureaucracy, empire films accrued many influences and markings on their journeys outward to the colonies and back again. Such signs and scars figure in the work Yervant Gianikian and Angela Ricci Lucchi have produced on the basis of Comerio's archive. Their 1985 film *Dal Polo all'Equatore*, which takes up Comerio's 1929 documentary of the same title, gathers the visual tropes of imperialism that we have seen throughout this book. The camera as an eye of war, violence as a masculine rite, the cameraman as an emblem of a mobile modernity: it is all there, but discernible only through a screen of ravaged, tinted footage that communicates the heaviness of its history and interrogates cinema's enmeshment in and mortification by this martial matrix. Robert Lumley's comment that the images presented by Ricci Lucchi and Gianikian "are themselves survivors and bear traces of the history of which they are fragmentary remnants" can apply as well to Fascist empire films, which were archived, along with and because of those traces, for most of the postwar period. Like the imperial past they purport to depict, they have been "less than accessible and perhaps hard to locate," and like the memories of that past, they have been "scattered, buried, and invisible": ruins, in Gabriel's definition. Yet Fascism's empire cinema has much to tell us, for the absences and presences within its stories, for its emphatic yet elusive relationship to its own times, and for its evocations of Italy's vexed relationship with Africa and the Mediterranean that continues to this day.[19]

NOTES

INTRODUCTION

I thank Michael Moore for translating the opening quote from Ennio Flaiano's "Aethiopia: Appunti per una canzonetta."

1. On these imperial tropes, see Shohat, "Gender and Culture of Empire."
2. On British and French empire cinema, see Grieveson and MacCabe, *Empire and Film*; Jaikumar, *Cinema at the End of Empire*; Chowdhry, *Colonial India*; Kennedy-Karpat, *Rogues, Romance, and Exoticism*; and Slavin, *Colonial Cinema and Imperial France*. On these themes in Nazi German cinema, see Koepnick, *Dark Mirror*; Hochscherf, "Nazis on the Ranch?"; von Moltke, *No Place Like Home*; and Langbehn, *German Colonialism*.
3. Ferbo, "Film coloniale."
4. Quote from Micciché, "Cadavere nell'armadio," 11. On empire films as part of longer colonial and postcolonial traditions, see Gili and Brunetta, *Ora d'Africa*; Ellena, *Film d'Africa*; Di Carmine, *Italy Meets Africa*; Greene, *Equivocal Subjects*; and Farassino, *Fuori di set*. For the 1935–1943 period, see Coletti, "Cinema coloniale"; Hay, *Popular Film Culture*, 181–200; Zinni, "L'Impero sullo grande schermo"; Landy, *Folkore of Consensus*, 157–161; and Argentieri's works: his edited volume *Schermi di guerra* and the authored books *Il cinema in guerra*, *L'occhio del regime*, and *L'asse cinematografico*.
5. *Lo squadrone bianco*, *Un pilota ritorna*, and *Luciano Serra, pilota* are available commercially in their original form. *L'Esclave blanc* has been released on DVD, but its Italian version, *Jungla nera*, cannot be viewed. The Cineteca di Bologna restored *Kif Tebbi* in 2004, but *Bengasi* still does not circulate in its original state: until 2000 only the 1955 remake (*Bengasi anno '41*) of Genina's work was commercially available; the 1942 version released commercially in 2000 had one of the four story lines excised. The Istituto Luce's digitalization of a good part of its holdings since the 2000s has rendered most of the nonfiction works I discuss consultable at www.archivioluce.com.
6. Lumley, *Entering the Frame*, 10.
7. Casetti, *Eye of the Century*, 170–171.
8. Labanca's *Guerra italiana* and *Oltremare*; Fuller, *Moderns Abroad*; Bosworth, *Italy, the Least of the Great Powers*; Gentile, "The Conquest of Modernity."

9. Quote from Ahmed et al., "Introduction," 7. See also Casetti, *Eye of the Century*; and Schwartz and Charney, *Cinema and the Invention of Modernity*, on this point.

10. Clifford, *Routes*. See also Leed, *Mind of the Traveller*; Larsen, Urry, and Axhausen, *Mobilities*; and, on the Italian case, Hom, "Empires of Tourism." For the nomadic as threat during Fascism, see Atkinson's "Embodied Resistance" and "Nomadic Strategies." On nomadic sensibilities, see Gabriel, "Thoughts on Nomadic Aesthetics."

11. Quotes from Fanchi and Mosconi, "Introduzione," 16; Il Super Revisore, "Lo dica a me"; and Farassino, *Fuori di set*, 13.

12. Mulvey, "Dislocations," 254.

13. Farassino, *Fuori di set*, 25 (italics in the original).

14. Bergfelder and Carter, "Introduction," 7. See also Higson, "Limiting Imagination."

15. O'Brien, "The 'Cinéma Colonial,'" 208.

16. For Luce's acquisition of the Museo Coloniale collection, see Laura, *Le stagioni dell'aquila*, 127. Leyda acknowledges the lack of information on the Italian case in *Films Beget Films*. See also Mulvey, "Dislocations"; and Kuehl, "Visual History Traduced."

17. Within the large bibliography on cinema and history I have relied particularly on Rosenstone, *Revisioning History*; Sorlin, *Film in History*; Ferro, *Cinéma et histoire*; Iaccio, *Cinema e storia*; de Baecque, *Histoire-Caméra*; Delage and Guigueno, *L'historien et le film*; Landy, *Cinematic Uses*; and White, "Historiography and Historiophony." On the Italian case, see Dalle Vacche, *Body in the Mirror*; and Zagarrio, *L'immagine del fascismo*.

18. Pavolini, *Disperata*, 66; Fogu, *The Historic Imaginary*.

19. Alberini, "Orientamenti del documentario"; Ferretti, "Il film documentario e gli altri"; U. d. f. [De Franciscis], "Il documentario deve documentare."

20. Quotes from Marks, *Skin of the Film*, 1; Zyrd, "Found Footage Film," 49; Gabriel, "Ruin and the Other," 217–218; Rosenstone, "Introduction," 7.

21. Millan, "The Institutionalization of *Squadrismo*"; Albanese, *La marcia su Roma*; Franzinelli, *Squadristi*; Reichardt, *Camicie nere, camicie brune*. On Fascist violence in general, see Ebner, *Ordinary Violence*; and Finchelstein, *Transatlantic Fascism*; on Ethiopia, Mattioli, *Experimentierfeld der Gewalt*; Brogini Künzi, *Italien und der Abessinienkrieg*; Mattioli and Asserate, *Erste faschistische Vernichtungskrieg*, which build on the work of Rochat, *Guerre italiane in Libia e in Etiopia*; and Del Boca, *Italiani in Africa Orientale*.

22. Pavolini (a former squadrist) noted the importance of such circulations in his Ethiopian war diary: "daggers and firecrackers that pass from hand to hand, stories that travel from mouth to mouth, badges and flags that spread from wave to wave [of Fascism]" (*Disperata*, 55).

23. Mulvey, "Dislocations," 254.

1. EMPIRE CINEMA

1. Quotes from Mussolini, "Discorso sulla mobilitazione generale," 218–220; Margalit, *Ethics of Memory*, esp. 107–146. See also IL, AC, "Adunata!," October 8, 1935, Giornale Luce B0761, www.archivioluce.com.

2. Mattioli, *Experimentierfeld der Gewalt*; Brogini Künzi, *Italien und der Abessinienkrieg*; Mattioli and Asserate, *Erste faschistische Vernichtungskrieg*; Rochat, *Guerre italiane*; Mack Smith, *Mussolini's Roman Empire*.

3. Quote from Burdett, "Italian Fascism and Utopia," 97. See also Fuller, *Moderns Abroad*, 39–62; Kallis, *Fascist Ideology*; and Arthurs, *Excavating Modernity*.

4. Quotes from Fuller, *Moderns Abroad,* 40; Chambers, *Mediterranean Crossings,* 28, 39. See also McGuire, "Fascism's Mediterranean Empire"; and McLaren, *Architecture and Tourism.* On Italy and/in the Mediterranean, see the special issue of *California Italian Studies* 1, no. 1 (2010), edited by Claudio Fogu and Lucia Re; and Trinchese, *Mare Nostrum.*

5. General studies include Zagarrio, *Cinema e fascismo;* Miccichè, "Cinema italiano sotto il fascismo"; Hay, *Popular Film Culture;* Reich and Garofalo, *Re-viewing Fascism;* Gili, *Le cinéma italien;* Ricci, *Cinema and Fascism;* Brunetta, *Storia del cinema italiano;* Quaresima, *Storia del cinema italiano;* Caldiron, *Storia del cinema italiano;* Laura, *Storia del cinema italiano;* Landy, *Folklore of Consensus* and *Fascism in Film.*

6. Quote from "Elementi per una nuova geografia italiana"; figures from Ben-Ghiat and Fuller, "Introduction," 5.

7. Figures from Ricci, *Cinema and Fascism,* 127; Forgacs and Gundle, *Mass Culture,* 126; Mosconi and Della Torre, "Consumo cinematografico," 27.

8. Fanchi, "Generi," 277–293. For the Western as paradigm for the Euro-American empire film, see Shohat and Stam, *Unthinking Eurocentrism,* 114–125.

9. Quote from Pavolini, *Disperata;* 241. See also Virilio, *War and Cinema* and *Machine de vision;* and Feldman, "Violence and Vision." On the trope of *bonifica,* or reclamation, see Ben-Ghiat, *Fascist Modernities;* Gentile, *La via italiana;* and Griffin, *Modernism and Fascism.*

10. Quotes from Alessandrini, interviewed by Savio, *Cinecittà anni trenta,* 1:33–34; Geyer, "Militarization of Europe," 101.

11. Quotes from Chow, "Where Have All the Natives Gone?," 132; and Cappelletti, "Attori primitivi." See also Terra, "Sentinelle di bronzo."

12. Quote from Fuller, *Moderns Abroad,* 58; Mattia, "Testimonianza di Ettore G. Mattias," 55; Quadrone, *Mudunda,* 49–59.

13. Quote from Cappelletti, "Attori primitivi." See also Quadrone, *Mudundu,* 97; and Ortner, "Resistance and Ethnographic Refusal."

14. Duvignand, untitled prefatory note, 9; Maggi, *Storia dei trasporti;* Baxa, *Roads and Ruins.*

15. Quote from Benjamin, *One-Way Street,* 59. See also Forgacs and Gundle, *Mass Culture,* 5–16; Atkinson, "Totalitarianism and the Street"; and Locatelli, "Beyond the Campo Cintato." On travel themes in 1930s cinema, see Hay, *Popular Film Culture;* Ricci, *Cinema and Fascism,* 104–124; and Farassino, *Fuori di set.*

16. Quotes from Fuller, *Moderns Abroad,* 38; Burdett, *Journeys through Fascism,* 13.

17. I reference Stefani, *Colonia per maschi;* Bellassai, "The Masculine Mystique," esp. 314–318. See also Wanrooij, *Storia del pudore;* Saraceno, "Costruzione"; Spackman, *Fascist Virilities;* Passerini, *Mussolini immaginario,* 99–121; and Kühberger, "'Il gallo delle oche.'" I also draw on Tosh, "Hegemonic Masculinity"; Kovitz, "Roots of Military Masculinity"; Nye, "Western Masculinities"; Mosse, *Image of Man;* Butler, *Gender Trouble;* and Bourdieu, *La domination masculine.*

18. Gundle, "Film Stars and Society," 315–340; Gundle, *Mussolini's Dream Factory;* Landy, *Stardom Italian Style,* 42–83.

19. Quotes from Boscaglia, *Eye of the Flesh,* 1; Pinkus, *Bodily Regimes,* 160. See also Paulicelli, *Fashion and Fascism,* 76–77; Falasca-Zamponi, "Peeking Underneath the Black Shirt"; 145–164; Nerenberg, *Prison Terms,* 50–57; Ribuoli, "Le uniforme civili," 35–39; and Bruzzi, *Undressing Cinema.*

20. Quotes from Hendrickson, "Introduction," 15; Di Lauro, *Governo delle genti di colore*, 86; Roberto Farinacci, writing to Mussolini in April 1938 after a trip to Ethiopia, cited in De Felice, *Storia degli ebrei*, 238n1.

21. Landy, *Folklore of Consensus*, 170; Bourdieu, *Distinction*.

22. Duncan, *Reading and Writing*, 40, 42.

23. de Certeau, *Practice of Everyday Life*, 127; Bellassai and Malatesta, *Genere e mascolinità*; Landy, *Folklore of Consensus*, 169–236; Landy, *Fascism in Film*, 118–174; Reich, *Beyond the Latin Lover*, 1–23.

24. Ciro Poggiali, "La donna italiana in A.O.," *Almanacco della donna italiana* (1939), cited in Pickering-Iazzi, "Mass-Mediated Fantasies," 261; Lombardi Diop, "Pioneering Female Modernity," 145–154.

25. Stefani notes that forty-seven of fifteen hundred prostitutes registered in East Africa in 1937 were white (*Maschi in colonia*, 132–133). See also Sbacchi, *Il colonialismo italiano in Etiopia*, 224–241; Sòrgoni, *Parole e corpi*; Iyob, "Madamismo and Beyond"; Tseggai, "Eritrean Women and Italian Soldiers"; Campassi, "Il madamato in Africa Orientale"; and Barrera, "Mussolini's Colonial Race Laws."

26. Quote from Bruno, *Atlas of Emotion*, 71. See also Bruno, *Streetwalking on a Ruined Map*; and Pickering-Iazzi's "Mass-Mediated Fantasies" and "Ways of Looking."

27. Quote from Bloom, *French Colonial Documentary*, 66; Kaplan, *Questions of Travel*; Marks, "Asphalt Nomadism," 125–148; Miller, *Nationalists and Nomads*, 171–208. For contemporary theorizations, see Deleuze and Guattari, *Nomadology*; and Braidotti, *Nuovi soggetti nomadi* and *Nomadic Subjects*. See also Shohat, "Gender and the Culture of Empire."

28. Quotes from Farassino, *Fuori di set*, 87; Falasca-Zamponi, "Fascism and Aesthetics," 353; Shaviro, *Cinematic Body*, 51. See also Sobchack, *Carnal Thoughts*, esp. 53–84; and Marks, *Skin of the Film*.

29. Quotes from Koepnick, *Dark Mirror*, 11; Altman, "Sound Space," 60; Mirjam Schaub, *Bilder aus dem Off* (Weimar: VDG, 2005), 76, cited in Elsaesser and Hagener, *Film Theory*, 131. See also on these issues Chion, *Audio-Vision*; Cartwright, *Moral Spectatorship*, 55; Gorbman, *Unheard Melodies*; van Leeuwen, *Speech, Music, Sound*, 125–155; Millet, *Bruit et cinéma*, 55–108; Weis and Belton, *Film Sound*; and, on the state of film sound studies, Beck and Grajeda, "Introduction," 1–22.

30. Quotes from Doane, "Voice in the Cinema," 341; Barthes, "Grain of the Voice," 181; Bertellini, "Colonial Autism," 257. For the notion of vocality, which includes non-verbal sounds, see Dunn and Jones, "Introduction."

31. On this larger imperial culture and Fascist political spectacle, see Stone, *Patron State*; Schnapp, *Staging Fascism*; Falasca-Zamponi, *Fascist Spectacle*; Crum and Lazzaro, *Donatello among the Blackshirts*; Labanca, *Africa in vetrina*; Arena, *Visioni d'oltremare*; Pinkus, *Bodily Regimes*; Arvidsson, *Marketing Italian Modernity*, 22–43; Polezzi, "The Circulation of Colonial Images"; Castelli and Laurenzi, *Permanenze e metamorfosi*; and Gabrielli, *Africa in giardino*. On colonial fiction, see Ricci, *La lingua dell'impero*, 104–151; Pagliara, *Romanzo coloniale*; and Tomasello, *Letteratura coloniale italiana*.

32. "Il cinema per l'impero"; Cappelletti, "Attori primitivi."

33. Quotes from Casetti, *Eye of the Century*, 11; Carter, *Dietrich's Ghosts*, 6; Gentile, "Fascism and the Italian Road to Totalitarianism," 291–302. I also reference here Ricci, *Cinema and Fascism*; Hay, *Popular Film Culture*; Hake, *Popular Cinema of the Third Reich*; Koepnick, *Dark Mirror*; and Rentschler, *Ministry of Illusion*.

34. Quote from Argentieri, *Occhio del regime*, 89. See also Brunetta, *Storia del cinema italiano*, 98–121; Cardillo, *Duce in moviola*; Bernagozzi, *Mito dell'immagine*, 102–116; and Della Pria, *Dittatura e immagine*. On the cult of Mussolini, see Passerini, *Mussolini immaginario*; and Bosworth, *Mussolini*. On Mussolini and Maciste, see Reich, *The Maciste Films*.

35. Segàla, *Muri del Duce*; Mosconi and Della Torre, *I manifesti tipografici del cinema*, 48–49; Argentieri, *Occhio del regime*, 92–93; Pinkus, *Bodily Regimes*, 16–18.

2. ITALIAN CINEMA AND THE COLONIES TO 1935

1. Brunetta, *Cinema muto*; Bernardini and Martinelli, *Cinema muto italiano*; Quaresimo, *Storia del cinema italiano*.

2. Bagnoni, "Cinema, occhio della guerra."

3. Kirby, *Parallel Tracks*. Georges Meliès, for example, made *Le Musulman rigolo/The Funny Muslim*, *Vente d'Esclaves au Harem/Slave-Trading in a Harem*, and *Danse au Sérail/Harem Dance* (all 1897).

4. Quotes from Oksiloff, *Picturing the Primitive*, 3; and Feldman, "Violence and Vision," 60. On geographic societies in Italy, see Atkinson, "Constructing Italian Africa"; and Monina, *Consenso coloniale*. On pre–World War I colonial film, see Griffiths, *Wondrous Difference*; Russell, *Experimental Ethnography*; Oksiloff, *Picturing the Primitive*; and Rony, *Third Eye*. On the modernity of the camera, see Moore, *Savage Theory*. On landscape in early film, see Sitney, "Landscape in the Cinema." Shohat, "Imperial Imaginary," recalls the genealogy from Etienne-Jules Marey's 1882 *fusil cinématographique* to the "aggressive use of the camera by colonial powers" (106).

5. Casetti, *Eye of the Century*, 143. I discuss the work of filmmakers Yervant Gianikian and Angela Ricci Lucchi with Comerio's archive in the epilogue. See, on Comerio, Lumley, *Entering the Frame*; and Degrada, Mosconi, and Paoli, *Moltiplicare l'istante*.

6. Pagliero, "Aeronautica Militare"; Whittam, *Politics of the Italian Army*, 165–177; Gentile, "Conquest of Modernity"; Fuller, *Moderns Abroad*, esp. 39–48.

7. Quotes from Behdad, *Belated Travelers*, 2; and Pascoli, "Grande proletaria," 239.

8. Bertellini, *Italy in Early American Cinema*; Greene, *Equivocal Subjects*, 14–42; Re, "Italians and the Invention of Race."

9. Quotes from Winter, "Under Cover of War," 194; Virilio, *Vision Machine*, 13; Marinetti, "Fondazione e Manifesto del Futurismo," 43; Weitz, *Century of Genocide*, 50; Bailey, "First World War," 134. From a vast bibliography, see Bartov, *Murder in Our Midst*; Fritzsche, "Nazi Modern," 1–21; Kershaw, "War and Political Violence," 107–123; Venturini, *La seduzione totalitaria*; and Gillis, *The Militarization of the Western World*.

10. Quotes from Bailey, "First World War," 135; Steimatsky, *Italian Locations*, 15; Hüppauf, "Modernism and Photographic Representation," 103. See also Virilio, *Vision Machine*, 12–13; and Bourke, *Intimate History of Killing*.

11. Quotes from Fantina, *Trincee dell'immaginario*, 92; Doane, *Emergence of Cinematic Time*, 33. See also Renzi, *Cinematografia al campo*; Alonge, "Occhio e cervello dell'esercito"; Gibelli, *Officina della guerra*, 174–175; and Venturini, *Seduzione totalitaria*.

12. Quotes from Marinetti et al., "Cinematografia futurista," 226, 228; Canosa and Carluccio, *Storia del cinema italiano, 1912–1923*.

13. Cerchi Usai, "Mario Camerini in Africa." Mario Camerini made *Maciste contro lo sceicco*, and Guido Brignone made *Maciste in Hell*, both in 1926. See Reich, *Maciste Films*; Ricci, *Cinema and Fascism*, 81–87; and Landy, *Stardom Italian Style*, 7–15.

14. Ricci, *Cinema and Fascism*, 57; Leprohon, *Italian Cinema*, 51.

15. Quote from Mussolini, "Quando il mito tramonta"; Ruffin and d'Agostino, *Dialoghi di regime*, 37, on literacy rates; Bertellini, "Dux/Divo"; Caprotti, "Information Management and Fascist Identity." On the IICE, see Taillibert, *Institut International du Cinéma Éducatif*; Maltby, "Cinema and the League of Nations," 82–116; and Laura, *Stagioni dell'aquila*, 51–55.

16. Quote from Laura, *Stagioni dell'aquila*, 14. See also Farassino, *Fuori di set*, 65–69; Bloom, *French Colonial Documentary*, 65–94; and Ruoff, *Virtual Voyages*.

17. Rochat, *Guerre italiane*, 35–38; Mattioli, *Experimentierfeld der Gewalt*, 41–54.

18. Quote from Graziani, *Cirenaica pacificata*, 119–122; Atkinson, "Embodied Resistance" and "Nomadic Strategies."

19. IL, AC, Giornale Luce A0805, "Il Sottosegretario dello Stato alle Colonie in Cirenaica," June 1931, www.archivioluce.com. Quote from Piccioli, *Nuova Italia dell'Oltremare*, 1:241; Labanca, "Italian Colonial Internment." Disease and malnourishment caused up to 40 percent of internees to perish over the next two years. See on these issues Moses, *Empire, Colony, Genocide*; and Moses and Stone, *Colonialism and Genocide*.

20. Quotes from Piccoli, *Nuova Italia d'Oltremare*, 1:240; and Raybaud, "Nomadism between the Archaic and the Modern," 150. On Libyan exiles, see Ahmida, *Forgotten Voices*; and Baldinetti, *Origins of the Libyan Nation*.

21. Quote from Bernstein, "Introduction," 5; Shohat, "Gender and the Culture of Empire"; Studlar, "'Out-Salomeing Salomé.'"

22. Hansen, "Pleasure, Ambivalence, Identification," 11. Quotes are from the film's intertitles.

23. Bertellini, "Duce/Divo."

24. Zùccoli, *Kif Tebbi*, ix. See Tamis, "*Kif Tebbi*"; and Di Carmine, *Italy Meets Africa*, 23–46.

25. Quote from Marks, *Skin of the Film*, 80. See also McDougall, *Transcultural Cinema*, 231–244.

26. Farassino, *Camerini*, 104. On the desert as a place for Europeans to go and Arabs to leave, see Marks, "Asphalt Nomadism," 130.

27. On the Turk as symbol of a backward and lascivious Orient, see Said, *Orientalism*, 59–60; and McGuire, "Fascism's Mediterranean Empire."

28. Quotation from *Kif Tebbi* titles. See IL, AC, Luce documentaries A0469, *Festa religiosa araba in Tripolitania*, November 1929, and A0934, *I Berberi e gli italiani*, March 1932, www.archivioluce.com. On such performances, see Oksiloff, *Picturing the Primitive*, 61–69.

29. On censorship of this film, see Ellena et al., *Film d'Africa*, 27.

30. On differences between film and novel, see Tamis, "*Kif Tebbi*."

31. Zùccoli, *Kif Tebbi*, 12.

32. Giuseppe Bini, review of *Kif Tebbi* in *La vita cinematografica* (June 10, 1929), anonymous review in *Cinematografo* (December 2, 1928), and review in *Rivista del cinematografo* (February 1929), all in Ellena et al., *Film d'Africa*, 27–31.

33. "Antonio Centa." See Martinelli's three essays: "Gastarbeiter fra le due guerre," "Cineasti italiani in Germania," and "Destinazione Parigi," 160–169; and Farassino, *Fuori di set*, esp. 83–106.

34. Duroviceva, "Translating America"; Vincendeau, "Hollywood Babel."

35. Ricci, *Cinema and Fascism*, 60–64, on the politics of dubbing in these years.

36. Quotes from Duroviceva, "Translating America," 147; and Farassino, *Fuori di set,* 17, 66. See also on these issues Schwartz, *It's So French!;* Koepnick, *Dark Mirror;* Farassino, *Fuori di set;* and Petrie, *Hollywood Destinies.*

37. On this legislation, see Gili, *Stato fascista.*

38. Quotes from Bottai, "Dichiarazione a favore della legge"; Alberti, "Cronaca del cinematografo." On the relation with foreign developments, see Ben-Ghiat, *Fascist Modernities,* esp. 70–92.

39. Luigi Freddi, report to Benito Mussolini, February 28, 1934, in ACS, PCM, 1934–36, 3.2.2.1397.

40. Gili, *Stato fascista e cinematografia,* 22–23, on censorship and 135–147 on the loans to filmmakers; Zagarrio, "Schizofrenie del modello fascista."

41. On the Mussolini-Laval accords of January 1935, see Strang, "Imperial Dreams," 799–809. On the March 1935 film festivities, see Mosconi, *Impressione del film,* 209–226; and IL, AC, Giornale Luce B0651, "Il 40° anniversario della cinematografia festeggiata nelle sale del Supercinema," www.archivioluce.com. See also Sottosegretariato di Stato per la Stampa e la Propaganda et al., *40° anniversario della cinematografia, 1895–1935.*

3. MAPPING EMPIRE CINEMA, 1935–1939

1. Quotes from Lombrassa, "Il senno dei Tigrini"; D'Errico, "Stile Luce"; Soldati, interview with Jean Gili, in Gili, *Le cinéma italien,* 86; Freddi, interviewed in G.us., "Guerre e guerrieri sullo schermo."

2. Dunn and Jones, "Introduction," 2; Doane, "The Voice in the Cinema."

3. The MCP also incorporated the Society for Italian Authors and Editors, which included many screenwriters and had a Film Distribution Service, as well as the Directorates for Press and Propaganda, for Tourism, and for Theater.

4. On these policies, see Zagarrio, "Schizofrenie del modello fascista"; and Gili, *Stato fascista e cinematografia,* 103. The studios were Metro-Goldwyn-Mayer, 20th Century Fox, Warner Brothers, and Paramount.

5. Figure from Spagnoletti, "Registi stranieri in Italia," 265. See also Grespi, "Cinecittà"; and Marino and Marino, *Ovra a Cinecittà.*

6. Quote from Paollela, "Cannes ovvero la storia di una mostra mancata." See also Argentieri, *L'asse cinematografico* and "Autarchia e internazionalità," 140–163; and Martin, "New Order for European Culture."

7. Camerini oversaw the German version of *Ma non è una cosa seria* (1936). Alessandrini's *Una donne tra due mondi* (1936), Brignone's *Mamma* (1941), and Genina's *Castelli in aria* (1939) were German-Italian co-productions. Genina made the feature *L'assedio dell'Alcazar* (1939) and Marcellini the documentary *Los novios de la muerte* (1938) in Spain.

8. Taillibert, *l'Institut International du Cinématografe Éducatif,* 316; Bono, "Mostra di Venezia."

9. Quotes from Argentieri, "Autarchia e internazionalità," 159; Aristarco, "Alba tragica." Jean Renoir, Pierre Chenal, Jean de Limur, Jean Epstein, Abel Gance, André Berthomieu, and Jeff Musso all made films in Italy in these years.

10. Figures from Forgacs and Gundle, *Mass Culture,* 63–91. See Argentieri, *L'asse cinematografico,* 38, on the Biennale. See also Ricci, *Cinema and Fascism,* 125–155; Hay, *Popular Film Culture,* 64–98; and Quaglietti, "Cinema americano, vecchio amore," 307–328.

11. Quote from Vittorio Mussolini, "Emancipazione del cinema italiano"; Chiarini, "Prefazione"; Chiarini, "Note." See Hay, *Popular Film Culture*, 260–261, and de Grazia, *Irresistible Empire*, 284–335, on this debate. Artisti Associati used the profits from its flourishing business (eleven offices throughout Italy) distributing United Artists films to fund its Italian productions, including *Il grande appello*.

12. Quotes from V. M. [V. Mussolini], "Un momento critico"; USMM, b.2820, f. "Compilazione di un film per la R. Marina," De Robertis, 1939 letter to unnamed navy official; Vittorio Mussolini, "Nuova situazione"; Casetti, *Eye of the Century*. Italian new releases took a 56.5 percent market share in 1942. Figures from Forgacs and Gundle, *Mass Culture*, 126.

13. Chion, *Audio-Vision*; Cicognini, interviewed by Savio, *Cinecittà anni trenta*, 1:238; Verretti, "Musicisti, produttori e registi"; Bassetti, "Musica per film." On Gabriel and the imperial in Italian musical culture, see Abbonizio, "Musica e colonialismo."

14. Chion, *Voice in Cinema*; Dunn and Jones, "Introduction"; Allodoli, "Cinema e lingua italiana."

15. Milano, "Italiano del cinema"; Allodoli, "Voi e lei"; Cicognini, "Abolizione del lei"; Migliorini, "Lei in soffitto"; Allodoli, "Cinema e lingua italiana." On these issues, see Raffaelli, *Parole proibite*; Klein, *Politica linguistica del fascismo*; Raffaelli, *Lingua filmata*; Valentini, *Presenze sonore*; and Rossi, *Lingua e cinema*.

16. Briareo [Giacomo Debenedetti], "Doppiaggio in Italia"; Maltby and Vesey, "'Temporary American Citizens,'" 49; Patuelli, "'Dipartimento dell'educazione.'"

17. Rossi, "Lingua doppiata," 408; Ruffin and D'Agostino, *Dialoghi del regime*, 84; Altichieri, "Lingua e il 'parlato.'" See also Migliorini, "Tradurre"; Menarini, *In margine della lingua*, 7–29; and Mereu Keating, "100% Italian."

18. Allodoli, "Cinema e lingua italiana"; Barthes, *Image, Text, Music*, 182.

19. Quotes from Rossi, "Lingua doppiata," 406; Chion, *Voice in Cinema*, 5. See also Menarini, *Ai margini della lingua*, 7–8; and Masso, "Proxemics of the Mediated Voice," 36–50.

20. Quotes from Simonini, *Linguaggio di Mussolini*, 40, 70–82; Chion, *Voice in Cinema*, 24. See also Argentieri, *Occhio del regime*, 92–97; Casetti and Mosconi, *Spettatori italiani*, 48–49; Desideri, "Linguaggio politico Mussoliniano," 41–42; and Spackman, *Fascist Virilities*, 119–132.

21. Quotes from Perbellini, "I meticci linguistici"; Apter, *Translation Zone*, 15; Foresti, "Problema linguistico." See also Pretelli, "Education in the Italian Colonies."

22. Doane, "Voice in the Cinema," 342; Millet, *Bruit et cinéma*, 12. See also O'Brien, "Cinéma coloniale."

23. Mosconi and Della Torre, "Consumo cinematografico"; Battistel, "Spettacolo cinematografico"; Bruno, *Atlas of Emotion*, 42–53; Mosconi and Osanna Cavadini, "Sala cinematografica."

24. Quote from Gemelli, "Psicologia al servizio della cinematografia." See also Tumiati, "Pazzia e cinematografo"; and Mosconi, "Chiesa cattolica e il cinema," 77–84.

25. Quote from Rava, "Popoli africani dinanzi allo schermo." See also Fiume, "L'Organizzazione cinematografica dell'AOI." Venue information from Ambrosino, "Cinema e propaganda in AOI." On the Miramare, see Abbonizio, "Musica e colonialismo," chap. 3.

26. Ambrosino, "Cinema e propaganda in AOI," esp.138–139.

27. Quote from Fiume, "L'organizzazione cinematografica dell'AOI." See also Mattia, "Cinema dei soldati in A.O.I."; and Ambrosino, "Cinema e propaganda," 147–150, on indigenous-only venues.

28. Quote from Roberti, "Corazzate con le rotelle..." See also Mattia, "Pubblico etiopico"; and Lombrassa, "Senno dei Tigrini." On mobile cinemas in British and French empires, see Chowdhry, *Colonial India*, 15–16; Larkin, *Signal and Noise*; Grieveson, "Cinema and the (Common) Wealth," 73–114; Levine, *Framing the Nation*, esp. 56–88; and Ambler, "Projecting the Modern Colonial State," 199–224.

29. Quote from Fiume, "L'organizzazione cinematografica dell'AOI." See also Mattia, "Cinema dei soldati in AOI"; and Ambrosini, "Cinema e propaganda," 145.

30. Rava, "I popoli africani dinanzi allo schermo"; Balestrazzi, "Il cinematografo e l'Impero"; V. M. [V. Mussolini], "Cinema per gli indigeni"; Mattia, "Pubblico etiopico"; Cappelletti, "Attori primitivi"; Colonel Gigante, letter to the Commando Truppe Regie, April 26, 1938, cited in Ambrosini, "Cinema e propaganda," 137. See also Fiume, "India contro il cinema."

31. Rava, "Popoli africani dinanzi allo schermo"; Mattia, "Pubblico etiopico."

32. Quote from Roberti, "Corrazzate con le rotelle." See also Mattia, "Pubblico etiopico"; Ambler, "Popular Films and Colonial Audiences," 89; and Vasudevan, "Addressing the Spectator."

33. Balestrazzi, "Il cinematografo e l'Impero"; Fiume, "L'India contro il cinema"; V. M. [V. Mussolini], "Cinema per gli indigeni." See also Diawara, "Black Spectatorship"; and Chowdhry, *Colonial India*.

34. Ricci, *Cinema and Fascism*, 70; Celli, "Guerre del Luce," 67; Argentieri, *L'occhio del regime*, 172–173; Laura, *Stagioni dell'aquila*.

35. Quote from MacDougall, *Transcultural Cinema*, 262. On these issues, see Renov, "Introduction"; Devereux and Hillman, *Fields of Vision*; Crawford and Turton, *Film as Ethnography*; and Ruby, *Picturing Culture*.

36. Virilio, *Vision Machine*, 5; USMM, f. 2824, "Servizio cinematografico e fotografico della R. Marina: Proposta per un Reparto per l'A.O.I.," pro-memoria by Captain A. Ginocchietti, head of the Press Office of the Royal Navy, June 23, 1934.

37. Bagnoni, "Cinema, occhio della guerra"; Spaino, "Organizzazione dell'Istituto Nazionale Luce"; D'Errico, "Luce A.O."; and USMM, f. 2824, pro-memoria of September 12, 1935. On Luce AOI, see Argentieri, *Occhio del regime*, 163–184; Laura, *Stagioni dell'aquila*, 125–138; and Celli, "Guerre del Luce," 62–70.

38. Quotes from Bagnoni, "Cinema, occhio della guerra"; Feldman, "Violence and Vision," 56. See also Volla, "Cinema e guerra aerea"; and Croce, "In A.O. col reparto fotocinematografico."

39. Dino Alfieri, quoted in Croce, "In A.O. col reparto fotocinematografico"; "Rassegna cinematografica"; Milani, "Da Adua ad Axum"; Argentieri, *Occhio del regime*, 165.

40. D'Errico, "Luce A.O."; Craveri, "Operatore fra guerre e rivoluzioni." On Craveri, see Laura, *Stagioni dell'aquila*, 104–106; Masi, *Storie della luce*, 91–94; and Guerri, "Operatori italiani," 450–459. See also Croce, "In AOI col reparto fotocinematografico"; and Méccoli, "Film d'aviazione."

41. McDougall, *Corporeal Images*; Yampolsky, "Reality at Second Hand"; D'Errico, "Stile Luce"; Brunetta, *Storia del cinema italiano*, 2:102.

42. Quotes from "Editoriale"; Giacomo Paulucci di Calboli, in Argentieri, *Occhio del regime*, 167–168. See also Celli, "Guerre del Luce," 68.

43. Quotes from Bhabha, "Dissemination," 145; Alberini, "Orientamenti del documentario." See also Ricci, *Cinema and Fascism*, 73.

44. Quotes from Comin, "Volto della realtà"; Pavolini, "Cinematografo"; "Un primato italiano." See also Antonioni, "Per un film sul fiume Po"; Tosti, "Cinema e l'esercito"; and Ferretti, "Film documentari e gli altri." On the documentary in these years, see Argentieri, *Occhio del regime;* Perniola, "Documentari fuori regime"; Bertozzi, *Storia del documentario italiano*, 59–96; and Steimatsky, *Italian Locations*, 1–14.

45. The eight films from 1937 listed under this rubric at www.archivioluce.com are *Governo dell'Amhara—Gondar* (5'48"), *Governo dei Galla e Sidamo—Lechenti* (5'), *Governo dei Galla e Sidamo—Gandela* (4'), *Amhara—Gorgorà* (4'10"), *Harar—Baccà* (1'31"), *Galla e Sidamo—Agheremariam* (6'50"), *Eritrea—Asmara* (7'), and *Galla e Sidamo—Uondo* (3'). For French and British imperial documentaries, see Bloom, *French Colonial Documentary;* Levine, *Framing the Nation*, esp. chaps. 4 and 6; and Grieveson and MacCabe, *Empire and Film*.

46. "Cronache dell'Impero."

47. Quote from Renov, *Subject of Documentary;* Tosti, "Il cinema e l'esercito"; S. a. p., "Un primato italiano." See on this double address Cowie, "Spectacle of Actuality," 19–45; and Smaill, *Documentary*.

48. Milani, "Sulle orme dei nostri pionieri"; IL, AC, *Sulle orme dei nostri pionieri* (Luciano De Feo, 1936), Luce D028702, www.archivioluce.com.

49. Quotes from "Rassegna Cinematografica"; Sobchack, *Carnal Thoughts*, 273; Mulvey, "Dislocations," 258; IL, AC, *Da Adua ad Axum: Le tappe dell'avanzata italiana in A.O.*, 1936, Luce D039001, www.archivioluce.com.

50. Cowie, "Spectacle of Actuality," 29; D'Errico, "Stile 'Luce'"; Burdett, *Journeys through Fascism*, 4–5.

51. Falconi, "*La freccia d'oro*"; IL, AC, *Ritmi di stazione* (Corrado D'Errico, 1933), Luce D062002, and *Il cammino degli eroi* (Corrado D'Errico, 1936), Luce D037101, www.archivioluce.com.

52. Quote from Paulucci di Calboli to Mussolini, March 1936, cited in Celli, "Guerre del Luce," 69. See also Perniola, "Documentari fuori regime," 371; Argentieri, *Occhio del regime*, 119; and Gili, *Stato fascista e cinematografia*, 86–87.

53. Alberini, "Orientamenti del documentario."

54. Bragaglia, "Narrazione e documentario"; De Franciscis, "Scenografia vera"; De Feo, "Elementi del film nazionale." See Ben-Ghiat, *Fascist Modernities,* on these experimentations.

55. Fiume, "Africa in bianco e nero"; V. N. N., "I lancieri del Bengala"; J. C., "I lancieri del Bengala."

56. Quote from O'Brien, "'Cinéma colonial,'" 223. See also Jaikumar, *Cinema at the End of Empire*, 124–133; and Andrew, "Praying Mantis."

57. Quotes from Di Carmine, *Italy Meets Africa*, 60–94; and the *Siliva Zulu* publicity reproduced in Ellena, *Film d'Africa*, 33.

58. Quotes from Fiume, "Africa in bianco e nero." See also his "Un'anno di cinema coloniale" and "Atmosfera e ambiente."

59. Hodeir and Pierre, *Exposition Coloniale;* Rice, "Exhibiting Africa"; Abbattista and Labanca, "Living Ethnological and Colonial Exhibitions"; Dore, "Ideologia coloniale." See also Jaikumar, *Cinema at the End of Empire*, 124–133; and O'Brien, "Cinéma colonial," 214–215.

60. Quote from Zyrd, "Found Footage Film," 49. See also Russell, *Experimental Ethnography*, 238–248; Triluzi, *Fotografia e storia dell'Africa*, 54–55; and Del Boca and Labanca, *Impero africano*.

4. COMING HOME TO THE COLONIES

1. Gabaccia, *Italy's Many Diasporas*, 134; Parini, *Italiani nel mondo*, 9; Mussolini, "La mobilitazione generale." See also Choate, *Emigrant Nation;* Gabaccia and Baldassar, *Intimacy and Italian Migration;* Verdicchio, *Bound by Distance;* Franzini, "'Varcare i confini,'" 115–152; and Tintori, "Cittadinanza e politiche," 52–106.

2. Quotes from Marks, *Skin of the Film*, 1; Longo, "Cultura sul piano imperiale"; Chambers, *Mediterranean Crossings*, 43; Scarpellini, *Material Nation*, 89–90. See Grespi, "Cinecittà," 130, on the General Cinema Directorate's financing of cinemas that showed movies in Italian abroad, such as New York City's Cinema Roma, which opened in 1936; and ACS, PCM, Direzione Generale Servizi della Propaganda, b.4 and 8, and b.30, on parallel initiatives planned for Argentina and Brazil, respectively. I thank David Aliano for supplying me with these documents.

3. Clifford, *Routes*, 249–250.

4. Figures from Gabaccia, *Italy's Many Diasporas*, 134; and Choate, "Identity Politics," 97–109.

5. Quotes from Soldati, *America primo amore*, 87, 15,18; G.us., interview with Freddi, "Guerre e guerrieri sullo schermo"; and Soldati, "Il grande appello." See also Marino and Marino, *Ovra a Cinecittà*, 105–108, 170–171; and De Berti, *Volo del cinema*, 167–182.

6. Reich, *Beyond the Latin Lover*, on the *inetto*.

7. Fink, "Où vont les autres," 68; Camerini, "Con spirito nuovo." See also Farassino, "Camerini, au-dela du cinéma italien," 11–32.

8. De Certeau, *Practice of Everyday Life*, 117.

9. Quotes from Mussolini, "Decidersi!"; Bertellini, "Colonial Autism," 268; and Chion, "Wasted Words,"106. See also Raffaelli, "Voci e iscrizioni."

10. Quotes from Longo, "Cultura sul piano imperiale"; and Apter, *Translation Zone*, 18. See also Campbell, *Wireless Writing*.

11. On the role of extra-textual visual knowledge in the spectator's response to documentary footage within fiction films, see Sobchack, *Carnal Thoughts*, 259–263.

12. Soldati, "*Il grande appello*" and "Con spirito nuovo." On Castellani, see Brunetta, "L'ora d'Africa del cinema italiano," 21–22.

13. On the Western, see Studlar, "Wider Horizons," 63–76; and Abel, "Our Country/Whose Country?" On Africa as a frontier, see Stefani, *Colonia per maschi*, 86–97.

14. Soldati, "*Il grande appello*."

15. I thank Roberto Scarcella Perino for his translation of the song's title.

16. On film as voicing the un-representable, see Ferro, *Cinema and History*, 29; and Marks, *Skin of the Film*, 26. See also Stefani, *Colonia per maschi*, 126–130, and Vickers, "'Good Fellow,'" 109–134, on the British case.

17. Niranjana, *Siting Translation*.

18. Soldati, "Con spirito nuovo"; Koepnick, *Dark Mirror*, 35.

19. Luigi Freddi mentions the use of Eritreans in G.us., "Guerre e guerrieri sullo schermo." On Fascist martyrology and mourning, see Suzzi Valli, "Culto dei martiri fascisti"; Labanca, "Morire per l'Imperol"; Berezin, *Making the Fascist Self;* and Wittman, *Tomb*.

20. Savarese, "Cinematografia italiana"; Bonfiglio, "Film coloniale"; [Interlandi], "La Patria ricorre in appello"; Càllari, "Cinematografo italiano e l'Impero"; "Cronache dei film nuovi"; Sacchi, *Il grande appello,* in *Film d'Africa,* 42; Falconi, *Il grande appello,* in *Ma l'amore no,* 164–165.

21. Freddi, *Cinema,* 377–341; Brunetta and Gili, *Ora d'Africa,* 50–58.

22. Soldati, "A Carte Scoperte." I thank Emiliano Morreale for enabling me to view the program. Camerini in Germani, "Avec Mario Camerini," 118; Soldati quoted in Gili, *Cinéma italien,* 68; Camerini, interview with Savio, *Cinecittà anni trenta,* 1:215.

23. Freddi, in G.us., "Guerre e guerrieri."

24. On *Luciano Serra, pilota,* see Gili, "Film dell'impero fascista," 64–76; and De Berti, *Dallo schermo alla carta,* 85–95.

25. On *Passaporto Rosso* and the emigrant drama *Porto* (Amleto Palermi, 1935), see Zambenedetti, "Italians on the Move," chap. 1. On Italians in Argentina, see Aliano, *Mussolini's National Project.* I reference here Verdicchio, *Bound by Distance;* Choate, *Emigrant Nation;* Pretelli, *Fascismo e gli italiani all'estero;* Sanfilippo and Franzina, *Fascismo e gli emigrati;* and Tintori and Luconi, *Ombra lunga del fascismo.*

26. IL, AC, Marcellini, *Legionari del Secondo Parallelo,* 1936, Luce D004601.

27. Marcellini, "Legioniari del 2° parallelo"; Favre, "Milizia nella documentazione Luce"; Cori, *Il cinema di Romolo Marcellini,* 40–44.

28. Marcellini, "Legioniari del 2° parallelo"; Favre, "Milizia nella documentario Luce." The rhyme is lost in the English translation: "Women and motors / Joy and Sadness. New York—USA."

29. Alessandrini, "15.000 Km. di preparazione."

30. Grandi, *Politica estera dell'Italia,* 132; Clifford, *Routes,* 255.

31. Vittorio Mussolini, "Emancipazione del cinema italiano" and "Momento critico"; IL, AC, Luce B1187, October 20, 1937, "Stati Uniti, Hollywood: La visita di Vittorio Mussolini," and Luce B1184 and B1189; Sedita, "Vittorio Mussolini."

32. Quotes from Vittorio Mussolini, in "Come abbiamo fatto *Luciano Serra, pilota*"; and "Cinema per l'impero." See also De Berti, "Figure e miti ricorrenti," 305.

33. Antonioni, "Luciano Serra italianissimo pilota," 28; Augé, *Non-Place;* Creswell, "Introduction."

34. On Nazzari, see Gundle, *Mussolini's Dream Factory,* 184–202. See also De Feo, "Elementi del film nazionale"; Ristori, "Ritorno all'attore"; and "Volto ed anima italiani." *Bianco e nero*'s special issue appeared as Chiarini and Barbaro, *Attore.*

35. Landy, *Stardom Italian Style,* 65, 66; Kezich, "Attori," 393.

36. Puck, "Galleria LIX"; Gubitosi, *Amedeo Nazzari,* 21, 57, 6.

37. Vittorio Mussolini in "Come abbiamo fatto *Luciano Serra, pilota.*" Alessandrini, in the same article, mentioned the early idea for a film without an on-screen father.

38. Pagliero, "Aeronautica Militare"; Ferrari, "Aviazione Italiana"; Esposito, *Mythische Moderne;* Maggi, *Storia dei trasporti,* 188, 271; Wohl, *Spectacle of Flight.*

39. On these trips, see Segre, *Italo Balbo,* 191–265; IL, AC, Craveri, *Stormo atlantico,* 1931, Luce D048805; Craveri, *Crociera aerea del decennale;* and Contiworth, *Chicago–New York Kartwright, Chicago–New York,* both 1933, Luce DO38801 and DO39801.

40. Guerri, "Italo Balbo," 108.

41. Bertozzi, *Storia del documentario italiano,* 72–73; Steimatsky, *Italian Locations,* 16–24; Miracco, *Futurist Skies;* De Berti, "Sguardo dall'altro," 175–180.

42. Quote from De Berti, *Il volo del cinema*, 9. See Hüppauf, "Modernism and the Photographic Representation"; and Deriu, "Picturing Ruinscapes."
43. Gili, "Film dell'impero," 64; Pavolini, *Disperata*, 131–132.
44. Marcellini lauded Craveri in "Mario Craveri"; Laura, *Stagioni dell'aquila*, 103–110. On the documentary to be made from Craveri's footage, see AA, Adriano Aprà and Marco Melani's interview with Franco Riganti in Rome, May 1983.
45. Vittorio Mussolini, *Voli sulle Ambe*, 28, 47–48, 34, 71; Shapiro, *Violent Cartographies*; Bourke, *Intimate History of Killing*, 4–15.
46. Quotes from Mosconi, "Goffredo Alessandrini," 236; Alessandrini interviewed by Doletti, "Dal cielo di Campoformido"; Alessandrini, "15000 Km. di preparazione"; a. b., "*Luciano Serra, pilota*." Alessandrini, in "Come abbiamo fatto *Luciano Serra, pilota*." *Don Bosco*, Alessandrini's 1935 portrait of the Salesian missionary, used location shoots and non-professional actors.
47. Roberto Villa, Mario Ferrari, and Amedeo Nazzari, in "Come abbiamo fatto *Luciano Serra, pilota*." Ferrari's past as a pilot contributed to his billing as a "proudly masculine" actor. See "Galleria: Mario Ferrari." Aldo Tonti recalled the set's martial tenor in *Odore di cinema*, 50–55.
48. Alessandrini, "Come abbiamo fatto"; Alessandrini, interview in Savio, *Cinecittà anni trenta*, 1:33–34; Alessandrini, "15000 Km. di preparazione."
49. Quotes from Alessandrini, "15000 Km. di preparazione"; "Primizie su *Luciano Serra, pilota*."
50. Quotes from Stefani, *Colonia per maschi*, 60–61; Favre, "Milizia nella documentazione Luce"; IL, AC, Luce B0911, "La sfilata militare alla presenza del Governatore della Libia Italo Balbo," 1936, www.archivioluce.com. On the Militia in Ethiopia, see Rochat, "Volontari di Mussolini," 123–140.
51. Puck, "Galleria: Amedeo Nazari." Dialogue from *La Bandera*. Ivo Perilli, author of an early version of the screenplay, recalls that Luciano was conceived as being "kind of crazy . . . one of those aviators who fought the war of '15/'18 and never demobilized, who could not stand the idea of returning to civilian life, and did crazy things." Perilli in Savio, *Cinecittà anni trenta*, 2:923–924.
52. Marks, *Skin of the Film*, 80.
53. Visentini, "Film di questi giorni: *Luciano Serra, pilota*"; Sacchi, "*Luciano Serra, pilota*"; De Feo, "*Luciano Serra, pilota*," *Il Messaggero* (August 29, 1938), cited in Gili, "I film dell'Impero fascista," 71.
54. Antonioni, "Luciano Serra italianissimo pilota"; Alessandrini interviewed in Doletti, "Dal cielo di Campoformido."
55. Quote from Segrè, *Italo Balbo*, 392. Nazzari garnered 19,020 votes in a 1939 *Cinema* viewer poll as opposed to 5,450 for Giachetti and 4,209 for De Sica. See Gubitosi, *Amedeo Nazzari*, 9. On the *cineromanzo*, see De Berti, *Dallo schermo alla carta*, 96–108.
56. Gabriel, "Ruin and the Other," 214; Ahmed et al., "Introduction," 2.

5. IMPERIAL BODIES, PART I

1. Mattia Mininni Caracciolo, "Le scuole nelle colonie italiane di dominio diretto," *Rivista pedagogica*, vol. 4 (1930), cited in Foresti, "Problema linguistico," 141; Rafael, *Promise of the Foreign*.

2. Ferbo, "Film coloniale."

3. Valdata, *"Kiff Tebby."* On *La figlia del deserto* and other Libya films, see Ellena, *Film d'Africa*, 19–32.

4. Guido Cortese, secretary of the *fascio* of Addis Ababa, 1937, cited in Le Houérou, *Epopée des soldats*, 95. On indigenous spectacle in Libya, see Abbonizio, "Ideologia, cultura, identità," 105–129.

5. Quadrone, *Mudundu*, 10; Marcellini, "Nostri negri." Luce's *Cronache dell'Impero* did not include Somalia.

6. Quote from Orano, "Una cinematografia coloniale" (article reprinted from *L'Italia d'oltremare* of February 20, 1939). See also Cogni, "Preliminari sul cinema"; Schneider, *Mussolini in Afrika*; Sbacchi, *Colonialismo italiano in Etiopia*; Sòrgoni, *Parole e corpi*; and Del Boca, "Leggi razziali."

7. Quotes from Volla, "Cinema"; and Feldman, "Violence and Vision," 60–61.

8. Quadrone, *Mudundu*, 96; *Lei* (February 1, 1935) quoted in Pinkus, *Bodily Regimes*, 55. On the tactile and film, see Elsaesser and Hagener, *Film Theory*, 108–128; Marks, *Skin of the Film*; and Barker, *Tactile Eye*.

9. Quote from Rao and Pierce, "Discipline and the Other Body," 12. See also Codell, "Blackface," 32–46; Lombardi-Diop, "Spotless Italy," 1–22; and Rogin, *Blackface, White Noise*. On fantasies of de-negrification, see Benthien, *Skin*, 145–184.

10. On Giachetti, see Gundle, *Mussolini's Dream Factory*, 203–223. Quotes from Landy, *Stardom Italian Style*, 69. The term *autarchic divo* is from Grazzini, "In memoria di Amedeo Nazzari."

11. "Antonio Centa." Centa later remembered his amazement that Genina did not dub him in *Lo squadrone bianco*. Interview with Savio, *Cinecittà anni trenta*, 1:306–322.

12. Duranti, *Romanzo della mia vita*, 61; Mattia, "Cinema dei soldati in A.O." See the results of the poll on the cover of *Cinema* (February 10, 1941). I reference here Butler, *Bodies That Matter*.

13. Quotes from Abler, *Hinterland Warriors*, 150; and Quirico, *Squadrone bianco*, 13. See also Volterra, *Sudditi coloniali*.

14. IL, AC, Giornale Luce B0861, "L'oasi di Gadames" (April 1, 1936); also the following Giornali Luce: B0845, "L'avanzata delle truppe italiane e dei Dubat sul fronte somalo" (March 4, 1936); B0848, "3000 guerrieri della tribù dei Galla Azebò . . ." (March 11, 1936); and D005109, "Al fronte somalo con i Dubat" (1936), all www.archivioluce.com.

15. Quotes from Stefani, *Maschi in colonia*, 123; Arvidsson, *Marketing Modernity*, 38–39; and Polezzi, "Imperial Reproductions," 40. See also Pinkus, *Bodily Regimes*, 22–81; Volterra, *Sudditi coloniali*, 96–97; and Quirico, *Squadrone bianco*, 13.

16. Quote from Wilson, "All the Rage," 36.

17. Farassino, *Fuori di set*, 117, 119. On Foreign Legion movies, see Slavin, *Colonial Cinema*, 138–171; and Farassino, *Legione straniera*.

18. Germani and Martinelli, *Cinema di Augusto Genina*; Costa, "Augusto Genina," 245–252.

19. Quotes from Umberto Masetti, in *Lo spettacolo d'Italia* (December 18, 1927), and the anonymous critic of *Ciné-monde* (January 31, 1935), cited in Germani and Martinelli, *Cinema di Augusto Genina*, 193, 229; and Ferdinando Di Bagno, "Sul cinema italiano," *Spettacolo* (June 16, 1935), cited in Fanchi, "Generi," 280. Genina had also directed the silent *Zuma* (1913), starring the diva Hesperia as a Sudanese gypsy who has an affair with an Italian count.

20. Dialogue here and henceforth from the film and from the matching dialogue script, in CSC, BLC, Sezione Sceneggiature, 10818, "*Squadrone bianco:* Dialoghi." On this film, see Hay, *Popular Film Culture,* 188–192; Gili and Brunetta, *Ora d'Africa,* 28–30; Boggio, "Black Shirts/Black Skins"; Bertellini, "Colonial Autism," 263–267; and Landy, *Folklore of Consensus,* 194–197.

21. Peyré, *L'Escadron blanc,* 40.

22. Paulicelli, *Fashion under Fascism;* Falasca-Zamponi, "Peeking under the Black Shirt"; Gundle, *"Bel paese."*

23. Peyré, *L'Escadron blanc,* 28, 19.

24. Quote from Gabriel, "Ruin and the Other," 215. On the ambiguities of Fascist homosocial discourse, see Benadusi, *Nemico dell'uomo nuovo;* and Stefani, *Colonia per maschi,* 126–130.

25. Boggi, "Black Shirts/Black Skins," 13.

26. Quote from Germani and Martinelli, *Cinema di Augusto Genina,* 21. See also, in the same volume, 208–210, Genina's "Il film muto è morto: Viva il film parlante," *Corriere dello Spettacolo* (June 18, 1929).

27. Genina, quoted in Fabrizio Saragoni, "*Lo squadrone bianco,*" *L'Ora* (undated but 1936), in CF, AC, Fondo Genina, *"Lo squadrone bianco"* clip file. See also "Si gira a Sinauen"; and Veretti, "Musicisti, produttori e registi."

28. Altman, "Sound Space," 60.

29. Quote from Shaviro, *Cinematic Body,* viii. See also Masso, "Proxemics." Germani and Martinelli, *Cinema di Augusto Genina,* comment that "the indigenous voices become integrated into a magmatic sound field" (28).

30. Bertellini, "Colonial Autism," 267; Pietro Lorenzo Patanè, cited in Stefani, *Colonia per maschi,* 114.

31. Quotes from Minister of Education Bottai, cited in Foresti, "Problema linguistico," 144–145; and Apter, *Translation Zone,* 3. The film credits Ianino Nahum (along with Mario Monicelli) as an assistant director; Nahum is also described in the press as the production's translator.

32. Genina in Saragoni, "*Squadrone bianco,*" in CF, AC, Fondo Genina, *Lo squadrone bianco,* clip file.

33. Balázs, "Theory of the Film," 117; Bertellini, "Colonial Autism," 265. On the nonneutrality of silence, see Chion, *Audio-Vision,* 57; and Bonitzer, "Silences de la voix," 22–33.

34. Quotes from Germani and Martinelli, *Cinema di Augusto Genina,* 27, 28–29; IL, AC, Giornale Luce B0465, "Esercitazioni di truppe indigene in Tripolitania" (1934); Giornale Luce B0973, "Un presidio di pattuglie di Meharisti . . ." (October14, 1936); *The Desert Patrol* (Fox Films, 1933), about Italian troops in Libya, all at www.archivioluce.com. On French Sahara documentaries, see Bloom, *French Colonial Documentary,* 65–94.

35. On rival soundscapes and auditory geographies, see Rodaway, *Sensuous Geographies,* 82–114; and Bruno, *Atlas of Emotion.* The sonnet from which Vivaldi's "Winter" is drawn speaks of finding shelter at the hearth from snow and icy wind.

36. Quote from Chion, *Voice in Cinema,* 77. See also Boggi, "Black Skins/Black Masks," 288–290; and Burdett, *Italian Journeys,* 133–134.

37. Puck, "Galleria: Augusto Genina"; Costa, "Augusto Genina," 247–248.

38. Giv., "Squadrone in Marcia."

39. "Notiziario internazionale"; Giv., "Squadrone in marcia"; "Si gira a Sinauen." See also "*Squadrone bianco,*" *Cinema illustrazione* (August 5, 1936), in *Film d'Africa,* edited by

Ellena et al., 44; Genina in Saragoni, "*Squadrone bianco,*" in CF, AC, Fondo Genina, *Lo Squadrone bianco* clip file; IL, AC, Giornale Luce B0907, "La lavorazione del film *Squadrone bianco*" (June 24, 1936); and Giornale Luce B0861, "L'oasi di Gadames" (April 1, 1936), both at www.archivioluce.com.

40. Sandro De Feo, "*Squadrone bianco*"; *Il Messaggero* (August 21, 1936), cited in Gili, "I film dell'impero fascista," 47–48; Sacchi, "*Squadrone bianco*"; Bonfiglio, "Film coloniale"; "Cronache di film nuovi: *Il grande appello, Lo Squadrone bianco.*" See also Genina in Saragoni, "*Squadrone bianco,*" in CF, AC, Fondo Genina, *Lo squadrone bianco,* clip file, which contains "*Squadrone bianco,*" review in *La Tribuna,* and many other reviews; and Maurice De Kobra to Genina, February 20, 1937, in Germani and Martinelli, *Cinema di Augusto Genina,* 247.

41. Quotes from Peyré, in "*L'Escadron Blanc,*" *Le Figaro* (February 19, 1936); Maurice Bardèche, "*L'Escadron blanc,*" *L'assaut* (March 2, 1937); and other French reviews, all in CF, AC, Fondo Genina, clip book "*Lo squadrone bianco:* Critiche francesi."

42. Angioletti, "Cinema italiano in Francia." See also Savarese, "Cinematografia italiana." A Ministry of Popular Culture telegram to Genina, November 16, 1938, noted that his film, projected both in the original and in a dubbed German version, was currently playing in thirteen different theaters in Berlin alone: in CF, AC, Fondo Genina, "*Lo squadrone bianco,*" which documents the film's foreign success.

43. Marcellini, "Avventura."

44. l. c. [Chiarini], "*I Lancieri del Bengala:* Il soggetto"; Marcellini, "Avventura." Figures on U.S. film intake from Fanchi, "Generi," 291.

45. Marcellini, "Avventura"; Marcellini in Savio, *Cinecittà anni trenta,* 705; Benthein, *Skin.*

46. Hess, *Italian Colonialism in Somalia,* 170, 186.

47. Figures from Pretelli, "Education in the Italian Colonies," 283; Buonaiuti, *Politica e religioni,* 431; and IL, AC, *Somalia italiana* (1932), Luce D033001, at www.archivioluce.com. Only 10 percent of *askaris* came from Somalia. See Moreno, "Politica e istruzione," 78.

48. Burdett, *Journeys through Fascism,* 134; Niranjana, *Siting Translation,* 11–35. My analysis of Italian-language speech in this English-dubbed film reflects my translations back into the original language, and I have been guided in this by criteria of conformity with the language commonly used in empire films and by the matching of gesture and body language to speech.

49. Labanca and Abbattista, "Living Ethnological and Colonial Exhibitions."

50. I am not arguing for a relation of influence here, since Sabu made his film debut the same year, in Robert Flaherty and Zoltan Korda's *Elephant Boy.* Both films are part of a larger European imperial discourse of labor exploitation predicated on the figure of the dark-skinned "boy" as servant, imperial court jester, and, at times, sexual surrogate.

51. Quote from Rao and Pierce, "Discipline and the Other Body," 22. On Indigenous Tribunals, see Buonaiuti, *Politica e religione,* 112–113; Hess, *Italian Colonialism in Somalia,* 109–112; and Martone, *Giustizia coloniale.*

52. Although the word "rape" is used on-screen (subtitles were used for Somali dialogue), I have used the word "kidnap." It is probable that the use of "rape" is a mistranslation from the Italian original *rapire,* which makes more sense in the context of the film, although rape is a distinct possibility, given Dabahò's presentation as war booty.

53. Silverman, *Acoustic Mirror,* 44. See also Chion, *Audio-Vision;* Doane, "Voice in the Cinema"; and Bourdieu, *Language and Symbolic Power.* I thank Igiaba Scego for her observations on the Somali language used in this film.

54. Quotes from synopsis in Cori, *Cinema di Romolo Marcellini*, 47–48; Duranti, *Romanzo della mia vita*, 71; and interview with Savio, *Cinecittà anni trenta*, 2:498. The character of Dahabò is not mentioned in the Ministry of Popular Culture's summary of the film. See the *nulla osta* of October 31, 1937, at www.italiataglia.it. On these issues, see Codell, "Blackface, Faciality, and Colony Nostalgia"; and Pickering-Iazzi, "Ways of Looking."

55. Duranti, *Romanzo della mia vita*, 72.

56. Quotes from Marks, *Skin of the Film*, xi; Marcellini, "I nostri negri"; and Pinkus, *Bodily Regimes*, 50. See also Sòrgoni, "'Defending the Race.'"

57. Quotes from Oksiloff, *Picturing the Primitive*, 4; Kracauer, *Theory of Film*, 303; and MacDougall, *Transcultural Cinema*, 69.

58. Duranti, *Romanzo della mia vita*, 70–71; Marcellini, "Nostri negri."

59. Marcellini, "Avventura"; Terra, "*Sentinelle di bronzo*"; Duranti, *Romanzo della mia vita*, 70–72; Niranjana, *Siting Translation*, 64–86, on ethnography as translation.

60. Marcellini, "Avventura."

61. Aumont, *Du visage au cinéma*; Doane, "Close-Up," 89–111; Deleuze, "Year Zero," 167–191.

62. Cori, *Cinema di Romolo Marcellini*, 47–48; Braidotti, *Nuovi soggetti nomadi*, 57.

63. First and last quote from "*Sentinelle di bronzo*," *Bianco e nero*; others from Deben [Giacomo Debenedetti], "In questi giorni: *Sentinelle di bronzo*"; and Sacchi, "*Sentinelle di bronzo*." The story's weakness is commented on by Bonfiglio, "Film coloniale"; and Savarese, "Cinematografia italiana."

64. Deben, "In questi giorni: *Sentinelle di bronzo*"; Ferbo, "Film coloniale"; Fiume, "Atmosfera e ambiente."

65. "La V Mostra d'Arte Cinematografica a Venezia: *Sentinelle di bronzo*"; Zunino, *L'ideologia del fascismo*, 124.

6. IMPERIAL BODIES, PART II

1. Quotes from Labanca, *Oltremare*, 355; Schwarz, "Colonial Disgust"; and Stoler, *Carnal Knowledge*.

2. Zewde, *History of Ethiopia*; Bestemann, *Unraveling Somalia*, 55–57.

3. Quotes from Greene, *Equivocal Subjects*, 53; and Triulzi, "Introduzione," 15–16.

4. Quadrone, *Mudundu*, 81–82; Duranti, *Romanzo della mia vita*, 78; Miran, *Red Sea Citizens*, 4.

5. Quotes from Podestà, *Il mito dell'impero*, 331. I thank Gian Luca Podestà for clarifying aspects of Fascist labor policies for me. Ciro Poggiali, "La nuova Addis Abeba," *Annali dell'Africa Italiana* 1, no. 2 (1938), cited in Fuller, *Moderns Abroad*, 199.

6. Locatelli, "Beyond the Campo Cintato"; Barrera, "Mussolini's Colonial Race Laws," 428; Le Houérou, *Épopée des soldats*, 89.

7. Labanca, *Oltremare*, 318; Locatelli, "Beyond the Campo Cintato"; Pankhurst, "Italian and Native Labour," 67, 60; Le Houérou, *Épopée des Soldats*, 115–136, 154–155.

8. Quotes from Giacomo Guiglia, *Lineamenti economici del nuovo Impero* (Genova: Emiliano degli Orfini, 1938), 341, cited in Pankhurst, "Italian and Native Labour," 67; figure on Asmara from Barrera, "Racial Hierarchies in Colonial Eritrea," 85; Le Houérou, *Épopée des Soldats*.

9. Quote from "Instruzioni di Lessona," in Podestà, *Il mito dell'impero*, 378; Locatelli, "Beyond the Campo Cintato" and her "'Ozioso, vagabondo, e prezioso.'"

10. Number of cohabitations from Matard-Bonucci, "Italian Fascism's Ethiopian Conquest," 104; Stefani, *Colonia per maschi*, 130–162; Trento, "Madamato and Colonial Concubinage," 184–205; Stoler, *Carnal Knowledge*, esp. 79–111, on these issues in French Indochina and the Dutch Indies.

11. Quote from Poggiali, "La donna italiana in A.O."; Le Houerou, *Épopée des Soldats*, 98. Figures from Pickering-Iazzi, "Mass-Mediated Fantasies," 206–207; Spadaro, "Intrepide Massaie," 27–52; Stefani, *Colonia per maschi*, 142–143; Martone, *Giustizia coloniale*, 300–312; Besteman, *Unraveling Somalia*, 55–56; RaiYouTube, "Montanelli, una moglie di 12 anni in Eritrea," at http://youtu.be/e_53KvZvTs8.

12. For Ethiopia, see Pankhurst, "Italian and Native Labour," 63–64; and Podestà, *Mito dell'impero*, 319–322. On Somalia, see Podestà, *Mito dell'impero*, 202–203; and Labanca, *Oltremare*, 311–330. For Libya, see Cresti, *Oasi di Italianità*; and Fuller, *Moderns Abroad*, 171–196. See Cooper, *Plantation Slavery*, for non-Italian East Africa.

13. Quotes from Besteman, *Unraveling Somalia*, 182; Ernesto Lama, "Presupposti corporative dell'economia coloniale," in Istituto Coloniale Fascista, *Atti del Terzo Congresso di Studi Coloniali* (Florence, 1937), 8:69, cited in Pankhurst, "Italian and Native Labour," 69. See also Bertizzolo and Pietrantonio, "Denied Reality?"

14. Quadrone, *Mudundu*,11, 9. In February 1934 Quadrone wrote a treatment with French director Gaston Biasini, entitled "Somalia," which was the basis for the untitled script Quadrone and Dreyer worked on together. Both can be consulted at the Danish Film Institute, Dreyer Archive, D I, B:14. The film's original title during the period of Dreyer's involvement was *Mudundu*,

15. Quadrone, *Mudundu*, 31.

16. Ibid., 56–58.

17. Ibid.,, 171, 205, 32.

18. The 2005 DVD produced by Les Documents Cinématographiques has interviews with Paulin's son and others and an audio reading of Quadrone and Dreyer's script illustrated with drawings by Denis Scoupe.

19. Quadrone, "*Mudundu* di Dreyer."

20. Georges Rigaud was credited as Giorgio Rigatti in the Italian version; Jeannette Ferney's role was played by Luisa Garrella. All dialogue is from *L'Esclave blanc*.

21. Fiume, "Atmosfera e ambiente."

22. Dubow, "From a View on the World," 96. On theatricality as an index of unstable identity, see Landy, *Folklore of Consensus*, xi.

23. The director's father, Paul Paulin, sculpted busts of friends such as Camille Pissarro, Auguste Renoir, Claude Monet, and Edgar Degas. Paulin Jr.'s first film, *La femme nue/The Nude Woman* (1932), features many naturalistic exterior shots of Paris (along with an African-themed artists' party).

24. Quotes from Quadrone, *Mudundu*, 13–14; and Harrison, *Forests*.

25. On cinema as window and frame, see Elsaesser and Hagener, *Film Theory*, 13–34.

26. Quotes from IL, AC, Luce D064901, "La fondazione della nuova Addis Abeba" (G. Martucci, 1939), which praises the removal of one hundred thousand indigenous to the periphery, at www.archivioluce.com; and Quadrone, *Mudundu*, 45. See also Fuller, *Moderns Abroad*, 197–213.

27. Quote from Pinkus, *Bodily Regimes*, 58; and Bazin, "Life and Death of Superimposition." See also IL, AC, Giornali Luce B0392, "Somalia: Una piantagione di cotone" (Janu-

ary 1934); B0600, "Somalia: Villaggio Duca degli Abbruzzi; La coltivazione del cotone" (January 1935), and B0603, "Italia Somala: La coltivazione delle banane" (January 1935), all at www.archivioluce.com.

28. Quotes from Quadrone, *Mudundu*, 111, 235, 128, 96–97; and Besteman, *Unraveling Somalia*, 182.

29. Quadrone, *Mudundu*, 50, 53–54, 127–128, 129.

30. Ibid., 20, 30; Quadrone, "*Mudundu* di Dreyer."

31. Bonfiglio, "Film coloniale"; Ferbo, "Film coloniale"; Savarese, "Cinematografia italiana"; Carancini, "*Jungla nera.*"

32. Quotes from Ministry of Popular Culture, Direzione Generale per la Cinematografia, *nulla osta* of July 8, 1937, searchable under *Jungla nera* at www.italiataglia.it; Sacchi, "*Jungla nera.*"

33. Duncan, *Reading and Writing*.

34. Wilson, "Decivilising Mission."

35. Quotes from Comin, "Propositi e realtà"; and Sabatello, "Si prepara *Sotto la Croce del Sud.*" See also "Primizie di *Sotto la Croce del Sud*"; and "*Sotto la Croce del Sud*, nuovo film d'Africa," for the role of Mailù and the wives in the original script. As in *Sentinelle di bronzo*, the producer Eugenio Fontana, Duranti's lover, mandated her presence and prominence.

36. Quotes from Comin, "Propositi e realtà"; and Cogni, "Prelminari sul cinema." See also Di Donno, "Razza Ario-Mediterranea"; and Gillette, *Racial Theories in Fascist Italy*.

37. Sabatello, "Si prepara *Sotto la Croce del Sud*," on emigranti in Comin's script.

38. "Il cinema per l'Impero."

39. Comin, "Propositi e realtà." I reference here Pickering-Iazzi, "Ways of Seeing" (whose analysis is otherwise exemplary); Greene, *Equivocal Subjects*, chap. 2; and Hay, *Popular Film Culture*, 192–196. Landy, *Folklore of Consensus*, 197–200, declines to label Mailù's ethnicity.

40. Quotes from Springer, "Newspaper Meets the Dime Novel," 34; Jaikumar, *Cinema at the End of Empire*, 135–164. See also Gledhill, *Home Is Where the Heart Is*; Mercer and Shingler, *Melodrama*; Williams, "Melodrama Revised"; and Elsaesser, "Tales of Sound and Fury." See Vasudevan, *Melodramatic Public*, for debates over melodrama as form and genre, and Landy, "Introduction," in *Imitations of Life*, 13–30.

41. Quote from Fiume, "Africa in bianco e nero." See also Gianni Canova, "Infiammazione della lacrima." Brignone's melodramas include *Corte d'assise* (1930), *La voce lontana* (1933), *Tenebre* (1934), and *Teresa Confalieri* (1934).

42. Quote from Gorbman, *Unheard Melodies*, 6. Duranti's "sharing" of a voice with Greta Garbo (both were dubbed by Tina Lattanzi) reinforced her association with metropolitan and foreign glamour—as *Bianco e nero*'s anonymous critic observed in ""La VI Mostra d'Arte Cinematografica di Venezia: *Sotto la Croce del Sud.*"

43. Cogni, "Preliminari sul cinema."

44. Greene, *Equivocal Subjects*, 70.

45. "La VI Mostra d'Arte Cinematografica di Venezia: *Sotto la Croce del Sud*"; Bazin, "Life and Death of Superimposition."

46. Vasudevan, *Melodramatic Public*, 19.

47. Quotes from Pickering-Iazzi, "Ways of Looking," 200–221; Canova, "Infiammazione della lacrima," 9: "*una storia mai del tutto dicibile.*"

48. Balázs, "Theory of the Film: Sound," 117.
49. Marks, *Skin of the Film*, 129.
50. Canova, "Infiammazione della lacrima," 8.
51. "La VI Mostra d'Arte Cinematografica di Venezia: *Sotto la Croce del Sud*"; De Feo, "*Sotto la Croce del Sud*," *Il Messaggero* (September 1, 1938); "*Sotto la Croce del Sud*, nuovo film d'Africa"; Vice, "*Sotto la Croce del Sud*"; Guido Brignone in Càllari, "Il cinematografo italiano e l'impero." D. [Mino Doletti], "Lettere," alludes to bad behavior by the viewing public at the Venice Biennale.
52. "La VI Mostra d'Arte Cinematografica di Venezia: *Sotto la Croce del Sud*"; McGuire, in "Fascism's Mediterranean Empire," notes "the foreign and potentially dangerous stranger in the midst was kept alive through the idea of the Levant" (131).
53. Fiume, "Bilancio di stagione"; Duranti, *Romanzo della mia vita*, 78, 82.
54. Quotes from Càlleri, "Il cinematografo italiano e l'Impero"; Balestrazzi, "Il cinematografo e l'Impero"; "Sottocenere: *Equatore*"; Visentini, "Film di questi giorni: *Equatore*"; Blasetti in Càllari, "Il cinematografo italiano e l'Impero." See also Fiume, "Due Afriche."
55. Quotes from Orano, "Una cinematografia coloniale"; and Fiume essays "Atmosfera e ambiente," "Le due Afriche," and "Inferno giallo e inferno nero"; and Càllari, "Cinematografia italiana e l'Impero."
56. Sobchack, *Carnal Thoughts*, 259, 267n16; Sobchack, "Toward a Phenomenology of Nonfictional Film Experience"; Noël Carroll, *Engaging the Moving Image*.
57. Balestrazzi, "Il cinematografo e l'Impero"; Càllari, "Il cinematografo italiano e l'Impero."
58. All of the above from Càllari, "Il cinematografo italiano e l'Impero."

7. FILM POLICIES AND CULTURES, 1940–1943

1. Mussolini, "Popolo italiano! Corri alle armi...," 403, 404; IL, AC, Mussolini, "1940: 10 giugno; Anno XVIII," Luce D035001, www.archivioluce.com.
2. Verdone, "Cinematografo e la guerra."
3. Quotes from De Santis, "Giarabub"; and Casiraghi and Viazzi, "Motivi di rinascita."
4. Quote from Farassino, *Fuori del set*, 145; and Alessandrini interview in Savio, *Cinecittà anni trenta*, 1:46. On *Harlem Knockout*, see Nazzari interview in Savio, *Cinecittà anni trenta*, 3:826.
5. Quotes from Ciano, *Diario*, entry of October 13, 1941; and "Vincere." See also "Guerra di principi." On these ambitions, see Rodogno, *Fascism's European Empire*; Burgwyn, *Empire on the Adriatic*; Knox, *Mussolini Unleashed*; and Burgwyn, *Mussolini Warload*. On initial popular consent for the war, see Imbriani, *Italiani e il Duce*, 82–97.
6. Quotes from "Umanità di nostra guerra"; Loffredo, "Nuovi caratteri del soldato italiano"; and Duvignand, "Esquisse pour le nomade," 19. See also Zavoli, "Spirito della modernità fascista"; and Curcio, "Guerra e dopoguerra." On the continuities between African and Balkan repressions, see Rodogno, *Fascism's European Empire*, 63, 333; and Mazower, *Hitler's Empire*, 349–350.
7. Quotes from Duranti, *Romanzo della mia vita*, 110; Ojetti, "Italia in mostra," 742; and Calvino, *Entry into the War*, 9. On bombings of Italy, see Baldoli and Knapp, *Forgotten Blitzes*; and Gribaudi, *Guerra totale*.
8. Pavolini cited in Martin, "A New Order for European Culture," 102–103; Pavolini, "Geografia cinematografica"; Pavolini, "Capi e popolo," 14–15; Giuliano, *Latinità e Ger-*

manesimo, 3, 152. On these issues, see Petersen, "Italia-Germania"; Ben-Ghiat, "Fascist Italy and Nazi Germany"; and Hoffend, *Zwischen Kultur-Asche und Kulturkampf.*

9. Quote from Elio Zorzi, "Collaborazione europea," *Primi piani* (August 1941), cited in Argentieri, *L'asse cinematografico,* 53 (figures from same source, 19); de Grazia, *Irresistible Empire,* 319–335.

10. Pietrangeli, "Mostra Veneziana." On the Biennale, see Marla Stone, "Last Film Festival."

11. Quote from Goebbels, *Tagebücher,* entry for June 13, 1941, 9:369–370; see also June 28, 1941, 9:409–410; and Michelangelo Antonioni cited in Spagnoletti, "Registi stranieri in Italia," 265. For period figures on export sales, see Pavolini, "Rapporto sulla cinematografia italiana"; and Argentieri, *L'asse cinematografico,* 111–149. On Italian-Romanian filmic relations, see Lazar and Spila, *Cineromit;* and Romano, *Giuseppe Volpi.*

12. Laura, *Stagioni dell'aquila,* 183; Argentieri, *L'asse cinematografico,* 111–149; Gili, "Distribution des film italiens," 166–167; Argentieri, *Cinema in guerra,* 222.

13. Argentieri, *Il cinema in guerra;* Forgacs and Gundle, *Mass Culture,* tables on 6 and 126. On mobile cinemas, see Virtue,"Royal Army, Fascist Empire"; Krimer, "Lettera dall'Africa settentrionale"; "Per i soldati in guerra"; and Canepelle and Rigon, *Fra luci e ombre,* 106.

14. "Disciplina, fantasia, intelligenza"; Argentieri, "Autarchia e internazionalità"; de Grazia, *Irresistible Empire,* 326–327; Forgacs and Gundle, *Mass Culture,* 208.

15. Quotes from Alberto Lattuada cited in Quaresima, "Parigi ci appartiene?," 448–449; Casiraghi, "Cinema e vita militare," reports on the "profound impression" left by Renoir's military drama. French films had 5.0 percent of the market in the late 1930s, but this rose to 17.6 percent for 1940 as opposed to 22.9 percent for American films. See Forgacs and Gundle, *Mass Culture,* 126.

16. Quote from *La Provincia di Bolzano* in Canepelle and Rigon, *Fra luci e ombre,* 224–225. I thank Dr. Alfonso Venturini for the Florence figures calculated from *La Nazione.*

17. Antonioni, "Vita impossibile del signor Clark Costa." The *Cinema* survey began with Umberto Barbaro and Luigi Chiarini, "Pro o contro? Inchiesta sul doppiato" (January 10, 1941), and ran to April 10, 1941, concluding with a summary by Antonioni, "Conclusioni sul doppiato" (April 25, 1941).

18. Fiume, "Un anno di cinema coloniale."

19. Quote from Cerchio, "Servizio di guerra"; and De Franciscis, "La guerra è protagonista." See also Laura, *Stagioni dell'aquila,* 178; and Argentieri, *L'occhio del regime.*

20. On these centers, see Argentieri, *Cinema in guerra.*

21. Quotes from Ferretti, "Il nuovo Luce"; Càllari, "L'arma più forte"; and De Franciscis, "La guerra è protagonista."

22. Quotes from "Operatori in prima linea"; U. d. f. [De Franciscis], "Documentari bellici"; and Cerchio, "Evoluzione del film-giornale." On camera operators as combatants, see also Cerchio, "Servizio di guerra"; Cenci, "Operatori della R. Aeronautica"; and Vittorio Calvino, "Operatori cinematografici della Reale Marina." On the remoteness of wartime newsreels, see Olivetti, "Cinegiornale e film di soggetto."

23. Fulks, "Walter Ruttmann"; Short, *Film and Radio Propaganda;* Chapman, *British at War;* Hoffmann, *Triumph of Propaganda,* 135–169; Argentieri, *Cinema in guerra.*

24. Quotes from F. C., "Fronte di guerra"; Cerchio, "Composizione e montaggio"; and "Come il popolo italiano." On these issues, see Argentieri, *L'occhio del regime,* 235–236, 242.

25. Review in *La Provincia di Bolzano* (July 27, 1940) cited in Caneppale and Rigon, *Fra luci e ombre*, 105–106; Isani, "Forza del documento bellico." See also V. Mussolini, "Cinema di Guerra."

26. Pavolini, "Cinema in guerra"; U. d. f. [De Franciscis], "Il documentario deve documentare"; Giuseppe Croce, "Documentari cinematografici della guerra italiana," in *Cinema italiano—Anno XIX* (Rome: Direzione Generale della Cinematografia, 1941), cited in Laura, *Stagioni dell'aquila*, 176.

27. IL, AC, cataloged as *Il primo colpo all'impero britannico: La conquista della Somalia inglese*, 1940 Luce D001001, www.archivioluce.com.

28. Doletti, "7 giorni a Roma"; "Operatori in prima linea."

29. Musu, "Parlano gli operatori"; Croce, "Documentari cinematografici," cited in Laura, *Stagioni dell'acquila*, 177; Bertozzi, *Storia del documentario italiano*, 91. *La battaglia dello Jonio* is cataloged as *La battaglia dello Ionio:* IL, AC, 1940, Luce D000304, www.archivioluce.com.

30. Musu, "Parlano gli operatori"; Càllari, "7 giorni a Roma: I documentari."

31. Quotes from "Cinematografo strumento"; and Reanda, "Cinematografia di guerra." *Cine-magazzino* (March 20, 1941) cited in Argentieri, *Il cinema in guerra*, 21.

32. Quotes from De Robertis, undated (but 1939) letter to undersecretary of the navy, in USMM, titolare 8, fasc. 2820; R. L., "Due Avvenimenti," *Cinema* (May 25, 1941). On Scalera, see Lughi, "La Scalera Film."

33. De Robertis, "Criteri di indirizzo," and the February 1, 1939, approval memorandum from the office of the navy undersecretary; and De Robertis, "Pro-memoria," January 18, 1939, all in USMM, titolare 8, f.2820.

34. Quotes from Casiraghi, "Cinema e vita militare"; De Santis, "Per un paesaggio italiano"; Casiraghi and Viazzi, "Presentazione postuma di un classico"; and Pietrangeli, "Mostra veneziana."

35. De Robertis, "Pro-memoria"; De Robertis, "Criteri di indirizzo"; and the February 1, 1939, approval memo from the office of the navy undersecretary, in USMM, titolare 8, f.2820. See also Giannini, "Fra realtà e finzione"; and Aprà, "Storie di guerra," 69–88.

36. Rondolino, *Rossellini*, 46; Gallagher, *Adventures of Roberto Rossellini*, 55–56; Caminati, *Roberto Rossellini documentarista*, 13–46.

37. Seknadje-Askenazi, *Roberto Rossellini et la seconde guerre mondiale*, 23–30, 39–45; Gallagher, *Adventures of Roberto Rossellini*, 66–72, 690; Brunette, *Roberto Rossellini*, 11–19.

38. De Robertis, "Criteri di indirizzo" and "Pro-memoria," January 18, 1939, all in USMM, titolario 8, f.2820; De Robertis, "Appunti per un film d'aviazione"; Macciocchi, *Femmes et leurs maîtres*, 81.

39. On the influence of Eisenstein in this movie, see Brunette, *Roberto Rossellini*, 13–15.

40. Craig, *Cinema after Fascism*, 17–26.

41. Information on screenings in USMM, titolario 8, f.2820, sf.2. See also Meccoli, "Nuovi registi"; Francisci, "Del 'puro' e del 'romanzato' nel documentario"; Alberini, "Rendiconto morale"; Pietro Bianchi [Volpone], "La nave bianca," *Bertoldo* (October 31, 1941), reprinted in Bianchi, *L'Occhio di vetro*, 94–95; Isani, review of *La nave bianca;* and Aristarco, "Scuola dei registi."

42. See Casiraghi, "Cinema e vita militare."

43. Isani, "Film di questi giorni: *La nave bianca*"; Fulchignani, "Film della Mostra di Venezia"; Aprà, *In viaggio con Rossellini*, 54. See also Bertozzi, *Storia del documentario italiano*, 97.

8. THE END OF EMPIRE

1. Quotes from "Cinema strumento"; and Pavolini, "Cinema in guerra." Information on censorship from Pavolini, "Rapporto della cinematografia"; and Ceroni, "Cinematografia nell'ora attuale." For the reframing of empire films as war films after 1941, see Freddi, "Gente dell'aria; and Casiraghi, "Cinema e vita militare."

2. Quotes from Pavolini, "Rapporto della cinematografia italiana"; Asvero Gravelli in *Film* (May 23, 1942), reprinted in *Film d'Africa,* edited by Ellena et al., 91; and Vice, "Film di questi giorni: *Giarabub*."

3. Vice, "Film di questi giorni: *Giarabub*"; Calcagno, "Sette giorni a Roma: *Giarabub.*" The phrase "war women" is from Fox, *Filming Women.*

4. Cannonieri, *Mia avventura fra gli Arussi,* 94–95, cited in Stefani, *Colonia per maschi,* 62–63.

5. Quotes from Deriu, "Picturing Ruinscapes," which discusses the British Royal Air Force's Central Interpretation Unit; L., "Fotocinematografia Aerea." See ASAM, Stato Maggiore dell'Aeronautica, 5th Reparto, Ufficio Storico: Album 80, "L'Aviazione italiana sul Fronte Greco-Albanese-Jugoslavo (anno XIX)—Effetti di mitragliamento e bombardamento," and Diario Storico, 1942, Sezione Autonoma Aerofotografica, "Relazione Rilievi aerofotogrammetrici Africa Settentrionale," March 10–May 17, 1942; IL, AC, *Ali fasciste/ Fascist Wings,* Giornale Luce C0081 (October 8, 1940), www.archivioluce.com.

6. R. G., "Momento aeronautico"; De Robertis, "Appunti per un film d'aviazione." I reference Ferroni, *L'ebbrezza del cielo/The Intoxication of the Air* (1940); Franciolini, *Giorni felici/Happy Days* (1942); Camerini, *Centomila dollari/One Hundred Thousand Dollars* (1939); Alessandrini, *Il ponte di vetro* (1939); Mattioli, *Mussolini aviatore;* and Ceroni, "Cinematografia nell'ora attuale."

7. R. G., "Momento aeronautico."

8. Quotes from L., "A Roberto Rossellini"; R. G., "Momento aeronautico"; and L., "*Un pilota ritorna*." Rossellini had intended to use a non-professional as lead, and he hired Massimo Girotti only when an open call produced no one suitable ("Concorso per il film *Un pilota ritorna*"). On Antonioni during this time, see Steimatsky, *Italian Locations,* 1–39.

9. Michael Curtiz, born Mario' Kertész Kaminer in Hungary, directed combat films such as *The Charge of the Light Brigade* and *Dive Bomber* before making *Casablanca.* See Basinger, *World War Two Combat Film;* Doherty, *Projections of War;* Koppes and Black, *Hollywood Goes to War;* and Mackenzie, *British War Films.*

10. AA, "*Un pilota ritorna*: Soggetto originale." On the Greek occupation, see Rodogno, *Fascism's European Empire;* Mazower, *Hitler's Empire,* 340–353; and Santarelli, "Muted Violence."

11. Apter, *Translation Zone,* 16.

12. Fiume, "Inferno giallo e inferno nero"; Aprà, "In viaggio con Rossellini," 33; Aprà, "Storie di Guerra: De Robertis e Rossellini"; Brunette, *Roberto Rossellini,* 19–24.

13. Gorbman, *Unheard Melodies,* 5.

14. On point of audition sound, see Altman, "Sound Space," 60–61.

15. Quotes from Seknadje-Askenazi, *Roberto Rossellini et la seconde guerre mondiale,* 90–91; and Altman, "Sound Space," 60. See also Aprà, "In viaggio con Rossellini," on this theme.

16. Benjamin, "Work of Art"; Buck-Morss, "Aesthetics and Anaesthetics."

17. Rao and Pierce, "Discipline and the Other Body," 5.

18. AA, "*Un pilota ritorna:* Soggetto originale."

19. Chion, *Voice in Cinema,* 153.

20. Quotes from L., "A Roberto Rossellini"; and L., "*Un pilota ritorna.*" Notice of the deaths during production in Gallagher, *Adventures of Roberto Rossellini,* 73. Rome figures from Argentieri, *Cinema in guerra,* 49. Florence figures from *La Nazione,* compiled by Alfonso Venturini. I thank Dr Venturini for these. Other 1942 Committee releases included De Robertis's *Alfa Tau* (fifty-eight days), Marcellini's *Mas* (twenty-six days), Genina's *Bengasi* (seventy-three days), and Alessandrini's *Giarabub* (sixty-eight days).

21. Calcagnò, "7 giorni a Roma: *Un pilota ritorna*"; Piovene, "*Un pilota ritorna.*"

22. Càllari, "Tre autentici registi."

23. Quotes from Alicata and De Santis, "Verità e poesia"; De Santis, "Film di questi giorni: *Un pilota ritorna.*" See also De Santis, "Linguaggio dei rapport" and "Per un paesaggio italiano." On these issues, see Scotto d'Ardino, *Revue Cinéma et le néo-realisme italien;* Steimatsky, *Italian Locations,* 79–86; and Minghelli, *Landscape and Memory,* 20–38.

24. De Santis, "Film di questi giorni: *Un pilota ritorna.*" On the different realisms in development during the war, see Argentieri, *Cinema in guerra,* 124–125, 269–296; and Marcus, *Italian Film,* 14–29.

25. Bonaffini, *Mare di paura;* Gabriel, "The Ruin and the Other."

26. Solv., "'Tempo nostro' e ambientazione dei film." On the film's gender politics, see Stone, "Last Film Festival"; and Argentieri, *Cinema in guerra,* 68–73.

27. Quotes from Giovannetti, "Registi"; and Puck, "Galleria: Augusto Genina."

28. Canella, "Tema libico"; Fellini cited in Gili, "I film dell'impero fascista," 41.

29. Quote from De Stefani, Alessandro (one of the film's screenwriters), "*Bengasi,* superbo documento di incrollabile fede italiana contro la prepotenza e le barbarie inglesi." *Il Lavoro Fascista* (October 29, 1942), in CF, AC, Fondo Genina, *Bengasi* clip file, along with Ingevelde Karwehl, "Ein Film mit 160 Rollen," *Volk-Zeitung* (September 13, 1942); CF, AC, Fondo Genina, *Bengasi* press book; and Germani and Martinelli, *Il cinema di Augusto Genina,* 267–268.

30. Rossellini, "Schermi sonori"; Pasinetti, "I film della Mostra di Venezia," CF, AC, Fondo Genina, *Bengasi* clip file, reviews of *Bengasi* in *Primi piani* (April 1942) and in *Cinemagazzino.*

31. Von Leeuwen, *Speech, Music, Sound,* 110–111, on such sound acts.

32. Quote from M. Caviglia, "Un grande film coloniale: *Bengasi,*" *La Tribuna* (October 25, 1942). See *Espansione Imperiale* (September 20, 1942), in CF, AC, Fondo Genina, *Bengasi* clip file, along with *Cine-magazzino's* review.

33. Gubitosi, *Amedeo Nazzari,* 5.

34. Stone, "Last Picture Show," 302. See Lombardi-Diop, "Pioneering Female Modernity," on the imperial journeys of professional women.

35. This scene presages the American-Italian encounter in the Sicilian episode of Rossellini's *Paisa,* where Joe teaches Carmela simple words like "milk."

36. The erasure of Libyan agency in the film stands in contrast to the actual violence that plagued Benghazi and other Libyan areas where the temporary evacuation of Italian authority led to Arab reprisal killings and vandalism (to which Italians responded with equal brutality, persecuting Libyan Jews for good measure and deporting many to the Giado concentration camp). See Bernhard, "Behind the Battle Lines," 425–446; and Salerno, *Uccideteli tutti.*

37. Denti di Pijano, *Cure for Serpents,* 264.

38. E. A. F. [Fiume], "Piloti e fanti nel deserto sirtico"; IL, AC, Marcellini, *Piloti a fanti nel deserto sirtico* (1941), Luce D007102; an uncredited film of the same title and length is listed as Luce D028203, both at www.archivioluce.com.

39. Quote from m. g. [Gromo], *"Bengasi"*; Fiume, *"Bengasi,"* and the following reviews in CF, AC, Fondo Genina, *Bengasi* clip file: Karwehl, "Film mit 160 Rollen"; Caviglia, "Un grande film italiano: *Bengasi*"; reviews of *Bengasi* in *Cinemagazzino* and *Primi piani*; and Giorgio Almirante, "*Bengasi*, il film che documenta la pattriotica passione del nostro popolo e l'inciviltà del barbaro nemico," *Il Tevere* (October 26, 1942).

40. Quotes from Vice, "Film di questi giorni: *Bengasi*"; Pietrangeli, "I film della Mostra di Venezia"; and the reviews in CF, AC, Fondo Genina, *Bengasi* clip file: Almirante, "*Bengasi*"; Mario Milani, *"Bengasi," Alba* (November 15, 1942); Raffaele Calzini, "Film quotidiano," *Venezia* (September 6, 1942).

41. Quotes from Pietrangeli, "La Mostra veneziana"; Vice, "Film di questi giorni: *Bengasi*"; and from reviews in CF, AC, Fondo Genina, *Bengasi* clip file: Piovene, review in *Primato*; Franci, Adolfo, *"Bengasi," L'Illustrazione Italiana* (November 1, 1942); "Alla decima mostra cinematografica veneziana," *La Voce Cattolica* (September 19, 1942).

42. CF, AC, Fondo Genina, *Bengasi* press book, "Dai tecnici"; quote from CF, AC, Fondo Genina, *Bengasi* clip file; A. Z., "*Bengasi*: Epopea della gente in Cirenaica," *Calabria Fascista* (November 5, 1942).

43. Florence figures compiled by Alfonso Venturini, from *La Nazione*. Franco Bassoli, telegram to Genina, October 23, 1942; and Direzione Generale di Cinematografia, telegram to Genina, October 24 1942, in CF, AC, Fondo Genina, *Bengasi*, clip file, which documents these Axis openings.

44. Bargelesi, *Bengasi città murata*, 94, 259, 267; Argentieri, *Cinema in guerra*, 52, on the theater adaptation.

45. Quotes from Tobino, "Deserts of Libya," undated entry (but 1941), 231; Calzini, "*Bengasi*."

46. Casetti, *Eye of the Century*, 170.

47. Fiume, "Inferno giallo e inferno nero"; and his "Atmosfera e ambiente del cinema coloniale."

48. Favre, "Film di Guerra"; Lattuada, *Occhio quadrato* (1941), reprinted in *Alberto Lattuada fotografo*, edited by Berengo Gardin, 15.

49. Figures from Rochat, *Guerre italiane*, 439–444; and Ballinger, "Borders of the Nation" and "Entangled or 'Extruded' Histories?"

EPILOGUE

1. Flaiano, *Tempo di uccidere*; Duncan, "Italian Identity," 109–116.

2. Figures from Ballinger, "On the Ruins of Empire," 6. On desires to return to Africa, see also Del Boca, *Italiani in Africa Orientale*, 3:582–593; Carlo Sforza cited in Labanca, *Oltremare*, 430; Brogi, *Question of Self-Esteem*; and Moreno, *Ultima Colonia*. On the aviation industry in the late 1940s, see Ferrari, "Trasformazioni e ridimensionamento."

3. Battini, *Missing Italian Nuremberg*; Petrusewicz, "Hidden Pages of Contemporary Italian History"; Conti, *Crimini di guerra italiani*; Focardi and Klinkhammer, "Questione dei criminali di guerra italiani."

4. Pavolini, *Disperata*, 305–306; Ponzanesi, "Beyond the Black Venus," 167–189; Iyob, "Madamismo and Beyond," 217–238.

5. Andall and Duncan, "Memories and Legacies," 21; Labanca, *Oltremare*, 427–470. On Montanelli's denial of the use of gas, see Del Boca, *I gas di Mussolini*.

6. IL, AC, *Notiziario Luce Nuova*, NL001 (1945), www.archivioluce.com; quotes by Ferruccio Parri and G.Sig., "Galleria: Giornali d'attualità," *Film Rivista* (July 15, 1946), cited in Laura, *Stagioni dell'aquila*, 224, 228; Frabotta, "Cammino dei cinegiornali italiani."

7. IL, AC, Notiziario Nuova Luce, *Un raro documento cinematografico sulla colonizzazione in Libia* (1946), NL020, www.archivioluce.com.

8. Figure from Brunetta, *Cinema neorealista italiano*, v; Forgacs and Gundle, *Mass Culture*, 130–142; Treveri Gennari, *Post-war Italian Cinema*.

9. Steimatsky, "Cinecittà Refugee Camp (1944–50)," 28, for the quote from "Sottoscrivete per i bambini di Cinecittà," *Film d'oggi* (June 16, 1945), and 42–45 on *Umanità*. See also Laura, *Stagioni dell'aquila*, 225–228; and IL, AC, *Umanità*, 1946, Luce DVD002, www.archivioluce.com.

10. Laura, "I reduci del cinema di Salò"; Ambrosinio, "Il cinema ricomincia," 61–66. The purge committee was chaired by Alfredo Guarini and was composed of Camerini, Soldati, Umberto Barbaro, Luchino Visconti, and Mario Chiari.

11. Alessandrini interviewed by Càllari in "Cinematografia italiana e l'Impero."

12. Brunetta, *Cent'anni di cinema italiano*, 274.

13. The Centro Cattolico Cinematografico produced *Pastor Angelicus*. Cori, *Cinema di Romolo Marcellini*, 72–88.

14. "L'assedio di Assisi," *Film d'oggi* (August 7, 1945), quoted in Germani, *Il cinema di Augusto Genina*, 274–276; Fink, "'Semo tutti Cristiani,'" 89.

15. Quote from Falasca-Zamponi, "Peeking under the Black Shirt," 164. See also Perinelli, *Fluchtlinien des Neorealismus*; and Brunetta, *Storia del cinema italiano*, 320.

16. On De Robertis, see Laura, "Reduci del cinema di Salò." This and subsequent quotes are from *Il mulatto*.

17. Quotes from Stoler, "Imperial Debris," 194, 193. Carlo José Bassoli, son of the original producer, argued that the war deprived the original *Bengasi* of a proper run in theaters. On these remakes and *Bengasi anno '41*, see Baratieri, *Memories and Silences*, 255–274; and Brunetta, *Cinema neorealista italiano*, 186–193. On the afterlife of the military genre, see Pesce, *Memoria e immaginario*.

18. Quote from Hunt, "Acoustic Register, Tenacious Images," 229. On Asmara, see Fuller, "Italy's Colonial Future." I thank Mark Brecke for information on cinemas in Somalia and reference his documentary film project *Somalia in the Picture*. On linguistic inheritances, see Ricci, *Lingua dell'impero*, 215–230; and Iyob, "From Mal d'Africa."

19. Quotes from Càllari, "L'arma più forte"; Lumley, *Entering the Frame*, 10; Fuller, "Italy's Colonial Future"; and Gabriel, "The Ruin and the Other," 214. See also Yervant Gianikian and Angela Ricci Lucchi, *Prigioneri di Guerra/Prisoners of War* (1995), *Su tutte le vette è pace/On the Heights All Is Peace* (1998), and *Oh! Uomo/Oh! Man* (2004).

BIBLIOGRAPHY

Archival Sources and Abbreviations

AA	Archivio Adriano Aprà
ACS	Archivio Centrale dello Stato
	MCP Ministero della Cultura Popolare
	PCM Presidenza del Consiglio dei Ministri
ASAM	Archivio Storico, Aeronautica Militare
CF	Cineteca dei Friuli
	AC Archivio Cinema
CSC	Centro Sperimentale di Cinematografia
	BLC Biblioteca Luigi Chiarini
IL	Istituto Luce
	AC Archivio Cinema
IWM	Imperial War Museum, Film and Video Archive
USMM	Ufficio Storico della Marina Militare

Unsigned Articles and Editorials

"Alla Patria." *Lo Schermo* (December 1935).
"Antonio Centa." *Lo Schermo* (March 1936).
"Il cinema per l'impero." *Lo Schermo* (June 1936).
"Il cinematografo strumento di lotta e di vittoria." *Lo Schermo* (May 1941).
"Come abbiamo fatto *Luciano Serra, Pilota*." *Film* (August 6, 1938).
"Come il popolo italiano ha 'visto' la sua guerra attraverso il cinematografo." *Lo Schermo* (June 1941).
"Concorso per il film *Un pilota ritorna*." *Cinema* (August 10, 1941).
"Cronache dei film nuovi: *Il grande appello, Lo squadrone bianco*." *Cinema* (October 25, 1936).
"Cronache dell'Impero." *Bianco e Nero* (September 1937).
"Disciplina, fantasia, intelligenza." *Lo Schermo* (January 1940).

"Editoriale." *Cinema* (June 25, 1937).
"Elementi per una nuova geografia italiana." *Critica Fascista* (September 1, 1937).
"Galleria: Mario Ferrari." *Cinema* (February 25, 1940).
"Guerra di principi." *Critica Fascista* (June 1, 1940).
"*Kif Tebbi.*" *Rivista del Cinematografo* (February 1929).
"Nota Editoriale." *Film* (February 8, 1941).
"Notiziario internazionale." *Lo Schermo* (March 1936).
"Operatori in prima linea." *Film* (September 18, 1940).
"Per i soldati in guerra." *Film* (February 8, 1941).
"Primizie di *Sotto la Croce del Sud*." *Cinema Illustrazione* (April 20, 1938).
"Primizie su *Luciano Serra, pilota*." *Cinema Illustrazione* (March 9, 1938).
"Pro-memoria." *Lo Schermo* (September 12, 1935).
"*Luciano Serra, pilota*." *Bianco e Nero* (September 1938).
"Rassegna cinematografica." *La Provincia di Bolzano* (November 22, 1935).
"Si gira a Sinauen *Lo squadrone bianco*." *L'Avvenire di Tripoli* (May 27, 1936).
"Sottocenere: *Equatore*." *Cinema* (November 10, 1937).
"*Sotto la Croce del Sud*, nuovo film d'Africa." *Film* (September 3, 1938).
"Umanità di nostra guerra." *Critica Fascista* (January 1, 1942).
"Vincere." *Critica Fascista* (June 15, 1940).
"La V Mostra d'Arte Cinematografica di Venezia: *Sentinelle di bronzo*." *Bianco e Nero* (September 1937).
"La VI Mostra d'Arte Cinematografica di Venezia: *Sotto la Croce del Sud*." *Bianco e Nero* (September 1938).
"Volto ed anima italiani per i film italiani." *Lo Schermo* (February 1938).

Books and Articles

A. A. V. V. *Italia e Germania, maggio XVI*. Rome: Stampatrice Novissima, 1938.

———. *Volare! Futurismo, aviomania, tecnica e cultura del volo, 1903–1940*. Rome: DeLuca Editore, 2003.

a. b. "*Luciano Serra, pilota*." *Lo Schermo* (July 1937).

Abbattista, Guido, and Nicola Labanca. "Living Ethnological and Colonial Exhibitions in Liberal and Fascist Italy." In *Human Zoos: Science and Spectacle in the Age of Colonial Empires*, edited by Pascal Blanchard, 341–352. Liverpool: Liverpool University Press, 2008.

Abbonizio, Isabella. "Ideologia, cultura, identità: Politica culturale e istituzioni musicali coloniali in Libia." *I sentieri della ricerca* 13 (September 2011): 105–129.

———. "Musica e colonialismo nell'Italia Fascista (1929–1943)." PhD, Università degli Studi di Roma "Tor Vergata," 2008–2009.

Abel, Richard. "Our Country/Whose Country? The 'American's' Project of Early Westerns." In *Back in the Saddle Again: New Essays on the Western*, edited by Edward Buscombe and Roberta E. Pearson, 77–95. London: British Film Institute, 1998.

Abler, Thomas S. *Hinterland Warriors and Military Dress: European Empires and Exotic Uniforms*. Oxford: Berg, 1999.

Ahmed, Sara. "Introduction." In *Uprootings/Regroundings: Questions of Home and Migration*, edited by Sara Ahmed, Claudia Castaneda, and Anne-Marie Fortier, 1–20. Oxford and New York: Berg, 2003.

Ahmida, Ali Abdullatif. *Forgotten Voices: Power and Agency in Colonial and Postcolonial Libya*. London: Routledge, 2005.
Albanese, Giulia. *La Marcia su Roma.*. Rome and Bari: Laterza, 2006.
Alberini, Massimo. "Orientamenti del documentario." *Cinema* (April 10, 1939).
———. "Rendiconto morale." *Cinema* (September 25, 1941).
Alberti, Guglielmo. "Cronaca del cinematografo." *Pègaso* (April 1932).
Alessandrini, Goffredo. "15.000 km. di preparazione a *Luciano Serra, pilota*." *Cinema* (June 25, 1937).
Aliano, David. *Mussolini's National Project in Argentina*. Madison, NJ: Fairleigh Dickinson University Press, 2012.
Alicata, Mario, and Giuseppe De Santis. "Verità e poesia: Verga e il cinema italiano." *Cinema* (October 10, 1941).
Allodoli, Ettore. "Cinema e lingua italiana." *Bianco e Nero* (April 1937).
———. "Voi e Lei." *La Lettura* (April 1938).
Alonge, Giaime. *Cinema e guerra: Il film, la Grande Guerra e l'immaginario bellico del Novecento*. Turin: UTET, 2001.
———. "L'occhio e il cervello dell'esercito: Tecnologia bellica e tecnologia cinematografica nelle riviste degli anni dieci." In *Cinema muto italiano: Tecnica e tecnologia*, edited by Michele Canosa and Giulia Carluccio, 1:25–29. Rome: Carocci, 2006.
Altichieri, Gilberto. "La lingua e il 'parlato.'" *Cinema* (February 25, 1938).
Altman, Rick. "Sound Space." In *Sound Theory, Sound Practice*, edited by Rick Altman, 46–64. New York: Routledge, 1992.
Ambler, Charles. "Popular Films and Colonial Audiences: The Movies in Northern Rhodesia." *American Historical Review* (February 2001): 81–105.
———. "Projecting the Modern Colonial State: The Mobile Cinema in Kenya." In *Film and the End of Empire*, edited by Lee Grieveson and Colin MacCabe, 199–224. New York: Palgrave Macmillan, 2011.
Ambrosino, Salvatore. "Cinema e propaganda in AOI." *Ventesimo Secolo* (January–April 1991): 127–150.
———. "Il cinema ricomincia: Attori e registi fra 'continuità' e 'frattura.'" In *Neorealismo: Cinema Italiano, 1945–1949*, edited by Alberto Farassino, 61–66. Turin: E. D. T., 1989.
Andall, Jacqueline, and Derek Duncan, eds. *Italian Colonialism: Legacy and Memory*. London and Oxford: Peter Lang, 2005.
———. "Memories and Legacies of Italian Colonialism." In *Italian Colonialism: Legacy and Memory*, edited by Jacqueline Andall and Derek Duncan, 9–28. London and Oxford: Peter Lang, 2005.
Andreoli, Annamaria, Giovanni Caprara, and Elena Fontanella, eds. *Volare! Futurismo, aviomania, tecnica e cultura del volo, 1903–1940*. Rome: De Luca, 2003.
Angioletti, G. B. "Cinema italiano in Francia." *Cinema* (April 10, 1938).
Antonioni, Michelangelo. "Conclusioni sul doppiato." *Cinema* (April 25, 1941).
———. "Luciano Serra italianissimo pilota." *Corriere Padano* (October 26, 1938).
———. "Per un film sul fiume Po." *Cinema* (April 25, 1939).
———. *Sul Cinema*. Edited by Giorgio Tinazzi and Carlo di Carlo. Venice: Marsilio, 2004.
———. "Vita impossibile del signor Clark Costa." *Cinema* (May 10, 1940).
Aprà, Adriano. *In viaggio con Rossellini*. Alessandria: Falsopiano, 2006.
———. "Storie di guerra: De Robertis e Rossellini." In *Storia del cinema italiano*, edited by Ernesto G. Laura, 6:69–88. Venice and Rome: Marsilio / Edizioni di Bianco & Nero, 2010.

Arena, Giovanni. *Visioni d'Oltremare: Allestimenti e politica dell'immagine nelle esposizioni coloniali del XX secolo.* Naples: Luogo, 2011.

Argentieri, Mino. *L'asse cinematografico Roma-Berlino.* Naples: Libreria Sapere, 1986.

———. "Autarchia e internazionalità." In *Storia del cinema italiano,* edited by Orio Caldiron, 5:140–163. Venice and Rome: Marsilio / Edizioni di Bianco & Nero, 2006.

———. *Il cinema in guerra: Arte, comunicazione e propaganda in Italia, 1940–1944.* Rome: Editori Riuniti, 1998.

———. *L'occhio del regime: Informazione e propaganda nel cinema del Fascismo.* Florence: Vallecchi, 1979.

———. *Schermi di guerra: Cinema italiano, 1939–1945.* Rome: Bulzoni, 1995.

Aristarco, Guido. "Alba tragica." *La Voce di Mantova* (August 26, 1939).

———. "La scuola dei registi." *Corriere Padano* (November 19, 1942).

Arthurs, Joshua. *Excavating Modernity: The Roman Past in Fascist Italy.* Ithaca, NY: Cornell University Press, 2012.

Arvidsson, Adam. *Marketing Modernity: Italian Advertising from Fascism to Postmodernity.* London and New York: Routledge, 2003.

Asserate, Asfa-Wossen, and Aram Mattioli, eds. *Der Erste Faschistische Vernichtungskrieg: Die Italienische Aggression Gegen Äthiopien, 1935–1941.* Cologne: SH-Verlag, 2006.

Atkinson, David. "Constructing Italian Africa: Geography and Geopolitics." In *Italian Colonialism,* edited by Ruth Ben-Ghiat and Mia Fuller, 15–26. New York: Palgrave Macmillan, 2005.

———. "Embodied Resistance, Italian Anxieties, and the Place of the Nomad in Colonial Cyrenaica." In *In Corpore: Bodies in Post-unification Italy,* edited by Loredana Polezzi and Charlotte Ross, 56–79. Madison, NJ: Fairleigh Dickinson University Press, 2007.

———. "Geopolitical Imaginations in Modern Italy." In *Geopolitical Traditions: A Century of Geopolitical Thought,* edited by Klaus Dodds and David Atkinson, 93–117. London: Routledge, 2000.

———. "Nomadic Strategies and Colonial Governance: Domination and Resistance in Cyrenaica, 1923–1932." In *Entanglements of Power: Geographies of Domination,* edited by Joanne P. Sharp et al., 93–121. London: Routledge, 2000.

———. "Totalitarianism and the Street in Fascist Rome." In *Images of the Street: Planning, Identity, and Control in Public Space,* edited by Nicholas R. Fyfe. London and New York: Routledge, 1998.

Augé, Marc. *Non-Places: Introduction to an Anthropology of Supermodernity.* London and New York: Verso, 1995.

Aumont, J. *Du visage au cinéma.* Paris: Editions de l'Etoile, 1992.

Bagnoni, Guido. "Cinema, occhio della guerra." *Cinema* (August 25, 1936).

Bahru, Zewde. *A History of Modern Ethiopia, 1855–1991.* Oxford and London: James Curry, 2001.

Bailey, Jonathan. "The First World War and the Birth of Modern Warfare." In *The Dynamics of Military Revolution, 1300–2050,* edited by MacGregor Knox and Murray Williamson, 132–153. Cambridge: Cambridge University Press, 2001.

Balázs, Béla. "Theory of the Film: Sound." In *Film Sound: Theory and Practice,* edited by Elisabeth Weis and John Belton. New York: Columbia University Press, 1985.

Baldassar, Loretta, and Donna R. Gabaccia, eds. *Intimacy and Italian Migration: Gender and Domestic Lives in a Mobile World.* New York: Fordham University Press, 2011.

Baldinetti, Anna. *The Origins of the Libyan Nation: Colonial Legacy, Exile, and the Emergence of a New Nation-State*. London: Routledge, 2010.

Baldoli, Claudia, and Andrew Knapp. *Forgotten Blitzes: France and Italy under Allied Air Attack, 1940–1945*. London and New York: Continuum, 2012.

Baldoli, Claudia, Andrew Knapp, and R. J. Overy. *Bombing, States, and Peoples in Western Europe, 1940–1945*. London and New York: Continuum, 2011.

Balestrazzi, Luigi. "Il cinematografo e l'Impero." *Rassegna sociale dell'Africa Italiana* (August 1939).

Ballinger, Pamela. "Borders of the Nation, Borders of Citizenship: Italian Repatriation and the Redefinition of National Identity after World War Two." *Comparative Studies in Society and History* 49, no. 3 (2007): 714–741.

———. "Entangled or 'Extruded' Histories? Displacement, National Refugees, and Repatriation after the Second World War." *Journal of Refugee Studies* 25, no. 3 (September 2012): 366–386.

———. "On the Ruins of Empire: Military Defeat, Violence, and the Fate of Italians in Africa and the Balkans." In *From Africa to the Balkans: New Perspectives on Colonialism and Material Culture in Fascist Italy*, edited by Jennie Hirsch and Lidia Santarelli (under review).

Balvetti, Mario. "Cambierà il cinema nel dopoguerra?" *Cinema* (August 10, 1942).

Baratieri, Daniela. *Memories and Silences Haunted by Fascism: Italian Colonialism, MCMXXX–MCMLX*. Bern: Peter Lang, 2010.

Barbaro, Umberto. "Nascita del film d'arte." In *40° anniversario della cinematografia italiana*. Rome: Sottosegretariato di Stato per la Stampa e la Propaganda, Direzione Generale per la cinematografia, e Segretariato dei Giovani Universitari Fascisti, 1935.

Barbaro, Umberto, and Luigi Chiarini. "Pro o contro? Inchiesta sul doppiato." *Cinema* (January 10, 1941).

Bargelesi, Alberto. *Bengasi città murata*. Milan: Istituto di Propaganda Libraria, 1942.

Barker, Jennifer M. *The Tactile Eye: Touch and the Cinematic Experience*. Berkeley: University of California Press, 2009.

Barrera, Giulia. "Mussolini's Colonial Race Laws and State-Settler Relations in Africa Orientale Italiana (1935–1941)." *Journal of Modern Italian Studies* 8, no. 3 (2003): 425–443.

———. "Racial Hierarchies in Colonial Eritrea." In *A Place in the Sun: Africa in Italian Colonial Culture from Post-unification to the Present*, edited by Patrizia Palumbo, 81–115. Berkeley: University of California Press, 2003.

Barthes, Roland. "The Grain of the Voice." In *Image, Text, Music*, by Roland Barthes, 179–189. New York: Macmillan, 1978.

———. *Image, Text, Music*. New York: Macmillan, 1978.

Bartov, Omer. *Murder in Our Midst: The Holocaust, Industrial Killing, and Representation*. New York and Oxford: Oxford University Press, 1996.

Basinger, Jeanine. *The World War II Combat Film: Anatomy of a Genre*. Middletown, CT: Wesleyan University Press, 2003.

Bassetti, Sergio. "Musica per film." In *Storia del cinema italiano*, edited by Orio Caldiron, 5:470–478. Venice and Rome: Marsilio / Edizioni di Bianco & Nero, 2006.

Battini, Michele. *The Missing Italian Nuremberg: Cultural Amnesia and Postwar Politics*. New York: Palgrave Macmillan, 2007.

Battistel, Cristina. "Lo spettacolo cinematografico." In *I manifesti tipografici del cinema: La collezione della Fondazione Cineteca Italiana, 1919–1939*, edited by Roberto Della Torre and Elena Mosconi, 70–87. Milan: Il castoro, 2001.

Baxa, Paul. *Roads and Ruins: The Symbolic Landscape of Fascist Rome*. Toronto: University of Toronto Press, 2010.

Bazin, André. "The Life and Death of Superimposition (1946)." *Film-Philosophy* 6, no. 1 (Summer 2002).

Beck, Jay, and Tony Grajeda. "Introduction: The Future of Sound Film Studies." In *Lowering the Boom: Critical Studies in Film Sound*, edited by Jay Beck and Tony Grajeda, 1–22. Urbana: University of Illinois Press, 2008.

Behdad, Ali. *Belated Travelers: Orientalism in the Age of Colonial Dissolution*. Durham, NC: Duke University Press, 1994.

Bellassai, Sandro. "The Masculine Mystique: Antimodernism and Virility in Fascist Italy." *Journal of Modern Italian Studies* 10, no. 3 (2005): 314–335.

Bellassai, Sandro, and Maria Malatesta. *Genere e mascolinità: Uno sguardo storico*. Rome: Bulzoni, 2000.

Benadusi, Lorenzo. *Il nemico dell'uomo nuovo: L'omosessualità nell'esperimento totalitario fascista*. Milan: Feltrinelli, 2005.

Ben-Ghiat, Ruth. "Fascist Italy and Nazi Germany: The Dynamics of an Uneasy Relationship." In *Art, Culture, and Media under the Third Reich*, edited by Richard A. Etlin, 257–286. Chicago: University of Chicago Press, 2002.

———. *Fascist Modernities: Italy, 1922–1945*. Berkeley: University of California Press, 2001.

———. "The Italian Colonial Cinema: Agendas and Audiences." *Modern Italy* 8, no. 1 (2003): 49–64.

Ben-Ghiat, Ruth, and Mia Fuller, eds. *Italian Colonialism*. New York: Palgrave Macmillan, 2005.

Benjamin, Walter. *One-Way Street, and Other Writings*. London and New York: Verso, 1992.

———. "The Work of Art in the Age of Mechanical Reproduction." In *Illuminations: Essays and Reflections*, by Walter Benjamin, edited by Hannah Arendt, 217–252. New York: Schocken Books, 1968.

Benthien, Claudia. *Skin: On the Cultural Border between Self and the World*. New York: Columbia University Press, 2002.

Berezin, Mabel. *Making the Fascist Self: The Political Culture of Interwar Italy*. Ithaca, NY: Cornell University Press, 1997.

Bergfelder, Tim, Erica Carter, and Deniz Göktürk, eds. *The German Cinema Book*. London: BFI, 2002.

Bernagozzi, Giampaolo. *Il mito dell'immagine*. Bologna: CLUEB, 1983.

Bernardini, Aldo, and Vittorio Martinelli. *Il cinema muto italiano*. 3 vols. Turin: Nuova ERI, 1991–1996.

Bernhard, Patrick. "Behind the Battle Lines: Italian Atrocities and Jewish Persecution in North Africa during World War Two." *Holocaust and Genocide Studies* 26, no. 3 (2012): 425–446.

Bernstein, Matthew. "Introduction." In *Visions of the East: Orientalism in Film*, edited by Matthew Bernstein and Gaylyn Studlar, 1–18. New Brunswick, NJ: Rutgers University Press, 1997.

Bernstein, Matthew, and Gaylyn Studlar, eds. *Visions of the East: Orientalism in Film*. New Brunswick, NJ: Rutgers University Press, 1997.

Bertellini, Giorgio. "The Atlantic Valentino: The 'Inimitable Lover' as Racialized and Gendered Italian." In *Intimacy and Italian Migration: Gender and Domestic Lives in a Mobile World*, edited by Loretta Baldassar and Donna R. Gabaccia, 37–48. New York: Fordham University Press, 2011.

———. "Colonial Autism: Whitened Heroes, Auditory Rhetoric, and National Identity in Interwar Italian Cinema." In *A Place in the Sun: Africa in Italian Colonial Culture from Post-Unification to the Present*, edited by Patrizia Palumbo, 255–278. Berkeley: University of California Press, 2003.

———. "Duce/Divo: Masculinity, Racial Identity, and Politics among Italian Americans in 1920s New York City." *Journal of Urban History* 31, no. 5 (2005): 685–726.

———. *Italy in Early American Cinema: Race, Landscape, and the Picturesque*. Bloomington: Indiana University Press, 2010.

Bertizzolo, Flora, and Silvia Pietrantonio. "A Denied Reality? Forced Labor in Italian Colonies in Northeast Africa." *Africana Studium* 7 (2004): 227–246.

Bertozzi, Marco. *Storia del documentario italiano: Immagini e culture dell'altro cinema*. Venice: Marsilio, 2008.

Besteman, Catherine Lowe. *Unraveling Somalia: Race, Violence, and the Legacy of Slavery*. Philadelphia: University of Pennsylvania Press, 1999.

Bhabha, Homi K. *The Location of Culture*. London and New York: Routledge, 2004.

Bianchi, Pietro. *L'occhio di vetro: Il cinema degli anni 1940–1943*. Milan: Il Formichiere, 1978.

Bini, Giuseppe. "*Kif Tebbi*." *La Vita Cinematografica* (June 10, 1929).

Bloom, Peter J. *French Colonial Documentary: Mythologies of Humanitarianism*. Minneapolis: University of Minnesota Press, 2008.

Boggio, Cecilia. "Black Shirts/Black Skins: Fascist Italy's Colonial Anxieties and *Lo Squadrone Bianco*." In *A Place in the Sun: Africa in Italian Colonial Culture from Post-Unification to the Present*, edited by Patrizia Palumbo, 279–298. Berkeley: University of California Press, 2003.

Bonaffini, Giuseppe. *Un mare di paura: Il Mediterraneo in età moderna*. Caltanissetta: S. Sciascia, 1997.

Bonfiglio, Ferruccio. "Il film coloniale." *L'Italia Coloniale* (September 1, 1937).

Bonitzer, Pascal. "Les silences de la voix." *Cahiers du Cinéma* 256 (February–March 1975): 22–33.

Bono, Francesco. "La mostra di Venezia." In *Storia del cinema italiano*, edited by Orio Caldiron, 5:183–192. Venice and Rome: Marsilio / Edizioni di Bianco & Nero, 2006.

Boscagli, Maurizia. *Eye on the Flesh: Fashions of Masculinity in the Early Twentieth Century*. Boulder, CO: Westview Press, 1996.

Bosworth, R. J. B. *Italy, the Least of the Great Powers: Italian Foreign Policy before the First World War*. Cambridge and New York: Cambridge University Press, 1979.

———. *Mussolini*. Oxford and New York: Oxford University Press, 2002.

Bottai, Giuseppe. "Dichiarazione a favore della legge." *Lo Spettacolo Italiano* (July–August 1931).

Bourdieu, Pierre. *La distinction: Critique sociale du jugement*. Paris: Éditions de Minuit, 1979.

———. *La domination masculine*. Paris: Seuil, 1998.
———. *Language and Symbolic Power*. Edited by John B. Thompson. Cambridge, MA: Harvard University Press, 1991.
Bourke, Joanna. *An Intimate History of Killing: Face-to-Face Killing in Twentieth Century Warfare*. London: Granta, 1998.
Bragaglia, Carlo Lodovico. "Narrazione e Documentario." *Cinema* (October 10, 1937).
Braidotti, Rosi. *Nuovi Soggetti Nomadi*. Rome: Luca Sossella, 2002.
Briareo, Gustavo [Giacomo Debenedetti]. "Il doppiaggio in Italia." *Cinema* (September 10, 1937).
Brogi, Alessandro. *A Question of Self-Esteem: The United States and the Cold War Choices in France and Italy, 1944–1958*. Westport, CT: Praeger, 2002.
Brogini Künzi, Giulia. *Italien und der Abessinienkrieg 1935/36: Kolonialkrieg Oder Totaler Krieg?* Paderborn: Ferdinand Schöningh, 2006.
Brunetta, Gian Piero. *Cent'anni di cinema italiano*. Rome and Bari: Laterza, 1991.
———. *Il cinema muto, 1895–1929*. Rome: Editori Riuniti, 1993.
———. *Il cinema neorealista italiano: Storia economica, politica e culturale*. Rome and Bari: Laterza, 2009.
———. "L'ora d'Africa del cinema italiano." In *L'ora d'Africa del cinema italiano, 1911–1989*, edited by Gian Piero Brunetta and Jean A. Gili, 9–37. Rovereto: Materiali di lavoro, 1990.
———. *Storia del cinema italiano: Dal 1945 agli anni ottanta*. Rome: Editori Riuniti, 1982.
———. *Storia del cinema italiano: Il cinema del regime, 1929–1945*. Rome: Editori Riuniti, 2000.
Brunetta, Gian Piero, and Jean A. Gili, eds. *L'ora d'Africa del cinema italiano, 1911–1989*. Rovereto: Materiali di lavoro, 1990.
Brunette, Peter. *Roberto Rossellini*. Oxford and New York: Oxford University Press, 1987.
Bruno, Edoardo. *Film come esperienza*. Rome: Bulzoni, 1986.
Bruno, Giuliana. *Atlas of Emotions: Journeys in Art, Architecture, and Film*. London: Verso, 2002.
———. *Streetwalking on a Ruined Map: Cultural Theory and the City Films of Elvira Notari*. Princeton, NJ: Princeton University Press, 1993.
Bruzzi, Stella. *Undressing Cinema: Clothing and Identity in the Movies*. London: Routledge, 1997.
Buck-Morss, Susan. "Aesthetics and Anaesthetics: Walter Benjamin's Artwork Essay Reconsidered." *October* 62 (Autumn 1992): 3–41.
Burdett, Charles. "Colonial Associations and the Memory of Italian East Africa." In *Italian Colonialism: Legacy and Memory*, edited by Jacqueline Andall and Derek Duncan, 125–142. London and Oxford: Peter Lang, 2005.
———. "Italian Fascism and Utopia." *History of the Human Sciences* 16, no. 1 (2003): 93–108.
———. *Journeys through Fascism: Italian Travel Writing between the Wars*. New York and Oxford: Berghahn Books, 2007.
Burgwyn, H. James. *Empire on the Adriatic: Mussolini's Conquest of Yugoslavia, 1941–1943*. New York: Enigma, 2005.
———. *Mussolini Warlord: Failed Dreams of Empire*. New York: Enigma Books, 2012.
Buscombe, Edward, and Roberta E. Pearson, eds. *Back in the Saddle Again: New Essays on the Western*. London: British Film Institute, 1998.

Butler, Judith. *Bodies That Matter: On the Discursive Limits of "Sex."* New York and London: Routledge, 1993.
———. *Gender Trouble: Feminism and the Subversion of Identity.* New York: Routledge, 1990.
Calcagnò, Diego. "7 Giorni a Roma: *Giarabub.*" *Film* (May 16, 1942).
———. "7 Giorni a Roma: *Un pilota ritorna.*" *Film* (April 18, 1942).
Caldiron, Orio, ed. *Storia del cinema italiano.* Vol. 5, *1934–1939.* Venice and Rome: Marsilio / Edizioni di Bianco & Nero, 2006.
Càllari, Francesco. "7 Giorni a Roma: I documentari." *Film* (July 27, 1940).
———. "L'arma più forte: Come si mettono iniseme i giornali di guerra." *Film* (June 15, 1940).
———. "Il cinematografo italiano e l'Impero." *Film* (May 11, 1940).
———. "Tre autentici registi." *Lo Schermo* (April 1942).
Calvino, Italo. *Into the War.* Translated by Martin McLaughlin. London and New York: Penguin, 2011.
Calvino, Vittorio. "Gli operatori cinematografici della Reale Marina." *Cinema* (October 10, 1942).
———. "Lo spettatore avido." *Cinema* (October 25, 1939).
Calzini, Raffaele. *"Bengasi."* *Film* (September 19, 1942).
Camerini, Mario. "Con spirito nuovo 'si gira' nei luoghi dell'Impero: Sbarco a Massaua." *Cinema* (August 25, 1936).
Caminati, Luca. *Roberto Rossellini documentarista: Una cultura della realtà.* Rome: Carocci, 2012.
Campassi, Gabriella. "Il madamato in Africa Orientale: Relazioni tra italiani e indigene come forma di aggressione coloniale." *Miscellanea di storie delle esplorazioni* 12 (1987): 219–260.
Campassi, Gabriella, and Maria Teresa Sega. "Uomo bianco, donna nera: L'immagine della donna nella fotografia coloniale." *Rivista di storia e critica della fotografia* 4, no. 5 (1983): 54–62.
Campbell, Timothy C. *Wireless Writing in the Age of Marconi.* Minneapolis: University of Minnesota Press, 2006.
Canella, A. "Tema Libico." *Cinema* (January 25, 1939).
Caneppale, Paolo, and Annalisa Rigon. *Fra luci e ombre: Intrattenimento e propaganda sugli schermi cinematografici di Bolzano, 1919–1945.* Bolzano: Provincia autonoma di Bolzano-Alto Adige, 2002.
Canosa, Michele, and Giulia Carluccio, eds. *Storia del cinema italiano, 1912–1923.* Venice and Rome: Marsilio / Edizioni di Bianco & Nero, forthcoming.
Canova, Gianni. "L'infiammazione della lacrima: Il paradosso del melò nel cinema italiano." In *Appassionatamente: Il melò nel cinema italiano,* edited by Orio Caldiron and Stefano Della Casa. Turin: Lindau, 1999.
Capone, Alfredo. "Corporeità maschile e modernità." In *Genere e mascolinità: Uno sguardo storico,* edited by Alessandro Bellassai and Maria Malatesta, 195–224. Rome: Bulzoni, 2000.
Cappelletti, Franco. "Attori primitivi." *Cinema* (August 25, 1939).
Caprotti, Federico. "Information Management and Fascist Identity: Newsreels in Fascist Italy." *Media History* 11, no. 3 (2005): 177–191.
Carancini, Gaetano. *"Jungla nera."* *Cine-Magazzino* (September 17, 1937).

Cardillo, Massimo. *Il Duce in moviola: Politica e divismo nei cinegiornali e documentari Luce.* Bari: Dedalo, 1983.
Carroll, Noël. *Engaging the Moving Image.* New Haven, CT: Yale University Press, 2003.
Carter, Erica. *Dietrich's Ghosts: The Sublime and the Beautiful in Third Reich Film.* London: British Film Institute, 2004.
Cartwright, Lisa. *Moral Spectatorship: Technologies of Voice and Affect in Postwar Representations of the Child.* Durham, NC: Duke University Press, 2008.
Casetti, Francesco. *Eye of the Century.* New York: Columbia University Press, 2008.
Casetti, Francesco, and Elena Mosconi. *Spettatori italiani: Riti e ambienti del consumo cinematografico (1900–1950).* Rome: Carocci, 2006.
Casiraghi, Ugo. "Cinema e vita militare." *Cinema* (July 25, 1941).
Casiraghi, Ugo, and Glauco Viazzi. "Motivi di rinascita." *Cinema* (May 10, 1941).
———. "Presentazione postuma di un classico." *Bianco e Nero* (April 1942).
Castelli, Enrico, and David Laurenzi, eds. *Permanenze e metamorfosi dell'immaginario coloniale in Italia.* Naples: Edizioni Scientifiche Italiane, 2000.
Celli, Silvio. "Le guerre del LUCE." In *Storia del cinema italiano,* edited by Orio Caldiron, 5:62–70. Venice and Rome: Marsilio / Edizioni di Bianco & Nero, 2006.
Cenci, Amerigo. "Operatori della R. Aeronautica." *Cinema* (October 10, 1942).
Cerchio, Fernando. "Composizione e montaggio dei film documentario di guerra." *Bianco e Nero* (February 1941).
———. "Evoluzione del film-giornale." *Cinema* (March 25, 1940).
———. "Servizio di guerra." *Cinema* (July 10, 1940).
Cerchi Usai, Paolo. "Mario Camerini in Africa." *Cinegrafie* 1, no. 2 (1989): 93–102.
Ceroni, Guglielmo. "La cinematografia nell'ora attuale: Nove film di guerra." *Lo Schermo* (August 1941).
Chambers, Iain. *Mediterranean Crossings: The Politics of an Interrupted Modernity.* Durham, NC: Duke University Press, 2008.
Chapman, James. *The British at War: Cinema, State, and Propaganda, 1939–1945.* London and New York: I. B. Tauris, 1998.
Charney, Leo, and Vanessa R. Schwartz. *Cinema and the Invention of Modern Life.* Berkeley: University of California Press, 1995.
Chelati Dirar, Uoldelul, Silvana Palma, Alessandro Triulzi, and Alessandro Volterra, eds. *Colonia e postcolonia come spazi diasporici: Attraversamenti di memorie, identità e confini nel corno d'Africa.* Rome: Carocci, 2011.
Chiarini, Luigi [l. c.]. "Il cinema e i giovani." *Lo Schermo* (August 1935).
———. "Introduzione." In *L'attore: Saggio di antologia critica,* edited by Luigi Chiarini and Umberto Barbaro, 5–28. Rome: Edizioni di Bianco e Nero, 1938.
———. "*I lancieri del Bengala:* Il soggetto." *Bianco e Nero* (January–April 1937).
——— [l. c.]. "Note." *Bianco e Nero* (March 31, 1937).
———. "Prefazione." *Bianco e Nero* (February 1939).
———. "Speranza ed esperienza." *Lo Schermo* (December 1935).
Chiarini, Luigi, and Umberto Barbaro, eds. *L'attore: Saggio di antologia critica.* Rome: Edizioni di Bianco e Nero, 1938.
Chion, Michel. *L'audio-vision: Son et image au cinéma.* Paris: Nathan, 2000.
———. *The Voice in Cinema.* Translated by Claudia Gorbman. New York: Columbia University Press, 1999.
———. "Wasted Words." In *Sound Theory, Sound Practice,* edited by Rick Altman, 104–110. New York: Routledge, 1992.

Choate, Mark I. *Emigrant Nation: The Making of Italy Abroad.* Cambridge, MA: Harvard University Press, 2008.

———. "Identity Politics and Political Perception in the European Settlement of Tunisia: The French Colony versus the Italian Colony." *French Colonial History* 8 (2007): 97–109.

Chow, Rey. "Where Have All the Natives Gone?" In *Contemporary Postcolonial Theory: A Reader,* edited by Padmini Mongia, 122–148. London: Arnold, 1996.

Chowdhry, Prem. *Colonial India and the Making of Empire Cinema: Image, Ideology, and Identity.* Manchester: Manchester University Press, 2000.

Ciano, Galeazzo. *Diario: 1939–1943.* Milan: Rizzoli, 1963.

Cicognini, Bruno. "L'abolizione del Lei." *Corriere della sera* (January 25, 1938).

Clifford, James. *Routes: Travel and Translation in the Late Twentieth Century.* Cambridge, MA: Harvard University Press, 1997.

Codell, Julie. "Blackface: Faciality and Colony Nostalgia in 1930s Empire Films." In *Postcolonial Cinema Studies,* edited by Sandra Ponzanesi and Marguerite R. Waller, 32–46. New York: Routledge, 2012.

Cogni, Giulio. "Preliminari sul cinema in difesa della razza." *Bianco e Nero* (January 31, 1938).

Coletti, Maria. "Il cinema coloniale tra propaganda e melò." In *Storia del cinema italiano,* edited by Orio Caldiron, 5:354–362. Venice and Rome: Marsilio / Edizioni di Bianco & Nero, 2006.

Comin, Jacopo. "Propositi e realtà." *Cinema* (March 10, 1938).

———. "Volto della realtà." *Bianco e Nero* (August 31, 1938).

Conley, Tom. *Film Hieroglyphs: Ruptures in Classical Cinema.* Minneapolis: University of Minnesota Press, 1991.

Conti, Davide. *Criminali di guerra italiani: Accuse, processi e impunità nel secondo dopoguerra.* Rome: Odradek, 2011.

Cori, Alessandra. *Il cinema di Romolo Marcellini: Tra storia e società dal colonialismo agli anni '70.* Recco, Genova: Le mani, 2009.

Costa, Antonio. "Augusto Genina, un regista europeo." In *Storia del cinema italiano,* edited by Orio Caldiron, 5:242–252. Venice and Rome: Marsilio / Edizioni di Bianco & Nero, 2006.

Cosulich, Callisto, ed. *Storia del cinema italiano.* Vol. 7, *1945–1948.* Venice and Rome: Marsilio / Edizioni di Bianco & Nero, 2003.

Cowie, Elizabeth. "The Spectacle of Actuality." In *Collecting Visible Evidence,* edited by Jane Gaines and Michael Renov, 19–45. Minneapolis: University of Minnesota Press, 1999.

Craig, Siobhan S. *Cinema after Fascism: The Shattered Screen.* New York: Palgrave Macmillan, 2010.

Craveri, Mario. "Un'operatore fra guerre e rivoluzioni." *Cinema* (October 10, 1936).

Cresswell, Tim. "Introduction: Theorizing Place." In *Mobilizing Place, Placing Mobility: The Politics of Representation in a Globalized World,* edited by Tim Cresswell and Ginette Verstraete, 11–32. Amsterdam: Rodopi, 2002.

Cresti, Federico. *Oasi di italianità: La Libia della colonizzazione agraria tra Fascismo, guerra e indipendenza (1935–1956).* Turin: Società editrice internazionale, 1996.

Croce, Giuseppe. "In A.O. col reparto fotocinematografico dell'Istituto Luce." *Lo Schermo* (July 1936).

Curcio, Carlo. "Guerra e dopoguerra." *Critica Fascista* (June 1, 1942).

Dagrada, Elena, Elena Mosconi, and Silvia Paoli. *Moltiplicare l'istante: Beltrami, Comerio e Pacchioni tra fotografia e cinema.* Milan: Il castoro, 2007.

Dalla Pria, Federica. *Dittatura e immagine: Mussolini e Hitler nei cinegiornali*. Rome: Edizioni di Storia e Letteratura, 2012.

Dalle Vacche, Angela. *The Body in the Mirror: Shapes of History in Italian Cinema*. Princeton, NJ: Princeton University Press, 1992.

Davico Bonino, Guido, ed. *Manifesti futuristi*. Milan: Rizzoli, 2009.

Debenedetti, Giacomo [Deben]. "In questi giorni: *Sentinelle di bronzo*." *Cinema* (December 25, 1937).

De Berti, Raffaele. *Dallo schermo alla carta: Romanzi, fotoromanzi, rotocalchi cinematografici: Il film e i suoi paratesti*. Milan: Vita e pensiero, 2000.

———. "Figure e miti ricorrenti." In *Storia del cinema italiano*, edited by Orio Caldiron, 5:294–311. Venice and Rome: Marsilio / Edizioni di Bianco & Nero, 2006.

———. "Lo sguardo dall'altro: Percorsi incrociati tra cinema e aeropittura." In *Volare! Futurismo, aviomania, tecnica e cultura del volo, 1903–1940*, edited by Annamaria Andreoli, Giovanni Caprara, and Elena Fontanella, 175–180. Rome: De Luca, 2003.

———. *Il volo del cinema: Miti moderni nell'Italia fascista*. Milan: Mimesis, 2012.

de Certeau, Michel. *The Practice of Everyday Life*. Berkeley: University of California Press, 1988.

De Felice, Renzo. *Mussolini: Il Duce*. Vol. 3. Turin: Einaudi, 1965.

———. *Storia degli ebrei italiani sotto il Fascismo*. Turin: Einaudi, 1993.

De Feo, Luciano. "Documento di vita nei programmi." *Cinema* (February 10, 1938).

———. "Elementi del film nazionale." *Lo Schermo* (January 1937).

De Franciscis, Umberto [U. d. f.]. "I documentari bellici dell'Istituto Nazionale L.U.C.E." *Cinema* (March 10, 1941).

——— [U. d. f.]. "Il documentario deve documentare." *Film* (February 14, 1942).

———. "La guerra è protagonista." *Film* (August 30, 1941).

———. "Scenografia vera." *Cinema* (February 25, 1940).

de Grazia, Victoria. *The Culture of Consent: Mass Organization of Leisure in Fascist Italy*. Cambridge and New York: Cambridge University Press, 1981.

———. *How Fascism Ruled Women*. Berkeley: University of California Press, 1992.

———. *Irresistible Empire: America's Advance through Twentieth-Century Europe*. Cambridge, MA: Belknap Press of Harvard University Press, 2005.

Delage, Christian, and Vincent Guigueno. *L'historien et le film*. Paris: Gallimard, 2004.

Del Boca, Angelo. *I gas di Mussolini: Il Fascismo e la Guerra d'Etiopia*. Rome: Editori riuniti, 2007.

———. *Gli Italiani in Africa Orientale*. 4 vols. Milan: Mondadori, 1992.

———. *Gli Italiani in Libia*. 2 vols. Rome and Bari: Laterza, 1986.

———. "Le leggi razziali nell'impero di Mussolini." In *Il regime fascista: Storia e storiografia*, edited by Angelo Del Boca, Massimo Legnani, and Mario G. Rossi, 329–351. Rome and Bari: Laterza, 1995.

Del Boca, Angelo, and Nicola Labanca. *L'impero africano del Fascismo: Nelle fotografie dell'Istituto Luce*. Rome: Riuniti, 2002.

Deleuze, Gilles. "Year Zero: Faciality." In *A Thousand Plateaus: Capitalism and Schizophrenia*, edited by Gilles Deleuze and Félix Guattari, 167–191. Minneapolis: University of Minnesota Press, 1987.

Della Torre, Roberto, and Elena Mosconi. *I manifesti tipografici del cinema: La collezione della Fondazione Cineteca Italiana, 1919–1939*. Milan: Il castoro, 2001.

Denti di Pijano, Alberto. *A Cure for Serpents*. New York: William Sloane, 1955.

Deriu, David. "Picturing Ruinscapes: The Aerial Photograph as Image of Historical Trauma." In *The Image and the Witness: Trauma, Memory, and Visual Culture,* edited by Frances Guerin and Roger Hallas, 189–206. London and New York: Wallflower Press, 2007.

De Robertis, Francesco. "Appunti per un film d'aviazione." *Cinema* (February 25, 1943).

D'Errico, Corrado. "Luce A.O." *Lo Schermo* (April 1936).

———. "Stile Luce." *Lo Schermo* (July 1936).

De Santis, Giuseppe. "Il linguaggio dei rapporti." *Cinema* (December 25, 1941).

———. "Per un paesaggio italiano." *Cinema* (April 25, 1941).

———. "*Un pilota ritorna.*" *Cinema* (April 25, 1942).

Desideri, Paola. "Il linguaggio politico mussoliniano: Procedure pragmatiche e configurazioni discursive." In "Parlare Fascista. Lingua del Fascismo, politica linguistica del Fascismo." Special issue, *Movimento Operaio e Socialista* 7, no. 1 (1984): 39–48.

Devereaux, Leslie, and Roger Hillman. *Fields of Vision: Essays in Film Studies, Visual Anthropology, and Photography.* Berkeley: University of California Press, 1995.

Diawara, Manthia. "Black Spectatorship: Problems of Identification and Resistance." *Screen* 29, no. 4 (1988): 66–79.

Di Carmine, Roberta. *Italy Meets Africa: Colonial Discourses in Italian Cinema.* New York: Peter Lang, 2011.

Di Donno, Fabrizio. "La razza Ario-Mediterranea." *Interventions* 8, no. 3 (2006): 394–412.

Di Lauro, Raffaele. *Il governo delle genti di colore.* Milan: Fratelli Bocca, 1940.

Doane, Mary Ann. "The Close-Up: Scale and Detail in the Cinema." *Differences* 14, no. 3 (2003): 89–111.

———. *The Emergence of Cinematic Time: Modernity, Contingency, the Archive.* Cambridge, MA: Harvard University Press, 2002.

———. "The Voice in the Cinema: The Articulation of Body and Space." In *Narrative, Apparatus, Ideology: A Film Theory Reader,* edited by Philip Rosen, 335–348. New York: Columbia University Press, 1986.

Doherty, Thomas Patrick. *Projections of War: Hollywood, American Culture, and World War II: [Revised and Updated to Include Recent World War II Films].* New York: Columbia University Press, 1999.

Doletti, Mino. "7 Giorni a Roma." *Film* (October 5, 1940).

——— [D.]. "Dal cielo di Campoformido al cielo d'Etiopia." *Cinema* (November 25, 1937).

——— [D.]. "Lettere: A Eugenio Fontana, produttore del *Sotto la Croce del Sud.*" *Film* (October 15, 1938).

Dore, Gianni. "Ideologia coloniale e senso comune etnografico nella Mostra delle terre d'Oltremare." In *L'Africa in vetrina: Storie di musei e di esposizioni coloniali in Italia,* edited by Nicola Labanca, 47–68. Paese, Treviso: Pagus, 1992.

Dubow, Jessica. "'From a View on the World to a Point of View in It': Rethinking Sight, Space, and the Colonial Subject." *Interventions* 2, no. 1 (2000): 87–102.

Dudley, Andrew. "Praying Mantis: Enchantment and Violence in French Cinema of the Exotic." In *Visions of the East: Orientalism in Film,* edited by Matthew Bernstein and Gaylyn Studlar, 232–252. New Brunswick, NJ: Rutgers University Press, 1997.

Duncan, Derek. "Italian Identity and the Risks of Contamination: The Legacies of Mussolini's Demographic Impulse in the Work of Comisso, Flaiano, and Dell'Oro." In *Italian Colonialism: Legacy and Memory,* edited by Jacqueline Andall and Derek Duncan, 99–123. London and Oxford: Peter Lang, 2005.

———. *Reading and Writing Italian Homosexuality: A Case of Possible Difference.* Aldershot, UK, and Burlington, VT: Ashgate, 2006.
Dunn, Leslie C., and Nancy A. Jones. "Introduction." In *Embodied Voices: Representing Female Vocality in Western Culture,* edited by Leslie C. Dunn and Nancy A. Jones, 1–13. Cambridge and New York: Cambridge University Press, 1994.
Duranti, Doris. *Il romanzo della mia vita.* Edited by Gianfranco Venè. Milan: Mondadori, 1987.
Duroviceva, Natasa. "Translating America: The Hollywood Multilinguals, 1919–1933." In *Sound Theory, Sound Practice,* edited by Rick Altman, 138–153. New York: Routledge, 1992.
Duvignand, Jean. "Esquisse pour le nomade." In *Nomades et vagabonds,* edited by Jacques Berque et al, 13–40. Paris: Union générale d'éditions, 1975.
———. "Untitled Prefatory Note." In *Nomades et vagabonds,* edited by Jacques Berque et al. Paris: Union générale d'éditions, 1975.
Ebner, Michael R. *Ordinary Violence in Mussolini's Italy.* New York: Cambridge University Press, 2011.
Ellena, Liliana. *Film d'Africa: Film italiani prima, durante e dopo l'avventura coloniale.* Turin: Archivio nazionale cinematografico della Resistenza, 1999.
Elsaesser, Thomas. "Tales of Sound and Fury: Observations on the Family Melodrama." *Monogram* 3 (1972): 2–15.
Elsaesser, Thomas, and Malte Hagener, eds. *Film Theory: An Introduction through the Senses.* New York: Routledge, 2010.
Esposito, Fernando, ed. *Mythische Moderne: Aviatik, Faschismus und die Sehnsucht nach Ordnung in Deutschland und Italien.* Munich: Oldenbourg, 2011.
F. C. "Fronte di guerra." *Film* (July 6, 1940).
Falasca-Zamponi, Simonetta. "Fascism and Aesthetics." *Constellations* 15, no. 3 (2008): 351–365.
———. *Fascist Spectacle: The Aesthetics of Power in Mussolini's Italy.* Berkeley: University of California Press, 1997.
———. "Peeking Underneath the Black Shirt." In *Fashioning the Body Politic: Dress, Gender, Citizenship,* edited by Wendy Parkins, 145–164. Oxford and New York: Berg, 2002.
Falconi, Dino. "Bengasi." *Il Popolo d'Italia* (October 24, 1942).
———. "La freccia d'oro." *Il Popolo d'Italia* (November 9, 1935).
———. "Il grande appello." *Il Popolo d'Italia* (November 27, 1936).
Fanchi, Mariagrazia. "I generi: Identità, trasformazioni e pratiche di consumo." In *Storia del cinema italiano,* edited by Orio Caldiron, 5:277–293. Venice and Rome: Marsilio / Edizioni di Bianco & Nero, 2006.
Fanchi, Mariagrazia, and Elena Mosconi. *Spettatori: Forme di consumo e pubblici del cinema in Italia, 1930–1960.* Venice: Marsilio, 2002.
Fantina, Livio. *Le trincee dell'immaginario: Spettacoli e spettatori nella Grande Guerra.* Verona: Cierre, 1998.
Farassino, Alberto. "Camerini, au-dela du cinéma italien." In *Mario Camerini,* edited by Alberto Farassino, 11–32. Locarno: Editions du Festival international du film de Locarno / Editions Yellow Now, 1992.
———. *Fuori di set: Viaggi, esplorazioni, emigrazioni, nomadismo.* Rome: Bulzoni, 2000.
———. *Legione straniera, l'immagine e il mito.* Rimini: Riminicinema, 1992.

———. *Mario Camerini*. Locarno: Editions du Festival international du film de Locarno / Editions Yellow Now, 1992.
Favre, Sisto. "Film di guerra." *Lo Schermo* (June 1943).
———. "La milizia nella documentazione 'Luce.'" *Lo Schermo* (February 1939).
Feldman, Allen. "Violence and Vision: The Prosthetics and Aesthetics of Terror." In *Violence and Subjectivity*, edited by Veena Das et al., 46–78. Berkeley: University of California Press, 2000.
Ferbo. "Il film coloniale." *Lo Schermo* (October 1937).
Ferrari, Massimo. "L'aviazione italiana nella Prima Guerra Mondiale." In *Volare! Futurismo, aviomania, tecnica e cultura del volo, 1903–1940*, edited by Annamaria Andreoli, Giovanni Caprara, and Elena Fontanella, 45–49. Rome: De Luca, 2003.
———. "Trasformazioni e ridimensionamento dell'industria aeronautica nel secondo dopoguerra." In *L'aeronautica italiana: Una storia del Novecento*, edited by Paolo Ferrari, 115–142. Milan: Franco Angeli, 2004.
Ferretti, Lando. "I film documentari e gli altri." *Lo Schermo* (February 1939).
———. "Il nuovo Luce." *Lo Schermo* (April 1940).
Ferro, Marc. *Cinema and History*. Detroit: Wayne State University Press, 1988.
Finchelstein, Federico. *Transatlantic Fascism: Ideology, Violence, and the Sacred in Argentina and Italy, 1919–1945*. Durham, NC: Duke University Press, 2010.
Fink, Guido. "Où vont les autres." In *Mario Camerini*, edited by Alberto Farassino, 62–76. Locarno: Editions du Festival international du film de Locarno / Editions Yellow Now, 1992.
———. "'Semo tutti Cristiani': Ebrei visibili e invisibili nel cinema italiano." In *In nome del cinema*, edited by Vito Zagarrio, 83–102. Milan: Il Ponte, 1999.
Fiume, Enrico. "Africa in bianco e nero." *Africa Italiana* (May 1940).
———. "Un anno di cinema coloniale." *Africa Italiana* (December 1940).
———. "Appunti sul film coloniale." *Rivista delle Colonie*, 1 (1939).
———. "Atmosfera e ambiente nel cinema coloniale." *Africa Italiana* (February–April 1943).
———. "Bengasi." *Africa Italiana* (November 1942–January 1943).
———. "Bilancio di stagione." *Africa Italiana* (August–October 1941).
———. "Le due Afriche." *Africa Italiana* (November 1940).
———. "L'India contro il cinema Anglo-Sassone." *Africa Italiana* (March 1941).
———. "Inferno giallo e inferno nero." *Africa Italiana* (May–July 1943).
———. "L'organizzazione cinematografica dell'AOI." *Africa Italiana* (April 1940).
——— [E.A.F.]. "Piloti e fanti nel deserto sirtico." *Africa Italiana* (May–June 1941).
Flaiano, Ennio. "Aethiopia: Appunti per una canzonetta." In *Opere scelte*, edited by Anna Longoni, 1427–1428. Milan: Adelphi, 2010.
———. "Tempo di uccidere." In *Opere scelte*, edited by Anna Longoni, 5–244. Milan: Adelphi, 2010.
Focardi, Filippo, and Lutz Klinkhammer. "La questione dei criminali di guerra italiani e una commissione d'inchiesta dimenticata." *Contemporanea* 4, no. 3 (2001): 497–528.
Fogu, Claudio. *The Historic Imaginary: Politics of History in Fascist Italy*. Toronto: University of Toronto Press, 2003.
Fogu, Claudio, and Lucia Re. "Italy in the Mediterranean." *California Italian Studies* 1, no. 1 (2010). http://escholarship.org/uc/ismrg_cisj?volume=1;issue=1.
Fonzi, Bruno. "Operatori L.U.C.E. nel divampare della battaglia." *Lo Schermo* (April 1942).

Foresti, Fabio. "Il problema linguistico nella 'politica indigena' del colonialismo fascista." In "Parlare fascista: Lingua del Fascismo, politica linguistica del Fascismo." Special issue, *Movimento operaio e socialista* 7, no. 1 (1984): 133–155.
Forgacs, David. "Sex in the Cinema: Regulation and Transgression in Italian Films, 1930–43." In *Re-viewing Fascism: Italian Cinema, 1922–1943*, edited by Jacqueline Reich and Piero Garofalo, 141–171. Bloomington: Indiana University Press, 2002.
Forgacs, David, and Stephen Gundle. *Mass Culture and Italian Society from Fascism to the Cold War*. Bloomington: Indiana University Press, 2007.
Fox, Jo. *Filming Women in the Third Reich*. Oxford: Berg, 2000.
Frabotta, Maria Adelaide. "Il cammino dei cinegiornali italiani del paese e in Europa." In *Identità italiana e identità europea nel cinema italiano dal 1945 al miracolo economico*, edited by Gian Piero Brunetta, 173–191. Turin: Edizioni della Fondazione Giovanni Agnelli, 1996.
Francisci, Pietro. "Del 'puro' e del 'romanzato' nel documentario." *Cinema* (February 25, 1943).
Franzina, Emilio, and Matteo Sanfilippo, eds. *Il Fascismo e gli emigrati: La parabola dei fasci italiani all'estero (1920–1943)*. Rome and Bari: Laterza, 2003.
Franzinelli, Mimmo. *Squadristi: Protagonisti e tecniche della violenza fascista, 1919–1922*. Milan: Mondadori, 2003.
Franzini, Emilio. "'Varcare i confini': Viaggi e passaggi degli emigranti; Il caso italiano e le teorie trasnazionali." In *Confini: Costruzioni, Attraversamenti, Rappresentazioni*, edited by Silvia Salvatici, 115–152. Soveria Mannelli: Rubbettino, 2005.
Freddi, Luigi. *Il Cinema: Miti, esperienze e realtà di un regime totalitario*. Rome: L'Arnia, 1949.
———. "Gente dell'aria." *Film* (February 14, 1942).
———. "Per il cinema italiano." *Intercine* (August–September 1935).
Fritzsche, Peter. "Nazi Modern." *Modernism/Modernity* 3 (January 1996): 1–31.
Fulchignani, Enrico. "I film della Mostra di Venezia." *Bianco e Nero* (October 1941).
Fulks, Barry. "Walter Ruttmann, the Avant-Garde Film, and Nazi Modernism." *Film and History* 14, no. 2 (1984): 26–35.
Fuller, Mia. "Italy's Colonial Future: Colonial Inertia and Postcolonial Capital in Asmara." *California Italian Studies* 2, no. 1 (2011). http://escholarship.org/uc/search?entity=ismrg_cisj;volume=2;issue=1.
———. *Moderns Abroad: Architecture, Cities, and Italian Imperialism*. London and New York: Routledge, 2007.
G.us. "Guerre e guerrieri sullo schermo."*Lo Schermo* (June 1936).
Gabaccia, Donna. *Italy's Many Diasporas*. Seattle: University of Washington Press, 2000.
Gabriel, Teshome. "The Ruin and the Other." In *Otherness and the Media: The Ethnography of the Imagined and the Imaged*, edited by Teshome Gabriel and Hamid Naficy, 211–220. Chur, Switzerland: Harwood Academic Publishers, 1993.
Gabrielli, Gianluca, ed. *L'Africa in giardino: Appunti sulla costruzione dell'immaginario coloniale*. Anzola dell'Emilia, Bologna: Zanini, 1998.
Gallagher, Tag. *The Adventures of Roberto Rossellini*. New York: Da Capo Press, 1998.
Gemelli, Agostino. "La psicologia al servizio della cinematografia." *Bianco e Nero* (September 1937).
Gentile, Emilio. "The Conquest of Modernity: From Modernist Nationalism to Fascism." *Modernism/Modernity* 1, no. 3 (1994): 55–87.

———. "Fascism and the Italian Road to Totalitarianism." *Constellations* 15, no. 3 (2008): 291–302.
———. *La via italiana al totalitarismo: Il partito e lo stato nel regime fascista*. Rome: La Nuova Italia scientifica, 1995.
Germani, Sergio Grmek. "Avec Mario Camerini." In *Mario Camerini*, edited by Alberto Farassino, 89–145. Locarno: Editions du Festival international du film de Locarno / Editions Yellow Now, 1992.
Germani, Sergio Grmek, and Vittorio Martinelli. *Il cinema di Augusto Genina*. Pasian di Prato, Ud: Edizioni biblioteca dell'immagine, 1989.
Geyer, Michael. "The Militarization of Europe, 1914–1945." In *The Militarization of the Western World*, edited by John Gillis, 65–102. New Brunswick, NJ: Rutgers University Press, 1989.
Giannini, Federico. "Fra realtà e finzione: De Robertis e il cinema di propaganda." *Bollettino d'archivio dell'ufficio storico della Marina Militare* (June 2005): 117–194.
Gibelli, Antonio. *L'officina della guerra: La Grande Guerra e le trasformazioni del mondo mentale*. Turin: Bollati Boringhieri, 1991.
Gili, Jean A. *Le cinéma italien a l'ombre des faisceaux, 1922–1945*. Perpignan, France: Institut Jean Vigo, 1990.
———. "La distribution des film italiens en France de 1930 a 1943." *Risorgimento* 2–3 (1981).
———. "I film dell'impero fascista." In *L'ora d'Africa nel cinema italiano*, edited by Gian Piero Brunetta and Jean A. Gili, 64–76. Rovereto: Materiali di lavoro, 1990.
———. *Stato fascista e cinematografia: Repressione e promozione*. Rome: Bulzoni, 1981.
Gillette, Aaron. *Racial Theories in Fascist Italy*. London and New York: Routledge, 2002.
Giovannetti, Eugenio. "I registi: Augusto Genina." *Film* (November 1, 1941).
Giuliano, Balbino. *Latinità e Germanesimo*. Bologna: Zanichelli, 1940.
Giv. "Squadrone in marcia." *Lo Schermo* (May 1936).
Gledhill, Christine. *Home Is Where the Heart Is: Studies in Melodrama and the Woman's Film*. London: British Film Institute, 1987.
Goebbels, Joseph. *Die Tagebücher von Joseph Goebbels: Sämtliche Fragmente*, edited by Elke Fröhlich. Vol. 14. Munich and New York: K. G. Saur, 1987.
Goglia, Luigi. *Colonialismo e fotografia: Il caso italiano*. Messina: Sicania, 1989.
Gorbman, Claudia. *Unheard Melodies: Narrative Film Music*. Bloomington: Indiana University Press, 1987.
Gorfinkel, Elena, and John David Rhodes. "Introduction." In *Taking Place: Location and the Moving Image*, edited by John David Rhodes and Elena Gorfinkel, vii–xxix. Minneapolis: University of Minnesota Press, 2011.
Grandi, Dino. *La politica estera dell'Italia dal 1929 al 1932*. Edited by Paolo Nello. Vol. 5. Rome: Bonacci, 1985.
Graziani, Rodolfo. *Cirenaica pacificata*. Milan: Mondadori, 1932.
———. *Pace romana in Libia*. Milan: Mondadori, 1937.
Grazzini, Giovanni. "In memoria di Amedeo Nazzari." *Corriere Della Sera* (November 7, 1969).
Green, Jared. "This Reality Which Is Not One." In *Docufictions: Essays on the Intersection of Documentary and Fictional Filmmaking*, edited by Gary Don Rhodes and John Parris Springer, 64–87. Jefferson, NC: McFarland, 2006.
Greene, Shelleen. *Equivocal Subjects: Between Italy and Africa Constructions of Racial and National Identity in the Italian Cinema*. New York: Continuum, 2012.

Grespi, Barbara. "Cinecittà: Utopia fascista e mito americano." In *Storia del cinema italiano*, edited by Orio Caldiron, 5:128–137. Venice and Rome: Marsilio / Edizioni di Bianco & Nero, 2006.

Gribaudi, Gabriella. *Guerra totale: Tra bombe alleate e violenze naziste; Napoli e il fronte meridionale, 1940–44*. Turin: Bollati Boringhieri, 2005.

Grieveson, Lee. "The Cinema and the (Common) Wealth of Nations." In *Empire and Film*, edited by Lee Grieveson and Colin MacCabe, 73–114. London: Palgrave Macmillan, 2011.

Grieveson, Lee, and Colin MacCabe, eds. *Empire and Film*. Cultural Histories of Cinema. London: Palgrave Macmillan, 2011.

———. *Film and the End of Empire*. New York: Palgrave Macmillan, 2011.

Griffin, Roger, ed. *Fascism, Totalitarianism, and Political Religion*. London and New York: Routledge, 2005.

———. *Modernism and Fascism: The Sense of a New Beginning under Mussolini and Hitler*. New York: Palgrave, 2010.

———. *The Nature of Fascism*. London and New York: Routledge, 1996.

Griffiths, Alison. *Wondrous Difference: Cinema, Anthropology & Turn-of-the-Century Visual Culture*. New York: Columbia University Press, 2002.

Gromo, Mario [m. g.]. "Bengasi." *La Stampa* (October 24, 1942).

Gubitosi, Giuseppe. *Amedeo Nazzari*. Bologna: Mulino, 1998.

Guerin, Frances, and Roger Hallas. *The Image and the Witness: Trauma, Memory, and Visual Culture*. London and New York: Wallflower Press, 2007.

Guerri, Alberto. "Gli operatori italiani." In *Storia del cinema italiano*, edited by Orio Caldiron, 5:450–459. Venice and Rome: Marsilio / Edizioni di Bianco & Nero, 2006.

Guerri, Giordano Bruno. "Italo Balbo e l'epopea delle trasvolate." In *Volare! Futurismo, aviomania, tecnica e cultura del volo, 1903–1940*, by A. A. V. V., 105–110. Rome: DeLuca Editore, 2003.

Gundle, Stephen. "*Il Bel Paese*: Art, Beauty, and the Cult of Appearance." In *The Politics of Italian National Identity*, edited by Gino Bedani and B. A. Haddock, 124–141. Cardiff: University of Wales Press, 2000.

———. "Film Stars and Society in Fascist Italy." In *Re-viewing Fascism: Italian Cinema, 1922–1943*, edited by Jacqueline Reich and Piero Garofalo, 315–340. Bloomington: Indiana University Press, 2002.

———. *Mussolini's Dream Factory: Film Stardom in Fascist Italy*. New York and Oxford: Berghahn, 2013.

Hake, Sabine. *Popular Cinema of the Third Reich*. Austin: University of Texas Press, 2001.

Hansen, Miriam. "Pleasure, Ambivalence, Identification: Valentino and Female Spectatorship." *Cinema Journal* 25, no. 4 (1986): 6–32.

Harrison, Robert Pogue. *Forests: The Shadow of Civilization*. Chicago: University of Chicago Press, 1992.

Hay, James. *Popular Film Culture in Fascist Italy: The Passing of the Rex*. Bloomington: Indiana University Press, 1987.

Hendrickson, Hildi. "Introduction." In *Clothing and Difference: Embodied Identities in Colonial and Post-colonial Africa*, edited by Hildi Hendrickson, 1–16. Durham, NC: Duke University Press, 1996.

Herzog, Dagmar. *Brutality and Desire: War and Sexuality in Europe's Twentieth Century*. New York: Palgrave Macmillan, 2009.

Hess, Robert L. *Italian Colonialism in Somalia*. Chicago: University of Chicago Press, 1966.
Higson, Andrew. "The Limiting Imagination of National Cinema." In *Transnational Cinema: The Film Reader*, edited by Elizabeth Ezra and Terry Rowden, 15–25. London and New York: Routledge, 2006.
Higson, Andrew, and Richard Maltby, eds. *"Film Europe" and "Film America": Cinema, Commerce, and Cultural Exchange, 1920–1939*. Exeter: University of Exeter Press, 1999.
Hochscherf, Tobias. "Nazis on the Ranch? Revisiting the Popular German Western *Der Kaiser Von Kalifornien* (1936) and the International Aspirations of Third Reich Cinema." *Postscript* 29, no. 2 (2010): 32–51.
Hodeir, Catherine, and Michel Pierre. *L'Exposition Coloniale*. Brussels: Editions Complexe, 1991.
Hoffend, Andrea. *Zwischen Kultur-Achse und Kulturkampf: Die Beziehungen zwischen "Drittem Reich" und faschistischem Italien in den bereichen Medien, Kunst, Wissenschaft und Rassenfragen*. Frankfurt and New York: Peter Lang, 1998.
Hoffmann, Hilmar. *The Triumph of Propaganda: Film and National Socialism, 1933–1945*. Providence, RI: Berghahn Books, 1995.
Hom, Stephanie Malia. "Empires of Tourism: Travel and Rhetoric in Italian Colonial Libya and Albania, 1911–1943." *Journal of Tourism History* 4, no. 3 (2012): 281–300.
Hunt, Nancy Rose. "Acoustic Register, Tenacious Images, and Congolose Scenes of Rape and Repetition." *Cultural Anthropology* 23, no. 2 (2008): 220–253.
Hüppauf, Bernd. "Modernism and the Photographic Representation of War and Destruction." In *Fields of Vision: Essays in Film Studies, Visual Anthropology, and Photography*, edited by Leslie Devereaux and Roger Hillman, 94–124. Berkeley: University of California Press, 1995.
Iaccio, Pasquale. *Cinema e Storia. Percorsi, immagini, testimonianze*. Naples: Liguori, 1998.
Imbriani, Angelo Michele. *Gli italiani e il Duce: Il mito e l'immagine di Mussolini negli ultimi anni del Fascismo (1938–1943)*. Naples: Liguori, 1992.
[Interlandi,Telesio]. "La Patria ricorre in appello." *Il Tevere* (November 29–30, 1936).
Isani, Giuseppe. "Film di questi giorni: *La nave bianca*." *Cinema* (October 10, 1941).
———. "Film di questi giorni: *Uomini sul fondo*." *Cinema* (February 25, 1941).
———. "Forza del documento bellico." *Cinema* (June 25, 1940).
Iyob, Ruth. "From Mal d'Africa to Mal d'Europa? The Ties That Bind." In *Italian Colonialism: Legacy and Memory*, edited by Derek Duncan and Jacqueline Andall, 255–282. London and Oxford: Peter Lang, 2005.
———. "*Madamismo* and Beyond: The Construction of Eritrean Women." *Nineteenth Century Contexts* 22, no. 2 (2000): 217–238.
J. C. "*I lancieri del Bengala*: La sceneggiatura." *Bianco e Nero* (January–April 1937).
Jaikumar, Priya. *Cinema at the End of Empire: A Politics of Transition in Britain and India*. Durham, NC: Duke University Press, 2006.
Janz, Oliver, Lutz Klinkhammer, and Roberto Balzani, eds. *La morte per la Patria: La celebrazione dei caduti dal Risorgimento alla repubblica*. Rome: Donzelli, 2008.
Kallis, Aristotle A. *Fascist Ideology: Territory and Expansionism in Italy and Germany, 1922–1945*. London and New York: Routledge, 2000.
Kaplan, Caren. *Questions of Travel: Postmodern Discourses of Displacement*. Durham, NC: Duke University Press, 1996.
Kennedy-Karpat, Colleen. *Rogues, Romance, and Exoticism in French Cinema of the 1930s*. Madison, NJ: Fairleigh Dickinson University Press, 2013.

Kershaw, Ian. "War and Political Violence in 20th Century Europe." *Contemporary European History* 14, no. 1 (2005): 107–123.

Kezich, Tullio. "Gli attori italiani dalla preistoria del divismo al monopolio." In *Storia del cinema italiano,* edited by Orio Caldiron, 5:383–403. Venice and Rome: Marsilio / Edizioni di Bianco & Nero, 2006.

Kirby, Lynne. *Parallel Tracks: The Railroad and Silent Cinema.* Durham, NC: Duke University Press, 1997.

Klein, Gabriella. *La politica linguistica del fascismo.* Bologna: Mulino, 1986.

Knox, MacGregor. *Mussolini Unleashed, 1939–1941.* Cambridge and New York: Cambridge University Press, 1982.

Knox, MacGregor, and Williamson Murray, eds. *The Dynamics of Military Revolution, 1300–2050.* Cambridge: Cambridge University Press, 2001.

Koepnick, Lutz P. *The Dark Mirror: German Cinema between Hitler and Hollywood.* Berkeley: University of California Press, 2002.

Koppes, Clayton R., and Gregory D. Black. *Hollywood Goes to War: How Politics, Profits, and Propaganda Shaped World War II Movies.* Berkeley: University of California Press, 1990.

Kovitz, Marcia. "The Roots of Military Masculinity." In *Military Masculinities: Identity and the State,* edited by Paul Higate, 1–14. Westport, CT: Praeger, 2003.

Kracauer, Siegfried. *Theory of Film: The Redemption of Physical Reality.* Princeton, NJ: Princeton University Press, 1997.

Krimer. "Lettera dall'Africa settentrionale: Soldati al cinema." *Film* (August 16, 1941).

Kuehl, Jerry. "Visual History Traduced: A Century of Compilation Films." *Journal of War and Culture Studies* (August 2007): 31–39.

Kühberger, Christoph. "'Il Gallo delle Oche': Mussolini als Vorbild für die faschistische Männlichkeit." In *Mascolinità italiane: Italienische Männlichkeiten im 20. Jahrhundert,* edited by Christoph Kühberger and Roman Reisinger, 63–76. Berlin: Logos, 2006.

L. "*Un pilota ritorna.*" *Cinema* (March 25, 1942).

———. "A Roberto Rossellini." *Cinema* (February 10, 1942).

———. "Fotocinematografia aerea." *Cinema* (April 10, 1942).

Labanca, Nicola. *L'Africa in vetrina: Storie di musei e di esposizioni coloniali in Italia.* Paese, Treviso: Pagus, 1992.

———. *La guerra italiana per la Libia, 1911–1931.* Bologna: Mulino, 2012.

———. "Italian Colonial Internment." In *Italian Colonialism,* edited by Ruth Ben-Ghiat and Mia Fuller, 27–36. New York: Palgrave Macmillan, 2005.

———. "Morire per l'Impero: Su cifre e parole per i caduti italiani di una guerra coloniale fascista." In *La morte per la patria,* edited by Oliver Janz, Lutz Klinkhammer, and Roberto Balzani, 121–156. Rome: Donzelli, 2008.

———. *Oltremare: Storia dell'espansione coloniale italiana.* Bologna: Mulino, 2002.

———. *Posti al sole: Diari e memorie di vita e di lavoro dalle colonie d'Africa.* Rovereto: Museo storico italiano della guerra, 2001.

Landy, Marcia. *Cinematic Uses of the Past.* Minneapolis: University of Minnesota Press, 1996.

———. *Fascism in Film: The Italian Commercial Cinema, 1931–1943.* Princeton, NJ: Princeton University Press, 1986.

———. *The Folklore of Consensus: Theatricality in the Italian Cinema, 1930–1943.* Albany: State University of New York Press, 1998.

———, ed. *Imitations of Life: A Reader on Film and Television Melodrama*. Detroit: Wayne State University Press, 1991.
———. *Stardom, Italian Style: Screen Performance and Personality in Italian Cinema*. Bloomington: Indiana University Press, 2008.
Langbehn, Volker, ed. *German Colonialism, Visual Culture, and Modern Memory*. New York: Routledge, 2012.
Larkin, Brian. *Signal and Noise: Media, Infrastructure, and Urban Culture in Nigeria*. Durham, NC: Duke University Press, 2008.
Larsen, Jonas, John Urry, and K. W. Axhausen. *Mobilities, Networks, Geographies*. Transport and Society. Aldershot, UK, and Burlington, VT: Ashgate, 2006.
Lattuada, Alberto. *Alberto Lattuada fotografo: Dieci anni di Occhio Quadrato, 1938–1948*, edited by Piero Berengo Gardin. Florence: Alinari, 1982.
Laura, Ernesto G. "I reduci del cinema di Salò." In *Storia del cinema italiano*, edited by Callisto Cosulich, 7:310–329. Venice and Rome: Marsilio / Edizioni di Bianco & Nero, 2003.
———. *Le stagioni dell'Aquila: Storia dell'Istituto Luce*. Rome: Ente dello spettacolo, 2000.
———, ed. *Storia del cinema italiano*. Vol. 6, *1940–1944*. Venice and Rome: Marsilio / Edizioni di Bianco & Nero, 2010.
Lazar, Veronica, and Piero Spila. *Cineromit: Il sogno della Cinecittà romena, 1941–1946*. Rome: Itaro Arte, 2003.
Lazzaro, Claudia, and Roger J. Crum, eds. *Donatello among the Blackshirts: History and Modernity in the Visual Culture of Fascist Italy*. Ithaca, NY: Cornell University Press, 2005.
Leed, Eric J. *The Mind of the Traveler: From Gilgamesh to Global Tourism*. New York: Basic Books, 1991.
Lefebvre, Martin. "Between Setting and Landscape in the Cinema." In *Landscape and Film*, edited by Martin Lefebvre, 19–60. New York: Routledge, 2006.
Le Houérou, Fabienne. *L'Épopée des soldats de Mussolini en Abyssinie, 1936–1938: Les "Ensablés."* Paris: L'Harmattan, 1994.
Leprohon, Pierre. *The Italian Cinema*. Edited by Roger Greaves, and Oliver Stallybrass. London: Secker and Warburg, 1972.
Levine, Alison J. Murray. *Framing the Nation: Documentary Film in Interwar France*. New York: Continuum, 2010.
Leyda, Jay. *Films Beget Films*. New York: Hill and Wang, 1964.
Liehm, Mira. *Passion and Defiance: Film in Italy from 1942 to the Present*. Berkeley: University of California Press, 1984.
Locatelli, Francesca. "Beyond the Campo Cintato: Prostitutes, Migrants, and 'Criminals' in Colonial Asmara (Eritrea), 1890–1941." In *African Cities: Competing Claims on Urban Spaces*, edited by Francesca Locatelli and Paul Nugent, 219–240. Leiden, Netherlands, and Biggleswade, UK: Brill, 2009.
———. "'Ozioso, vagabondo, e prezioso': Labour, Law, and Crime in Colonial Asmara, 1890–1941." *International Journal of African Historical Studies* 40, no. 2 (2007): 225–250.
Loffredo, Ferdinando. "Nuovi caratteri del soldato italiano." *Critica Fascista* (September 15, 1940).
Lombardi-Diop, Cristina. "Pioneering Female Modernity: Fascist Women in Colonial Africa." In *Italian Colonialism*, edited by Ruth Ben-Ghiat and Mia Fuller, 145–154. New York: Palgrave Macmillan, 2005.

———. "Spotless Italy: Hygiene, Domesticity, and the Ubiquity of Whiteness in Fascist and Postwar Consumer Culture." *California Italian Studies* 2, no. 1 (2011): 1–22.

Lombardi-Diop, Cristina, and Caterina Romeo, eds. *Postcolonial Italy: Challenging National Homogeneity*. London and New York: Palgrave Macmillan, 2012.

Lombrassa, Giuseppe. "Il senno dei tigrini." *Lo Schermo* (November 1935).

Longo, Giuseppe. "La cultura sul piano imperiale." *Critica Fascista* (May 15, 1937).

Luconi, Stefano, and Guido Tintori. *L'ombra lunga del fascio: Canali di propaganda fascista per gli italiani d'America*. Milan: M&B, 2004.

Lughi, Paolo. "La Scalera Film: Lo studio system all'italiana." In *Storia del cinema italiano*, edited by Ernesto G. Laura, 6:392–399. Venice and Rome: Marsilio / Edizioni di Bianco & Nero, 2010.

Lumley, Robert. *Entering the Frame: Cinema and History in the Films of Yervant Gianikian and Angela Ricci Lucchi*. Oxford and New York: Peter Lang, 2011.

Macciocchi, Maria Antonietta. *Les femmes et leurs maîtres*. Paris: Christian Bourgeois, 1978.

MacDougall, David. *The Corporeal Image: Film, Ethnography, and the Senses*. Princeton, NJ: Princeton University Press, 2006.

———. *Transcultural Cinema*. Edited by Lucien Castaing-Taylor. Princeton, NJ: Princeton University Press, 1998.

Mackenzie, S. P. *British War Films, 1939–1945: The Cinema and the Services*. London: Hambledon and London, 2001.

Mack Smith, Denis. *Mussolini's Roman Empire*. New York: Viking Press, 1976.

Maggi, Stefano. *Colonialismo e comunicazioni: Le strade ferrate nell'Africa Italiana, 1887–1943*. Naples: Edizioni scientifiche italiane, 1996.

———. *Storia dei trasporti in Italia*. Bologna: Il Mulino, 2005.

Maltby, Richard. "The Cinema and the League of Nations." In *"Film Europe" and "Film America": Cinema, Commerce, and Cultural Exchange, 1920–1939*, edited by Andrew Higson and Richard Maltby, 82–116. Exeter: University of Exeter Press, 1999.

Maltby, Richard, and Ruth Vesey. "'Temporary American Citizens' Cultural Anxieties and Industrial Strategies in the Americanization of European Cinema." In *"Film Europe" and "Film America": Cinema, Commerce, and Cultural Exchange, 1920–1939*, edited by Andrew Higson and Richard Maltby. Exeter: University of Exeter Press, 1999.

Marcellini, Romolo. "Avventura: Come è nato 'Sentinelle di bronzo' e come ... sta per nascere un altro film." *Lo Schermo* (October 1937).

———. "I legionari del 2° parallelo." *Lo Schermo* (September 1936).

———. "Mario Craveri: Operatore di grande avventura." *Film* (May 28, 1938).

———. "I nostri negri." *Lo Schermo* (October 1936).

Marcus, Millicent. *Italian Film in the Light of Neorealism*. Princeton, NJ: Princeton University Press, 1986.

Margalit, Avishai. *The Ethics of Memory*. Cambridge, MA: Harvard University Press, 2002.

Marinetti, Filippo Tommaso. "Fondazione e manifesto del Futurismo" (February 20, 1909). In *Manifesti futuristi*, edited by Guido Davico Bonino. Milan: Rizzoli, 2009.

Marinetti, Filippo Tommaso, et al. "La cinematografia futurista" (September 11–November 15, 1916). In *Manifesti futuristi*, edited by Guido Davico Bonino, 225–231. Milan: Rizzoli, 2009.

Marino, Natalia, and Emanuele Valerio Marino. *L'Ovra a Cinecittà: Polizia politica e spie in camicia nera*. Turin: Bollati Boringhieri, 2005.

Marks, Laura U. "Asphalt Nomadism: The New Desert in Arab Independent Cinema." In *Landscape and Film*, edited by Martin Lefebvre, 125–148. New York: Routledge, 2006.

———. *The Skin of the Film: Intercultural Cinema, Embodiment, and the Senses*. Durham, NC: Duke University Press, 2000.

Marongiu Buonaiuti, Cesare. *Politica e religioni nel colonialismo italiano, 1882–1941*. Rome: Giuffrè, 1982.

Martin, Benjamin. "A New Order for European Culture: The German-Italian Axis and the Reordering of International Cultural Exchange, 1936–1943." PhD diss., Columbia University, 2006.

Martinelli, Vittorio. "Cineasti italiani in Germania tra le due guerre." In *Cinema italiano in Europa, 1907–1929*, edited by Vittorio Martinelli, 131–159. Rome: Associazione italiana per le ricerche di storia del cinema, 1992.

———, ed. *Cinema italiano in Europa, 1907–1929*. Rome: Associazione italiana per le ricerche di storia del cinema, 1992.

———. "Destinazione Parigi." In *Cinema italiano in Europa, 1907–1929*, edited by Vittorio Martinelli, 160–169. Rome: Associazione italiana per le ricerche di storia del cinema, 1992.

———. "I Gastarbeiter fra le due guerre." *Bianco e Nero* 39, no. 3 (1978): 3–39.

Martone, Luciano. *Giustizia coloniale: Modelli e prassi penale per i sudditi d'Africa dall'età giolittiana al Fascismo*. Naples: Jovene, 2002.

Masetti, Enzo. "La musica e la guerra." *Film* (February 14, 1942).

Masi, Stefano. *Storie della luce: I film, la vita, le avventure, le idee di 200 operatori italiani*. Rome: Savelli Gaumont, 1983.

Masso, Arnt. "The Proxemics of the Mediated Voice." In *Lowering the Boom*, edited by Jay Beck and Tony Grajeda, 36–50. Urbana: University of Illinois Press, 2008.

Matard-Bonucci, Marie-Anne. "Italian Fascism's Ethiopian Conquest and the Dream of a Prescribed Sexuality." In *Brutality and Desire*, edited by Dagmar Herzog, 91–108. New York: Palgrave Macmillan, 2009.

Mattia, Ettore G. "Il cinema dei soldati in A.O.I." *Cinema* (June 25, 1940).

———. "Pubblico etiopico." *Cinema* (March 25, 1940).

———. "Testimonianza di Ettore G. Mattia." In *Pratiche basse e telefoni bianchi: Cinema italiano, 1923–1943*, edited by Gianfranco Graziani. Pescara: Tracce, 1986

Mattioli, Aram. *Experimentierfeld der Gewalt: Der Abessinienkrieg und seine internationale Bedeutung, 1935–1941*. Zurich: Orell Füssli, 2005.

Mazower, Mark. *Hitler's Empire: How the Nazis Ruled Europe*. New York: Penguin Press, 2008.

McGuire, Valerie. "Fascism's Mediterranean Empire." PhD diss., New York University, 2013.

McLaren, Brian. *Architecture and Tourism in Italian Colonial Libya: An Ambivalent Modernism*. Studies in Modernity and National Identity. Seattle: University of Washington Press, 2006.

Meccoli, Domenico. "Film d'aviazione." *Cinema* (February 10, 1938).

———. "I nuovi registi." *Cinema* (December 25, 1941).

Menarini, Alberto. *In margine della lingua*. Florence: Sansoni, 1947.

Mercer, John, and Martin Shingler. *Melodrama: Genre, Style, Sensibility*. London and New York: Wallflower, 2004.

Mereu Keating, Carla. "'100% Italian': The Coming of Sound Cinema in Italy and State Regulation on Dubbing." *California Italian Studies* 4, no. 1 (2013): 1–24.

Micciché, Lino. "Il cadavere nell'armadio." In *Cinema italiano sotto il Fascismo*, edited by Riccardo Redi, 9–18. Venice: Marsilio, 1979.

———. "Il cinema italiano sotto il Fascismo: Elementi per un ripensamento possible." In *Risate di regime: La commedia italiana, 1930–1944*, edited by Mino Argentieri, 37–64. Venice: Marsilio, 1991.

Migliorini, Bruno. "Il Lei in soffitto." *Critica Fascista* (March 1, 1938).

———. "Tradurre." *Critica Fascista* (February 15, 1938).

Milani, Mario. "Da Adua ad Axum." *Rivista del Cinematografo* (October 1935).

———. "Sulle orme dei nostri pionieri." *Rivista del Cinematografo* (March 1936).

Milano, Paolo. "L'italiano del cinema." *Cinema* (July 10, 1938).

Millan, Matteo. "The Institutionalization of *Squadrismo*: Disciplining Paramilitary Violence in the Fascist Dictatorship." *Contemporary European History* 22, no. 4 (2013): 551–574.

Miller, Monica L. *Slaves to Fashion: Black Dandyism and the Styling of Black Diasporic Identity*. Durham, NC: Duke University Press, 2009.

Millet, Thierry. *Bruit et cinéma*. Aix-en-Provence, France: Publications de l'Université de Provence, 2007.

Minghelli, Giuliana. *Landscape and Memory in Post-Fascist Italian Film: Cinema Year Zero*. London: Routledge, 2013.

Miracco, Renato. "Futurist Skies: The Turns, Ups, and Downs, of Aeropainting." In *Futurist Skies: Italian Aeropainting*, edited by Renato Miracco, 11–23. Milan: Mazzotta, 2005.

Miran, Jonathan. *Red Sea Citizens: Cosmopolitan Society and Cultural Change in Massawa*. Bloomington: Indiana University Press, 2009.

Monina, Giancarlo. *Il consenso coloniale: Le società geografiche e l'Istituto Coloniale Italiano, 1896–1914*. Rome: Carocci, 2002.

Moore, Rachel. *Savage Theory: Cinema as Modern Magic*. Durham, NC: Duke University Press, 1999.

Morandini, Mario. "Del film militare." *Lo Schermo* (December 1935).

Moreno, Antonio. "Politica e istruzione nella Somalia sotto tutela italiana." In *Colonia e postcolonia come spazi diasporici: Attraversamenti di memorie, identità e confini nel corno d'Africa*, edited by Uoldelul Chelati Dirar, Silvana Palma, Alessandro Triulzi, and Alessandro Volterra, 75–92. Rome: Carocci, 2011.

———. *L'ultima colonia: Come l'Italia è tornata in Africa, 1950–1960*. Rome and Bari: Laterza, 2011.

Mosconi, Elena. "La Chiesa Cattolica e il cinema." In *Storia del cinema italiano*, edited by Orio Caldiron, 5:77–84. Venice and Rome: Marsilio / Edizioni di Bianco & Nero, 2006.

———. "Goffredo Alessandrini." In *Storia del cinema italiano*, edited by Orio Caldiron, 5:236–244. Venice and Rome: Marsilio / Edizioni di Bianco & Nero, 2006.

———. *L'impressione del film: Contributi per una storia culturale del cinema italiano, 1895–1945*. Milan: V&P, 2006.

Mosconi, Elena, and Roberto Della Torre. "Consumo cinematografico e funzioni sociali del cinema." In *Spettatori: Forme di consumo e pubblici del cinema in Italia, 1930–1960*, edited by Mariagrazia Fanchi and Elena Mosconi, 23–61. Venice: Marsilio, 2002.

Mosconi, Elena, and Nicoletta Ossanna Cavadini. "La sala cinematografica tra le due guerre: Spazio architettonico e spazio sociale." In *Spettatori italiani: Riti e ambienti del consumo cinematografico (1900–1950)*, edited by Francesco Casetti and Elena Mosconi, 63–68. Rome: Carocci, 2006.

Moses, A. Dirk. *Empire, Colony, Genocide: Conquest, Occupation, and Subaltern Resistance in World History*. New York and Oxford: Berghahn, 2008.

Moses, A. Dirk, and Dan Stone, eds. *Colonialism and Genocide*. London and New York: Routledge, 2006.

Mosse, George L. *The Image of Man: The Creation of Modern Masculinity*. Oxford and New York: Oxford University Press, 1996.

Mulvey, Laura. "Dislocations: Some Reflections on the Colonial Compilation Film." In *Film at the End of Empire*, edited by Lee Grieveson and Colin MacCabe, 251–264. New York: Palgrave Macmillan, 2011.

Mussolini, Benito. "1940: 10 Giugno Anno XVIII." In *Opera Omnia*, edited by Edoardo Susmel and Duilio Susmel, 29:403–405. Florence: La Fenice, 1951.

———. "Decidersi!" *Il Popolo d'Italia* (January 12, 1932).

———. "La mobilitazione generale: Discorso del 2 ottobre 1935." In *Scritti e discorsi*, 9:217–220. Milan: Hoepli, 1934.

———. "Quando il mito tramonta." *Il Popolo d'Italia* (December 23, 1932).

Mussolini, Vittorio [V. M.]. "Cinema di guerra." *Cinema* (June 25, 1940).

———. "Cinema per gli indigeni." *Cinema* (February 25, 1939).

———. "Emancipazione del cinema italiano." *Cinema* (September 25, 1936).

———. "Un momento critico." *Cinema* (November 25, 1938).

———. "Nuova situazione." *Cinema* (December 25, 1941).

———. *Voli sulle ambe*. Florence: Sansoni, 1936.

Musu, Angelo. "Parlano gli operatori dell'Istituto Luce: Come abbiamo girato il documentario *Battaglia navale nello Jonio*." *Film* (July 20, 1940).

Nerenberg, Ellen Victoria. *Prison Terms: Representing Confinement during and after Italian Fascism*. Toronto: University of Toronto Press, 2001.

Niranjana, Tejaswini. *Siting Translation: History, Post-Structuralism, and the Colonial Context*. Berkeley: University of California Press, 1992.

Nye, Robert. "Western Masculinities in War and Peace." *American Historical Review* 112, no. 2 (2007): 417–438.

O'Brien, Charles. "The 'Cinéma Colonial' of 1930s France: Film Narration as Spatial Practice." In *Visions of the East: Orientalism in Film*, edited by Matthew Bernstein and Gaylyn Studlar, 207–231. New Brunswick, NJ: Rutgers University Press, 1997.

O'Healy, Aine. "Mediterranean Passages: Abjection and Belonging in Contemporary Italian Cinema." *California Italian Studies* 1, no. 1 (2010): 1–19.

———. "Screening Intimacy and Racial Difference in Contemporary Italy." In *Postcolonial Italy: Challenging National Homogeneity*, edited by Cristina Lombardi-Diop and Caterina Romeo, 205–220. London and New York: Palgrave Macmillan, 2012.

Ojetti, Ugo. "L'Italia in Mostra." *Pègaso* (May–June 1933).

Oksiloff, Assenka. *Picturing the Primitive: Visual Culture, Ethnography, and Early German Cinema*. New York: Palgrave, 2001.

Olivetti, Paola. "Cinegiornale e film di soggetto, 1940–1943: Strutture linguistiche a confronto." *L'impegno* 13, no. 1 (1993). http://www.storia900bivc.it/pagine/editoria/olivetti193.html.

Orano, Emanuele. "Una cinematografia coloniale." *Bianco e Nero* (May 1939).

Ortner, Sherry. "Resistance and the Problem of Ethnographic Refusal." *Comparative Studies in Society and History* 37, no. 1 (1995): 173–193.
Pagliara, Maria. *Il romanzo coloniale: Tra imperialismo e rimorso*. Rome and Bari: Laterza, 2001.
Pagliero, Maurizio. "L'aeronautica militare dall'Eritrea alla Spagna." In *Volare! Futurismo, aviomania, tecnica e cultura del volo, 1903–1940*, edited by Annamaria Andreoli, Giovanni Caprara, Elena Fontanella, 39–43. Rome: De Luca, 2003.
Palumbo, Patrizia, ed. *A Place in the Sun: Africa in Italian Colonial Culture from Post-Unification to the Present*. Berkeley: University of California Press, 2003.
Pankhurst, Richard. "Italian and Native Labour during the Italian Fascist Occupation of Ethiopia." *Ghana Social Science Journal* 2, no. 2 (1972): 42–73.
Paollela, Roberto. "Cannes ovvero la storia di una mostra mancata." *Cinema* (February 10, 1939).
Parini, Piero. *Gli italiani nel mondo*. Rome: Fasci all'estero, 1935.
Pascoli, Giovanni. "La grande proletaria si è mossa." In *Patria e umanità. Raccolta di scritti e discorsi*. Bologna: Zanichelli, 1911.
Pasinetti, Francesco. "I film della Mostra di Venezia." *Cinema* (September 25, 1942).
Passerini, Luisa. *Mussolini immaginario: Storia di una biografia, 1915–1939*. Rome and Bari: Laterza, 1991.
Patuelli, Raffaello. "Il 'Dipartimento dell'educazione,' ovvero il gergo dei film tradotti." *Lo Schermo* (May 1936).
Paulicelli, Eugenia. *Fashion under Fascism: Beyond the Black Shirt*. Oxford and New York: Berg, 2004.
Pavolini, Alessandro. "Capi e popolo." In *Italia e Germania, maggio XVI*, by A. A. V. V. Rome: Stampatrice Novissima, 1938.
———. "Cinema di guerra." *Film* (February 14, 1942).
———. *Disperata*. Florence: Vallecchi, 1937.
———. "Geografia cinematografica." *Cinema* (September 10, 1942).
———. "Rapporto sulla cinematografia italiana." *Bianco e Nero* (August 1942).
Pavolini, Corrado. "Cinematografo: Nuove terre." *L'Orto* (May 2, 1937).
Pellegrini, Glauco. "Il documentario: Ieri, oggi, domani." *Bianco e Nero* (September 1942).
Perbellini, A. M. "I meticci linguistici: Del parlare italiano con gli indigeni." *Etiopia* 1, no. 1 (1937).
Perinelli, Massimo. *Fluchtlinien des Neorealismus: Der organlose Körper den Italienischen Nachkriegszeit, 1943–1949*. Bielefeld, Germany: Transcript, 2008.
Perniola, Ivelise. "Documentari fuori regime." In *Storia del cinema italiano*, edited by Orio Caldiron, 5:372–380. Venice and Rome: Marsilio / Edizioni di Bianco & Nero, 2006.
Pesce, Sara. *Memoria e immaginario: La Seconda Guerra Mondiale nel cinema italiano*. Recco, Genova: Le mani, 2008.
Petersen, Jens. "Italia-Germania: Percezioni, stereotipi, pregiudizi, immagini d'inimicizia." In *L'emigrazione tra Italia e Germania*, edited by Jens Petersen, 199–219. Manduria: P. Lacaita, 1993.
Petrie, Graham. *Hollywood Destinies: European Directors in America, 1922–1931*. London: Routledge & Kegan Paul, 1985.
Petrusewicz, Marta, ed. "The Hidden Pages of Contemporary Italian History: War Crimes, War Guilt, Collective Memory." Special issue, *Journal of Modern Italian Studies* 9, no. 3 (2004).

Peyré, Joseph. *L'Escadron Blanc*. Paris: Bernard Grasset, 1934.
Piccioli, Angelo, ed. *La Nuova Italia d'oltremare: L'opera del Fascismo nelle colonie italiane*. 2 vols. Milan: Mondadori, 1933.
Pickering-Iazzi, Robin. "Mass-Mediated Fantasies of Feminine Conquest, 1930–1940." In *A Place in the Sun: Africa in Italian Colonial Culture from Post-Unification to the Present*, edited by Patrizia Palumbo, 197–224. Berkeley: University of California Press, 2003.
———. "Ways of Looking in Black and White: Female Spectatorship and the Miscege-National Body in *Sotto la Croce del Sud*." In *Re-viewing Fascism: Italian Cinema, 1922–1943*, edited by Jacqueline Reich and Piero Garofalo, 194–222. Bloomington: Indiana University Press, 2002.
Pierce, Steven, and Anupama Rao, eds. *Discipline and the Other Body: Correction, Corporeality, Colonialism*. Durham, NC: Duke University Press, 2006.
Pietrangeli, Antonio. "I film della Mostra di Venezia." *Film* (September 6, 1942).
———. "La mostra veneziana." *Bianco e Nero* (September 1942).
Pinkus, Karen. *Bodily Regimes: Italian Advertising under Fascism*. Minneapolis: University of Minnesota Press, 1995.
Piovene, Guido [G. P.]. "*Un pilota ritorna*." *Corriere della sera* (April 18, 1942).
Podestà, Gian Luca. *Il mito dell'Impero: Economia, politica e lavoro nelle colonie italiane dell'Africa Orientale, 1898–1941*. Turin: G. Giappichelli, 2004.
Poggiali, Ciro. "La donna italiana in A.O." *Almanacco della donna italiana* (1939): 53–73.
Polezzi, Loredana. "Imperial Reproductions: The Circulation of Colonial Images across Popular Genres and Media in the 1920s and 1930s." *Modern Italy* 8, no. 1 (2003): 31–47.
Ponzanesi, Sandra. "Beyond the Black Venus: Colonial Sexual Politics and Contemporary Visual Practices." In *Italian Colonialism: Legacy and Memory*, edited by Jacqueline Andall and Derek Duncan, 167–189. London and Oxford: Peter Lang, 2005.
Pretelli, Matteo. "Education in the Italian Colonies during the Interwar Period." *Modern Italy* 16, no. 3 (2011): 275–293.
———. *Il Fascismo e gli italiani all'estero*. Bologna: Clueb, 2010.
Puck [Gianni Puccini]. "Galleria: Amedeo Nazzari." *Cinema* (December 10, 1938).
———. "Galleria: Augusto Genina." *Cinema* (November 10, 1941).
Quadrone, Ernesto. *Mudundu: Cacciatori d'ombre all'Equatore*. Milan: Marangoni, 1935.
———. "*Mudundu* di Dreyer ucciso dalla malaria." *Cinema* (August 1, 1951).
Quaglietti, Lorenzo. "Cinema americano, vecchio amore." In *Schermi di guerra: Cinema italiano, 1939–1945*, edited by Mino Argentieri, 307–328. Rome: Bulzoni, 1995.
Quaresima, Leonardo. "Parigi ci appartiene? Modelli francesi nel cinema italiano del dopoguerra." In *Identità italiana e identità europea nel cinema italiano dal 1945 al miracolo economico*, edited by Gian Piero Brunetta, 441–468. Turin: Edizioni della Fondazione Giovanni Agnelli, 1996.
———, ed. *Storia del cinema italiano, 1924–1929*. Venice and Rome: Marsilio, 2014.
Quirico, Domenico. "*Squadrone bianco*": *Storia delle truppe coloniali italiane*. Milan: Mondadori, 2002.
R. G. "Momento aeronautico." *Cinema* (February 10, 1942).
Rafael, Vicente L. *The Promise of the Foreign: Nationalism and the Technics of Translation in the Spanish Philippines*. Durham, NC: Duke University Press, 2005.
Raffaelli, Sergio. *La lingua filmata: Didascalia e dialoghi nel cinema italiano*. Florence: Le lettere, 1992.

———. *Le parole proibite: Purismo di stato e regolamentazione della pubblicità in Italia, 1812–1945*. Bologna: Il Mulino, 1983.

———. "Voci e iscrizioni nel *Grande appello* di Camerini (1936)." *Lingua nostra* 70, nos. 1–2 (2009): 12–17.

RAI Youtube Channel. "Montanelli, una moglie di 12 anni in Eritrea." http://www.youtube.com/watch?v=e_53KvZvTs8.

Rava, Maurizio. "I popoli africani dinanzi allo schermo." *Cinema* (July 10, 1936).

Raybaud, Antoine. "Nomadism between the Archaic and the Modern." *Yale French Studies* 82, no. 1 (1993): 146–157.

Re, Lucia. "Italians and the Invention of Race: The Poetics and Politics of Difference in the Struggle over Libya, 1890–1913." *California Italian Studies* 1, no. 1 (2010): 1–58.

Reich, Jacqueline. *Beyond the Latin Lover: Marcello Mastroianni, Masculinity, and Italian Cinema*. Bloomington: Indiana University Press, 2004.

———. *The Maciste Films of Early Italian Cinema*. Bloomington: Indiana University Press, forthcoming.

Reich, Jacqueline, and Piero Garofalo, eds. *Re-viewing Fascism: Italian Cinema, 1922–1943*. Bloomington: Indiana University Press, 2002.

Reichardt, Sven. *Camicie nere, camicie brune: Milizie fasciste in Italia e in Germania*. Bologna: Il Mulino, 2009.

Renov, Michael. "Introduction: The Truth about Non-Fiction." In *Theorizing Documentary*, edited by Michael Renov, 1–11. New York: Routledge, 1993.

———. *The Subject of Documentary*. Minneapolis: University of Minnesota Press, 2004.

Rentschler, Eric. *The Ministry of Illusion: Nazi Cinema and Its Afterlife*. Cambridge, MA: Harvard University Press, 1996.

Renzi, Renzo, Gian Luca Farinelli, and Nicola Mazzanti. *Il cinematografo al campo: L'arma nuova nel primo conflitto mondiale*. Ancona: Transeuropa, 1993.

Ribuoli, Patrizia. "Le uniformi civili nel regime fascista." In *1922–1943, Vent'anni di moda italiana: Proposta per un museo della moda a Milano*, edited by Grazietta Butazzi, 35–39. Florence: Centro Di, 1980.

Ricci, Laura. *La lingua dell'Impero: Comunicazione, letteratura e propaganda nell'età del colonialismo italiano*. Rome: Carocci, 2005.

Ricci, Steven. *Cinema and Fascism: Italian Film and Society, 1922–1943*. Berkeley: University of California Press, 2008.

Rice, Tim. "Exhibiting Africa: British Instructional Film and the Empire Series (1925–8)." In *Empire and Film*, edited by Lee Grieveson and Colin MacCabe, 115–134. London: Palgrave Macmillan, 2011.

Ristori, Rodolfo Jacuzio. "Ritorno all'attore." *Lo Schermo* (August 1938).

Roberti, Vero. "Le corazzate con le rotelle . . ." *Lo Schermo* (April 1938).

Rochat, Giorgio. *Le guerre italiane, 1935–1943: Dall'Impero d'Etiopia alla disfatta*. Turin: Einaudi, 2005.

———. *Guerre italiane in Libia e in Etiopia: Studi militari, 1921–1939*. Paese, Treviso: Pagus, 1991.

———. "I volontari di Mussolini." In *Fare il soldato: Storie del reclutamento militare in Italia*, edited by Nicola Labanca, 123–140. Milan: Unicopli, 2007.

Rodaway, Paul. *Sensuous Geographies: Body, Sense, and Place*. London and New York: Routledge, 1994.

Rodogno, Davide. *Fascism's European Empire: Italian Occupations during World War Two*. Cambridge: Cambridge University Press, 2006.

Rogin, Michael Paul. *Blackface, White Noise: Jewish Immigrants in the Hollywood Melting Pot.* Berkeley: University of California Press, 1996.
Romano, Sergio. *Giuseppe Volpi: Industria e finanza tra Giolitti e Mussolini.* Milan: Bompiani, 1979.
Rondolino, Gianni. *Roberto Rossellini.* Turin: UTET, 2006.
Rony, Fatimah Tobing. *The Third Eye: Race, Cinema, and Ethnographic Spectacle.* Durham, NC: Duke University Press, 1996.
Rosenstone, Robert A. *Revisioning History: Film and the Construction of a New Past.* Princeton, NJ: Princeton University Press, 1995.
Rossellini, Renzo. "Schermi sonori." *Cinema* (November 25, 1942).
Rossi, Fabio. "La lingua doppiata." In *Storia del cinema italiano*, edited by Orio Caldiron, 5:404–412. Venice and Rome: Marsilio / Edizioni di Bianco & Nero, 2006.
———. *Lingua italiana e cinema.* Rome: Carocci, 2007.
Ruby, Jay. *Picturing Culture: Explorations of Film & Anthropology.* Chicago: University of Chicago Press, 2000.
Ruffin, Valentina, and Patrizia D'Agostino. *Dialoghi di regime: La lingua del cinema degli anni trenta.* Rome: Bulzoni, 1997.
Ruoff, Jeffrey, ed. *Virtual Voyages: Cinema and Travel.* Durham, NC: Duke University Press, 2006.
Russell, Catherine. *Experimental Ethnography: The Work of Film in the Age of Video.* Durham, NC: Duke University Press, 1999.
S. a. p. "Un primato italiano: Il documentario." *Lo Schermo* (July 1939).
Sabatello, Dario. "Si prepara *Sotto la Croce del Sud*." *Cinema Illustrazione* (March 2, 1938).
Sacchi, Filippo [f. s.]. "Cavalleria." *Corriere della sera* (December 12, 1935).
———. "Il grande appello." *Corriere della sera* (November 27, 1936).
———. "Jungla nera." *Corriere della sera* (August 15, 1937).
———. "Luciano Serra, pilota." *Corriere della sera* (August 29, 1938).
———. "Sentinelle di bronzo." *Corriere della sera* (May 26, 1938).
———. "Lo squadrone bianco." *Corriere della sera* (October 28, 1936).
Said, Edward W. *Orientalism.* New York: Vintage Books, 1994.
Salerno, Eric. *Uccideteli tutti, Libia 1943: Gli ebrei nel campo di concentramento fascista di Giado; Una Storia Italiana.* Milan: Il saggiatore, 2008.
Sampieri, G. V. "Divismo." *Lo Schermo* (July 1939).
Santarelli, Lidia. "Muted Violence: Fascist War Crimes in Occupied Greece." *Journal of Modern Italian Studies* 9, no. 3 (2004): 280–299.
Savarese, Roberto. "La cinematografia italiana sullo sfondo luminoso dell'Impero." *L'Italia Coloniale* (November 1937).
Savio, Francesco. *Cinecittà anni trenta: Parlano 116 protagonisti del secondo cinema italiano, 1930–1943.* 3 vols. Rome: Bulzoni, 1979.
———. *Ma l'amore no.* Milan: Sonzogno, 1975.
Sbacchi, Alberto. *Il Colonialismo Italiano in Etiopia, 1936–1940.* Milan: Mursia, 1980.
———. "Poison Gas and Atrocities in the Italo-Ethiopian War, 1935–1936." In *Italian Colonialism,* edited by Ruth Ben-Ghiat and Mia Fuller, 47–56. New York: Palgrave Macmillan, 2005.
Scarpellini, Emanuela. *Material Nation: A Consumer's History of Modern Italy.* Oxford and New York: Oxford University Press, 2011.
Schnapp, Jeffrey T. *Staging Fascism: 18 BL and the Theater of Masses for Masses.* Stanford, CA: Stanford University Press, 1996.

Schneider, Gabriele. *Mussolini in Afrika: Die faschistische Rassenpolitik in den italienischen Kolonien, 1936–1941*. Cologne: SH-Verlag, 2000.

Schwartz, Vanessa R. *It's So French! Hollywood, Paris, and the Making of Cosmopolitan Film Culture*. Chicago: University of Chicago Press, 2007.

Schwarz, Thomas. "Colonial Disgust: The Colonial Master's Emotion of Superiority." In *German Colonialism, Visual Culture, and Modern Memory*, edited by Volker Max Langbehn, 182–196. New York: Routledge, 2010.

Scotto d'Ardino, Laurent. *La revue Cinema et le néo-réalisme italien: Autonomisation d'un champ esthétique*. Saint-Denis, France: Presses universitaires de Vincennes, 1999.

Sedita, Giovanni. "Vittorio Mussolini, Hollywood, and Neorealism." *Journal of Modern Italian Studies* 15, no. 3 (2010): 431–457.

Segàla, Ariberto. *I muri del Duce*. Gardolo, Trentino: Edizioni Arca, 2001.

Segrè, Claudio G. *Italo Balbo: A Fascist Life*. Berkeley: University of California Press, 1987.

Seknadje-Askenazi, Enrique. *Roberto Rossellini et la Seconde Guerre Mondiale: Un cinéaste entre propagande et réalisme*. Paris: Harmattan, 2000.

Serandrei, Mario. "Films italiani." *Cinematografo* (December 2, 1928).

Shapiro, Michael J. *Violent Cartographies: Mapping Cultures of War*. Minneapolis: University of Minnesota Press, 1997.

Shaviro, Steven. *The Cinematic Body*. Minneapolis: University of Minnesota Press, 1993.

Shohat, Ella. "Gender and the Culture of Empire: Toward a Feminist Ethnography of the Cinema." In *Visions of the East: Orientalism in Film*, edited by Matthew Bernstein and Gaylyn Studlar, 19–68. New Brunswick, NJ: Rutgers University Press, 1997.

———. "The Imperial Imaginary." In *Unthinking Eurocentrism*, edited by Ella Shohat and Robert Stam, 100–136. London and New York: Routledge, 1994.

Shohat, Ella, and Robert Stam. *Unthinking Eurocentrism: Multiculturalism and the Media*. London and New York: Routledge, 1994.

Short, K. R. M., ed. *Film & Radio Propaganda in World War II*. Knoxville: University of Tennessee Press, 1983.

Silverman, Kaja. *The Acoustic Mirror: The Female Voice in Psychoanalysis and Cinema*. Bloomington: Indiana University Press, 1988.

Simonini, Augusto. *Il linguaggio di Mussolini*. Milan: Bompiani, 1978.

Sitney, P. Adams. "Landscape in the Cinema: The Rhythms of the World and the Camera." In *Landscape: Natural Beauty and the Arts*, edited by Ivan Gaskell and Salim Kemal, 103–126. Cambridge and New York: Cambridge University Press, 1993.

Slavin, David Henry. *Colonial Cinema and Imperial France, 1919–1939: White Blind Spots, Male Fantasies, Settler Myths*. Baltimore: Johns Hopkins University Press, 2001.

Smaill, Belinda. *The Documentary: Politics, Emotion, Culture*. Basingstoke, UK, and New York: Palgrave Macmillan, 2010.

Sobchack, Vivian Carol. *Carnal Thoughts: Embodiment and Moving Image Culture*. Berkeley: University of California Press, 2004.

———. "Toward a Phenomenology of Nonfictional Film Experience." In *Collecting Visible Evidence*, edited by Jane Gaines and Michael Renov, 241–254. Minneapolis: University of Minnesota Press, 1999.

Soldati, Mario. *America primo amore*. Florence: Bemporad, 1935.

———. *A Carte Scoperte*. Radiotelevisione Italiana, aired June 18, 1974.

———. "Con spirito nuovo 'si gira' nei luoghi dell'Impero: Primo ricordo del nostro film in A.O." *Cinema* (August 25, 1936).

———. "Il grande appello." *Lo Schermo* (November 1936).
Solmi, Vittorio. "Cronache della produzione italiana: *Un pilota ritorna*." *Lo Schermo* (January 1942).
Solv. "'Tempo nostro' e ambientazione dei film." *Lo Schermo* (April 1942).
Sòrgoni, Barbara. "'Defending the Race': The Italian Reinvention of the Hottentot Venus during Fascism." *Journal of Modern Italian Studies* 8, no. 3 (2003): 411–424.
———. *Parole e corpi: Antropologia, discorso giuridico e politiche sessuali interrazziali nella colonia Eritrea, 1890–1941*. Naples: Liguori, 1998.
Sorlin, Pierre. *The Film in History: Restaging the Past*. Totowa, NJ: Barnes & Noble, 1980.
Sottosegretariato di Stato per la Stampa e la Propaganda, et al., eds. *40° anniversario della cinematografia, 1895–1935*. Rome: Poligrafo della Stato, 1935.
Spackman, Barbara. *Fascist Virilities: Rhetoric, Ideology, and Social Fantasy in Italy*. Minneapolis: University of Minnesota Press, 1996.
Spadaro, Barbara. "Intrepide massaie: Genere, imperialismo e totalitarismo nella preparazione coloniale femminile durante il Fascismo (1937–1943)." *Contemporanea* 13, no. 1 (2010): 27–52.
Spagnoletti, Giovanni. "Registi stranieri in Italia." In *Storia del cinema italiano*, edited by Orio Caldiron, 5:265–274. Venice and Rome: Marsilio / Edizioni di Bianco & Nero, 2006.
Spaino, Alberto. "L'organizzazione dell'Istituto Nazionale Luce." *Lo Schermo* (July 1936).
Springer, John Parris. "The Newspaper Meets the Dime Novel: Docudrama in Early Cinema." In *Docufictions*, edited by Gary Don Rhodes and John Parris Springer, 27–42. Jefferson, NC: McFarland, 2006.
Stefani, Giulietta. *Colonia per maschi: Italiani in Africa Orientale, una storia di genere*. Verona: Ombre corte, 2007.
Steimatsky, Noa. "The Cinecittà Refugee Camp (1944–50)." *October* 128 (Spring 2009): 22–50.
———. *Italian Locations: Reinhabiting the Past in Postwar Cinema*. Minneapolis: University of Minnesota Press, 2008.
Stoler, Ann Laura. *Carnal Knowledge and Imperial Power: Race and the Intimate in Colonial Rule*. Berkeley: University of California Press, 2002.
———. "Imperial Debris: Reflections on Ruins and Ruination." *Cultural Anthropology* 23, no. 2 (2008): 191–219.
Stone, Marla. "The Last Film Festival: The Venice Biennale Goes to War." In *Re-viewing Fascism: Italian Cinema, 1922–1943*, edited by Jacqueline Reich and Piero Garofalo, 293–314. Bloomington: Indiana University Press, 2002.
———. *The Patron State: Culture & Politics in Fascist Italy*. Princeton, NJ: Princeton University Press, 1998.
Strang, G. Bruce. "Imperial Dreams: The Mussolini-Laval Accord of January 1935." *Historical Journal* 44, no. 3 (2001): 799–809.
Studlar, Gaylyn. "Discourses of Gender and Ethnicity: The Construction and De(Con) Struction of Rudolph Valentino as Other." *Film Criticism* 13, no. 2 (1989): 18–36.
———. "'Out-Salomeing Salome': Dance, the New Woman, and Fan Magazine Orientalism." In *Visions of the East: Orientalism in Film*, edited by Matthew Bernstein and Gaylyn Studlar, 99–129. New Brunswick, NJ: Rutgers University Press, 1997.
———. "Wider Horizons: Douglas Fairbanks and Nostalgic Primitivism." In *Back in the Saddle Again: New Essays on the Western*, edited by Edward Buscombe and Roberta E. Pearson, 63–76. London: British Film Institute, 1998.
Super Revisore, Il. "Lo dica a me e mi dica tutto." *Cinema Illustrazione* (March 2, 1938).

Suzzi Valli, Roberta. "Il culto dei martiri fascisti." In *La morte per la patria*, edited by Oliver Janz, Lutz Klinkhammer, and Roberto Balzani, 102–120. Rome: Donzelli, 2008.
Taddia, Irma. *Autobiografie africane: Il colonialismo nelle memorie orali*. Milan: Franco Angeli, 1996.
Taillibert, Christel. *L'Institut International du Cinématographe Éducatif: Regards sur le rôle du cinéma éducatif dans la politique internationale du fascisme italien*. Paris: Harmattan, 1999.
Tamis, Anne Marie. "*Kif Tebbi:* Visions of Colonial Libya in Novel and Film." *Journal of Romance Studies* 12, no. 2 (2012): 75–92.
Terhoeven, Petra. *Oro alla patria: Donne, guerra e propaganda nella giornata della fede fascista*. Bologna: il Mulino, 2006.
Terra, Giorgio. "*Sentinelle di bronzo.*" *Cinema* (May 10, 1937).
Tintori, Guido. "Cittadinanza e politiche di emigrazione nell'Italia liberale e fascista." In *Familismo legale: Come (non) diventare italiani*, edited by Giovanna Zincone, 52–106. Rome and Bari: Laterza, 2006.
Tobino, Mario. "The Deserts of Libya." In *The Lost Legions: Three Italian War Novels*, translated by Archibald Colquohon, 149–302. New York: Alfred Knopf, 1967.
Tomasello, Giovanna. *La letteratura coloniale italiana dalle avanguardie al Fascismo*. Palermo: Sellerio, 1984.
Tonti, Aldo. *Odore di cinema*. Florence: Vallecchi, 1964.
Tosh, John. "Hegemonic Masculinity and the History and Gender." In *Masculinities in Politics and War: Gendering Modern History*, edited by Stefan Dudink, Karen Hagemann, and John Tosh, 22–40. Manchester: Manchester University Press, 2004.
Tosti, A. "Il cinema e l'esercito." *Lo Schermo* (February 1939).
Trento, Giovanna. "Madamato and Colonial Concubinage in Ethiopia: A Comparative Perspective." *Aethiopica* 14 (2011): 184–205.
Treveri Gennari, Daniela. *Post-war Italian Cinema: American Intervention, Vatican Interests*. London and New York: Routledge, 2009.
Trinchese, Stefano. *Mare Nostrum: Percezione ottomana e mito Mediterraneo in Italia all'alba del '900*. Milan: Guerini studio, 2005.
Triulzi, Alessandro. "Fotografia e storia dell'Africa: Atti del convegno internazionale, Napoli, Roma, 9–11 Settembre 1992." Naples and Rome: Istituto Universitario Orientale, 1992, 1995.
———. "Introduzione." In *Colonia e postcolonia come spazi diasporici: Attraversamenti di memorie, identità e confini nel corno d'Africa*, edited by Uoldelul Chelati Dirar, Silvana Palma, Alessandro Triulzi, and Alessandro Volterra, 11–20. Rome: Carocci, 2011.
Tseggai, Araia. "Eritrean Women and Italian Soldiers: Status of Eritrean Women under Italian Rule." *Journal of Eritrean Studies* (1990): 7–12.
Tumiati, Corrado. "Pazzia e cinematografo." *Cinema* (May 10, 1937).
Turton, David, and Peter Ian Crawford, eds. *Film as Ethnography*. Manchester: Manchester University Press, 1992.
V. N. N. "*I lancieri del Bengala:* La scenografia." *Bianco e Nero* (January–April 1937).
Valentini, Paola. *Presenze sonore: Il passaggio al sonoro in Italia tra cinema e radio*. Florence: Le lettere, 2007.
Van Leeuwen, Theo. *Speech, Music, Sound*. Basingstoke, UK, and New York: Macmillan Press / St. Martin's Press, 1999.
Vasudevan, Ravi. "Addressing the Spectator of a 'Third World' National Cinema: The Bombay 'Social' Films of the 1940s and 1950s." *Screen* 36, no. 4 (1995): 305–324.

———. *The Melodramatic Public: Film Form and Spectatorship in Indian Cinema.* Ranikhet and Bangalore: Permanent Black, 2010.
Vecchietti, Giorgio. "Il documentario fa da sé." *Cinema* (March 10, 1938).
Ventrone, Angelo. *La seduzione totalitaria: Guerra, modernità, violenza politica, 1914–1918.* Rome: Donzelli, 2003.
Verdicchio, Pasquale. *Bound by Distance: Rethinking Nationalism through the Italian Diaspora.* Madison, NJ: Fairleigh Dickinson University Press, 1997.
Verdone, Mario. "Il cinematografo e la guerra." *Bianco e Nero* (November–December 1942).
Veretti, Antonio. "Musicisti, produttori e registi davanti alla musica nel film." *Lo Schermo* (October 1935).
Vice. "Film di questi giorni: *Alfa Tau!*" *Cinema* (October 10, 1942).
———. "Film di questi giorni: *Bengasi.*" *Cinema* (November 10, 1942).
———. "Film di questi giorni: *Giarabub.*" *Cinema* (May 25, 1942).
———. "*Sotto la Croce del Sud.*" *Il Popolo d'Italia* (October 8, 1938).
Vickers, Emma. "'The Good Fellow': Negotiation, Remembrance, and Recollection—Homosexuality in the British Armed Forces, 1939–1945." In *Brutality and Desire: War and Sexuality in Europe's Twentieth Century,* edited by Dagmar Herzog, 109–134. New York: Palgrave Macmillan, 2009.
Vincendeau, Ginette. "Hollywood Babel: The Coming of Sound and the Multiple-Language Version (1929–1932)." In *"Film Europe" and "Film America,"* edited by Andrew Higson and Richard Maltby, 207–224. Exeter: University of Exeter Press, 1999.
Virilio, Paul. *La machine de vision.* Paris: Éditions Galilée, 1988.
———. *War and Cinema: The Logistics of Perception.* London and New York: Verso, 1989.
Virtue, Nicolas. "Royal Army, Fascist Empire: The *Regio Esercito* on Occupation Duty, 1936–43." PhD thesis, Western University, in progress.
Visentini, Gino. "Film di questi giorni: *Equatore.*" *Cinema* (July 25, 1939).
———. "Film di questi giorni: *Luciano Serra, pilota.*" *Cinema* (November 10, 1938).
Volla, Bernardo. "Cinema: Arma di guerra aerea." *Cinema* (July 25, 1936): 53–56.
Volterra, Alessandro. *Sudditi coloniali: Ascari Eritrei, 1935–1941.* Milan: F. Angeli, 2005.
von Moltke, Johannes. *No Place Like Home: Locations of Heimat in German Cinema.* Berkeley: University of California Press, 2005.
Wanrooij, Bruno P. F. *Storia del pudore: La questione sessuale in Italia, 1860–1940.* Venice: Marsilio, 1990.
Weis, Elisabeth, and John Belton, eds. *Film Sound: Theory and Practice.* New York: Columbia University Press, 1985.
Weitz, Eric D. *A Century of Genocide: Utopias of Race and Nation.* Princeton, NJ: Princeton University Press, 2003.
White, Hayden. "Historiography and Historiophony." *American Historical Review* 93 (1988): 1193–1199.
Whittam, John. *The Politics of the Italian Army, 1861–1918.* London and Hamden, CT: Croom Helm / Archon Books, 1977.
Williams, Linda. "Melodrama Revised." In *Refiguring American Film Genres: History and Theory,* edited by Nick Browne, 42–88. Berkeley: University of California Press, 1998.
Wilson, Elizabeth. "All the Rage." In *Fabrications: Costume and the Female Body,* edited by Charlotte Herzog and Jane Gaines, 28–38. New York: Routledge, 1989.
Wilson, Owen. "The Decivilizing Mission: Auguste Dupuis-Yakouba and French Timbuktu." *French Historical Studies* 27, no. 3 (2004): 541–568.

Winter, Jay. "Under Cover of War: The Armenian Genocide in the Context of Total War." In *The Specter of Genocide: Mass Murder in Historical Perspective,* edited by Robert Gellately and Ben Kiernan, 189–214. Cambridge and New York: Cambridge University Press, 2003.

Wittman, Laura. *The Tomb of the Unknown Soldier, Modern Mourning, and the Reinvention of the Mystical Body.* Toronto: University of Toronto Press, 2011.

Wohl, Robert. *The Spectacle of Flight: Aviation and the Western Imagination, 1920–1950.* New Haven, CT: Yale University Press, 2005.

Yampolsky, Mikhail. "Reality at Second Hand." *Historical Journal of Film, Radio, and Television* 11, no. 2 (1991): 161–171.

Zagarrio, Vito. *Cinema e Fascismo: Film, modelli, immaginari.* Venice: Marsilio, 2004.

———. *L'immagine del Fascismo: La re-visione del cinema e dei media nel regime.* Rome: Bulzoni, 2009.

———. "Schizofrenie del modello fascista." In *Storia del cinema italiano,* edited by Orio Caldiron, 5:37–61. Venice and Rome: Marsilio / Edizioni di Bianco & Nero, 2006.

Zambenedetti, Alberto. "Italians on the Move: Toward a History of Italian Migration Cinema." PhD thesis, New York University, 2012.

Zavoli, Sergio. "Spirito della modernità fascista." *Critica Fascista* (January 1, 1941).

Zinni, Maurizio. *Fascisti di celluloide: La memoria del ventennio nel cinema italiano, 1945–2000.* Venice: Marsilio, 2010.

———. "L'Impero sullo grande schermo: Il cinema di finzione fascista e la conquista coloniale, 1936–1942." *Mondo contemporaneo* 3 (2011): 5–38. http://host.uniroma3.it/uffici/stampa/ecostampa/pdf/1GHM/1GHM0Y.PDF.

Zùccoli, Luciano. *"Kif Tebbi": Romanzo Africano.* Milan: Garzanti, 1923.

Zyrd, Michael. "Found Footage Film as Discursive Metahistory: Craig Baldwin's *Tribulation 99.*" *Moving Image* 49 (Fall 2003): 40–61.

FILMOGRAPHY

1860, dir. Alessandro Blasetti. Italy, Società Anonima Stefano Pittaluga, 1934.
1940: 10 giugno; Anno XVIII (Luce D035001). Italy, Istituto Nazionale Luce, 1940.
A nous la liberté / Freedom for Us, dir. René Clair. France, Socièté des Films Sonores Tobis, 1931.
Abuna Messias, dir. Goffredo Alessandrini. Italy, Romana Editrice Film, 1939.
Aethiopia, dir. Franco Martini. Italy, Sindicato Istruzione Cinematografica, 1924.
Aldebaran, dir. Alessandro Blasetti. Italy, Manenti Film, 1935.
Ali fasciste: Attività della nostra aviazione nel Mediterraneo orientale/Fascist Wings: Our Aviation's Activity in the Eastern Mediterranean (Giornale Luce C0081), dir. Basilio Franchina. Italy, Istituto Nazionale Luce, 1940.
Alima, dir. Gino Cerruti. Italy, Cito-Cinema, 1921.
Amhara-Gorgorà (Cronache dell'impero CI003). Italy, Istituto Nazionale Luce, 1937.
L'assedio dell'Alcazar/The Siege of Alcazar, dir. Augusto Genina. Italy, Bassoli Film, 1940.
L'Atlantide/Atlantis, dir. Jacques Feyder. France, Thalman et Cie, 1921.
I bambini ci guardano/The Children Are Watching Us, dir. Vittorio de Sica. Italy, Scalera Film, 1942.
La Bandera/Escape from Yesterday, dir. Julien Duvivier. France, Société Nouvelle de Cinématographie, 1935.
La battaglia delle due palme/The Battle of Two Palms, dir. Luca Comerio. Italy, Milano Film, 1912.
La battaglia dello Jonio/The Battle of Jonio (Luce D000304). Italy, Istituto Nazionale Luce, 1940.
Bengasi, dir. Augusto Genina. Italy, Bassoli Film, 1942.
Bengasi, anno '41, dir. Augusto Genina. Italy, Bassoli Film, 1955.
I berberi e gli italiani/The Berbers and the Italians (Giornale Luce A0934), dir. Arnaldo Ricotti. Italy, Istituto Nazionale Luce, 1932.
Berlin: The Symphony of a Great City, dir. Walter Ruttmann. Germany, Deutsche-Vereins Film, 1927.
Bianco contro negro/The White against the Black, dir. Ubaldo Maria Del Colle. Italy, Pasquali e C., 1913.

Bidoni e l'araba/Bidoni and the Negress. Italy, Società Italiana Cines, 1914.
Cabiria, dir. Giovanni Pastrone. Italy, Itala Film, 1914.
Camicia nera/Black Shirt, dir. Giovacchino Forzano. Italy, Istituto Nazionale Luce, 1933.
Il cammino degli eroi/The Path of the Heroes, dir. Corrado d'Errico (Luce D037101). Italy, Istituto Nazionale Luce, 1936.
Canto, ma sottovoce/I Am Singing Softly, dir. Guido Brignone. Italy, Itala Film, 1946.
Casablanca, dir. Michael Curtiz. United States, Warner Bros., 1942.
I cavalieri del deserto/The Cavaliers of the Desert, dir. Gino Talamo and Osvaldo Talenti. Italy, Alleanza Cinematografica Italiana, 1942.
Il cavaliere di Kruja/The Knight of Kruja, dir. Carlo Campogalliani. Italy, Capitani Film, 1940.
Cavalleria, dir. Goffredo Alessandrini. Italy, Iniziative Cinematografiche Internazionale, 1936.
Chi l'ha visto?/Who Has Seen Him?, dir. Goffredo Alessandrini. Italy, Industrie Cinematografiche Artistiche Romane, 1945.
Un chien andalou/An Andalusian Dog, dir. Luis Buñuel. France, Paris Studios Billancourt, 1928.
Il cielo sulla palude/Heaven over the Marshes, dir. Augusto Genina. Italy, Bassoli Film, 1949.
Les Cinq Gentlemen Maudits/Moon over Morocco, dir. Julien Duvivier. France, Les Films Marcel Vandal et Charles Delac, 1931.
The Conquest of the Air, dir. Zoltan Korda. United Kingdom, London Film Productions, 1936.
La conquista dell'aria, dir. Romolo Marcellini. Italy, Manderfilm, 1939.
Da Adua ad Axum: Le tappe dell'avanzata italiana nell'A.O./From Adwa to Axum: The Stages of the Italian Advance in East Africa (Luce D039001). Italy, Istituto Nazionale Luce, 1936.
Dall'Italia all'Equatore, dir. Massimo Terzano. Italy, Società Anonima Stefano Pittaluga, 1923.
Dal Polo all'Equatore/From the Pole to the Equator, dir. Luca Comerio. Italy, Lab 80 Film, 1929.
Dal Polo all'Equatore/From the Pole to the Equator, dir. Yervant Gianikian and Angela Ricci Lucchi. Germany, Zweites Deutsches Fernsehen, 1985.
Desperate Journey, dir. Raoul Walsh. United States, Warner Bros., 1942.
Dive Bomber, dir. Michael Curtiz. United States, Warner Bros., 1941.
Due lettere anonime/Two Anonymous Letters, dir. Mario Camerini. Italy, Lux Film, 1945.
Dux. Italy, Istituto Nazionale Luce, 1926.
L'ebreo errante/The Wandering Jew, dir. Goffredo Alessandrini. Italy, Cinematografica Distributori Indipendenti, 1948.
Equatore/Equator, dir. Gino Valori. Italy, Roma Film, 1939.
Eritrea-Asmara (*Cronache dell'impero* CI004). Italy, Istituto Nazionale Luce, 1937.
L'eroica fanciulla da Derna/The Heroine from Derna, dir. Gennaro Righelli. Italy, Vesuvio-Films, 1912.
L'Esclave blanc/Jungla nera, dir. Carl Theodore Dryer and Jean-Paul Paulin. France-Italy, Artisti Associati, 1936.
L'Esclave blanche/The White Slave, dir. Augusto Genina. France-Germany, Lothar-Stark Film/Wolfe Productions, 1927.
Eskimo, dir. W. S. Van Dyke. United States, Metro-Goldwyn-Mayer, 1933.

¡España, una, grande, libre!/¡Spain, United, Great, Free!, dir. Giorgio Ferroni. Italy, Istituto Nazionale Luce, 1939.
Ettore Fieramosca, dir. Alessandro Blasetti. Italy, Nembo-Film, 1938.
Fantasmi del mare/Phantoms of the Sea, dir. Francesco De Robertis. Italy, Centro Cinematografiche Italiano, 1948.
Festa religiosa araba in Tripolitania/Arabic Religious Festival in Tripolitania (Giornale Luce A0469). Italy, Istituto Nazionale Luce, 1929.
Feuertaufe/Baptism of Fire, dir. Hans Bertram. Germany, Tobis Filmkunst, 1940.
Fiamme abissine/Abyssinian Flames, dir. Gino Cerruti. Italy, Cito-Cinema, 1921.
La figlia del deserto/The Daughter of the Desert, dir. A. Di Natale. Italy, Libia Film, 1923.
La freccia d'oro/The Golden Arrow, dir. Corrado d'Errico and Piero Ballerini. Italy, Colosseum Film, 1935.
Il fu Mattia Pascal/He Was Mattia Pascal, dir. Pierre Chenal. France, Général Productions, 1937.
Galla e Sidamo-Agheremariam (*Cronache dell'impero* CI003). Italy, Istituto Nazionale Luce, 1937.
Galla e Sidamo-Uondo (*Cronache dell'impero* CI004). Italy, Istituto Nazionale Luce, 1937.
The Garden of Allah, dir. Richard Boleslawksi. United States, Selznick International Pictures, 1936.
Giarabub, dir. Goffredo Alessandrini. Italy, Scalera Film, 1942.
Giungla/Jungle, dir. Nunzio Malasomma. Italy, Industrie Cinematografiche Italiane, 1942.
Governo dei Galla e Sidamo-Gambela (*Cronache dell'impero* CI001). Italy, Istituto Nazionale Luce, 1937.
Governo dei Galla e Sidamo-Lechenti (*Cronache dell'impero* CI001). Italy, Istituto Nazionale Luce, 1937.
Governo dell'Amhara-Gondar (*Cronache dell'impero* CI001). Italy, Istituto Nazionale Luce, 1937.
Il grande appello/The Last Roll Call, dir. Mario Camerini. Italy, ADIA Films, 1936.
La grande illusion/Grand Illusion, dir. Jean Renoir. France, Réalisations d'Art Cinématographique, 1937.
Grand Hotel, dir. Edmund Goulding. United States, Metro-Goldwyn-Mayer, 1932.
Il gruppo meharista al commando del Duca d'Aosta/The Meharist Group at the Command of the Duke of Aosta. Italy, Istituto Nazionale Luce, 1928.
Guerra alla guerra/War on War, dir. Romolo Marcellini. Italy, Orbis Film, 1946.
Guerra italo-turca tra "scugnizzi" napoletani/The Italian-Turkish War among the Neapolitan Street Urchins, dir. Elvira Notari. Italy, Film Dora, 1912.
Harar-Baccà (*Cronache dell'impero* CI003). Italy, Istituto Nazionale Luce, 1937.
Harlem Knockout, dir. Carmine Gallone. Italy, Cines, 1943.
L'inaugurazione della stazione radiotelegrafica di Tripoli/The Inauguration of the Radio-Telegraphy Station in Tripoli, dir. Luca Comerio. Italy, Milano Film, 1912.
Inferno giallo/Yellow Inferno, dir. Géza von Radványi. Italy, Colosseum Film, 1942.
Intolerance, dir. D.W. Griffith. United States, Triangle Distributing Corporation, 1916.
The Iron Horse, dir. John Ford. United States, Fox Film Corporation, 1924.
I Wanted Wings, dir. Mitchell Leisen. United States, Paramount Pictures, 1941.
Le jour se lève/Daybreak, dir. Marcel Carné. France, Productions Sigma, 1939.
Jud Süss, dir. Veit Harlan. Germany, Terra Film, 1940.

Kif tebbi, dir. Mario Camerini. Italy, ADIA Films, 1928.
Kri kri reduce d'Africa/Kri kri Veteran of Africa, dir. Giuseppe Gambardella. Italy, Società Italiana Cines, 1914.
Lacrime di sangue/Tears of Blood, dir. Guido Brignone. Italy, Industrie Nazionale Associate Cinematografiche, 1944.
Legionari del secondo parallelo: Diario di un milite/Legionaires of the Second Parallel: Diary of a Militiaman, dir. Romolo Marcellini (Luce D004601). Italy, Istituto Nazionale Luce, 1936.
The Lives of a Bengal Lancer, dir. Henry Hathaway. United States, Paramount Pictures, 1935.
The Lost Patrol, dir. John Ford. United States, RKO Radio Pictures, 1934.
Luciano Serra, pilota, dir. Goffredo Alessandrini. Italy, Aquila Films, 1938.
Maciste all'inferno/Maciste in Hell, dir. Guido Brignone. Italy, Itala Film, 1926.
Maciste contro lo sceicco/Maciste against the Sheik, dir. Mario Camerini. Italy, Fert Film, 1926.
Mädchen in Uniform/Girls in Uniform, dir. Leontine Sagan. Germany, Deutsche Film-Gemeinschaft, 1931.
Marinai senza stelle/Sailors without Stars, dir. Francesco De Robertis. Italy, Scalera Film, 1949.
Maschiaccio/The Boyish Girl, dir. Augusto Genina. Italy, Società Anonima Ambrosio, 1917.
Men of the Lightship, dir. David MacDonald. United Kingdom, Crown Film Unit, 1940.
Morocco, dir. Josef von Sternberg. United States, Paramount Pictures, 1930.
Il mulatto/The Mulatto, dir. Francesco De Robertis. Italy, Scalera Film, 1950.
Myriam, dir. Enrico Guazzoni. Italy, Suprema Film, 1929.
La nave bianca/The White Ship, dir. Roberto Rossellini. Italy, Scalera Film, 1941.
Negri comici/Comic Negroes. Italy, Società Italiana Cines, 1912.
Noi vivi—Addio Kira/We the Living—Goodbye Kira, dir. Goffredo Alessandrini. Italy, Scalera Film, 1942.
Non ti scordar di me/Forget Me Not, dir. Zoltan Korda. United Kingdom, London Film Productions, 1935.
Il nostro esercito coloniale/Our Colonial Army. Italy, Istituto Nazionale Luce, 1928.
Los Novios de la Muerte/The Grooms of Death, dir. Romolo Marcellini. Italy, Istituto Nazionale Luce, 1937.
Ohm Krüger/Uncle Krüger, dir. Hans Steinhoff. Germany, Tobis Filmkunst, 1941.
Olympia, dir. Leni Riefenstahl. Germany, Tobis Filmkunst, 1938.
One of Our Aircraft Is Missing, dir. Michael Powell. United Kingdom, Archers Film Productions, 1942.
Ossessione, dir. Luchino Visconti. Italy, Industrie Cinematografiche Italiane, 1943.
Paisà, dir. Roberto Rossellini. Italy, Organizzazione Film Internazionali, 1946.
Partire/Departure, dir. Amleto Palermi. Italy, Astra Film, 1938.
Passaporto Rosso/The Red Passport, dir. Guido Brignone. Italy, Società Anonima Stefano Pittaluga, 1935.
The Passion of Jeanne d'Arc, dir. Carl Theodor Dreyer. France, Société générale des films, 1927.
Pastor Angelicus, dir. Romolo Marcellini. Italy, Centro Cattolico Cinematografico, 1942.
Un pilota ritorna/A Pilot Returns, dir. Roberto Rossellini. Italy, Alleanza Cinematografica Italiana, 1942.
Piloti e fanti nel deserto sirtico/Pilots and Infantrymen in the Sirte Desert, dir. Romolo Marcellini. Italy, Istituto Nazionale Luce, 1941.

Poil de carotte/The Red Head, dir. Julien Duvivier. France, Les Films Marcel Vandal et Charles Delac, 1932.
Il ponte di vetro/Bridge of Glass, dir. Goffredo Alessandrini. Italy, Scalera Film, 1939.
Il primo colpo all'impero britannico: La conquista della Somalia Britannica/The First Blow to the British Empire: The Conquest of British Somalia. Italy, Istituto Nazionale Luce, 1940.
Princesse Tam-Tam, dir. Edmond Gréville. France, Productions Arys, 1935.
Prix de beauté/Miss Europa, dir. Augusto Genina. France, Sofar-Film, 1930.
Quelli della montagna/Men of the Mountain, dir. Aldo Vergano. Italy, Lux Film, 1943.
Rien que les heures/Nothing but Time, dir. Alberto Cavalcanti. France, Néo Film, 1926.
Ritmi di stazione/Rhythms of the Station, dir. Corrado d'Errico (Luce D062002). Italy, Istituto Nazionale Luce, 1933.
Roma città aperta/Rome Open City, dir. Roberto Rossellini. Italy, Excelsa Film, 1945.
Rotaie/Rails, dir. Mario Camerini. Italy, S.A.C.I.A. Cines, 1930.
S.O.S. Sahara, dir. Jacques de Baroncelli. Germany, L'Alliance Cinématographique Européene, 1938.
Sanders of the River, dir. Zoltan Korda. United Kingdom, London Film Productions, 1935.
San Francesco, giullare di Dio/The Flowers of Saint Francis, dir. Roberto Rossellini. Italy, Rizzoli Film, 1950.
Scipione l'Africano, dir. Carmine Gallone. Italy, Ente Nazionale Industrie Cinematografiche, 1937.
Seconda B, dir. Goffredo Alessandrini. Italy, Industrie Cinematografiche Artistiche Romane, 1934.
La segretaria privata/The Private Secretary, dir. Goffredo Alessandrini. Italy, Cines, 1931.
Sentinelle di bronzo/Dusky Sentinels, dir. Romolo Marcellini. Italy, Generalcine-Fono Roma, 1937.
The Sheik, dir. George Melford. United States, Paramount Pictures, 1921.
Sieg im Westen/Victory in the West, dir. Svend Noldan. Germany, Oberkommando der Wehrmacht Wehrpropaganda V, 1941.
Siliva Zulu, dir. Attilio Gatti. Italy, Explorator Film, 1927.
Sotto la Croce del Sud/Under the Southern Cross, dir. Guido Brignone. Italy, Mediterranea Film, 1938.
Il Sottosegretario di Stato alle Colonie in Cirenaica (Giornale Luce A0805). Italy, Istituto Nazionale Luce, 1931.
La spedizione Franchetti nella Dancalia etiopica/The Franchetti Expedition to Ethiopian Dancalia, dir. Mario Craveri. Italy, Istituto Nazionale Luce, 1929.
La sperduta di Allah/Allah's Lost Soul, dir. Enrico Guazzoni. Italy, Suprema Film, 1929.
Lo squadrone bianco/The White Squadron, dir. Augusto Genina. Italy, Roma Film, 1936.
Lo stormo Atlantico/The Atlantic Flock, dir. Mario Craveri (Luce D048805). Italy, Istituto Nazionale Luce, 1931.
Stramilano/Supermilan, dir. Corrado d'Errico (Luce M016101). Italy, Istituto Nazionale Luce, 1929.
Sulle orme dei nostri pionieri/On the Tracks of Our Pioneers, dir. Luciano de Feo (Luce D028702). Italy, Istituto Nazionale Luce, 1936.
T'amerò sempre/I Will Love You Always, dir. Mario Camerini. Italy, Cines, 1933.
Tosca, dir. Carlo Koch and Jean Renoir. Italy, Scalera Film, 1941.
Trader Horn, dir. W.S. Van Dyke. United States, Metro-Goldwyn-Mayer, 1931.

I trecento della settima/The Three Hundred of the Seventh, dir. Mario Baffico. Italy, Nettunia Film, 1943.
Treno popolare/The Popular Train, dir. Raffaello Materazzo. Italy, Amato Film, 1933.
Ultimo Amore/The Last Love, dir. Luigi Chiarini. Italy, Pan Film, 1947.
L'Ultimo Lord/The Last Lord, dir. Augusto Genina. Italy, Cinés-Pittaluga, 1926.
Umanità/Humanity, dir. Jack Salvatori (Luce DVD002). Italy, Istituto Nazionale Luce and UNRRA, 1946.
Gli uomini, che mascalzoni!/What Scoundrels Men Are!, dir. Mario Camerini. Italy, Società Italiana Cines, 1932.
Uomini sul fondo/Men on the Bottom, dir. Francesco De Robertis. Italy, Scalera Film, 1941.
L'uomo della croce/The Man with the Cross, dir. Roberto Rossellini. Italy, Continentalcine, 1943.
Uragano ai tropici/Hurricane in the Tropics, dir. Pier Luigi Faraldo and Gino Talamo. Italy, Ponzano Film, 1939.
Vampyr, dir. Carl Theodor Dreyer. Germany, Tobis Filmkunst, 1932.
Villafranca, dir. Giovacchino Forzano. Italy, Fono Roma, 1934.
La vita degli ascari eritrei/The Life of the Eritrean Ascari, dir. Luca Comerio. Italy, Milano Films, 1912.
Vivere in pace/To Live in Peace, dir. Luigi Zampa. Italy, Lux Film, 1947.

INDEX

Italicized page numbers refer to figures.

A nous la liberté/Freedom for Us (Clair, 1931), 51
Abuna Messias (Alessandrini, 1939), 6, 7–8, 54, 301, 305
ADIA consortium, 131
Aethiopia (Martini, 1924), 27–28
"Aethiopia: Notes for a Little Song" (Flaiano), 296
African actors and extras, 6–9; in *L'Esclave blanc* (1936), 9, 159; in *Il grande appello* (1936), 93; in *Luciano Serra, pilota* (1938), 110–111, 114–115; in *Sentinelle di bronzo* (1937), 15, 60, 152–158; soldiers as, 7, 110–111, 114–115
African women: casting and, 188–190; in empire films, 125, 127; in *L'Esclave blanc* (1936), 182–190; in Fascist empire cinema, 14–15; in *Il grande appello* (1936), 83; interracial sex and, 8, 14; in *Kif Tebbi* (1928), 34–36; *mal d'Africa* and, 298; in *Sotto la Croce del Sud* (1938), 202–204
Africans: as interpreters, translators and guides, 9, 111, 119; as spectators, 56–62
Ala Littoria (commercial airline), 105–106, 117
Albania, 214–215, 246
Alberini, Massimo, 240
Aldebaran (Blasetti, 1935), 120, 125, 148

Alessandrini, Goffredo: aerial themes and, 246; after the fall of Fascism, 301, 302; denounced, 46; in Hollywood, 38, 39, 47, 101, 249, 301; indigenous extras and, 6; Scalera and, 231
Alessandrini, Goffredo, films: *Abuna Messias* (1939), 6, 7–8, 54, 301, 305; *Cavalleria* (1936), 100, 101, 103, 105; *Chi l'ha visto?* (1945), 302; *Una donna tra due mondi*, 315n7; *L'ebreo errante* (1948), 302–303; *Giarabub* (1942), 15, 125, 215, 244–245, 305; *Noi vivi—Addio Kira* (1942), 290; *Il ponte di vetro* (1939), 117; *Seconda B* (1934), 109; *La segretaria privata* (1931), 109. See also *Luciano Serra, pilota*
Alfieri, Dino, 44, 45, 48, 64, 66
Ali, Mohamed Agi, 152–153
Ali fasciste: Attività della nostra aviazione nel Mediterraneo orientale/Fascist Wings: Alima (Istituto Luce, 1940), 246
Alicata, Mario, 264
Alima (Cerruti, 1921), 74
Allied Commission for the Purge of Directors, Assistant Directors, and Screenwriters, 301
Allied Psychological War Board, 305
Allodoli, Ettore, 50
Almirante, Giorgio, 288

Alpine mysticism, xiv
Altichieri, Gilberto, 51–52
Altman, Rick, 256
America, primo amore/America, First Love (Soldati), 82
American cinema and film industry: Alessandrini and, 38, 39, 47, 101, 249, 301; consumption of in Italy, 4, 46, 48, 58, 221; consumption of in the colonies, 58; ENIC and, 45; European cinema and, 47–48, 249; Fascist empire cinema and, 4–5, 73–74; *Luciano Serra, pilota* (1938) and, 101–102; models of masculinity in, 11
American Westerns: European cinema and, xiv; Fascist empire cinema and, 210–211; *Il grande appello* (1936) and, 88–89; *Luciano Serra, pilota* (1938) and, 99; popularity of, 58; *Sentinelle di bronzo* (1937) and, 160–162
Andall, Jacqui, 298
Angioletti, G. B., 146
anti-Semitic sentiments and legislation, 48, 122, 198–199, 209, 243, 291. *See also* Jews
Antonioni, Michelangelo: on dubbing, 222; empire films and, xv; on Italian film industry, 220; on *Luciano Serra, pilota* (1938), 102; *Un pilota ritorna* (1942) and, 247–248
Aprà, Adriano, 242, 253
Apter, Emily, 54, 139, 250
Arata, Ubaldo, 107, 110
Argentieri, Mino, 47
Argentina, 97, 194, 218–219
Aristarco, Guido, 240
askari soldiers: *1860* (1934) and, 60; Ethiopian War and, 127; as film extras, 7, 77, 111, 127; roles of, 127–129; in *Lo squadrone bianco* (1936), 139; World War II and, 127
L'assedio dell'Alcazar/The Siege of Alcazar (Genina, 1940), 268–269, 315n7
L'Atlantide/Atlantis (Feyder, 1921), 30
Augustus (Asmara cinema), 56
Autonomous Aerophotographic Section, 246
Autry, Gene, 90
aviation: aerial photography and film and, 25, 68, 76, 96, 105–107, 224, 245–247; aerial warfare and, 6, 23–24, 25, 66, 105–107; Balbo and, xvii–xviii, 105, 106, 112–113; Fascist propaganda and, 105–110, 245; in *Luciano Serra, pilota* (1938), 105, 107–110, 112–113, 224, 246, 251; Paris Peace Treaty and, 297
L'Avvenire di Tripoli (Italian Libyan newspaper), 144
Axis Alliance: as cinematographic Axis, 46; co-productions and, 300; De Robertis and, 236; empire films and, 43, 80, 218–220, 269, 288, 290; Libya and, 268; military engagements and, 2; *Un pilota ritorna* (1942) and, 249–250, 253; Rossellini and, 236, 239; World War II and, xiv

Baffico, Mario: *I trecento della settima* (1943), 291
Bagnoni, Guido, 63
Baker, Josephine, 15
Balázs, Béla, 140, 204
Balbo, Italo: aviation and, xvii–xviii, 105, 106, 112–113; as governor of Libya, 120, 268; *Luciano Serra, pilota* (1938) and, 97, 112–113; *Lo squadrone bianco* (1936) and, 143
Balestrazzi, Luigi, 210, 211–212
Ballerini, Piero: *La freccia d'oro* (with D'Errico, 1935), 71–72
I bambini ci guardano/The Children Are Watching Us (De Sica, 1942), 287
Banco Nazionale del Lavoro, 41
La bandera/Escape fom Yesterday (Duvivier, 1935): *Il grande appello* (1936) and, 83, 85, 87–88, 93; *Luciano Serra, pilota* (1938) and, 113; reception of, 209; *Lo squadrone bianco* (1936) and, 144
Baratieri, Daniela, 305
Bardèche, Maurice, 146
Bargelesi, Alberto, 290–291
Baroncelli, Jacques de: *S.O.S. Sahara* (1938), 209
Barrera, Giulia, 170–171
Barthes, Roland, 52
Bassoli, Franco, 290
La battaglia delle due palme/The Battle of Two Palms (Comerio, 1912), 22

La battaglia dello Jonio/The Battle of Jonio (Istituto Nazionale Luce, 1940), 229–230, 232, 234, 235, 239
battle scenes, 5, 76; in *Bengasi* (1942), 289; in *Il grande appello* (1936), 94; in *Luciano Serra, pilota* (1938), 111–115, *114–115;* in *Lo squadrone bianco* (1936), 140–141
Baum, Vicki, 71–72
Bazin, André, 187
Behdad, Ali, 23
Bellassai, Alessandro, 10
belly dancing, 120
Belmonte, Michaela, 248
Benadir (Mogadishu cinema), 56, 57, 306
Bengasi (Genina, 1942): Committee for War and Political Cinema and, 290; companion text for, 290–291; current availability of, 309n5; *Due lettere anonime* (1945) and, 303; ending of, 283–285; Fascist ideology in, 301; financial incentives and assistance for, 4; foreign speech in, 50–51; Italian soldiers as extras in, 216; language and silence in, 280–282; masculinity in, 244, 275–279, 284–285; music in, 270; *Un pilota ritorna* (1942) and, 254; press book for, 291–292, *292;* production of, 215, 266–268, 269–270; publicity for, 288; realism and melodrama in, 270–272, 282; reception of, 222, 288–290; sets in Cinecittà for, 300; as transition from empire films, 287–288; translation in, 280–282, 284; Veretti and, 49; witness in, 303; women in, 245, 271–275, 279–280, 283
Bengasi, anno '41 (Genina, 1955), 305–306, 309n5
Bengasi. La città murata (Bargelesi), 290–291
Benjamin, Walter, 9–10, 257
I berberi e gli italiani/The Berbers and the Italians (Ricotti, 1932), 34
Berclè Zaitù Taclè, 7–8
Berlin: Die Sinfonie der Grosstadt/Berlin: The Symphony of a Great City (Ruttmann, 1927), 226
Bertellini, Giorgio, 17, 139, 140
Bertram, Hans: *Feuertaufe* (1940), 226

Bianchi, Giorgio, 232
Bianco contro negro/The White against the Black (Del Colle, 1913), 24
Bianco e nero (magazine): anti-Semitic sentiments and, 198–199; on *Cronache dell'impero* (1937), 68; on *The Lives of a Bengal Lancer* (1935), 74; on masculinity and Italianness, 102; on *Sentinelle di bronzo* (1937), 165, 166; on *Sotto la Croce del Sud* (1938), 209
Biancoli, Oreste, 213
Biasini, Gaston, 326n14
Bidoni e l'araba/Bidoni and the Negress (Società Italiana Cines, 1914), 24
Blasetti, Alessandro, 210; *Aldebaran* (1935), 120, 125, 148; *1860* (1934), 51, 60, 100, 283–284; *Ettore Fieramosca* (1938), 100
Boggi, Cecilia, 136, 143
Boleslawksi, Richard: *The Garden of Allah* (1936), 15
bombings: Comerio and, 22–23; Fascist propaganda and, 23–24, 105–106, 246; in Italy, 217; in *Luciano Serra, pilota* (1938), 96, 112–113; V. Mussolini and, 108; in *Un pilota ritorna* (1942), 248–249, 250–251, 256, 261, 266
Bonfiglio, Ferruccio, 145–146, 190
Boscaglia, Maurizia, 11
Bottai, Giuseppe, 40
Bourdieu, Pierre, 12
Bragaglia, C. L., 73
Braidotti, Rosy, 164
Brazil, 79, 84, 97, 102, 106, 112
Brignone, Guido, 26, 231; *Canto, ma sottovoce* (1946), 303; *Lacrime di sangue* (1944), 303; *Mamma* (1941), 315n7; *Passaporto rosso* (1935), 97, 194. See also *Sotto la Croce del Sud*
British cinema and film industry: Crown Film Unit and, 226, 233; imperial agenda and, xiv
Brooks, Louise, 131
Brunetta, Gian Piero, 301–302
Bruno, Giuliana, 14–15
Bulgaria, 219, 220
Buñuel, Luis: *Un chien andalou* (1928), 236
Burdett, Charles, 10

Cabiria (Pastrone, 1914), 26, 42
Càllari, Francesco: on *La battaglia dello Jonio* (1940), 230; on history of Fascist empire films, 212–213; on Luce war films, 307; on *Un pilota ritorna* (1942), 263–264; on *Sotto la Croce del Sud* (1938), 209
Calvino, Italo, 218, 295
Camerini, Mario: ADIA consortium and, 131; aerial themes and, 246; after the fall of Fascism, 301; career abroad of, 38, 39; on colonial films, 212–213; Maciste films and, 26, 30–31, 120
Camerini, Mario, films: *Due lettere anonime* (1945), 303; *Ma non è una cosa seria* (1936), 315n7; *Maciste contro lo sceicco* (1926), 30–31, 120; *Rotaie* (1930), 71; *T'amerò sempre* (1933), 73; *Gli uomini, che mascalzoni!* (1932), 73. See also *Il grande appello*; *Kif Tebbi*
Camicia nera/Black Shirt (Forzano, 1933), 73
Il cammino degli eroi/The Path of the Heroes (D'Errico, 1936), 63–64, 71, 72–73, 251
Campogalliani, Carlo: *Il cavaliere di Kruja* (1940), 125–127, 215
Cannes Film Festival, 46–47
Cannonieri, Giorgio, 245
Canto, ma sottovoce/I Am Singing Softly (Brignone, 1946), 303
Cappelletti, Franco, 8
Caproni precision bombers, 105, 109
Carné, Marcel, 47, 198, 221; *Le jour se lève* (1939), 47
Carnera, Primo, 102
Carroll, Noël, 211
Casablanca (Curtiz, 1942), 85
case del fascio, 56
Casetti, Francesco, xvi, 18, 23
Casiraghi, Ugo, 234, 329n15
Castellani, Renato, xv, 88
Castelli in aria (1939), 315n7
Catholic Church, 55, 94, 291
Cavalcanti, Alberto, 233; *Rien que les heures* (1926), 226
Il cavaliere di Kruja/The Knight of Kruja (Campogalliani, 1940), 125–127, 215
I cavalieri del deserto/The Cavaliers of the Desert (Talamo and Talenti, 1942), 268

Cavalleria (Alessandrini, 1936), 100, 101, 103, 105
censorship, 41, 44–45, 51, 190, 243
Centa, Antonio: Paramount and, 38; in *Sotto la Croce del Sud* (1938), 125, 195, 200–201; in *Lo squadrone bianco* (1936), 125, 126, 131–132
Centro Cattolico Cinematografico (Catholic Center for Cinematography), 55
Centro Sperimentale di Cinematografia (CSC), 299
Cerchi Usai, Paolo, 26
Cerchio, Fernando, 225, 226–227
Cerruti, Gino: *Alima* (1921), 74; *Fiamme abissine* (1922), 74
Chambers, Iain, 80
chemical weapons, 2, 23, 66, 247
Chenal, Pierre: *Il fu Mattia Pascal* (1937), 198
Chi l'ha visto?/Who Has Seen Him? (Alessandrini, 1945), 302
Chiarini, Luigi, 47–48, 147–148; *Ultimo Amore* (1947), 297
Un chien andalou/An Andalusian Dog (Buñuel, 1928), 236
Chion, Michel, 49, 53, 143, 261
Christian humanism, 239
Christina, Alima, 189
Ciano, Galeazzo, 70, 73, 113, 216
Il cielo sulla palude/Heaven over the Marshes (Genina, 1949), 302
Cigoli, Emilio, 52
Cinecittà (studio complex): *Bengasi* (1942) and, 266, 269; "cinematographic axis" and, 219–220; creation of, 45; Fascist spies in, 45–46; Freddi and, xxii; Istituto Luce and, 45; Italian soldiers as extras in, 216; as refugee camp, 300
cinema: consumption of in Italy, 4, 26; Fascist laws on, 39–40, 48; fortieth anniversary of the invention of, 41–42; origins of, 22. See also American cinema and film industry; British cinema and film industry; Fascist empire cinema; French cinema and film industry
Cinema (review): Bagnoni and, 63; on cinemas in the colonies, 58, 61; on co-

lonial adventure film, 192; on dubbing, 222; on Duranti, 127; French cinema and, 47; on *Giarabub* (1942), 245; on *Il grande appello* (1936), 94–95; on Luce newsreels, 66; on *Luciano Serra, pilota* (1938), 109, 110, 116; V. Mussolini and, 4, 48, 55–56; on *La nave bianca* (1941), 238; on operators in war units, 223; on *Un pilota ritorna* (1942), 247, 264; on racial masquerade, 123; on the role of cinema, 18; on *Sotto la Croce del Sud* (1938), 210; on *Lo squadrone bianco* (1936), 145

Cinema Centers of the Armed Forces, 223, 224

Cinema dell'Impero (Asmara), 306

Cinema Eel Gaab (Somalia), 306

Cinema Illustrazione (magazine), xviii, 111, 144, 192–193

Cinema Italia (later Cinema Hamar) (Somalia), 306

Cinema Roma (Somalia), 306

cinemamitragliatrice ("cinema-machine gun"), 63

cinemas: in Italian East African Empire, 56–58, 57, 306; in Italy, 55, 220–221

Cines (Società Italiana Cines), 26, 38

Les Cinq Gentlemen Maudits/Moon over Morocco (Duvivier, 1931), 34

Cinque Maggio (cinema in Addis Ababa), 56, 57, 58

"Cinque Minuti O Di Piacer/Oh, Five Minutes of Pleasure" (popular song), 90

Cipriani, Lidio, 74

Civinini, Guelfo, 27–28

Clair, René, 131; *A nous la liberté* (1931), 51

Clifford, James, xvii

Cogni, Giulio, 198–199

Colonial Museum of Rome, xx

Come si seducono le donne e si tradiscono gli uomini/ How to Seduce Women and Betray Men (Marinetti), 83

Comerio, Luca, 22–23, 24, 25, 246; *La battaglia delle due palme* (1912), 22; *Dal Polo all'Equatore* (1929), 23, 307; *L'inaugurazione della stazione radiotelegrafica di Tripoli* (1912), 22; *La vita degli ascari eritrei* (1912), 22

Comin, Jacopo: on American cinema, 74; on colonial adventure film, 192; *La conquista dell'aria* (1939) and, 246; on documentaries, 67; *Sotto la Croce del Sud* (1938) and, 192, 194, 208

Committee for War and Political Cinema: *Bengasi* (1942) and, 290; creation of, 243; *La nave bianca* (1941) and, 231, 239; *Un pilota ritorna* (1942) and, 247, 251, 263, 265; Rossellini and, 301

The Conquest of the Air (Z. Korda, 1936), 246

La conquista dell'aria (Marcellini, 1939), 246

Cooper, Gary, 52, 58, 124

Corriere della sera (newspaper), 145, 165

Craveri, Mario: *La conquista dell'aria* (1939) and, 246; documentary films and, 62; *L'Esclave blanc* (1936) and, 174, 188–189; *La figlia del deserto* (1923) and, 120; Istituto Luce and, 65, 223–224; *Lacrime di sangue* (1944) and, 303; *Luciano Serra, pilota* (1938) and, 107–108, 109; popularity of, 65; Sinistri and, 228

Craveri, Mario, films: *La spedizione Franchetti nella Dancalia etiopica* (1929), 28; *Lo stormo atlantico* (1931), 106

Croce, Benedetto, 297

Croce, Giuseppe, 228

Cronache dell'impero/Chronicles of Empire (Istituto Nazionale Luce, 1937), 62, 67–68

Crown Film Unit (UK), 226, 233

A Cure for Serpents (Denti di Pirjano), 284

Curtiz, Michael, 249; *Casablanca* (1942), 85; *Dive Bomber* (1941), 247

Da Adua ad Axum: Le tappe dell'avanzata italiana nell'A.O./From Adwa to Axum: The Stages of the Italian Advance in East Africa (Istituto Nazionale Luce, 1936), 64–65, 69

Dal Polo all'Equatore/From the Pole to the Equator (Comerio, 1929), 23, 307

Dal Polo all'Equatore/From the Pole to the Equator (Gianikian and Ricci Lucchi, 1985), 307

Dall'Italia all'Equatore/From Italy to the Equator (Terzano, 1923), 148

D'Annunzio, Gabriele, 23–24
Davis, Bette, 58
de Certeau, Michel, 13, 84–85
De Feo, Luciano, 69, 102, 115; *Sulle orme dei nostri pionieri* (1936), 63–64, 69, 72–73
De Feo, Sandro, 145
De Franciscis, Umberto, 228
De Kobra, Maurice, 145
De Robertis, Francesco: after the fall of Fascism, 303–304; on American cinema, 48; aviation and, 247; Genina and, 288; masculinity and, 255; *Il mulatto* (1950), 304–305; *La nave bianca* (1941) and, 234, 235, 236, 238–239; Rossellini and, 224
De Robertis, Francesco, films: *Fantasmi del mare* (1948), 304; *Marinai senza stelle* (1949), 304; *Uomini sul fondo* (1941), 231–234, 234, 235, 238, 240–242
De Santis, Giuseppe, 257, 264, 265–266
De Sarno (army major), 110–111
De Sica, Vittorio, 58, 264; *I bambini ci guardano* (De Sica, 1942), 287
De Tasnady, Maria, 267
Debenedetti, Giacomo, 51, 165–166
Del Colle, Ubaldo Maria: *Bianco contro negro* (1913), 24
Deleuze, Gilles, 164
Denti di Pirjano, Alberto, 284
D'Errico, Corrado: anniversary of the invention of cinema and, 42; *La battaglia dello Jonio* (1940) and, 229; documentary films and, 62, 212; Istituto Luce and, 224; *Kif Tebbi* (1928) and, 33–34, 71; on Luce cameramen, 65; "Luce style" and, 66, 71; Scalera and, 231
D'Errico, Corrado, films: *Il cammino degli eroi* (1936), 63–64, 71, 72–73, 251; *La freccia d'oro* (with Ballerini, 1935), 71–72; *Ritmi di stazione* (1933), 71; *Stramilano* (1929), 71
Desperate Journey (Walsh, 1942), 249
Di Natale, A.: *La figlia del deserto* (1923), 120
dialects and regional accents, 51, 92–93
Dietrich, Marlene, 15, 52
Direzione Generale di Cinematografia (General Directorate for Cinematography), 41, 44–45, 193
Disperata bomb squad, 107, *108*, 113

Dive Bomber (Curtiz, 1941), 247
Doane, Mary Ann, 17
documentari romanzati (novelized documentaries): Scalera and, 231. See also *La nave bianca*; *Uomini sul fondo*
documentary films: on Ethiopian war, 62, 63, 66; Fascist propaganda and, 26–28, 67–73; feature film programming and, 225–226; feature films and, 62, 69, 215; in Germany, 221, 226, 227–228; recycled footage in, 27, 63; as technologies of imperial conquest, 5–6; World War I and, 62; World War II and, 214, 223–242, 253, 288
Dodecanese Islands, 3, 54, 249, 297
Doletti, Mino, 229
Una donna tra due mondi (Alessandrini, 1936), 315n7
Douhet, Giulio, 105
The Dreamer (H. Rousseau), 184
Dreyer, Carl Theodor: *L'Homme ensablé* and, 174–177
Dreyer, Carl Theodor, films: *The Passion of Jeanne d'Arc* (1927), 176; *Vampyr* (1932), 176, 184. See also *L'Esclave blanc*
dubat, 118, 128, 149, 151–152, 162
dubbing and dubbing industry: African audiences and, 61; Chion on, 261; decrees on, 39–40; Italian films and, 222; origins of, 39; *Un pilota ritorna* (1942) and, 261; role of, 51–52; *Sentinelle di bronzo* (1937) and, 161
Dubow, Jessica, 180
Duce. *See* Mussolini, Benito
Due lettere anonime/Two Anonymous Letters (Camerini, 1945), 303
Duncan, Derek, 13, 191, 298
Dupuis-Yakouba, Auguste, 192
Duranti, Doris: on Addis Ababa, 170; in *Il cavaliere di Kruja* (1940), 215; denounced, 46; female nomad roles and, 125–127, 244–245; in *Giarabub* (1942), 244–245; popularity of, 222; in *Sentinelle di bronzo* (1937), 148, 152, 155, *156*, 157, 158, 160, 189; in *Sotto la Croce del Sud* (1938), 192–193, 208, 209–210, 244–245; on World War II, 217
Duvignand, Jean, 9, 217

Duvivier, Julien: *Les Cinq Gentlemen Maudits* (1931), 34; *Poil de carotte* (1932), 42. See also *La bandera*
Dux (Istituto Nazionale Luce, 1926), 27

L'ebreo errante/The Wandering Jew (Alessandrini, 1948), 302–303
1860 (Blasetti, 1934), 51, 60, 100, 283–284
emigrants and emigration, 78–80; to Argentina, 194; to French colonies, 81; in *Il grande appello* (1936), 79, 80–81, 116–117; as Italians abroad, 97; in *Legionari del secondo parallelo: Diario di un milite* (1936) and, 97–99; in *Luciano Serra, pilota* (1938), 79, 80, 96–97, 99–100, 116–117
Ente Nazionale Industrie Cinematografiche (ENIC, National Agency for Cinematographic Industries), 41, 45, 48, 220, 299
Equatore/Equator (Valori, 1939), 210
Eritrea: cinemas in, 61; filmmaking in, 121; mixed-race relationships in, 172
Eritrea-Asmara (Istituto Nazionale Luce, 1937), 68
Eritrean foot soldiers, 128
L'eroica fanciulla da Derna/The Heroine from Derna (Righelli, 1912), 24
L'Escadron blanc (Peyré), 5, 130, 132–133, 134–136, 140, 146
L'Esclave blanche/The White Slave (Genina, 1927), 131; music in, 181–183, *182–183*
L'Esclave blanc/Jungla nera (Dreyer and Paulin, 1936): Africa as sensory paradise in, 167–168; African actors and extras in, 9, 159; bodily control in, 124; Craveri and, 107; current availability of, 309n5; endings of, 186–188, 192; Fascist ideology in, 177–178; father figures in, 167, 178; foreign funding for, 243, 300; *insabbiamento* in, 184–186, *185*; masculinity in, 280; nomadism in, 118, 186; nude screen tests for, 8; nudity in, 123; Orientalism and, 30, 181; the Other in, 253; picturesque in, 180–182; production of, 173–177, 188–190; Quadrone and, 121; reception of, 75, 190–191; as set in Somalia, 173, 174; *Sotto la Croce del Sud* (1938) and, 195, 199, 200, 205–207; sound in, 181–183, *182–183*; violence in, 186; women in, 14, 118, 167, 179–180, 182–186, *185*, 202, 233; woundings in, 259
Eskimo (Van Dyke, 1933), 147, 148
¡España, una, grande, libre!/¡Spain, United, Great, Free! (Ferroni, 1939), 69
Ethiopia: cinemas in, 61; filmmaking in, 6–7, 7, 121, 167; invasion of, xx–xxi, 1–2, 42, 43, 44; labor shortages in, 172–173; in *Legionari del secondo parallelo: Diario di un milite* (1936) and, 98–99; occupation of, 3–4; slavery in, 168–169
Ethiopian War: *askari* soldiers and, 127; documentary films on, xv–xvi, 62, 63, 66, 212; emigration and, 78–79; V. Mussolini on, 108; photography and, 76; slavery and, 168–169
ethnographic elements: in *L'Esclave blanc* (1936), 181–182, 184–186; in *Kif Tebbi* (1928), 34; role of, 74–76, 119, 122–123; in *Sentinelle di bronzo* (1937), 155–158; in *Sotto la Croce del Sud* (1938), 202–205
Etrusca Films (production company), 73
Ettore Fieramosca (Blassetti, 1938), 100

"Faccetta nera" (song), 168, 172–173, 191, 306
Fai (Somali actress), 190
Fantasmi del mare/Phantoms of the Sea (De Robertis, 1948), 304
Faraldo, Luigi: *Uragano ai tropici* (with Talamo, 1939), 268
Farassino, Alberto, xix, 130, 216
fasci all'estero (Fascist groups abroad), 97
Fascist empire cinema: camera as weapon in, 7, 23, 63–65, *64*, 72, 225; "cinematographic axis" and, 218–223; documentary films and, xix–xx, 62, 69, 215; end of empire and, 292–294; ethnographic elements in, 74–76, 119, 122–123; as experiences of vision and audition, 16–20; as eye of the war, 21–28, 63, *64*; films as "machines of war" and, 43, 63–65; Italian technologies in, xvi; mobility and gender in, xvi–xviii, 9–16; nonfiction film and, 73–77; propagandistic agendas of, xvii–xviii, 2–5; *romanzesco* in, 210–211; as "skeleton in the closet," xiv–xv; spectators and, 44, 55–62; as technologies

of imperial conquest, 5–9; use of term, xv–xvi; as weapon of propaganda in the colonies, 57–58
Favre, Sisto, 98, 294
Fejos, Paul, 39
Fellini, Federico, xv, 268–269, 302
Ferney, Jeannette, 178, *179*, 179–180
Ferrari, Mario, 97, 100–101
Ferretti, Lando, 224–225
Ferroni, Giorgio, 246; *¡España, una, grande, libre!* (1939), 69
Festa religiosa araba in Tripolitania/Arabic Religious Festival in Tripolitania (Istituto Nazionale Luce, 1929), 34
Feuertaufe/Baptism of Fire (Bertram, 1940), 226
Feyder, Jacques, 198; *L'Atlantide* (1921), 30
Fiamme abissine/Abyssinian Flames (Cerruti, 1922), 74
La figlia del deserto/The Daughter of the Desert (Di Natale, 1923), 120
Film (review), 111, 227, 229, 230, 288–289
Film d'oggi (magazine), 300
Fink, Guido, 84, 303
Fiume, Enrico: on actors in empire films, 180; on American cinema, 73–74; on authenticity, 211; on cinemas in the colonies, 58–60, 61–62; on colonial films, 293–294; on documentaries and feature films, 75, 223; on effective propaganda in films, 253
Flaiano, Ennio, xiii, 296, 297–298
Flynn, Errol, 11, 249
Fontana, Eugenio, 148
forced labor, 173, 199–200
Ford, John: *The Iron Horse* (1924), 112; *The Lost Patrol* (1934), 130, 144, 146
Foreign Language Versions (FLVs), 38–39, 45
Foreign Legion, 83, 88, 93, 100, 113, 130
foreign speech, 50–51, 54, 119, 139, 222–223
Forzano, Giovacchino: *Camicia nera* (1933), 73; *Villafranca* (1934), 100
Four Seasons (Vivaldi), 141
France: colonial culture in, 81, 129–131; invasion of, 215; Italian cinema in, 220; Paramount studio complex in, 38–39; World War II and, 216. *See also* French cinema and film industry

Franchetti, Raimondo, 22–23, 65
Franciolini, Gianni, 246
Francis, Saint, 302
La freccia d'oro/The Golden Arrow (D'Errico and Ballerini, 1935), 71–72
Freddi, Luigi: Cinecittà and, xxii; *La conquista dell'aria* (1939) and, 246; denounced, 46; Direzione Generale di Cinematografia and, 41, 45; film music and, 49; *Il grande appello* (1936) and, 82–83, 85, 95–96; in Hollywood, 41; on military and colonial films, 43
French cinema and film industry: consumption of in Italy, 46–47, 220, 221; imperial agenda and, xiv; interracial unions in, 121
Il fu Mattia Pascal/He Was Mattia Pascal (Chenal, 1937), 198
Fulchignani, Enrico, 242
Fuller, Mia, 3, 8
Futurism, 23–24, 26, 107
Futurist Cinematography (manifesto), 26

Gabaccia, Donna, 78
Gabin, Jean, 87–88
Gable, Clark, 58
Gabriel, Gavino, 49
Gabriel, Teshome, xxii, 116, 266, 307
Gallone, Carmine, 62, 301; *Harlem Knockout* (1943), 216; *Scipione l'Africano* (1937), xxi, 147
Gambardella, Giuseppe: *Kri kri reduce d'Africa* (1914), 24
Gance, Abel, 198
Garbo, Greta, 52, 71–72, 327n42
The Garden of Allah (Boleslawksi, 1936), 15
Gassman, Vittorio, 302–303
Gatti, Attilio: *Siliva Zulu* (1927), 74–75, 148
Gemelli, Agostino, 55
Genina, Augusto: after the fall of Fascism, 301; career abroad of, 38, 39, 249, 301; denounced, 46; Italianness and, 120–121; religion and, 302; Verretti and, 49; WWI military documentaries by, 62
Genina, Augusto, films: *L'assedio dell'Alcazar* (1940), 269, 315n7; *Bengasi, anno '41* (1955), 305–306, 309n5; *I cavalieri del deserto* (1942) and, 268–269; *Il*

cielo sulla palude (1949), 302; *L'Esclave blanche* (1927), 131; *Maschiaccio* (1917), 280; *Prix de beauté* (1930), 131; *L'Ultimo Lord* (1926), 280. See also *Bengasi*; *Lo squadrone bianco*
Gentile, Emilio, 18–19
Gentile, Felice, 267
Germani, Sergio Grmek, 141
Germany: Alessandrini and, 109; "cinematographic axis" and, 218–223; consumption of in Italy, 221–222; documentaries and, 221, 226, 227–228; imperial agenda and, xiv; Italy and, 46–47; Nazi film propaganda corps and, 223; Reich Film Chamber and, 40–41, 46; UFA and, 224
Geyer, Michael, 6
Giachetti, Fosco: acting style of, 124–125, 126; in *Bengasi* (1942), 267, 277, 287, 288; as model of masculinity, 11; in *Sentinelle di bronzo* (1937), 149, 151, 160, 161; in *Lo squadrone bianco* (1936), 133–134, 151
Giacosi, Luigi, 247
Gianikian, Yervant: *Dal Polo all'Equatore* (with Ricci Lucchi, 1985), 307
Giarabub (Alessandrini, 1942), 15, 125, 215, 244–245, 305
Gigli, Beniamino, 19, 20
Gioi, Vivi, 267
Giovannetti, Eugenio, 268
Gioventù Araba del Littorio, 54
Gioventù Universitaria Fascista (GUF, Young University Fascist), 40, 42, 67
"Giovinezza" (song), 87–88
Girotti, Massimo, 331n8
Giungla/Jungle (Malasomma, 1942), 218
Giunta, Francesco, xxii, 143–144, 210
Glori, Enrico, 198
Goebbels, Joseph, 40–41, 46, 219, 220
Goretti, Maria, 302
Goulding, Edmund: *Grand Hotel* (1932), 71–72
Governo dell'Amhara-Gondar (Istituto Nazionale Luce, 1937), 68
Grand Hotel (Goulding, 1932), 71–72
Il grande appello/The Last Roll Call (Camerini, 1936): aviation and, 224; bodily control in, 124; dialects in, 51, 92–93; emigration in, 79, 80–81, 116–117; Ethiopia in, 121; financial incentives and assistance for, 4, 82, 94; foreign speech in, 50–51; Freddi and, xxii, 82–83; funding of, 243; homosociality in, 191, 201; Hotel Orient in, 83–85, 86, 170; male comradeship in, 124; masculinity in, 88–89; music in, 201; natural setting of, 88–89; reception of, 94–95; representation of Africans in, 93; Soldati and, 82–83, 88, 89, 95; *Sotto la Croce del Sud* (1938) and, 194; sound in, 85–88, 90–93; *Lo squadrone bianco* (1936) and, 135; Terzano and, 148; Villa in, 136; women in, 233; woundings in, 235–236
La grande illusion/Grand Illusion (Renoir, 1937), 221, 265
Grandi, Dino, 97, 100
Grant, Cary, 52
Grasso, Giovanni, 152, 194, 198
Gravelli, Asvero, 244
Graziani, Rodolfo, 28–29, 32, 99
Greece, 215, 217, 246, 249–250
Greene, Shelleen, 200
Gréville, Edmond: *Princesse Tam-Tam* (1935), 15
Grierson, John, 226
Griffith, D. W.: *Intolerance* (1916), 42, 284–285
Grinieff, Jacques, 176
Il gruppo meharista al commando del Duca d'Aosta/The Meharist Group at the Command of the Duke of Aosta (Istituto Nazionale Luce, 1928), 28
Guazzoni, Enrico: *Myriam* (1929), 120; *La sperduta di Allah* (1929), 30, 120, 212
Gubitosi, Giuseppe, 103–104
Guerra alla guerra/War on War (Marcellini, 1946), 302
Guerra italo-turca tra "scugnizzi" napoletani/The Italian-Turkish War among the Neapolitan Street Urchins (Notari, 1912), 24
Guiglia, Giacomo, 171

Harlan, Veit: *Jud Süss* (1940), 209, 221–222
Harlem Knockout (Gallone, 1943), 216
Hathaway, Henry: *The Lives of a Bengal Lancer* (1935), 74, 124

Hawks, Howard, 247
Hayworth, Rita, 52
Henrickson, Hildi, 12
Hess, Robert, 149
Hitler, Adolf, 41, 193, 216
Hoffman, Hilmar, 226
homoeroticism, 13, 79, 129, 168; in *Sentinelle di bronzo* (1937), 162, 163; in *Sotto la Croce del Sud* (1938), 205–208
homosociality, 11, 13, 14–15, 79, 191, 201
Hungary, 219, 220
Hunt, Nancy Rose, 306
Hüppauf, Bernd, 25
Hussein, Muhammed, 304–305

I Wanted Wings (Leisen, 1941), 247
Imperial Cinema (Assab), 56–58
Impero (Asmara cinema), 56
L'inaugurazione della stazione radiotelegrafica di Tripoli/The Inauguration of the Radio-Telegraphy Station in Tripoli (Comerio, 1912), 22
Incom (Industria Corti Metraggi), 67, 70, 223, 299
Inferno giallo/Yellow Inferno (von Radványi, 1942), 294
insabbiamento, 171, 175, 184, 207
Institute for Book Propaganda, 290
Interlandi, Telesio, 95
International Film Chamber (IFC), 46–47, 219
International Institute of Educational Cinema (IICE), 27, 69
International Union of Catholics, 304
Intolerance (Griffith, 1916), 42, 284–285
The Iron Horse (Ford, 1924), 112
Isani, Giuseppe, 227
Istituto Luce: African audiences and, 61; after the fall of Fascism, 299; archives of, 309n5; *Bengasi* (1942) and, 269; Cinecittà and, 45; *cinegiornale* by, 220; cinemas in the colonies and, 56, 58; commercial film industry and, 41; East Africa Unit (Luce AOI) and, 63, 64–65, 72, 107, 223, 228; founding of, 27; inauguration of, 28; Ministry of Popular Culture and, 44–45; B. Mussolini and, 214; newsreels and, 27,

40, 223, 224–226; recycled footage and, xx, 63; traveling cinemas and, 221
Itala Film, 46
Italian Air Force (Regia Aeronautica Italiana): embedded operators in, 63, 223; Ethiopian War and, 224; Italo-Turkish War and, 23; in *Luciano Serra, pilota* (1938), 100–101, 105–106, 107, 109, 110; Marcellini and, 147; Masoero and, 269; in *Un pilota ritorna* (1942), 245–246, 263
Italian Army (Regio Esercito): cinema center and, 224; documentaries on mass mobilization by, 69; embedded operators in, 63, 223; in empire films, 127; *Giarabub* (1942) and, 244; in Greece and Yugoslavia, 217; *Luciano Serra, pilota* (1938) and, 110, 111; in *Sentinelle di bronzo* (1937), 150
Italian East African Empire (A.O.I.): cinemas in, 56–58, 57, 306; defeat of, 215; establishment of, 2; filmmaking in, xiii–xiv, 121; Italians in, 170–171; slavery in, 168–169. *See also* Eritrea; Ethiopia; Somalia
Italian Navy (Regia Marina): in *La battaglia dello Jonio* (1940), 229; cinema center and, 224, 231, 235; embedded operators in, 63, 223; in *Uomini sul fondo* (1941), 238
Italian Socialist Party, 23–24
Italian women: in *Bengasi* (1942), 271–280, 283–285; in colonies, 13–14; in *L'Esclave blanc* (1936), 179–180; in Fascist empire cinema, 13–15; in *Un pilota ritorna* (1942), 245, 250; in *Sotto la Croce del Sud* (1938), 194–195; in *Lo squadrone bianco* (1936), 136; in *Uomini sul fondo* (1941), 233, 238
Italian-German Cinema Exhibition, 219
Italian-German Cultural Accord (1938), 46
Italo-Turkish War (1911–1912): aviation in, 105; documentary films on, 211; importance of, 23–24; in *Kif Tebbi* (1928), 32; silent features and, 120
Iyob, Ruth, 298

Jaikumar, Priya, 195–196
Jannarelli, Angelo, 268
Jannings, Emil, 222
Jews: after the fall of Fascism, 295; anti-

Semitic sentiments and, 198–199, 209, 243; in *Bengasi. La città murata,* 291; in *L'ebreo errante* (1948), 302–303; Hollywood and, 48; racial legislation and, 122, 198–199
Le jour se lève/Daybreak (Carné, 1939), 47
Jud Süss (Harlan, 1940), 209, 221–222

Kif Tebbi (Camerini, 1928): ADIA consortium and, 131; as based on Zùccoli's novel, 18, 32; bodily control in, 124; current availability of, 309n5; D'Errico and, 33–34, 71; female nomadism in, 15, 34–36, 125; gramophone in, 196; as historical film, xxi; Orientalism in, 21, 30–38, 33, 37, 149; reception of, 212; representation of Africans in, 93; *The Sheik* (1921) and, 30–31, 34; as shot in Libya, 120; Turks in, 193; violence in, 77
Kines (review), 120
Koch, Carlo: *Tosca* (with Renoir, 1941), 220, 231
Korda, Alexander, 143; *Non ti scordar di me/Forget Me Not* (1935), 19, 20
Korda, Zoltan: *The Conquest of the Air* (1936), 246; *Sanders of the River* (1935), 143
Kracauer, Sigfried, 158
Kri kri reduce d'Africa/Kri kri Veteran of Africa (Gambardella, 1914), 24

Lacrime di sangue/Tears of Blood (Brignone, 1944), 303
Landy, Marcia, 12, 103
language, 92, 200, 280–282, 284; in *Bengasi* (1942), 280–282, 284; in empire films, 53–55, 61, 119; Fascist ideology and, 50; in *Il grande appello* (1936), 88–93; illiteracy and, 27; in *Luciano Serra, pilota* (1938), 100; in *Un pilota ritorna* (1942), 250, 254–255; in *Sentinelle di bronzo* (1937), 151, 153–155; in *Uomini sul fondo* (1941), 222–223. *See also* foreign speech; linguistic autarchy; pidgin Italian
Lanzi, Fulvia, 131–132
Lattanzi, Tina, 52, 327n42
Lattuada, Alberto, 47, 221, 224, 294–295
Laval, Pierre, 42

Le Houérou, Fabienne, 171
League of Nations, 1–2, 19–20, 27, 69
Legionari del secondo parallelo: Diario di un milite/Legionaires of the Second Parallel: Diary of a Militiaman (Marcellini, 1936), 97–98, 113, 147, 201
Leisen, Mitchell: *I Wanted Wings* (1941), 247
Leone, Rosario, 263
Lessona, Alessandro, 29, 171
L'Herbier, Marcel, 39
Libya: aviation in, 105; British Empire and, 215; cinemas in, 56–58; concentration camps in, 29; education in, 54; filmmaking in, xiii, 6–7, 120–121, 268; films and documentaries set in, 24, 28–29, 29–30, 34; mass transfer to, 3–4; *mehariasti* in, 118, 128, 134, 283; newsreels on, 299–300; traveling cinemas in, 58. *See also* Italo-Turkish War
Libya Films (production company), 120
Licati, Giovanni, 58
linguistic autarchy, 50, 92, 100, 222
linguistic imperialism, 92, 280–282
The Lives of a Bengal Lancer (Hathaway, 1935), 74, 124
Loffredo, Ferdinando, 217
Lombrassa, Giuseppe, 43
London Film, 143
Long, Lotus, 148
The Lost Patrol (Ford, 1934), 130, 144, 146
Louis, Joe, 102
Loy, Myrna, 58
Luciano Serra, pilota (Alessandrini, 1938): Alessandrini on, 109–110, 212; aviation in, 105, 107–110, 112–113, 224, 246, 251; aviation movies and, 247; battle scenes in, 111–115; bodily control in, 124; *cineromanzo* version of, 290; current availability of, 309n5; *documentari romanzati* and, 240–241; emigration in, 79, 80, 96–97, 99–100, 116–117; Ethiopia in, 121; financial incentives and assistance for, 4; funding of, 243; indigenous actors and extras in, 110–111, 114–115; influence of American cinema in, 101–102; Italian soldiers in, 110–111, 114–115; *Legionari del secondo parallelo: Diario di*

un milite (1936) and, 97–99; marketing for, 115–116; Masoero and, 269; Nazzari in, 96, 102–105, *104*, 106, 110, 113, 114, 116, 279; Pavolini on, 227–228; Rossellini and, 235; Sinistri and, 228; smoke clouds in, 230; *Sotto la Croce del Sud* (1938) and, 194; sound in, 138–139; *Lo squadrone bianco* (1936) and, 130; Venice Biennale and, 46–47, 208; Villa in, 136; violence in, 77; vocality in, 50; woundings in, 235–236, 258

Lumière, Louis, 22, 42

Lux (production house), 47

Lyons Exhibition (1897), 22

Ma non è una cosa seria (Camerini, 1936), 315n7

MacDonald, David: *Men of the Lightship* (1940), 233–234

MacDougall, David, 65, 158

Maciste (Bartolomeo Pagano), 19, 26

Maciste contro lo sceicco/Maciste against the Sheik (Camerini, 1926), 30–31, 120

Mädchen in Uniform/Girls in Uniform (Sagan, 1931), 109

La Maitresse noire (Royer), 175

mal d'Africa: African women and, 298; in empire films, 118, 168, 169, 208; Pavolini on, 298; Quadrone on, 175, 182–183

Mala, Ray, 148

Malasomma, Nunzio: *Giungla* (1942), 218

Mamma (Brignone, 1941), 315n7

Marcellini, Romolo: documentary films and, 62, 253; filmmaking in Somalia and, 121; military service in Africa and, 6; Photocinematographic Center and, 224; *Scipione l'Africano* (1937) and, 147

Marcellini, Romolo, films: *La conquista dell'aria* (Marcellini, 1939), 246; *Guerra alla guerra* (1946), 302; *Legionari del secondo parallelo: Diario di un milite* (1936), 97–99, 113, 147, 201; *Los novios de la muerte* (1937), 107, 246, 315n7; *Pastor Angelicus* (1942), 302; *Piloti e fanti nel deserto sirtico* (1941), 288. See also *Sentinelle di bronzo*

Margalit, Avishai, 2

Marinai senza stelle/Sailors without Stars (De Robertis, 1949), 304

Marinetti, Filippo Tommaso, 83

Marks, Laura, 80, 157

Martinelli, Vittorio, 141

Martini, Franco: *Aethiopia* (1924), 27–28

Maschiaccio/The Boyish Girl (Genina, 1917), 280

masculinity: in *Bengasi* (1942), 274–280; in *L'Esclave blanc* (1936), 167, 178–179, 191; in Fascist empire cinema, 10–13, 79, 124–125, 128–129, 244, 275–279, 284–285; in *Il grande appello* (1936), 88–90; in *Kif Tebbi* (1928), 31–34; in *Luciano Serra, pilota* (1938), 102–104, 109–110; B. Mussolini as model of, 10, 11, 19, 27, 36; in *Sentinelle di bronzo* (1937), 151–152, 192; in *Sotto la Croce del Sud* (1938), 205–207; in *Lo squadrone bianco* (1936), 132–135, 140; in *Uomini sul fondo* (1941), 232–233; vocality and, 52–53

Masoero, Filippo, 107, 224, 269

Matarazzo, Raffaele: *Treno popolare* (1933), 73

Mattia, Ettore, 8, 58, 60, 127

Mazower, Mark, 217

McBride, John, 45

Mediterranean: after the fall of Fascism, 296–297; in empire films, 10, 141, 208; Fascist imperial agendas and, xvii–xviii, 2–3, 23, 35, 69, 81, 214; nomadism and, 125

meharisti, 118, 128, 134, 283

Melford, George: *The Sheik* (1921), 30–31, 34

Meliès, Georges, 22

Men of the Lightship (MacDonald, 1940), 233–234

Il Messaggero (newspaper), 145

Metro-Goldwyn-Mayer (MGM), 39

Micciché, Lino, xiv–xv

Mida, Massimo, 248

Milan Triennale, 221

Milani, Mario, 69

Milano, Paolo, 50

Militia: documentaries on, xxii; embedded operators in, 63; in Greece and Yugoslavia, 217; in *Luciano Serra, pilota* (1938), 96–97, 113–115, 130; Marcellini and, 147

Millet, Thierry, 55
Ministry of Aeronautics, 82
Ministry of Colonies, 82, 95
Ministry of Italian Africa, 61
Ministry of Popular Culture (MCP):
 Bengasi (1942) and, 291; censorship and, 190; Committee for War and Political Cinema and, 243; documentary films and, 223; Istituto Luce and, 44–45, 66
Ministry of Press and Propaganda, 82
Ministry of War, 82, 94, 223
Miramare (Tripoli cinema), 56
miscegenation, 168, 171–172, 174. *See also* racial legislation
Mohamed, Hassan, 7–8, 148, 149, 164
Monicelli, Mario, xv, 210
Montanelli, Indro, 172, 298
Morocco (von Sternberg, 1930), 15, 85
Mudundu (Quadrone): Africa as sensory paradise in, 173–174, 183–184; on casting, 188–190; on promiscuity in the colonies, 169–170; on slavery, 188; on violence, 186
al-Mukhtar, 'Umar, 29
Il mulatto/The Mulatto (De Robertis, 1950), 304–305
Mulvey, Laura, xviii
music: in *La battaglia dello Jonio* (1940), 230; in *Bengasi* (1942), 270; in *L'Esclave blanche* (1927), 181–184; in *Il grande appello* (1936), 201; in *La nave bianca* (1941), 236, 239, 264; in *Un pilota ritorna* (1942), 256, 264; in *Il primo colpo all'impero britannico. La conquista della Somalia Britannica* (1940), 229; role of in films, 49; in *Sotto la Croce del Sud* (1938), 196, 201, 236, 264; in *Lo squadrone bianco* (1936), 136–138, 141; in *L'uomo della croce* (1943), 264. *See also* sound
Mussolini, Benito: aviation and, 246–247; in *Il cammino degli eroi* (1936), 72; on cinema, 26–27; cult of Italian victimhood and, 12; ENIC and, 48; as father in fascist ideology, 79; Freddi and, 41; *Il grande appello* (1936) and, 82; Hitler and, 46; invasion of Ethiopia and, 1–2, 42; Italians abroad and, 96; *Luciano Serra, pilota* (1938) and, 99; military operations in Libya and, 28; mobility and, 9; as model of masculinity, 10, 11, 19, 27, 36, 102, 103–104; modernity and, xvi; represented in *Bengasi* (1942), 285; on role of Fascism, 85; *Sentinelle di bronzo* (1937) and, 158–159, 162, 163; style of speaking of, 17, 19, 53, 136; on transmigrants, 78; World War II and, 214; writing style of, 19
Mussolini, Vittorio: on American cinema, 47–48, 101; anti-Semitic statements and, 48; aviation and, 108–109; *I cavalieri del deserto* (1942) and, 268–269; on cinema's dangers, 55–56; on documentaries, 62; on Hollywood's boycott, 48; on indigenous audiences, 60; *Luciano Serra, pilota* (1938) and, 99, 104, 108–109; Photocinematographic Center and, 224; pilot chronicles by, 108, 112; *Un pilota ritorna* (1942) and, 247, 266; role in empire cinema culture of, 4; Rossellini and, 235; visit to Hollywood, 101
Myriam (Guazzoni, 1929), 120

Nahum, Sanino, 144
National Association of Industrial Motors and Aircraft, 107
La nave bianca/The White Ship (Rossellini, 1941), 230, 231, 234–242, 237, 240–241, 250, 264
Navy Cinema Center, 229, 231, 235
Nazzari, Amedeo: acting style of, 124; in *Bengasi* (1942), 267, 277, 279, 282, 287; in *Cavalleria* (1936), 101, 103, 105; in *Luciano Serra, pilota* (1938), 96, 102–105, 104, 106, 110, 113, 114, 116, 279; as model of masculinity, 11, 79; popularity of, 58
Negri comici/Comic Negroes (Società Italiana Cines, 1912), 24
New York Times (newspaper), 37–38
newsreels: after the fall of Fascism, 299; *askari* soldiers in, 128; foreign news services and, 40; Istituto Luce and, 223, 224–226; on Libya, 299–300; "Luce style" and, 65–67; B. Mussolini and, 27; recycled footage in, 63; World War II and, 224–226

Ninchi, Carlo, 244
Noi vivi—Addio Kira/We the Living—Goodbye Kira (Alessandrini, 1942), 290
Noldan, Svend: *Sieg im Westen* (1941), 226
nomads and nomadism: in *L'Esclave blanc* (1936), 118, 186; Fascist Militia and army forces as, 217; in *Kif Tebbi* (1928), 15, 34–36; in Libya, 28–29, 150; prostitution and, 171–172; in *Sentinelle di bronzo* (1937), 118, 150, 164; in Somalia, 150; in *Sotto la Croce del Sud* (1938), 118; in *Lo squadrone bianco* (1936), 118; women and, 15, 34–36, 125, 125–127
Non ti scordar di me/Forget Me Not (Korda, 1935), 19, 20
nonfiction film: Fascist empire cinema and, 73–77; Fascist propaganda and, 26–28, 44; B. Mussolini and, 26–27; recycled footage in, 27, 224; World War II and, 223–228. *See also* documentary films; newsreels
Il nostro esercito coloniale/Our Colonial Army (Istituto Nazionale Luce, 1928), 28
Notari, Elvira: *Guerra italo-turca tra "scugnizzi" napoletani* (1912), 24
Notari, Guido, 229, 230, 285, 299
Notiziario Luce Nuova/New Luce News Digest, 299
Novarro, Ramon, 109–110
Los novios de la muerte/The Grooms of Death (Marcellini, 1937), 107, 246, 315n7
La nuova Italia d'oltremare/The New Italy Overseas (Piccioli), 29

O'Brien, Charles, xix, 74
Ohm Krüger/Uncle Krüger (Steinhoff, 1941), 221–222
Ojetti, Ugo, 217–218
Oliveri, Egisto, 178
Olympia (Riefenstahl, 1938), 46–47
Omar, Abdul, 149
Omegna, Roberto, 22
One of Our Aircraft Is Missing (Powell, 1942), 249
Opera Nazionale Dopolavoro (National Leisure Organization), 58, 221

Orientalism: African women and, 14; in *L'Esclave blanc* (1936), 30, 181; in *L'Esclave blanche* (1927), 131; in *Kif Tebbi* (1928), 21, 30–38, 33, 37, 149; in *Sentinelle di bronzo* (1937), 148–149, 160; in *Siliva Zulu* (1927), 74–75
Osman (Ethiopian translator), 111
Ossessione (Visconti, 1943), 287

Pabst, Georg Wilhem, 131
Pagano, Bartolomeo (Maciste), 19, 26
Paisà (Rossellini, 1946), 256
Palermi, Amleto, 212–213; *Partire/Departure* (1938), 10
Paolella, Domenico, 246
Paramount (U.S. production company), 38–39
Paris Peace Treaty (1947), 297, 305
Parri, Ferruccio, 299
Partire/Departure (Palermi, 1938), 10
Pascoli, Giovanni, 23–24
Pasinetti, Francesco, 270
Passaporto rosso/The Red Passport (Brignone, 1935), 97, 194
The Passion of Jeanne d'Arc (Dreyer, 1927), 176
Pastor Angelicus (Marcellini, 1942), 302
Pastrone, Giovanni: *Cabiria* (1914), 26, 42
Patti, Ercole, 86
Paulin, Jean-Paul. See *L'Esclave blanc*
Paulucci di Calboli, Giacomo, 41, 66, 72
Pavolini, Alessandro: on aerial warfare, 6, 107; on bombing of Adwa, xxi; Disperata squad bombs and, 113; Duranti and, 127; on German documentaries and, 227–228; on Italian film industry, 243–244; on *mal d'Africa*, 298
Pavolini, Corrado, 67
Perilli, Ivo, 321n51
Peyré, Joseph. See *L'escadron blanc*
Pickering-Iazzi, Robin, 14–15, 202
pidgin Italian: Alessandrini and, 111; in *Il mulatto* (1950), 304–305; role of, 53–54, 139, 306; in *Sotto la Croce del Sud* (1938), 200
Pietrangeli, Antonio, 219, 289
Un pilota ritorna/A Pilot Returns (Rossel-

lini, 1942): aviation and, 224; *Bengasi* (1942) and, 277; bombers in, 248–249, 261; Committee for War and Political Cinema and, 247, 251, 263, 265; ending of, 261–263; as filmed near Viterbo, 215–216, 248; financial incentives and assistance for, 4; Greek scenes in, 287; humanitarianism in, 258–259; Italianness in, 283; local power politics in, 285; masculinity in, 244; music in, 256, 264; vs. *La nave bianca* (1941), 236, 239; occupation of Greece in, 249–250; publicity for, 263; reception of, 222, 247–248, 263–266; temporality and history in, 250–253, 292; unconventional storytelling in, 253–258; violence in, 77; witness in, 303; women in, 245, 250; woundings in, 258–259
Piloti e fanti nel deserto sirtico/Pilots and Infantrymen in the Sirte Desert (Marcellini, 1941), 288
Pilotto, Camillo, 79, 81, 88, 194
Pinkus, Karen, 12, 122
Piovene, Guido, 289
Pittaluga, Stefano, 26
Pius XI (Pope), 55
Podestà, Gian Luca, 170
Poil de carotte/The Red Head (Duvivier, 1932), 42
Polacco, Cesare, 54, 139
Il ponte di vetro/Bridge of Glass (Alessandrini, 1939), 117
Ponzanesi, Sandra, 298
Il Popolo d'Italia (newspaper), 71
positivism, 12
post-synchronized sound, 222
Powell, Michael: *One of Our Aircraft Is Missing* (1942), 249
Premio Strega, 296
Il primo colpo all'impero britannico. La conquista della Somalia Britannica/The First Blow at the British Empire: The Conquest of British Somalia (1940), 228–229
Princesse Tam-Tam (Gréville, 1935), 15
Prix de beauté/Miss Europa (Genina, 1930), 131

prostitution, 8, 14, 171–172
La Provincia di Bolzano (newspaper), 65, 69, 221, 330n25
Puck (Gianni Puccini), 103, 268

Quadrone, Ernesto: *L'Esclave blanc* (1936) and, 121, 181, 300; *L'Homme ensablé* and, 174–177; on *mal d'Africa*, 175, 182–183; on Somalis, 123. See also *Mudundu*
Quelli della montagna/Men of the Mountain (Vergano, 1943), 291

racial legislation, xv, 8, 57, 75, 122, 170–172, 198–199
racisms: in empire films, 54, 121–122, 298, 304–305; in *Luciano Serra, pilota* (1938), 102, 110–111; as manifested in Fascist colonial ideologies, 54, 56–58, 83, 110–111, 121–123, 170–173; in *Sentinelle di bronzo* (1937), 151–153, 155–160; in *Sotto la Croce del Sud* (1938), 193–195, 196–199, 200–205
radio, 27, 76, 80, 86–87, 92, 232
Radvanyi, Géza von: *Inferno giallo* (1942), 294
Rava, Maurizio, 55–56, 60, 188–189
Redy, Laura, 267
Reich Film Chamber (Germany), 40–41, 46
religion, 302
Renoir, Jean, 47; *La grande illusion* (1937), 221, 265; *Tosca* (with Koch, 1941), 220, 231
Renov, Michael, 68–69
revisori (linguistic censors), 50
Ricci, Steven, 62
Ricci Lucchi, Angela: *Dal Polo all'Equatore* (with Gianikian, 1985), 307
Ricotti, Arnaldo: *I berberi e gli italiani* (1932), 34
Riefenstahl, Leni: *Olympia*, 46–47
Rien que les heures/Nothing but Time (Cavalcanti, 1926), 226
Riganti, Franco, 109, 110, 235, 247
Rigaud, Georges, 178, 179
Righelli, Gennaro: *L'eroica fanciulla da Derna* (1912), 24
Ritmi di stazione/Rhythms of the Station (D'Errico, 1933), 71

Rivista del cinematografo (magazine), 65
Roach, Hal, 101
Rodogno, Davide, 217
Roma città aperta/Rome Open City (Rossellini, 1945), 236, 257–258, 264, 303
Roman salute, 140
Romance, Viviane, 222
Romania, 219, 220
romanità, 3
Romano, Marisa, 208
romanzesco, 210–211
Rosenstone, Robert, xxii
Rossellini, Renzo: on *Bengasi* (1942), 270; *I cavalieri del deserto* (1942) and, 268; *La nave bianca* (1941) and, 236, 264; *Un pilota ritorna* (1942) and, 264; *Sotto la Croce del Sud* (1938) and, 196, 207, 264; *L'uomo della croce* (1943) and, 264
Rossellini, Roberto: after the fall of Fascism, 301; career abroad of, 46; *Cinema* on, 247; De Robertis and, 224; empire films and, xv; Genina and, 288; *Luciano Serra, pilota* (1938) and, 108, 251–253
Rossellini, Roberto, films: *La nave bianca* (1941), 230, 231, 234–242, 237, 240–241, 250, 264; *Paisà* (1946), 256; *Roma città aperta* (1945), 236, 257–258, 264, 303; *San Francesco, giullare di Dio* (1950), 302; *L'uomo della croce* (1943), 222, 264, 291. See also *Un pilota ritorna*
Rossi, Amelia, 267
Rossi, Fabio, 51
Rotaie/Rails (Camerini, 1930), 71
Rousseau, Henri, 184
Rousseau, Jean-Jacques, 184
Royal Italian Academy, 50
Royer, Louis-Charles, 175
Ruttmann, Walter: *Berlin: Die Sinfonie der Grosstadt* (1927), 226

Sacchi, Filippo, 145, 191
Sagan, Leontine: *Mädchen in Uniform* (1931), 109
Salgari, Emilio, 268
Salvatori, Jack: *Umanità* (1946), 300–301
San Francesco, giullare di Dio/The Flowers of Saint Francis (Rossellini, 1950), 302

Sanders of the River (Z. Korda, 1935), 143
Savarese, Roberto, 190
Scalera (production house): after the fall of Fascism, 299; *Bengasi* (1942) and, 267, 268; *documentari romanzati* and, 231; French film industry and, 47; funding of, 9; *Il mulatto* (1950) and, 304–305; Rossellini and, 235
Schaub, Mirjan, 17
Lo Schermo (magazine): on Centa, 125; on Etrusca Films, 73; on *Il grande appello* (1936), 82; on Italian films, 221; Mussolini in, 11; on newsreels, 224–225; on the role of cinema, 18, 101; on *Sotto la Croce del Sud* (1938), 194; on *Lo squadrone bianco* (1936), 144; on war cinema, 231
Scheuemann, Franz, 46
Schomburgk, Hans, 22
Scipione l'Africano (Gallone, 1937), xxi, 147
Scoupe, Denis, 176
Seconda B (Alessandrini, 1934), 109
Segrè, Claudio, 116
La segretaria privata/The Private Secretary (Alessandrini, 1931), 109
Seknadje-Askenazi, Enrique, 236, 256
Selassie, Haile, 95, 168, 243
Sentinelle di bronzo/Dusky Sentinels (Marcellini, 1937): African actors in, 60; African women in, 189; American Westerns and, 160–162; *askaris* in, 127; bodily control in, 124; casting and, 148, 158; current availability of, xv; Duranti in, 148, 152, 155, 156, 157, 158, 160, 189; endings of, 163–164; *L'Esclave blanc* (1936) and, 174, 178, 180, 190; ethnographic elements in, 155–158; Fascist technology in, 162–163; female nomadism in, 15; Grasso in, 194, 198; male body in, 191; masculinity in, 244; Mohamed in, 7–8; nomadism in, 118, 125; nudity in, 123; production of, 158–160; prostitutes for crew of, 8; reception of, 164–166; silence in, 232; Somali *dubat* in, 118, 149, 151–152, 162; sound in, 153–155; translators in, 200; women in, 125, 193; woundings in, 152–153, 154, 235–236, 258
sex police (*squadra del madamismo*), 172

Sforza, Carlo, 297
The Sheik (Melford, 1921), 30–31, 34
Shub, Esther, xx
Sieg im Westen/Victory in the West (Noldan, 1941), 226
silence: in *Bengasi* (1942), 280–282; in *Sentinelle di bronzo* (1937), 232; in *Lo squadrone bianco* (1936), 136–138, 139–140; in *Uomini sul fondo* (1941), 232
silent cinema, 232
Siliva Zulu (Gatti, 1927), 74–75, 148
Silverman, Kaja, 155
Simonini, Augusto, 53
Sinistri, Renato, 228
slavery, 168–169, 171–174, 188–189, 191, 195
Sobchack, Vivian Carol, 70, 211
Society for Italian Authors and Editors, 315n3
Solari, Piero, 82
Soldati, Mario: denounced, 46; empire films and, xv; *Il grande appello* (1936) and, 82–83, 88, 89, 95; on invasion of Ethiopia, 43
soldiers, as actors and extras, 5, 76–77, 94, 110–111, 114–115, 216. See also *askari* soldiers
Soliman, Zainù, 111
Somali women, 123
Somalia: cinemas in, 61, 306; conquest of, 149–150; education in, 150–151; filmmaking in, 6–7, 121, 167; labor shortages in, 173; Paris Peace Treaty and, 297; slavery in, 168–169
S.O.S. Sahara (Baroncelli, 1938), 209
Sotto la Croce del Sud/Under the Southern Cross (Brignone, 1938): Africa as sensory paradise in, 167–168; bodily control in, 124; Centa in, 125, 195, 200–201; Comin and, 192, 194; Duranti in, 192–193, 208, 209–210, 244–245; *L'esclave blanc* (1936) and, 177; ethnographic elements in, 202–205; father figures in, 167; funding of, 243; homoeroticism in, 205–207; homosociality in, 191; Italian women in, 194–195; labor in, 195, 199–200; Levantines in, 193, 196–199, 197; male attire in, 279; melodrama in, 195–196, 207–208;

music in, 196, 201, 236, 264; nomadism in, 118, 125; nudity in, 123; the Other in, 253; reception of, 75, 208–210, 213; as re-released after the war, 305; women in, 14, 15, 118, 125, 167, 192–193, 201–203, 233, 275; woundings in, 259
sound: in *La battaglia dello Jonio* (1940), 230; in *Bengasi* (1942), xx; in documentary films, 68; in empire features, xx; in *L'esclave blanche* (1927), 181–184, 182–183; in *Il grande appello* (1936), 85–88, 90–93; in *Luciano Serra, pilota*, 138–139; in *La nave bianca* (1941), 236; in *Un pilota ritorna* (1942), xx; role of, 16–17, 44, 49–55, 80; in *Sentinelle di bronzo* (1937), 153–155; in *Lo squadrone bianco* (1936), 136–140, 141; in *Uomini sul fondo* (1941), 232. See also dubbing and dubbing industry; music; voice and vocality
Spada, Marcello, 31–32, 34, 109–110
Spanish cinema and film industry, 46
spectators, 44, 55–62
La spedizione Franchetti nella Dancalia etiopica/The Franchetti Expedition to Ethiopian Dancalia (Craveri, 1929), 28
La sperduta di Allah/Allah's Lost Soul (Guazzoni, 1929), 30, 120, 212
Springer, John Parris, 195
squadrism, xxii, 79, 116, 144, 163, 217
Lo squadrone bianco/The White Squadron (Genina, 1936): African sojourn in, 168; *askaris* in, 127; aviation and, 224; battle scenes in, 140–141; *Bengasi* (1942) and, 274, 277; bodily control in, 124; Centa in, 125, 126, 131–132; D'Errico and, 212; desert in, 288; *documentari romanzati* and, 240–241; *L'Esclave blanc* (1936) and, 186; financial incentives and assistance for, 4; foreign funding for, 243; French colonial culture and, 129–131; Giachetti in, 151; Giunta and, xxii; homosociality in, 191; Italian colonial style and, 133–134; *meharisti* in, 118, 134, 283; music in, 136–138, 141; nomadism in, 118, 125; Peyré's novel and, 5, 18, 130, 132–133, 134–136, 140, 146; pidgin Italian in, 54; publicity for, 143–145; reception of, 145–146, 268; as shot in

Libya, 120; silence in, 232; smoke clouds in, 230; sound in, 136–140, 141; Terzano and, 148; translation in, 280–282; translators in, 200; Venice Biennale Film Festival and, 5, 145, 146; Veretti and, 49; vocality in, 50; watching and being watched in, 141–143; women in, 14, 15, 125, 131–132, *133*, 193, 202, 233

La Stampa (newspaper), 176

Stefani, Giulietta, 10, 128, 312n25

Steinhoff, Hans: *Ohm Krüger* (1941), 221–222

Sternberg, Josef von: *Morocco* (1930), 15, 85

Lo stormo atlantico/The Atlantic Flock (Craveri, 1931), 106

Stramilano/Supermilan (D'Errico, 1929), 71

subtitles and subtitling, 52, 61. *See also* dubbing and dubbing industry

Sue, Eugène, 302

Sulle orme dei nostri pionieri/On the Tracks of Our Pioneers (De Feo, 1936), 63–64, 69, 72–73

Supercinema Teatro Italia (Addis Ababa), 56, 57

Talamo, Gino: *Uragano ai tropici* (with Faraldo, 1939), 268

Tamberlani, Carlo, 267

T'amerò sempre/I Will Love You Always (Camerini, 1933), 73

"Tammurriata nera" (popular song), 304

Tempo di uccidere/A Time to Kill (Flaiano), 296, 297–298

Terzano, Massimo, 148, 165; *Dall'Italia all'Equatore* (1923), 148

Thiele, Wilhelm, 109

Tobino, Mario, 291

Tobis (German production house), 46

Togliatti, Palmiro, 297

Tosca (Koch and Renoir, 1941), 220, 231

tourist films, 67–68

Trader Horn (Van Dyke, 1931), 147

translation and translators, 200, 280–282, 284

traveling cinemas, 58, 59, 220–221

I trecento della settima/The Three Hundred of the Seventh (Baffico, 1943), 291

Treno popolare/The Popular Train (Materazzo, 1933), 73

Tryan, Cecyl, 31

UFA (German production house), 224

Ultimo Amore/The Last Love (Chiarini, 1947), 297

L'Ultimo Lord/The Last Lord (Genina, 1926), 280

Umanità/Humanity (Salvatori, 1946), 300–301

"Under the Southern Cross" (song), 196

uniforms: in *Bengasi* (1942), 267, 275–279, 290; in *La nave bianca* (1941), 239, 250; role of, 11–12, 79, 129, 301, 303; in *Sentinelle di bronzo* (1937), 200; in *Lo squadrone bianco* (1936), 134, 145, 152, 200

Unione Cinematografica Italiana (Italian Cinematographic Union), 26

United Nations Relief and Rehabilitation Administration (UNRRA), 300–301

Gli uomini, che mascalzoni!/What Scoundrels Men Are! (Camerini, 1932), 73

Uomini sul fondo/Men on the Bottom (De Robertis, 1941), 231–234, 234, 235, 238, 240–242

L'uomo della croce/The Man with the Cross (Rossellini, 1943), 222, 264, 291

Uragano ai tropici/Hurricane in the Tropics (Faraldo and Talamo, 1939), 268

Valentino, Rodolfo: Giachetti compared to, 124; B. Mussolini compared to, 27; Navarro and, 109–110; in *The Sheik* (1921), 30–31, 34, 35; Spada and, 109–110

Valli, Alida, 127

Valori, Gino: *Equatore* (1939), 210

Vampyr (Dreyer, 1932), 176, 184

Van Dyke, W. S.: *Eskimo* (1933), 147, 148; *Trader Horn* (1931), 147

varietà, 55, 56

Vatican, 55, 94, 302

Venice Biennale Film Festival: after the fall of Fascism, 299; American cinema and,

47; *Bengasi* (1942) and, 288; creation of, 40; Fulchignani on, 242; *La grande illusion* (1937) and, 221; IFC and, 46–47; as Italian-German Cinema Exhibition, 219; *La nave bianca* (1941) and, 239; *Sotto la Croce del Sud* (1938) and, 208; *Lo squadrone bianco* (1936) and, 5, 145, 146
Veretti, Antonio, 49, 137, 246, 270
Verga, Giovanni, 264
Vergano, Aldo: *Quelli della montagna* (1943), 291
verismo, 264
Vertov, Dziga, 72–73
Vice, 289–290
Victor Emanuel II, King of Italy, 27
Vidor, King, 247
Vigilanti cura (encyclical), 55
Villa, Roberto, 81, 96, 110, 116–117, 136
Villafranca (Forzano, 1934), 100
Virilio, Paul, 24, 63, 76
Visconti, Luchino, 47; *Ossessione* (1943), 287
La vita degli ascari eritrei/The Life of the Eritrean Ascari (Comerio, 1912), 22
Vitrotti, Giovanni, 22, 74
Vivaldi, Antonio, 141
Vivere in pace/To Live in Peace (Zampa, 1947), 296–297
voice and vocality: masculinity and, 52–53; role of, 17, 44, 49–50, 54; in *Sentinelle di bronzo* (1937), 153–155; in *Lo squadrone bianco* (1936), 136–137, 138–139. *See also* dubbing and dubbing industry; foreign speech; language
Voli sulle Ambe/Flights over the Mountains (V. Mussolini), 108
Volpi di Misurata, Giuseppe, 219

Walsh, Raoul: *Desperate Journey* (1942), 249
Winter, Jay, 24
Western. *See* American Western
women: in *Bengasi* (1942), 245, 271–275, 279–280, 283; in desert spaces, 15; in *L'Esclave blanc* (1936), 14, 118, 167, 179–180, 182–186, *185*, 202, 233; in *Il grande appello* (1936), 233; in *La nave bianca* (1941), 238, 239; nomadism and, 15, 34–36, 125, 125–127; in *Un pilota ritorna* (1942), 245, 250; in *Sotto la Croce del Sud* (1938), 14, 15, 118, 125, 167, 192–193, 201–203, 233; in *Uomini sul fondo* (1941), 233. *See also* African women; Italian women
World War I, 21, 24–26, 62, 63, 105
World War II: *askari* soldiers and, 127; empire films and, xiv; Ethiopian invasion and, 2; Italy's participation in, 214, 216–218, 243; nonfiction film and, 223–228; in *Vivere in pace* (1947), 296–297
woundings: in *Bengasi* (1942), 272, 274–275; in *L'Esclave blanc* (1936), 259; in *Il grande appello* (1936), 235–236; in *Luciano Serra, pilota* (1938), 235–236, 258; in *La nave bianca* (1941), 235–236; in *Un pilota ritorna* (1942), 251, 254–259, 261; in *Sentinelle di bronzo* (1937), 152–153, *154*, 235–236, 258; World War II and, 235–236

Yugoslavia, 215, 217, 246, 297

Zampa, Luigi: *Vivere in pace* (1947), 296–297
Zùccoli, Luciano, 32, 35–36
Zyrd, Michael, 76

RUTH BEN-GHIAT

is Professor of Italian Studies and History at New York University. The recipient of Guggenheim, National Endowment for the Humanities, Fulbright, and other fellowships, she is the author of *Fascist Modernities: Italy, 1922–45* (2001, 2004), the editor of *Gli imperi: Dall'antichità all'età contemporanea* (2009), the editor (with Mia Fuller) of *Italian Colonialism* (2005, 2008), and the editor (with Stephanie Malia Hom) of *Italian Mobilities* (forthcoming). Her current book project is *Prisoners of War: Italians in French, German, and British Captivity, 1940–1950*.

www.ingramcontent.com/pod-product-compliance
Lightning Source LLC
Chambersburg PA
CBHW050427240426
43661CB00055B/2299